TODAY'S MORAL PROBLEMS

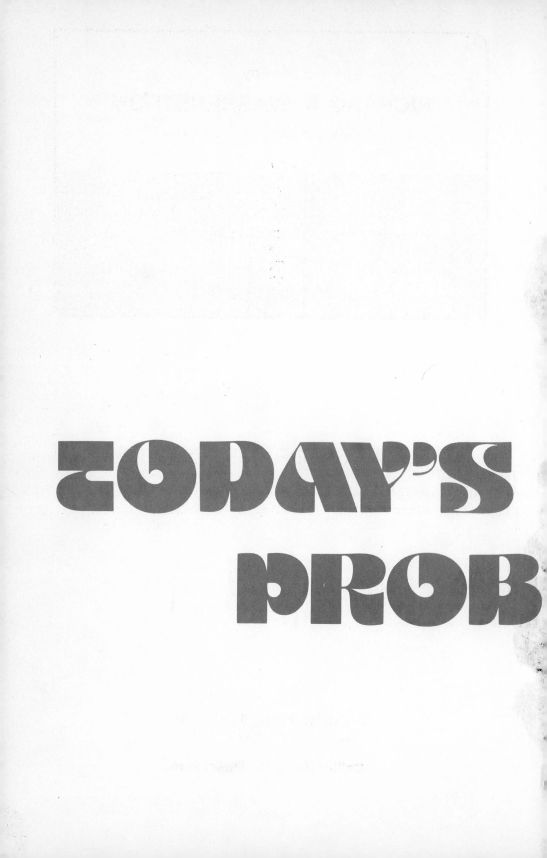

Edited by
RICHARD A. WASSERSTROM
University of California, Los Angeles

SECOND EDITION

MORAL LEMS

Macmillan Publishing Co., Inc.
New York

Collier Macmillan Publishers
London

Macmillan Publishing Co., Inc.
866 Third Avenue, New York, New York 10022

Collier Macmillan Canada, Ltd.

Library of Congress Cataloging in Publication Data

Wasserstrom, Richard A. (date)
Today's moral problems.

Includes bibliographies.
1. United States—Moral conditions.   I. Title.
HN90.M6W37   1979   301.41'7973   78–6975
ISBN 0–02–424820–7

Printing: 1 2 3 4 5 6 7 8   Year: 9 0 1 2 3 4

PREFACE

The writings in this collection deal with moral issues that have been of special concern to people living in the United States in recent years. In addition, almost all of the selections were written during the past decade. It is worth asking why this latter fact is so. Part of the explanation, of course, is the problems selected for inclusion. Because such things as abortion, preferential treatment, and sexual morality have been among the particular worries of this generation, it is not surprising that contemporary moral philosophers have turned their attention to issues such as these.

But this is not the whole answer. The problems considered in this collection are hardly new problems, or even problems that have only acquired a particular urgency in our own time. Nor have philosophers just become aware of moral issues such as these; morality has been a concern of philosophers for as long as there has been philosophy. So, the recent vintage of most of these pieces does not reflect either a new-found philosophical concern for morality or the rise to prominence of new moral problems. What it does reflect, at least, is a change of sorts in Anglo-American academic philosophy.

For some time philosophers who were interested in moral philosophy were interested primarily in what have been called the problems of metaethics. They were concerned with such things as the analysis and examination of the way moral concepts and moral arguments worked and, sometimes, the development of general theories about the meaning and characteristics of fundamental moral ideas. Their philosophical inquiries were about ethical statements and judgments.

Many of the writings found in this collection are not metaethics but rather normative ethics. That is to say, they are philosophical attempts to elucidate and assess what is to be said for and against particular ways of behaving in respect to particular moral problems. The distinction between metaethics and normative ethics is anything but precise. And even if it were, no philosophical inquiry worthy of respect could help engaging in substantial metaethical activity. Nonetheless, what distinguishes these writings from the writings in moral philosophy of the recent past is this immersion in specific moral issues and this willingness to move to the presentation of more particular moral assessments.

The legal cases and philosophical writings reproduced in this book are arranged in accordance with the particular topics to which they are directly addressed. There is, however, a certain degree of arbitrariness to the organization by topics, and there are themes discussed in the writings that cut across the topics. For example, some of the issues dealt with in the final section, "The World at Large," are also relevant to the subjects of abortion and sexual morality. And the question of who is a person and why that question matters is a theme that runs through most, if not all, of the topics considered. For this reason, the readings can certainly be approached in ways different from that suggested by the arrangement presented here. The reader should, in any event, be prepared to integrate the ideas discussed under any of the headings wherever they are elsewhere relevant.

I think that the inquiries collected here are exciting both because of what they teach about the moral problems they examine and because of what they show about this additional aspect of philosophical activity. I hope that those who read these philosophical writings will find them exhilarating. I hope that they will serve to introduce people to some of the important, but less traditional, types of philosophical explorations that can take place in respect to morality. And I hope, as well, that these writings reveal to them some of the ways in which philosophy can make an important contribution to an adequate and informed understanding of serious, live moral issues.

R. A. W.

CONTENTS

three

PREFERENTIAL TREATMENT

four

SEXUAL MORALITY

five

PRIVACY

six

PUNISHMENT

seven

THE WORLD AT LARGE

TODAY'S MORAL PROBLEMS

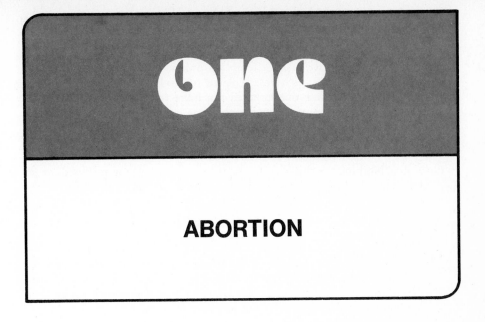

one

ABORTION

Roe v. Wade 410 U.S. 113, 93 S.Ct. 705 (1973)

One of the plaintiffs in this case was a pregnant single woman who sued under the fictitious name of Jane Roe to challenge the constitutionality of various Texas criminal statutes relating to abortion. The sections of the Texas Penal Code under attack read as follows:

1. "Article 1191. Abortion

"If any person shall designedly administer to a pregnant woman or knowingly procure to be administered with her consent any drug or medicine, or shall use towards her any violence or means whatever externally or internally applied, and thereby procure an abortion, he shall be confined in the penitentiary not less than two nor more than five years; if it be done without her consent, the punishment shall be doubled. By 'abortion' is meant that the life of the fetus or embryo shall be destroyed in the woman's womb or that a premature birth thereof be caused.

"Art. 1192. Furnishing the means

"Whoever furnishes the means for procuring an abortion knowing the purpose intended is guilty as an accomplice.

"Art. 1193. Attempt at abortion

"If the means used shall fail to produce an abortion, the offender is nevertheless guilty of an attempt to produce abortion, provided it be shown that such means were calculated to produce that result, and shall be fined not less than one hundred nor more than one thousand dollars.
"Art. 1194. Murder in producing abortion
"If the death of the mother is occasioned by an abortion so pro-duced or by an attempt to effect the same it is murder.
"Art. 1196. By medical advice
"Nothing in this chapter applies to an abortion procured or at-tempted by medical advice for the purpose of saving the life of the mother."

In addition, Article 1195, not challenged in the lawsuit read:

"Art. 1195. Destroying unborn child
"Whoever shall during parturition of the mother destroy the vi-tality or life in a child in a state of being born and before actual birth, which child would otherwise have been born alive, shall be confined in the penitentiary for life or for not less than five years."

In her lawsuit Jane Roe asked the federal district court for a declara-tory judgment that the statutes were unconstitutional and for an in-junction against their enforcement. She claimed that she was unable to secure a safe abortion performed by a competent physician under clinical conditions because her life was not threatened by the preg-nancy. She also claimed that she lacked the funds to travel to any other state where safe abortions for persons such as herself were legal.

What follows are portions of the majority opinion by Justice Blackmun, the concurring opinion of Justice Douglas, and the dis-senting opinion of Justice White. The concurring opinion of Justice Stewart and the dissenting opinion of Justice Rehnquist have been omitted and the remaining footnotes have been renumbered.

· · ·

Mr. Justice Blackmun delivered the opinion of the Court.
Three reasons have been advanced to explain historically the enact-ment of criminal abortion laws in the 19th century and to justify their continued existence.
It has been argued occasionally that these laws were the product of a Victorian social concern to discourage illicit sexual conduct. Texas, however, does not advance this justification in the present case, and it appears that no court or commentator has taken the argument seriously. The appellants and *amici* contend, moreover, that this is not a proper state purpose at all and suggest that, if it were, the Texas statutes are overbroad in protecting it since the law fails to distinguish between mar-ried and unwed mothers.

A second reason is concerned with abortion as a medical procedure. When most criminal abortion laws were first enacted, the procedure was a hazardous one for the woman.[1] This was particularly true prior to the development of antisepsis. Antiseptic techniques, of course, were based on discoveries by Lister, Pasteur, and others first announced in 1867, but were not generally accepted and employed until about the turn of the century. Abortion mortality was high. Even after 1900, and perhaps until as late as the development of antibiotics in the 1940's, standard modern techniques such as dilation and curettage were not nearly so safe as they are today. Thus it has been argued that a State's real concern in enacting a criminal abortion law was to protect the pregnant woman, that is, to restrain her from submitting to a procedure that placed her life in serious jeopardy.

Modern medical techniques have altered this situation. Appellants and various *amici* refer to medical data indicating that abortion in early pregnancy, that is, prior to the end of first trimester, although not without its risk, is now relatively safe. Mortality rates for women undergoing early abortions, where the procedure is legal, appear to be as low as or lower than the rates for normal childbirth.[2] Consequently, any interest of the State in protecting the woman from an inherently hazardous procedure, except when it would be equally dangerous for her to forgo it, has largely disappeared. Of course, important state interests in the area of health and medical standards do remain. The State has a legitimate interest in seeing to it that abortion, like any other medical procedure, is performed under circumstances that insure maximum safety for the patient. This interest obviously extends at least to the performing physician and his staff, to the facilities involved, to the availability of aftercare, and to adequate provision for any complication or emergency that might arise. The prevalence of high mortality rates at illegal "abortion mills" strengthens, rather than weakens, the State's interest in regulating the conditions under which abortions are performed. Moreover, the risk to the woman increases as her pregnancy continues. Thus the State retains a definite interest in protecting the woman's own health and safety when an abortion is proposed at a late stage of pregnancy.

The third reason is the State's interest—some phrase it in terms of duty—in protecting prenatal life. Some of the argument for this justifica-

[1] See C. Haagensen & W. Lloyd, A Hundred Years of Medicine 19 (1943).
[2] Potts, Postconception Control of Fertility, 8 Int'l J. of G. & O. 957, 967 (1970) (England and Wales); Abortion Mortality, 20 Morbidity and Morality, 208, 209 (July 12, 1971) (U.S. Dept. of HEW, Public Health Service) (New York City); Tietze, United States: Therapeutic Abortions, 1963–1968, 59 Studies in Family Planning 5, 7 (1970); Tietze, Mortality with Contraception and Induced Abortion, 45 Studies in Family Planning 6 (1969) (Japan, Czechoslovakia, Hungary); Tietze & Lehfeldt, Legal Abortion in Eastern Europe, 175 J.A.M.A. 1149, 1152 (April 1961). Other sources are discussed in Lader 17–23[L. Lader, Abortion, 1966].

tion rests on the theory that a new human life is present from the moment of conception.[3] The State's interest and general obligation to protect life then extends, it is argued, to prenatal life. Only when the life of the pregnant mother herself is at stake, balanced against the life she carries within her, should the interest of the embryo or fetus not prevail. Logically, of course, a legitimate state interest in this area need not stand or fall on acceptance of the belief that life begins at conception or at some other point prior to live birth. In assessing the State's interest, recognition may be given to the less rigid claim that as long as at least *potential* life is involved, the State may assert interests beyond the protection of the pregnant woman alone.

Parties challenging state abortion laws have sharply disputed in some courts the contention that a purpose of these laws, when enacted, was to protect prenatal life. Pointing to the absence of legislative history to support the contention, they claim that most state laws were designed solely to protect the woman. Because medical advances have lessened this concern, at least with respect to abortion in early pregnancy, they argue that with respect to such abortions the laws can no longer be justified by any state interest. There is some scholarly support for this view of original purpose. The few state courts called upon to interpret their laws in the 19th and early 20th centuries did focus on the State's interest in protecting the woman's health rather than in preserving the embryo and fetus. Proponents of this view point out that in many States, including Texas, by statute or judicial interpretation, the pregnant woman herself could not be prosecuted for self-abortion or for cooperating in an abortion performed upon her by another. They claim that adoption of the "quickening" distinction through received common law and state statutes tacitly recognizes the greater health hazards inherent in late abortion and impliedly repudiates the theory that life begins at conception.

It is with these interests, and the weight to be attached to them, that this case is concerned.

The Constitution does not explicitly mention any right of privacy. In a line of decisions, however, going back perhaps as far as Union Pacific R. Co. v. Botsford, 141 U.S. 250, 251, 11 S.Ct. 1000, 1001, 35 L.Ed. 734 (1891), the Court has recognized that a right of personal privacy, or a guarantee of certain areas or zones of privacy, does exist under the Constitution. In varying contexts the Court or individual Justices have indeed found at least the roots of that right in the First Amendment . . .; in

---

[3] See Brief of Amicus National Right to Life Foundation; R. Drinan, The Inviolability of the Right to Be Born, in Abortion and the Law 107 (D. Smith, editor, 1967); Louisell, Abortion, The Practice of Medicine, and the Due Process of Law, 16 UCLA L.Rev. 233 (1969); Noonan 1[J. Noonan, ed. The Morality of Abortion, 1970].

the Fourth and Fifth Amendments, . . . in the penumbras of the Bill of Rights, . . . in the Ninth Amendment, or in the concept of liberty guaranteed by the first section of the Fourteenth Amendment, . . . These decisions make it clear that only personal rights that can be deemed "fundamental" or "implicit in the concept of ordered liberty," . . . are included in this guarantee of personal privacy. They also make it clear that the right has some extension to activities relating to marriage, . . . procreation, . . . contraception, . . . family relationships, . . . and child rearing and education, . . .

This right of privacy, whether it be founded in the Fourteenth Amendment's concept of personal liberty and restrictions upon state action, as we feel it is, or, as the District Court determined, in the Ninth Amendment's reservation of rights to the people, is broad enough to encompass a woman's decision whether or not to terminate her pregnancy. The detriment that the State would impose upon the pregnant woman by denying this choice altogether is apparent. Specific and direct harm medically diagnosable even in early pregnancy may be involved. Maternity, or additional offspring, may force upon the woman a distressful life and future. Psychological harm may be imminent. Mental and physical health may be taxed by child care. There is also the distress, for all concerned, associated with the unwanted child, and there is the problem of bringing a child into a family already unable, psychologically and otherwise, to care for it. In other cases, as in this one, the additional difficulties and continuing stigma of unwed motherhood may be involved. All these are factors the woman and her responsible physician necessarily will consider in consultation.

On the basis of elements such as these, appellants and some *amici* argue that the woman's right is absolute and that she is entitled to terminate her pregnancy at whatever time, in whatever way, and for whatever reason she alone chooses. With this we do not agree. Appellants' arguments that Texas either has no valid interest at all in regulating the abortion decision, or no interest strong enough to support any limitation upon the woman's sole determination, is unpersuasive. The Court's decisions recognizing a right of privacy also acknowledge that some state regulation in areas protected by that right is appropriate. As noted above, a state may properly assert important interests in safeguarding health, in maintaining medical standards, and in protecting potential life. At some point in pregnancy, these respective interests become sufficiently compelling to sustain regulation of the factors that govern the abortion decision. The privacy right involved, therefore, cannot be said to be absolute. In fact, it is not clear to us that the claim asserted by some *amici* that one has an unlimited right to do with one's body as one pleases bears a close relationship to the right of privacy previously articulated in the Court's decisions. The Court has refused to recognize an unlimited right of this kind in the past. Jacobson v. Massachusetts, 197 U.S. 11, 25 S.Ct. 358,

49 L.Ed. 643 (1905) (vaccination); Buck v. Bell, 274 U.S. 200, 47 S.Ct. 584, 71 L.Ed. 1000 (1927) (sterilization).

We therefore conclude that the right of personal privacy includes the abortion decision, but that this right is not unqualified and must be considered against important state interests in regulation.

We note that those federal and state courts that have recently considered abortion law challenges have reached the same conclusion. A majority, in addition to the District Court in the present case, have held state laws unconstitutional, at least in part, because of vagueness or because of overbreadth and abridgement of rights. . . .

Although the results are divided, most of these courts have agreed that the right of privacy, however based, is broad enough to cover the abortion decision; that the right, nonetheless, is not absolute and is subject to some limitations; and that at some point the state interests as to protection of health, medical standards, and prenatal life, become dominant. We agree with this approach.

Where certain "fundamental rights" are involved, the Court has held that regulation limiting these rights may be justified only by a "compelling state interest," . . . and that legislative enactments must be narrowly drawn to express only the legitimate state interests at stake. . . .

In the recent abortion cases, cited above, courts have recognized these principles. Those striking down state laws have generally scrutinized the State's interest in protecting health and potential life and have concluded that neither interest justified broad limitations on the reasons for which a physician and his pregnant patient might decide that she should have an abortion in the early stages of pregnancy. Courts sustaining state laws have held that the State's determinations to protect health or prenatal life are dominant and constitutionally justifiable.

The District Court held that the appellee failed to meet his burden of demonstrating that the Texas statute's infringement upon Roe's rights was necessary to support a compelling state interest, and that, although the defendant presented "several compelling justifications for state presence in the area of abortions," the statutes outstripped these justifications and swept "far beyond any areas of compelling state interest." . . . Appellant and appellee both contest that holding. Appellant, as has been indicated, claims an absolute right that bars any state imposition of criminal penalties in the area. Appellee argues that the State's determination to recognize and protect prenatal life from and after conception constitutes a compelling state interest. As noted above, we do not agree fully with either formulation.

A. The appellee and certain *amici* argue that the fetus is a "person" within the language and meaning of the Fourteenth Amendment. In support of this they outline at length and in detail the well-known facts of fetal development. If this suggestion of personhood is established, the appellant's case, of course, collapses, for the fetus' right to life is then guaranteed specifically by the Amendment. The appellant conceded as much on reargument. On the other hand, the appellee conceded on re-argument that no case could be cited that holds that a fetus is a person within the meaning of the Fourteenth Amendment.

The Constitution does not define "person" in so many words. Section 1 of the Fourteenth Amendment contains three references to "person." The first, in defining "citizens," speaks of "persons born or naturalized in the United States." The word also appears both in the Due Process Clause and in the Equal Protection Clause. "Person" is used in other places in the Constitution: in the listing of qualifications for representatives and senators, Art. I, § 2, cl. 2, and § 3, cl. 3; in the Apportionment Clause, Art. I, § 2, cl. 3;[4] in the Migration and Importation provision, Art. I, § 9, cl. 1; in the Emolument Clause, Art. I, § 9, cl. 8; in the Electors provisions, Art. II, § 1, cl. 2, and the superseded cl. 3; in the provision outlining qualifications for the office of President, Art. II, § 1, cl. 5; in the Extradition provisions, Art. IV, § 2, cl. 2, and the super-seded Fugitive Slave cl. 3; and in the Fifth, Twelfth, and Twenty-second Amendments as well as in §§ 2 and 3 of the Fourteenth Amendment. But in nearly all these instances, the use of the word is such that it has application only postnatally. None indicates, with any assurance, that it has any possible pre-natal application.[5]

[12] All this, together with our observation, *supra*, that throughout the major portion of the 19th century prevailing legal abortion practices were far freer than they are today, persuades us that the word "person," as used in the Fourteenth Amendment, does not include the unborn.[6] This is in accord with the results reached in those few cases where the

---

[4] We are not aware that in the taking of any census under this clause, a fetus has ever been counted.

[5] When Texas urges that a fetus is entitled to Fourteenth Amendment protection as a person, it faces a dilemma. Neither in Texas nor in any other State are all abortions prohibited. Despite broad proscription, an exception always exists. The exception contained in Art. 1196, for an abortion procured or attempted by medical advice for the purpose of saving the life of the mother, is typical. But if the fetus is a person who is not to be deprived of life without due process of law, and if the mother's condition is the sole determinant, does not the Texas exception appear to be out of line with the Amendment's command?

There are other inconsistencies between Fourteenth Amendment status and the typical abortion statute. It has already been pointed out, . . . that in Texas the woman is not a principal or an accomplice with respect to an abortion upon her. If the fetus is a person, why is the woman not a principal or an accomplice? Further, the penalty for criminal abortion specified by Art. 1195 is significantly less than the maximum penalty for murder prescribed by Art. 1257 of the Texas Penal Code. If the fetus is a person, may the penalties be different?

[6] Cf. the Wisconsin abortion statute, defining "unborn child" to mean "a human being from the time of conception until it is born alive," Wis.Stat. § 940.04(6) (1969), and the new Connecticut statute, Public Act No. 1, May 1972 Special Session, declaring it to be the public policy of the State and the legislative intent "to protect and preserve human life from the moment of conception."

issue has been squarely presented. . . . Indeed, our decision in United States v. Vuitch, 402 U.S. 62, 91 S.Ct. 1294, 28 L.Ed.2d 601 (1971), inferentially is to the same effect, for we there would not have indulged in statutory interpretation favorable to abortion in specified circumstances if the necessary consequence was the termination of life entitled to Fourteenth Amendment protection.

This conclusion, however, does not of itself fully answer the contentions raised by Texas, and we pass on to other considerations.

B. The pregnant woman cannot be isolated in her privacy. She carries an embryo and, later, a fetus, if one accepts the medical definitions of the developing young in the human uterus. See Dorland's *Illustrated Medical Dictionary*, 478–479, 547 (24th ed. 1965). The situation therefore is inherently different from marital intimacy, or bedroom possession of obscene material, or marriage, or procreation, or education, with which *Eisenstadt, Griswold, Stanley, Loving, Skinner, Pierce,* and *Meyer* were respectively concerned. As we have intimated above, it is reasonable and appropriate for a State to decide that at some point in time another interest, that of health of the mother or that of potential human life, becomes significantly involved. The woman's privacy is no longer sole and any right of privacy she possesses must be measured accordingly.

Texas urges that, apart from the Fourteenth Amendment, life begins at conception and is present throughout pregnancy, and that, therefore, the State has a compelling interest in protecting that life from and after conception. We need not resolve the difficult question of when life begins. When those trained in the respective disciplines of medicine, philosophy, and theology are unable to arrive at any consensus, the judiciary, at this point in the development of man's knowledge, is not in a position to speculate as to the answer.

It should be sufficient to note briefly the wide divergence of thinking on this most sensitive and difficult question. There has always been strong support for the view that life does not begin until live birth. This was the belief of the Stoics. It appears to be the predominant, though not the unanimous, attitude of the Jewish faith.[7] It may be taken to represent also the position of a large segment of the Protestant community, insofar as that can be ascertained; organized groups that have taken a formal position on the abortion issue have generally regarded abortion as a matter for the conscience of the individual and her family. As we have noted, the common law found greater significance in quickening. Physicians and their scientific colleagues have regarded that event with less interest and have tended to focus either upon conception or upon live birth or upon the interim point at which the fetus becomes "viable," that is, potentially

---

[7] Lader 97–99; D. Feldman, Birth Control in Jewish Law 251–294 (1968). For a stricter view, see I. Jakobovits, Jewish Views on Abortion, in Abortion and the Law 124 (D. Smith ed. 1967).

able to live outside the mother's womb, albeit with artificial aid.[8] Viability is usually placed at about seven months (28 weeks) but may occur earlier, even at 24 weeks.[9] The Aristotelian theory of "mediate animation," that held sway throughout the Middle Ages and the Renaissance in Europe, continued to be official Roman Catholic dogma until the 19th century, despite opposition to this "ensoulment" theory from those in the Church who would recognize the existence of life from the moment of conception.[10] The latter is now, of course, the official belief of the Catholic Church. As one of the briefs *amicus* discloses, this is a view strongly held by many non-Catholics as well, and by many physicians. Substantial problems for precise definition of this view are posed, however, by new embryological data that purport to indicate that conception is a "process" over time, rather than an event, and by new medical techniques such as menstrual extraction, the "morning-after" pill, implantation of embryos, artificial insemination, and even artificial wombs.[11]

In areas other than criminal abortion the law has been reluctant to endorse any theory that life, as we recognize it, begins before live birth or to accord legal rights to the unborn except in narrowly defined situations and except when the rights are contingent upon live birth. For example, the traditional rule of tort law had denied recovery for prenatal injuries even though the child was born alive.[12] That rule has been changed in almost every jurisdiction. In most States recovery is said to be permitted only if the fetus was viable, or at least quick, when the injuries were sustained, though few courts have squarely so held. In a recent development, generally opposed by the commentators, some States permit the parents of a stillborn child to maintain an action for wrongful death because of prenatal injuries. Such an action, however, would appear to be one to vindicate the parents' interest and is thus consistent with the view that the fetus, at most, represents only the potentiality of life. Similarly, unborn children have been recognized as acquiring rights or interests by way of inheritance or other devolution of property, and have been repre-

---

[8] L. Hellman & J. Pritchard, Williams Obstetrics 493 (14th ed. 1971); Dorland's Illustrated Medical Dictionary 1689 (24th ed. 1965).

[9] Hellman & Pritchard, *supra*, n. 58, at 493.

[10] For discussions of the development of the Roman Catholic position, see D. Callahan, Abortion: Law, Choice and Morality 409–447 (1970); Noonan 1.

[11] See D. Brodie, The New Biology and the Prenatal Child, 9 J.Fam. L. 391, 397 (1970); R. Gorney, The New Biology and the Future of Man, 15 UCLA L.Rev. 273 (1968); Note, Criminal Law—Abortion—The "Morning-After" Pill and Other Pre-Implantation Birth-Control Methods and the Law, 46 Ore.L.Rev. 211 (1967); G. Taylor, The Biological Time Bomb 32 (1968); A. Rosenfeld, The Second Genesis 138–139 (1969); G. Smith, Through a Test Tube Darkly: Artificial Insemination and the Law, 67 Mich.L.Rev. 127 (1968); Note, Artificial Insemination and the Law, U.Ill.L.F. 203 (1968).

[12] Prosser, Handbook of the Law of Torts 335–338 (1971); 2 Harper & James, The Law of Torts 1028–1031 (1956); Note, 63 Harv.L.Rev. 173 (1949).

sented by guardians *ad litem*.[13] Perfection of the interests involved, again, has generally been contingent upon live birth. In short, the unborn have never been recognized in the law as persons in the whole sense.

In view of all this, we do not agree that, by adopting one theory of life, Texas may override the rights of the pregnant woman that are at stake. We repeat, however, that the State does have an important and legitimate interest in preserving and protecting the health of the pregnant woman, whether she be a resident of the State or a non-resident who seeks medical consultation and treatment there, and that it has still *another* important and legitimate interest in protecting the potentiality of human life. These interests are separate and distinct. Each grows in substantiality as the woman approaches term and, at a point during pregnancy, each becomes "compelling."

With respect to the State's important and legitimate interest in the health of the mother, the "compelling" point, in the light of present medical knowledge, is at approximately the end of the first trimester. This is so because of the now established medical fact, referred to above . . . that until the end of the first trimester mortality in abortion is less than mortality in normal childbirth. It follows that, from and after this point, a State may regulate the abortion procedure to the extent that the regulation reasonably relates to the preservation and protection of maternal health. Examples of permissible state regulation in this area are requirements as to the qualifications of the person who is to perform the abortion; as to the licensure of that person; as to the facility in which the procedure is to be performed, that is, whether it must be a hospital or may be a clinic or some other place of less-than-hospital status; as to the licensing of the facility; and the like.

This means, on the other hand, that, for the period of pregnancy prior to this "compelling" point, the attending physician, in consultation with his patient, is free to determine, without regulation by the State, that in his medical judgment the patient's pregnancy should be terminated. If that decision is reached, the judgment may be effectuated by an abortion free of interference by the State.

With respect to the State's important and legitimate interest in potential life, the "compelling" point is at viability. This is so because the fetus then presumably has the capability of meaningful life outside the mother's womb. State regulation protective of fetal life after viability thus has both logical and biological justifications. If the State is interested in protecting fetal life after viability, it may go so far as to proscribe abortion during that period except when it is necessary to preserve the life or health of the mother.

[13] D. Louisell, Abortion, The Practice of Medicine, and the Due Process of Law, 16 UCLA L.Rev. 233, 235–238 (1969); Note, 56 Iowa L.Rev. 994, 999–1000 (1971; Note, The Law and the Unborn Child, 46 Notre Dame Law, 349, 351–354 (1971).

Measured against these standards, Art. 1196 of the Texas Penal Code, in restricting legal abortions to those "procured or attempted by medical advice for the purpose of saving the life of the mother," sweeps too broadly. The statute makes no distinction between abortions performed early in pregnancy and those performed later, and it limits to a single reason, "saving" the mother's life, the legal justification for the procedure. The statute, therefore, cannot survive the constitutional attack made upon it here.

This conclusion makes it unnecessary for us to conder the additional challenge to the Texas statute asserted on grounds of vagueness. . . .

. . .

MR. JUSTICE DOUGLAS, concurring. [Mr. Justice Douglas' concurrence applied both to this case and to the companion case from Georgia, Doe v. Bolton, 410 U.S. 179.]

While I join the opinion of the court, I add a few words.

The questions presented in the present cases go far beyond the issues of vagueness, which we considered in United States v. Vuitch, 402 U.S. 62, 91 S.Ct. 1294, 28 L.Ed.2d 601. They involve the right of privacy, one aspect of which we considered in Griswold v. Connecticut, 381 U.S. 479, 484, 85 S.Ct. 1678, 1681, 14 L.Ed.2d 510, when we held that various guarantees in the Bill of Rights create zones of privacy.[14]

The *Griswold* case involved a law forbidding the use of contraceptives. We held that law as applied to married people unconstitutional:

> We deal with a right of privacy older than the Bill of Rights—older than
> our political parties, older than our school system. Marriage is a coming

---

[14] There is no mention of privacy in our Bill of Rights but our decisions have recognized it as one of the fundamental values those amendments were designed to protect. The fountainhead case is Boyd v. United States, 116 U.S. 616, 6 S.Ct. 524, 29 L.Ed. 746, holding that a federal statute which authorized a court in tax cases to require a taxpayer to produce his records or to concede the Government's allegations offended the Fourth and Fifth Amendments. Justice Bradley, for the Court, found that the measure unduly intruded into the "sanctity of a man's home and the privacies of life." *Id.*, 630, 6 S.Ct., 532. Prior to *Boyd*, in Kilbourn v. Thompson, 103 U.S. 168, 195, 26 L.Ed. 377, Mr. Justice Miller held for the Court that neither House of Congress "possesses the general power of making inquiry into the private affairs of the citizen." Of *Kilbourn* Mr. Justice Field later said, "This case will stand for all time as a bulwark against the invasion of the right of the citizen to protection in his private affairs against the unlimited scrutiny of investigation by a congressional committee." In re Pacific Ry. Comm'n, C.C., 32 F. 241, 253 (cited with approval in Sinclair v. United States, 279 U.S. 263, 293, 49 S.Ct. 268, 271, 73 L.Ed. 692). Mr. Justice Harlan, also speaking for the Court, in Interstate Commerce Comm'n v. Brimson, 154 U.S. 447, 478, 14 S.Ct. 1125, 1134, 38 L.Ed. 1047, thought the same was true of administrative inquiries, saying the Constitution did not permit a "general power of making inquiry into the private affairs of the citizen." . . .

together for better or for worse, hopefully enduring, and intimate to the degree of being sacred. *Id.*, 486, 85 S.Ct., 1682.

The District Court in *Doe* held that *Griswold* and related cases "establish a Constitutional right to privacy broad enough to encompass the right of a woman to terminate an unwanted pregnancy in its early stages, by obtaining an abortion." . . .

The Supreme Court of California expressed the same view in People v. Belous,[15] 71 Cal.2d 954, 963, 80 Cal.Rptr. 354, 458 P.2d 194.

The Ninth Amendment obviously does not create federally enforceable rights. It merely says, "The enumeration in the Constitution of certain rights, shall not be construed to deny or disparage others retained by the people." But a catalogue of these rights includes customary, traditional, and time-honored rights, amenities, privileges, and immunities that come within the sweep of "the Blessings of Liberty" mentioned in the preamble to the Constitution. Many of them in my view come within the meaning of the term "liberty" as used in the Fourteenth Amendment.

First is the autonomous control over the development and expression on one's intellect, interests, tastes, and personality.

These are rights protected by the First Amendment and in my view they are absolute, permitting of no exceptions. . . . The Free Exercise Clause of the First Amendment is one facet of this constitutional right. The right to remain silent as respects one's own beliefs, . . . is protected by the First and the Fifth. The First Amendment grants the privacy of first-class mail, . . . All of these aspects of the right of privacy are "rights retained by the people" in the meaning of the Ninth Amendment.

Second is freedom of choice in the basic decisions of one's life respecting marriage, divorce, procreation, contraception, and the education and upbringing of children.

These rights, unlike those protected by the First Amendment, are subject to some control by the police power. Thus the Fourth Amendment speaks only of "unreasonable searches and seizures" and of "probable cause." These rights are "fundamental" and we have held that in order to support legislative action the statute must be narrowly and precisely drawn and that a "compelling state interest" must be shown in support of the limitation. . . .

The liberty to marry a person of one's own choosing, . . . the right of procreation, . . . the liberty to direct the education of one's children, . . . and the privacy of the marital relation, . . . are in this category. Only last Term in Eisenstadt v. Baird, 405 U.S. 438, 92 S.Ct.

[15] The California abortion statute, held unconstitutional in the *Belous* case made it a crime to perform or help perform an abortion "unless the same is necessary to preserve [the mother's] life." . . .

1029, 31 L.Ed.2d 349, another contraceptive case, we expanded the concept of *Griswold* by saying:

> It is true that in Griswold the right of privacy in question inhered in the marital relationship. Yet the marital couple is not an independent entity with a mind and heart of its own, but an association of two individuals each with a separate intellectual and emotional make up. If the right of privacy means anything, it is the right of the *individual*, married or single, to be free from unwarranted governmental intrusion into matters so fundamentally affecting a person as the decision whether to bear or beget a child.

This right of privacy was called by Mr. Justice Brandeis the right "to be let alone." Olmstead v. United States, 277 U.S. 438, 478, 48 S.Ct. 564, 572, 72 L.Ed. 944. That right includes the privilege of an individual to plan his own affairs, for "outside areas of plainly harmful conduct, every American is left to shape his own life as he thinks best, do what he pleases, go where he pleases." Kent v. Dulles, 357 U.S. 116, 126, 78 S.Ct. 1113, 1118, 2 L.Ed.2d 1204.

> *Third is the freedom to care for one's health and person, freedom from bodily restraint or compulsion, freedom to walk, stroll, or loaf.*

These rights, though fundamental, are likewise subject to regulation on a showing of "compelling state interest." We stated in Papachristou v. City of Jacksonville, 405 U.S. 156, 164, 92 S.Ct. 839, 844, 31 L.Ed.2d 110, that walking, strolling, and wandering "are historically part of the amenities of life, as we have known [them]." As stated in Jacobson v. Massachusetts, 197 U.S. 11, 29, 25 S.Ct. 358, 362, 49 L.Ed. 643:

> There is, of course, a sphere within which the individual may assert the supremacy of his own will and rightfully dispute the authority of any human government,—especially of any free government existing under a written constitution, to interfere with the exercise of that will.

In Union Pac. Ry. Co. v. Botsford, 141 U.S. 250, 252, 11 S.Ct. 1000, 1001, 35 L.Ed. 734, the Court said,

> The inviolability of the person is as much invaded by a compulsory stripping and exposure as by a blow.

In Terry v. Ohio, 392 U.S. 1, 8–9, 88 S.Ct. 1868, 1873, 20 L.Ed.2d 889, the Court in speaking of the Fourth Amendment stated

> This inestimable right of personal security belongs as much to the citizen on the streets of our cities as to the [Governor] closeted in his study to dispose of his secret affairs.

Katz v. United States, 389 U.S. 347, 350, 88 S.Ct. 507, 510, 19 L.Ed.2d 576, emphasizes that the Fourth Amendment

> protects individual privacy against certain kinds of governmental intrusion.

In Meyer v. Nebraska, 262 U.S. 390, 399, 43 S.Ct. 625, 626, 67 L.Ed. 1042, the Court said:

> Without doubt, it [liberty] denotes not merely freedom from bodily restraint but also the right of the individual to contract, to engage in any of the common occupations of life, to acquire useful knowledge, to marry, establish a home and bring up children, to worship God according to the dictates of his own conscience, and generally to enjoy those privileges long recognized at common law as essential to the orderly pursuit of happiness by free men.

The Georgia statute is at war with the clear message of these cases— that a woman is free to make the basic decision whether to bear an unwanted child. Elaborate argument is hardly necessary to demonstrate that childbirth may deprive a woman of her preferred life style and force upon her a radically different and undesired future. For example, rejected applicants under the Georgia statute are required to endure the discomforts of pregnancy; to incur the pain, higher mortality rate, and aftereffects of childbirth; to abandon educational plans; to sustain loss of income; to forgo the satisfactions of careers; to tax further mental and physical health in providing childcare; and, in some cases, to bear the lifelong stigma of unwed motherhood, a badge which may haunt, if not deter, later legitimate family relationships.

Such a holding is, however, only the beginning of the problem. The State has interests to protect. Vaccinations to prevent epidemics are one example, as *Jacobson* holds. The Court held that compulsory sterilization of imbeciles afflicted with hereditary forms of insanity or imbecility is another. . . . Abortion affects another. While childbirth endangers the lives of some women, voluntary abortion at any time and place regardless of medical standards would impinge on a rightful concern of society. The woman's health is part of that concern; as is the life of the fetus after quickening. These concerns justify the State in treating the procedure as a medical one.

One difficulty is that this statute as construed and applied apparently does not give full sweep to the "psychological as well as physical well-being" of women patients which saved the concept "health" from being void for vagueness in United States v. Vuitch, *supra*, 402 U.S. at 72, 91 S.Ct. at 1299. But apart from that, Georgia's enactment has a constitutional infirmity because, as stated by the District Court, it "limits the number of reasons for which an abortion may be sought." I agree with the holding of the District Court, "This the State may not do, because such action unduly restricts a decision sheltered by the Constitutional right to privacy." . . .

The vicissitudes of life produce pregnancies which may be unwanted, or which may impair "health" in the broad *Vuitch* sense of the term, or which may imperil the life of the mother, or which in the full setting of the case may create such suffering, dislocations, misery, or tragedy as to make an early abortion the only civilized step to take. These hardships may be properly embraced in the "health" factor of the mother as appraised by a person of insight. Or they may be part of a broader medical judgment based on what is "appropriate" in a given case, though perhaps not "necessary" in a strict sense.

The "liberty" of the mother, though rooted as it is in the Constitution, may be qualified by the State for the reasons we have stated. But where fundamental personal rights and liberties are involved, the corrective legislation must be "narrowly drawn to prevent the supposed evil," . . . and not be dealt with in an "unlimited and indiscriminate" manner. . . . Unless regulatory measures are so confined and are addressed to the specific areas of compelling legislative concern, the police power would become the great leveller of constitutional rights and liberties.

There is no doubt that the State may require abortions to be performed by qualified medical personnel. The legitimate objective of preserving the mother's health clearly supports such laws. Their impact upon the woman's privacy is minimal. But the Georgia statute outlaws virtually all such operations—even in the earliest stages of pregnancy. In light of modern medical evidence suggesting that an early abortion is safer healthwise than childbirth itself,[16] it cannot be seriously urged that so comprehensive a ban is aimed at protecting the woman's health. Rather, this expansive proscription of all abortions along the temporal spectrum can rest only on a public goal of preserving both embryonic and fetal life.

The present statute has struck a balance between the woman and the State's interests wholly in favor of the latter. I am not prepared to hold that a State may equate, as Georgia has done, all phases of maturation preceding birth. We held in *Griswold* that the States may not preclude spouses from attempting to avoid the joinder of sperm and egg. If this is true, it is difficult to perceive any overriding public necessity which might attach precisely at the moment of conception. As Mr. Justice Clark has said: [17]

> To say that life is present at conception is to give recognition to the potential, rather than the actual. The unfertilized egg has life, and if

[16] Many studies show that it is safer for a woman to have a medically induced abortion than to bear a child. In the first 11 months of operation of the New York abortion law, the mortality rate associated with such operations was six per 100,000 operations. Abortion Mortality, 20 Morbidity and Mortality 208, 209 (1971) (U.S. Department of Health, Education, and Welfare, Public Health Service). On the other hand, the maternal mortality rate associated with childbirths other than abortions was 18 per 100,000 live births. Tietze, Mortality with Contraception and Induced Abortion, 45 Studies in Family Planning 6 (1969). See also C. Tietze & H. Lehfeldt, Legal Abortion in Eastern Europe 175 J.A.M.A. 1149, 1152 (1961); V. Kolblova, Legal Abortion in Czechoslovakia, 196 J.A.M.A. 371 (1966); Mehland, Combating Illegal Abortion in the Socialist Countries of Europe, 13 World Med.J. 84 (1966).

[17] Religion, Morality and Abortion: A Constitutional Appraisal, 2 Loy.U. (L.A.) L.Rev. 1, 10 (1969).

fertilized, it takes on human proportions. But the law deals in reality, not obscurity—the known rather than the unknown. When sperm meets egg, life may eventually form, but quite often it does not. The law does not deal in speculation. The phenomenon of life takes time to develop, and until it is actually present, it cannot be destroyed. Its interruption prior to formation would hardly be homicide, and as we have seen, society does not regard it as such. The rites of Baptism are not performed and death certificates are not required when a miscarriage occurs. No prosecutor has ever returned a murder indictment charging the taking of the life of a fetus.[18] This would not be the case if the fetus constituted human life.

In summary, the enactment is overbroad. It is not closely correlated to the aim of preserving pre-natal life. In fact, it permits its destruction in several cases, including pregnancies resulting from sex acts in which unmarried females are below the statutory age of consent. At the same time, however, the measure broadly proscribes aborting other pregnancies which may cause severe mental disorders. Additionally, the statute is overbroad because it equates the value of embryonic life immediately after conception with the worth of life immediately before birth.

Under the Georgia Act the mother's physician is not the sole judge as to whether the abortion should be performed. Two other licensed physicians must concur in his judgment. Moreover, the abortion must be performed in a licensed hospital; and the abortion must be approved in advance by a committee of the medical staff of that hospital.

Physicians, who speak to us in *Doe* through an *amicus* brief, complain of the Georgia Act's interference with their practice of their profession.

The right of privacy has no more conspicuous place than in the physician-patient relationship, unless it be in the priest-penitent relation.

It is one thing for a patient to agree that her physician may consult with another physician about her case. It is quite a different matter for the State compulsorily to impose on that physician-patient relationship another layer or, as in this case, still a third layer of physicians. The right of privacy—the right to care for one's health and person and to seek out a physician of one's own choice protected by the Fourteenth Amendment—becomes only a matter of theory not a reality, when a multiple physician approval system is mandated by the State.

The State licenses a physician. If he is derelict or faithless, the procedures available to punish him or to deprive him of his license are well

18 In Keeler v. Superior Court of Amador County, 2 Cal.3d 619, 87 Cal.Rptr. 481, 470 P.2d 617, the California Supreme Court held in 1970 that the California murder statute did not cover the killing of an unborn fetus, even though the fetus be "viable" and that it was beyond judicial power to extend the statute to the killing of an unborn. It held that the child must be "born alive before a charge of homicide can be sustained." 2 Cal.3d, at 639, 87 Cal.Rptr., at 494, 470 P2d, at 630.

known. He is entitled to procedural due process before professional disciplinary sanctions may be imposed. . . . Crucial here, however, is state-imposed control over the medical decision whether pregnancy should be interrupted. The good-faith decision of the patient's chosen physician is overridden and the final decision passed on to others in whose selection the patient has no part. This is a total destruction of the right of privacy between physician and patient and the intimacy of relation which that entails.

The right to seek advice on one's health and the right to place his reliance on the physician of his choice are basic to Fourteenth Amendment values. We deal with fundamental rights and liberties, which, as already noted, can be contained or controlled only by discretely drawn legislation that preserves the "liberty" and regulates only those phases of the problem of compelling legislative concern. The imposition by the State of group controls over the physician-patient relation is not made on any medical procedure apart from abortion, no matter how dangerous the medical step may be. The oversight imposed on the physician and patient in abortion cases denies them their "liberty," viz., their right of privacy, without any compelling, discernable state interest.

Georgia has constitutional warrant in treating abortion as a medical problem. To protect the woman's right of privacy, however, the control must be through the physician of her choice and the standards set for his performance.

The protection of the fetus when it has acquired life is a legitimate concern of the State. Georgia's law makes no rational, discernible decision on that score.[19] For under the Act the developmental stage of the fetus is irrelevant when pregnancy is the result of rape or when the fetus will very likely be born with a permanent defect or when a continuation of the pregnancy will endanger the life of the mother or permanently injure her health. When life is present is a question we do not try to resolve. While basically a question for medical experts, as stated by Mr. Justice Clark,[20] it is, of course, caught up in matters of religion and morality.

In short, I agree with the Court that endangering the life of the woman or seriously and permanently injuring her health are standards too narrow for the right of privacy that are at stake.

I also agree that the superstructure of medical supervision which Georgia has erected violates the patient's right of privacy inherent in her choice of her own physician.

· · ·

Mr. Justice White, with whom Mr. Justice Rehnquist joins, dissenting.

[19] See Rochat, Tyler, and Schoenbucher, An Epidemiological Analysis of Abortion in Georgia, 61 Am.J. of Public Health 541 (1971).
[20] Religion, Morality and Abortion: A Constitutional Appraisal, 2 Loy.U. (L.A.) L.Rev. 1, 10 (1969).

At the heart of the controversy in these cases are those recurring pregnancies that pose no danger whatsoever to the life or health of the mother but are nevertheless unwanted for any one or more of a variety of reasons—convenience, family planning, economics, dislike of children, the embarrassment of illegitimacy, etc., The common claim before us is that for any one of such reasons, or for no reason at all, and without asserting or claiming any threat to life or health, any woman is entitled to an abortion at her request if she is able to find a medical advisor willing to undertake the procedure.

The Court for the most part sustains this position: During the period prior to the time the fetus becomes viable, the Constitution of the United States values the convenience, whim or caprice of the putative mother more than the life or potential life of the fetus; the Constitution, therefore, guarantees the right to an abortion as against any state law or policy seeking to protect the fetus from an abortion not prompted by more compelling reasons of the mother.

With all due respect, I dissent. I find nothing in the language or history of the Constitution to support the Court's judgment. The Court simply fashions and announces a new constitutional right for pregnant mothers and, with scarcely any reason or authority for its action, invests that right with sufficient substance to override most existing state abortion statutes. The upshot is that the people and the legislatures of the 50 States are constitutionally disentitled to weigh the relative importance of the continued existence and development of the fetus on the one hand against a spectrum of possible impacts on the mother on the other hand. As an exercise of raw judicial power, the Court perhaps has authority to do what it does today; but in my view its judgment is an improvident and extravagant exercise of the power of judicial review which the Constitution extends to this Court.

The Court apparently values the convenience of the pregnant mother more than the continued existence and development of the life or potential life which she carries. Whether or not I might agree with that marshalling of values, I can in no event join the Court's judgment because I find no constitutional warrant for imposing such an order of priorities on the people and legislatures of the States. In a sensitive area such as this, involving as it does issues over which reasonable men may easily and heatedly differ, I cannot accept the Court's exercise of its clear power of choice by interposing a constitutional barrier to state efforts to protect human life and by investing mothers and doctors with the constitutionally protected right to exterminate it. This issue, for the most part, should be left with the people and to the political processes the people have devised to govern their affairs.

It is my view, therefore, that the Texas statute is not constitutionally infirm because it denies abortions to those who seek to serve only their convenience rather than to protect their life or health. Nor is this plaintiff,

who claims no threat to her mental or physical health, entitled to assert
the possible rights of those women whose pregnancy assertedly implicates
their health. This, together with United States v. Vuitch, 402 U.S. 62, 91
S.Ct. 1294, 28 L.Ed.2d 601 (1971), dictates reversal of the judgment of
the District Court.

Likewise, because Georgia may constitutionally forbid abortions to
putative mothers who, like the plaintiff in this case, do not fall within the
reach of § 26–1202(a) of its criminal code, I have no occasion, and the
District Court had none, to consider the constitutionality of the procedural requirements of the Georgia statute as applied to those pregnancies posing substantial hazards to either life or health. I would reverse the
judgment of the District Court in the Georgia case.

——————————————————— **JUDITH JARVIS THOMSON**

A Defense of Abortion[1]

Most opposition to abortion relies on the premise that the fetus is a
human being, a person, from the moment of conception. The premise is
argued for, but, as I think, not well. Take, for example, the most common
argument. We are asked to notice that the development of a human being
from conception through birth into childhood is continuous; then it is
said that to draw a line, to choose a point in this development and say
"before this point the thing is not a person, after this point it is a person"
is to make an arbitrary choice, a choice for which in the nature of things
no good reason can be given. It is concluded that the fetus is, or anyway
that we had better say it is, a person from the moment of conception. But
this conclusion does not follow. Similar things might be said about the
development of an acorn into an oak tree, and it does not follow that
acorns are oak trees, or that we had better say they are. Arguments of this
form are sometimes called "slippery slope arguments"—the phrase is perhaps self-explanatory—and it is dismaying that opponents of abortion rely
on them so heavily and uncritically.

I am inclined to agree, however, that the prospects for "drawing a
line" in the development of the fetus look dim. I am inclined to think

Reprinted from *Philosophy and Public Affairs*, Vol. 1, No. 1 (1971), 47–66.
Copyright © 1971 by Princeton University Press. Reprinted by permission of the
author and Princeton University Press.

[1] I am very much indebted to James Thomson for discussion, criticism, and many
helpful suggestions.

also that we shall probably have to agree that the fetus has already become a human person well before birth. Indeed, it comes as a surprise when one first learns how early in its life it begins to acquire human characteristics. By the tenth week, for example, it already has a face, arms and legs, fingers and toes; it has internal organs, and brain activity is detectable.[2] On the other hand, I think that the premise is false, that the fetus is not a person from the moment of conception. A newly fertilized ovum, a newly implanted clump of cells, is no more a person than an acorn is an oak tree. But I shall not discuss any of this. For it seems to me to be of great interest to ask what happens if, for the sake of argument, we allow the premise. How, precisely, are we supposed to get from there to the conclusion that abortion is morally impermissible? Opponents of abortion commonly spend most of their time establishing that the fetus is a person, and hardly any time explaining the step from there to the impermissibility of abortion. Perhaps they think the step too simple and obvious to require much comment. Or perhaps instead they are simply being economical in argument. Many of those who defend abortion rely on the premise that the fetus is not a person, but only a bit of tissue that will become a person at birth; and why pay out more arguments than you have to? Whatever the explanation, I suggest that the step they take is neither easy nor obvious, that it calls for closer examination than it is commonly given, and that when we do give it this closer examination we shall feel inclined to reject it.

I propose, then, that we grant that the fetus is a person from the moment of conception. How does the argument go from here? Something like this, I take it. Every person has a right to life. So the fetus has a right to life. No doubt the mother has a right to decide what shall happen in and to her body; everyone would grant that. But surely a person's right to life is stronger and more stringent than the mother's right to decide what happens in and to her body, and so outweighs it. So the fetus may not be killed; an abortion may not be performed.

It sounds plausible. But now let me ask you to imagine this. You wake up in the morning and find yourself back to back in bed with an unconscious violinist. A famous unconscious violinist. He has been found to have a fatal kidney ailment, and the Society of Music Lovers has canvassed all the available medical records and found that you alone have the right blood type to help. They have therefore kidnapped you, and last night the violinist's circulatory system was plugged into yours, so that your kidneys can be used to extract poisons from his blood as well

---

[2] Daniel Callahan, *Abortion: Law, Choice and Morality* (New York, 1970), p. 373. This book gives a fascinating survey of the available information on abortion. The Jewish tradition is surveyed in David M. Feldman, *Birth Control in Jewish Law* (New York, 1968), Part 5, the Catholic tradition in John T. Noonan, Jr., "An Almost Absolute Value in History," in *The Morality of Abortion*, ed. John T. Noonan, Jr. (Cambridge, Mass., 1970).

as your own. The director of the hospital now tells you, "Look, we're sorry the Society of Music Lovers did this to you—we would never have permitted it if we had known. But still, they did it, and the violinist now is plugged into you. To unplug you would be to kill him. But never mind, it's only for nine months. By then he will have recovered from his ailment, and can safely be unplugged from you." Is it morally incumbent on you to accede to this situation? No doubt it would be very nice of you if you did, a great kindness. But do you *have* to accede to it? What if it were not nine months, but nine years? Or longer still? What if the director of the hospital says, "Tough luck, I agree, but you've now got to stay in bed, with the violinist plugged into you, for the rest of your life. Because remember this. All persons have a right to life, and violinists are persons. Granted you have a right to decide what happens in and to your body, but a person's right to life outweighs your right to decide what happens in and to your body. So you cannot ever be unplugged from him." I imagine you would regard this as outrageous, which suggests that something really is wrong with that plausible-sounding argument I mentioned a moment ago.

In this case, of course, you were kidnapped; you didn't volunteer for the operation that plugged the violinist into your kidneys. Can those who oppose abortion on the ground I mentioned make an exception for a pregnancy due to rape? Certainly. They can say that persons have a right to life only if they didn't come into existence because of rape; or they can say that all persons have a right to life, but that some have less of a right to life than others, in particular, that those who came into existence because of rape have less. But these statements have a rather unpleasant sound. Surely the question of whether you have a right to life at all, or how much of it you have, shouldn't turn on the question of whether or not you are the product of a rape. And in fact the people who oppose abortion on the ground I mentioned do not make this distinction, and hence do not make an exception in case of rape.

Nor do they make an exception for a case in which the mother has to spend the nine months of her pregnancy in bed. They would agree that would be a great pity, and hard on the mother; but all the same, all persons have a right to life, the fetus is a person, and so on. I suspect, in fact, that they would not make an exception for a case in which, miraculously enough, the pregnancy went on for nine years, or even the rest of the mother's life.

Some won't even make an exception for a case in which continuation of the pregnancy is likely to shorten the mother's life; they regard abortion as impermissible even to save the mother's life. Such cases are nowadays very rare, and many opponents of abortion do not accept this extreme view. All the same, it is a good place to begin: a number of points of interest come out in respect to it.

1. Let us call the view that abortion is impermissible even to save

the mother's life "the extreme view." I want to suggest first that it does
not issue from the argument I mentioned earlier without the addition of
some fairly powerful premises. Suppose a woman has become pregnant,
and now learns that she has a cardiac condition such that she will die if
she carries the baby to term. What may be done for her? The fetus, being
a person, has a right to life, but as the mother is a person too, so has she
a right to life. Presumably they have an equal right to life. How is it
supposed to come out that an abortion may not be performed? If mother
and child have an equal right to life, shouldn't we perhaps flip a coin?
Or should we add to the mother's right to life her right to decide what
happens in and to her body, which everybody seems to be ready to grant
—the sum of her rights now outweighing the fetus' right to life?

The most familiar argument here is the following. We are told that
performing the abortion would be directly killing [3] the child, whereas
doing nothing would not be killing the mother, but only letting her die.
Moreover, in killing the child, one would be killing an innocent person,
for the child has committed no crime, and is not aiming at his mother's
death. And then there are a variety of ways in which this might be continued. (1) But as directly killing an innocent person is always and absolutely impermissible, an abortion may not be performed. Or, (2) as
directly killing an innocent person is murder, and murder is always and
absolutely impermissible, an abortion may not be performed.[4] Or, (3) as
one's duty to refrain from directly killing an innocent person is more
stringent than one's duty to keep a person from dying, an abortion may
not be performed. Or, (4) if one's only options are directly killing an
innocent person or letting a person die, one must prefer letting the person
die, and thus an abortion may not be performed.[5]

Some people seem to have thought that these are not further premises which must be added if the conclusion is to be reached, but that they

[3] The term "direct" in the arguments I refer to is a technical one. Roughly, what is
meant by "direct killing" is either killing as an end in itself, or killing as a means
to some end, for example, the end of saving someone else's life. See note 6, below,
for an example of its use.

[4] Cf. *Encyclical Letter of Pope Pius XI on Christian Marriage*, St. Paul Editions (Boston, n.d.), p. 32: "however much we may pity the mother whose health and
even life is gravely imperiled in the performance of the duty allotted to her by
nature, nevertheless what could ever be a sufficient reason for excusing in any way
the direct murder of the innocent? This is precisely what we are dealing with
here." Noonan (*The Morality of Abortion*, p. 43) reads this as follows: "What
cause can ever avail to excuse in any way the direct killing of the innocent? For
it is a question of that."

[5] The thesis in (4) is in an interesting way weaker than those in (1), (2), and (3):
they rule out abortion even in cases in which both mother *and* child will die if
the abortion is not performed. By contrast, one who held the view expressed in
(4) could consistently say that one needn't prefer letting two persons die to
killing one.

follow from the very fact that an innocent person has a right to life.[6] But this seems to me to be a mistake, and perhaps the simplest way to show this is to bring out that while we must certainly grant that innocent persons have a right to life, the theses in (1) through (4) are all false. Take (2), for example. If directly killing an innocent person is murder, and thus is impermissible, then the mother's directly killing the innocent person inside her is murder, and thus is impermissible. But it cannot seriously be thought to be murder if the mother performs an abortion on herself to save her life. It cannot seriously be said that she *must* refrain, that she *must* sit passively by and wait for her death. Let us look again at the case of you and the violinist. There you are, in bed with the violinist, and the director of the hospital says to you, "It's all most distressing, and I deeply sympathize, but you see this is putting an additional strain on your kidneys, and you'll be dead within the month. But you *have* to stay where you are all the same. Because unplugging you would be directly killing an innocent violinist, and that's murder, and that's impermissible." If anything in the world is true, it is that you do not commit murder, you do not do what is impermissible, if you reach around to your back and unplug yourself from that violinist to save your life.

The main focus of attention in writings on abortion has been on what a third party may or may not do in answer to a request from a woman for an abortion. This is in a way understandable. Things being as they are, there isn't much a woman can safely do to abort herself. So the question asked is what a third party may do, and what the mother may do, if it is mentioned at all, is deduced, almost as an afterthought, from what it is concluded that third parties may do. But it seems to me that to treat the matter in this way is to refuse to grant to the mother that very status of person which is so firmly insisted on for the fetus. For we cannot simply read off what a person may do from what a third party may do. Suppose you find yourself trapped in a tiny house with a growing child. I mean a very tiny house, and a rapidly growing child—you are already up against the wall of the house and in a few minutes you'll be crushed to death. The child on the other hand won't be crushed to death; if nothing is done to stop him from growing he'll be hurt, but in the end he'll simply burst open the house and walk out a free man. Now I could well understand it if a bystander were to say, "There's nothing

[6] Cf. the following passage from Pius XII, *Address to the Italian Catholic Society of Midwives*: "The baby in the maternal breast has the right to life immediately from God.—Hence there is no man, no human authority, no science, no medical, eugenic, social, economic or moral 'indication' which can establish or grant a valid juridical ground for a direct deliberate disposition of an innocent human life, that is a disposition which looks to its destruction either as an end or as a means to another end perhaps in itself not illicit.—The baby, still not born, is a man in the same degree and for the same reason as the mother" (quoted in Noonan, *The Morality of Abortion*, p. 45).

we can do for you. We cannot choose between your life and his, we cannot be the ones to decide who is to live, we cannot intervene." But it cannot be concluded that you too can do nothing, that you cannot attack it to save your life. However innocent the child may be, you do not have to wait passively while it crushes you to death. Perhaps a pregnant woman is vaguely felt to have the status of house, to which we don't allow the right of self-defense. But if the woman houses the child, it should be remembered that she is a person who houses it.

I should perhaps stop to say explicitly that I am not claiming that people have a right to do anything whatever to save their lives. I think, rather, that there are drastic limits to the right of self-defense. If someone threatens you with death unless you torture someone else to death, I think you have not the right, even to save your life, to do so. But the case under consideration here is very different. In our case there are only two people involved, one whose life is threatend, and one who threatens it. Both are innocent: the one who is threatened is not threatened because of any fault, the one who threatens does not threaten because of any fault. For this reason we may feel that we bystanders cannot intervene. But the person threatened can.

In sum, a woman surely can defend her life against the threat to it posed by the unborn child, even if doing so involves its death. And this shows not merely that the theses in (1) through (4) are false; it shows also that the extreme view of abortion is false, and so we need not canvass any other possible ways of arriving at it from the argument I mentioned at the outset.

2. The extreme view could of course be weakened to say that while abortion is permissible to save the mother's life, it may not be performed by a third party, but only by the mother herself. But this cannot be right either. For what we have to keep in mind is that the mother and the unborn child are not like two tenants in a small house which has, by an unfortunate mistake, been rented to both: the mother *owns* the house. The fact that she does adds to the offensiveness of deducing that the mother can do nothing from the supposition that third parties can do nothing. But it does more than this: it casts a bright light on the supposition that third parties can do nothing. Certainly it lets us see that a third party who says "I cannot choose between you" is fooling himself if he thinks this is impartiality. If Jones has found and fastened on a certain coat, which he needs to keep him from freezing, but which Smith also needs to keep him from freezing, then it is not impartiality that says "I cannot choose between you" when Smith owns the coat. Women have said again and again "This body is *my* body!" and they have reason to feel angry, reason to feel that it has been like shouting into the wind. Smith, after all, is hardly likely to bless us if we say to him, "Of course it's your coat, anybody would grant that it is. But no one may choose between you and Jones who is to have it."

We should really ask what it is that says "no one may choose" in the face of the fact that the body that houses the child is the mother's body. It may be simply a failure to appreciate this fact. But it may be something more interesting, namely the sense that one has a right to refuse to lay hands on people, even where it would be just and fair to do so, even where justice seems to require that somebody do so. Thus justice might call for somebody to get Smith's coat back from Jones, and yet you have a right to refuse to be the one to lay hands on Jones, a right to refuse to do physical violence to him. This, I think, must be granted. But then what should be said is not "no one may choose," but only "I cannot choose," and indeed not even this, but "I will not act," leaving it open that somebody else can or should, and in particular that anyone in a position of authority, with the job of securing people's rights, both can and should. So this is no difficulty. I have not been arguing that any given third party must accede to the mother's request that he perform an abortion to save her life, but only that he may.

I suppose that in some views of human life the mother's body is only on loan to her, the loan not being one which gives her any prior claim to it. One who held this view might well think it impartiality to say "I cannot choose." But I shall simply ignore this possibility. My own view is that if a human being has any just, prior claim to anything at all, he has a just, prior claim to his own body. And perhaps this needn't be argued for here anyway, since, as I mentioned, the arguments against abortion we are looking at do grant that the woman has a right to decide what happens in and to her body.

But although they do grant it, I have tried to show that they do not take seriously what is done in granting it. I suggest the same thing will reappear even more clearly when we turn away from cases in which the mother's life is at stake, and attend, as I propose we now do, to the vastly more common cases in which a woman wants an abortion for some less weighty reason than preserving her own life.

3. Where the mother's life is not at stake, the argument I mentioned at the outset seems to have a much stronger pull. "Everyone has a right to life, so the unborn person has a right to life." And isn't the child's right to life weightier than anything other than the mother's own right to life, which she might put forward as ground for an abortion?

This argument treats the right to life as if it were unproblematic. It is not, and this seems to me to be precisely the source of the mistake.

For we should now, at long last, ask what it comes to, to have a right to life. In some views having a right to life includes having a right to be given at least the bare minimum one needs for continued life. But suppose that what in fact *is* the bare minimum a man needs for continued life is something he has no right at all to be given? If I am sick unto death, and the only thing that will save my life is the touch of Henry Fonda's cool hand on my fevered brow, then all the same, I have no right to be given the touch of Henry Fonda's cool hand on my fevered brow. It would be frightfully nice of him to fly in from the West Coast to provide it. It would be less nice, though no doubt well meant, if my friends flew out to the West Coast and carried Henry Fonda back with them. But I have no right at all against anybody that he should do this for me. Or again, to return to the story I told earlier, the fact that for continued life that violinist needs the continued use of your kidneys does not establish that he has a right to be given the continued use of your kidneys. He certainly has no right against you that *you* should give him continued use of your kidneys. For nobody has any right to use your kidneys unless you give him such a right; and nobody has the right against you that you shall give him this right—if you do allow him to go on using your kidneys, this is a kindness on your part, and not something he can claim from you as his due. Nor has he any right against anybody else that *they* should give him continued use of your kidneys. Certainly he had no right against the Society of Music Lovers that they should plug him into you in the first place. And if you now start to unplug yourself, having learned that you will otherwise have to spend nine years in bed with him, there is nobody in the world who must try to prevent you, in order to see to it that he is given something he has a right to be given.

Some people are rather stricter about the right to life. In their view, it does not include the right to be given anything, but amounts to, and only to, the right not to be killed by anybody. But here a related difficulty arises. If everybody is to refrain from killing that violinist, then everybody must refrain from doing a great many different sorts of things. Everybody must refrain from slitting his throat, everybody must refrain from shooting him—and everybody must refrain from unplugging you from him. But does he have a right against everybody that they shall refrain from unplugging you from him? To refrain from doing this is to allow him to continue to use your kidneys. It could be argued that he has a right against us that *we* should allow him to continue to use your kidneys. That is, while he had no right against us that we should give him the use of your kidneys, it might be argued that he anyway has a right against us that we shall not now intervene and deprive him of the use of your kidneys. I shall come back to third-party interventions later. But certainly the violinist has no right against you that *you* shall allow him to continue to use your kidneys. As I said, if you do allow him to use them, it is a kindness on your part, and not something you owe him.

The difficulty I point to here is not peculiar to the right to life. It reappears in connection with all the other natural rights; and it is something which an adequate account of rights must deal with. For present purposes it is enough just to draw attention to it. But I would stress that I am not arguing that people do not have a right to life—quite to the contrary, it seems to me that the primary control we must place on the acceptability of an account of rights is that it should turn out in that account to be a truth that all persons have a right to life. I am arguing only that having a right to life does not guarantee having either a right to be given the use of or a right to be allowed continued use of another person's body—even if one needs it for life itself. So the right to life will not serve the opponents of abortion in the very simple and clear way in which they seem to have thought it would.

4. There is another way to bring out the difficulty. In the most ordinary sort of case, to deprive someone of what he has a right to is to treat him unjustly. Suppose a boy and his small brother are jointly given a box of chocolates for Christmas. If the older boy takes the box and refuses to give his brother any of the chocolates, he is unjust to him, for the brother has been given a right to half of them. But suppose that, having learned that otherwise it means nine years in bed with that violinist, you unplug yourself from him. You surely are not being unjust to him, for you gave him no right to use your kidneys, and no one else can have given him any such right. But we have to notice that in unplugging yourself, you are killing him; and violinists, like everybody else, have a right to life, and thus in the view we are considering just now, the right not to be killed. So here you do what he supposedly has a right you shall not do, but you do not act unjustly to him in doing it.

The emendation which may be made at this point is this: the right to life consists not in the right not to be killed, but rather in the right not to be killed unjustly. This runs a risk of circularity, but never mind: it would enable us to square the fact that the violinist has a right to life with the fact that you do not act unjustly toward him in unplugging yourself, thereby killing him. For if you do not kill him unjustly, you do not violate his right to life, and so it is no wonder you do him no injustice.

But if this emendation is accepted, the gap in the argument against abortion stares us plainly in the face: it is by no means enough to show that the fetus is a person, and to remind us that all persons have a right to life—we need to be shown also that killing the fetus violates its right to life, i.e., that abortion is unjust killing. And is it?

I suppose we may take it as a datum that in a case of pregnancy due to rape the mother has not given the unborn person a right to the use of her body for food and shelter. Indeed, in what pregnancy could it be supposed that the mother has given the unborn person such a right? It is not as if there were unborn persons drifting about the world, to whom a woman who wants a child says "I invite you in."

But it might be argued that there are other ways one can have acquired a right to the use of another person's body than by having been invited to use it by that person. Suppose a woman voluntarily indulges in intercourse, knowing of the chance it will issue in pregnancy, and then she does become pregnant; is she not in part responsible for the presence, in fact the very existence, of the unborn person inside her? No doubt she did not invite it in. But doesn't her partial responsibility for its being there itself give it a right to the use of her body? [7] If so, then her aborting it would be more like the boy's taking away the chocolates, and less like your unplugging yourself from the violinist—doing so would be depriving it of what it does have a right to, and thus would be doing it an injustice.

And then, too, it might be asked whether or not she can kill it even to save her own life: If she voluntarily called it into existence, how can she now kill it, even in self-defense?

The first thing to be said about this is that it is something new. Opponents of abortion have been so concerned to make out the independence of the fetus, in order to establish that it has a right to life, just as its mother does, that they have tended to overlook the possible support they might gain from making out that the fetus is *dependent* on the mother, in order to establish that she has a special kind of responsibility for it, a responsibility that gives it rights against her which are not possessed by any independent person—such as an ailing violinist who is a stranger to her.

On the other hand, this argument would give the unborn person a right to its mother's body only if her pregnancy resulted from a voluntary act, undertaken in full knowledge of the chance a pregnancy might result from it. It would leave out entirely the unborn person whose existence is due to rape. Pending the availability of some further argument, then, we would be left with the conclusion that unborn persons whose existence is due to rape have no right to the use of their mothers' bodies, and thus that aborting them is not depriving them of anything they have a right to and hence is not unjust killing.

And we should also notice that it is not at all plain that this argument really does go even as far as it purports to. For there are cases and cases, and the details make a difference. If the room is stuffy, and I therefore open a window to air it, and a burglar climbs in, it would be absurd to say, "Ah, now he can stay, she's given him a right to the use of her house—for she is partially responsible for his presence there, having voluntarily done what enabled him to get in, in full knowledge that there are such things as burglars, and that burglars burgle." It would be still more absurd to say this if I had had bars installed outside my windows, precisely to prevent burglars from getting in, and a burglar got in only because of a defect in the bars. It remains equally absurd if we imagine it is not a burglar who climbs in, but an innocent person who blunders or falls in. Again, suppose it were like this: people-seeds drift about in the air like pollen, and if you open your windows, one may drift in and take root in your carpets or upholstery. You don't want children, so you fix up your windows with fine mesh screens, the very best you can buy. As can happen,

---

[7] The need for a discussion of this argument was brought home to me by members of the Society for Ethical and Legal Philosophy, to whom this paper was originally presented.

however, and on very, very rare occasions does happen, one of the screens
is defective; and a seed drifts in and takes root. Does the person–plant
who now develops have a right to the use of your house? Surely not—
despite the fact that you voluntarily opened your windows, you knowingly
kept carpets and upholstered furniture, and you knew that screens were
sometimes defective. Someone may argue that you are responsible for its
rooting, that it does have a right to your house, because after all you
could have lived out your life with bare floors and furniture, or with
sealed windows and doors. But this won't do—for by the same token anyone can avoid a pregnancy due to rape by having a hysterectomy, or anyway by never leaving home without a (reliable!) army.

It seems to me that the argument we are looking at can establish at
most that there are *some* cases in which the unborn person has a right to
the use of its mother's body, and therefore *some* cases in which abortion
is unjust killing. There is room for much discussion and argument as to
precisely which, if any. But I think we should sidestep this issue and leave
it open, for at any rate the argument certainly does not establish that all
abortion is unjust killing.

5. There is room for yet another argument here, however. We surely
must all grant that there may be cases in which it would be morally indecent to detach a person from your body at the cost of his life. Suppose
you learn that what the violinist needs is not nine years of your life, but
only one hour: all you need do to save his life is to spend one hour in
that bed with him. Suppose also that letting him use your kidneys for that
one hour would not affect your health in the slightest. Admittedly you
were kidnapped. Admittedly you did not give anyone permission to plug
him into you. Nevertheless it seems to me plain you *ought* to allow him to
use your kidneys for that hour—it would be indecent to refuse.

Again, suppose pregnancy lasted only an hour, and constituted no
threat to life or health. And suppose that a woman becomes pregnant as
a result of rape. Admittedly she did not voluntarily do anything to bring
about the existence of a child. Admittedly she did nothing at all which
would give the unborn person a right to the use of her body. All the same
it might well be said, as in the newly emended violinist story, that she
ought to allow it to remain for that hour—that it would be indecent in
her to refuse.

Now some people are inclined to use the term "right" in such a way
that it follows from the fact that you ought to allow a person to use your
body for the hour he needs, that he has a right to use your body for the
hour he needs, even though he has not been given that right by any person
or act. They may say that it follows also that if you refuse, you act unjustly toward him. This use of the term is perhaps so common that it
cannot be called wrong; nevertheless it seems to me to be an unfortunate
loosening of what we would do better to keep a tight rein on. Suppose that
box of chocolates I mentioned earlier had not been given to both boys

jointly, but was given only to the older boy. There he sits, stolidly eating his way through the box, his small brother watching enviously. Here we are likely to say "You ought not to be so mean. You ought to give your brother some of those chocolates." My own view is that it just does not follow from the truth of this that the brother has any right to any of the chocolates. If the boy refuses to give his brother any, he is greedy, stingy, callous—but not unjust. I suppose that the people I have in mind will say it does follow that the brother has a right to some of the chocolates, and thus that the boy does act unjustly if he refuses to give his brother any. But the effect of saying this is to obscure what we should keep distinct, namely the difference between the boy's refusal in this case and the boy's refusal in the earlier case, in which the box was given to both boys jointly, and in which the small brother thus had what was from any point of view clear title to half.

A further objection to so using the term "right" that from the fact that A ought to do a thing for B, it follows that B has a right against A that A do it for him, is that it is going to make the question of whether or not a man has a right to a thing turn on how easy it is to provide him with it; and this seems not merely unfortunate, but morally unacceptable. Take the case of Henry Fonda again. I said earlier that I had no right to the touch of his cool hand on my fevered brow, even though I needed it to save my life. I said it would be frightfully nice of him to fly in from the West Coast to provide me with it, but that I had no right against him that he should do so. But suppose he isn't on the West Coast. Suppose he has only to walk across the room, place a hand briefly on my brow— and lo, my life is saved. Then surely he ought to do it, it would be in- decent to refuse. Is it to be said "Ah, well, it follows that in this case she has a right to the touch of his hand on her brow, and so it would be an injustice in him to refuse"? So that I have a right to it when it is easy for him to provide it, though no right when it's hard? It's rather a shocking idea that anyone's rights should fade away and disappear as it gets harder and harder to accord them to him.

So my own view is that even though you ought to let the violinist use your kidneys for the one hour he needs, we should not conclude that he has a right to do so—we would say that if you refuse, you are, like the boy who owns all the chocolates and will give none away, self-centered and callous, indecent in fact, but not unjust. And similarly, that even supposing a case in which a woman pregnant due to rape ought to allow the unborn person to use her body for the hour he needs, we should not conclude that he has a right to do so; we should conclude that she is self-centered, callous, indecent, but not unjust, if she refuses. The complaints are no less grave; they are just different. However, there is no need to insist on this point. If anyone does wish to deduce "he has a right" from "you ought," then all the same he must surely grant that there are cases in which it is not morally required of you that you allow that violinist to use your kidneys, and in which he does not have a right to use them, and in which you do not do him an injustice if you refuse. And so also for mother and unborn child. Except in such cases as the unborn person has a right to demand it—and we were leaving open the possibility that there may be such cases—nobody is morally *required* to make large sacrifices, of health, of all other interests and concerns, of all other duties and commitments, for nine years, or even for nine months, in order to keep another person alive.

6. We have in fact to distinguish between two kinds of Samaritan: the Good Samaritan and what we might call the Minimally Decent Samaritan. The story of the Good Samaritan, you will remember, goes like this:

> A certain man went down from Jerusalem to Jericho, and fell among thieves, which stripped him of his raiment, and wounded him, and departed, leaving him half dead.
>
> And by chance there came down a certain priest that way; and when he saw him, he passed by on the other side.
>
> And likewise a Levite, when he was at the place, came and looked on him, and passed by on the other side.
>
> But a certain Samaritan, as he journeyed, came where he was; and when he saw him he had compassion on him.
>
> And went to him, and bound up his wounds, pouring in oil and wine, and set him on his own beast, and brought him to an inn, and took care of him.
>
> And on the morrow, when he departed, he took out two pence, and gave them to the host, and said unto him, "Take care of him; and whatsoever thou spendest more, when I come again, I will repay thee."
>
> *(Luke 10:30–35)*

The Good Samaritan went out of his way, at some cost to himself, to help one in need of it. We are not told what the options were, that is, whether or not the priest and the Levite could have helped by doing less than the Good Samaritan did, but assuming they could have, then the fact they did nothing at all shows they were not even Minimally Decent Samaritans, not because they were not Samaritans, but because they were not even minimally decent.

These things are a matter of degree, of course, but there is a difference, and it comes out perhaps most clearly in the story of Kitty Genovese, who, as you will remember, was murdered while thirty-eight people watched or listened, and did nothing at all to help her. A Good Samaritan would have rushed out to give direct assistance against the murderer. Or perhaps we had better allow that it would have been a Splendid Samaritan who did this, on the ground that it would have involved a risk of death for himself. But the thirty-eight not only did not do this, they did not even trouble to pick up a phone to call the police. Minimally Decent Samaritanism would call for doing at least that, and their not having done it was monstrous.

After telling the story of the Good Samaritan, Jesus said "Go, and do thou likewise." Perhaps he meant that we are morally required to act as the Good Samaritan did. Perhaps he was urging people to do more than is morally required of them. At all events it seems plain that it was not morally required of any of the thirty-eight that he rush out to give direct assistance at the risk of his own life, and that it is not morally required of anyone that he give long stretches of his life—nine years or nine months—to sustaining the life of a person who has no special right (we were leaving open the possibility of this) to demand it.

Indeed, with one rather striking class of exceptions, no one in any country in the world is *legally* required to do anywhere near as much as this for anyone else. The class of exceptions is obvious. My main concern here is not the state of the law in respect to abortion, but it is worth drawing attention to the fact that in no state in this country is any man compelled by law to be even a Minimally Decent Samaritan to any person; there is no law under which charges could be brought against the thirty-eight who stood by while Kitty Genovese died. By contrast, in most states in this country women are compelled by law to be not merely Minimally Decent Samaritans, but Good Samaritans to unborn persons inside them. This doesn't by itself settle anything one way or the other, because it may well be argued that there should be laws in this country—as there are in many European countries—compelling at least Minimally Decent Samaritanism.[8] But it does show that there is a gross injustice in the existing state of the law. And it shows also that the groups currently working against liberalization of abortion laws, in fact working toward having it declared unconstitutional for a state to permit abortion, had better start working for the adoption of Good Samaritan laws generally, or earn the charge that they are acting in bad faith.

I should think, myself, that Minimally Decent Samaritan laws would be one thing, Good Samaritan laws quite another, and in fact highly improper. But we are not here concerned with the law. What we should ask is not whether anybody should be compelled by law to be a Good Samaritan, but whether we must accede to a situation in which somebody is being compelled—by nature, perhaps—to be a Good Samaritan. We have, in other words, to look now at third-party interventions. I have been arguing that no person is morally required to make large sacrifices to sustain the life of another who has no right to demand them, and this even where the sacrifices do not include life itself; we are not morally required to be Good Samaritans or anyway Very Good Samaritans to one another. But what if a man cannot extricate himself from such a situation? What if he appeals to us to extricate him? It seems to me plain that there are cases in which we can, cases in which a Good Samaritan would extricate him. There you are,

[8] For a discussion of the difficulties involved, and a survey of the European experience with such laws, see *The Good Samaritan and the Law*, ed. James M. Ratcliffe (New York, 1966).

you were kidnapped, and nine years in bed with that violinist lie ahead of you. You have your own life to lead. You are sorry, but you simply cannot see giving up so much of your life to the sustaining of his. You cannot extricate yourself, and ask us to do so. I should have thought that—in light of his having no right to the use of your body—it was obvious that we do not have to accede to your being forced to give up so much. We can do what you ask. There is no injustice to the violinist in our doing so.

7. Following the lead of the opponents of abortion, I have throughout been speaking of the fetus merely as a person, and what I have been asking is whether or not the argument we began with, which proceeds only from the fetus' being a person, really does establish its conclusion. I have argued that it does not.

But of course there are arguments and arguments, and it may be said that I have simply fastened on the wrong one. It may be said that what is important is not merely the fact that the fetus is a person, but that it is a person for whom the woman has a special kind of responsibility issuing from the fact that she is its mother. And it might be argued that all my analogies are therefore irrelevant—for you do not have that special kind of responsibility for that violinist, Henry Fonda does not have that special kind of responsibility for me. And our attention might be drawn to the fact that men and women both *are* compelled by law to provide support for their children.

I have in effect dealt (briefly) with this argument in section 4 above; but a (still briefer) recapitulation now may be in order. Surely we do not have any such "special responsibility" for a person unless we have assumed it, explicitly or implicitly. If a set of parents do not try to prevent pregnancy, do not obtain an abortion, and then at the time of birth of the child do not put it out for adoption, but rather take it home with them, then they have assumed responsibility for it, they have given it rights, and they cannot *now* withdraw support from it at the cost of its life because they now find it difficult to go on providing for it. But if they have taken all reasonable precautions against having a child, they do not simply by virtue of their biological relationship to the child who comes into existence have a special responsibility for it. They may wish to assume responsibility for it, or they may not wish to. And I am suggesting that if assuming responsibility for it would require large sacrifices, then they may refuse. A Good Samaritan would not refuse—or anyway, a Splendid Samaritan, if the sacrifices that had to be made were enormous. But then so would a Good Samaritan assume responsibility for that violinist; so would Henry Fonda, if he is a Good Samaritan, fly in from the West Coast and assume responsibility for me.

8. My argument will be found unsatisfactory on two counts by many of those who want to regard abortion as morally permissible. First, while I do argue that abortion is not impermissible, I do not argue that it is always permissible. There may well be cases in which carrying the child

to term requires only Minimally Decent Samaritanism of the mother, and this is a standard we must not fall below. I am inclined to think it a merit of my account precisely that it does *not* give a general yes or a general no. It allows for and supports our sense that, for example, a sick and desperately frightened fourteen-year-old schoolgirl, pregnant due to rape, may *of course* choose abortion, and that any law which rules this out is an insane law. And it also allows for and supports our sense that in other cases resort to abortion is even positively indecent. It would be indecent in the woman to request an abortion, and indecent in a doctor to perform it, if she is in her seventh month, and wants the abortion just to avoid the nuisance of postponing a trip abroad. The very fact that the arguments I have been drawing attention to treat all cases of abortion, or even all cases of abortion in which the mother's life is not at stake, as morally on a par ought to have made them suspect at the outset.

Secondly, while I am arguing for the permissibility of abortion in some cases, I am not arguing for the right to secure the death of the unborn child. It is easy to confuse these two things in that up to a certain point in the life of the fetus it is not able to survive outside the mother's body; hence removing it from her body guarantees its death. But they are importantly different. I have argued that you are not morally required to spend nine months in bed, sustaining the life of that violinist; but to say this is by no means to say that if, when you unplug yourself, there is a miracle and he survives, you then have a right to turn round and slit his throat. You may detach yourself even if this costs him his life; you have no right to be guaranteed his death, by some other means, if unplugging yourself does not kill him. There are some people who will feel dissatisfied by this feature of my argument. A woman may be utterly devastated by the thought of a child, a bit of herself, put out for adoption and never seen or heard of again. She may therefore want not merely that the child be detached from her, but more, that it die. Some opponents of abortion are inclined to regard this as beneath contempt—thereby showing insensitivity to what is surely a powerful source of despair. All the same, I agree that the desire for the child's death is not one which anybody may gratify, should it turn out to be possible to detach the child alive.

At this place, however, it should be remembered that we have only been pretending throughout that the fetus is a human being from the moment of conception. A very early abortion is surely not the killing of a person, and so is not dealt with by anything I have said here.

—————————————————————————————MARY ANNE WARREN

On the Moral and
Legal Status of Abortion

We will be concerned with both the moral status of abortion, which for
our purposes we may define as the act which a woman performs in voluntarily terminating, or allowing another person to terminate, her pregnancy,
and the legal status which is appropriate for this act. I will argue that,
while it is not possible to produce a satisfactory defense of a woman's right
to obtain an abortion without showing that a fetus is not a human being,
in the morally relevant sense of that term, we ought not to conclude that
the difficulties involved in determining whether or not a fetus is human
make it impossible to produce any satisfactory solution to the problem of
the moral status of abortion. For it is possible to show that, on the basis
of intuitions which we may expect even the opponents of abortion to
share, a fetus is not a person, and hence not the sort of entity to which it
is proper to ascribe full moral rights.

Of course, while some philosophers would deny the possibility of any
such proof,[1] others will deny that there is any need for it, since the moral
permissibility of abortion appears to them to be too obvious to require
proof. But the inadequacy of this attitude should be evident from the fact
that both the friends and the foes of abortion consider their position to be
morally self-evident. Because pro-abortionists have never adequately come
to grips with the conceptual issues surrounding abortion, most if not all, of
the arguments which they advance in opposition to laws restricting access
to abortion fail to refute or even weaken the traditional antiabortion argument, i.e., that a fetus is a human being, and therefore abortion is murder.

These arguments are typically of one of two sorts. Either they point
to the terrible side effects of the restrictive laws, e.g., the deaths due to
illegal abortions, and the fact that it is poor women who suffer the most
as a result of these laws, or else they state that to deny a woman access

Reprinted from *The Monist*, Volume 57, No. 1 (January 1973), 43–61, La
Salle, Illinois, with the permission of the publisher and the author. The "Postscript on Infanticide" by Mary Anne Warren was added especially for this
volume.

[1] For example, Roger Wertheimer, who in "Understanding the Abortion Argument"
(*Philosophy and Public Affairs*, 1, No. 1 [Fall, 1971], 67–95), argues that the
problem of the moral status of abortion is insoluble, in that the dispute over the
status of the fetus is not a question of fact at all, but only a question of how
one responds to the facts.

to abortion is to deprive her of her right to control her own body. Unfortunately, however, the fact that restricting access to abortion has tragic side effects does not, in itself, show that the restrictions are unjustified, since murder is wrong regardless of the consequences of prohibiting it; and the appeal to the right to control one's body, which is generally construed as a property right, is at best a rather feeble argument for the permissibility of abortion. Mere ownership does not give me the right to kill innocent people whom I find on my property, and indeed I am apt to be held responsible if such people injure themselves while on my property. It is equally unclear that I have any moral right to expel an innocent person from my property when I know that doing so will result in his death.

Furthermore, it is probably inappropriate to describe a woman's body as her property, since it seems natural to hold that a person is something distinct from her property, but not from her body. Even those who would object to the identification of a person with his body, or with the conjunction of his body and his mind, must admit that it would be very odd to describe, say, breaking a leg, as damaging one's property, and much more appropriate to describe it as injuring one*self*. Thus it is probably a mistake to argue that the right to obtain an abortion is in any way derived from the right to own and regulate property.

But however we wish to construe the right to abortion, we cannot hope to convince those who consider abortion a form of murder of the existence of any such right unless we are able to produce a clear and convincing refutation of the traditional antiabortion argument, and this has not, to my knowledge, been done. With respect to the two most vital issues which that argument involves, i.e., the humanity of the fetus and its implication for the moral status of abortion, confusion has prevailed on both sides of the dispute.

Thus, both proabortionists and antiabortionists have tended to abstract the question of whether abortion is wrong to that of whether it is wrong to destroy a fetus, just as though the rights of another person were not necessarily involved. This mistaken abstraction has led to the almost universal assumption that if a fetus is a human being, with a right to life, then it follows immediately that abortion is wrong (except perhaps when necessary to save the woman's life), and that it ought to be prohibited. It has also been generally assumed that unless the question about the status of the fetus is answered, the moral status of abortion cannot possibly be determined.

Two recent papers, one by B. A. Brody,[2] and one by Judith Thomson,[3] have attempted to settle the question of whether abortion ought to be prohibited apart from the question of whether or not the fetus is hu-

---

[2] B. A. Brody, "Abortion and the Law," *The Journal of Philosophy*, 68, No. 12 (June 17, 1971), 357–69.

[3] Judith Thomson, "A Defense of Abortion," *Philosophy and Public Affairs*, 1, No. 1 (Fall, 1971), 47–66.

man. Brody examines the possibility that the following two statements are compatible: (1) that abortion is the taking of innocent human life, and therefore wrong; and (2) that nevertheless it ought not to be prohibited by law, at least under the present circumstances.[4] Not surprisingly, Brody finds it impossible to reconcile these two statements, since, as he rightly argues, none of the unfortunate side effects of the prohibition of abortion is bad enough to justify legalizing the *wrongful* taking of human life. He is mistaken, however, in concluding that the incompatibility of (1) and (2), in itself, shows that "the legal problem about abortion cannot be resolved independently of the status of the fetus problem" (p. 369).

What Brody fails to realize is that (1) embodies the questionable assumption that if a fetus is a human being, then of course abortion is morally wrong, and that an attack on *this* assumption is more promising, as a way of reconciling the humanity of the fetus with the claim that laws prohibiting abortion are unjustified, than is an attack on the assumption that if abortion is the wrongful killing of innocent human beings then it ought to be prohibited. He thus overlooks the possibility that a fetus may have a right to life and abortion still be morally permissible, in that the right of a woman to terminate an unwanted pregnancy might override the right of the fetus to be kept alive. The immorality of abortion is no more demonstrated by the humanity of the fetus, in itself, than the immorality of killing in self-defense is demonstrated by the fact that the assailant is a human being. Neither is it demonstrated by the *innocence* of the fetus, since there may be situations in which the killing of innocent human beings is justified.

It is perhaps not surprising that Brody fails to spot this assumption, since it has been accepted with little or no argument by nearly everyone who has written on the morality of abortion. John Noonan is correct in saying that "the fundamental question in the long history of abortion is, How do you determine the humanity of a being?" [5] He summarizes his own antiabortion argument, which is a version of the official position of the Catholic Church, as follows:

> . . . it is wrong to kill humans, however poor, weak, defenseless, and lacking in opportunity to develop their potential they may be. It is therefore morally wrong to kill Biafrans. Similarly, it is morally wrong to kill embryos.[6]

Noonan bases his claim that fetuses are human upon what he calls the theologians' criterion of humanity: that whoever is conceived of human

---

[4] I have abbreviated these statements somewhat, but not in a way which affects the argument.

[5] John Noonan, "Abortion and the Catholic Church: A Summary History," *Natural Law Forum*, 12 (1967), 125.

[6] John Noonan, "Deciding Who is Human," *Natural Law Forum*, 13 (1968), 134.

beings is human. But although he argues at length for the appropriateness of this criterion, he never questions the assumption that if a fetus is human then abortion is wrong for exactly the same reason that murder is wrong.

Judith Thomson is, in fact, the only writer I am aware of who has seriously questioned this assumption; she has argued that, even if we grant the antiabortionist his claim that a fetus is a human being, with the same right to life as any other human being, we can still demonstrate that, in at least some and perhaps most cases, a woman is under no moral obligation to complete an unwanted pregnancy.[7] Her argument is worth examining, since if it holds up it may enable us to establish the moral permissibility of abortion without becoming involved in problems about what entitles an entity to be considered human, and accorded full moral rights. To be able to do this would be a great gain in the power and simplicity of the pro-abortion position, since, although I will argue that these problems can be solved at least as decisively as can any other moral problem, we should certainly be pleased to be able to avoid having to solve them as part of the justification of abortion.

On the other hand, even if Thomson's argument does not hold up, her insight, i.e., that it requires *argument* to show that if fetuses are human then abortion is properly classified as murder, is an extremely valuable one. The assumption she attacks is particularly invidious, for it amounts to the decision that it is appropriate, in deciding the moral status of abortion, to leave the rights of the pregnant woman out of consideration entirely, except possibly when her life is threatened. Obviously, this will not do; determining what moral rights, if any, a fetus possesses is only the first step in determining the moral status of abortion. Step two, which is at least equally essential, is finding a just solution to the conflict between whatever rights the fetus may have, and the rights of the woman who is unwillingly pregnant. While the historical error has been to pay far too little attention to the second step, Ms. Thomson's suggestion is that if we look at the second step first we may find that a woman has a right to obtain an abortion *regardless* of what rights the fetus has.

Our own inquiry will also have two stages. In Section I, we will consider whether or not it is possible to establish that abortion is morally permissible even on the assumption that a fetus is an entity with a full-fledged right to life. I will argue that in fact this cannot be established, at least not with the conclusiveness which is essential to our hopes of convincing those who are skeptical about the morality of abortion, and that we therefore cannot avoid dealing with the question of whether or not a fetus really does have the same right to life as a (more fully developed) human being.

In Section II, I will propose an answer to this question, namely, that a fetus cannot be considered a member of the moral community, the set of beings with full and equal moral rights, for the simple reason that it is not

[7] "A Defense of Abortion."

a person, and that it is personhood, and not genetic humanity, i.e., humanity as defined by Noonan, which is the basis for membership in this community. I will argue that a fetus, whatever its stage of development,
satisfies none of the basic criteria of personhood, and is not even enough
like a person to be accorded even some of the same rights on the basis of
this resemblance. Nor, as we will see, is a fetus's *potential* personhood a
threat to the morality of abortion, since, whatever the rights of potential
people may be, they are invariably overridden in any conflict with the
moral rights of actual people.

I

We turn now to Professor Thomson's case for the claim that even if a fetus
has full moral rights, abortion is still morally permissible, at least sometimes, and for some reasons other than to save the woman's life. Her argument is based upon a clever, but I think faulty, analogy. She asks us to
picture ourselves waking up one day, in bed with a famous violinist. Imagine that you have been kidnapped, and your bloodstream hooked up to
that of the violinist, who happens to have an ailment which will certainly
kill him unless he is permitted to share your kidneys for a period of nine
months. No one else can save him, since you alone have the right type of
blood. He will be unconscious all that time, and you will have to stay in
bed with him, but after the nine months are over he may be unplugged,
completely cured, that is provided that you have cooperated.

 Now then, she continues, what are your obligations in this situation?
The antiabortionist, if he is consistent, will have to say that you are obligated to stay in bed with the violinist: for all people have a right to life,
and violinists are people, and therefore it would be murder for you to dis-
connect yourself from him and let him die (p. 49). But this is outrageous,
and so there must be something wrong with the same argument when it is
applied to abortion. It would certainly be commendable of you to agree to
save the violinist, but it is absurd to suggest that your refusal to do so
would be murder. His right to life does not obligate you to do whatever is
required to keep him alive; nor does it justify anyone else in forcing you
to do so. A law which required you to stay in bed with the violinist would
clearly be an unjust law, since it is no proper function of the law to force
unwilling people to make huge sacrifices for the sake of other people
toward whom they have no such prior obligation.

 Thomson concludes that, if this analogy is an apt one, then we can
grant the antiabortionist his claim that a fetus is a human being, and still
hold that it is at least sometimes the case that a pregnant woman has the
right to refuse to be a Good Samaritan towards the fetus, i.e., to obtain an
abortion. For there is a great gap between the claim that *x* has a right to
life, and the claim that *y* is obligated to do whatever is necessary to keep *x*

alive, let alone that he ought to be forced to do so. It is y's duty to keep x alive only if he has somehow contracted a *special* obligation to do so; and a woman who is unwillingly pregnant, e.g., who was raped, has done nothing which obligates her to make the enormous sacrifice which is necessary to preserve the conceptus.

This argument is initially quite plausible, and in the extreme case of pregnancy due to rape it is probably conclusive. Difficulties arise, however, when we try to specify more exactly the range of cases in which abortion is clearly justifiable even on the assumption that the fetus is human. Professor Thomson considers it a virtue of her argument that it does not enable us to conclude that abortion is *always* permissible. It would, she says, be "indecent" for a woman in her seventh month to obtain an abortion just to avoid having to postpone a trip to Europe. On the other hand, her argument enables us to see that "a sick and desperately frightened schoolgirl pregnant due to rape may *of course* choose abortion, and that any law which rules this out is an insane law" (p. 65). So far, so good; but what are we to say about the woman who becomes pregnant not through rape but as a result of her own carelessness, or because of contraceptive failure, or who gets pregnant intentionally and then changes her mind about wanting a child? With respect to such cases, the violinist analogy is of much less use to the defender of the woman's right to obtain an abortion.

Indeed, the choice of a pregnancy due to rape, as an example of a case in which abortion is permissible even if a fetus is considered a human being, is extremely significant; for it is only in the case of pregnancy due to rape that the woman's situation is adequately analogous to the violinist case for our intuitions about the latter to transfer convincingly. The crucial difference between a pregnancy due to rape and the *normal* case of an unwanted pregnancy is that in the normal case we cannot claim that the woman is in no way responsible for her predicament; she could have remained chaste, or taken her pills more faithfully, or abstained on dangerous days, and so on. If, on the other hand, you are kidnapped by strangers, and hooked up to a strange violinist, then you are free of any shred of responsibility for the situation, on the basis of which it could be argued that you are obligated to keep the violinist alive. Only when her pregnancy is due to rape is a woman clearly just as nonresponsible.[8]

Consequently, there is room for the antiabortionist to argue that in the normal case of unwanted pregnancy a woman has, by her own actions, assumed responsibility for the fetus. For if x behaves in a way which he could have avoided, and which he knows involves, let us say, a 1 percent

---

[8] We may safely ignore the fact that she might have avoided getting raped, e.g., by carrying a gun, since by similar means you might likewise have avoided getting kidnapped, and in neither case does the victim's failure to take all possible precautions against a highly unlikely event (as opposed to reasonable precautions against a rather likely event) mean that he is morally responsible for what happens.

chance of bringing into existence a human being, with a right to life, and does so knowing that if this should happen then that human being will perish unless x does certain things to keep him alive, then it is by no means clear that when it does happen x is free of any obligation to what he knew in advance would be required to keep that human being alive.

The plausibility of such an argument is enough to show that the Thomson analogy can provide a clear and persuasive defense of a woman's right to obtain an abortion only with respect to those cases in which the woman is in no way responsible for her pregnancy, e.g., where it is due to rape. In all other cases, we would almost certainly conclude that it was necessary to look carefully at the particular circumstances in order to determine the extent of the woman's responsibility, and hence the extent of her obligation. This is an extremely unsatisfactory outcome, from the viewpoint of the opponents of restrictive abortion laws, most of whom are convinced that a woman has a right to obtain an abortion regardless of how and why she got pregnant.

Of course a supporter of the violinist analogy might point out that it is absurd to suggest that forgetting her pill one day might be sufficient to obligate a woman to complete an unwanted pregnancy. And indeed it *is* absurd to suggest this. As we will see, the moral right to obtain an abortion is not in the least dependent upon the extent to which the woman is responsible for her pregnancy. But unfortunately, once we allow the assumption that a fetus has full moral rights, we cannot avoid taking this absurd suggestion seriously. Perhaps we can make this point more clear by altering the violinist story just enough to make it more analogous to a normal unwanted pregnancy and less to a pregnancy due to rape, and then seeing whether it is still obvious that you are not obligated to stay in bed with the fellow.

Suppose, then, that violinists are peculiarly prone to the sort of illness the only cure for which is the use of someone else's bloodstream for nine months, and that because of this there has been formed a society of music lovers who agree that whenever a violinist is stricken they will draw lots and the loser will, by some means, be made the one and only person capable of saving him. Now then, would you be obligated to cooperate in curing the violinist if you had voluntarily joined this society, knowing the possible consequences, and then your name had been drawn and you had been kidnapped? Admittedly, you did not promise ahead of time that you would, but you did deliberately place yourself in a position in which it might happen that a human life would be lost if you did not. Surely this is at least a prima facie reason for supposing that you have an obligation to stay in bed with the violinist. Suppose that you had gotten your name drawn deliberately; surely *that* would be quite a strong reason for thinking that you had such an obligation.

It might be suggested that there is one important disanalogy between the modified violinist case and the case of an unwanted pregnancy, which makes the woman's responsibility significantly less, namely, the fact that the fetus *comes into existence* as the result of the result of the woman's actions. This fact might give her a right to refuse to keep it alive, whereas she would not have had this right had it existed previously, independently, and then as a result of her actions become dependent upon her for its survival.

My own intuition, however, is that x has no more right to bring into existence, either deliberately or as a foreseeable result of actions he could have avoided, a being with full moral rights (y), and then refuse to do what he knew beforehand would be required to keep that being alive, than he has to enter into an agreement with an existing person, whereby he may be called upon to save that person's life, and then refuse to do so when so called upon. Thus, x's responsibility for y's existence does not seem to lessen his obligation to keep y alive, if he is also responsible for y's being in a situation in which only he can save him.

Whether or not this intuition is entirely correct, it brings us back once again to the conclusion that once we allow the assumption that a fetus has full moral rights it becomes an extremely complex and difficult question whether and when abortion is justifiable. Thus the Thomson analogy cannot help us produce a clear and persuasive proof of the moral permissibility of abortion. Nor will the opponents of the restrictive laws thank us for anything less; for their conviction (for the most part) is that abortion is obviously *not* a morally serious and extremely unfortunate, even though sometimes justified act, comparable to killing in self-defense or to letting the violinist die, but rather is closer to being a morally neutral act, like cutting one's hair.

The basis of this conviction, I believe, is the realization that a fetus is not a person, and thus does not have a full-fledged right to life. Perhaps the reason why this claim has been so inadequately defended is that it seems self-evident to those who accept it. And so it is, insofar as it follows from what I take to be perfectly obvious claims about the nature of personhood, and about the proper grounds for ascribing moral rights, claims which ought, indeed, to be obvious to both the friends and foes of abortion. Nevertheless, it is worth examining these claims, and showing how they demonstrate the moral innocuousness of abortion, since this apparently has not been adequately done before.

II

The question which we must answer in order to produce a satisfactory solution to the problem of the moral status of abortion is this: How are we to define the moral community, the set of beings with full and equal moral rights, such that we can decide whether a human fetus is a member of this community or not? What sort of entity, exactly, has the inalienable rights to life, liberty, and the pursuit of happiness? Jefferson attributed these rights to all *men*, and it may or may not be fair to suggest that he intended to attribute them *only* to men. Perhaps he ought to have attributed them to all human beings. If so, then we arrive, first, at Noonan's problem of defining what makes a being human, and, second, at the equally vital question which Noonan does not consider, namely, What reason is there for identifying the moral community with the set of all human beings, in whatever way we have chosen to define that term?

1. On the Definition of 'Human'

One reason why this vital second question is so frequently overlooked in the debate over the moral status of abortion is that the term 'human' has two distinct, but not often distinguished, senses. This fact results in a slide of meaning, which serves to conceal the fallaciousness of the traditional argument that since (1) it is wrong to kill innocent human beings, and (2) fetuses are innocent human beings, then (3) it is wrong to kill fetuses. For if 'human' is used in the same sense in both (1) and (2) then, whichever of the two senses is meant, one of these premises is question-begging. And if it is used in two different senses then of course the conclusion doesn't follow.

Thus, (1) is a self-evident moral truth,[9] and avoids begging the question about abortion, only if 'human being' is used to mean something like 'a full-fledged member of the moral community.' (It may or may not also be meant to refer exclusively to members of the species *Homo sapiens*.) We may call this the *moral* sense of 'human.' It is not to be confused with what we will call the *genetic* sense, i.e., the sense in which *any* member of the species is a human being, and no member of any other species could be. If (1) is acceptable only if the moral sense is intended, (2) is non-question-begging only if what is intended is the genetic sense.

In "Deciding Who Is Human," Noonan argues for the classification of fetuses with human beings by pointing to the presence of the full genetic code, and the potential capacity for rational thought (p. 135). It is clear that what he needs to show, for his version of the traditional argument to be valid, is that fetuses are human in the moral sense, the sense in which it is analytically true that all human beings have full moral rights. But, in the absence of any argument showing that whatever is genetically human is also morally human, and he gives none, nothing more than genetic humanity can be demonstrated by the presence of the human genetic code. And, as we will see, the *potential* capacity for rational

---

[9] Of course, the principle that it is (always) wrong to kill innocent human beings is in need of many modifications, e.g., that it may be permissible to do so to save a greater number of other innocent human beings, but we may safely ignore these complications here.

thought can at most show that an entity has the potential for *becoming* human in the moral sense.

2. Defining the Moral Community

Can it be established that genetic humanity is sufficient for moral humanity? I think that there are very good reasons for not defining the moral community in this way. I would like to suggest an alternative way of defining the moral community, which I will argue for only to the extent of explaining why it is, or should be, self-evident. The suggestion is simply that the moral community consists of all and only *people*, rather than all and only human beings; [10] and probably the best way of demonstrating its self-evidence is by considering the concept of personhood, to see what sorts of entity are and are not persons, and what the decision that a being is or is not a person implies about its moral rights.

What characteristics entitle an entity to be considered a person? This is obviously not the place to attempt a complete analysis of the concept of personhood, but we do not need such a fully adequate analysis just to determine whether and why a fetus is or isn't a person. All we need is a rough and approximate list of the most basic criteria of personhood, and some idea of which, or how many, of these an entity must satisfy in order to properly be considered a person.

In searching for such criteria, it is useful to look beyond the set of people with whom we are acquainted, and ask how we would decide whether a totally alien being was a person or not. (For we have no right to assume that genetic humanity is necessary for personhood.) Imagine a space traveler who lands on an unknown planet and encounters a race of beings utterly unlike any he has ever seen or heard of. If he wants to be sure of behaving morally toward these beings, he has to somehow decide whether they are people, and hence have full moral rights, or whether they are the sort of thing which he need not feel guilty about treating as, for example, a source of food.

How should he go about making this decision? If he has some anthropological background, he might look for such things as religion, art, and the manufacturing of tools, weapons, or shelters, since these factors have been used to distinguish our human from our prehuman ancestors, in what seems to be closer to the moral than the genetic sense of 'human.' And no doubt he would be right to consider the presence of such factors as good evidence that the alien beings were people, and morally human. It would, however, be overly anthropocentric of him to take the absence of these things as adequate evidence that they were not, since we can

---

[10] From here on, we will use 'human' to mean genetically human, since the moral sense seems closely connected to, and perhaps derived from, the assumption that genetic humanity is sufficient for membership in the moral community.

imagine people who have progressed beyond, or evolved without ever developing, these cultural characteristics.

I suggest that the traits which are most central to the concept of personhood, or humanity in the moral sense, are, very roughly, the following:

1. consciousness (of objects and events external and/or internal to the being), and in particular the capacity to feel pain;
2. reasoning (the *developed* capacity to solve new and relatively complex problems);
3. self-motivated activity (activity which is relatively independent of either genetic or direct external control);
4. the capacity to communicate, by whatever means, messages of an indefinite variety of types, that is, not just with an indefinite number of possible contents, but on indefinitely many possible topics;
5. the presence of self-concepts, and self-awareness, either individual or racial, or both.

Admittedly, there are apt to be a great many problems involved in formulating precise definitions of these criteria, let alone in developing universally valid behavioral criteria for deciding when they apply. But I will assume that both we and our explorer know approximately what (1)–(5) mean, and that he is also able to determine whether or not they apply. How, then, should he use his findings to decide whether or not the alien beings are people? We needn't suppose that an entity must have *all* of these attributes to be properly considered a person; (1) and (2) alone may well be sufficient for personhood, and quite probably (1)–(3) are sufficient. Neither do we need to insist that any one of these criteria is *necessary* for personhood, although once again (1) and (2) look like fairly good candidates for necessary conditions, as does (3), if 'activity' is construed so as to include the activity of reasoning.

All we need to claim, to demonstrate that a fetus is not a person, is that any being which satisfies *none* of (1)–(5) is certainly not a person. I consider this claim to be so obvious that I think anyone who denied it, and claimed that a being which satisfied none of (1)–(5) was a person all the same, would thereby demonstrate that he had no notion at all of what a person is—perhaps because he had confused the concept of a person with that of genetic humanity. If the opponents of abortion were to deny the appropriateness of these five criteria, I do not know what further arguments would convince them. We would probably have to admit that our conceptual schemes were indeed irreconcilably different, and that our dispute could not be settled objectively.

I do not expect this to happen, however, since I think that the concept of a person is one which is very nearly universal (to people), and that it is common to both proabortionists and antiabortionists, even though neither group has fully realized the relevance of this concept to the resolution of their dispute. Furthermore, I think that on reflection even the antiabortionists ought to agree not only that (1)–(5) are central to the concept of personhood, but also that it is a part of this concept that all and only people have full moral rights. The concept of a person is in part a moral concept; once we have admitted that x is a person we have recognized, even if we have not agreed to respect, x's right to be treated as a member of the moral community. It is true that the claim that x is a *human being* is more commonly voiced as part of an appeal to treat x decently than is the claim that x is a person, but this is either because 'human being' is here used in the sense which implies personhood, or because the genetic and moral senses of 'human' have been confused.

Now if (1)–(5) are indeed the primary criteria of personhood, then it is clear that genetic humanity is neither necessary nor sufficient for establishing that an entity is a person. Some human beings are not people, and there may well be people who are not human beings. A man or woman whose consciousness has been permanently obliterated but who remains alive is a human being which is no longer a person; defective human beings, with no appreciable mental capacity, are not and presumably never will be people; and a fetus is a human being which is not yet a person, and which therefore cannot coherently be said to have full moral rights. Citizens of the next century should be prepared to recognize highly advanced, self-aware robots or computers, should such be developed, and intelligent inhabitants of other worlds, should such be found, as people in the fullest sense, and to respect their moral rights. But to ascribe full moral rights to an entity which is not a person is as absurd as to ascribe moral obligations and responsibilities to such an entity.

3. Fetal Development and the Right to Life

Two problems arise in the application of these suggestions for the definition of the moral community to the determination of the precise moral status of a human fetus. Given that the paradigm example of a person is a normal adult human being, then (1) How like this paradigm, in particular how far advanced since conception, does a human being need to be before it begins to have a right to life by virtue, not of being fully a person as of yet, but of being *like* a person? and (2) To what extent, if any, does the fact that a fetus has the *potential* for becoming a person endow it with some of the same rights? Each of these questions requires some comment.

In answering the first question, we need not attempt a detailed consideration of the moral rights of organisms which are not developed enough, aware enough, intelligent enough, etc., to be considered people, but which resemble people in some respects. It does seem reasonable to suggest that the more like a person, in the relevant respects, a being is, the stronger is the case for regarding it as having a right to life, and indeed the stronger its right to life is. Thus we ought to take seriously the suggestion that, insofar as "the human individual develops biologically in a continuous fashion . . . the rights of a human person might develop in the same way." [11] But we must keep in mind that the attributes which are relevant in determining whether or not an entity is enough like a person to be regarded as having some of the same moral rights are no different from those which are relevant to determining whether or not it is fully a person—i.e., are no different from (1)–(5)—and that being genetically human, or having recognizably human facial and other physical features, or detectable brain activity, or the capacity to survive outside the uterus, are simply not among these relevant attributes.

Thus it is clear that even though a seven- or eight-month fetus has features which make it apt to arouse in us almost the same powerful protective instinct as is commonly aroused by a small infant, nevertheless it is not significantly more personlike than is a very small embryo. It is *somewhat* more personlike; it can apparently feel and respond to pain, and it may even have a rudimentary form of consciousness, insofar as its brain is quite active. Nevertheless, it seems safe to say that it is not fully conscious, in the way that an infant of a few months is, and that it cannot reason, or communicate messages of indefinitely many sorts, does not engage in self-motivated activity, and has no self-awareness. Thus, in the *relevant* respects, a fetus, even a fully developed one, is considerably less personlike than is the average mature mammal, indeed the average fish. And I think that a rational person must conclude that if the right to life of a fetus is to be based upon its resemblance to a person, then it cannot be said to have any more right to life than, let us say, a newborn guppy (which also seems to be capable of feeling pain), and that a right of that magnitude could never override a woman's right to obtain an abortion, at any stage of her pregnancy.

There may, of course, be other arguments in favor of placing legal limits upon the stage of pregnancy in which an abortion may be performed. Given the relative safety of the new techniques of artificially inducing labor during the third trimester, the danger to the woman's life or health is no longer such an argument. Neither is the fact that people tend to respond to the thought of abortion in the later stages of pregnancy with emotional repulsion, since mere emotional responses cannot take the place of moral reasoning in determining what ought to be permitted. Nor, finally, is the frequently heard argument that legalizing abortion, especially late in the pregnancy, may erode the level of respect for human life, leading, perhaps, to an increase in unjustified euthanasia and other

11 Thomas L. Hayes, "A Biological View," *Commonweal*, 85 (March 17, 1967), 677–78; quoted by Daniel Callahan, in *Abortion, Law, Choice, and Morality* (London: Macmillan & Co., 1970).

crimes. For this threat, if it is a threat, can be better met by educating people to the kinds of moral distinctions which we are making here than by limiting access to abortion (which limitation may, in its disregard for the rights of women, be just as damaging to the level of respect for human rights).

Thus, since the fact that even a fully developed fetus is not person-like enough to have any significant right to life on the basis of its person-likeness shows that no legal restrictions upon the stage of pregnancy in which an abortion may be performed can be justified on the grounds that we should protect the rights of the older fetus; and since there is no other apparent justification for such restrictions, we may conclude that they are entirely unjustified. Whether or not it would be *indecent* (whatever that means) for a woman in her seventh month to obtain an abortion just to avoid having to postpone a trip to Europe, it would not, in itself, be *immoral*, and therefore it ought to be permitted.

4. Potential Personhood and the Right to Life

We have seen that a fetus does not resemble a person in any way which can support the claim that it has even some of the same rights. But what about its *potential*, the fact that if nurtured and allowed to develop naturally it will very probably become a person? Doesn't that alone give it at least some right to life? It is hard to deny that the fact that an entity is a potential person is a strong prima facie reason for not destroying it; but we need not conclude from this that a potential person has a right to life, by virtue of that potential. It may be that our feeling that it is better, other things being equal, not to destroy a potential person is better explained by the fact that potential people are still (felt to be) an invaluable resource, not to be lightly squandered. Surely, if every speck of dust were a potential person, we would be much less apt to conclude that every potential person has a right to become actual.

Still, we do not need to insist that a potential person has no right to life whatever. There may well be something immoral, and not just imprudent, about wantonly destroying potential people, when doing so isn't necessary to protect anyone's rights. But even if a potential person does have some prima facie right to life, such a right could not possibly outweigh the right of a woman to obtain an abortion, since the rights of any actual person invariably outweigh those of any potential person, whenever the two conflict. Since this may not be immediately obvious in the case of a human fetus, let us look at another case.

Suppose that our space explorer falls into the hands of an alien culture, whose scientists decide to create a few hundred thousand or more human beings, by breaking his body into its component cells, and using these to create fully developed human beings, with, of course, his genetic code. We may imagine that each of these newly created men will have all of the original man's abilities, skills, knowledge, and so on, and also have an individual self-concept, in short that each of them will be a bona fide (though hardly unique) person. Imagine that the whole project will take only seconds, and that its chances of success are extremely high, and that our explorer knows all of this, and also knows that these people will be treated fairly. I maintain that in such a situation he would have every right to escape if he could, and thus to deprive all of these potential people of their potential lives; for his right to life outweighs all of theirs together, in spite of the fact that they are all genetically human, all innocent, and all have a very high probability of becoming people very soon, if only he refrains from acting.

Indeed, I think he would have a right to escape even if it were not his life which the alien scientists planned to take, but only a year of his freedom, or, indeed, only a day. Nor would he be obligated to stay if he had gotten captured (thus bringing all these people-potentials into existence) because of his own carelessness, or even if he had done so deliberately, knowing the consequences. Regardless of how he got captured, he is not morally obligated to remain in captivity for *any* period of time for the sake of permitting any number of potential people to come into actuality, so great is the margin by which one actual person's right to liberty outweighs whatever right to life even a hundred thousand potential people have. And it seems reasonable to conclude that the rights of a woman will outweigh by a similar margin whatever right to life a fetus may have by virtue of its potential personhood.

Thus, neither a fetus's resemblance to a person, nor its potential for becoming a person provides any basis whatever for the claim that it has any significant right to life. Consequently, a woman's right to protect her health, happiness, freedom, and even her life,[12] by terminating an unwanted pregnancy, will always override whatever right to life it may be appropriate to ascribe to a fetus, even a fully developed one. And thus, in the absence of any overwhelming social need for every possible child, the laws which restrict the right to obtain an abortion, or limit the period of pregnancy during which an abortion may be performed, are a wholly unjustified violation of a woman's most basic moral and constitutional rights.[13]

Postscript on Infanticide

Since the publication of this article, many people have written to point out that my argument appears to justify not only abortion, but infanticide as well. For a new-born infant is not significantly more person-like than an advanced fetus, and consequently it would seem that if the destruction

---

[12] That is, insofar as the death rate, for the woman, is higher for childbirth than for early abortion.

[13] My thanks to the following people, who were kind enough to read and criticize an earlier version of this paper: Herbert Gold, Gene Glass, Anne Lauterbach, Judith Thomson, Mary Mothersill, and Timothy Binkley.

of the latter is permissible so too must be that of the former. Inasmuch as most people, regardless of how they feel about the morality of abortion, consider infanticide a form of murder, this might appear to represent a serious flaw in my argument.

Now, if I am right in holding that it is only people who have a full-fledged right to life, and who can be murdered, and if the criteria of personhood are as I have described them, then it obviously follows that killing a new-born infant isn't murder. It does *not* follow, however, that infanticide is permissible, for two reasons. In the first place, it would be wrong, at least in this country and in this period of history, and other things being equal, to kill a new-born infant, because even if its parents do not want it and would not suffer from its destruction, there are other people who would like to have it, and would, in all probability, be deprived of a great deal of pleasure by its destruction. Thus, infanticide is wrong for reasons analogous to those which make it wrong to wantonly destroy natural resources, or great works of art.

Secondly, most people, at least in this country, value infants and would much prefer that they be preserved, even if foster parents are not immediately available. Most of us would rather be taxed to support orphanages than allow unwanted infants to be destroyed. So long as there are people who want an infant preserved, and who are willing and able to provide the means of caring for it, under reasonably humane conditions, it is, *ceteris parabis*, wrong to destroy it.

But, it might be replied, if this argument shows that infanticide is wrong, at least at this time and in this country, doesn't it also show that abortion is wrong? After all, many people value fetuses, are disturbed by their destruction, and would much prefer that they be preserved, even at some cost to themselves. Furthermore, as a potential source of pleasure to some foster family, a fetus is just as valuable as an infant. There is, however, a crucial difference between the two cases: so long as the fetus is unborn, its preservation, contrary to the wishes of the pregnant woman, violates her rights to freedom, happiness, and self-determination. Her rights override the rights of those who would like the fetus preserved, just as if someone's life or limb is threatened by a wild animal, his right to protect himself by destroying the animal overrides the rights of those who would prefer that the animal not be harmed.

The minute the infant is born, however, its preservation no longer violates any of its mother's rights, even if she wants it destroyed, because she is free to put it up for adoption. Consequently, while the moment of birth does not mark any sharp discontinuity in the degree to which an infant possesses the right to life, it does mark the end of its mother's right to determine its fate. Indeed, if abortion could be performed without killing the fetus, she would never possess the right to have the fetus destroyed, for the same reasons that she has no right to have an infant destroyed.

On the other hand, it follows from my argument that when an unwanted or defective infant is born into a society which cannot afford and/or is not willing to care for it, then its destruction is permissible. This conclusion will, no doubt, strike many people as heartless and immoral; but remember that the very existence of people who feel this way, and who are willing and able to provide care for unwanted infants, is reason enough to conclude that they should be preserved.

RICHARD WERNER

Abortion: The Ontological and Moral Status of the Unborn

It is one of the ironies of history that the issues most in need of cool and dispassionate thinking for their resolution emerge during the course of human events at just those times when this is most difficult to achieve; notably during times of crisis, when emotions are running high and the fires of irrationalism are most likely to have been kindled.[1]

So it is with the abortion problem in contemporary American society. Often, when one is asked about the abortion issue, the inquirer is only interested in one's conclusions; rarely are good reasons considered relevant. The primary concern is, "Whose side are you on, are you with 'us' or are you one of 'them?'" Hence, we have the highly volatile, political character of the abortion issue in contemporary society.

In this paper, I will be attempting what several philosophers have attempted previously, namely, to give reasoned arguments to examine the moral issue of abortion. My concern will be with justification rather than motivation. Accordingly, my arguments will be philosophical rather than political. It is my hope, as unlikely as it may be, that in the end it will be justification rather than mere emotion or blind allegiance that will move us. It is to that end that my paper is directed.

I will argue the following points. First, one is a bona fide human

Reprinted from *Social Theory and Practice*, Vol. 3, No. 4 (1974), 201–222, with the permission of the author and the publisher. Revised by the author for this volume.

[1] R. L. Holmes, "Violence and Nonviolence," *Violence*, ed. J. Shaffer (New York: David McKay Co., 1971), p. 103.

being from the point of conception onward. Second, the position advanced by some philosophers, which bases full membership in the moral community on the criterion of personhood such that being a person entails having certain advanced conceptual capacities, is incapable of capturing our considered moral judgments concerning the moral treatment of nonperson humans. Thus, the criterion is defective. Third, being a sentient human being is the relevant criterion for being a fully fledged member of the moral community. Fourth, my arguments lead to the conclusion that abortion wrongs neither directly nor morally the nonsentient unborn, although it is sometimes morally bad. But after sentiency is attained by the fetus, in most actual and probable cases of pregnancy arising as the result of the actions of consenting adults and where the mother's life is not endangered, abortion is unjustifiable.

I

Before I begin to show that one is a human being from conception onward, I want to make the following observations. When I claim that the unborn are human beings, I am not merely stipulating what I will take the sign "human being" to mean, nor am I giving the results of a random sample poll conducted among ordinary language users. What I claim to show is that if you and I are paradigms of human beings, then there is every reason to believe and no good reason to deny that the unborn are also human. I intend to show that one cannot refuse to grant that the unborn are human without either (a) contradicting our present concept of a human being or (b) radically changing our present concept of a human being. I will show this by arguing that there are no relevant dissimilarities between us as human beings and the unborn as human beings. All proposed cut-off points in the development of the unborn will be shown to lead to unacceptable consequences and, as such, will be deemed arbitrary.

Additionally, in partial agreement with M. Tooley and M. A. Warren, I want to distinguish between a human being and a person. By "human being" I mean a bona fide member of the biological species Homo sapiens. By "person" I mean a fully fledged member of a human community, someone having a developed concept of self, memories, a language and/or moral obligations as well as moral rights (if one wants to keep the notion of a person morally neutral, then ignore this last criterion).

This distinction, I believe, saves us from arguing at cross-purposes in the abortion issue such as when one side means "person" when they claim that the unborn are not human and the other side means "human being" when they argue that the unborn are human. Disputes like this are common. Others have generated confusion concerning the abortion issue by failing to make this distinction, R. Wertheimer and R. M. Hare, for instance.[2] Further, the distinction allows us to speak first to those who believe that only persons have full moral rights and, then, to those adherents of abortion who want to deny that personhood is a necessary condition for having rights, all without begging the question against either side. Finally, the distinction itself does not beg any substantive questions concerning the abortion issue. That is, the distinction does not beg any questions its denial would not equally beg.

The justification for my proposed distinction is that it is useful in clarifying important issues and does so without begging any substantive questions. It saves us from engaging in purely verbal disputes by "dividing at the proper joints" as Plato would say. Simply put, the distinction is justified pragmatically; it is instrumental in clarifying or resolving some problem at hand. This is, I believe, the only legitimate justification for any philosophical distinction, e.g., the philosophical distinctions between inductive and deductive arguments, deontological and teleological theories of obligation, the subject and the object in perception.

Finally, if one finds one's ordinary language sensibilities stripped by my use of the words "human being" and "person," please substitute "human being$_1$," wherever the former appears and "human being$_2$," for the latter. It will not affect the outcome of my arguments in any way. My arguments are not parasitic upon any moral meanings of "person" or "human being," at least not in any illegitimate way.

Here is my argument:

1. An adult human being is the end result of the continuous growth of the organism from conception.
2. From conception to adulthood, there is no break in this development which is relevant to the ontological status of the organism.
3. If k is related to k' such that k is the end result of the continuous growth of the organism k' and there is no break in this growth which is relevant to the ontological status of the organism, then k' shares the same ontological status as does k.
4. Therefore, one is a human being from the point of conception onward.

OBJECTION A.   Certainly the most troublesome premise in this argument is 2. It assumes that if one is a human being at time $t + 1$, one must also have been human at time t (given that t is not prior in time to conception). Why accept this premise at all?

REPLY TO A.   Unless one has good reasons for believing that some significant change has occurred to a human being between t and $t + 1$,

---

[2] See my "Hare on Abortion," *Analysis*, 36, No. 1 (June 1976), 177–181, for an explanation and elaboration on this claim at least with regard to Hare.

there is no reason to believe that such an entity would have changed its ontological status. So, to support *Objection A* one needs to show that premise 2 is false. One must show that k had some significant characteristic(s) that made k a human being at time $t + 1$ but that k lacked at time t. In other words, one must be prepared to (i) give some nonarbitrary, non-ad hoc criterion for being human; and (ii) show that this criterion is not met by k at some time t but is met at time $t + 1$.

Let us consider some of the more popular attempts to provide such a necessary condition for being human. We will consider in turn each of the following conditions: (a) attainment of human form, (b) quickening or the achievement of spontaneous movement, (c) the achievement of consciousness as evidenced by an EEG, (d) viability, (e) birth.

Clearly, neither (a) nor (b) will do as necessary conditions since people who become severely disfigured and totally paralyzed are still considered human. Indeed, a disfigured or a paralyzed newborn is considered human even though failing to have attained these supposedly necessary conditions.

Condition (c), the ability to evidence an EEG, seems a more likely candidate than the first two. However, one's EEG may cease and then be revived some short time later after which one continues living one's normal life. Such entities are deemed human both during the lapse of the EEG and after its reappearance.

A more realistic attempt at a condition for being human is the following:

(c') k is a human being · only if · (c) *or* (k has been a human being before)

                & (k will have an EEG in the future)

Besides the fact that the addition of the clause "one has been a human being before" seems totally ad hoc (the only function it serves is to rule out embryos and fetuses as humans), (c') also has some rather undesirable consequences. For instance, if a doctor were working to revive the EEG of a patient and someone came into the room and shot the patient in the head, we could not say that the patient, qua human being, was killed by the gun shot wound. Since the patient neither had an EEG, nor would have one in the future, the patient would, by this criterion, have ceased to be a human being prior to the time of the gun shot. Also, even if someone never evidenced a human EEG but had all of the attributes we normally count as human—they looked and acted human, had a personality, could talk, think, remember, move about and so on—we would undoubtedly consider them human. Examples such as these show that there is neither a necessary nor a conceptual connection between EEGs and being human even though, in fact, the two may appear together most frequently.

Condition (d), viability or the ability to survive as an independent organism, is perhaps the most popular pro-abortionist position at the present time. The difficulty with this criterion is that it rules out as human the man on the heart-lung machine, the woman on the pace-maker, or the old person or baby who is totally dependent on others for their continued existence. In modern times it is more and more common for one to rely on some outside device or entity for one's continued existence. And, since the beginning of human life, some members of society have always been dependent on others for the continuance of their life. Yet condition (d) would be unable to account for the humanity of either of these groups.

Even if one were able to spell out the notion of viability in such a way as to capture the above groups but to exclude embryos and fetuses, perhaps by tacking on the notion of not being directly dependent on another human body for continued existence, it would still fall prey to the following sort of counterexample. In some cases of Siamese twins one member of the pair could be parted from his sibling and go on to live a normal life. However, the second twin is directly dependent on the first twin's body for his existence such that a separation would cause this second twin's death. Now this dependent twin is certainly not viable in any sense in which an embryo or fetus is not. Yet he is surely a human being. Hence, even the modified version of (d) lacks credibility as a criterion for being human.

Condition (e), birth, is totally arbitrary. There is no relevant biological, moral or conceptual difference between the newborn and the almost delivered fetus. The fact that during the last two months of pregnancy we could deliver the fetus at any time shows that birth is a totally ad hoc criterion for being human, since when birth occurs is totally arbitrary and even controllable by outside means.

Further, if it were possible to raise test-tube babies from the point of conception on, just what if anything would count as birth? Suppose in such cases it was necessary to keep the entity in an incubator six months longer than in the case of normal pregnancy, when then is birth? Suppose it was necessary to change the type of incubator every two weeks during this 15-month period, and then to return the child to a controlled environment every night for the first two years of life, when then is birth? Again the arbitrary nature of when birth occurs makes any attempt at drawing a line seem ludicrous.

Unless one is capable of providing a nonarbitrary, non-ad hoc necessary condition for being human that rules out embryos and fetuses as human, *Objection* A does not hold.

OBJECTION B.   One might hold that the concept of a human being has vague boundaries. During pregnancy the fetus gradually moves from a nonhuman state into a human one; there is a hazy period in pregnancy during which a fetus gradually becomes a human being.[3] One might defend this position by pointing out that the concept of a human being is so complex that the addition of no one property makes one human. So, the transformation into a human being is a gradual one, taking place over a period of time and requiring the addition of a cluster of properties.

REPLY TO B.   If we attempt something like the following, which makes the best possible cluster concept for the pro-abortionist given the properties we stated earlier, we still run into difficulties.

k is a human being · only if · (a) or (b) or (c) or (d) or (e)

One can imagine a severely disfigured, totally paralyzed, nonviable Siamese twin who was conceived and developed in a test tube and whose EEG has ceased during an operation but which will be revived in the next minute and who will then go on to live his life. We would still consider such a twin to be a human being even though he satisfies none of the above criteria.

Another possibility would be to attempt to construct a cluster concept out of the properties suggested by M. A. Warren.[4] Basically, these are the following: (f) consciousness, (g) reasoning ability, (h) self-motivated activity, (i) capacity to communicate, (j) presence of self-concepts. This then, would give us the following sort of analysis.

k is a human being · only if · (f) or (g) or (h) or (i) or (j)

First, it should be noted, according to this criterion a perfectly normal six-month-old child would fail to be human. However, such a child is counted as human by everyone save, perhaps, adherents of infanticide. If this is incapable of convincing the reader, one can easily imagine a society where suspended animation had been developed to a very high degree of sophistication. In this society people could be instantly frozen and then, years later, slowly revived over a two-year period. Further, while in this state of suspended animation, the frozen entity would have none of the properties (f) through (j). Nevertheless, after going through the two-year revitalization period, one's normal bodily functions and abilities would be restored. It is clear that during the state of suspended animation, one would still be a human being. For instance, if someone entered the frozen room housing the bodies and in full possession of his wits, willfully began to destroy the bodies, we would certainly hold him responsible for murder. These frozen persons show that even Warren's list of properties cannot provide the foundation for a cluster concept for being human.

[3] M. A. Warren, "On the Moral and Legal Status of Abortion," *The Monist*, 57, No. 1 (January 1973), 43–61 and reprinted in *Today's Moral Problems*, 2nd ed., Richard Wasserstrom, ed. (New York: Macmillan Publishing Co., Inc., 1979), 35–51, with an added postcript. Following page references will be to the latter publication.
[4] Warren, 45.

Like the proponents of *Objection A*, those of *Objection B* must be able to give some nonarbitrary, non-ad hoc criteria for being human and then show that a fetus or embryo fails to satisfy them at time *t*, but does satisfy them at time $t + 1$. In neither case can I see any way of carrying that out.

Furthermore, one can agree that the concept of human being, like most interesting notions, is indeed a cluster concept, but deny that fetuses and embryos fall within the hazy boundaries of the concept. For instance, if monkeys throughout the world began giving birth to creatures that looked and behaved much more like humans than monkeys, then we may well be perplexed as to whether these entities were human. Cases like these illustrate the unclear boundaries of the concept of a human being rather than cases like embryos and fetuses.

OBJECTION C.   One can construct an argument of exactly the same form as the one I constructed in sec. I, but which would yield the absurd conclusion that if a zygote is a human being, then gametes are human beings and always have been. Such a conclusion illustrates the perversity of using a "slippery slope" type of argument to deal with the complex concept of a human being. Just as an acorn is not an oak, an embryo is not a human.[5]

REPLY TO C.   The difficulty with the argument proposed in *Objection C* is that it must assume that conception is an irrelevant change in genetic human development. But unlike the fetus immediately prior to birth and the baby immediately afterward, there is a significant and important difference between the ovum or sperm immediately before fertilization and the zygote immediately afterward. Given the proper environment the embryo, qua itself, is a growing, developing organism. All things being equal, the zygote will grow into a person. On the other hand, the ovum or sperm qua itself is neither growing nor developing no matter in what sort of environment one should find it or put it into. A gamete will not, by itself, grow into anything other than what it already is—a gamete. In this sense it is inert and, thereby, nonhuman. A necessary condition of the ovum becoming human is that it begin to grow and develop into a person, that it be fertilized by a sperm cell. Otherwise, it remains inert, never developing or growing into anything whatever and, as such, is no more a human being than is one of my red blood cells. Admittedly an acorn is not an oak, nor is an ovum or sperm cell a human, but an acorn germinated in the soil is indeed an oak and so is the impregnated ovum a human.[6]

[5] This point is J. J. Thomson's objection to the type of argument I have presented. "A Defense of Abortion," *Philosophy and Public Affairs* 1, No. 1 (Fall 1977), 47–66.

[6] See J. Finnis, "The Rights and Wrongs of Abortion," *Philosophy and Public Affairs* 2, No. 2 (Winter 1973), 144–156, who uses a similar line of argument and the same analogy as the one I have presented.

In addition, the zygote is the beginning of the spatiotemporal identity of the creature we call a human being. Clearly, any two separate biological units are at least numerically distinct and, accordingly, could not be the same human. We simply are not the sorts of creatures that can be divided over space and time into distinct biological units, such as ovum and sperm are, with all disjoints remaining one and the same human being. Prior to conception there simply is nothing that could count as a *single* growing and developing human being. The zygote is the first link in the spatiotemporal chain of identity we know as a human being.[7]

Basically what my original argument comes to is the following:

k is a human being · *iff* · k belongs to a spatiotemporal chain of identity m such that m is an instance of at least a portion of the archetypal human spatiotemporal chain of identity l.

l is the archetypal human spatiotemporal chain of identity · *iff* · l is that spatiotemporal chain of identity some portion of which is commonly recognized as being paradigmatic of belonging to the human species *and* the rest of the chain l is such that there is no break in the chain l which is relevant to the human ontological status of the organism.

The following diagram illustrates what I mean.

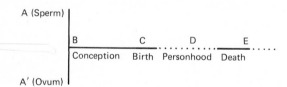

Now, clearly, C through E is that portion of the archetypal spatiotemporal chain of identity that is commonly recognized as being paradigmatic of belonging to the human species. Further, A and A' through B fail to be portions of the archetypal human spatiotemporal chain of identity because (a) prior to conception the characteristic humanness of the chain, evidenced by the growing developing nature of the human organism from B through E, is lacking, (b) the chain of identity breaks down at B since, prior to that moment, there is no single organism that k might be. My rejection of other proposed cutoff points is taken as evidence that the archetypal chain of identity extends as far back as B, that there is no break in the chain from B onward that is relevant to the human

---

[7] See R. Wertheimer, "Understanding the Abortion Argument," *Philosophy and Public Affairs* 1, No. 1 (Fall 1971), 67–95, who uses a similar line of argument to the one I have presented.

ontological status of the organism. So, the archetypal human chain of identity would be constituted by B through E. All that is needed for my criterion to hold is that k evidence some chain of identity m such that m exemplifies at least a portion of this archetypal human chain of identity l.[8]

J. Narveson has proposed two types of counterexamples to my proposed analysis. First,

> Now, suppose that we have a particular embryo which is aborted. Does Werner intend that his embryo be accounted a human being by his definition, or doesn't he? Prima facie, he oughtn't. For this embryo does not belong to such a continuum. There are no later stages, from birth to death, in the spatiotemporal entity in question: it never gets that far. So, prima facie, it is not a human being. . . .[9]

My rewording of my originally proposed analysis of a human being clears up this point rather nicely. An aborted embryo is human at the time of the abortion if it belongs to a spatiotemporal chain of identity that is an instance of at least a portion of the *archetypal* (and not merely the paradigmatic) human spatiotemporal chain that extends from conception to death. A normal human embryo meets this condition even if it is eventually aborted.

Second,

> . . . consider what would be said by a proponent of Werner's position about an embryo, apparently normal in all respects, which unhappily does not turn into a paradigmatic human being but instead into a zombie or humanoid, lacking consciousness, personality, moral capacities, and so on.[10]

A human embryo that becomes a zombie or humanoid rather than a person evidences a spatiotemporal chain of identity that, at some point in its development, departed from being an instance of the archetypal human spatiotemporal chain. The zombie's or humanoid's spatiotemporal chain would not be an instance of a portion of the archetypal one from that time at which it became a zombie or a humanoid. Hence, by my proposed analysis, it would cease to be human at that time at which it became nonhuman.

With the case of the zombie, Narveson also raises the question of how do we *know* that the human embryo is indeed human and won't develop into a zombie? [11] My answer is that we know it in the same way

[8] Now that we have answered C we can return to an objection similar to B. One might claim that my arguments are like those which use mathematical induction to show that one cannot draw a clear line between being bald and not and, hence, no one could ever become bald. Unlike the baldness argument, however, we have drawn a clear and sharp line and have given arguments to show why this is the relevant cut-off point. Unlike the baldness argument, our argument is neither slippery nor sophistic.

[9] J. Narveson, "Semantics, Future Generations, and the Abortion Problem: Comments on a Fallacious Case Against the Morality of Abortion," *Social Theory and Practice*, 3, No. 4 (Fall 1975), 478.

[10] Narveson, 479.

[11] Narveson, 479.

we *know* that you or I won't turn into zombies, rabbits, or washing machines. That is, we have every reason to believe that a normal human embryo will develop in accord with the archetypal spatiotemporal chain and no good reason to doubt it. Likewise with you, myself, and our development. If we have evidence to the contrary in the case of the embryo or ourselves, then perhaps we have good reason to believe that it or us is not human.

OBJECTION D.   It might be charged that all that I have done is to focus on one single aspect of the abortion issue. That is, the strong similarities between each set of successive stages of fetal development are singled out for consideration. The pro-abortionist, on the other hand, points to the gross differences between widely separated stages of development.

> The arguments are equally strong and equally weak, for they are the *same* argument, an argument that can be pointed in either of two directions . . . If you are led in one direction rather than the other, that is not because of logic, but because you respond in a certain way to certain facts.[12]

REPLY TO D.   As a matter of logic, one can construct a valid argument as we have done, from the strong similarities between each set of successive stages of human development. But when one turns to the gross differences between widely separated stages, there is no valid argument form to be found. Just as one can point to a zygote and a full-grown adult human and say "See, they are *so* different they cannot possibly both be human beings belonging to the same species," so one can point to a guppy in an aquarium and a sting ray in the ocean and say "See, they are *so* different they cannot both be fish." But of course both organisms *are* fish just as both the zygote and adult *are* human. The argument Wertheimer attributes to the pro-abortionist is no argument at all. As a matter of logic, it is vacuous. The fact that both the pro- and anti-abortionist can agree on all the same facts and still disagree on their conclusions to the abortion issue, does not show that the abortion question is insolvable. What it does show is that at least one of the parties is involved in a case of faulty reasoning, just as we have found.

II

In the previous section I tried to establish only that one is human from the point of conception onward. In this section I will be concerned with one particular type of argument that has been advanced to establish the morality of abortion. Proponents of this position claim or hold positions that entail that the morally relevant stage in human development begins

[12] Wertheimer, p. 85. This objection is one of the main points of Wertheimer's article.

when one realizes the status of personhood. This type of argument has taken several forms and I will explain each briefly in turn.

First, M. A. Warren holds that the concept of a person is in part a *moral* concept; to be recognized as a person is, *eo ipso*, to be recognized as an entity who is a fully fledged member of the moral community, having all of the rights such membership entails. Having at least one of the characteristics (f) through (j) (mentioned earlier) is a necessary condition of being a person. On the other hand, the concept of a human being in the biological sense is not a moral concept. Hence, simply being human entitles one to no moral rights or considerations. However, other persons may have an interest in having children who are unwanted by their natural parents or an interest in not having their moral sensibilities shocked by infanticide. Infanticide is wrong for reasons analogous to those which make it wrong to wantonly destroy natural resources or great works of art. So long as there are people who want an infant preserved, and who are willing and able to provide the means to care for it, it is wrong to destroy it. Other persons' interest in the unborn does not, however, render abortion wrong. The rights of the mother to freedom, happiness, and self-determination plus the unborn's dependence on the mother override other's interests.[13]

Second, M. Tooley holds that one has a right to life if there is some time at which one is or will be capable of wishing that one had such a right and at which time one *would* so wish if one had all of the relevant information and had not been subjected to influences that distorted one's preferences. Only the unborn and future generations who will have an actual existence as persons have rights and can be wronged.[14]

Third, J. Narveson holds that the reason it is wrong to kill innocent human being V is because V values or desires V's continued existence. Accordingly, at least in the case of persons in Tooley's sense, having values or desires is a necessary condition for a person to have a right not to be killed. Clearly, fetuses lack values and desires of the appropriate sort since they are conceptually incapable of either valuing or desiring to lead a full life. Narveson argues that in the case of the unborn, it is the values or desires of its mother or appropriate parent(s) that are the relevant factor in deciding whether the act of abortion should be performed. Although Narveson does not apply this reasoning to infants, it seems clear where his arguments would lead. Small infants are as conceptually incapable as a fetus of valuing their existence or desiring to lead a full life. As such, the values and desires of the child's parents or those interested in adopting or providing support for the child are the relevant factor in deciding whether the act of infanticide should be performed. As with Warren, the

---

13 Warren, 44–51.

14 M. Tooley, "Abortion and Infanticide," *Philosophy and Public Affairs*, 2, No. 1 (Fall 1971), 37–65. Also, "Michael Tooley Replies," *Philosophy and Public Affairs*, 2, No. 4 (Summer 1973), 419–432.

child or the unborn *itself* is due neither moral rights nor moral consideration since it lacks the characteristics necessary for such consideration.[15]

There is one type of counterexample that I believe demonstrates the
unacceptable consequences of adopting any of the three positions sketched
previously. Let us imagine a society that accepts that full moral rights and
amenability to moral consideration applies only to persons in the senses
prescribed by Warren or Tooley or to humans with values or desires as
prescribed by Narveson. Let us suppose further that in such a society no
one desires or has an interest in stepping in as parents, trustees, or guardians for infants and the unborn. Such a society could legitimately declare
a national open hunting season on infant orphans and other unwanted
nonpersons such as the grossly retarded or insane. They could develop a
new gourmet delight "roast unwanted infant." They could begin to establish farms such that one buys live abortuses, raises them for food, experimentation, or sport. They could take such young children raised from live
abortuses, perform brain operations on them so as to ensure that they will
never develop characteristics (f) through (j) or desires or values of the
appropriate sort and then use them as pets, servants, slaves, lab animals,
and so on. Indeed, it seems that we could not rule out the wanton killing
of or medical experimentation upon infants, severely retarded humans,
the extremely mentally ill, certain possible future generations and all other
nonperson humans.

One might attempt to discount all of this by appealing to Warren's
notion of the rights of actually existing persons not to have their values
defamed by such goings on, or by bringing in J. Feinberg's notion of
guardians or trustees who represent the interests of such beings. [16] But,
by hypothesis, in our example these considerations are irrelevant. Further,
even if we drop the requirement in our example that states that there are
no guardians or morally shocked people available, we can, I believe, take
an ideal observer's view, ignore any violations of the rights of actually
existing persons, and *still* we would find such activities as I have just
described morally repugnant and wrong. What this shows is that it is these
human creatures who are being *directly* wronged rather than the mere
indirect harm to some trustee or other person. They, the nonperson humans, ought not to be so treated *because of who they are* and regardless

---

[15] Narveson, 461–485.

[16] J. Feinberg, "Is There a Right To Be Born?" *Understanding Moral Philosophy*, ed.
James Rachels (Enrico and Belmont California: Dickenson Publishing Co., Inc.:
1976), 346–357. The counterexample used here would also apply to Feinberg's
analysis. At least the last part of the counterexample would also be telling against
L. S. Carrier, "Abortion and the Right to Life," *Social Theory and Practice*, 3,
No. 4 (Fall 1975), 381–401, who holds that ". . . an individual who possesses
both consciousness *and the potentiality for a heightened consciousness* does have
a distinctive right to life." (My emphasis) Carrier, 397. And, "where there is no
right to life, then—all else being equal—there is no moral case to be made
against abortion as such. . . ." Carrier, 381.

of how others' senses are shocked and so on. Neither of the three positions sketched earlier can account for this fact.

Narveson's point that abortion is allowed and widely practiced in North America and elsewhere, yet people still raise children with love, dedication, and enthusiasm, at best provides cold comfort for the non-person humans in our example. My concern is with what a moral theory actually entails and not with the inconsistency of actual practices. If one adopts the position that a necessary condition of x having a right to A is x's valuing or desiring such a right or x's having one or more of character-istics (f) through (j), then one's position entails that none of the afore-mentioned beings in our imaginary society has rights in and of himself. One has adopted a moral theory that, at least in instances where no actual person's values or desires are frustrated, cannot disallow as immoral the practices I have sketched.

Similarly unhelpful is Narveson's point that to deny that x has a right to life is not the same as saying we may do anything we like to x. One could kill or alter all of the creatures in question in a painless and kind manner, one could then treat them with kindness and care, again not causing them pain (perhaps even destroying their capacity for pain in the original alterations), and still, I would think, we would find such killings or alterations morally repugnant. The real question is: Do the human creatures of which I just wrote have *the right* not to be so treated? If one admits that *for their own sake* they ought morally not to be so treated, and ought morally not to be so treated even when no actual person's values or desires are frustrated, then I do not see how one can deny that they, qua themselves, have the right not to be so treated. And this is, after all, the question at issue. I believe that my example shows rather conclusively that we cannot capture our considered moral judg-ments concerning the treatment of nonperson humans by granting rights only to persons or only to humans with the appropriate values and desires. Accordingly, the three positions sketched all derive from defective moral theories.

III

In this section I will argue that being a sentient human being is the relevant criterion for being a fully fledged member of the moral commu-nity, for having full moral rights and obligations compatible with the stage of one's development. Let me begin by arguing that sentiency is a neces-sary condition for a creature to have any rights. My thinking on this issue is expressed well by W. K. Frankena.

> . . . we do not have any moral obligations, prima facie or actual, to do anything that does not, directly or indirectly, have some connection with what makes somebody's life good or bad, better or worse. . . . To say

this is to say not only that we have no obligations except when some improvement or impairment of someone's life is involved but also that we have a prima facie obligation *whenever* this is involved.[17]

. . .

Reflecting on the . . . intrinsic values myself, I come to the following conclusions. It seems to me that . . . it is the *experience* of them that is good in itself.[18]

Simply put, one cannot make a creature's life good or bad, better or worse unless that creature is capable of experiencing and, in particular, capable of experiencing pleasure, satisfaction, happiness, pain, dissatisfaction, or anguish. One cannot help or harm another creature unless that creature is capable of help or harm, capable of having experiences consonant with help or harm. Clearly, a creature that has no experiences is not capable of having experiences consonant with helping or harming the creature. If the creature is destroyed before it becomes sentient, appeal to the better or worse condition of its future experiences is irrelevant. Hence, one cannot have moral obligations to a being that is not sentient and will not become sentient and, thereby, such a being cannot have moral rights.

In the case of a being that is not yet sentient but will become sentient, certainly we can help or harm this being by an action we perform today that will affect the future experiences of the being. However, it would seem that our moral obligations are not to the nonsentient being that now exists. So, a being would not have rights until it became sentient. Let me explain. Suppose that person A, purely out of malice and for no good reason, sets a death trap for person B's future child C, who is not yet conceived. Suppose further that C will be a normal human being and that the trap will not be effected until C's eighteenth birthday. We shall imagine that the trap will be effective and that it kills C on his eighteenth birthday. Now, clearly, A has harmed C directly and ought morally not to have done so. Yet A did not wrong an existent C when he set the trap, for, at that time, C did not exist. Setting the trap was wrong and primarily at least, it was wrong because of what it would do to C on his eighteenth birthday. At the time of setting the trap, A violated his moral obligations to the future C, to the future sentient C. It was the future sentient C's rights that were violated. Hence, one can, through a present act, violate the rights of a future being that does not yet exist, assuming that the being will exist. It seems, then, perfectly reasonable to assume that the same type of reasoning would apply to presently nonsentient beings who will become sentient. Our present action may violate the future sentient being's rights but not the rights of the present nonsentient being since it has no rights. Also, if we grant rights to nonsentient beings

---

[17] W. K. Frankena, *Ethics*, 2nd ed. (Englewood Cliffs, New Jersey: Prentice-Hall Inc.: 1973), 44–45.
[18] Frankena, 89.

who will become sentient but not to nonsentient beings who will never attain sentiency, we will allow situations that are both contradictory and unjust. Imagine D and E who, at time t, are both nonsentient and also identical in all relevant respects. Suppose that D will be aborted prior to sentiency while E will survive to personhood. If we grant rights to non-sentient beings who will become sentient but not to nonsentient beings who will not become sentient, then at time t, E has rights but D does not, even though E and D are identical in all relevant respects at time t. Quite obviously, parity of reason is contradicted by granting rights to non-sentient beings who will become sentient but not to nonsentient beings who will never attain sentiency. Also, a necessary condition for any legitimate theory of justice has been denied, namely, that similar cases are to be treated similarly. Hence, justice is denied. For these reasons, it seems to me that we should not grant rights directly to nonsentient beings who will become sentient. Sentiency is a necessary condition for having rights.

In addition, it seems that being a sentient human is a sufficient condition for being a fully fledged member of the moral community. My reasoning is that if we choose some other criterion, such as being a person in one of the previous three senses discussed or being a human with one or more of the characteristics discussed in sec. I, we are led to refrain from granting full moral rights to humans whom we normally deem worthy of such consideration. I believe that my previous examples establish this fact. In other words, I believe that sentiency is the weakest criterion capable of capturing our considered moral judgments concerning which humans are fully fledged members of the moral community.

I refrain from making sentient humanness a necessary condition of being a fully fledged member of the moral community on the grounds that if we found that porpoises or whales had a sophisticated consciousness, language, moral insight, personalities, and so on, we might include them as full moral entities. Likewise with nonhuman alien life forms or sophisticated robots.

Also, I should point out that being a sentient human does not presuppose that one is sentient all of the time. It does presuppose either that one is now sentient or that one has been sentient in the past and would be sentient in the future, *ceteris paribus*. One can be a healthy human being even though one is not always healthy, e.g., one could be a healthy human even though one is now experiencing one's first cold in twenty years. Similar examples can be given of being a wise, happy, or kind human. In each of these cases one is the x-kind of human because one has had the characteristic x most frequently in the past and would go on to exhibit this same characteristic, other things being equal. That is, assuming that the individual does not die, is not killed, or greatly physically or psychologically impaired in the meantime. This same pattern of analysis is true of the human characteristic of sentiency. One is a sentient human if one is now sentient or one has been sentient in the past and would be so in the future, *ceteris paribus,* i.e., assuming that one does not die, is not killed, and is not greatly physically or psychologically impaired in the meantime. This analysis of sentiency can handle the type of counterexamples I posed earlier to the claim that consciousness or some highbred version of consciousness is a necessary condition of being human. One can be a sentient human, according to the present analysis, even if one's sentiency is gappy rather than a smooth-flowing stream.

At this point, one might object that my criterion for being a sentient human is indeed the criterion for being human. This, I believe, would be a mistake. One can be a dead human as opposed to a live human, and dead humans are one sort of human who lack sentiency or the capacity for sentiency given the present technological state of society. Given that one is still a human being when one is a dead human, being sentient is not a necessary condition for being human.

One might also argue that humans prior to sentiency are potentially sentient and, accordingly, should be fully fledged members of the moral community. However, the very notion of potentiality is a very vague and nefarious one. A single sperm cell or ovum is also a potentially sentient human; yet I doubt we want to grant full moral rights and give full moral consideration to each sperm and ovum, particularly if it entails seeing each one realize its potential as an actually existing sentient human. Moreover, if cloning is technologically possible, each and every one of each and every individual's cells may be a potentially sentient human. I doubt very much that we want to grant full membership to each and every human cell in the universe. But reliance upon the notion of potentiality would seem to commit us to such an absurd conclusion. This is sufficient to show that reliance upon the notion of potentiality leads us quickly to a *reductio ad absurdum.*

One cautionary note: To say that nonsentient humans do not have moral rights and are not fully fledged members of the moral community, is not to say that they are not in any way due moral consideration. If our present action will, in a good or bad way, affect the future experiences of a presently nonsentient human, then we may be violating the creature's future rights. Clearly, this is worthy of moral consideration. Also, an individual human life, even nonsentient, is intrinsically valuable in the same way as the environment or great works of art. Hence, the destruction of a nonsentient human life, the environment, or a great work of art is bad in itself and, all things being equal, worthy of avoidance. Even though we have no direct moral obligations to nonsentient humans, the environment, or great works of art, their destruction is an evil worthy of avoidance and, consequently, due moral consideration.

This fact explains why many women, even some feminists, find early abortions upsetting and even anguishing. It is also why many people find the raping of the environment by modern industrial society or the wanton destruction of great books and works of art by the Nazis or similar groups

such evil acts. There is something intrinsically valuable about each of these entities even though they themselves lack rights and are not due any moral obligations directly.

Further, the intrinsic value of a human life, sentient or otherwise, explains why the sort of counterexample I used in sec. II could not be turned against my position. To wantonly defame human lives in the way the example requires would be like wantonly defaming the environment or great works of art. This is wrong morally, *ceteris paribus*, whether or not any existing people have an interest in the intrinsic value of these entities, since future generations, when they become existing persons, may have an interest in and value these entities which have long since been destroyed. We are obligated morally not to violate the future rights of these individuals given that the entities in question are intrinsically good. Furthermore, in agreement with Plato, Aristotle, John Dewey, and W. K. Frankena,[19] I hold that x is good just in case x would be found to be desirable upon rational reflection. Consequently, I hold that rational inquirers would concur that human life, nature, and great art are all desirable both for their own sake and because of what they accomplish and, accordingly, that they are intrinsically good. Lastly, it would be necessary to render the nonsentient humans permanently nonsentient, which would, I believe, make them very poor objects for experimentation, sport, or slavery. A totally nonsentient human simply could not function in the ways required for the example to go through.

So, then, my central points in this section have been that being a sentient human is a sufficient condition for being a fully fledged member of the moral community, while being sentient is a necessary condition for a human to be such a member. In the next section, I will go on to develop the consequences of the arguments of the first three sections for the morality of abortion.

IV

Given that prior to sentiency, which the best science of the time places at between 8 to 10 weeks of pregnancy,[20] we have no moral obligations directly to the unborn, abortions during these early stages would not morally wrong the unborn. Even though other persons may place a high intrinsic value on such nonsentient humans, the preservation of the un-

---

[19] Frankena, 87–92.

[20] Although very little is now known about the mental life of the unborn, the brain is functioning at 6 weeks and there is some reason to believe that at between 8 and 10 weeks the first feelings or experiences are had by the fetus. It should be pointed out that at present there is great difficulty in establishing the beginnings of sentiency in the fetus and further investigation, both conceptual and empirical, is required.

born contrary to the wishes of the pregnant woman violates her rights to freedom, self-determination, and, in particular, her right to choose and pursue her own life plan. A parallel case would be a situation where the preservation of a section of the environment, a forest for instance, threatens to endanger the rights of its owner to freedom and self-determination. For example, in order to finance his career goals he may need the money obtainable by chopping down and selling the forest. Clearly his rights to freedom and self-determination override the rights of others who would prefer that the forest be maintained because of its intrinsic value, particularly if the others are unwilling or unable to purchase the forest from the owner. The owner, then, would be justified morally in chopping down and selling the forest for profit. Hence, considerations of the intrinsic value of a human life, given that we have no moral obligations directly to the nonsentient unborn, would not be great enough to override the rights of the mother.

However, abortion in and of itself would always be the destruction of an intrinsic value, a human life. It just so happens that given the physical connection between the mother and the unborn, it is a lesser of two evils when the mother desires an abortion. My claim is based on the mother's rights to freedom and self-determination and the fact that we have no moral obligations directly to the nonsentient unborn. Indeed, we may count a woman who willfully became pregnant and then had an early abortion so that she could be in the "in-group" who had had abortions, as insensitive, cruel, and callous—perhaps even as an evil person. But I do not see how we could count her as morally wronging the nonsentient fetus, since the nonsentient fetus is not yet capable of being harmed or wronged.[21]

On the other hand, a college student who obtains an early abortion to terminate an unwanted pregnancy so that she might continue to pursue her future plans to become a lawyer without a possibly dangerous interruption to these plans, may be seen as a woman caught between a rock and a hard place. She must choose between her own future life plans and the life of a nonsentient human. In such a case, I believe, an early abortion is not morally wrong, nor is it callous, cruel, or indicative of an evil personality. An abortion in such a situation would be morally justifiable as well as morally permissible. It is making the best of a bad situation, given that the pregnancy might have been avoided by proper birth-control methods or even by abstinence on the particular occasion. Such a person deserves our support in obtaining an abortion, even our help, but I doubt that she deserves moral praise for her action.

[21] I do believe, however, that the woman in our example was morally wrong to willfully become pregnant for the sole purpose of obtaining an abortion. But she is wrong because she violated the rights of others who value human life, not because of a violation of the rights of the unborn. This is similar to someone who purchases a great work of art or a particularly valuable part of the environment for the sole purpose of destroying it.

In order to examine cases of the abortion of a sentient fetus, I would like first to discuss the complex issue of the justifiable killing of a sentient human. In so doing, I will be borrowing heavily from Onora O'Neill's excellent analysis of this issue.[22] I will assume that each sentient human has a basic prima facie right not to be killed as well as a corresponding obligation not to kill other sentient humans. I will also assume that this rights and its corresponding obligation are among the weightiest and most fundamental rights and obligations anyone can have.

As O'Neill points out, there seems to be two general types of justifiable killings. The first of these is the case of unavoidable killings. These occur in situations where a person doing some act causes some death(s) that could not have been avoided. A death as a result of an automobile accident where neither party is morally at fault would be an example of an unavoidable killing.

The second type of justifiable killing, and the one most interesting for our purposes, is the case of self-defense. The right of self-defense is a corollary of the right not to be killed; it is a right to take action to prevent killings.

> If I have a right not to be killed then I have a right to prevent others from endangering my life, though I may endanger their lives in so doing only if that is the only available way to prevent the danger to my own life. Similarly if another has the right not to be killed then I should, if possible, do something to prevent others from endangering his life, but I may endanger their lives in so doing only if that is the only available way to prevent danger to his life.[23]

. . .

> The right not to be killed . . . is a right to take action against others who endanger our lives whether or not they do so intentionally. A's right not to be killed entitles him to take action not only against aggressors but also against those "innocent threats" who endanger lives without being aggressors.[24]

I take it that this characterization of justifiable killings sketches the standard of minimumly decent behavior and that pacifism of whatever degree or kind would be consistent with the right of self-defense.[25] Indeed, it may be that pacifism is the morally best behavior, the most ideal behavior morally. But, I believe, it would be expecting too much of humanity to equate minimal decency with ideal moral behavior.

[22] Onora O'Neill, "Lifeboat Earth," *Philosophy and Public Affairs*, 4, No. 3 (Spring 1975), 273–292.

[23] O'Neill, 274.

[24] O'Neill, 275.

[25] On this point I believe that I diverge from O'Neill's analysis. She holds that "this duty to defend others is not a general duty of beneficence but a very restricted duty to enforce others' rights not to be killed." O'Neill, 274.

With this characterization of the justifiable killing of sentient humans, I will go on next to deal with some specific cases of the morality of the abortion of sentient fetuses. Given a normal unwanted pregnancy, which is having no calamitous effects such as endangering other people's lives, one's basic prima facie obligation not to take the life of a sentient human is not overridden. Such a situation presents us neither with an unavoidable killing nor with an act of self-defense. Hence, aborting the sentient unborn in such a case would be an instance of an unjustified killing and, thereby, would be morally wrong.

In such a circumstance both partners, when they engaged in intercourse, knew that the foreseeable and natural consequences of their actions was a pregnancy. Just as a man who goes into his backyard to fire his gun, knowing full well that the consequences of his actions may result in the death of some innocent person, is indeed responsible if he kills someone no matter how much he may have desired not to do so, so are the two responsible if they cause an unwanted pregnancy. Even if the two take the best possible precautions against pregnancy, they still know or are accountable for knowing that these precautions are not 100 per cent effective and that the foreseeable and natural consequences of their actions may still be an unwanted pregnancy. So, by engaging in intercourse, they are responsible for and obligated to accept the consequences of their actions. This situation is analogous to that of a man who derives great satisfaction from taking target practice with his gun. Unfortunately, he lives in a very crowded community; so he builds the most elaborately protective shooting range possible in the basement of his home. He is, nevertheless, aware that it is only 99 per cent effective in stopping bullets and that the use of the range could eventually result in the death of some innocent human. But, because of the great satisfaction he derives, he begins firing his gun in the basement anyway. Now if this man eventually kills someone, surely he is morally responsible for their death. In firing the gun he knew that one of the foreseeable and natural consequences of his actions may be the killing of an innocent human. Like the two engaging in intercourse, this man has created a special obligation through his actions, they by engaging in intercourse, he by firing his gun in a crowed community.[26] Or, to quote M. A. Warren:

> . . . x has no moral right to bring into existence, either deliberately or as a foreseeable result of actions which he could have avoided, a being with full moral rights (y), and then refuse to do what he knew beforehand would be required to keep that being alive, than he has to enter

[26] W. D. Ross, *The Right and the Good* (Oxford: Oxford University Press: 1930), 27, points out that a "special obligation" is an implicit promise we make through "modes of behavior in which without explicit verbal promise we intentionally create an expectation that we can be counted on to behave in a certain way in the interests of another person."

into an agreement with an existing person, whereby he may be called upon to save that person's life, and then refuse to do so when called upon.[27]

J. J. Thomson attempts to provide two counterexamples to the type of claim I have just made.[28] I will consider each in turn. If a room is stuffy, and x opens a window which allows a burglar to enter, it is absurd to say that x is responsible for the burglar's presence, even though x voluntarily did what enabled the burglar to enter and did so in full knowledge that there are burglars. Similarly, having willfully engaged in intercourse does not make one responsible for any resulting pregnancy, especially if one took precautions to prevent it.

There is not only a difference of degree here, the likelihood of the two different consequences of their respective actions actually occurring, but also a decisive difference of kind. In Thomson's case, the burglar is acting immorally by entering the window whether it be opened or closed, locked or unlocked, barred or unbarred. It is this fact which makes us decide that the burglar, rather than the window opener who has every right to open his window, is responsible for his own wrongdoing. On the other hand, the embryo cannot be held responsible for its conception nor is it under any moral obligation not to be conceived. Whether it is conceived is *entirely* dependent on the actions of its parents. It is this fact that should make us conclude that the parents are responsible for the conception and existence of the unborn, but that the window opener is not responsible for the entry of the burglar.

Thomson also offers another possible counterexample. Suppose that people-seeds drift about in the air like pollen and if one opens one's window, such a seed may drift in and take root in the carpets. Suppose further that you do not want children so you fix your windows with fine mesh screens. But, as happens, one screen is defective and a seed drifts in and takes root. Surely the person–plant that now develops has no right to the use of your house. Similarly, when one uses contraceptives and they fail, one is not responsible for the ensuing pregnancy.

Suppose that this is the natural and foreseen cause of a new life in this society. Then, assuming that this society has the same notion of human rights and obligations that we have, if this germinated people–seed is sentient, it would have both a right and a claim to your house. Either keep your windows closed, do away with your rugs, or accept your responsibilities. If in this society opening your window does have the natural and foreseen consequences of begetting new sentient life or this society has a different regard for human life, then the analogy simply does not apply.

Next, I will consider cases where continuance of the pregnancy will

---

[27] Warren, 42.
[28] Thomson, "A Defense of Abortion," 58–59.

result in the death of the mother. There are two possibilities. First, continuance of the pregnancy will result in the death of both mother and fetus, while there is no possible way to save the sentient fetus but a successful abortion will save the mother. The second case is when the mother will die if an abortion is not performed, however, the sentient fetus will survive if the abortion is not performed. In both cases, the mother's request for an abortion is a clear instance of self-defense provoked by an innocent threat. In both cases, the actions of those around the mother designed to help her attain her desired abortion (the doctor, the father, etc.) are, thereby, legitimate cases of others protecting the mother's right not to be killed. Thus, in either instance where the mother's life is threatened by the continued existence of the fetus, abortion is morally justified as an act of self-defense provoked by an innocent threat.

The situation of rape provides another hard case for abortion. But it would seem that unless the mother's life is threatened, once again one's basic prima facie moral obligation to refrain from the unjustified killing of sentient humans is not overridden. Even the fact that the sentient fetus has no claim against the mother for the use of her body, since the mother did not consent to intercourse in the first place, certainly does not by itself override one's basic obligation to refrain from killing sentient humans. Nor does this claim depend, as Thomson implies, on any sort of "Good Samaritanism." Even in the case of a pregnancy resulting from rape where the fetus has no claim upon the mother for the use of her body, abortion is still the premeditated killing of an otherwise living sentient human and not an unavoidable killing, an act of self-defense, or even the disinterested turning of one's head to allow an avoidable death to occur. It should be remembered, however, that abortion prior to the 8-to-10-week period would be morally justified and not merely morally permissible given that the unborn has no claim against the mother, the heinous nature of rape, the one of a kind relationship between the mother, father, and child, and the possible bad consequences for the mother, the child, and society at large.[29]

Discussing fully the remaining instances of proposed abortions after the 8-to-10-week period of pregnancy is far beyond the province of this

---

[29] Thomson, "A Defense of Abortion," 62–66, argues that in a pregnancy resulting from rape an abortion would be merely failing to save the life of the fetus rather than actively killing it. In her reply to Finnis, "Rights and Deaths," *Philosophy and Public Affairs*, 2, No. 2 (Winter 1973), 146–159, she argues that there is no morally relevant difference between similar cases of killing x and failing to save the life of x. Hence, even according to Thomson, a woman who obtains an abortion solely because she has been raped is as morally responsible as if she had actively killed the unborn. This is all that my argument need assume. This point also applies to Thomson's now famous example of the violinist. Only if killing the violinist would be unavoidable or a justifiable act of self-defense would it be morally permissible.

paper. But it seems that cases of rape and pregnancy that will lead to severe psychological damage to the mother, "psychological death," can justify abortion given that the fetus has no claim against the mother due to the nature of rape. Also, abortion for a very young pregnant girl can, I believe, be justified in much the same way. Abortion in the case of a potentially future retarded human raises hard questions about the quality of the life of the future child. Given that I am not convinced that the life of such humans is inferior to our own, since such arguments, I believe, rest on rather perverse and chauvinistic presuppositions of psychological normalcy, I do not see that our obligations to the future sentient but retarded human justify or require abortion. This is particularly so given that such arguments would probably justify as well the killing of presently retarded people. Last, even in cases where due to financial poverty the future prospects of the sentient fetus seem dismal, again I am not convinced that abortion is justified or required by an appeal to our obligations to the future child.[30] Adoption is always a possibility. Also, such reasoning would probably justify infanticide or the killing of other humans, if we deemed that their future prospects were poor. The real cause of the evil here is poverty itself and not the unwanted child. If we want to right the situation, our efforts should, I believe, be directed toward overcoming poverty and its effects, not to killing unwanted children.

So, then, to summarize my conclusions: Abortion during the first 8 to 10 weeks of pregnancy is never morally wrong because of the moral effects on the unborn. In some situations, however, an abortion may be bad morally and indicative of an insensitive, cruel, or evil personality. After the 8-to-10-week period, in most actual or probable cases of pregnancy arising as the result of actions of consenting adults, unless an abortion can be justified by appeal to an unavoidable death or to self-defense, abortion is unjustified. It is my belief that such considerations would justify an abortion whenever the mother's life was endangered by a continued pregnancy, in cases of rape where continuance of the pregnancy would have severe psychological effects on the mother, and in cases of the pregnancy of a young girl.

Selected Bibliography

CALLAHAN, DANIEL. *Abortion: Law, Choice and Morality.* New York: Macmillan Publishing Co., Inc., 1970.

ENGLISH, JANE. "Abortion and the Concept of a Person," *Canadian Journal of Philosophy,* Vol. V, no. 2 (1975), 233.

FEINBERG, JOEL (ed.). *The Problem of Abortion.* Belmont, Calif.: Wadsworth Publishing Co., Inc., 1973.

FOOT, PHILIPPA. "The Problem of Abortion and the Doctrine of Double Ef-

---

30 This position is advanced by Feinberg, *op. cit.*

fect," *Oxford Review*, 5 (1967). Reprinted in James Rachel (ed.), *Moral Problems*. New York: Harper & Row Publishers, 1971, p. 28.

GRISEZ, GERMAIN. *Abortion: The Myths, the Realities, and the Arguments*. New York: Corpus Books, 1970.

HARE, R. M. "Abortion and the Golden Rule," *Philosophy and Public Affairs*, Vol. 4, no. 3 (1975), 201.

JAGGAR, ALISON, "Abortion and a Woman's Right to Decide," *Philosophical Forum*, Vol. 5 (1973–74), 347.

NOONAN, JOHN T., JR. (ed). *The Morality of Abortion: Legal and Historical Perspectives*. Cambridge, Mass.: Harvard University Press, 1970.

TOOLEY, MICHAEL. "Abortion and Infanticide," *Philosophy and Public Affairs*, Vol. 2, no. 1 (1972), 37.

WERTHEIMER, ROGER. "Understanding the Abortion Argument," *Philosophy and Public Affairs*, Vol. 1, no. 1 (1971), 67.

two

RACISM AND SEXISM

RICHARD A. WASSERSTROM

On Racism and Sexism

Introduction

Racism and sexism are two central issues that engage the attention of many persons living within the United States today. But while there is relatively little disagreement about their importance as topics, there is substantial, vehement, and apparently intractable disagreement about what individuals, practices, ideas, and institutions are either racist or sexist— and for what reasons. In dispute are a number of related questions concerning how individuals ought to regard and respond to matters relating to race or sex.

There are, I think, a number of important similarities between issues of racism and issues of sexism, but there are also some significant differences. More specifically, while the same general method of analysis can usefully be employed to examine a number of the issues that arise in re-

This is a somewhat revised version of Parts I and II of "Racism, Sexism, and Preferential Treatment: An Approach to the Topics" published in *UCLA Law Review* Vol. 24, 581–622 (1977), © 1977 by Richard A. Wasserstrom. Some footnotes have been deleted and the remaining ones renumbered.

spect to either, the particular topics of controversy often turn out to be rather different. What I want to do in this essay is first propose a general way of looking at issues of racism and sexism, then look at several of the respects in which racism and sexism are alike and different, and then, finally, examine one somewhat neglected but fundamental issue; namely that of what a genuinely nonracist or nonsexist society might look like.

There are, I think, at least four questions that anyone interested in issues of racism and sexism ought to see as both distinct and worth asking. The first is what I call the question of the social realities. That question is concerned with rendering a correct description of the existing social arrangements, including the existing institutional structures, practices, attitudes and ideology. The second is devoted to the question of explanation. Given a correct understanding of what the existing social reality is, there can be a variety of theories to explain how things got that way and by what mechanisms they tend to be perpetuated. Much of the feminist literature, for example, is concerned with the problem of explanation. Complex and sophisticated accounts have been developed which utilize the theories of Freud, Levi-Strauss, and Marx to explain the oppression of women. Other, equally complex accounts have insisted on the non-reductionist character of the nature and causes of the present sexual arrangements. Although important in their own right, as well as for the solution of other problems, I will have virtually nothing else to say about these explanatory issues in this essay.

The third question, and one that I will concentrate upon, is what I term the question of ideals. I see it as concerned with asking: If we had the good society, if we could change the social reality so that it conformed to some vision of what a nonracist or nonsexist society would be like, what would that society's institutions, practices, and ideology be in respect to matters of racial or sexual differentiation? Here, what I find especially interesting, is the question of whether anything like the ideal that is commonly accepted as a very plausible one for a nonracist society can be as plausibly proposed for a conception of a nonsexist society.

The fourth and final question is that of instrumentalities. Once one has developed the correct account of the social realities, and the most defensible conception of what the good society would look like, and the most comprehensive theory of how the social realities came about and are maintained, then the remaining question is the instrumental one of social change: How, given all of this, does one most effectively and fairly move from the social realities to a closer approximation of the ideal. This, too, is a question with which I will not be concerned in what follows, although it is, for instance, within this context and this perspective that, it seems to me, all of the significant questions concerning the justifiability of programs of preferential treatment arise. That is to say, the way to decide whether such programs are justifiable is to determine whether they are appropriate means by which to bring about a particular, independently justifiable end.

These, then, are four central questions which any inquiry into sexism, racism or any other comparable phenomenon must distinguish and examine. I turn first to an examination of this question of the social realities and then to a consideration of ideals and the nature of a nonracist or a nonsexist society.

I. Social Realities

A. The Position of Blacks and Women

Methodologically, the first thing it is important to note is that to talk about social realities is to talk about a particular social and cultural context. And in our particular social and cultural context race and sex are socially very important categories. They are so in virtue of the fact that we live in a culture which has, throughout its existence, made race and sex extremely important characteristics of and for all the people living in the culture.[1]

It is surely possible to imagine a culture in which race would be an unimportant, insignificant characteristic of individuals. In such a culture race would be largely if not exclusively a matter of superficial physiology; a matter, we might say, simply of the way one looked. And if it were, then any analysis of race and racism would necessarily assume very different dimensions from what they do in our society. In such a culture, the meaning of the term "race" would itself have to change substantially. This can be seen by the fact that in such a culture it would literally make no sense to say of a person that he or she was "passing."[2] This is something that

[1] In asserting the importance of one's race and sex in our culture I do not mean to deny the importance of other characteristics—in particular, socioeconomic class. I do think that in our culture race and sex are two very important facts about a person, and I am skeptical of theories which "reduce" the importance of these features to a single, more basic one, e.g., class. But apart from this one bit of skepticism I think that all of what I have to say is compatible with several different theories concerning why race and sex are so important—including, for instance, most versions of Marxism. See, e.g., the account provided in J. MITCHELL, WOMAN'S ESTATE (1971). The correct causal explanation for the social realities I describe is certainly an important question, both in its own right and for some of the issues I address. It is particularly significant for the issue of how to alter the social realities to bring them closer to the ideal. Nonetheless, I have limited the scope of my inquiry to exclude a consideration of this large, difficult topic.

[2] Passing is the phenomenon in which a person who in some sense knows himself or herself to be black "passes" as white because he or she looks white. A version of this is described in Sinclair Lewis' novel KINGSBLOOD ROYAL (1947), where the protagonist discovers when he is an adult that he, his father, and his father's mother are black (or, in the idiom of the late 1940's, Negro) in virtue of the fact that his great grandfather was black. His grandmother knew this and was consciously passing. When he learns about his ancestry, one decision he has to make is whether to continue to pass, or to acknowledge to the world that he is in fact "Negro."

can be said and understood in our own culture and it shows at least that to talk of race is to talk of more than the way one looks.[3]

Sometimes when people talk about what is wrong with affirmative action programs, or programs of preferential hiring, they say that what is wrong with such programs is that they take a thing as superficial as an individual's race and turn it into something important.[4] They say that a person's race doesn't matter; other things do, such as qualifications. Whatever else may be said of statements such as these, as descriptions of the social realities they seem to be simply false. One complex but true empirical fact about our society is that the race of an individual is much more than a fact of superficial physiology. It is, instead, one of the dominant characteristics that affects both the way the individual looks at the world and the way the world looks at the individual. As I have said, that need not be the case. It may in fact be very important that we work toward a society in which that would not be the case, but it is the case now and it must be understood in any adequate and complete discussion of racism. That is why, too, it does not make much sense when people sometimes say, in talking about the fact that they are not racists, that they would not care if an individual were green and came from Mars, they would treat that individual the same way they treat people exactly like themselves. For part of *our* social and cultural history is to treat people of certain races in a certain way, and we do not have a social or cultural history of treating green people from Mars in any particular way. To put it simply, it is to misunderstand the social realities of race and racism to think of them simply as questions of how some people respond to other people whose skins are of different hues, irrespective of the social context.

I can put the point another way: Race does not function in our culture as does eye color. Eye color is an irrelevant category; nobody cares what color people's eyes are; it is not an important cultural fact; nothing turns on what eye color you have. It is important to see that race is not like that at all. And this truth affects what will and will not count as cases of racism. In our culture to be nonwhite—especially to be black [5]—is to be

---

[3] That looking black is not in our culture a necessary condition for being black can be seen from the phenomenon of passing. That it is not a sufficient condition can be seen from the book BLACK LIKE ME (1960), by John Howard Griffin, where "looking black" is easily understood by the reader to be different from being black. I suspect that the concept of being black is, in our culture, one which combines both physiological and ancestral criteria in some moderately complex fashion.

[4] Mr. Justice Douglas suggests something like this in his dissent in *DeFunis*: "The consideration of race as a measure of an applicant's qualification normally introduces a capricious and irrelevant factor working an invidious discrimination." DeFunis v. Odegaard, 416 U.S. 312, 333 (1974).

[5] There are significant respects in which the important racial distinction is between being white and being nonwhite, and there are other significant respects in which the fact of being black has its own special meaning and importance. My analysis is conducted largely in terms of what is involved in being black. To a consid-

treated and seen to be a member of a group that is different from and inferior to the group of standard, fully developed persons, the adult white males. To be black is to be a member of what was a despised minority and what is still a disliked and oppressed one.[6] That is simply part of the awful truth of our cultural and social history, and a significant feature of the social reality of our culture today.

We can see fairly easily that the two sexual categories, like the racial ones, are themselves in important respects products of the society. Like one's race, one's sex is not merely or even primarily a matter of physiology. To see this we need only realize that we can understand the idea of a transsexual. A transsexual is someone who would describe himself or herself as a person who is essentially a female but through some accident of nature is trapped in a male body, or a person who is essentially a male but through some accident of nature is trapped in the body of a female. His (or her) description is some kind of a shorthand way of saying that he (or she) is more comfortable with the role allocated by the culture to people who are physiologically of the opposite sex. The fact that we regard this assertion of the transsexual as intelligible seems to me to show how deep the notion of sexual identity is in our culture and how little it has to do with physiological differences between males and females. Because people do pass in the context of race and because we can understand what passing means; because people are transsexuals and because we can understand what transsexuality means, we can see that the existing social categories of both race and sex are in this sense creations of the culture.

It is even clearer in the case of sex than in the case of race that one's sexual identity is a centrally important, crucially relevant category within our culture. I think, in fact, that it is more important and more fundamental than one's race. It is evident that there are substantially different role expectations and role assignments to persons in accordance with their sexual physiology, and that the positions of the two sexes in the culture are distinct. We do have a patriarchal society in which it matters enormously

---

erable extent, however, what I say directly applies to the more inclusive category of being nonwhite. To the extent to which what I say does not apply to the other nonwhite racial distinctions, the analysis of those distinctions should, of course, be undertaken separately.

6 *See, e.g.,* J. BALDWIN, THE FIRE NEXT TIME (1963); W. E. B. DuBOIS, THE SOULS OF BLACK FOLKS (1903); R. ELLISON, INVISIBLE MAN (1952); J. FRANKLIN, FROM SLAVERY TO FREEDOM (3d ed. 1968); C. HAMILTON & S. CARMICHAEL, BLACK POWER (1967); REPORT OF THE U.S. COMMISSION ON CIVIL DISORDERS 1968); Kilson, *Whither Integration?*, 45 AM SCHOLAR 360 (1976); and hundreds, if not thousands of other books and articles, both literary and empirical. These sources describe a great variety of features of the black experience in America: such things as the historical as well as the present day material realities, and the historical as well as present day ideological realities, the way black people have been and are thought about within the culture. In KINGSBLOOD ROYAL, *supra* note 2, Lewis provides a powerful account of what he calls the "American Credo" about the Negro, circa 1946. *Id.* at 194–97.

whether one is a male or a female.[7] By almost all important measures it is more advantageous to be a male rather than a female.

Women and men are socialized differently. We learn very early and forcefully that we are either males or females and that much turns upon which sex we are. The evidence seems to be overwhelming and well-documented that sex roles play a fundamental role in the way persons think of themselves and the world—to say nothing of the way the world thinks of them.[8] Men and women are taught to see men as independent, capable,

[7] The best general account I have read of the structure of patriarchy and of its major dimensions and attributes is that found in SEXUAL POLITICS in the chapter, "Theory of Sexual Politics." K. MILLETT, SEXUAL POLITICS 23–58 (1970). The essay seems to me to be truly a major contribution to an understanding of the subject. Something of the essence of the thesis is contained in the following:

"[A] disinterested examination of our system of sexual relationship must point out that the situation between the sexes now, and throughout history, is a case of that phenomenon Max Weber defined as *herrschaft*, a relationship of dominance and subordinance. What goes largely unexamined, often even unacknowledged (yet is institutionalized nonetheless) in our social order, is the birthright priority whereby males rule females. Through this system a most ingenious form of 'interior colonization' has been achieved. It is one which tends moreover to be sturdier than any form of segregation and more rigorous than class stratification, more uniform, certainly more enduring. However muted its present appearance may be, sexual dominion obtains nevertheless as perhaps the most pervasive ideology of our culture and provides its most fundamental concept of power.

"This is so because our society, like all other historical civilizations, is a patriarchy. The fact is evident at once if one recalls that the military, industry, technology, universities, science, political office, and finance—in short, every avenue of power within the society, including the coercive force of the police, is entirely in male hands. . . .

"Sexual politics obtains consent through the 'socialization' of both sexes to basic patriarchal politics with regard to temperament, role, and status. As to status, a pervasive assent to the prejudice of male superiority guarantees superior status in the male, inferior in the female. The first item, temperament, involves the formation of human personality along stereotyped lines of sex category ('masculine' and 'feminine'), based on the needs and values of the dominant group and dictated by what its members cherish in themselves and find convenient in subordinates: aggression, intelligence, force and efficacy in the male; passivity, ignorance, docility, 'virtue,' and ineffectuality in the female. This is complemented by a second factor, sex role, which decrees a consonant and highly elaborate code of conduct, gesture and attitude for each sex. In terms of activity, sex role assigns domestic service and attendance upon infants to the female, the rest of human achievement, interest and ambition to the male. . . . Were one to analyze the three categories one might designate status as the political component, role as the sociological, and temperament as the psychological—yet their interdependence is unquestionable and they form a chain." *Id.* at 24–26 (footnotes omitted).

[8] *See, e.g.* Hochschild, *A Review of Sex Role Research*, 78 AM. J. Soc. 1011 (1973), which reviews and very usefully categorizes the enormous volume of literature on this topic. *See also* Stewart, *Social Influences on Sex Differences in Behavior*, in SEX DIFFERENCES 138 (M. Teitelbaum ed. 1976); Weitzman, *Sex Role Socialization*, in WOMEN: A FEMINIST PERSPECTIVE 105 (J. Freeman ed. 1975). A

and powerful; men and women are taught to see women as dependent, limited in abilities, and passive. A woman's success or failure in life is defined largely in terms of her activities within the family. It is important for her that she marry, and when she does she is expected to take responsibility for the wifely tasks: the housework, the child care, and the general emotional welfare of the husband and children.[9] Her status in society is determined in substantial measure by the vocation and success of her husband.[10] Economically, women are substantially worse off than men. They do not receive any pay for the work that is done in the home. As members of the labor force their wages are significantly lower than those paid to men, even when they are engaged in similar work and have similar educational backgrounds.[11] The higher the prestige or the salary of the job, the less present women are in the labor force. And, of course, women are conspicuously absent from most positions of authority and power in the major economic and political institutions of our society.

As is true for race, it is also a significant social fact that to be a female is to be an entity or creature viewed as different from the standard,

---

number of the other pieces in WOMEN: A FEMINIST PERSPECTIVE also describe and analyze the role of women in the culture, including the way they are thought of by the culture.

9 "For the married woman, her husband and children must always come first; her own needs and desires, last. When the children reach school age, they no longer require constant attention. The emotional-expressive function assigned to the woman is still required of her. Called the 'stroking function' by sociologist Jessie Bernard, it consists of showing solidarity, raising the status of others, giving help, rewarding, agreeing, concurring, complying, understanding, and passively accepting. The woman is expected to give emotional support and comfort to other family members, to make them feel like good and worthwhile human beings." B. DECKARD, THE WOMEN'S MOVEMENT 59 (1975), *citing* J. BERNARD, WOMEN AND THE PUBLIC INTEREST 88 (1971).

"Patriarchy's chief institution is the family. It is both a mirror of and a connection with the larger society: a patriarchal unit within a patriarchal whole. Mediating between the individual and the social structure, the family effects control and conformity where political and other authorities are insufficient." K. MILLETT, *supra* note 7, at 33.

10 "Even if the couple consciously try to attain an egalitarian marriage, so long as the traditional division of labor is maintained, the husband will be 'more equal.' He is the provider not only of money but of status. Especially if he is successful, society values what he does; she is just a housewife. Their friends are likely to be his friends and co-workers; in their company, she is just his wife. Because his provider function is essential for the family's survival, major family decisions are made in terms of how they affect his career. He need not and usually does not act like the authoritarian paterfamilius [sic] of the Victorian age. His power and status are derived from his function in the family and are secure so long as the traditional division of labor is maintained." B. DECKARD, *supra* note 9, at 62.

11 In 1970, women workers were, on the average, paid only 59 percent of men's wages. And when wages of persons with similar educational levels are compared, women still were paid over 40 percent less than men. *Id.* at 79–81.

fully developed person who is male as well as white. But to be female, as opposed to being black, is not to be conceived of as simply a creature of less worth. That is one important thing that differentiates sexism from racism: The ideology of sex, as opposed to the ideology of race, is a good deal more complex and confusing. Women are both put on a pedestal and deemed not fully developed persons. They are idealized; their approval and admiration is sought; and they are at the same time regarded as less competent than men and less able to live fully developed, fully human lives—for that is what men do.[12] At best, they are viewed and treated as having properties and attributes that are valuable and admirable for humans of this type. For example, they may be viewed as especially empathetic, intuitive, loving, and nurturing. At best, these qualities are viewed as good properties for women to have, and, provided they are properly muted, are sometimes valued within the more well-rounded male. Because the sexual ideology is complex, confusing, and variable, it does not unambiguously proclaim the lesser value attached to being female rather than being male, nor does it unambiguously correspond to the existing social realities. For these, among other reasons, sexism could plausibly be regarded as a deeper phenomenon than racism. It is more deeply embedded in the culture, and thus less visible. Being harder to detect, it is harder to eradicate. Moreover, it is less unequivocally regarded as unjust and unjustifiable. That is to say, there is less agreement within the dominant ideology that sexism even implies an unjustifiable practice or attitude. Hence, many persons announce, without regret or embarrassment, that they are sexists or male chauvinists; very few announce openly that they are racists.[13] For all of these reasons sexism may be a more insidious evil than racism, but there is

[12] "It is generally accepted that Western patriarchy has been much softened by the concepts of courtly and romantic love. While this is certainly true, such influence has also been vastly overestimated. In comparison with the candor of 'machismo' or oriental behavior, one realizes how much of a concession traditional chivalrous behavior represents—a sporting kind of reparation to allow the subordinate female certain means of saving face. While a palliative to the injustice of woman's social position, chivalry is also a technique for disguising it. One must acknowledge that the chivalrous stance is a game the master group plays in elevating its subject to pedestal level. Historians of courtly love stress the fact that the raptures of the poets had no effect upon the legal or economic standing of women, and very little upon their social status. As the sociologist Hugo Beigel has observed, both the courtly and the romantic versions of love are 'grants' which the male concedes out of his total powers. Both have the effect of obscuring the patriarchal character of Western culture and in their general tendency to attribute impossible virtues to women, have ended by confining them in a narrow and often remarkably conscribing sphere of behavior. It was a Victorian habit, for example, to insist the female assume the function of serving as the male's conscience and living the life of goodness he found tedious but felt someone ought to do anyway."
K. MILLETT, supra note 7, at 36–37.

[13] Thus, even after his "joke" about black persons became known to the public, the former Secretary of Agriculture, Earl Butz, took great pains to insist that this in no way showed that he was a racist. This is understandable, given the strongly condemnatory feature of being described as a racist.

little merit in trying to decide between two seriously objectionable practices which one is worse.

While I do not think that I have made very controversial claims about either our cultural history or our present-day culture, I am aware of the fact that they have been stated very imprecisely and that I have offered little evidence to substantiate them. In a crude way we ought to be able both to understand the claims and to see that they are correct if we reflect seriously and critically upon our own cultural institutions, attitudes, and practices. But in a more refined, theoretical way, I am imagining that a more precise and correct description of the social reality in respect to race and sex would be derivable from a composite, descriptive account of our society which utilized the relevant social sciences to examine such things as the society's institutions, practices, attitudes and ideology [14]—if the social sciences could be value-free and unaffected in outlook or approach by the fact that they, themselves, are largely composed of persons who are white and male.[15]

Equally illuminating was the behavior of Butz's associates and superiors. Then-President Ford, for example, critized Butz for the joke, but did not demand Butz's removal until there was a strong public outcry. It was as though Butz's problem was that he had been indiscreet; he had done something rude like belching in public. What Ford, Butz, and others apparently failed to grasp is that it is just as wrong to tell these jokes in private because to tell a joke of this sort is to have a view about what black people are like: that they can appropriately be ridiculed as being creatures who care only about intercourse, shoes, and defecation. What these persons also failed to grasp is how implausible it is to believe that one can hold these views about black people and at the same time deal with them in a nonracist fashion.

[14] At a minimum, this account would include: (1) a description of the economic, political, and social positions of blacks and whites, males and females in the culture; (2) a description of the sexual and racial roles, *i.e.*, the rules, conventions and expectations concerning how males and females, blacks and whites, should behave, and the attitudes and responses produced by these roles; and (3) a description of the de facto ideology of racial and sexual differences. This would include popular beliefs about how males and females, blacks and whites, differ, as well as the beliefs as to what accounts for these differences, roles, and economic, political and social realities.

[15] The problem of empirical objectivity is compounded by the fact that part of the dominant, white male ideology is that white males are the one group in society whose members are able to be genuinely detached and objective when it comes to things like an understanding of the place of race and sex in the culture. Thus, for example, when a sex-discrimination suit was brought against a law firm and the case was assigned to Judge Constance Motley, the defendant filed a motion that she be disqualified partly because, as a woman judge, she would be biased in favor of the plaintiff. Judge Motley denied the motion. Blank v. Sullivan & Cromwell, 418 F. Supp. 1 (S.D.N.Y. 1975), *writ of mandamus denied sub nom.* Sullivan & Cromwell v. Motley, No. 75–3045 (2d Cir. Aug. 26, 1975). Explaining her decision, Judge Motley stated: "[I]f background or sex or race of each judge were, *by definition*, sufficient grounds for removal, no judge on this court could hear this case, or many others, by virtue of the fact that all of them were attorneys, of a sex, often with distinguished law firm or public service backgrounds." 418 F. Supp. at 4 (emphasis added).

Viewed from the perspective of social reality it should be clear, too, that racism and sexism should not be thought of as phenomena that consist simply in taking a person's race or sex into account, or even simply in taking a person's race or sex into account in an arbitrary way. Instead, racism and sexism consist in taking race and sex into account in a certain way, in the context of a specific set of institutional arrangements and a specific ideology which together create and maintain a specific *system* of institutions, role assignments, beliefs and attitudes. That system is one, and has been one, in which political, economic, and social power and advantage is concentrated in the hands of those who are white and male.

The evils of such systems are, however, not all of a piece. For instance, sometimes people say that what was wrong with the system of racial discrimination in the South was that it took an irrelevant characteristic, namely race, and used it systematically to allocate social benefits and burdens of various sorts. The defect was the irrelevance of the characteristic used, i.e., race, for that meant that individuals ended up being treated in a manner that was arbitrary and capricious.

I do not think that was the central flaw at all—at least of much of the system. Take, for instance, the most hideous of the practices, human slavery. The primary thing that was wrong with the institution was not that the particular individuals who were assigned the place of slaves were assigned there arbitrarily because the assignment was made in virtue of an irrelevant characteristic, i.e., their race. Rather, it seems to me clear that the primary thing that was and is wrong with slavery is the practice itself— the fact of some individuals being able to own other individuals and all that goes with that practice. It would not matter by what criterion individuals were assigned; human slavery would still be wrong. And the same can be said for many of the other discrete practices and institutions that comprised the system of racial discrimination even after human slavery was abolished. The practices were unjustifiable—they were oppressive— and they would have been so no matter how the assignment of victims had been made. What made it worse, still, was that the institutions and ideology all interlocked to create a system of human oppression whose effects on those living under it were as devastating as they were unjustifiable.

Some features of the system of sexual oppression are like this and others are different. For example, if it is true that women are socialized to play the role of servers of men and if they are in general assigned that position in the society, what is objectionable about that practice is the practice itself. It is not that women are being arbitrarily or capriciously assigned the social role of server, but rather that such a role is at least *prima facie* unjustifiable as a role in a decent society. As a result, the assignment on any basis of individuals to such a role is objectionable.

The assignment of women to primary responsibility for child rearing and household maintenance may be different; it may be objectionable on grounds of unfairness of another sort. That is to say, if we assume that these are important but undesirable aspects of social existence—if we assume that they are, relatively speaking, unsatisfying and unfulfilling ways to spend one's time, then the objection is that women are unduly and unfairly allocated a disproportionate share of unpleasant, unrewarding work. Here the objection, if it is proper, is to the degree to which the necessary burden is placed to a greater degree than is fair on women, rather than shared equally by persons of both sexes.

Even here, though, it is important to see that the essential feature of both racism and sexism consists in the fact that race or sex is taken into account in the context of a specific set of arrangements and a specific ideology which is systemic and which treats and regards persons who are nonwhite or female in a comprehensive, systemic way. Whether it would be capricious to take either a person's race or a person's sex into account in the good society, because race and sex were genuinely irrelevant characteristics is a question that can only be answered after we have a clearer idea of what the good society would look like in respect either to race or sex.

Another way to bring this out, as well as to show another respect in which racism and sexism are different, concerns segregated bathrooms. We know, for instance, that it is wrong, clearly racist, to have racially segregated bathrooms. There is, however, no common conception that it is wrong, clearly sexist, to have sexually segregated ones. How is this to be accounted for? The answer to the question of why it was and is racist to have racially segregated bathrooms can be discovered through a consideration of the role that this practice played in that system of racial segregation we had in the United States—from, in other words, an examination of the social realities. For racially segregated bathrooms were an important part of that system. And that system had an ideology; it was complex and perhaps not even wholly internally consistent. A significant feature of the ideology was that blacks were not only less than fully developed humans, but that they were also dirty and impure. They were the sorts of creatures who could and would contaminate white persons if they came into certain kinds of contact with them—in the bathroom, at the dinner table, or in bed, although it was appropriate for blacks to prepare and handle food, and even to nurse white infants. This ideology was intimately related to a set of institutional arrangements and power relationships in which whites were politically, economically, and socially dominant. The ideology supported the institutional arrangements, and the institutional arrangements reinforced the ideology. The net effect was that racially segregated bathrooms were both a part of the institutional mechanism of oppression and an instantiation of this ideology of racial taint. The point of maintaining racially segregated bathrooms was not in any simple or direct sense to keep both whites and blacks from using each other's bathrooms; it was to make sure that blacks would not contaminate bathrooms used by whites. The practice also taught both whites and blacks that certain kinds of contacts were forbidden because whites would be degraded by the contact with the blacks.

The failure to understand the character of these institutions of racial oppression is what makes some of the judicial reasoning about racial discrimination against blacks so confusing and unsatisfactory. At times when the courts have tried to explain what is constitutionally wrong with racial segregation, they have said that the problem is that race is an inherently suspect category. What they have meant by this, or have been thought to mean, is that any differentiation among human beings on the basis of racial identity is inherently unjust, because arbitrary, and therefore any particular case of racial differentiation must be shown to be fully rational and justifiable.[16] But the primary evil of the various schemes of racial segregation against blacks that the courts were being called upon to assess was not that such schemes were a capricious and irrational way of allocating public benefits and burdens. That might well be the primary wrong with racial segregation if we lived in a society very different from the one we have. The primary evil of these schemes was instead that they designedly and effectively marked off all black persons as degraded, dirty, less than fully developed persons who were unfit for full membership in the political, social, and moral community.[17]

It is worth observing that the social reality of sexually segregated bathrooms appears to be different. The idea behind such sexual segregation seems to have more to do with the mutual undesirability of the use by both sexes of the same bathroom at the same time. There is no notion

[16] Thus, in Bolling v. Sharpe, 347 U.S. 497 (1953), the Supreme Court said that what was wrong with preventing black children from attending the all white schools of the District of Columbia was that "[s]egregation in public education is not reasonably related to any proper governmental objective, and thus it imposes on Negro children of the District of Columbia a burden that constitutes an arbitrary deprivation of their liberty in violation of the Due Process Clause." *Id.* at 500. I ignore those cases in which the courts decline to formulate a view about racial differentiation because the behavior involved is not the sort that the law thinks it appropriate to deal with, *e.g.*, "private" racial discrimination.

[17] Others have made this general point about the nature of the evil of racial segregation in the United States. *See, e.g.,* Fiss, *Groups and Equal Protection,* 5 PHIL. & PUB. AFF. 107 (1976); Thalberg, *Reverse Discrimination and the Future,* 5 PHIL. F. 268 (1973).

The failure fully to understand this general point seems to me to be one of the things wrong with Weschler's famous article, *Toward Neutral Principles of Constitutional Interpretation,* 73 HARV. L. REV. 1 (1959). Near the very end of the piece Weschler reports, "In the days when I joined with Charles H. Houston [a well-known black lawyer] in a litigation in the Supreme Court, before the present building was constructed, he did not suffer more than I in knowing that we had to go to Union Square to lunch together during the recess." *Id.* at 34. If the stress in that sentence is wholly on the fact of *knowing,* no one can say for certain that Weschler is wrong. But what is certain is that Charles H. Houston suffered more than Weschler from *living* in a system in which he could only lunch at Union Station.

of the possibility of contamination; or even directly of inferiority and superiority. What seems to be involved—at least in part—is the importance of inculcating and preserving a sense of secrecy concerning the genitalia of the opposite sex. What seems to be at stake is the maintenance of that same sense of mystery or forbiddenness about the other sex's sexuality which is fostered by the general prohibition upon public nudity and the unashamed viewing of genitalia.

Sexually segregated bathrooms simply play a different role in our culture than did racially segregated ones. But that is not to say that the role they play is either benign or unobjectionable—only that it is different. Sexually segregated bathrooms may well be objectionable, but here too, the objection is not on the ground that they are prima facie capricious or arbitrary. Rather, the case against them now would rest on the ground that they are, perhaps, one small part of that scheme of sex-role differentiation which uses the mystery of sexual anatomy, among other things, to maintain the primacy of heterosexual sexual attraction central to that version of the patriarchal system of power relationships we have today.[18] Once again, whether sexually segregated bathrooms would be objectionable, because irrational, in the good society depends once again upon what the good society would look like in respect to sexual differentiation.

B. Types of Racism or Sexism

Another recurring question that can profitably be examined within the perspective of social realities is whether the legal system is racist or sexist. Indeed, it seems to me essential that the social realities of the relationships and ideologies concerning race and sex be kept in mind whenever one is trying to assess claims that are made about the racism or sexism of important institutions such as the legal system. It is also of considerable importance in assessing such claims to understand that even within the perspective of social reality, racism or sexism can manifest itself, or be understood, in different ways. That these are both important points can be seen through a brief examination of the different, distinctive ways in which our own legal system might plausibly be understood to be racist. The mode of analysis I propose serves as well, I believe, for an analogous analysis of the sexism of the legal system, although I do not undertake the latter analysis in this paper.

The first type of racism is the simplest and the least controversial. It is the case of overt racism, in which a law or a legal institution expressly takes into account the race of individuals in order to assign benefits and

---

[18] This conjecture about the role of sexually segregated bathrooms may well be inaccurate or incomplete. The sexual segregation of bathrooms may have more to do with privacy than with patriarchy. However, if so, it is at least odd that what the institution makes relevant is sex rather than merely the ability to perform the eliminatory acts in private.

burdens in such a way as to bestow an unjustified benefit upon a member or members of the racially dominant group or an unjustified burden upon members of the racial groups that are oppressed. We no longer have many, if any, cases of overt racism in our legal system today, although we certainly had a number in the past. Indeed, the historical system of formal, racial segregation was both buttressed by, and constituted of, a number of overtly racist laws and practices. At different times in our history, racism included laws and practices which dealt with such things as the exclusion of nonwhites from the franchise, from decent primary and secondary schools and most professional schools, and the prohibition against interracial marriages.

The second type of racism is very similar to overt racism. It is covert, but intentional, racism, in which a law or a legal institution has as its purpose the allocation of benefits and burdens in order to support the power of the dominant race, but does not use race specifically as a basis for allocating these benefits and burdens. One particularly good historical example involves the use of grandfather clauses which were inserted in statutes governing voter registration in a number of states after passage of the fifteenth amendment.[19]

Covert racism within the law is not entirely a thing of the past. Many instances of de facto school segregation in the North and West are cases of covert racism. At times certain school boards—virtually all of which are overwhelmingly white in composition—quite consciously try to maintain exclusively or predominantly white schools within a school district. The classifications such school boards use are not ostensibly racial, but are based upon the places of residence of the affected students. These categories provide the opportunity for covert racism in engineering the racial composition of individual schools within the board's jurisdiction.[20]

What has been said so far is surely neither novel nor controversial. What is interesting, however, is that a number of persons appear to believe that as long as the legal system is not overtly or covertly racist, there is nothing to the charge that it is racist. So, for example, Mr. Justice Powell said in a speech a few years ago:

[19] *See, e.g.,* Guinn v. United States, 238 U.S. 347 (1915). Such statutes provided that the grandchild of someone who had been registered to vote in the state was permitted to vote in that state; but the grandchild of somebody who had never been registered to vote in the state had to take a special test in order to become qualified to vote. It does not take much knowledge of history to know that in most of the southern states few if any black people had grandparents who before the Civil War were registered to vote. And the persons who enacted these laws knew it too. So even though race was not made a category by the described laws, they effectively divided people on grounds of race into those who were qualified to vote without more, and those who had to submit to substantially more rigorous tests before they could exercise the franchise. All of this was done, as is well known, so as to perpetuate the control of the franchise by whites.

[20] *See, e.g.,* Crawford v. Board of Educ., 17 Cal. 3d 280 (1976); Jackson v. Pasadena City School Dist., 59 Cal. 2d 876, 382 P.2d 878, 31 Cal. Rptr. 606 (1963).

It is of course true that we have witnessed racial injustice in the past, as has every other country with significant racial diversity. But no one can fairly question the present national commitment to full equality and justice. Racial discrimination, by state action, is now proscribed by laws and court decisions which protect civil liberties more broadly than in any other country. But laws alone are not enough. Racial prejudice in the hearts of men cannot be legislated out of existence; it will pass only in time, and as human beings of all races learn in humility to respect each other—a process not furthered by recrimination or undue self-accusation.[21]

I believe it is a mistake to think about the problem of racism in terms of overt or covert racial discrimination by state action, which is now banished, and racial prejudice, which still lingers, but only in the hearts of persons. For there is another, more subtle kind of racism—unintentional, perhaps, but effective—which is as much a part of the legal system as are overt and covert racist laws and practices. It is what some critics of the legal system probably mean when they talk about the "institutional racism" of the legal system.[22]

There are at least two kinds of institutional racism. The first is the racism of sub-institutions within the legal system such as the jury, or the racism of practices built upon or countenanced by the law. These institutions and practices very often, if not always, reflect in important and serious ways a variety of dominant values in the operation of what is apparently a neutral legal mechanism. The result is the maintenance and reenforcement of a system in which whites dominate over nonwhites. One relatively uninteresting (because familiar) example is the case of de facto school segregation. As observed above, some cases of de facto segregation are examples of covert racism. But even in school districts where there is no intention to divide pupils on grounds of race so as to maintain existing power relationships along racial lines, school attendance zones are utilized which are based on the geographical location of the pupil. Because it is a fact in our culture that there is racial discrimination against black people in respect to housing, it is also a fact that any geographical allocation of

---

21 N.Y. Times, Aug. 31, 1972, § 1, at 33, col. 3.

22 All of the laws, institutional arrangements, etc., that I analyze are, I think, cases of racism and not, for example, cases of prejudice. The latter concept I take to refer more specifically to the defective, incomplete or objectionable beliefs and attitudes of individuals. Prejudiced individuals often engage in racist acts, enact racist laws and participate in racist institutions. But they need not. Nor is it true that the only persons connected with racist acts, laws, or institutions need be prejudiced individuals.

A perceptive account of the differences between prejudice and racism, and of the different kinds of racism, including institutional racism of the sorts I discuss below, can be found in M. JONES, PREJUDICE AND RACISM (1972). See especially id. at 60–115 (ch. 4, "Perspectives on Prejudice"); id. at 116–67 (ch. 5, "Realities of Racism"). A somewhat analogous set of distinctions concerning sexism is made in Jaggar, On Sexual Equality, 84 ETHICS 275, 276–77 (1974).

pupils—unless one pays a lot of attention to housing patterns—will have the effect of continuing to segregate minority pupils very largely on grounds of race. It is perfectly appropriate to regard this effect as a case of racism in public education.[23]

A less familiar, and hence perhaps more instructive, example concerns the question of the importance of having blacks on juries, especially in cases in which blacks are criminal defendants. The orthodox view within the law is that it is unfair to try a black defendant before an all-white jury if blacks were overtly or covertly excluded from the jury rolls used to provide the jury panel, but not otherwise.[24] One reason that is often given is that the systematic exclusion of blacks increases too greatly the chance of racial prejudice operating against the black defendant.[25] The problem with this way of thinking about things is that it does not make much sense. If whites are apt to be prejudiced against blacks, then an all-white jury is just as apt to be prejudiced against a black defendant, irrespective of whether blacks were systematically excluded from the jury rolls. I suspect that the rule has developed in the way it has because the courts think that many, if not most, whites are not prejudiced against blacks, unless, perhaps, they happen to live in an area where there is systematic exclusion of blacks from the jury rolls. Hence prejudice is the chief worry, and a sectional, if not historical, one at that.

White prejudice against blacks is, I think, a problem, and not just a sectional one. However, the existence or nonexistence of prejudice against blacks does not go to the heart of the matter. It is a worry, but it is not the chief worry. A black person may not be able to get a fair trial from an all-white jury even though the jurors are disposed to be fair and impartial,

[23] One example of what may have been an instance of genuine de facto racism in a non-educational setting is found in Gregory v. Litton Systems, Inc., 316 F. Supp. 401 (C.D. Cal. 1970), *modified*, 472 F.2d 631 (9th Cir. 1972). Litton Systems had a policy of refusing to employ persons who had been frequently arrested. The court found this to violate Title VII of the Civil Rights Act of 1964, 42 U.S.C. § 2000e (1970):

"Negroes are arrested substantially more frequently than whites in proportion to their numbers. The evidence on this question was overwhelming and utterly convincing. For example, negroes nationally comprise some 11% of the population and account for 27% of reported arrests and 45% of arrests reported as 'suspicious arrests.' Thus, any policy that disqualifies prospective employees because of having been arrested once, or more than once, discriminates in fact against negro applicants. This discrimination exists even though such a policy is objectively and fairly applied as between applicants of various races. A substantial and disproportionately large number of negroes are excluded from employment opportunities by Defendant's policy."
316 F. Supp. at 403.

[24] Whitus v. Georgia, 385 U.S. 545 (1967), Avery v. Georgia, 345 U.S. 559 (1953), and Strauder v. West Virginia, 100 U.S. 303 (1880), are three of the many cases declaring it unconstitutional to exclude blacks systematically from the jury rolls when the defendant is black. Swain v. Alabama, 380 U.S. 202 (1965), is one of the many cases declaring that it is not unconstitutional that no blacks were in fact on the jury that tried the defendant.

[25] *See, e.g.,* Peters v. Kiff, 407 U.S. 493, 508–509 (Burger, C. J., dissenting).

because the whites may unknowingly bring into the jury box a view about a variety of matters which affects in very fundamental respects the way they will look at and assess the facts. Thus, for example, it is not, I suspect, part of the experience of most white persons who serve on juries that police often lie in their dealings with people and the courts. Indeed, it is probably not part of their experience that persons lie about serious matters except on rare occasions. And they themselves tend to take truth telling very seriously. As a result, white persons for whom these facts about police and lying are a part of their social reality will have very great difficulty taking seriously the possibility that the inculpatory testimony of a police witness is a deliberate untruth. However, it may also be a part of the social reality that many black persons, just because they are black, have had encounters with the police in which the police were at best indifferent to whether they, the police, were speaking the truth. And even more black persons may have known a friend or a relative who has had such an experience. As a result, a black juror would be more likely than his or her white counterpart to approach skeptically the testimony of ostensibly neutral, reliable witnesses such as police officers. The point is not that all police officers lie; nor is the point that all whites always believe everything police say, and blacks never do. The point is that because the world we live in is the way it is, it is likely that whites and blacks will on the whole be disposed to view the credibility of police officers very differently. If so, the legal system's election to ignore this reality, and to regard as fair and above reproach the common occurrence of all-white juries (and white judges) passing on the guilt or innocence of black defendants is a decision in fact to permit and to perpetuate a kind of institutional racism within the law.[26]

[26] I discuss this particular situation in somewhat more detail in Wasserstrom, *The University and the Case for Preferential Treatment*, 13 AM. PHIL. Q. 165, 169–70 (1976). Mr. Justice Marshall expresses a view that I take to be reasonably close to mine in Peters v. Kiff, 407 U.S. 493 (1972). The case involved the question of whether a white defendant could challenge the systematic exclusion of blacks from the jury rolls. Mr. Justice Marshall held that he could:

"[W]e are unwilling to make the assumption that the exclusion of Negroes has relevance only for issues involving race. When any large and identifiable segment of the community is excluded from jury service, the effect is to remove from the jury room qualities of human nature and varieties of human experience, the range of which is unknown and perhaps unknowable. It is not necessary to assume that the excluded group will consistently vote as a class in order to conclude, as we do, that its exclusion deprives the jury of a perspective on human events that may have unsuspected importance in any case that may be presented."

Id. at 503–04 (footnote omitted).

Given my analysis, I think any defendant is disadvantaged by the absence of blacks from the jury, where, for instance, the testimony of a police officer is a significant part of the prosecution case. Because police are more apt to lie about black defendants, and because black jurors are more apt to be sensitive to this possibility, black defendants are, I think, especially likely to be tried unfairly by many all-white juries. What matters in terms of fairness is that blacks be represented on particular juries; nonexclusion from the jury rolls is certainly not obviously sufficient.

The second type of institutional racism is what I will call "conceptual" institutional racism. We have a variety of ways of thinking about the legal system, and we have a variety of ways of thinking within the legal system about certain problems. We use concepts. Quite often without realizing it, the concepts used take for granted certain objectionable aspects of racist ideology without our being aware of it. The second *Brown* case (*Brown II*) provides an example.[27] There was a second *Brown* case because, having decided that the existing system of racially segregated public education was unconstitutional (*Brown I*),[28] the Supreme Court gave legitimacy to a second issue—the nature of the relief to be granted—by treating it as a distinct question to be considered and decided separately. That in itself was striking because in most cases, once the Supreme Court has found unconstitutionality, there has been no problem about relief (apart from questions of retroactivity): The unconstitutional practices and acts are to cease. As is well known, the Court in *Brown II* concluded that the desegregation of public education had to proceed "with all deliberate speed." [29] The Court said that there were "complexities arising from the transition to a system of public education freed from racial discrimination." [30] More specifically, time might be necessary to carry out the ruling because of

> problems related to administration, arising from the physical condition of the school plant, the school transportation system personnel, revision of school districts and attendance areas into compact units to achieve a system of determining admission to the public school on a non-racial basis, and revision of local laws and regulations which may be necessary in solving the foregoing problems.[31]

Now, I do not know whether the Court believed what it said in this passage, but it is a fantastic bit of nonsense that is, for my purposes, most instructive. Why? Because there was nothing complicated about most of the dual school systems of the southern states. Many counties, especially the rural ones, had one high school, typically called either "Booker T. Washington High School" or "George Washington Carver High School," where all the black children in the county went; another school, often called "Sidney Lanier High School" or "Robert E. Lee High School," was attended by all the white children in the county. There was nothing difficult about deciding that—as of the day after the decision—half of the children in the county, say all those who lived in the southern part of the county, would go to Robert E. Lee High School, and all those who lived in the northern half would go to Booker T. Washington High School. *Brown* I could have been implemented the day after the Court reached its decision. But it was also true that the black schools throughout the South

[27] Brown v. Board of Educ., 349 U.S. 294 (1955).
[28] Brown v. Board of Educ., 347 U.S. 483 (1954).
[29] 349 U.S. at 301.
[30] *Id.* at 299.
[31] *Id.* at 300–01.

were utterly wretched when compared to the white schools. There never had been any system of separate but equal education. In almost every measurable respect, the black schools were inferior. One possibility is that, without being explicitly aware of it, the members of the Supreme Court made use of some assumptions that were a significant feature of the dominant racist ideology. If the assumptions had been made explicit, the reasoning would have gone something like this: Those black schools are wretched. We cannot order white children to go to those schools, especially when they have gone to better schools in the past. So while it is unfair to deprive blacks, to make them go to these awful, segregated schools, they will have to wait until the black schools either are eliminated or are sufficiently improved so that there are good schools for everybody to attend.

What seems to me to be most objectionable, and racist, about *Brown II* is the uncritical acceptance of the idea that during this process of change, black schoolchildren would have to suffer by continuing to attend inadequate schools. The Supreme Court's solution assumed that the correct way to deal with this problem was to continue to have the black children go to their schools until the black schools were brought up to par or eliminated. That is a kind of conceptual racism in which the legal system accepts the dominant racist ideology, which holds that the claims of black children are worth less than the claims of white children in those cases in which conflict is inevitable.[32] It seems to me that any minimally

---

[32] The unusual character of *Brown II* was recognized by Mr. Justice Goldberg in Watson v. City of Memphis, 373 U.S. 526 (1963):

"Most importantly, of course, it must be recognized that even the delay countenanced by *Brown* was a necessary, albeit significant, adaptation of the usual principle that any deprivation of constitutional rights calls for prompt rectification. The rights here asserted are, like all such rights, *present* rights; they are not merely hopes to some *future* enjoyment of some formalistic constitutional promise. The basic guarantees of our Constitution are warrants for the here and now and, unless there is an overwhelmingly compelling reason, they are to be promptly fulfilled. The second *Brown* decision is but a narrowly drawn, and carefully limited, qualification upon usual precepts of constitutional adjudication. . . ."

Id. at 532–33 (emphasis in original; footnote omitted). As I have indicated, the problem with *Brown II* is that there was no "overwhelmingly compelling reason" to delay. It might be argued though, that the Court deliberately opted for "all deliberate speed" and all that meant about the dreary pace of desegregation because it believed the country would not accept full, immediate implementation of *Brown I*. If this was the reasoning, it is equally pernicious. It is sound, only if the country is identified with white people; blacks were surely willing to accept the immediate elimination of the system of racial segregation.

But someone might still say that the Court was just dealing sensibly with the political realities. The white power structure would not have accepted anything more drastic. Arguments such as these are developed at considerable length by A. Bickel, The Least Dangerous Branch 247–54 (1962). The problem with this is twofold. First, what is deemed a drastic solution has a lot to do with whether whites or blacks are being affected, and how. It was and is thought to be drastic for force and the criminal law to be used against whites to secure

fair solution would have required that during the interim process, if anybody had to go to an inadequate school, it would have been the white
children, since they were the ones who had previously had the benefit of
the good schools. But this is simply not the way racial matters are thought
about within the dominant ideology.

A study of *Brown II* is instructive because it is a good illustration of
conceptual racism within the legal system. It also reflects another kind of
conceptual racism—conceptual racism about the system. *Brown I* and *II*
typically are thought of by our culture, and especially by our educational
institutions, as representing one of the high points in the legal system's
fight against racism. The dominant way of thinking about the desegregation cases is that the legal system was functioning at its very best. Yet, as I
have indicated, there are important respects in which the legal system's
response to the then existing system of racially segregated education was
defective and hence should hardly be taken as a model of the just, institutional way of dealing with this problem of racial oppression. But the fact
that we have, as well as inculcate, these attitudes of effusive praise toward
Brown I and *II* and its progeny reveals a kind of persistent conceptual
racism in talk about the character of the legal system, and what constitutes
the right way to have dealt with the social reality of American racial oppression of black people.[33]

In theory, the foregoing analytic scheme can be applied as readily to
the social realities of sexual oppression as to racism. Given an understanding of the social realities in respect to sex—the ways in which the system of

---

compliance with laws relating to segregation. It was and is thought to be much
less drastic to use force and the criminal law against blacks who object vigorously
and sometimes violently to the system of racial oppression. The simple truth is
that when the executive branch, as well as the judiciary, thought about these
issues it typically weighed the claims of whites very differently from the
claims of blacks. The history of the enforcement of civil rights by the federal
government in the 1950's and early 1960's is largely a history of the consistent
overvaluation of the claims and concerns of whites vis-à-vis blacks. I have suggested some of the ways this was true of the Civil Rights Division of the Department of Justice. *See* Wasserstrom, Book Review, 33 U. CHI. L. REV. 406,
409–13 (1966); Wasserstrom, *Postscript: Lawyers and Revolution*, 30 U. PITT.
L. REV. 125, 131 (1968).

Second, whether the decision would have been "accepted" is in large
measure a function of what the United States government would have been
prepared to do to get the decision implemented. During this same era things
that were viewed as absolutely unacceptable or as not feasible suddenly became
acceptable and feasible without any substantial change in material circumstances,
e.g., the passage of the 1965 Voting Rights Act, 42 U.S.C. §§ 1973 *et seq.*
(1970). It mysteriously became acceptable to the Congress, enforceable by the
government and accepted by the South when Reverend Reeb and Mrs. Liuzzo
were murdered during the time of the Selma march, and former President Johnson
declared his determination to see the law enacted and enforced.

[33] A discussion of some of these same kinds of issues concerning ideology can be found
in Thalberg, *Justifications for Institutional Racism*, 5 PHIL. F. 243 (1973).

patriarchy inequitably distributes important benefits and burdens for the benefit of males, and the ideology which is a part of that patriarchal system and supportive of it—one can examine the different types of sexism that exist within the legal system. In practice the task is more difficult because we are inclined to take as appropriate even overt instances of sexist laws, e.g., that it is appropriately a part of the definition of rape that a man cannot rape his wife.[34] The task is also more difficult because sexism is, as I have suggested, a "deeper" phenomenon than racism.[35] As a result, there is less awareness of the significance of much of the social reality, e.g., that the language we use to talk about the world and ourselves has embedded within it ideological assumptions and preferences that support the existing patriarchal system.[36] Cases of institutional sexism will therefore be systematically harder to detect. But these difficulties to one side, the mode of analysis seems to me to be in principle equally applicable to sexism, although, as I indicate in the next section on ideals, a complete account of the sexism of the legal system necessarily awaits a determination of what is the correct picture of the good society in respect to sexual differences.

II. Ideals

The second perspective, described at the outset, which is also important for an understanding and analysis of racism and sexism, is the perspective of the ideal. Just as we can and must ask what is involved today in our culture in being of one race or of one sex rather than the other, and how individuals are in fact viewed and treated, we can also ask different questions: namely, what would the good or just society make of race and sex, and to what degree, if at all, would racial and sexual distinctions ever be taken into account? Indeed, it could plausibly be argued that we could not have an adequate idea of whether a society was racist or sexist unless we had some conception of what a thoroughly nonracist or nonsexist society would look like. This perspective is an extremely instructive as well as an often neglected one. Comparatively little theoretical

[34] In California, rape is defined as "an act of sexual intercourse, accomplished with a female *not the wife of the perpetrator*, under either of the following circumstances. . . ." CAL. PENAL CODE § 261 (West Supp. 1976) (emphasis added).

[35] For an example of a kind of analysis that is beginning to show some of the ways in which the law builds upon and supports the patriarchal system of marriage, see Johnston, *Sex and Property: The Common Law Tradition, The Law School Curriculum, and Developments Toward Equality,* 47 N.Y.U. L. REV. 1033, 1071–89 (1972). Another very rich source is the recent casebook on sex discrimination by B. BABCOCK, A. FREEDMAN, E. NORTON & S. ROSS, SEX DISCRIMINATION AND THE LAW—CAUSES AND REMEDIES (1975).

[36] *See, e.g.,* R. LAKOFF, LANGUAGE AND WOMAN'S PLACE (1975); Baker, *"Pricks" and "Chicks": A Plea for "Persons,"* in PHILOSOPHY AND SEX 45 (R. Baker & F. Elliston eds. 1975); Moulton, *Sex and Reference* in *id.* at 34.

literature that deals with either racism or sexism has concerned itself in a systematic way with this perspective.

In order to ask more precisely what some of the possible ideals are of desirable racial or sexual differentiation, it is necessary to see that we must ask: "In respect to what?" And one way to do this is to distinguish in a crude way among three levels or areas of social and political arrangements and activities. These correspond very roughly to the matters of status, role, and temperament identified earlier. First, there is the area of basic political rights and obligations, including the rights to vote and to travel, and the obligation to pay income taxes. Second, there is the area of important, nongovernmental institutional benefits and burdens. Examples are access to and employment in the significant economic markets, the opportunity to acquire and enjoy housing in the setting of one's choice, the right of persons who want to marry each other to do so, and the duties (nonlegal as well as legal) that persons acquire in getting married. And third, there is the area of individual, social interaction, including such matters as whom one will have as friends, and what aesthetic preferences one will cultivate and enjoy.

As to each of these three areas we can ask, for example, whether in a nonracist society it would be thought appropriate ever to take the race of the individuals into account. Thus, one picture of a nonracist society is that which is captured by what I call the assimilationist ideal: a nonracist society would be one in which the race of an individual would be the functional equivalent of the eye color of individuals in our society today.[37] In our society no basic political rights and obligations are determined on the basis of eye color. No important institutional benefits and burdens are connected with eye color. Indeed, except for the mildest sort of aesthetic preferences, a person would be thought odd who even made private, social decisions by taking eye color into account. And for reasons that we could fairly readily state we could explain why it would be wrong to permit anything but the mildest, most trivial aesthetic preference to turn on eye color. The reasons would concern the irrelevance of eye color for any political or social institution, practice or arrangement. According to the assimilationist ideal, a nonracist society would be one in which an individual's race was of no more significance in any of these three areas than is eye color today.

The assimilationist ideal in respect to sex does not seem to be as readily plausible and obviously attractive here as it is in the case of race. In fact, many persons invoke the possible realization of the assimilationist ideal as a reason for rejecting the Equal Rights Amendment and indeed

---

[37] There is a danger in calling this ideal the "assimilationist" ideal. That term suggests the idea of incorporating oneself, one's values, and the like into the dominant group and its practices and values. I want to make it clear that no part of that idea is meant to be captured by my use of this term. Mine is a stipulative definition.

the idea of women's liberation itself. My own view is that the assimilationist ideal may be just as good and just as important an ideal in respect
to sex as it is in respect to race. But many persons think there are good
reasons why an assimilationist society in respect to sex would not be
desirable.

To be sure, to make the assimilationist ideal a reality in respect to
sex would involve more profound and fundamental revisions of our institutions and our attitudes than would be the case in respect to race. On the
institutional level we would have to alter radically our practices concerning
the family and marriage. If a nonsexist society is a society in which one's
sex is no more significant than eye color in our society today, then laws
that require the persons who are getting married to be of different sexes
would clearly be sexist laws.

And on the attitudinal and conceptual level, the assimilationist ideal
would require the eradication of all sex-role differentiation. It would never
teach about the inevitable or essential attributes of masculinity or femin-
ity; it would never encourage or discourage the ideas of sisterhood or
brotherhood; and it would be unintelligible to talk about the virtues as
well as disabilities of being a woman or a man. Were sex like eye color,
these things would make no sense. Just as the normal, typical adult is
virtually oblivious to the eye color of other persons for all major interpersonal relationships, so the normal, typical adult in this kind of nonsexist society would be indifferent to the sexual, physiological differences
of other persons for all interpersonal relationships.

To acknowledge that things would be very different is, of course,
hardly to concede that they would be undesirable. But still, perhaps the
problem is with the assimilationist ideal. And the assimilationist ideal is
certainly not the only possible, plausible ideal.

There are, for instance, two others that are closely related, but distinguishable. One I call the ideal of diversity; the other, the ideal of
tolerance. Both can be understood by considering how religion, rather
than eye color, tends to be thought about in our culture. According to the
ideal of diversity, heterodoxy in respect to religious belief and practice is
regarded as a positive good. On this view there would be a loss—it would
be a worse society—were everyone to be a member of the same religion.
According to the other view, the ideal of tolerance, heterodoxy in respect
to religious belief and practice would be seen more as a necessary, lesser
evil. On this view there is nothing intrinsically better about diversity in
respect to religion, but the evils of achieving anything like homogeneity
far outweigh the possible benefits.

Now, whatever differences there might be between the ideals of
diversity and tolerance, the similarities are more striking. Under neither
ideal would it be thought that the allocation of basic political rights and
duties should take an individual's religion into account. And we would
want equalitarianism even in respect to most important institutional bene-

fits and burdens—for example, access to employment in the desirable vocations. Nonetheless, on both views it would be deemed appropriate to have
some institutions (typically those that are connected in an intimate way
with these religions) that do in a variety of ways take the religion of
members of the society into account. For example, it might be thought
permissible and appropriate for members of a religious group to join
together in collective associations which have religious, educational and
social dimensions. And on the individual, interpersonal level, it might be
thought unobjectionable, or on the diversity view, even admirable, were
persons to select their associates, friends, and mates on the basis of their
religious orientation. So there are two possible and plausible ideals of what
the good society would look like in respect to religion in which religious
differences would be to some degree maintained because the diversity of
religions was seen either as an admirable, valuable feature of the society,
or as one to be tolerated. The picture is a more complex, less easily
describable one than that of the assimilationist ideal.

It may be that in respect to sex (and conceivably, even in respect to
race) something more like either of these ideals in respect to religion is
the right one. But one problem then—and it is a very substantial one—is to
specify with a good deal of precision and care what that ideal really comes
to. Which legal, institutional and personal differentiations are permissible
and which are not? Which attitudes and beliefs concerning sexual identification and difference are properly introduced and maintained and which
are not? Part, but by no means all, of the attractiveness of the assimilationist ideal is its clarity and simplicity. In the good society of the assimilationist sort we would be able to tell easily and unequivocally whether
any law, practice, or attitude was in any respect either racist or sexist. Part,
but by no means all, of the unattractiveness of any pluralistic ideal is that
it makes the question of what is racist or sexist a much more difficult and
complicated one to answer. But although simplicity and lack of ambiguity
may be virtues, they are not the only virtues to be taken into account in
deciding among competing ideals. We quite appropriately take other
considerations to be relevant to an assessment of the value and worth of
alternative nonracist and nonsexist societies.

Nor do I even mean to suggest that all persons who reject the assimilationist ideal in respect to sex would necessarily embrace either something
like the ideal of tolerance or the ideal of diversity. Some persons might
think the right ideal was one in which substantially greater sexual differentiation and sex-role identification was retained than would be the case
under either of these conceptions. Thus, someone might believe that the
good society was, perhaps, essentially like the one they think we now
have in respect to sex: equality of political rights, such as the right to vote,
but all of the sexual differentiation in both legal and nonlegal institutions
that is characteristic of the way in which our society has been and still is
ordered. And someone might also believe that the usual ideological justifications for these arrangements are the correct and appropriate ones.

This could, of course, be regarded as a version of the ideal of diversity, with the emphasis upon the extensive character of the institutional and personal difference connected with sexual identity. Whether it is a kind of ideal of diversity or a different ideal altogether turns, I think, upon two things: First, how pervasive the sexual differentiation is, second, whether the ideal contains a conception of the appropriateness of significant institutional and interpersonal inequality, e.g., that the woman's job is in large measure to serve and be dominated by the male. The more this latter feature is present, the clearer the case for regarding this as ideal, distinctively different from any of those described by me so far.

The next question, of course, is that of how a choice is rationally to be made among these different, possible ideals. One place to begin is with the empirical world. For the question of whether something is a plausible and attractive ideal does turn in part on the nature of the empirical world. If it is true, for example, that any particular characteristic, such as sex, is not only a socially significant category in our culture but that it is largely a socially created one as well, then many ostensible objections to the assimilationist ideal appear immediately to disappear.

What I mean is this: It is obvious that we could formulate and use some sort of a crude, incredibly imprecise physiological concept of race. In this sense we could even say that race is a naturally occurring rather than a socially created feature of the world. There are diverse skin colors and related physiological characteristics distributed among human beings. But the fact is that except for skin hue and the related physiological characteristics, race is a socially created category. And skin hue, as I have shown, is neither a necessary nor a sufficient condition for being classified as black in our culture. Race as a naturally occurring characteristic is also a socially irrelevant category. There do not in fact appear to be any characteristics that are part of this natural concept of race and that are in any plausible way even relevant to the appropriate distribution of any political, institutional, or interpersonal concerns in the good society. Because in this sense race is like eye color, there is no plausible case to be made on this ground against the assimilationist ideal.[38]

There is, of course, the social reality of race. In creating and tolerating a society in which race matters, we must recognize that we have created a vastly more complex concept of race which includes what might be called the idea of ethnicity as well—a set of attitudes, traditions, beliefs, etc., which the society has made part of what it means to be of a race. It may be, therefore, that one could argue that a form of the pluralist ideal ought to be preserved in respect to race, in the socially created sense, for reasons

[38] This is not to deny that certain people believe that race is linked with characteristics that prima facie are relevant. Such beliefs persist. They are, however, unjustified by the evidence. *See, e.g.,* Block & Dworkin, *IQ, Heritability and Inequality* (pts. 1–2), 3 PHIL. & PUB. AFF. 331, 4 *id.* 40 (1974). More to the point, even if it were true that such a linkage existed, none of the characteristics suggested would require that political or social institutions, or interpersonal relationships, would have to be structured in a certain way.

similar to those that might be offered in support of the desirability of some version of the pluralist ideal in respect to religion. As I have indicated, I am skeptical, but for the purposes of this essay it can well be left an open question.

Despite appearances, the case of sex is more like that of race than is often thought. What opponents of assimilationism seize upon is that sexual difference appears to be a naturally occurring category of obvious and inevitable social relevance in a way, or to a degree, which race is not. The problems with this way of thinking are twofold. To begin with, an analysis of the social realities reveals that it is the socially created sexual differences which tend in fact to matter the most. It is sex-role differentiation, not gender per se,[39] that makes men and women as different as they are from each other, and it is sex-role differences which are invoked to justify most sexual differentiation at any of the levels of society.[40]

More importantly, even if naturally occurring sexual differences were of such a nature that they were of obvious prima facie social relevance, this would by no means settle the question of whether in the good society

[39] The term "gender" may be used in a number of different senses. I use it to refer to those anatomical, physiological, and other differences (if any) that are naturally occurring in the sense described above. Some persons refer to these differences as "sex differences," but that seems to me confusing. In any event, I am giving a stipulative definition to "gender."

[40] See, e.g., authorities cited in note 8 supra; M. MEAD, SEX AND TEMPERAMENT IN THREE PRIMITIVE SOCIETIES (1935):

"These three situations [the cultures of the Anapesh, the Mundugumor, and the Tchambuli] suggest, then, a very definite conclusion. If those temperamental attitudes which we have traditionally regarded as feminine—such as passivity, responsiveness, and a willingness to cherish children—can so easily be set up as the masculine pattern in one tribe, and in another to be outlawed for the majority of women as well as for the majority of men, we no longer have any basis for regarding such aspects of behaviour as sex-linked. . . .

". . . We are forced to conclude that human nature is almost unbelievably malleable, responding accurately and contrastingly to contrasting cultural conditions. . . . Standardized personality differences between the sexes are of this order, cultural creations to which each generation, male and female is trained to conform."

Id. at 190–91.

A somewhat different view is expressed in J. SHERMAN, ON THE PSYCHOLOGY OF WOMEN (1971). There, the author suggests that there are "natural" differences of a psychological sort between men and women, the chief ones being aggressiveness and strength of sex drive. See id. at 238. However, even if she is correct as to these biologically based differences, this does little to establish what the good society should look like. See pp. 611–15 infra.

Almost certainly the most complete discussion of this topic is E. MACOBY & C. JACKLIN, THE PSYCHOLOGY OF SEX DIFFERENCES (1974). The authors conclude that the sex differences which are, in their words, "fairly well established," are: (1) that girls have greater verbal ability than boys; (2) that boys excel in visual-spacial ability; (3) that boys excel in mathematical ability; and (4) that males are more aggressive. Id at 351–52. They conclude, in respect to the etiology of these psychological sex differences, that there appears to be a biological component to the greater visual-spacial ability of males and to their greater aggressiveness. Id. at 360.

sex should or should not be as minimally significant as eye color. Even though there are biological differences between men and women in nature, this fact does not determine the question of what the good society can and should make of these differences. I have difficulty understanding why so many persons seem to think that it does settle the question adversely to anything like the assimilationist ideal. They might think it does settle the question for two different reasons. In the first place, they might think the differences are of such a character that they substantially affect what would be possible within a good society of human persons. Just as the fact that humans are mortal necessarily limits the features of any possible good society, so, they might argue, the fact that males and females are physiologically different limits the features of any possible good society.

In the second place, they might think the differences are of such a character that they are relevant to the question of what would be desirable in the good society. That is to say, they might not think that the differences *determine* to a substantial degree what is possible, but that the differences ought to be taken into account in any rational construction of an ideal social existence.

The second reason seems to me to be a good deal more plausible than the first. For there appear to be very few, if any, respects in which the ineradicable, naturally occurring differences between males and females *must* be taken into account. The industrial revolution has certainly made any of the general differences in strength between the sexes capable of being ignored by the good society in virtually all activities.[41] And it is sex-

---

[41] As Sherman observes:

"Each sex has its own special physical assets and liabilities. The principal female liability of less muscular strength is not ordinarily a handicap in a civilized, mechanized, society. . . . There is nothing in the biological evidence to prevent women from taking a role of equality in a civilized society."

J. SHERMAN, *supra* note 40, at 11.

There are, of course, some activities that would be sexually differentiated in the assimilationist society; namely, those that were specifically directed toward, say, measuring unaided physical strength. Thus, I think it likely that even in this ideal society, weight lifting contests and boxing matches would in fact be dominated, perhaps exclusively so, by men. But it is hard to find any *significant* activities or institutions that are analogous. And it is not clear that such insignificant activities would be thought worth continuing, especially since sports function in existing patriarchal societies to help maintain the dominance of males. *See* K. MILLETT, *supra* note 7, at 48–49.

It is possible that there are some nontrivial activities or occupations that depend sufficiently directly upon unaided physical strength that most if not all women would be excluded. Perhaps being a lifeguard at the ocean is an example. Even here, though, it would be important to see whether the way lifeguarding had traditionally been done could be changed to render such physical strength unimportant. If it could be changed, then the question would simply be one of whether the increased cost (or loss of efficiency) was worth the gain in terms of equality and the avoidance of sex-role differentiation. In a nonpatriarchal society very different from ours, where sex was not a dominant social category, the argument from efficiency might well prevail. What is important, once again, is to see how infrequent and peripheral such occupational cases are.

role acculturation, not biology, that mistakenly leads many persons to the view that women are both naturally and necessarily better suited than men to be assigned the primary responsibilities of child rearing. Indeed, the only fact that seems required to be taken into account is the fact that reproduction of the human species requires that the fetus develop *in utero* for a period of months. Sexual intercourse is not necessary, for artificial insemination is available. Neither marriage nor the family is required for conception or child rearing. Given the present state of medical knowledge and the natural realities of female pregnancy, it is difficult to see why any important institutional or interpersonal arrangements *must* take the existing gender difference of *in utero* pregnancy into account.

But, as I have said, this is still to leave it a wholly open question to what degree the good society *ought* to build upon any ineradicable gender differences to construct institutions which would maintain a substantial degree of sexual differentiation. The arguments are typically far less persuasive for doing so than appears upon the initial statement of this possibility. Someone might argue that the fact of menstruation, for instance, could be used as a premise upon which to predicate different social roles for females than for males. But this could only plausibly be proposed if two things were true: first, that menstruation would be debilitating to women and hence relevant to social role even in a culture which did not teach women to view menstruation as a sign of uncleanliness or as a curse;[42]

---

[42] *See, e.g.,* Paige, Women Learn to Sing the Menstrual Blues, in THE FEMALE EXPERIENCE 17 (C. Tavis ed. 1973).

"I have come to believe that the 'raging hormones' theory of menstrual distress simply isn't adequate. All women have the raging hormones, but not all women have menstrual symptoms, nor do they have the same symptoms for the same reasons. Nor do I agree with the 'raging neurosis' theory, which argues that women who have menstrual symptoms are merely whining neurotics, who need only a kind pat on the head to cure their problems.

"We must instead consider the problem from the perspective of women's subordinate social position, and of the cultural ideology that so narrowly defines the behaviors and emotions that are appropriately 'feminine.' Women have perfectly good reasons to react emotionally to reproductive events. Menstruation, pregnancy and childbirth—so sacred, yet so unclean—are the woman's primary avenues of achievement and self-expression. Her reproductive abilities define her femininity; other routes to success are only second-best in this society. . . .

• • •

". . . My current research on a sample of 114 societies around the world indicates that ritual observances and taboos about menstruation are a method of controlling women and their fertility. Men apparently use such rituals, along with those surrounding pregnancy and childbirth, to assert their claims to women and their children.

". . . The hormone theory isn't giving us much mileage, and it's time to turn it in for a better model, one that looks to our beliefs about menstruation and women. It is no mere coincidence that women get the blue meanies along with an event they consider embarrassing, unclean—and a curse."
Id. at 21.

and second, that the way in which menstruation necessarily affected some or all women was in fact related in an important way to the role in question. But even if both of these were true, it would still be an open question whether any sexual differentiation ought to be built upon these facts. The society could still elect to develop institutions that would nullify the effect of the natural differences. And suppose, for example, what seems implausible—that some or all women will not be able to perform a particular task while menstruating, *e.g.*, guard a border. It would be easy enough, if the society wanted to, to arrange for substitute guards for the women who were incapacitated. We know that persons are not good guards when they are sleepy, and we make arrangements so that persons alternate guard duty to avoid fatigue. The same could be done for menstruating women, even given these implausibly strong assumptions about menstruation. At the risk of belaboring the obvious, what I think it important to see is that the case against the assimilationist ideal—if it is to be a good one—must rest on arguments concerned to show why some other ideal would be preferable; it cannot plausibly rest on the claim that it is either necessary or inevitable.

There is, however, at least one more argument based upon nature, or at least the "natural," that is worth mentioning. Someone might argue that significant sex-role differentiation is natural not in the sense that it is biologically determined but only in the sense that it is a virtually universal phenomenon in human culture. By itself, this claim of virtual universality, even if accurate, does not directly establish anything about the desirability or undesirability of any particular ideal. But it can be made into an argument by the addition of the proposition that where there is a virtually universal social practice, there is probably some good or important purpose served by the practice. Hence, given the fact of sex-role differentiation in all, or almost all, cultures, we have some reason to think that substantial sex-role differentiation serves some important purpose for and in human society.

This is an argument, but I see no reason to be impressed by it. The premise which turns the fact of sex-role differentiation into any kind of a strong reason for sex-role differentiation is the premise of conservatism. And it is no more convincing here than elsewhere. There are any number of practices that are typical and yet upon reflection seem without significant social purpose. Slavery was once such a practice; war perhaps still is.

More to the point, perhaps, the concept of "purpose" is ambiguous. It can mean in a descriptive sense "plays some role" or "is causally relevant." Or it can mean in a prescriptive sense "does something desirable" or "has some useful function." If "purpose" is used descriptively in the conservative premise, then the argument says nothing about the continued desirability of sex-role differentiation or the assimilationist ideal. If "purpose" is used prescriptively in the conservative premise, then there is no reason to think that premise is true.

To put it another way, the question is whether it is desirable to have a society in which sex-role differences are to be retained at all. The straight-forward way to think about that question is to ask what would be good and what would be bad about a society in which sex functioned like eye color does in our society. We can imagine what such a society would look like and how it would work. It is hard to see how our thinking is sub-stantially advanced by reference to what has typically or always been the case. If it is true, as I think it is, that the sex-role differentiated societies we have had so far have tended to concentrate power in the hands of males, have developed institutions and ideologies that have perpetuated that concentration and have restricted and prevented women from living the kinds of lives that persons ought to be able to live for themselves, then this says far more about what may be wrong with any nonassimilationist ideal than does the conservative premise say what may be right about any nonassimilationist ideal.

Nor is this all that can be said in favor of the assimilationist ideal. For it seems to me that the strongest affirmative moral argument on its behalf is that it provides for a kind of individual autonomy that a non-assimilationist society cannot attain. Any nonassimilationist society will have sex roles. Any nonassimilationist society will have some institutions that distinguish between individuals by virtue of their gender, and any such society will necessarily teach the desirability of doing so. Any sub-stantially nonassimilationist society will make one's sexual identity an important characteristic, so that there are substantial psychological, role, and status differences between persons who are males and those who are females. Even if these could be attained without systemic dominance of one sex over the other, they would, I think, be objectionable on the ground that they necessarily impaired an individual's ability to develop his or her own characteristics, talents and capacities to the fullest extent to which he or she might desire. Sex roles, and all that accompany them, necessarily impose limits—restrictions on what one can do, be or become. As such, they are, I think, at least prima facie wrong.

To some degree, all role-differentiated living is restrictive in this sense. Perhaps, therefore, all role-differentiation in society is to some degree troublesome, and perhaps all strongly role-differentiated societies are objectionable. But the case against sexual differentiation need not rest upon this more controversial point. For one thing that distinguishes sex roles from many other roles is that they are wholly involuntarily assumed. One has no choice whatsoever about whether one shall be born a male or female. And if it is a consequence of one's being born a male or a female that one's subsequent emotional, intellectual, and material develop-ment will be substantially controlled by this fact, then substantial, permanent, and involuntarily assumed restraints have been imposed on the most central factors concerning the way one will shape and live one's life. The point to be emphasized is that this would necessarily be the case, even in the unlikely event that substantial sexual differentiation could be maintained without one sex or the other becoming dominant and developing institutions and an ideology to support that dominance.

I do not believe that all I have said in this section shows in any conclusive fashion the desirability of the assimilationist ideal in respect to sex. I have tried to show why some typical arguments against the assimilationist ideal are not persuasive,[43] and why some of the central ones in support of that ideal are persuasive. But I have not provided a complete account, or a complete analysis. At a minimum, what I have shown is how thinking about this topic ought to proceed, and what kinds of arguments need to be marshalled and considered before a serious and informed discussion of alternative conceptions of a nonsexist society can even take place. Once assembled, these arguments need to be individually and carefully assessed before any final, reflective choice among the competing ideals can be made. There does, however, seem to me to be a strong presumptive case for something very close to, if not identical with, the assimilationist ideal.

--- **ALISON JAGGAR**

Political Philosophies of Women's Liberation

Feminists are united by a belief that the unequal and inferior social status of women is unjust and needs to be changed. But they are deeply divided about what changes are required. The deepest divisions are not differences about strategy or the kinds of tactics that will best serve women's interests; instead, they are differences about what *are* women's interests, what constitutes women's liberation.

Within the women's liberation movement, several distinct ideologies can be discerned. All [1] believe that justice requires freedom and equality for women, but they differ on such basic philosophical questions as the proper account of freedom and equality, the functions of the state, and the notion of what constitutes human, and especially female, nature. In

---

[43] Still other arguments against something like the assimilationist ideal and in favor of something like the idea of diversity are considered by Jaggar and shown by her to be unpersuasive. *See* Jagger, *supra* note 22, at 281–91.

[1] All except one: as we shall see later, Lesbian separatism is evasive on the question whether men should, even ultimately, be equal with women.

what follows, I shall outline the feminist ideologies which are currently most influential and show how these give rise to differences on some particular issues. Doing this will indicate why specific debates over feminist questions cannot be settled in isolation but can only be resolved in the context of a theoretical framework derived from reflection on the fundamental issues of social and political philosophy.

The Conservative View

This is the position against which all feminists are in reaction. In brief, it is the view that differential treatment of women, as a group, is not unjust. Conservatives admit, of course, that some individual women do suffer hardships, but they do not see this suffering as part of the systematic social oppression of women. Instead, the clear differences between women's and men's social roles are rationalized in one of two ways. Conservatives either claim that the female role is not inferior to that of the male, or they argue that women are inherently better adapted than men to the traditional female sex role. The former claim advocates a kind of sexual apartheid, typically described by such phrases as "complementary but equal"; the latter postulates an inherent inequality between the sexes.[2]

All feminists reject the first claim, and most feminists, historically, have rejected the second. However, it is interesting to note that, as we shall see later, some modern feminists have revived the latter claim.

Conservative views come in different varieties, but they all have certain fundamentals in common. All claim that men and women should fulfill different social functions, that these differences should be enforced by law where opinion and custom are insufficient, and that such action may be justified by reference to innate differences between men and women. Thus all sexual conservatives presuppose that men and women are inherently unequal in abilities, that the alleged difference in ability implies a difference in social function and that one of the main tasks of the state is to ensure that the individual perform his or her proper social function. Thus, they argue, social differentiation between the sexes is not unjust, since justice not only allows but requires us to treat unequals unequally.

[2] The inequalities between the sexes are said to be both physical and psychological. Alleged psychological differences between the sexes include women's emotional instability, greater tolerance for boring detail, incapacity for abstract thought, and less aggression. Writers who have made such claims range from Rousseau (*Émile, or Education* [1762; translation, London: J. M. Dent, 1911]; see especially Book 5 concerning the education of "Sophie, or Woman"), through Schopenhauer (*The World As Will and Idea* and his essay "On Women"), Fichte (*The Science of Rights*), Nietzsche (*Thus Spake Zarathustra*), and Freud down to, in our own times, Steven Goldberg with *The Inevitability of Patriarchy* (New York: William Morrow, 1973–74).

Liberal Feminism

In speaking of liberal feminism, I am referring to that tradition which received its classic expression in J. S. Mill's *The Subjection of Women* and which is alive today in various "moderate" groups, such as the National Organization for Women, which agitate for legal reform to improve the status of women.

The main thrust of the liberal feminist's argument is that an individual woman should be able to determine her social role with as great freedom as does a man. Though women now have the vote, the liberal sees that we are still subject to many constraints, legal as well as customary, which hinder us from success in the public worlds of politics, business and the professions. Consequently the liberal views women's liberation as the elimination of those constraints and the achievement of equal civil rights.

Underlying the liberal argument is the belief that justice requires that the criteria for allocating individuals to perform a particular social function should be grounded in the individual's ability to perform the tasks in question. The use of criteria such as "race, sex, religion, national origin or ancestry" [3] will normally not be directly relevant to most tasks. Moreover, in conformity with the traditional liberal stress on individual rights, the liberal feminist insists that each person should be considered separately in order that an outstanding individual should not be penalized for deficiencies that her sex as a whole might possess.[4]

This argument is buttressed by the classic liberal belief that there should be a minimum of state intervention in the affairs of the individual. Such a belief entails rejection of the paternalistic view that women's weakness requires that we be specially protected.[5] Even if relevant differences between women and men in general could be demonstrated, the existence of those differences still would not constitute a sufficient reason for allowing legal restrictions on women as a group. Even apart from the possibility of penalizing an outstanding individual, the liberal holds that women's own good sense or, in the last resort, our incapacity to do the job will render legal prohibitions unnecessary.[6]

From this sketch it is clear that the liberal feminist interprets equality to mean that each individual, regardless of sex, should have an equal opportunity to seek whatever social positions she or he wishes. Freedom is primarily the absence of legal constraints to hinder women in this enterprise. However, the modern liberal feminist recognizes that equality and freedom, construed in the liberal way, may not always be compatible.

---

[3] This is the language used by Title VII of the Civil Rights Act with Executive Order 11246, 1965, and Title IX.

[4] J. S. Mill, *The Subjection of Women* (1869; reprint ed., London: J. M. Dent, 1965), p. 236.

[5] Ibid., p. 243.

[6] Ibid, p. 235.

Hence, the modern liberal feminist differs from the traditional one in believing not only that laws should not discriminate against women, but that they should be used to make discrimination illegal. Thus she would outlaw unequal pay scales, prejudice in the admission of women to job-training programs and professional schools, and discrimination by employers in hiring practices. She would also outlaw such things as discrimination by finance companies in the granting of loans, mortgages, and insurance to women.

In certain areas, the modern liberal even appears to advocate laws which discriminate in favor of women. For instance, she may support the preferential hiring of women over men, or alimony for women unqualified to work outside the home. She is likely to justify her apparent inconsistency by claiming that such differential treatment is necessary to remedy past inequalities—but that it is only a temporary measure. With regard to (possibly paid) maternity leaves and the employer's obligation to reemploy a woman after such a leave, the liberal argues that the bearing of children has at least as good a claim to be regarded as a social service as does a man's military or jury obligation, and that childbearing should therefore carry corresponding rights to protection. The liberal also usually advocates the repeal of laws restricting contraception and abortion, and may demand measures to encourage the establishment of private day-care centers. However, she points out that none of these demands, nor the father's payment of child support, should really be regarded as discrimination in favor of women. It is only the customary assignment of responsibility for children to their mothers which it makes it possible to overlook the fact that fathers have an equal obligation to provide and care for their children. Women's traditional responsibility for child care is culturally determined, not biologically inevitable—except for breast-feeding, which is now optional. Thus the liberal argues that if women are to participate in the world outside the home on equal terms with men, not only must our reproductive capacity come under our own control but, if we have children, we must be able to share the responsibility for raising them. In return, as an extension of the same principle of equal responsibility, the modern liberal supports compulsory military service for women so long as it is obligatory for men.

Rather than assuming that every apparent difference in interests and abilities between the sexes is innate, the liberal recognizes that such differences, if they do not result entirely from our education, are at least greatly exaggerated by it. By giving both sexes the same education, whether it be cooking or carpentry, the liberal claims that she is providing the only environment in which individual potentialities (and, indeed, genuine sexual differences) can emerge. She gives little weight to the possible charge that in doing this she is not liberating women but only imposing a different kind of conditioning. At the root of the liberal tradition is a deep faith in the autonomy of the individual which is incapable of being challenged within that framework.

In summary, then, the liberal views liberation for women as the freedom to determine our own social role and to compete with men on terms that are as equal as possible. She sees every individual as being engaged in constant competition with every other in order to maximize her or his own self-interest, and she claims that the function of the state is to see that such competition is fair by enforcing "equality of opportunity." The liberal does not believe that it is necessary to change the whole existing social structure in order to achieve women's liberation. Nor does she see it as being achieved simultaneously for all women; she believes that individual women may liberate themselves long before their condition is attained by all. Finally, the liberal claims that her concept of women's liberation also involves liberation for men, since men are not only removed from a privileged position but they are also freed from having to accept the entire responsibility for such things as the support of their families and the defense of their country.

Classical Marxist Feminism

On the classical Marxist view, the oppression of women is, historically and currently, a direct result of the institution of private property; therefore, it can only be ended by the abolition of that institution. Consequently, feminism must be seen as part of a broader struggle to achieve a communist society. Feminism is one reason for communism. The long-term interests of women are those of the working class.

For Marxists, everyone is oppressed by living in a society where a small class of individuals owns the means of production and hence is enabled to dominate the lives of the majority who are forced to sell their labor power in order to survive. Women have an equal interest with men in eliminating such a class society. However, Marxists also recognize that women suffer special forms of oppression to which men are *not* subject, and hence, insofar as this oppression is rooted in capitalism, women have additional reasons for the overthrow of that economic system.

Classical Marxists believe that the special oppression of women results primarily from our traditional position in the family. This excludes women from participation in "public" production and relegates us to domestic work in the "private" world of the home. From its inception right up to the present day, monogamous marriage was designed to perpetuate the consolidation of wealth in the hands of a few. Those few are men. Thus, for Marxists, an analysis of the family brings out the inseparability of class society from male supremacy. From the very beginning of surplus production, "the sole exclusive aims of monogamous marriage were to make the man supreme in the family, and to propagate, as the future heirs to his wealth, children indisputably his own." [7] Such marriage is "founded on the open or concealed domestic slavery of the wife," [8] and is char-

---

[7] Friedrich Engels, *The Origin of the Family, Private Property and the State* (1884; reprint ed., New York: International Publishers, 1942), pp. 57–58.

[8] Ibid., p. 65.

acterized by the familiar double standard which requires sexual fidelity from the woman but not from the man.

Marxists do not claim, of course, that women's oppression is a creation of capitalism. But they do argue that the advent of capitalism intensified the degradation of women and that the continuation of capitalism requires the perpetuation of this degradation. Capitalism and male supremacy each reinforce the other. Among the ways in which sexism benefits the capitalist system are: by providing a supply of cheap labor for industry and hence exerting a downward pressure on all wages; by increasing the demand for the consumption goods on which women are conditioned to depend; and by allocating to women, for no direct pay, the performance of such socially necessary but unprofitable tasks as food preparation, domestic maintenance and the care of the children, the sick and the old.[9]

This analysis indicates the directions in which classical Marxists believe that women must move. "The first condition for the liberation of the wife is to bring the whole female sex back into public industry." [10] Only then will a wife cease to be economically dependent on her husband. But for woman's entry into public industry to be possible, fundamental social changes are necessary: all the work which women presently do—food preparation, child care, nursing, etc.—must come within the sphere of public production. Thus, whereas the liberal feminist advocates an egalitarian marriage, with each spouse shouldering equal responsibility for domestic work and economic support, the classical Marxist feminist believes that the liberation of women requires a more radical change in the family. Primarily, women's liberation requires that the economic functions performed by the family should be undertaken by the state. Thus the state should provide child care centers, public eating places, hospital facilities, etc. But all this, of course, could happen only under socialism. Hence it is only under socialism that married women will be able to participate fully in public life and end the situation where "within the family [the husband] is the bourgeois and the wife represents the proletariat." [11]

It should be noted that "the abolition of the monogamous family as the economic unit of society" [12] does not necessitate its disappearance as a social unit. Since "sexual love is by its nature exclusive," [13] marriage will continue, but now it will no longer resemble an economic contract, as it has done hitherto in the property-owning classes. Instead, it will be based solely on "mutual inclination" [14] between a woman and a man who are now in reality, and not just formally, free and equal.

[9] This is, of course, very far from being a complete account of the ways in which Marxists believe that capitalism benefits from sexism.
[10] Engels, op. cit., p. 66.
[11] Ibid., pp. 65–66.
[12] Ibid., p. 66.
[13] Ibid., p. 72.
[14] Ibid.

It is clear that classical Marxist feminism is based on very different philosophical presuppositions from those of liberal feminism. Freedom is viewed not just as the absence of discrimination against women but rather as freedom from the coercion of economic necessity. Similarly, equality demands not mere equality of opportunity to compete against other individuals but rather approximate equality in the satisfaction of material needs. Hence, the classical Marxist feminist's view of the function of the state is very different from the view of the liberal feminist. Ultimately, the Marxist pays at least lip service to the belief that the state is an instrument of class oppression which eventually will wither away. In the meantime, she believes that it should undertake far more than the minimal liberal function of setting up fair rules for the economic race. Instead, it should take over the means of production and also assume those economic responsibilities that capitalism assigned to the individual family and that placed that woman in a position of dependence on the man. This view of the state presupposes a very different account of human nature from that held by the liberal. Instead of seeing the individual as fundamentally concerned with the maximization of her or his own self-interest, the classical Marxist feminist believes that the selfish and competitive aspects of our natures are the result of their systematic perversion in an acquisitive society. Viewing human nature as flexible and as reflecting the economic organization of society, she argues that it is necessary for women (indeed for everybody) to be comprehensively reeducated, and to learn that ultimately individuals have common rather than competing goals and interests.

Since she sees women's oppression as a function of the larger socioeconomic system, the classical Marxist feminist denies the possibility, envisaged by the liberal, of liberation for a few women on an individual level. However, she does agree with the liberal that women's liberation would bring liberation for men, too. Men's liberation would now be enlarged to include freedom from class oppression and from the man's traditional responsibility to "provide" for his family, a burden that under liberalism the man merely lightens by sharing it with his wife.

Radical Feminism

Radical feminism is a recent attempt to create a new conceptual model for understanding the many different forms of the social phenomenon of oppression in terms of the basic concept of sexual oppression. It is formulated by such writers as Ti-Grace Atkinson and Shulamith Firestone.[15]

Radical feminism denies the liberal claim that the basis of women's

[15] Ti-Grace Atkinson, "Radical Feminism" and "The Institution of Sexual Intercourse" in *Notes from the Second Year: Major Writings of the Radical Feminists*, ed. S. Firestone (N.Y., 1970); and Shulamith Firestone, *The Dialectic of Sex: The Case for Feminist Revolution* (N.Y.: Bantam Books; 1970).

oppression consists in our lack of political or civil rights; similarly, it rejects the classical Marxist belief that basically women are oppressed because they live in a class society. Instead, in what seems to be a startling regression to conservatism, the radical feminist claims that the roots of women's oppression are biological. She believes that the origin of women's subjection lies in the fact that, as a result of the weakness caused by childbearing, we became dependent on men for physical survival. Thus she speaks of the origin of the family in apparently conservative terms as being primarily a biological rather than a social or economic organization.[16] The radical feminist believes that the physical subjection of women by men was historically the most basic form of oppression, prior rather than secondary to the institution of private property and its corollary, class oppression.[17] Moreover, she believes that the power relationships which develop within the biological family provide a model for understanding all other types of oppression such as racism and class society. Thus she reverses the emphasis of the classical Marxist feminist by explaining the development of class society in terms of the biological family rather than explaining the development of the family in terms of class society. She believes that the battles against capitalism and against racism are both subsidiary to the more fundamental struggle against sexism.

Since she believes that the oppression of women is basically biological, the radical feminist concludes that our liberation requires a biological revolution. She believes that only now, for the first time in history, is technology making it possible for women to be liberated from the "fundamental inequality of the bearing and raising of children." It is achieving this through the development of techniques of artificial reproduction and the consequent possibility of diffusing the childbearing and child-raising role throughout society as a whole. Such a biological revolution is basic to the achievement of those important but secondary changes in our political, social and economic systems which will make possible the other prerequisites for women's liberation. As the radical feminist sees them, those other prerequisites are: the full self-determination, including economic independence, of women (and children); the total integration of women (and children) into all aspects of the larger society; and the freedom of all women (and children) to do whatever they wish to do sexually.[18]

[16] Engels recognizes that early forms of the family were based on what he calls "natural" conditions, which presumably included the biological, but he claims that monogamy "was the first form of the family to be based, not on natural, but on economic conditions—on the victory of private property over primitive, natural communal property." Engels, op. cit., p. 57.

[17] Atkinson and Firestone do talk of women as a "political class," but not in Marx's classic sense where the criterion of an individual's class membership is her/his relationship to the means of production. Atkinson defines a class more broadly as a group treated in some special manner by other groups: in the case of women, the radical feminists believe that women are defined as a "class" in virtue of our childbearing capacity. "Radical Feminism," op. cit., p. 24.

[18] These conditions are listed and explained in The Dialectic of Sex, pp. 206–9.

Not only will technology snap the link between sex and reproduction and thus liberate women from our childbearing and child-raising function; the radical feminist believes that ultimately technology will liberate both sexes from the necessity to work. Individual economic burdens and dependencies will thereby be eliminated, along with the justification for compelling children to attend school. So both the biological and economic bases of the family will be removed by technology. The family's consequent disappearance will abolish the prototype of the social "role system," [19] the most basic form, both historically and conceptually, of oppressive and authoritarian relationships. Thus, the radical feminist does not claim that women should be free to determine their own social roles: she believes instead that the whole "role system" must be abolished, even in its biological aspects.

The end of the biological family will also eliminate the need for sexual repression. Male homosexuality, lesbianism, and extramarital sexual intercourse will no longer be viewed in the liberal way as alternative options, outside the range of state regulation, in which the individual may or may not choose to participate. Nor will they be viewed, in the classical Marxist way, as unnatural vices, perversions resulting from the degrading influence of capitalist society.[20] Instead, even the categories of homosexuality and heterosexuality will be abandoned; the very "institution of sexual intercourse," where male and female each play a well-defined role, will disappear.[21] "Humanity could finally revert to its natural 'polymorphously perverse' sexuality." [22]

For the radical feminist, as for other feminists, justice requires freedom and equality for women. But for the radical feminist "equality" means not just equality under the law nor even equality in satisfaction of basic needs; rather, it means that women, like men, should not have to bear children. Correspondingly, the radical feminist conception of freedom requires not just that women should be free to compete, nor even that we should be free from material want and economic dependence on men; rather, freedom for women means that any woman is free to have close relationships with children without having to give birth to them. Politically, the radical feminist envisions an eventual "communistic anarchy," [23] an ultimate abolition of the state. This will be achieved gradually, through an intermediate state of "cybernetic socialism" with household licenses to raise children and a guaranteed income for all. Perhaps surprisingly, in view of Freud's reputation among many feminists, the radical feminist concep-

[19] "Radical Feminism," op. cit., p. 36.
[20] Engels often expresses an extreme sexual puritanism in *The Origin of the Family, Private Property and the State*. We have already seen his claim that "sexual love is by its nature exclusive." Elsewhere (p. 57) he talks about "the abominable practice of sodomy." Lenin is well known for the expression of similar views.
[21] "The Institution of Sexual Intercourse," op. cit.
[22] *The Dialectic of Sex*, p. 209.
[23] Ibid., final chart, pp. 244–45.

tion of human nature is neo-Freudian. Firestone believes, with Freud, that "the crucial problem of modern life [is] sexuality." [24] Individuals are psychologically formed through their experience in the family, a family whose power relationships reflect the underlying biological realities of female (and childhood) dependence. But technology will smash the universality of Freudian psychology. The destruction of the biological family, never envisioned by Freud, will allow the emergence of new women and men, different from any people who have previously existed.

The radical feminist theory contains many interesting claims. Some of these look almost factual in character: they include the belief that pregnancy and childbirth are painful and unpleasant experiences, that sexuality is not naturally genital and heterosexual, and that technology may be controlled by men and women without leading to totalitarianism. Other presuppositions are more clearly normative: among them are the beliefs that technology should be used to eliminate all kinds of pain, that hard work is not in itself a virtue, that sexuality ought not to be institutionalized and, perhaps most controversial of all, that children have the same rights to self-determination as adults.

Like the other theories we have considered, radical feminism believes that women's liberation will bring benefits for men. According to this concept of women's liberation, not only will men be freed from the role of provider, but they will also participate on a completely equal basis in childbearing as well as child-rearing. Radical feminism, however, is the only theory which argues explicitly that women's liberation also necessitates children's liberation. Firestone explains that this is because "The heart of woman's oppression is her childbearing and child-rearing roles. And in turn children are defined in relation to this role and are psychologically formed by it; what they become as adults and the sorts of relationships they are able to form determine the society they will ultimately build." [25]

New Directions

Although the wave of excitement about women's liberation which arose in the late '60's has now subsided, the theoretical activity of feminists has continued. Since about 1970, it has advanced in two main directions: lesbian separatism and socialist feminism.

Lesbian separatism is less a coherent and developed ideology than an emerging movement, like the broader feminist movement, within which different ideological strains can be detected. All lesbian separatists believe that the present situation of male supremacy requires that women should refrain from heterosexual relationships. But for some lesbian separatists, this is just a temporary necessity, whereas for others, lesbianism will always be required.

[24] Ibid., p. 43.
[25] Ibid., p. 72.

Needless to say, all lesbian separatists reject the liberal and the classical Marxist beliefs about sexual preferences; but some accept the radical feminist contention that ultimately it is unimportant whether one's sexual partner be male or female.[26] However, in the immediate context of a male-supremacist society, the lesbian separatist believes that one's sexual choice attains tremendous political significance. Lesbianism becomes a way of combating the overwhelming heterosexual ideology that perpetuates male supremacy.

> Women . . . become defined as appendages to men so that there is a coherent ideological framework which says it is natural for women to create the surplus to take care of men and that men will do other things. Reproduction itself did not have to determine that. The fact that male supremacy developed the way it has and was institutionalized is an ideological creation. The ideology of heterosexuality, not the simple act of intercourse, is the whole set of assumptions which maintains the ideological power of men over women.[27]

Although this writer favors an ultimate de-institutionalization of sexual activity, her rejection of the claim that reproduction as such does not determine the inferior status of women clearly places her outside the radical feminist framework; indeed, she would identify her methodological approach as broadly Marxist. Some lesbian separatists are more radical, however. They argue explicitly for a matriarchal society which is "an affirmation of the power of female consciousness of the Mother." [28] Such matriarchists talk longingly about ancient matriarchal societies where women were supposed to have been physically strong, adept at self-defense, and the originators of such cultural advances as: the wheel, pottery, industry, leather working, metal working, fire, agriculture, animal husbandry, architecture, cities, decorative art, music, weaving, medicine, communal child care, dance, poetry, song, etc.[29] They claim that men were virtually excluded from these societies. Women's culture is compared favorably with later patriarchal cultures as being peaceful, egalitarian, vegetarian, and intellectually advanced. Matriarchal lesbian separatists would like to re-create a similar culture which would probably imitate the earlier ones in its exclusion of men as full members. Matriarchal lesbian separatists do not

---

[26] "In a world devoid of male power and, therefore, sex roles, who you lived with, loved, slept with and were committed to would be irrelevant. All of us would be equal and have equal determination over the society and how it met our needs. Until this happens, how we use our sexuality and our bodies is just as relevant to our liberation as how we use our minds and time." Coletta Reid, "Coming Out in the Women's Movement," in *Lesbianism and the Women's Movement*, ed. Nancy Myron and Charlotte Buch (Baltimore: Diana Press, 1975), p. 103.

[27] Margaret Small, "Lesbians and the Class Position of Women," in *Lesbianism and the Women's Movement*, p. 58.

[28] Jane Alpert, "Mother Right: A New Feminist Theory," *Ms.*, August 1973, p. 94.

[29] Alice, Gordon, Debbie, and Mary, *Lesbian Separatism: An Amazon Analysis*, typescript, 1973, p. 5. (To be published by Diana Press, Baltimore.)

claim unequivocally that "men are genetically predisposed towards destruction and dominance," [30] but, especially given the present research on the behavioral effects of the male hormone testosterone,[31] they think it is a possibility that lesbians must keep in mind.

Socialist feminists believe that classical Marxism and radical feminism each have both insights and deficiencies. The task of socialist feminism is to construct a theory that avoids the weaknesses of each but incorporates its (and other) insights. There is space here for only a brief account of some of the main points of this developing theory.

Socialist feminists reject the basic radical feminist contention that liberation for women requires the abolition of childbirth. Firestone's view is criticized as ahistorical, anti-dialectical, and utopian. Instead, socialist feminists accept the classical Marxist contention that socialism is the main precondition for women's liberation. But though socialism is necessary, socialist feminists do not believe that it is sufficient. Sexism can continue to exist despite public ownership of the means of production. The conclusion that socialist feminists draw is that it is necessary to resort to direct cultural action in order to develop a specifically feminist consciousness in addition to transforming the economic base. Thus their vision is totalistic, requiring "transformation of the entire fabric of social relationships." [32]

In rejecting the radical feminist view that the family is based on biological conditions, socialist feminists turn toward the classical Marxist account of monogamy as being based "not on natural but on economic conditions." [33] But they view the classical Marxist account as inadequate, overly simple. Juliet Mitchell [34] argues that the family should be analyzed in a more detailed, sophisticated, and historically specific way in terms of the separate, though interrelated, functions that women perform within it: production, reproduction, sexuality, and the socialization of the young.

Socialist feminists agree with classical Marxists that women's liberation requires the entry of women into public production. But this in itself is not sufficient. It is also necessary that women have access to the more prestigious and less deadening jobs and to supervisory and administrative positions. There should be no "women's work" within public industry.[35]

In classical Marxist theory, "productive labor" is viewed as the production of goods and services within the market economy. Some socialist

---

[30] Ibid., p. 23.

[31] It is interesting that this is the same research on which Steven Goldberg grounds his thesis of "the inevitability of patriarchy"; see note 2 above.

[32] Barbara Ehrenreich, "Socialist/Feminism and Revolution" (unpublished paper presented to the National Socialist-Feminist Conference, Antioch College, Ohio, July 1975), p. 1.

[33] Engels, op. cit., p. 57.

[34] Juliet Mitchell, *Woman's Estate* (New York: Random House, 1971). Lively discussion of Mitchell's work continues among socialist feminists.

[35] For one socialist feminist account of women's work in public industry see Sheila Rowbotham, *Woman's Consciousness, Man's World* (Baltimore: Penguin Books, 1973), chap. 6, "Sitting Next to Nellie."

feminists believe that this account of productiveness obscures the socially vital character of the labor that women perform in the home. They argue that, since it is clearly impossible under capitalism to bring all women into public production, individuals (at least as an interim measure) should be paid a wage for domestic work. This reform would dignify the position of housewives, reduce their dependence on their husbands and make plain their objective position, minimized by classical Marxists, as an integral part of the working class.[36] Not all socialist feminists accept this position, however, and the issue is extremely controversial at the time of this writing.

One of the main insights of the feminist movement has been that "the personal is political." Socialist feminists are sensitive to the power relations involved in male/female interaction and believe that it is both possible and necessary to begin changing these, even before the occurrence of a revolution in the ownership of the means of production. Thus, socialist feminists recognize the importance of a "subjective factor" in revolutionary change and reject the rigid economic determinism that has characterized many classical Marxists. They are sympathetic to attempts by individuals to change their life styles and to share responsibility for each other's lives, even though they recognize that such attempts can never be entirely successful within a capitalist context. They also reject the sexual puritanism inherent in classical Marxism, moving closer to the radical feminist position in this regard.

Clearly there are sharp differences between socialist feminism and most forms of lesbian separatism. The two have been dealt with together in this section only because each is still a developing theory and because it is not yet clear how far either represents the creation of a new ideology and how far it is simply an extension of an existing ideology. One suspects that at least the matriarchal version of lesbian separatism may be viewed as a new ideology: after all, the interpretation of "freedom" to mean "freedom from men" is certainly new, as is the suggestion that women are innately superior to men. Socialist feminism, however, should probably be seen as an extension of classical Marxism, using essentially similar notions of human nature, of freedom and equality, and of the role of the state, but attempting to show that women's situation and the sphere of personal relations in general need more careful analysis by Marxists.[37]

---

[36] One influential exponent of wages for housework is Mariarosa Dalla Costa, *The Power of Women and the Subversion of Community* (Bristol, England: Falling Wall Press, 1973).

[37] Since I wrote this section, I have learned of some recent work by socialist feminists which seems to provide an excitingly new theoretical underpinning for much socialist feminist practice. An excellent account of these ideas is given by Gayle Rubin in "The Traffic in Women: Notes on the 'Political Economy' of Sex." This paper appears in *Toward an Anthropology of Women*, ed. Rayna R. Reiter (New York: Monthly Review Press, 1975). If something like Rubin's account is accepted by socialist feminists, it will be a difficult and important question to work out just how far they have moved from traditional Marxism and how much they still share with it.

This sketch of some new directions in feminism completes my outline of the main contemporary positions on women's liberation. I hope that I have made clearer the ideological presuppositions at the root of many feminist claims and also shed some light on the philosophical problems that one needs to resolve in order to formulate one's own position and decide on a basis for action. Many of these philosophical questions, such as the nature of the just society, the proper account of freedom and equality, the functions of the state and the relation between the individual and society, are traditional problems which now arise in a new context; others, such as the role of technology in human liberation, are of more recent origin. In either case, feminism adds a fresh dimension to our discussion of the issues and points to the need for the so-called philosophy of man to be transformed into a comprehensive philosophy of women and men and their social relations.

SHARON BISHOP HILL

Self-Determination and Autonomy

Some have spoken as if the sexual revolution amounts to greatly increased liberality about sex. Recently there is talk that it will not be accomplished until there is an end to sexual discrimination and women as well as men are liberated. Not a few are certain that they know what changes are required to liberate women. Many are content with things as they are, and some are merely complacent about this revolution. Others are perplexed though not unwilling to change, for those they love seem unhappy. In winding a way through an unreal but not unlikely dispute, I suggest a way of allaying these perplexities and justifying some of these demands. If what I say about how to set aside certain doubts about women's liberation is plausible, then I imagine radical changes are in order, not just about how we view and treat women, but also about how we view and treat men and children. What these changes are is difficult to say. In any case, my interest here is primarily in principles and arguments which might be used to explain and justify some of the demands now being made in the name of women's liberation. But to begin with, the dispute.

Used with the permission of the author.

I wish to thank Thomas Hill, Jr., and Richard Wasserstrom who read earlier versions of this paper and made many helpful comments and suggestions.

I. The Dispute

Over the years, John and Harriet have had long arguments about women's liberation. Both have come a long way. When Harriet first decided that she could not find self-fulfillment without a paying job, John felt threatened and protested that it would not be proper. But now he is reconciled and even insists that women get equal pay for equal work. He supports the Equal Rights Amendment and urges his company to give talented and well-trained women an equal chance at job opportunities. He has given up as muddled his old belief that women are naturally inferior to men in intelligence, objectivity, emotional stability and the like. He acknowledges that women have often been treated in degrading ways, and like many liberals, he has tried hard to purge his vocabulary of such words as "chick," "broad," and "piece." He even tries, not always successfully, to avoid references like "the girls in the office." Women, he says, have as much right to happiness as men, and so he is ready to oppose any social scheme which makes them, relative to men, systematically discontent or unhappy. But this is as far as he will go.

Harriet says that this is not far enough. And the dispute came to a head when she protested to the school principal and finally to the school board about their daughter's education. Harriet was distressed that girls were encouraged in numerous ways to accept the traditional feminine role. For example, the practice at most school dances was for girls to wait to be asked by boys. The school had well-developed and financed athletic programs for boys, but few for girls, and very little staff to help girls to develop their skills. The counselors were comparatively uninterested in advising girls about their futures. When they did, they assumed that, for the most part, appropriate careers for girls were as secretaries, decorators, teachers, nurses or medical assistants. Students' programs were then tailored for these vocations. These, in turn, were viewed as stop-gap or carry-over measures to enable girls to get through any periods in which they were not married or supported by someone. If they did marry, it was assumed that there would be children and a home to which the woman should devote herself.

Harriet gradually came to see that her objections to these practices arose as she faced her own feelings of resentment and betrayal at the kinds of opportunities and counseling she had early in life. Though she acknowledged the occasion of her objections, she also became convinced that her complaints were well founded. She was less clear how to support them, but her way of life seemed unnecessarily restrictive and she believed that she had interests and capacities which should have been developed but were not. She was irked, too, that she had never had a genuine opportunity to choose the way of life in which she and other women were so deeply involved. Whatever she might have chosen and whether or not she liked having a family and the feminine virtues, she felt that she had never really had any choice. She realized that part of the problem was that she herself had not regarded these as proper objects of her own choice. This failure she thought was the result of a complicated and overlapping set of teachings which had it that women were almost inevitably unfulfilled without having children, that normally they were better at raising children than men and men better suited for earning a living. Consequently, as the story went, the current division of labor is really most efficient, better for almost everyone and thus best. Both men and women were said to have duties associated with these roles. She now resents these teachings, justifiably she believes. She became especially anxious as she saw her daughter falling into the patterns of behavior and belief to which she now objects and so she complained to the school board.

John found Harriet less than convincing on these matters. It is important to oppose sex roles, he argued, if the roles function in a way which humiliates or degrades women or deprives them of political or economic rights. If these abuses could be avoided, he thinks the current standard division of labor and roles would not only be legitimate but quite a good way to arrange things. Someone, after all, needs to care for children and most women seem quite content. These arrangements seem natural to him. He suspects that women are naturally more sensitive and so make better parents for the very young; moreover, those he knows who have either not married or not had children seem to be weak and stunted characters or else hostile and aggressive. These observations suggest to him that most people, including women, are well off under something like the current division of labor and role. He acknowledges some, at least, of the difficulties about his belief that women are naturally suited for the domestic role. He does not, for example, rely on personality inventories of women versus men, because the traits they test for are bound to be influenced by the culture in which people grow up including, of course, some of the practices Harriet finds obnoxious. He does not appeal to the obvious physical differences between men and women, and he regards as irrelevant, at least in the modern world, appeals to differences in brute strength. Still he believes that some of the relevant differences are natural. He supports his suspicion by appeals to anthropological evidence about widely divergent groups in which women have almost invariably had the domestic role and quite often the traits which suit them for raising children and managing households. Were this not natural, he thinks it would not be so frequent. He has been known to remark that estrogen is associated with passive as opposed to aggressive personality traits, reminding Harriet that women maintain a higher level of this hormone than men. He suspects that the thwarted and hostile women he finds among the unmarried and childless result from frustration of the natural capacities of women for close emotional relations. There are, he admits, extraordinarily ambitious women who would be frustrated in following the traditional pattern; but a society which grants full political and economic rights to all adults can accommodate these exceptional people. Consequently, he resists the idea that there is something wrong with encouraging in young girls the feminine traits he so likes. He wants his daughter to be ladylike in figure and personality and hopes, for her sake, that she will never choose a career at the expense of having a family. He communicates this to her in innumerable, sometimes subtle, sometimes direct ways.

It is at this point that Harriet becomes most exasperated and even despairing. By all the conventional criteria, John seems liberal enough. He believes in equal pay for equal work and equal opportunities for those of equal achievement, motivation and talent. He acknowledges that women have been deprived of income, opportunities, power and their associated satisfactions by unfair social practices of various sorts. What he envisages is a world in which these injustices are eradicated but one in which women remain sensitive, understanding and charming, and in which most take up a domestic life while most men take up a paying vocation. Since he thinks it only efficient to prepare people for these likely different but quite natural futures, he thinks sound educational policy calls for certain subtle differences in the training of males and females. Harriet, on the other hand, believes that her resentment is justified, that she has been wronged in some way and would continue to be wronged if the world were magically transformed to match John's dreams. She becomes most desperate when she thinks of her daughter who is being similarly wronged.

The perplexed, like John, may say, "But where is the difficulty?" They understand complaints about violations of political and economic rights, like the right to vote, hold office and receive equal pay for equal work. They admit that a person would be wronged if gratuitously insulted or deliberately injured. But none of these seem to fit the case of Harriet or her daughter at least in the world John wants. There is no reason to believe they will be insulted, and it is difficult to pick out any political or economic right which we could confidently claim would be violated. Even if we think that Harriet and her daughter have been injured by the workings of the social system in this world, it is not clear that the harm was deliberate. No definite person designed the social system for the purpose of keeping women down, much less for the purpose of harming Harriet; it, like Topsy, just growed. If that is the case, whatever harm they may have suffered seems in important respects like a natural misfortune and not a deliberate wrong. If Harriet's objections to John's views can be defended, it must be on some other pattern of reasoning.

In the following, I shall try to isolate and explain some principles which could be used to justify Harriet's feelings about her own life and her protests of school practices. Roughly, I shall argue that if adults are viewed as having a right to self-determination, then Harriet and other adult women do nothing inappropriate in eschewing a traditional role nor do they have duties directly associated with such a role. Moreover, if as adults, we are to have a right of self-determination which is meaningful, we ought not be treated in ways which distort or prevent the development of the capacity for autonomous choice. I do not attempt to justify the claim that adults have a right of self-determination nor the claim that viewing adults as having such a right is better than any of a variety of other ways of regarding them, for example, as potential contributors to the general welfare or to some social or economic ideal. I hope that some of what I say will make respect for a right of self-determination attractive, but here I only set out to explain something about the right.

I try this line of argument, first, because I think it a promising one to explain the depth and kind of feeling generated in women who begin thinking seriously about their lives and their daughters' prospects. In the end, it may help explain why such pervasive changes are required and why some of them must be changes in attitude. Secondly, it seems possible with this reasoning to avoid some philosophical and empirical difficulties involved in more familiar arguments. For example, a number of people argue for sweeping changes in the treatment of women on the grounds that the resulting system will be more efficient in turning out happy individuals or in using the available pool of natural abilities. One problem here, of course, is to determine what is to count as being happy and so what is to count as evidence that some new system will be more efficient producing it than the present one. Others suggest that there has been a deliberate male conspiracy to keep women in the kitchen and out of the most lucrative and satisfying jobs. There are innumerable problems about what could be meant by "deliberate conspiracy" in this case; there does not seem to have been a conspiratorial meeting attended by anyone much less by most men or by representative men. It does not even seem plausible that some rather large number of men have consciously intended to keep women out of the mainstream of social and economic life at least in recent history. Even if some clear sense can be given to the notion, successful completion of the argument would require complicated empirical inquiries. Although it is true that a deliberate conspiracy to do wrong makes things rather worse, what seems important here is rather the wrong that has been done. If questions about the deliberateness of the wrongs are important at all, they seem to belong rather with attempts to decide to whom the burdens of change may legitimately fall. Finally, the line of reasoning I propose directly undercuts two of the kinds of arguments John suggested against Harriet. In the end, he claimed that his views about women and educational policy could be supported by appeals to efficient ways of arranging for child rearing as well as the natural suitability of current sex roles and the division of labor. Once a right of self-determination is granted, however, it does not matter whether the complex facts John appeals to are true or not, that is, it does not matter whether current sex roles are efficient means of rearing children or whether women, on the average, are better at domestic affairs than men. There are other considerations having to do with self-determination and autonomy which make these alleged facts irrelevant and which do justice to Harriet's response. She does not need to await empirical evidence about what is suitable for women and what makes women and children happy in order to know that something is wrong.

II. The Right of Self-Determination

To say that persons or states have a right of self-determination is to say minimally that they and only they have the authority to determine certain sorts of things. This does not necessarily mean that they have the power or capacity to determine these things, but rather that they have the title to. Sovereign states, for example, are widely regarded as having rather extensive authority to choose for themselves; they are said to have a right to determine how and who shall govern them, to have rights to determine for themselves what their ideals shall be, how they will allocate funds, what forms of culture they will support and devote themselves to, and the like. Having title to make these choices means that they have a right to expect others not to interfere with the legitimate exercise of their authority and a right to protect themselves from interference. It means, too, that they have a right to expect to carry on the processes of their government without foreign interest groups bribing their officials, and without being flooded with propaganda designed to influence the outcome of elections and the like. All this seems rather uncontroversial. More controversially, a small dependent state might claim that its right of self-determination was violated by threats of loss of essential support just because it failed to adopt the policies its larger, more affluent neighbor wanted. Withdrawal of such support makes it impossible to exercise its right of self-determination, consequently, threatening such withdrawal may be counted as incompatible with respecting the small nation's right. This may seem especially plausible where the support is well established, and where the threat is given for failure, say, to give up some local ritual or some trading policy mildly contrary to the interests of the affluent. Mature adults are often said to have a similar right, for example, to determine for themselves what their vocations shall be, whether to use their money for steaks or tennis balls, their leisure time for concerts or back-packing, and so on. Again, what is meant is that only they have the authority to make such choices, that others ought to refrain from interfering with the legitimate exercise of the title, and that they have the right to protect themselves from interference. Individuals may, if they wish, delegate parts of that authority. They give up some of it when they take a job, put themselves under the tutelage of an instructor or decide to let a friend choose the day's activities. Even in these cases, however, it is only they who may decide not to exercise the right.

Like other rights, this one is limited. Sovereign states do not have a right to make war on their neighbors for profit. Individuals do not have the right to harm or restrain one another simply for the fun of it however much they may want to. The limitations on this right will be roughly what is prohibited by other moral principles. Although these limitations cannot be spelled out here, we could get agreement about a number of cases like injuring another for one's own pleasure. While this does not give us a satisfactory criterion for what morality forbids, it is enough to permit us to focus on the right of self-determination confident that it need not commit us to silly views about the rights of sadists.

Obviously the right is not in fact granted or guaranteed to everyone by the state or culture in which they live. Like the rights to life, liberty and security, it is a natural right, that is, it is thought of as belonging to everyone simply by virtue of their being human and so it is a right which everyone has equally. Society can and should protect us in exercising it in some ways, for example, in choosing a vocation. A state should not, however, enforce all the behavior and attitudes which might be appropriate in someone who believes in the right of self-determination. For example, I suspect that some committed to honoring the right of self-determination would regard themselves as bound not to influence those close to them by exploiting any emotional dependence they might have. If this is a reasonable attitude, it does not seem that it would be wise for a society to protect us from the influence of those on whom we are dependent emotionally. The right of self-determination does not, in general, determine a particular outcome as the just or only acceptable one. It rather outlines a range of considerations which should come into play whenever we are trying to adjust our behavior or attitudes to persons making permissible choices. I call it a right because it is thought of as a title and because the considerations it picks out as relevant mark off an area in which we do not allow conclusions about either the general good or an individual's good to be decisive. The point of the right of self-determination is to enable people to work out their own way of life in response to their own assessments of current conditions and their own interests, capacities and needs, rather than to secure the minimal conditions for living or to maximize a person's expectations for satisfaction. In respecting an individual's right of self-determination, one expresses a certain view about that person which is not a belief that one is acting for the good of that person (at least in some narrow sense of the person's good having to do with his or her welfare or happiness). The rough idea is that persons are, among other things, creatures who have title to select what they will do from among the permitted options. This establishes a presumption that other people should refrain from interfering with our selections whatever their content. They should refrain even if they do not like the particular choice or if they correctly believe that it is not in the chooser's or society's long-term interests.

Applying the right of self-determination to questions about the treatment of women, John and Harriet readily agree on a number of conclusions. First, bending the will of a woman by force is wrong. Conquering nations violate the right of self-determination and so does the man who keeps a woman or harem in servitude however nice he may make their lives. The man who prevents his wife from attending her therapy session or sky-diving lessons by force also violates this right. He does not allow her to do what she has a right to do. He violates the right whether he prevents her because he fears the changes in her personality, or is jealous of her handsome teacher, or because he correctly and sincerely believes the group is harming her or that sky-diving is dangerous. So long as we are talking about a mature woman who is choosing nothing prohibited by morality, it does not matter whether he acts in her own interests or not, he will still have violated her right to determine on her own what she will do.

The husband who achieves similar results by threatening to divorce his wife who has no other means of support may also violate her right to self-determination. This would be like a powerful state that threatens to cut off aid whenever a dependent state acts contrary to its wishes. Some may feel more certain that the threatening husband makes a mistake than that the powerful state violates the right of self-determination of the smaller state. Someone may note that it is quite accepted that relations among nations proceed by threat and counter threat. Things do not go all that well when carried on in this manner, but they go on. When husband, wife, parents or friends resort to such tactics, the relation of friendship or love is effectively off. Someone who is prepared to use such tactics displays special callousness toward the friendship. If they care about maintaining it at all, they will have made a grave blunder. They will also have indicated that they are indifferent to the feelings of the individual they threaten. They show a willingness to harm them, and this may be considered a moral fault for which there is no analogue in the threatening state. These observations can be accepted, I think, without weakening the original claim. We began by saying that states and persons have a right to make certain sorts of choices for themselves without interference by force or threat of force or withdrawal of essential support. This implies in both the case of states and individuals that there is a special wrong in threatening those who are making perfectly permissible policy, namely the violation of this right; that other wrongs and blunders may also be involved is beside the point.

Finally, if a group of men were to conspire together to discourage their wives from taking jobs or joining groups where women work through their problems together, they would violate the women's right of self-determination. These conclusions are not a problem for a liberal like John. He is not tempted to prevent his wife from going anywhere by force. Nor is he tempted to use the threat of loss of support in order to win a battle. He knows that would be to lose the war, and he wants her love and respect, not simply her presence and obedience. He knows, too, that his wife could find other means of support in this world. She is able, and this is not the nineteenth century where his support may well have been essential. Moreover, he has always been inclined to resist the temptation to adjust his relation to his wife in response to or in concert with others. So far the right of self-determination adds nothing startling to the list of legitimate complaints that women might have.

It does, however, add something to the reasons we may have for objecting to a variety of policies. For example, it means that some wrong is involved in the above cases apart from the objectionable techniques used to bring about the desired result. The wrong is not either simply that someone made a conscious attempt to interfere with someone's legitimate choice, but rather that someone's selections were blocked or interfered with. In addition, the right of self-determination takes us a good way toward directly undermining John's views about women. He seemed to think that it was perfectly all right to advise adult women to engage in and stick with traditional domestic life styles on the grounds that it was efficient and natural for women to have them. What appears to be the case now, is that, even if it is efficient and natural, enticing women to take this role for these reasons is likely to interfere with their right of self-determination. It is likely to do this because it encourages the false belief that these reasons are or should be decisive in determining an important lifetime commitment. Instead the right of self-determination establishes a presumption that within the range of permissible selections a person's uncoerced, unforced spontaneous responses to her own interests and circumstances are or should be decisive. It does not matter whether the interference is deliberate or non-deliberate or whether it is well-intended guidance. Once it is known that a practice, policy or teaching interferes, there is good reason to believe it should be revised. That is not to say that there is always sufficient reason, for this presumption like others can be rebutted. If the rebuttal is to work, however, it must give something like an equally important reason, for example, that revising the policy will cause perpetual or irremediable disaster, that it represents the only possible way for anyone to have a decent life, that some other natural right would be violated or that some particular person is not capable of exercising the right for some special reason. While this is not an adequate account of what will rebut the presumption established by the right of self-determination, it does suggest that John's arguments were simply beside the point if he was trying to justify policies which encourage a group of people to take up some lifetime role.

It is even difficult to see why the argument from efficiency should be effective in persuading a particular person like Harriet to exercise her right of self-determination by choosing a traditional domestic role. It seemed to be an argument that society in general will run more efficiently under the current role division, and it is not obvious that it is wise to make important lifetime commitments on the grounds that society in general is likely to run more efficiently. If the argument is rather that Harriet's life would work more smoothly and efficiently if she has a domestic role, then the right of self-determination says that it is up to her whether to take these facts (supposing them to be determinate) as decisive. If she does not want to struggle or if she does not fancy some other definite way of life, she may prefer the so-called efficient way. At the same time, it should be noted that it is a little difficult to determine what is meant by saying that her life would be more efficient, for surely that will depend to some very great extent on what her ends are. If her ends are to develop some talents she has or even to remain a lively and developing person, this may not be an efficient route at all. Nor is the evidence clear that this is the most efficient way for her to raise healthy children; that will depend to some extent on whom she thinks of raising them with, how that is likely to work, and so on.

The argument that the current division of labor and role is in some deep and important sense natural is also beside the point. If these roles are "natural," then persons who are taught that they have a right of self-determination will tend to choose them. There is, then, no need to worry about what it might mean to say that the sex roles are natural, nor to await the empirical evidence about whether they are before we decide whether it is justifiable to encourage them or not. Moreover, taking the perspective of someone committed to the right of self-determination accords nicely with a reasonable suspicion that what is natural for persons is not determinate. Sometimes when people talk about a person being a natural in a role, they have in mind that given the person's background, achievement and current interests, he or she would do well at it and flourish in it. Sometimes, however, they attempt to tie success and satisfaction with a role more closely to a person's genetic heritage. In this sense, a role is natural for persons if because of their genetic endowment, they have certain special capacities which enable them to play the role well, the role does not frustrate some deep need and it provides opportunities for them to express their central interests. In the former sense, it is probably true that the domestic role is a natural for most women now, but it is the latter sense that plays a part in arguments that the current division of labor and role is natural and therefore justifiable. In a modern industrial community, however, there must be at the very least several life styles which could be natural in this sense for most any normal person. That is, there must be several ways of life in which their natural talents could be used and which would provide circumstances for the expression of a range of strong human interests without tending to frustrate deep needs. What the right of self-determination gives people is the title to let their own preferences put together a way of life. If these preferences are properly weighted by themselves and others, then the style they put together is very likely to be one which makes use of their special capacities, does not frustrate and provides opportunities for the expression of central interests.

Unfortunately, it is not clear that the right of self-determination will complete the job Harriet hoped it would; that is, adjudicate in her favor the dispute with John over their daughter's education. John, we may suppose, says that it will not do this because the right of self-determination is a right of adults and not of children. He says that it would be absurd if not impossible and immoral to treat young children as if they had the right to make major choices regarding their futures. Either we would give the children no guidance at all, in which case they may well feel lost and have too little discipline to gain what they will want as adults, or we would be required to use the techniques of rational persuasion that we use with adults. This, too, is likely to have disastrous consequences. At best it leads children to confuse the forms of reasoning with reasonable choosing and tends to make them overrate their capacities and status. Guidance must be given to children for their own sakes, and it will be guidance which inevitably will influence what they want later in life. The question is what kind of guidance to give. John wants to encourage in his daughter the feminine virtues. He wants her to be graceful in figure and movement, he is afraid that too much concentration on competitive athletic games will spoil her development. He thinks the modern dance and figure control programs the school has for girls are all that is important for them. He wants her to remain sweet and coy, affectionate and sensitive, and to develop feminine interests in cooking, sewing and children. Not only does he do what he can to encourage these traits in her, but he wants the school to. He thinks that Harriet and her friends have gone too far in complaining about the fact that only a few exceptionally talented or stubborn women are presented as professionals, and in demanding that the girls be taught the manual arts as well as home economics.

In the following section, I argue that even if the right of self-determination is reserved for adults, John's arguments about his daughter's education do not succeed. Even if the right of self-determination does not itself directly limit the kinds of guidance we may give our children, it does in an indirect way.

III. The Importance of Autonomy

Let us say that parents have the authority to make certain decisions affecting the welfare of their offspring. They have this authority because children lack the know-how and the physical and psychological resources to make it on their own. Typically parents are supposed to exercise this authority in the interests of their children though sometimes they may exercise it for their own peace of mind, especially after nine and on weekends. Even given this picture of legitimate parental authority, there is something wrong with John's educational policies. There are, I think, two objections to teaching girls the traditional feminine virtues and role. First (A), such teaching interferes subtly with their exercise of the right of self-determination as mature women. Second (B), anyone committed to the right of self-determination and its importance has reasons for attaching special significance to the development of the capacity to exercise it autonomously.

(A) To begin with, when we say that mature persons have a right of self-determination, we mean that they are entitled to decide for themselves which career they will attempt, whether or whom to marry, whether to have children, how to spend their leisure time and the like. We all know that deciding for oneself is incompatible with being coerced at the time of choice, but there are subtle influences which may occur earlier and which interfere with the exercise of the right of self-determination.

Let us imagine that a school system has the following practices. First, the system leads girls to take up domestic activities and keeps them from others like competitive games and mechanics. Then, when women reach the age to choose how to spend their time, they have already developed the skills to enjoy cooking and sewing at a high level and discover, not surprisingly, that they like domestic tasks, and not car repair, carpentry or basketball. Surely the possibility that these latter might have been the objects of their choice is virtually extinguished. By hypothesis, home economics training for the girls has been successful, that is, many of them really have learned to manage themselves in the kitchen or sewing room so that they are creative and effective, and they have not made similar progress in the workroom. People tend to prefer doing what they are good at, and so women will tend to prefer cooking.

It might be said that at the age of reason, women have the right of self-determination, to choose, for example, to learn carpentry or mechanics, but the right to choose these things will not be worth much if at that time they do not have the possibility of getting satisfaction from these activities at some fairly advanced level because whatever original interest they might have had was never exposed. Not, of course, that everyone should be forced to take home economics, mechanics, and so on, but adults would have a reason to complain if they were systematically deprived of the opportunity to develop some legitimate interest; whereas, if the opportunity had been there and they failed to take it, they would not.

Secondly, the schools do not provide girls with information about women's capacities except for domestic affairs like mothering and cooking. If this occurs, then when the girls become women, they will be unlikely to imagine alternatives and choose intelligently between them. If this were to happen, then women could not even freely choose a domestic life, since they would be likely to see it as the only possibility instead of one among several. Alternatively, suppose that girls are presented with a few examples of women professionals, but these are always presented as rare, extraordinary persons who had to pay a high price for their aspirations. They either gave up the possibility of developing a marriage or they withstood criticism and ostracism for their strange ambitions or both. This makes the cost of choosing another way of life seem so high that most would be unwilling to select it.

Imagine next that girls are rewarded for being patient, sensitive, responsive and obedient, but that displays of ambition and curiosity are met with frowns or silence. The result is that the girls learn to be passive, understanding and sensitive, and not at the same time confident, interested and active. What has happened is that the pattern of traits they develop suit them for domestic life, and when they come to choose between being a housewife and a doctor, they may judge quite correctly that given their current wants and temperament, housewifery is a better prospect for them. If, however, they had been rewarded for curiosity and ambition, the pattern of their personalities would have been different, and it might have been worthwhile for them to develop interests they have in, say, some science, and so to choose another style of life. The difficulty with the training they in fact had is that it has made such a choice unreasonable and done so without attending to the spontaneous and quite legitimate preferences of girls as they developed.

Finally, suppose that certain styles of dress and standards of etiquette are insisted upon for girls and that boys are encouraged to expect girls to meet these and admire those who meet them well. Anyone who deviates from the norm is made to feel uneasy or embarrassed. Imagine, too, that style of dress, while insignificant in itself, is associated with certain career roles and basic life styles. Dress in such a world serves to symbolize the career role and set up important expectations. When the time comes for a woman to choose what she will do, her expectations tend to be fixed not just with regard to the otherwise insignificant matter of dress, but also with regard to what role she will take up. When this happens, it is difficult for her to choose any unexpected role, for any deviation from expectations about her will produce stress and recall the uneasiness she felt upon breaking the dress code.

If the above practices in fact have the effects I envisage, they interfere with the right of self-determination of mature women. To believe that mature persons have a right of self-determination and that such practices are justifiable is rather like believing that Southern Blacks have a right to vote, but that Whites may legitimately ostracize those who exercise it. It would be like believing that Blacks have a right to eat where Whites do and that it would be merely impolite for Whites to stare as if they did not. In some important respects, it would be like a government maintaining that its citizens have a right to travel wherever they choose, but confiscating the passports of those who go to Cuba. If these analogies are acceptable, then even though the educational policies described above do not violate the right of self-determination, they should be changed. Or rather they should be revised unless it can be argued reasonably that each proposed revision would cause disaster or violate some equally important right.

(B) So far Harriet's commitment to the right of self-determination inclines her to prevent and avoid violations and to minimize interferences like those described above. If, however, she is also committed to the importance of the right, she will want those she cares about to exercise it and to exercise it in a worthwhile way. It is not in general true that belief that one has a right means that one cares about having it or exercising it; for example, the right to travel or to marry do not seem to be rights that one need care about exercising or having. The right of self-determination, however, seems importantly different at least when it is accepted for the suggested rationale. The right was granted to persons to enable them to work out their own way of life in response to their own assessment of their situation, interests and capacities because it was thought appropriate and important that persons work out their own way of life believing that they have a right to. We may ask why this is important, but that is beyond the scope of the present inquiry. It would require explaining the advantages of regarding persons in part as creators of their own way of life rather than merely contributors to the general welfare or some other social ideal.

Assuming, then, that Harriet is also committed to the importance of the right of self-determination, she will want those she loves to exercise it and that its exercise be worthwhile for them. The right of self-determination tends to be worth less to mature persons the fewer opportunities and more interferences they are confronted with and the more they have been trained to have personality traits which make them suited for some definite life role. To say further what tends to make the right worth more, it helps to ask what one would want for persons one loves as they exercise the right of self-determination. Using this device, we are blocked from regarding ourselves as proper determiners of their life style. We do, however, want their good, but partly because we cannot properly determine it and partly because we do not know what will confront them, we do not know what in particular will be good or best for them. Still something can be said about what we want for them.

First, talking of our children and not knowing what they will face, we shall want them to develop the kind of personality which will enable them to respond well to their circumstances whatever they are. We shall want them to have what might be called broadly useful traits, that is, traits which will be helpful whatever their interests and circumstances, traits like confidence, intelligence and discipline. Self-confidence is, for example, a trait which it is good to have because it is useful in a wide variety of ways and inevitably satisfying. Broadly useful traits are the kinds which make a wider range of alternatives feasible for those who have them and so are important for exercising the right of self-determination. We should set about teaching these, then, rather than those associated with some culturally variable sex role.

Secondly, given that our children when mature will have a right of self-determination and given our ignorance of what they will face, it is not in general reasonable for us to aim for a particular outcome of our children's choices, but rather to develop their capacity to make choices in a certain way, namely, autonomously. That is, at least we want them to make the selections free from certain kinds of pressure. We do not want their selections to be coerced, threatened or bribed, and we do not want them to succumb easily to seductive advice or the bare weight of tradition. Neither do we want their preferences to be neurotic or self-destructive even though there are admittedly circumstances in which neurotic responses pay. In short, we want them to have certain psychological strengths which will enable them to make sensible use of the right of self-determination.

To want our children's choices to be autonomous is also to want their selections to express genuine interests of theirs which arise spontaneously under certain conditions. These are the circumstances in which they have the above psychological strengths and as they are making rational assessments of their capacities and situation. The selections should be spontaneous under these conditions because those are the choices we think of as expressive of us as individuals, and those in turn are the selections we tend to find most deeply satisfying and with which we feel most comfortable. Although we do not usually know what in particular these interests will be, we do know that there are certain basic human interests which anyone might have regardless of their sex or other peculiarities about them. Basic human interests are those taken in the kinds of activities which typically individuals find satisfying and which are potentially healthy. For example, people are capable of gaining satisfaction directly in their work or indirectly because it provides them with income, they find successful friendships and love relations satisfying, they enjoy play and developing their talents. The capacities to enjoy each of these interests, unlike other human capacities—for example, for self-destruction, enmity, hostility, envy and so on—are potentially healthy. They are potentially healthy in that they can be coordinated in one person to produce a satisfying way of life and styles of life in which these capacities are exploited (and the others minimized) are styles which can be coordinated together in a smooth way. What we can legitimately want and hope that our children have, then, are the satisfactions associated with each of these kinds of interests, and more rather than less. These are legitimate aspirations for us to have for our children because they are the kinds they would want to build their lives around if they were mature and reasonable and if the background conditions of life were decent. Given that these are legitimate aspirations, we should set about helping children understand these potential satisfactions vividly and not to suiting them for some particular lifetime role. Then when people are of an age to warrant saying they have a right of self-determination, ideally they will have psychological strengths and a vivid appreciation of the range of enjoyments possible for them so that they are able to work out a satisfying way of life which is an expression of their spontaneous preferences. This does not require that each be equally capable of fitting in anywhere, but only that there is for everyone some array of feasible options.

According to the preceding argument, young persons should be treated in whatever ways give them the strength and imagination to make use of their right of self-determination autonomously when they reach maturity. Treating them in ways which are believed to do this is a way of respecting the right they will have when they reach maturity. In addition, if one is to respect someone's right of self-determination fully, one must be willing to allow its exercise even when one believes it is being done badly. This suggests that some importance should be attached to the choices of people simply because they are attempts to arrive at the available alternative most in line with their autonomous preferences. For the most part, this will probably amount to keeping out of others' business. In those we care about and love, however, it will mean valuing and appreciating what they choose simply because it is their choice. This is, perhaps, one way of expressing our love. If so, then Harriet may have taken John's reticence about some of her projects as signs that he did not love her. Equally, of course, he may have believed that Harriet was a bit wacky and irresponsible, or he may not be committed to the right of self-determination or its importance. None of these is likely to sit well with Harriet, who we might imagine really has reached a vision about the moral life which is incompatible with John's view and with which she feels quite comfortable.

THOMAS E. HILL, JR.

Servility and Self-Respect

Several motives underlie this paper.[1] In the first place, I am curious to see if there is a legitimate source for the increasingly common feeling that servility can be as much a vice as arrogance. There seems to be something morally defective about the Uncle Tom and the submissive housewife; and yet, on the other hand, if the only interests they sacrifice are their own, it seems that we should have no right to complain. Secondly, I have some sympathy for the now unfashionable view that each person has duties to himself as well as to others. It does seem absurd to say that a person could literally violate his own rights or owe himself a debt of gratitude, but I suspect that the classic defenders of duties to oneself had something different

Reprinted from *The Monist*, Vol. 57, No. 1 (January 1973), 87–104, La Salle, Illinois, with the permission of the publisher and the author.

[1] An earlier version of this paper was presented at the meetings of the American Philosophical Association, Pacific Division. A number of revisions have been made as a result of the helpful comments of others, especially Norman Dahl, Sharon Hill, Herbert Morris, and Mary Mothersill.

in mind. If there are duties to oneself, it is natural to expect that a duty to avoid being servile would have a prominent place among them. Thirdly, I am interested in making sense of Kant's puzzling, but suggestive, remarks about respect for persons and respect for the moral law. On the usual reading, these remarks seem unduly moralistic; but, viewed in another way, they suggest an argument for a kind of self-respect which is incompatible with a servile attitude.

My procedure will not be to explicate Kant directly. Instead I shall try to isolate the defect of servility and sketch an argument to show why it is objectionable, noting only in passing how this relates to Kant and the controversy about duties to oneself. What I say about self-respect is far from the whole story. In particular, it is not concerned with esteem for one's special abilities and achievements or with the self-confidence which characterizes the especially autonomous person. Nor is my concern with the psychological antecedents and effects of self-respect. Nevertheless, my conclusions, if correct, should be of interest; for they imply that, given a common view of morality, there are nonutilitarian moral reasons for each person, regardless of his merits, to respect himself. To avoid servility to the extent that one can is not simply a right but a duty, not simply a duty to others but a duty to oneself.

I

Three examples may give a preliminary idea of what I mean by *servility*. Consider, first, an extremely deferential black, whom I shall call the *Uncle Tom*. He always steps aside for white men; he does not complain when less qualified whites take over his job; he gratefully accepts whatever benefits his all-white government and employers allot him, and he would not think of protesting its insufficiency. He displays the symbols of deference to whites, and of contempt towards blacks; he faces the former with bowed stance and a ready 'sir' and 'Ma'am'; he reserves his strongest obscenities for the latter. Imagine, too, that he is not playing a game. He is not the shrewdly prudent calculator, who knows how to make the best of a bad lot and mocks his masters behind their backs. He accepts without question the idea that, as a black, he is owed less than whites. He may believe that blacks are mentally inferior and of less social utility, but that is not the crucial point. The attitude which he displays is that what he values, aspires for, and can demand is of less importance than what whites value, aspire for, and can demand. He is far from the picture book's carefree, happy servant, but he does not feel that he has a right to expect anything better.

Another pattern of servility is illustrated by a person I shall call the *Self-Deprecator*. Like the Uncle Tom, he is reluctant to make demands. He says nothing when others take unfair advantage of him. When asked for his preferences or opinions, he tends to shrink away as if what he said should make no difference. His problem, however, is not a sense of racial inferiority but rather an acute awareness of his own inadequacies and failures as an individual. These defects are not imaginary: he has in fact done poorly by his own standards and others'. But, unlike many of us in the same situation, he acts as if his failings warrant quite unrelated mal-treatment even by strangers. His sense of shame and self-contempt make him content to be the instrument of others. He feels that nothing is owed him until he has earned it and that he has earned very little. He is not simply playing a masochist's game of winning sympathy by disparaging himself. On the contrary, he assesses his individual merits with painful accuracy.

A rather different case is that of the *Deferential Wife*. This is a woman who is utterly devoted to serving her husband. She buys the clothes *he* prefers, invites the guests *he* wants to entertain, and makes love when-ever *he* is in the mood. She willingly moves to a new city in order for him to have a more attractive job, counting her own friendships and geographi-cal preferences insignificant by comparison. She loves her husband, but her conduct is not simply an expression of love. She is happy, but she does not subordinate herself as a means to happiness. She does not simply defer to her husband in certain spheres as a trade-off for his deference in other spheres. On the contrary, she tends not to form her own interests, values, and ideals; and, when she does, she counts them as less important than her husband's. She readily responds to appeals from Women's Liberation that she agrees that women are mentally and physically equal, if not superior, to men. She just believes that the proper role for a woman is to serve her family. As a matter of fact, much of her happiness derives from her belief that she fulfills this role very well. No one is trampling on her rights, she says; for she is quite glad, and proud, to serve her husband as she does.

Each one of these cases reflects the attitude which I call servility.[2] It betrays the absence of a certain kind of self-respect. What I take this attitude to be, more specifically, will become clearer later on. It is im-portant at the outset, however, not to confuse the three cases sketched above with other, superficially similar cases. In particular, the cases I have sketched are not simply cases in which someone refuses to press his rights, speaks disparagingly of himself, or devotes himself to another. A black, for

[2] Each of these cases is intended to represent only one possible pattern of servility. I make no claims about how often these patterns are exemplified, nor do I mean to imply that only these patterns could warrant the labels "Deferential Wife," "Uncle Tom," etc. All the more, I do not mean to imply any comparative judg-ments about the causes or relative magnitude of the problems of racial and sexual discrimination. One person, e.g., a self-contemptuous woman with a sense of racial inferiority, might exemplify features of several patterns at once; and, of course, a person might view her being a woman the way an Uncle Tom views his being black, etc.

example, is not necessarily servile because he does not demand a just wage; for, seeing that such a demand would result in his being fired, he might forbear for the sake of his children. A self-critical person is not necessarily servile by virtue of bemoaning his faults in public; for his behavior may be merely a complex way of satisfying his own inner needs quite independent of a willingness to accept abuse from others. A woman need not be servile whenever she works to make her husband happy and prosperous; for she might freely and knowingly choose to do so from love or from a desire to share the rewards of his success. If the effort did not require her to submit to humiliation or maltreatment, her choice would not mark her as servile. There may, of course, be grounds for objecting to the attitudes in these cases; but the defect is not servility of the sort I want to consider. It should also be noted that my cases of servility are not simply instances of deference to superior knowledge or judgment. To defer to an expert's judgment on matters of fact is not to be servile; to defer to his every wish and whim is. Similarly, the belief that one's talents and achievements are comparatively low does not, by itself, make one servile. It is no vice to acknowledge the truth, and one may in fact have achieved less, and have less ability, than others. To be servile is not simply to hold certain empirical beliefs but to have a certain attitude concerning one's rightful place in a moral community.

II

Are there grounds for regarding the attitudes of the Uncle Tom, the Self-Deprecator, and the Deferential Wife as morally objectionable? Are there moral arguments we could give them to show that they ought to have more self-respect? None of the more obvious replies is entirely satisfactory.

One might, in the first place, adduce utilitarian considerations. Typically the servile person will be less happy than he might be. Moreover, he may be less prone to make the best of his own socially useful abilities. He may become a nuisance to others by being overly dependent. He will, in any case, lose the special contentment that comes from standing up for one's rights. A submissive attitude encourages exploitation, and exploitation spreads misery in a variety of ways. These considerations provide a prima facie case against the attitudes of the Uncle Tom, the Deferential Wife, and the Self-Deprecator, but they are hardly conclusive. Other utilities tend to counterbalance the ones just mentioned. When people refuse to press their rights, there are usually others who profit. There are undeniable pleasures in associating with those who are devoted, understanding, and grateful for whatever we see fit to give them—as our fondness for dogs attests. Even the servile person may find his attitude a source of happiness, as the case of the Deferential Wife illustrates. There may be comfort and security in thinking that the hard choices must be made by others, that what I would say has little to do with what ought to be done. Self-condemnation may bring relief from the pangs of guilt even if it is not deliberately used for that purpose. On balance, then, utilitarian considerations may turn out to favor servility as much as they oppose it.

For those who share my moral intuitions, there is another sort of reason for not trying to rest a case against servility on utilitarian considerations. Certain utilities seem irrelevant to the issue. The utilitarian must weight them along with others, but to do so seems morally inappropriate. Suppose, for example, that the submissive attitudes of the Uncle Tom and the Deferential Wife result in positive utilities for those who dominate and exploit them. Do we need to tabulate *these* utilities before conceding that servility is objectionable? The Uncle Tom, it seems, is making an error, a moral error, quite apart from consideration of how much others in fact profit from his attitude. The Deferential Wife may be quite happy; but if her happiness turns out to be contingent on her distorted view of her own rights and worth as a person, then it carries little moral weight against the contention that she ought to change that view. Suppose I could cause a woman to find her happiness in denying all her rights and serving my every wish. No doubt I could do so only by nonrational manipulative techniques, which I ought not to use. But is this the only objection? My efforts would be wrong, it seems, not only because of the techniques they require but also because the resultant attitude is itself objectionable. When a person's happiness stems from a morally objectionable attitude, it ought to be discounted. That a sadist gets pleasure from seeing others suffer should not count even as a partial justification for his attitude. That a servile person derives pleasure from denying her moral status, for similar reasons, cannot make her attitude acceptable. These brief intuitive remarks are not intended as a refutation of utilitarianism, with all its many varieties; but they do suggest that it is well to look elsewhere for adequate grounds for rejecting the attitudes of the Uncle Tom, the Self-Deprecator, and the Deferential Wife.

One might try to appeal to meritarian considerations. That is, one might argue that the servile person *deserves* more than he allows himself. This line of argument, however, is no more adequate than the utilitarian one. It may be wrong to deny others what they deserve, but it is not so obviously wrong to demand less for oneself than one deserves. In any case, the Self Deprecator's problem is not that he underestimates his merits. By hypothesis, he assesses his merits quite accurately. We cannot reasonably tell him to have more respect for himself because he *deserves* more respect; he knows that he has not *earned* better treatment. His problem, in fact, is that he thinks of his moral status with regard to others as entirely dependent upon his merits. His interests and choices are important, he feels, only if he has earned the right to make demands; or if he had rights by birth, they were forfeited by his subsequent failures and misdeeds. My Self-Deprecator is no doubt an atypical person, but nevertheless he illustrates an important point. Normally when we find a self-contemptuous person, we can plausibly argue that he is not so bad as he thinks, that his self-contempt is an overreaction prompted more by inner needs than by objective assessment of his merits. Because this argument cannot work with the Self-Deprecator, his case draws attention to a distinction, applicable in other cases as well, between saying that someone deserves respect for his merits and saying that he is owed respect as a person. On meritarian grounds we can only say 'You deserve better than this,' but the defect of the servile person is not merely failure to recognize his merits.

Other common arguments against the Uncle Tom, et al., may have some force but seem not to strike to the heart of the problem. For example, philosophers sometimes appeal to the value of human potentialities. As a human being, it is said, one at least has a capacity for rationality, morality, excellence, or autonomy, and this capacity is worthy of respect. Although such arguments have the merit of making respect independent of a person's actual deserts, they seem quite misplaced in some cases. There comes a time when we have sufficient evidence that a person is not ever going to *be* rational, moral, excellent, or autonomous even if he still has a capacity, in some sense, for being so. As a person approaches death with an atrocious record so far, the chances of his realizing his diminishing capacities become increasingly slim. To make these capacities the basis of his self-respect is to rest it on a shifting and unstable ground. We do, of course, respect persons for capacities which they are not exercising at the moment; for example, I might respect a person as a good philosopher even though he is just now blundering into gross confusion. In these cases, however, we respect the person for an active capacity, a ready disposition, which he has displayed on many occasions. On this analogy, a person should have respect for himself only when his capacities are developed and ready, needing only to be triggered by an appropriate occasion or the removal of some temporary obstacle. The Uncle Tom and the Deferential Wife, however, may in fact have quite limited capacities of this sort, and, since the Self-Deprecator is already overly concerned with his own inadequacies, drawing attention to his capacities seems a poor way to increase his self-respect. In any case, setting aside the Kantian nonempirical capacity for autonomy, the capacities of different persons vary widely; but what the servile person seems to overlook is something by virtue of which he is equal with every other person.

III

Why, then, is servility a moral defect? There is, I think, another sort of answer which is worth exploring. The first part of this answer must be an attempt to isolate the objectionable features of the servile person; later we can ask why these features are objectionable. As a step in this direction, let us examine again our three paradigm cases. The moral defect in each case, I suggest, is a failure to understand and acknowledge one's own moral rights. I assume, without argument here, that each person has moral rights.[3] Some of these rights may be basic human rights; that is, rights for which a person needs only to be human to qualify. Other rights will be derivative and contingent upon his special commitments, institutional affiliations, etc. Most rights will be prima facie ones; some may be absolute. Most can be waived under appropriate conditions; perhaps some cannot. Many rights can be forfeited; but some, presumably, cannot. The servile person does not, strictly speaking, violate his own rights. At least in our paradigm cases he fails to acknowledge fully his own moral status because he does not fully understand what his rights are, how they can be waived, and when they can be forfeited.

The defect of the Uncle Tom, for example, is that he displays an attitude that denies his moral equality with whites. He does not realize, or apprehend in an effective way, that he has as much right to a decent wage and a share of political power as any comparable white. His gratitude is misplaced; he accepts benefits which are his by right as if they were gifts. The Self-Deprecator is servile in a more complex way. He acts as if he has forfeited many important rights which in fact he has not. He does not understand, or fully realize in his own case, that certain rights to fair and decent treatment do not have to be earned. He sees his merits clearly enough, but he fails to see that what he can expect from others is not merely a function of his merits. The Deferential Wife *says* that she understands her rights vis-à-vis her husband, but what she fails to appreciate is that her consent to serve him is a valid waiver of her rights only under certain conditions. If her consent is coerced, say, by the lack of viable options for women in her society, then her consent is worth little. If socially fostered ignorance of her own talents and alternatives is responsible for her consent, then her consent should not count as a fully legitimate waiver of her right to equal consideration within the marriage. All the more, her consent to defer constantly to her husband is not a legitimate setting aside of her rights if it results from her mistaken belief that she has a moral duty to do so. (Recall: "The *proper* role for a woman is to serve her family.") If she believes that she has a *duty* to defer to her husband, then, whatever she may say, she cannot fully understand that she has a *right* not to defer to him. When she says that she freely gives up such a right, she is confused. Her confusion is rather like that of a person who has been persuaded by an unscrupulous lawyer that it is legally incumbent on him

---

[3] As will become evident, I am also presupposing some form of cognitive or "naturalistic" interpretation of rights. If, to accommodate an emotivist or prescriptivist, we set aside talk of moral knowledge and ignorance, we might construct a somewhat analogous case against servility from the point of view of those who adopt principles ascribing rights to all; but the argument, I suspect, would be more complex and less persuasive.

to refuse a jury trial but who nevertheless tells the judge that he understands that he has a right to a jury trial and freely waives it. He does not
really understand what it is to have and freely give up the right if he thinks
that it would be an offense for him to exercise it.

Insofar as servility results from moral ignorance or confusion, it need
not be something for which a person is to blame. Even self-reproach may
be inappropriate; for at the time a person is in ignorance he cannot feel
guilty about his servility, and later he may conclude that his ignorance
was unavoidable. In some cases, however, a person might reasonably believe
that he should have known better. If, for example, the Deferential Wife's
confusion about her rights resulted from a motivated resistance to drawing
the implications of her own basic moral principles, then later she might
find some ground for self-reproach. Whether blameworthy or not, servility
could still be morally objectionable at least in the sense that it ought to be
discouraged, that social conditions which nourish it should be reformed,
and the like. Not all morally undesirable features of a person are ones for
which he is responsible, but that does not mean that they are defects
merely from an esthetic or prudential point of view.

In our paradigm cases, I have suggested, servility is a kind of deferential attitude towards others resulting from ignorance or misunderstanding
of one's moral rights. A sufficient remedy, one might think, would be
moral enlightenment. Suppose, however, that our servile persons come to
know their rights but do not substantially alter their behavior. Are they
not still servile in an objectionable way? One might even think that reproach is more appropriate now because they know what they are doing.

The problem, unfortunately, is not as simple as it may appear. Much
depends on what they tolerate and why. Let us set aside cases in which a
person merely refuses to *fight* for his rights, chooses not to exercise certain
rights, or freely waives many rights which he might have insisted upon.
Our problem concerns the previously servile person who continues to display the same marks of deference even after he fully knows his rights.
Imagine, for example, that even after enlightenment our Uncle Tom per-
sists in his old pattern of behavior, giving all the typical signs of believing
that the injustices done to him are not really wrong. Suppose, too, that the
newly enlightened Deferential Wife continues to defer to her husband,
refusing to disturb the old way of life by introducing her new ideas. She
acts as if she accepts the idea that she is merely doing her duty though
actually she no longer believes it. Let us suppose, further, that the Uncle
Tom and the Deferential Wife are not merely generous with their time
and property; they also accept without protest, and even appear to sanction,
treatment which is humiliating and degrading. That is, they do not simply
consent to waive mutually acknowledged rights; they tolerate violations of
their rights with apparent approval. They pretend to give their permission
for subtle humiliations which they really believe no permission can make
legitimate. Are such persons still servile despite their moral knowledge?

The answer, I think, should depend upon why the deferential role is played. If the motive is a morally commendable one, or a desire to avert dire consequences to oneself, or even an ambition to set an oppressor up for a later fall, then I would not count the role player as servile. The Uncle Tom, for instance, is not servile in my sense if he shuffles and bows to keep the Klan from killing his children, to save his own skin, or even to buy time while he plans the revolution. Similarly, the Deferential Wife is not servile if she tolerates an abusive husband because he is so ill that further strain would kill him, because protesting would deprive her of her only means of survival, or because she is collecting atrocity stories for her book against marriage. If there is fault in these situations, it seems inappropriate to call it *servility*. The story is quite different, however, if a person continues in his deferential role just from laziness, timidity, or a desire for some minor advantage. He shows too little concern for his moral status as a person, one is tempted to say, if he is willing to deny it for a small profit or simply because it requires some effort and courage to affirm it openly. A black who plays the Uncle Tom merely to gain an advantage over other blacks is harming them, of course; but he is also displaying disregard for his own moral position as an equal among human beings. Similarly, a woman throws away her rights too lightly if she continues to play the subservient role because she is used to it or is too timid to risk a change. A Self-Deprecator who readily accepts what he knows are violations of his rights may be indulging his peculiar need for punishment at the expense of denying something more valuable. In these cases, I suggest, we have a kind of servility independent of any ignorance or confusion about one's rights. The person who has it may or may not be blameworthy, depending on many factors; and the line between servile and nonservile role playing will often be hard to draw. Nevertheless, the objectionable feature is perhaps clear enough for present purposes: it is a willingness to disavow one's moral status, publicly and systematically, in the absence of any strong reason to do so.

My proposal, then, is that there are at least two types of servility: one resulting from misunderstanding of one's rights and the other from placing a comparatively low value on them. In either case, servility manifests the absence of a certain kind of self-respect. The respect which is missing is not respect for one's merits but respect for one's rights. The servile person displays this absence of respect not directly by acting contrary to his own rights but indirectly by acting as if his rights were nonexistent or insignificant. An arrogant person ignores the rights of others, thereby arrogating for himself a higher status than he is entitled to; a servile person denies his own rights, thereby assuming a lower position than he is entitled to. Whether rooted in ignorance or simply lack of concern for moral rights, the attitudes in both cases may be incompatible with a proper regard for morality. That this is so obvious in the case of arrogance; but to see it in the case of servility requires some further argument.

IV

The objectionable feature of the servile person, as I have described him, is his tendency to disavow his own moral rights either because he misunderstands them or because he cares little for them. The question remains: why should anyone regard this as a moral defect? After all, the right which he denies are his own. He may be unfortunate, foolish, or even distasteful; but why *morally* deficient? One sort of answer, quite different from those reviewed earlier, is suggested by some of Kant's remarks. Kant held that servility is contrary to a perfect nonjuridical duty to oneself.[4] To say that the duty is perfect is roughly to say that it is stringent, never overridden by other considerations (e.g. beneficence). To say that the duty is non-juridical is to say that a person cannot legitimately be coerced to comply. Although Kant did not develop an explicit argument for this view, an argument can easily be constructed from materials which reflect the spirit, if not the letter, of his moral theory. The argument which I have in mind is prompted by Kant's contention that respect for persons, strictly speaking, is respect for moral law.[5] If taken as a claim about all sorts of respect, this seems quite implausible. If it means that we respect persons only for their moral character, their capacity for moral conduct, or their status as "authors" of the moral law, then it seems unduly moralistic. My strategy is to construe the remark as saying that at least one sort of respect for persons is respect for the rights which the moral law accords them. If one respects the moral law, then one must respect one's own moral rights; and this amounts to having a kind of self-respect incompatible with servility.

The premises for the Kantian argument, which are all admittedly vague, can be sketched as follows:

First, let us assume, as Kant did, that all human beings have equal basic human rights. Specific rights vary with different conditions, but all must be justified from a point of view under which all are equal. Not all rights need to be earned, and some cannot be forfeited. Many rights can be waived but only under certain conditions of knowledge and freedom. These conditions are complex and difficult to state; but they include something like the condition that a person's consent releases others from obligation only if it is autonomously given, and consent resulting from underestimation of one's moral status is not autonomously given. Rights can be

---

[4] See Immanuel Kant, *The Doctrine of Virtue*, Part II of *The Metaphysics of Morals*, ed. by M. J. Gregor (New York: Harper & Row, 1964), pp. 99–103; Prussian Academy edition, Vol. VI, pp. 434–37.

[5] Immanuel Kant, *Groundwork of the Metaphysics of Morals*, ed. by H. J. Paton (New York: Harper & Row, 1964), p. 69; Prussian Academy edition, Vol. IV, p. 401; *The Critique of Practical Reason*, ed. by Lewis W. Beck (New York: Bobbs-Merrill, 1956), pp. 81, 84; Prussian Academy edition, Vol. V, pp. 78, 81. My purpose here is not to interpret what Kant meant but to give a sense to his remark.

objects of knowledge, but also of ignorance, misunderstanding, deception, and the like.

Second, let us assume that my account of servility is correct; or, if one prefers, we can take it as a definition. That is, in brief, a servile person is one who tends to deny or disavow his own moral rights because he does not understand them or has little concern for the status they give him.

Third, we need one formal premise concerning moral duty, namely, that each person ought, as far as possible, to respect the moral law. In less Kantian language, the point is that everyone should approximate, to the extent that he can, the ideal of a person who fully adopts the moral point of view. Roughly, this means not only that each person ought to do what is morally required and refrain from what is morally wrong but also that each person should treat all the provisions of morality as valuable—worth preserving and prizing as well as obeying. One must, so to speak, take up the spirit of morality as well as meet the letter of its requirements. To keep one's promises, avoid hurting others, and the like, is not sufficient; one should also take an attitude of respect towards the principles, ideals, and goals of morality. A respectful attitude towards a system of rights and duties consists of more than a disposition to conform to its definite rules of behavior; it also involves holding the system in esteem, being unwilling to ridicule it, and being reluctant to give up one's place in it. The essentially Kantian idea here is that morality, as a system of equal fundamental rights and duties, is worthy of respect and hence a completely moral person would respect it in word and manner as well as in deed. And what a completely moral person would do, in Kant's view, is our duty to do so far as we can.

The assumptions here are, of course, strong ones, and I make no attempt to justify them. They are, I suspect, widely held though rarely articulated. In any case, my present purpose is not to evaluate them but to see how, if granted, they constitute a case against servility. The objection to the servile person; given our premises, is that he does not satisfy the basic requirement to respect morality. A person who fully respected a system of moral rights would be disposed to learn his proper place in it, to affirm it proudly, and not to tolerate abuses of it lightly. This is just the sort of disposition that the servile person lacks. If he does not understand the system, he is in no position to respect it adequately. This lack of respect may be no fault of his own, but it is still a way in which he falls short of a moral ideal. If, on the other hand, the servile person knowingly disavows his moral rights by pretending to approve of violations of them, barring special explanations, he shows an indifference to whether the provisions of morality are honored and publicly acknowledged. This avoidable display of indifference, by our Kantian premises, is contrary to the duty to respect morality. The disrespect in this second case is somewhat like the disrespect a religious believer might show toward his religion if, to avoid embarrassment, he laughed congenially while nonbelievers were mocking the beliefs which he secretly held. In any case, the servile person, as such, does not express disrespect for the system of moral rights in the obvious way by violating the rights of others. His lack of respect is more subtly manifested by his acting before others as if he did not know or care about his position of equality under that system.

The central idea may be illustrated by an analogy. Imagine a club, say, an old German dueling fraternity. By the rules of the club, each member has certain rights and responsibilities. These are the same for each member regardless of what titles he may hold outside the club. Each has, for example, a right to be heard at meetings, a right not to be shouted down by the others. Some rights cannot be forfeited: for example, each may vote regardless of whether he has paid his dues and satisfied other rules. Some rights cannot be waived: for example, the right to be defended when attacked by several members of the rival fraternity. The members show respect for each other by respecting the status which the rules confer on each member. Now one new member is careful always to allow the others to speak at meetings; but when they shout him down, he does nothing. He just shrugs as if to say, 'Who am I to complain?' When he fails to stand up in defense of a fellow member, he feels ashamed and refuses to vote. He does not deserve to vote, he says. As the only commoner among illustrious barons, he feels that it is his place to serve them and defer to their decisions. When attackers from the rival fraternity come at him with swords drawn, he tells his companions to run and save themselves. When they defend him, he expresses immense gratitude—as if they had done him a gratuitous favor. Now one might argue that our new member fails to show respect for the fraternity and its rules. He does not actually violate any of the rules by refusing to vote, asking others not to defend him, and deferring to the barons, but he symbolically disavows the equal status which the rules confer on him. If he ought to have respect for the fraternity, he ought to change his attitude. Our servile person, then, is like the new member of the dueling fraternity in having insufficient respect for a system of rules and ideals. The difference is that everyone ought to respect morality whereas there is no comparable moral requirement to respect the fraternity.

The conclusion here is, of course, a limited one. Self-sacrifice is not always a sign of servility. It is not a duty always to press one's rights. Whether a given act is evidence of servility will depend not only on the attitude of the agent but also on the specific nature of his moral rights, a matter not considered here. Moreover, the extent to which a person is responsible, or blameworthy, for his defect remains an open question. Nevertheless, the conclusion should not be minimized. In order to avoid servility, a person who gives up his rights must do so with a full appreciation for what they are. A woman, for example, may devote herself to her husband if she is uncoerced, knows what she is doing, and does not pretend that she has no decent alternative. A self-contemptuous person may decide not to press various unforfeited rights but only if he does not take the attitude that he is too rotten to deserve them. A black may demand less than is due to him provided he is prepared to acknowledge that no one has a right to expect this of him. Sacrifices of this sort, I suspect, are extremely rare. Most people, if they fully acknowledged their rights, would not autonomously refuse to press them.

An even stronger conclusion would emerge if we could assume that some basic rights cannot be waived. This is, if there are some rights that others are bound to respect regardless of what we say, then, barring special explanation, we would be obliged not only to acknowledge these rights but also to avoid any appearance of consenting to give them up. To act as if we could release others from their obligation to grant these rights, apart from special circumstances, would be to fail to respect morality. Rousseau, held, for example, that at least a minimal right to liberty cannot be waived. A man who consents to be enslaved, giving up liberty without *quid pro quo*, thereby displays a conditioned slavish mentality that renders his consent worthless. Similarly, a Kantian might argue that a person cannot release others from the obligation to refrain from killing him: consent is no defense against the charge of murder. To accept principles of this sort is to hold that rights to life and liberty are, as Kant believed, rather like a trustee's rights to preserve something valuable entrusted to him: he has not only a right but a duty to preserve it.

Even if there are no specific rights which cannot be waived, there might be at least one formal right of this sort. This is the right to some minimum degree of respect from others. No matter how willing a person is to submit to humiliation by others, they ought to show him some respect as a person. By analogy with self-respect, as presented here, this respect owed by others would consist of a willingness to acknowledge fully, in word as well as action, the person's basically equal moral status as defined by his other rights. To the extent that a person gives even tacit consent to humiliations incompatible with this respect, he will be acting as if he waives a right which he cannot in fact give up. To do this, barring special explanations, would mark one as servile.

V

Kant held that the avoidance of servility is a duty to oneself rather than a duty to others. Recent philosophers, however, tend to discard the idea of a duty to oneself as a conceptual confusion. Although admittedly the analogy between a duty to oneself and a duty to others is not perfect, I suggest that something important is reflected in Kant's contention.

Let us consider briefly the function of saying that a duty is *to* someone. *First,* to say that a duty is *to* a given person sometimes merely indicates who is the object of that duty. That is, to tell us that the duty is concerned with how that person is to be treated, how his interests and wishes are to be taken into account, and the like. Here we might as well say that we have a duty *towards*, or *regarding* that person. Typically the person in question is the beneficiary of the fulfillment of the duty. For example, in this sense I have a duty to my children and even a duty to a distant stranger if I promised a third party that I would help that stranger. Clearly a duty to avoid servility would be a duty to oneself at least in this minimal sense, for it is a duty to avoid, so far as possible, the denial of one's own moral status. The duty is concerned with understanding and affirming one's rights, which are, at least as a rule, for one's own benefit.

Second, when we say that a duty is *to* a certain person, we often indicate thereby the person especially entitled to complain in case the duty is not fulfilled. For example, if I fail in my duty to my colleagues, then it is they who can most appropriately reproach me. Others may sometimes speak up on their behalf, but, for the most part, it is not the business of strangers to set me straight. Analogously, to say that the duty to avoid servility is a duty to oneself would indicate that, though sometimes a person may justifiably reproach himself for being servile, others are not generally in the appropriate position to complain. Outside encouragement is sometimes necessary, but, if any blame is called for, it is primarily self-recrimination and not the censure of others.

Third, mention of the person to whom a duty is owed often tells us something about the source of that duty. For example, to say that I have a duty to another person may indicate that the argument to show that I have such a duty turns upon a promise to that person, his authority over me, my having accepted special benefits from him, or, more generally, his rights. Accordingly, to say that the duty to avoid servility is a duty to oneself would at least imply that it is not entirely based upon promises to others, their authority, their beneficence, or an obligation to respect their rights. More positively, the assertion might serve to indicate that the source of the duty is one's own rights rather than the rights of others, etc. That is, one ought not to be servile because, in some broad sense, one ought to respect one's own rights as a person. There is, to be sure, an asymmetry: one has certain duties to others because one ought not to violate their rights, and one has a duty to oneself because one ought to affirm one's own rights. Nevertheless, to dismiss duties to oneself out of hand is to overlook significant similarities.

Some familiar objections to duties to oneself, moreover, seem irrelevant in the case of servility. For example, some place much stock in the idea that a person would have no duties if alone on a desert island. This can be doubted, but in any case is irrelevant here. The duty to avoid servility is a duty to take a certain stance towards others and hence would be inapplicable if one were isolated on a desert island. Again, some suggest that if there were duties to oneself then one could make promises to oneself or owe oneself a debt of gratitude. Their paradigms are familiar ones.

Someone remarks, 'I promised myself a vacation this year' or 'I have been such a good boy I owe myself a treat'. Concentration on these facetious cases tends to confuse the issue. In any case the duty to avoid servility, as presented here, does not presuppose promises to oneself or debts of gratitude to oneself. Other objections stem from the intuition that a person has no duty to promote his own happiness. A duty to oneself, it is sometimes assumed, must be a duty to promote one's own happiness. From a utilitarian point of view, in fact, this is what a duty to oneself would most likely be. The problems with such alleged duties, however, are irrelevant to the duty to avoid servility. This is a duty to understand and affirm one's rights, not to promote one's own welfare. While it is usually in the interest of a person to affirm his rights, our Kantian argument against servility was not based upon this premise. Finally, a more subtle line of objection turns on the idea that, given that rights and duties are correlative, a person who acted contrary to a duty to oneself would have to be violating his own rights, which seems absurd.[6] This objection raises issues too complex to examine here. One should note, however, that I have tried to give a sense to saying that servility is contrary to a duty to oneself without presupposing that the servile person violates his own rights. If acts contrary to duties to others are always violations of their rights, then duties to oneself are not parallel with duties to others to that extent. But this does not mean that it is empty or pointless to say that a duty is to oneself.

My argument against servility may prompt some to say that the duty is "to morality" rather than "to oneself." All this means, however, is that the duty is derived from a basic requirement to respect the provisions of morality; and in this sense every duty is a duty "to morality". My duties to my children are also derivative from a general requirement to respect moral principles, but they are still duties *to* them.

Kant suggests that duties to oneself are a precondition of duties to others. On our account of servility, there is at least one sense in which this is so. Insofar as the servile person is ignorant of his own rights, he is not in an adequate position to appreciate the rights of others. Misunderstanding the moral basis for his equal status with others, he is necessarily liable to underestimate the rights of those with whom he classifies himself. On the other hand, if he plays the servile role knowingly, then, barring special explanation, he displays a lack of concern to see the principles of morality acknowledged and respected and thus the absence of one motive which can move a moral person to respect the rights of others. In either case, the servile person's lack of self-respect necessarily puts him in a less than ideal position to respect others. Failure to fulfill one duty to oneself, then, renders a person liable to violate duties to others. This, however, is a consequence of our argument against servility, not a presupposition of it.

[6] This, I take it, is part of M. G. Singer's objection to duties to oneself in *Generalization in Ethics* (New York: Alfred A. Knopf, 1961), pp. 311–18. I have attempted to examine Singer's arguments in detail elsewhere.

Selected Bibliography

BOXILL, BARNARD. "Self-Respect and Protest," *Philosophy and Public Affairs*, Vol. 6, no. 1 (1976), 58.

CARMICHAEL, STOKELY, and CHARLES HAMILTON. *Black Power*. New York: Random House, Inc., 1967.

ENGLISH, JANE (ed.). *Sex Equality*. Englewood Cliffs, N.J.: Prentice-Hall, Inc., 1977.

GOULD, CAROL C., and MARX W. WARTOFSKY (eds.). *Women and Philosophy*. New York: G. P. Putnam's Sons, 1976.

JAGGAR, ALISON M., and PAULA ROTHENBERG STRUHL (eds.). *Feminist Frameworks*. New York: McGraw-Hill Book Company, 1978.

MELDEN, A. I. (ed.). *Human Rights*. Belmont, Calif.: Wadsworth Publishing Co., Inc., 1970.

MILL, JOHN STUART. *The Subjection of Women*. London: Longman's, 1869.

PHILOSOPHIA, Vol. 8, nos. 1–2 (1978) (Philosophical Essays on Racism).

THALBERG, IRVING. "Justifications of Institutional Racism," *The Philosophical Forum*, Vol. III, no. 2 (1972), 243.

THALBERG, IRVING. "Visceral Racism," *The Monist*, Vol. 56, no. 4 (1972), 43.

VETTERLING-BRAGGIN, MARY, FREDERICK A. ELLISTON, and JANE ENGLISH (eds.). *Feminism and Philosophy*. Totowa, N.J.: Littlefield, Adams & Co., 1977.

three

PREFERENTIAL TREATMENT

Regents of the University of California v. Allan Bakke __ U.S. __ , 98 S.Ct. 2733, 46 L.W. 4896 (1978)

Mr. Justice Powell announced the judgment of the Court.

This case presents a challenge to the special admissions program of the petitioner, the Medical School of the University of California at Davis, which is designed to assure the admission of a specified number of students from certain minority groups. The Superior Court of California sustained respondent's challenge, holding that petitioner's program violated the

Editor's Note: Six of the nine Justices of the Supreme Court wrote opinions in the Bakke case. The opinions of Mr. Justice White and Mr. Justice Stevens have been omitted. The opinion of Mr. Justice Powell has been edited, as has the opinion of Mr. Justice Brennan. Page references to *The Record* have been deleted. A number of footnotes have been deleted from the opinions of Mr. Justice Powell and Mr. Justice Brennan, and those that remain have been renumbered.

California Constitution, Title VI of the Civil Rights Act of 1964, 42 U.S.C. § 2000d, and the Equal Protection Clause of the Fourteenth Amendment. The court enjoined petitioner from considering respondent's race or the race of any other applicant in making admissions decisions. It refused, however, to order respondent's admission to the Medical School, holding that he had not carried his burden of proving that he would have been admitted but for the constitutional and statutory violations. The Supreme Court of California affirmed those portions of the trial court's judgment declaring the special admissions program unlawful and enjoining petitioner from considering the race of any applicant. It modified that portion of the judgment denying respondent's requested injunction and directed the trial court to order his admission.

For the reasons stated in the following opinion, I believe that so much of the judgment of the California court as holds petitioner's special admissions program unlawful and directs that respondent be admitted to the Medical School must be affirmed. For the reasons expressed in a separate opinion, my Brothers THE CHIEF JUSTICE, MR. JUSTICE STEWART, MR. JUSTICE REHNQUIST, and MR. JUSTICE STEVENS concur in this judgment.

I also conclude for the reasons stated in the following opinion that the portion of the court's judgment enjoining petitioner from according any consideration to race in its admissions process must be reversed. For reasons expressed in separate opinions, my Brothers MR. JUSTICE BRENNAN, MR. JUSTICE WHITE, MR. JUSTICE MARSHALL, and MR. JUSTICE BLACKMUN concur in this judgment.

Affirmed in part and reversed in part.

I

The Medical School of the University of California at Davis opened in 1968 with an entering class of 50 students. In 1971, the size of the entering class was increased to 100 students, a level at which it remains. No admissions program for disadvantaged or minority students existed when the school opened, and the first class contained three Asians but no blacks, no Mexican-Americans, and no American Indians. Over the next two years, the faculty devised a special admissions program to increase the representation of "disadvantaged" students in each medical school class. The special program consisted of a separate admissions system operating in coordination with the regular admissions process.

Under the regular admissions procedure, a candidate could submit his application to the medical school beginning in July of the year preceding the academic year for which admission was sought. Because of the large number of applications,[1] the admissions committee screened each one to select candidates for further consideration. Candidates whose overall undergraduate grade point averages fell below 2.5 on a scale of 4.00 were summarily rejected. About one out of six applicants was invited for a personal interview. Following the interviews, each candidate was rated on a scale of 1 to 100 by his interviewers and four other members of the admissions committee. The rating embraced the interviewers' summaries, the candidate's overall grade point average, grade point average in science courses, and scores on the Medical College Admissions Test (MCAT), letters of recommendation, extracurricular activities, and other biographical data. The ratings were added together to arrive at each candidate's "benchmark" score. Since five committee members rated each candidate in 1973, a perfect score was 500; in 1974, six members rated each candidate, so that a perfect score was 600. The full committee then reviewed the file and scores of each applicant and made offers of admission on a "rolling" basis. The chairman was responsible for placing names on the waiting list. They were not placed in strict numerical order; instead, the chairman had discretion to include persons with "special skills."

The special admissions program operated with a separate committee, a majority of whom were members of minority groups. On the 1973 application form, candidates were asked to indicate whether they wished to be considered as "economically and/or educationally disadvantaged" applicants; on the 1974 form the question was whether they wished to be considered as members of a "minority group," which the medical school apparently viewed as "Blacks," "Chicanos," "Asians," and "American Indians." If these questions were answered affirmatively, the application was forwarded to the special admissions committee. No formal definition of "disadvantaged" was ever produced, but the chairman of the special committee screened each application to see whether it reflected economic or educational deprivation. Having passed this initial hurdle, the applications then were rated by the special committee in a fashion similar to that used by the general admissions committee, except that special candidates did not have to meet the 2.5 grade point average cut-off applied to regular applicants. About one-fifth of the total number of special applicants were invited for interviews in 1973 and 1974.[2] Following each interview, the special committee assigned each special applicant a benchmark score. The special committee then presented its top choices to the general admissions committee. The latter did not rate or compare the special candidates against the general applicants but could reject recommended special candi-

---

[1] For the 1973 entering class of 100 seats, the Davis medical school received 2,464 applications. For the 1974 entering class, 3,737 applications were submitted.

[2] For the class entering in 1973, the total number of special applicants was 297, of whom 73 were white. In 1974, 628 persons applied to the special committee, of whom 172 were white. Record 133–134.

dates for failure to meet course requirements or other specific deficiencies. The special committee continued to recommend special applicants until a number prescribed by faculty vote were admitted. While the overall class size was still 50, the prescribed number was eight; in 1973 and 1974, when the class size had doubled to 100, the prescribed number of special admissions also doubled, to 16.

From the year of the increase in class size—1971—through 1974, the special program resulted in the admission of 21 black students, 30 Mexican-Americans, and 12 Asians, for a total of 63 minority students. Over the same period, the regular admissions program produced one black, six Mexican-Americans, and 37 Asians, for a total of 44 minority students.[3] Although disadvantaged whites applied to the special program in large numbers, none received an offer of admission through that process. Indeed, in 1974, at least, the special committee explicitly considered only "disadvantaged" special applicants who were members of one of the designated minority groups.

Allan Bakke is a white male who applied to the Davis Medical School in both 1973 and 1974. In both years Bakke's application was considered by the general admissions program, and he received an interview. His 1973 interview was with Dr. Theodore H. West, who considered Bakke "a very desirable applicant to [the] medical school." Despite a strong benchmark score of 468 out of 500, Bakke was rejected. His application had come late in the year, and no applicants in the general admissions process with scores below 470 were accepted after Bakke's application was completed. There were four special admissions slots unfilled at that time, however, for which Bakke was not considered. After his 1973 rejection, Bakke wrote to Dr. George H. Lowrey, Associate Dean and Chairman of the Admissions Committee, protesting that the special admissions program operated as a racial and ethnic quota.

Bakke's 1974 application was completed early in the year. His student interviewer gave him an overall rating of 94, finding him "friendly, well tempered, conscientious and delightful to speak with." His faculty inter-

---

[3] The following table provides a year-by-year comparison of minority admissions at the Davis Medical School:

	Special Admissions Program				*General Admissions*				
	Blacks	Chi-canos	Asians	Total	Blacks	Chi-canos	Asians	Total	*Total*
1970	5	3	0	8	0	0	4	4	12
1971	4	9	2	15	1	0	8	9	24
1972	5	6	5	16	0	0	11	11	27
1973	6	8	2	16	0	2	13	15	31
1974	6	7	3	16	0	4	5	9	25

Sixteen persons were admitted under the special program in 1974 but one Asian withdrew before the start of classes, and the vacancy was filled by a candidate from the general admissions waiting list.

viewer was, by coincidence, the same Dr. Lowrey to whom he had written in protest of the special admissions program. Dr. Lowrey found Bakke "rather limited in his approach" to the problems of the medical profession and found disturbing Bakke's "very definite opinions which were based more on his personal viewpoints than upon a study of the total problem." *Id.*, at 226. Dr. Lowrey gave Bakke the lowest of his six ratings, an 86; his total was 549 out of 600. Again, Bakke's application was rejected. In neither year did the chairman of the admissions committee, Dr. Lowrey, exercise his discretion to place Bakke on the waiting list. In both years, applicants were admitted under the special program with grade point averages, MCAT scores, and benchmark scores significantly lower than Bakke's.[4]

After the second rejection, Bakke filed the instant suit in the Superior Court of California.[5] He sought mandatory, injunctive, and declaratory

[4] The following table compares Bakke's science grade point average, overall grade point average, and MCAT Scores with the average scores of regular admittees and of special admittees in both 1973 and 1974. Record 210, 223, 231, 234:

Class Entering in 1973

				MCAT (Percentiles)		
	SGPA	OGPA	Verbal	Quanti-tative	Science	Gen. Infor.
Bakke	3.44	3.51	96	94	97	72
Average of Regular Admittees	3.51	3.49	81	76	83	69
Average of Special Admittees	2.62	2.88	46	24	35	33

Class Entering in 1974

				MCAT (Percentiles)		
	SGPA	OGPA	Verbal	Quanti-tative	Science	Gen. Infor.
Bakke	3.44	3.51	96	94	97	72
Average of Regular Admittees	3.36	3.29	69	67	82	72
Average of Special Admittees	2.42	2.62	34	30	37	18

Applicants admitted under the special program also had benchmark scores significantly lower than many students, including Bakke, rejected under the general admissions program, even though the special rating system apparently gave credit for overcoming "disadvantage."

[5] Prior to the actual filing of the suit, Bakke discussed his intentions with Peter C. Storandt, Assistant to the Dean of Admissions at the Davis Medical School. Storandt expressed sympathy for Bakke's position and offered advice on litigation strategy. Several *amici* imply that these discussions render Bakke's suit "collusive." There is no indication, however, that Storandt's views were those of the medical school or that anyone else at the school even was aware of Storandt's correspondence and conversations with Bakke. Storandt is no longer with the University.

relief compelling his admission to the Medical School. He alleged that the Medical School's special admissions program operated to exclude him from the school on the basis of his race, in violation of his rights under the Equal Protection Clause of the Fourteenth Admendment,[6] Art. I, § 21 of the California Constitution,[7] and § 601 of Title VI of the Civil Rights Act of 1964, 42 U.S.C. § 2000d.[8] The University cross-complained for a declaration that its special admissions program was lawful. The trial court found that the special program operated as a racial quota, because minority applicants in the special program were rated only against one another, Record 388, and 16 places in the class of 100 were reserved for them. Declaring that the University could not take race into account in making admissions decisions, the trial court held the challenged program violative of the Federal Constitution, the state constitution and Title VI. The court refused to order Bakke's admission, however, holding that he had failed to carry his burden of proving that he would have been admitted but for the existence of the special program.

Bakke appealed from the portion of the trial court judgment denying him admission, and the University appealed from the decision that its special admissions program was unlawful and the order enjoining it from considering race in the processing of applications. The Supreme Court of California transferred the case directly from the trial court, "because of the importance of the issues involved." 18 Cal. 3d 34, 39, 553 P. 2d 1152, 1156 (1976). The California court accepted the findings of the trial court with respect to the University's program.[9] Because the special admissions program involved a racial classification, the supreme court held itself bound to apply strict scrutiny. *Id.*, at 49, 553 P. 2d, at 1162–1163. It then turned to the goals the University presented as justifying the special program. Although the court agreed that the goals of integrating the medical profession and increasing the number of physicians willing to serve members of minority groups were compelling state interests, *id.*, at 53, 553 P. 2d, at 1165, it concluded that the special admissions program was not the

---

[6] ". . . [N]or shall any State . . . deny to any person within its jurisdiction the equal protection of the laws."

[7] "No special privileges or immunities shall ever be granted which may not be altered, revoked, or repealed by the Legislature; nor shall any citizen, or class of citizens, be granted privileges, or immunities which, upon the same terms, shall not be granted to all citizens."

This section was recently repealed and its provisions added to Art. § 7 of the state constitution.

[8] Section 601 of Title VI provides as follows:

"No person in the United States shall, on the ground of race, color, or national origin, be excluded from participation in, be denied the benefits of, or be subjected to discrimination under any program or activity receiving Federal financial assistance."

[9] Indeed, the University did not challenge the finding that applicants who were not members of a minority group were excluded from consideration in the special admissions process. 18 Cal. 3d, at 44, 553 P. 2d, at 1159.

least intrusive means of achieving those goals. Without passing on the state constitutional or the federal statutory grounds cited in the trial court's judgment, the California court held that the Equal Protection Clause of the Fourteenth Amendment required that "no applicant may be rejected because of his race, in favor of another who is less qualified, as measured by standards applied without regard to race." *Id.*, at 55, 553 P. 2d, at 1166.

Turning to Bakke's appeal, the court ruled that since Bakke had established that the University had discriminated against him on the basis of his race, the burden of proof shifted to the University to demonstrate that he would not have been admitted even in the absence of the special admissions program. *Id., at* 63–64, 553 P. 2d, at 1172. The court analogized Bakke's situation to that of a plaintiff under Title VII to the Civil Rights Act of 1964, 42 U. S. C. §§ 200e–17, see, *e.g., Franks* v. *Bowman Transportation Co.*, 424 U.S. 747, 772 (1976). *Ibid.* On this basis, the court initially ordered a remand for the purpose of determining whether, under the newly allocated burden of proof, Bakke would have been admitted to either the 1973 or the 1974 entering class in the absence of the special admissions program. In its petition for rehearing below, however, the University conceded its inability to carry that burden. The California court thereupon amended its opinion to direct that the trial court enter judgment ordering Bakke's admission to the medical school. 18 Cal. 3d, at 64, 553 P. 2d, at 1172. That order was stayed pending review in this Court. 429 U.S. 953 (1976). We granted certiorari to consider the important constitutional issue. 429 U.S. 1090 (1977).

· · ·

III

A

Petitioner does not deny that decisions based on race or ethnic origin by faculties and administrations of state universities are reviewable under the Fourteenth Amendment. See *e.g., Missouri ex rel. Gaines* v. *Canada,* 305 U.S. 337 (1938); *Sipuel* v. *Board of Regents,* 332 U.S. 631 (1948); *Sweatt* v. *Painter,* 339 U.S. 629 (1950); *McLaurin* v. *Oklahoma State Regents,* 339 U.S. 637 (1950). For his part, respondent does not argue that all racial or ethnic classifications are *per se* invalid. See, *e.g., Hirabayashi* v. *United States,* 320 U.S. 31 (1943); *Korematsu* v. *United States,* 323 U.S. 214 (1944); *Lee* v. *Washington,* 390 U.S. 333, 334 (1968) (Black, Harlan, and STEWART, JJ., concurring); *United Jewish Organizations* v. *Carey,* 430 U.S. 144 (1977). The parties do disagree as to the level of judicial scrutiny to be applied to the special admissions program. Petitioner argues that the court below erred in applying strict scrutiny, as this inexact term has been applied in our cases. That level of review, petitioner asserts, should be reserved for classifications that disadvantage "discrete and insular minorities." See *United States* v. *Carolene Products Co.*, 304 U.S. 144, 152 n. 4 (1938). Respondent, on the other hand, contends that the California court correctly rejected the notion that the degree of judicial scrutiny accorded a particular racial or ethnic classification hinges upon membership in a discrete and insular minority and duly recognized that the "rights established [by the Fourteenth Amendment] are personal rights." *Shelley* v. *Kraemer*, 334 U.S. 1, 22 (1948).

En route to this crucial battle over the scope of judicial review,[10] the parties fight a sharp preliminary action over the proper characterization of the special admissions program. Petitioner prefers to view it as establishing a "goal" of minority representation in the medical school. Respondent, echoing the courts below, labels it a racial quota.[11]

This semantic distinction is beside the point: the special admissions program is undeniably a classification based on race and ethnic background. To the extent that there existed a pool of at least minimally qualified minority applicants to fill the 16 special admissions seats, white applicants could compete only for 84 seats in the entering class, rather than the 100 open to minority applicants. Whether this limitation is

---

[10] That issue has generated a considerable amount of scholarly controversy. See, *e.g.*, Ely, The Constitutionality of Reverse Racial Discrimination, 41 U. Chi. L. Rev. 723 (1974); Greenawalt, Judicial Scrutiny of "Benign" Racial Preferences in Law School Admissions, 75 Colum. L. Rev. 559 (1975); Kaplan, Equal Justice in an Unequal World: Equality for the Negro, 61 Nw. U. L. Rev. 363 (1966); Karst & Horowitz, Affirmative Action and Equal Protection, 60 Va. L. Rev. 955 (1974); O'Neil, Racial Preference and Higher Education: The Larger Context, 60 Va. L. Rev. 925 (1974); Posner, The DeFunis Case and the Constitutionality of Preferential Treatment of Racial Minorities, 1974 Sup. Ct. Rev. 1; Redish, Preferential Law School Admissions and the Equal Protection Clause: An Analysis of the Competing Arguments, 22 U. C. L. A. L. Rev. 343 (1974); Sandalow, Racial Preferences in Higher Education: Political Responsibility and the Judicial Role, 42 U. Chi. L. Rev. 536 (1975); Sedler, Racial Preference, Reality and the Constitution: Bakke v. Regents of the University of California, 17 Santa Clara L. Rev. 329 (1977); Seeburger, A Heuristic Argument Against Preferential Admissions, 39 U. Pitt. L. Rev. 285 (1977).

[11] Petitioner defines "quota" as a requirement which must be met but can never be exceeded, regardless of the quality of the minority applicants. Petitioner declares that there is no "floor" under the total number of minority students admitted; completely unqualified students will not be admitted simply to meet a "quota." Neither is there a "ceiling," since an unlimited number could be admitted through the general admissions process. On this basis the special admissions program does not meet petitioner's definition of a quota.

The court below found—and petitioner does not deny—that white applicants could not compete for the 16 places reserved solely for the special admissions program. 18 Cal. 3d, at 44, 553 P. 2d, at 1159. Both courts below characterized this as a "quota" system.

described as a quota or a goal, it is a line drawn on the basis of race and ethnic status.[12]

The guarantees of the Fourteenth Amendment extend to persons. Its language is explicit: "No state shall . . . deny to any person within its jurisdiction the equal protection of the laws." It is settled beyond question that the "rights created by the first section of the Fourteenth Amendment are, by its terms, guaranteed to the individual. They are personal rights," *Shelley* v. *Kraemer, supra,* at 22. Accord, *Missouri ex rel. Gaines* v. *Canada, supra,* at 351; *McCabe* v. *Atchison, T. & S. F. R. Co.,* 235 U.S. 151, 161–162 (1914). The guarantee of equal protection cannot mean one thing when applied to one individual and something else when applied to a person of another color. If both are not accorded the same protection, then it is not equal.

Nevertheless, petitioner argues that the court below erred in applying strict scrutiny to the special admissions programs because white males, such as respondent, are not a "discrete and insular minority" requiring extraordinary protection from the majoritarian political process. *Carolene Products Co., supre,* at 152–153, n. 4. This rationale, however, has never been invoked in our decisions as prerequisite to subjecting racial or ethnic distinctions to strict scrutiny. Nor has this Court held that discreteness and insularity constitute necessary preconditions to a holding that a particular classification is invidious.[13] See, *e.g., Skinner* v. *Oklahoma,* 316 U.S. 535, 541 (1942); *Carrington* v. *Rash,* 380 U.S. 89, 94–97 (1965). These characteristics may be relevant in deciding whether or not to add new types of classifications to the list of "suspect" categories or whether a particular classification survives close examination. See, *e.g., Massachusetts Bd. of Retirement* v. *Murgia,* 427 U.S. 307, 313 (1976) (age); *San Antonio Indep. School Dist.* v. *Rodriquez,* 411 U.S. 1, 28 (1973) (wealth); *Graham* v. *Richardson,* 403 U.S. 365, 372 (1971) (aliens). Racial and ethnic classifications, however, are subject to stringent examination without regard to these additional characteristics. We declared as much in the first cases explicitly to recognize racial distinctions as suspect:

[12] Moreover, the University's special admissions program involves a purposeful, acknowledged use of racial criteria. This is not a situation in which the classification on its face is racially neutral, but has a disproportionate racial impact. In that situation, plaintiff must establish an intent to discriminate. *Village of Arlington Heights* v. *Metropolitan Housing Devel. Corp.,* 429 U.S. 252, 264–265 (1977); *Washington* v. *Davis,* 426 U.S. 229, 242 (1976); see *Yick Wo* v. *Hopkins,* 118 U.S. 356 (1886).

[13] After *Carolene Products,* the first specific reference in our decisions to the elements of "discreteness and insularity" appears in *Minersville School District* v. *Gobitis,* 310 U.S. 586, 606 (1940) (Stone, J., dissenting). The next does not appear until 1970. *Oregon* v. *Mitchell,* 400 U.S. 112, 295 n. 14 (1970) (STEWART, J., concurring in part and dissenting in part). These elements have been relied upon in recognizing a suspect class in only one group of cases, those involving aliens. E.g., *Graham* v. *Richardson,* 403 U.S. 365, 372 (1971).

"Distinctions between citizens solely because of their ancestry are by their very nature odious to a free people whose institutions are founded upon the doctrine of equality." *Hirabayashi*, 320 U.S., at 100.

". . . [A]ll legal restrictions which curtail the rights of a single racial group are immediately suspect. That is not to say that all such restrictions are unconstitutional. It is to say that courts must subject them to the most rigid scrutiny." *Korematsu*, 323 U.S., at 216.

The Court has never questioned the validity of those pronouncements. Racial and ethnic distinctions of any sort are inherently suspect and thus call for the most exacting judicial examination.

B

This perception of racial and ethnic distinctions is rooted in our Nation's constitutional and demographic history. The Court's initial view of the Fourteenth Amendment was that its "one pervading purpose" was "the freedom of the slave race, the security and firm establishment of that freedom, and the protection of the newly-made freeman and citizen from the oppressions of those who had formerly exercised dominion over him." *Slaughter-House Cases*, 16 Wall. 36, 71 (1873). The Equal Protection Clause, however, was "[v]irtually strangled in its infancy by post-civil-war judicial reactionism." [14] It was relegated to decades of relative desuetude while the Due Process Clause of the Fourteenth Amendment, after a short germinal period, flourished as a cornerstone in the Court's defense of property and liberty of contract. See, *e.g., Mugler* v. *Kansas*, 123 U.S. 623, 661 (1887); *Allgeyer* v. *Louisiana*, 165 U.S. 578 (1897); *Lochner* v. *New York*, 198 U.S. 45 (1905). In that cause, the Fourteenth Amendment's "one pervading purpose" was displaced. See, *e.g., Plessy* v. *Ferguson*, 163 U.S. 537 (1896). It was only as the era of substantive due process came to a close, see, *e.g., Nebbia* v. *New York*, 291 U.S. 502 (1934); *West Coast Hotel* v. *Parrish*, 300 U.S. 379 (1937), that the Equal Protection Clause began to attain a genuine measure of vitality, see, *e.g., Carolene Products, supra; Skinner* v. *Oklahoma, supra.*

By that time it was no longer possible to peg the guarantees of the Fourteenth Amendment to the struggle for equality of one racial minority. During the dormancy of the Equal Protection Clause, the United States had become a nation of minorities.[15] Each had to struggle [16]—and to some

---

[14] Tussman & tenBroek, The Equal Protection of the Laws, 37 Calif. L. Rev. 341, 381 (1949).

[15] M. Jones, American Immigration 177–246 (1960).

[16] J. Higham, Strangers in the Land (1955); G. Abbott, The Immigrant and the Community (1917); P. Roberts, The New Immigration 66–73, 86–91, 248–261 (1912). See also E. Fenton, Immigrants and Unions: A Case Study 561–562 (1975).

extent struggles still [17]—to overcome the prejudices not of a monolithic majority, but of a "majority" composed of various minority groups of whom it was said—perhaps unfairly in many cases—that a shared characteristic was a willingness to disadvantage other groups.[18] As the Nation filled with the stock of many lands, the reach of the Clause was gradually extended to all ethnic groups seeking protection from official discrimination. See *Strauder* v. *West Virginia*, 100 U.S. 303, 308 (1880). (Celtic Irishmen) (dictum); *Yick Wo* v. *Hopkins*, 118 U.S. 356 (1886) (Chinese); *Truax* v. *Raich*, 239 U.S. 33, 41 (1915) (Austrian resident aliens); *Korematsu, supra* (Japanese); *Hernandez* v. *Texas*, 347 U.S. 475 (1954) (Mexican-Americans). The guarantees of equal protection, said the Court in *Yick Wo*, "are universal in their application, to all persons within the territorial jurisdiction, without regard to any differences of race, of color, or of nationality; and the equal protection of the laws is a pledge of the protection of equal laws." 118 U.S., at 369.

Although many of the Framers of the Fourteenth Amendment conceived of its primary function as bridging the vast distance between members of the Negro race and the white "majority," *Slaughter-House Cases, supra*, the Amendment itself was framed in universal terms, without reference to color, ethnic origin, or condition of prior servitude. As this Court recently remarked in interpreting the 1866 Civil Rights Act to extend to claims of racial discrimination against white persons, "the 39th Congress was intent upon establishing in federal law a broader principle than would have been necessary to meet the particular and immediate plight of the newly freed Negro slaves." *McDonald* v. *Santa Fe Trail Transp. Co.*, 427 U.S. 273, 296 (1976). And that legislation was specifically broadened in 1870 to ensure that "all persons,' not merely "citizens," would enjoy equal rights under the law. See *Runyon* v. *McCrary*, 427 U.S. 160, 192–202 (1976) (WHITE, J., dissenting). Indeed, it is not unlikely that among the Framers were many who would have applauded a reading of the Equal Protection Clause which states a principle of universal application and is responsive to the racial, ethnic and cultural diversity of the Nation. See, e.g., Cong. Globe, 39th Cong., 1st Sess., 1056 (1866) (remarks of Rep. Niblack); *id.*, at 2891–2892 (remarks of Sen. Corness); *id.*, 40th Cong., 2d Sess., 883 (1868) (remarks of Sen. Howe) (Fourteenth Amendment "protect[s] classes from class legislation"). See also Bickel, The Original Understanding and the Segregation Decision, 69 Harv. L. Rev. 1, 60–63 (1955).

---

[17] "Members of various religious and ethnic groups, primarily but not exclusively of eastern, and middle and southern European ancestry, such as Jews, Catholics, Italians, Greeks and Slavic groups [continue] to be excluded from executive, middle-management and other job levels because of discrimination based upon their religion and/or national origin." 41 CFR § 60–50.1 (b) (1977).

[18] E.g., P. Roberts, The New Immigration 75 (1912); G. Abbott, The Immigrant and the Community 270–271 (1917).

Over the past 30 years, this Court has embarked upon the crucial mission of interpreting the Equal Protection Clause with the view of assuring to all persons "the protection of equal laws," *Yick Wo, supra,* at 369, in a Nation confronting a legacy of slavery and racial discrimination. See, *e.g., Shelley* v. *Kraemer,* 334 U.S. 1 (1948); *Brown* v. *Board of Education,* 347 U.S. 483 (1954); *Hills* v. *Gautreaux,* 425 U.S. 284 (1976). Because the landmark decisions in this area arose in response to the continued exclusion of Negroes from the mainstream of American society, they could be characterized as involving discrimination by the "majority" white race against the Negro minority. But they need not be read as depending upon that characterization for their results. It suffices to say that "[o]ver the years, this Court consistently repudiated '[d]istinctions between citizens solely because of their ancestry' as being 'odious to a free people whose institutions are founded upon the doctrine of equality.'" *Loving* v. *Virginia,* 388 U.S. 1, 11 (1967), quoting *Hirabayashi,* 320 U.S., at 100.

Petitioner urges us to adopt for the first time a more restrictive view of the Equal Protection Clause and hold that discrimination against members of the white "majority" cannot be suspect if its purpose can be characterized as "benign." [19] The clock of our liberties, however, cannot be turned back to 1868. *Brown* v. *Board of Education, supra,* at 492; accord, *Loving* v. *Virginia, supra,* at 9. It is far too late to argue that the guarantee of equal protection to *all* persons permits the recognition of special wards entitled to a degree of protection greater than that accorded others.[20] "The

---

[19] In the view of MR. JUSTICE BRENNAN, MR. JUSTICE WHITE, MR. JUSTICE MARSHALL, and MR. JUSTICE BLACKMUN, the pliable notion of "stigma" is the crucial element in analyzing racial classifications. The Equal Protection Clause is not framed in terms of "stigma." Certainly the word has no clearly defined constitutional meaning. It reflects a subjective judgment that is standardless. *All* state-imposed classifications that rearrange burdens and benefits on the basis of race are likely to be viewed with deep resentment by the individuals burdened. The denial to innocent persons of equal rights and opportunities may outrage those so deprived and therefore may be perceived as invidious. These individuals are likely to find little comfort in the notion that the deprivation they are asked to endure is merely the price of membership in the dominant majority and that its imposition is inspired by the supposedly benign purpose of aiding others. One should not lightly dismiss the inherent unfairness of, and the perception of mistreatment that accompanies, a system of allocating benefits and privileges on the basis of skin color and ethnic origin. Moreover, MR. JUSTICE BRENNAN, MR. JUSTICE WHITE, MR. JUSTICE MARSHALL, and MR. JUSTICE BLACKMUN offer no principle for deciding whether preferential classification reflect a benign remedial purpose or a malevolent stigmatic classification, since they are willing in this case to accept mere *post hoc* declarations by an isolated state entity—a medical school faculty—unadorned by particularized findings of past discrimination, to establish such a remedial purpose.

[20] Professor Bickel noted the self-contradiction of that view:

"The lesson of the great decisions of the Supreme Court and the lesson of contemporary history have been the same for at least a generation: discrimination

Fourteenth Amendment is not directed solely against discrimination due to a 'two-class theory'—that is, based upon differences between 'white' and Negro." *Hernandez, supra,* at 478.

Once the artificial line of a "two-class theory" of the Fourteenth Amendment is put aside, the difficulties entailed in varying the level of judicial review according to a perceived "preferred" status of a particular racial or ethnic minority are intractable. The concepts of "majority" and "minority" necessarily reflect temporary arrangements and political judgments. As observed above, the white "majority" itself is composed of various minority groups, most of which can lay claim to a history of prior discrimination at the hands of the state and private individuals. Not all of these groups can receive preferential treatment and corresponding judicial tolerance of distinctions drawn in terms of race and nationality, for then the only "majority" left would be a new minority of White Anglo-Saxon Protestants. There is no principled basis for deciding which groups would merit "heightened judicial solicitude" and which would not.[21] Courts

---

on the basis of race is illegal, immoral, unconstitutional, inherently wrong, and destructive of democratic society. Now this is to be unlearned and we are told that this is not a matter of fundamental principle but only a matter of whose ox is gored. Those for whom racial equality was demanded are to be more equal than others. Having found support in the Constitution for equality, they now claim support for inequality under the same Constitution." A. Bickel, The Morality of Consent 133 (1975).

[21] As I am in agreement with the view that race may be taken into account as a factor in an admissions program, I agree with my Brothers BRENNAN, WHITE, MARSHALL, and BLACKMUN that the portion of the judgment that would prescribe all consideration of race must be reversed. See Part V, *infra.* But I disagree with much that is said in their opinion.

They would require as a justification for a program such as petitioner's, only two findings: (i) that there has been some form of discrimination against the preferred minority groups "by society at large," (it being conceded that petitioner had no history of discrimination), and (ii) that "there is reason to believe" that the disparate impact sought to be rectified by the program is the "product" of such discrimination:

"If it was reasonable to conclude—as we hold that it was—that the failure of Negroes to qualify for admission at Davis under regular procedures was due principally to the effects of past discrimination, then there is a reasonable likelihood that, but for pervasive racial discrimination, respondent would have failed to qualify for admission even in the absence of Davis's special admission program."

The breadth of this hypothesis is unprecedented in our constitutional system. The first step is easily taken. No one denies the regrettable fact that there has been societal discrimination in this country against various racial and ethnic groups. The second step, however, involves a speculative leap: but for this discrimination by society at large, Bakke "would have failed to qualify for admission" because Negro applicants—nothing is said about Asians, would have made better scores. Not one word in the record supports this conclusion, and the plurality offers no standard for courts to use in applying such a presumption of causation to other racial or ethnic classifications. This failure is a grave one, since

would be asked to evaluate the extent of the prejudice and consequent harm suffered by various minority groups. Those whose societal injury is thought to exceed some arbitrary level of tolerability then would be entitled to preferential classifications at the expense of individuals belonging to other groups. Those classifications would be free from exacting judicial scrutiny. As these preferences began to have their desired effect, and the consequences of past discrimination were undone, new judicial rankings would be necessary. The kind of variable sociological and political analysis necessary to produce such rankings simply does not lie within the judicial competence—even if they otherwise were politically feasible and socially desirable.[22]

---

if it may be concluded *on this record* that each of the minority groups preferred by the petitioner's special program is entitled to the benefit of the presumption, it would seem difficult to determine that any of the dozens of minority groups that have suffered "societal discrimination" cannot also claim it, in any area of social intercourse. See Part IV-B, *infra*.

[22] Mr. Justice Douglas has noted the problems associated with such inquiries:

"The reservation of a proportion of the law school class for members of selected minority groups is fraught with . . . dangers, for one must immediately determine which groups are to receive such favored treatment and which are to be excluded, the proportions of the class that are to be allocated to each, and even the criteria by which to determine whether an individual is a member of a favored group. [Cf. *Plessy* v. *Ferguson*, 163 U.S. 537, 549, 552 (1896).] There is no assurance that a common agreement can be reached, and first the schools, and then the courts, will be buffeted with the competing claims. The University of Washington included Filipinos, but excluded Chinese and Japanese; another school may limit its program to blacks, or to blacks and Chicanos. Once the Court sanctioned racial preferences such as these, it could not then wash its hands of the matter, leaving it entirely in the discretion of the school, for then we would have effectively overruled *Sweatt* v. *Painter*, 339 U.S. 629, and allowed imposition of a "zero" allocation. But what standard is the Court to apply when a rejected applicant of Japanese ancestry brings suit to require the University of Washington to extend the same privileges to his group? The Committee might conclude that the population of Washington is now 2% Japanese, and that Japanese also constitute 2% of the Bar, but that had they not been handicapped by a history of discrimination, Japanese would now constitute 5% of the Bar, or 20%. Or, alternatively, the Court could attempt to assess how grievously each group has suffered from discrimination, and allocate proportions accordingly; if that were the standard the current University of Washington policy would almost surely fall, for there is no Western state which can claim that it has always treated Japanese and Chinese in a fair and evenhanded manner. See, *e.g.*, *Yick Wo* v. *Hopkins*, 118 U.S. 356; *Terrace* v. *Thompson*, 263 U.S. 197; *Oyama* v. *California*, 332 U.S. 633. This Court has not sustained a racial classification since the wartime cases of *Korematsu* v. *United States*, 323 U.S. 214, and *Hirabayashi* v. *United States*, 320 U.S. 81, involving curfews and relocations imposed upon Japanese-Americans.

"Nor obviously will the problem be solved if next year the Law School included only Japanese and Chinese, for then Norwegians and Swedes, Poles and Italians, Puerto Ricans and Hungarians, and all other groups which form this diverse Nation would have just complaints." *DeFunis* v. *Odegaard*, 416 U.S. 312, 337–340 (1974) (Douglas, J., dissenting) (footnotes omitted).

Moreover, there are serious problems of justice connected with the idea of preference itself. First, it may not always be clear that a so-called preference is in fact benign. Courts may be asked to validate burdens imposed upon individual members of particular groups in order to advance the group's general interest. See *United Jewish Organizations* v. *Carey*, 430 U.S. 144, 172–173 (BRENNAN, J., concurring in part). Nothing in the Constitution supports the notion that individuals may be asked to suffer otherwise impermissible burdens in order to enhance the societal standing of their ethnic groups. Second, preferential programs may only reinforce common stereotypes holding that certain groups are unable to achieve success without special protection based on a factor having no relationship to individual worth. See *DeFunis* v. *Odegaard*, 416 U.S. 312, 343 (Douglas, J., dissenting). Third, there is a measure of inequity in forcing innocent persons in respondent's position to bear the burdens of redressing grievances not of their making.

By hitching the meaning of the Equal Protection Clause to these transitory considerations, we would be holding, as a constitutional principle, that judicial scrutiny of classifications touching on racial and ethnic background may vary with the ebb and flow of political forces. Disparate constitutional tolerance of such classifications well may serve to exacerbate racial and ethnic antagonisms rather than alleviate them. *United Jewish Organizations, supra,* at 173–174 (BRENNAN, J., concurring). Also, the mutability of a constitutional principle, based upon shifting political and social judgments, undermines the chances for consistent application of the Constitution from one generation to the next, a critical feature of its coherent interpretation. *Pollock* v. *Farmers Loan & Trust Co.*, 157 U.S. 429, 650–651 (1895) (White, J., dissenting). In expounding the Constitution, the Court's role is to discern "principles sufficiently absolute to give them roots throughout the community and continuity over significant periods of time, and to lift them above the level of the pragmatic political judgments of a particular time and place." A. Cox, The Role of the Supreme Court in American Government 114 (1976).

If it is the individual who is entitled to judicial protection against classifications based upon his racial or ethnic background because such distinctions impinge upon personal rights, rather than the individual only because of his membership in a particular group, then constitutional standards may be applied consistently. Political judgments regarding the necessity for the particular classification may be weighed in the constitutional balance, *Korematsu* v. *United States*, 323 U.S. 214 (1944), but the standard of justification will remain constant. This is as it should be, since those political judgments are the product of rough compromise struck by contending groups within the democratic process.[23] When they touch

---

[23] R. Dahl, A Preface to Democratic Theory (1956); Posner, The DeFunis Case and the Constitutionality of Preferential Treatment of Minorities, 1974 Sup. Ct. Rev. 1, 27; cf. Stewart, The Reformation of American Administrative Law, 88 Harv. L. Rev. 1683–1685, and nn. 64–67 (1975) and sources cited therein.

upon an individual's race or ethnic background, he is entitled to a judicial determination that the burden he is asked to bear on that basis is precisely tailored to serve a compelling governmental interest. The Constitution guarantees that right to every person regardless of his background. *Shelley v. Kraemer*, 334 U.S. 1, 22 (1948); *Missouri ex rel. Gaines v. Canada*, 305 U.S. 337, 351 (1938).

C

Petitioner contends that on several occasions this Court has approved preferential classifications without applying the most exacting scrutiny. Most of the cases upon which petitioner relies are drawn from three areas: school desegregation, employment discrimination, and sex discrimination. Each of the cases cited presented a situation materially different from the facts of this case.

The school desegregation cases are inapposite. Each involved remedies for clearly determined constitutional violations. E. g., *Swann v. Charlotte-Mecklenburg Board of Education*, 402 U.S. 1 (1971); *McDaniel v. Barresi*, 402 U.S. 39 (1971); *Green v. County School Board*, 391 U.S. 430 (1968). Racial classifications thus were designed as remedies for the vindication of constitutional entitlement.[24] Moreover, the scope of the remedies was not permitted to exceed the extent of the violations. E. g., *Dayton Board of Education v. Brinkman*, 433 U.S. 406 (1977); *Milliken v. Bradley*, 418 U.S. 717 (1974); see *Pasadena City Board of Education v. Spangler*, 427 U.S. 424 (1976). See also *Austin Indep. School Dist. v. United States*, 429 U.S. 990, 991–995 (1976) (POWELL, J., concurring). Here, there was no judicial determination of constitutional violation as a predicate for the formulation of a remedial classification.

[24] Petitioner cites three lower court decisions allegedly deviating from this general rule in school desegregation cases; *Offermann v. Nitkowski*, 378 F. 2d 22 (CA2 1967); *Warner v. County School Board*, 357 F. 2d 452 (CA4 1966); *Springfield School Committee v. Barksdale*, 348 F. 2d 261 (CA1 1965). Of these, *Warner* involved a school system held to have been *de jure* segregated and enjoined from maintaining segregation; racial districting was deemed necessary. 357 F. 2d, at 454. Cf. *United Jewish Organizations v. Carey*, 430 U.S. 144 (1977). In *Barksdale* and *Offermann*, courts did approve voluntary districting designed to eliminate discriminatory attendance patterns. In neither, however, was there any showing that the school board planned extensive pupil transportation that might threaten liberty or privacy interests. See *Keyes v. School District No. 1*, 413 U.S. 189, 240–250 (1973) (POWELL, J., concurring in part and dissenting in part). Nor were white students deprived of an equal opportunity for education.

Respondent's position is wholly dissimilar to that of a pupil bused from his neighborhood school to a comparable school in another neighborhood in compliance with a desegregation decree. Petitioner did not arrange for respondent to attend a different medical school in order to desegregate Davis Medical School; instead, it denied him admission and may have deprived him altogether of a medical education.

The employment discrimination cases also do not advance petitioner's cause. For example, in *Franks* v. *Bowman Transportation Co.*, 424 U.S. 747 (1975), we approved a retroactive award of seniority to a class of Negro truck drivers who had been the victims of discrimination—not just by society at large, but by the respondent in that case. While this relief imposed some burdens on other employees, it was held necessary " 'to make [the victims] whole for injuries suffered on account of unlawful employment discrimination.' " *Id.*, at 771, quoting *Albemarle Paper Co.* v. *Moody*, 422 U.S. 405, 418 (1975). The courts of appeals have fashioned various types of racial preferences as remedies for constitutional or statutory violations resulting in identified, race-based injuries to individuals held entitled to the preference. *E. g.*, *Bridgeport Guardians, Inc.* v. *Civil Service Commission*, 482 F. 2d 1333 (CA2 1973); *Carter* v. *Gallagher*, 452 F. 2d 15, modified on rehearing en banc, 452 F. 2d 327 (CA8 1972). Such preferences also have been upheld where a legislative or administrative body charged with the responsibility made determinations of past discrimination by the industries affected, and fashioned remedies deemed appropriate to rectify the discrimination. *E. g.*, *Contractors Association of Eastern Pennsylvania* v. *Secretary of Labor*, 442 F. 2d 159 (CA3), cert. denied, 404 U.S. 954 (1971); *Associated General Contractors of Massachusetts, Inc.* v. *Altschuler*, 490 F. 2d 9 (CA1 1973), cert. denied, 416 U.S. 957 (1974); cf. *Katzenbach* v. *Morgan*, 384 U.S. 641 (1966). But we have never approved preferential classifications in the absence of proven constitutional or statutory violations.

Nor is petitioner's view as to the applicable standard supported by the fact that gender-based classifications are not subjected to this level of scrutiny. *E. g.*, *Califano* v. *Webster*, 430 U.S. 313, 316–317 (1977); *e.g.*, *Craig* v. *Boren*, 429 U.S. 190, 211 n.* (1976) (POWELL, J., concurring). Gender-based distinctions are less likely to create the analytical and practical problems present in preferential programs premised on racial or ethnic criteria. With respect to gender there are only two possible classifications. The incidence of the burdens imposed by preferential classifications is clear. There are no rival groups who can claim that they, too, are entitled to preferential treatment. Classwide questions as to the group suffering previous injury and groups which fairly can be burdened are relatively manageable for reviewing courts. See, *e.g.*, *Califano* v. *Goldfarb*, 430 U.S. 199, 212–217 (1977); *Weinberger* v. *Wiesenfeld*, 420 U.S. 636, 645 (1975). The resolution of these same questions in the context of racial and ethnic preferences presents far more complex and intractable problems than gender-based classifications. More importantly, the perception of racial classifications as inherently odious stems from a lengthy and tragic history that gender-based classifications do not share. In sum, the Court has never viewed such classification as inherently suspect or as comparable to racial or ethnic classifications for the purpose of equal-protection analysis.

Petitioner also cites *Lau* v. *Nichols*, 414 U.S. 563 (1974), in support of the proposition that discrimination favoring racial or ethnic minorities has received judicial approval without the exacting inquiry ordinarily accorded "suspect" classifications. In *Lau*, we held that the failure of the San Francisco school system to provide remedial English instruction for some 1,800 students of oriental ancestry who spoke no English amounted to a violation of Title VI of the Civil Rights Act of 1964, 42 U. S. C. § 2000d, and the regulations promulgated thereunder. Those regulations required remedial instruction where inability to understand English excluded children of foreign ancestry from participation in educational programs. *Id.*, at 568. Because we found that the students in *Lau* were denied "a meaningful opportunity to participate in the educational program," *ibid.*, we remanded for the fashioning of a remedial order.

Lau provides little support for petitioner's argument. The decision rested solely on the statute, which had been construed by the responsible administrative agency to reach educational practices "which have the effect of subjecting individuals to discrimination," *id.*, at 568. We stated: "Under these state-imposed standards there is no equality of treatment merely by providing students with the same facilities, textbooks, teachers and curriculum; for students who do not understand English are effectively foreclosed from any meaningful education." *Id.*, *at* 566. Moreover, the "preference" approved did not result in the denial of the relevant benefit —"meaningful participation in the educational program"—to anyone else. No other student was deprived by that preference of the ability to participate in San Francisco's school system, and the applicable regulations required similar assistance for all students who suffered linguistic deficiencies. *Id.*, at 570–571 (STEWART, J., concurring).

In a similar vein,[25] petitioner contends that our recent decision in *United Jewish Organizations* v. *Carey*, 430 U.S. 144 (1977), indicates a willingness to approve racial classifications designed to benefit certain minorities, without denominating the classifications as "suspect." The State of New York had redrawn its reapportionment plan to meet objections of the Department of Justice under § 5 of the Voting Rights Act of 1965, 42 U. S. C. § 1973c. Specifically, voting districts were redrawn to enhance the electoral power of certain "nonwhite" voters found to have been the victims of unlawful "dilution" under the original reapportionment plan. *United Jewish Organizations*, like *Lau*, properly is viewed as a case in which the remedy for an administrative finding of discrimination

[25] Petitioner also cites our decision in *Morton* v. *Mancari*, 417 U.S. 535 (1974), for the proposition that the State may prefer members of traditionally disadvantaged groups. In *Mancari*, we approved a hiring preference for qualified Indians in the Bureau of Indian Affairs of the Department of the Interior (BIA). We observed in that case, however, that the legal status of BIA is *sui generis*. *Id.*, at 554. Indeed, we found that the preference was not racial at all, but "an employment criterion reasonably designed to further the cause of Indian self-government and to make the BIA more responsive to groups[,] . . . whose lives are governed by the BIA in a unique fashion." *Ibid.*

encompassed measures to improve the previously disadvantaged group's ability to participate, without excluding individuals belonging to any other group from enjoyment of the relevant opportunity—meaningful participation in the electoral process.

In this case, unlike *Lau* and *United Jewish Organizations*, there has been no determination by the legislature or a responsible administrative agency that the University engaged in a discriminatory practice requiring remedial efforts. Moreover, the operation of petitioner's special admissions program is quite different from the remedial measures approved in those cases. It prefers the designated minority groups at the expense of other individuals who are totally foreclosed from competition for the 16 special admission seats in every medical school class. Because of that foreclosure, some individuals are excluded from enjoyment of a state-provided benefit —admission to the medical school—they otherwise would receive. When a classification denies an individual opportunities or benefits enjoyed by others solely because of his race or ethnic background, it must be regarded as suspect. *E. g., McLaurin v. Oklahoma State Regents*, 339 U.S. 637, 641–642 (1950).

IV

We have held that in "order to justify the use of a suspect classification, a State must show that its purpose or interest is both constitutionally permissible and substantial, and that its use of the classification is 'necessary . . . to the accomplishment' of its purpose or the safeguarding of its interest." *In re Griffiths*, 413 U.S. 717, 722–723 (1973) (footnotes omitted); *Loving v. Virginia*, 388 U.S. 1, 11 (1967); *McLaughlin v. Florida*, 379 U.S. 184, 196 (1964). The special admissions program purports to serve the purposes of: (i) "reducing the historic deficit of traditionally disfavored minorities in medical schools and the medical professions," Brief for Petitioner 32; (ii) countering the effects of societal discrimination; [26] (iii)

---

[26] A number of distinct sub-goals have been advanced as falling under the rubric of "compensation for past discrimination." For example, it is said that preferences for Negro applicants may compensate for harm done them personally, or serve to place them at economic levels they might have attained but for discrimination against their forebears. Greenawalt, *supra*, n. 1, at 581– 586. Another view of the "compensation" goal is that it serves as a form of reparation by the "majority" to a victimized group as a whole. B. Bittker, The Case for Black Reparations (1973). That justification for racial or ethnic preference has been subjected to much criticism. *E.g.*, Greenawalt, *supra*, at 581; Posner, *supra*, n. 25, at 16–17, and n. 33. Finally it has been argued that ethnic preferences "compensate" the group by providing examples of success whom other members of the group will emulate, thereby advancing the group's interest and society's interest in encouraging new generations to overcome the barriers and frustrations of the past. Redish, *supra*, n. 25, at 391. For purposes of analysis these sub-goals need not be considered separately.

increasing the number of physicians who will practice in communities currently underserved; and (iv) obtaining the educational benefits that flow from an ethnically diverse student body. It is necessary to decide which, if any, of these purposes is substantial enough to support the use of a suspect classification.

A

If petitioner's purpose is to assure within its student body some specified percentage of a particular group merely because of its race or ethnic origin, such a preferential purpose must be rejected not as insubstantial but as facially invalid. Preferring members of any one group for no reason other than race or ethnic origin is discrimination for its own sake. This the Constitution forbids. E. g., Loving v. Virginia, supra, at 11; McLaughlin v. Florida, supra, at 196; Brown v. Board of Education, 347 U.S. 483 (1954.)

B

The State certainly has a legitimate and substantial interest in ameliorating, or eliminating where feasible, the disabling effects of identified discrimination. The line of school desegregation cases, commencing with Brown, attests to the importance of this state goal and the commitment of the judiciary to affirm all lawful means towards its attainment. In the school cases, the States were required by court order to redress the wrongs worked by specific instances of racial discrimination. That goal was far more focused than the remedying of the effects of "societal discrimination," an amorphous concept of injury that may be ageless in its reach into the past.

We have never approved a classification that aids persons perceived as members of relatively victimized groups at the expense of other innocent individuals in the absence of judicial, legislative, or administrative findings of constitutional or statutory violations. See, e.g., Teamsters v. United States, 431 U.S. 324, 367–376 (1977); United Jewish Organizations, 430 U.S., at 155–156; South Carolina v. Katzenbach, 383 U.S. 308 (1966). After such findings have been made, the governmental interest in preferring members of the injured groups at the expense of others is substantial, since the legal rights of the victims must be vindicated. In such a case, the

---

Racial classifications in admissions conceivably could serve a fifth purpose, one which petitioner does not articulate: fair appraisal of each individual's academic promise in the light of some cultural bias in grading or testing procedures. To the extent that race and ethnic background were considered only to the extent of curing established inaccuracies in predicting academic performance, it might be argued that there is no "preference" at all. Nothing in this record, however, suggests either that any of the quantitative factors considered by the Medical School were culturally biased or that petitioner's special admissions program was formulated to correct for any such biases. Furthermore, if race or ethnic background were used solely to arrive at an unbiased prediction of academic success, the reservation of fixed numbers of seats would be inexplicable.

extent of the injury and the consequent remedy will have been judicially, legislatively, or administratively defined. Also, the remedial action usually remains subject to continuing oversight to assure that it will work the least harm possible to other innocent persons competing for the benefit. Without such findings of constitutional or statutory violations, it cannot be said that the government has any greater interest in helping one individual than in refraining from harming another. Thus, the government has no compelling justification for inflicting such harm.

Petitioner does not purport to have made, and is in no position to make, such findings. Its broad mission is education, not the formulation of any legislative policy or the adjudication of particular claims of illegality. For reasons similar to those stated in Part III of this opinion, isolated segments of our vast governmental structures are not competent to make those decisions, at least in the absence of legislative mandates and legislatively determined criteria.[27] Cf. *Hampton* v. *Mow Sun Wong*, 426 U.S. 88 (1976). Before relying upon these sorts of findings in establishing a racial classification, a governmental body must have the authority and capability to establish, in the record, that the classification is responsive to identified discrimination. See, *e.g., Califano* v. *Webster*, 430 U.S. 313, 316–321 (1977); *Califano* v. *Goldfarb*, 430 U.S. 199, 212–217 (1977). Lacking this capability, petitioner has not carried its burden of justification on this issue.

Hence, the purpose of helping certain groups whom the faculty of the Davis Medical School perceived as victims of "societal discrimination" does not justify a classification that imposes disadvantages upon persons like respondent, who bear no responsibility for whatever harm the beneficiaries of the special admissions program are thought to have suffered. To hold otherwise would be to convert a remedy heretofore reserved for violations of legal rights into a privilege that all institutions throughout the Nation could grant at their pleasure to whatever groups are perceived as victims of societal discrimination. That is a step we have never approved. Cf. *Pasadena City Board of Education* v. *Spangler*, 427 U.S. 424 (1976).

C

Petitioner identifies, as another purpose of its program, improving the delivery of health care services to communities currently underserved. It may be assumed that in some situations a State's interest in facilitating the health care of its citizens is sufficiently compelling to support the use of a suspect classification. But there is virtually no evidence in the record indicating that petitioner's special admissions program is either needed

---

[27] For example, the University is unable to explain its selection of only the three favored groups—Negroes, Mexican-Americans, and Asians—for preferential treatment. The inclusion of the last group is especially curious in light of the substantial numbers of Asians admitted through the regular admissions process.

or geared to promote that goal.[28] The court below addressed this failure of proof:

> "The University concedes it cannot assure that minority doctors who entered under the program, all of whom express an 'interest' in participating in a disadvantaged community, will actually do so. It may be correct to assume that some of them will carry out this intention, and that it is more likely they will practice in minority communities than the average white doctor. (See Sandalow, *Racial Preferences in Higher Education: Political Responsibility and the Judicial Role* (1975) 42 U. Chi. L. Rev. 653, 688). Nevertheless, there are more precise and reliable ways to identify applicants who are genuinely interested in the medical problems of minorities than by race. An applicant of whatever race who has demonstrated his concern for disadvantaged minorities in the past and who declares that practice in such a community is his primary professional goal would be more likely to contribute to alleviation of the medical shortage than one who is chosen entirely on the basis of race and disadvantage. In short, there is [sic] no empirical data to demonstrate that any one race is more selflessly socially oriented or by contrast that another is more selfishly acquisitive." 18 Cal. 3d, at 56, 553 P. 2d, at 1167.

Petitioner simply has not carried its burden of demonstrating that it must prefer members of particular ethnic groups over all other individuals in order to promote better health care delivery to deprived citizens. Indeed, petitioner has not shown that its preferential classification is likely to have any significant effect on the problem.[29]

D

The fourth goal asserted by petitioner is the attainment of a diverse student body. This clearly is a constitutionally permissible goal for an institution of higher education. Academic freedom, though not a specifically enumerated constitutional right, long has been viewed as a special concern of the First Amendment. The freedom of a university to make its own judgments as to education includes the selection of its student body. Mr. Justice Frankfurter summarized the "four essential freedoms" that comprise academic freedom:

> " '. . . It is the business of a university to provide that atmosphere which is most conducive to speculation, experiment and creation. It is an at-

[28] The only evidence in the record with respect to such underservice is a newspaper article.

[29] It is not clear that petitioner's two-track system, even if adopted throughout the country, would substantially increase representation of blacks in the medical profession. That is the finding of a recent study by Sleeth & Mishell, Black Under-Representation in United States Medical Schools, New England J. of Med. 1146 (Nov. 24, 1977). Those authors maintain that the cause of black underrepresentation lies in the small size of the national pool of qualified black applicants. In their view, this problem is traceable to the poor premedical experiences of black undergraduates, and can be remedied effectively only by developing remedial programs for black students before they enter college.

mosphere, in which there prevail 'the four essential freedoms' of a university—to determine for itself on academic grounds who may teach, what may be taught, how it shall be taught, and who may be admitted to study.' " *Sweezy* v. *New Hampshire*, 354 U.S. 234, 263 (1957) (Frankfurter, J., concurring).

Our national commitment to the safeguarding of these freedoms with university communities was emphasized in *Keyishian* v. *Board of Regents*, 385 U.S. 589, 603 (1967):

> "Our Nation is deeply committed to safeguarding academic freedom which is of transcendent value to all of us and not merely to the teachers concerned. That freedom is therefore a special concern of the First Amendment. . . . The Nation's future depends upon leaders trained through wide exposure to that robust exchange of ideas which discovers truth 'out of a multitude of tongues, rather than through any kind of authoritative selection.' *United States* v. *Associated Press*, 52 F. Supp. 362, 372."

The atmosphere of "speculation, experiment and creation"—so essential to the quality of a higher education—is widely believed to be promoted by a diverse student body.[30] As the Court noted in *Keyishian*, it is not too much to say that the "nation's future depends upon leaders trained through wide exposure" to the ideas and mores of students as diverse as this Nation of many peoples.

Thus, in arguing that its universities must be accorded the right to select those students who will contribute the most to the "robust exchange of ideas," petitioner invokes a countervailing constitutional interest, that of the First Amendment. In this light, petitioner must be viewed as seeking

---

[30] The president of Princeton University has described some of the benefits derived from a diverse student body:

". . . [A] great deal of learning occurs informally. It occurs through interactions among students of both sexes; of different races, religions, and backgrounds; who come from cities and rural areas, from various states and countries; who have a wide variety of interests and perspectives; and who are able, directly or indirectly, to learn from their differences and to stimulate one another to reexamine even their most deeply held assumptions about themselves and their world. As a wise graduate of ours once observed in commenting on this aspect of the educational process, 'People do not learn very much when they are surrounded only by the likes of themselves.'

. . .

"In the nature of things, it is hard to know how, and when, and even if, this informal 'learning through diversity' actually occurs. It does not occur for everyone. For many, however, the unplanned, casual encounters with roommates, fellow sufferers in an organic chemistry class, student workers in the library, teammates on a basketball squad, or other participants in class affairs or student government can be subtle and yet powerful sources of improved understanding and personal growth." Bowen, Admissions and the Relevance of Race, Princeton Alumni Weekly 7, 9 (Sept. 26, 1977).

to achieve a goal that is of paramount importance in the fulfillment of its mission.

It may be argued that there is greater force to these views at the undergraduate level than in a medical school where the training is centered primarily on professional competency. But even at the graduate level, our tradition and experience lend support to the view that the contribution of diversity is substantial. In *Sweatt v. Painter*, 339 U.S. 629, 634 (1950), the Court made a similar point with specific reference to legal education:

> "The law school, the proving ground for legal learning and practice, cannot be effective in isolation from the individuals and institutions with which the law interacts. Few students and no one who has practiced law would choose to study in an academic vacuum, removed from the interplay of ideas and the exchange of views with which the law is concerned."

Physicians serve a heterogeneous population. An otherwise qualified medical student with a particular background—whether it be ethnic, geographic, culturally advantaged or disadvantaged—may bring to a professional school of medicine experiences, outlooks and ideas that enrich the training of its student body and better equip its graduates to render with understanding their vital service to humanity.[31]

Ethnic diversity, however, is only one element in a range of factors a university properly may consider in attaining the goal of a heterogeneous student body. Although a university must have wide discretion in making the sensitive judgments as to who should be admitted, constitutional limitations protecting individual rights may not be disregarded. Respondent urges—and the courts below have held—that petitioner's dual admissions program is a racial classification that impermissibly infringes his rights under the Fourteenth Amendment. As the interest of diversity is compelling in the context of a university's admissions program, the question remains whether the program's racial classification is necessary to promote this interest. *In re Griffiths*, 413 U.S. 717, 721–722 (1973).

V

A

It may be assumed that the reservation of a specified number of seats in each class for individuals from the preferred ethnic groups would contri-

---

[31] Graduate admissions decisions, like those at the undergraduate level, are concerned with "assessing the potential contributions to the society of each individual candidate following his or her graduation—contributions defined in the broadest way to include the doctor and the poet, the most active participant in business or government affairs and the keenest critic of all things organized, the solitary scholar and the concerned parent." Bowen, *supra*, n. 48, at 10.

bute to the attainment of considerable ethnic diversity in the student body. But petitioner's argument that this is the only effective means of serving the interest of diversity is seriously flawed. In a most fundamental sense the argument misconceives the nature of the state interest that would justify consideration of race or ethnic background. It is not an interest in simple ethnic diversity, in which a specified percentage of the student body is in effect guaranteed to be members of selected ethnic groups, with the remaining percentage an undifferentiated aggregation of students. The diversity that furthers a compelling state interest encompasses a far broader array of qualifications and characteristics of which racial or ethnic origin is but a single though important element. Petitioner's special admissions program, focused *solely* on ethnic diversity, would hinder rather than further attainment of genuine diversity.[32]

Nor would the state interest in genuine diversity be served by expanding petitioner's two-track system into a multitrack program with a prescribed number of seats set aside for each identifiable category of applicants. Indeed, it is inconceivable that a university would thus pursue the logic of petitioner's two-track program to the illogical end of insulating each category of applicants with certain desired qualifications from competition with all other applicants.

The experience of other university admissions programs, which take race into account in achieving the educational diversity valued by the First Amendment, demonstrates that the assignment of a fixed number of places to a minority group is not a necessary means toward that end. An illuminating example is found in the Harvard College program:

> "In recent years Harvard College has expanded the concept of diversity to include students from disadvantaged economic, racial and ethnic groups. Harvard College now recruits not only Californians or Louisianans but also blacks and Chicanos and other minority students.
>
> • • •
>
> "In practice, this new definition of diversity has meant that race has been a factor in some admission decisions. When the Committee on Admissions reviews the large middle group of applicants who are 'admissible' and deemed capable of doing good work in their courses, the race of an applicant may tip the balance in his favor just as geographic origin or a life spent on a farm may tip the balance in other candidates' cases. A farm boy from Idaho can bring something to Harvard College that a Bostonian cannot offer. Similarly, a black student can usually bring something that a white person cannot offer." See Appendix hereto.
>
> • • •

[32] See Manning, The Pursuit of Fairness in Admissions to Higher Education, in Carnegie Council on Policy Studies in Higher Education, Selective Admissions in Higher Education 19, 57–59 (1977).

"In Harvard college admissions the Committee has not set target-quotas for the number of blacks, or of musicians, football players, physicists or Californians to be admitted in a given year. . . . But that awareness [of the necessity of including more than a token number of black students] does not mean that the Committee sets the minimum number of blacks or of people from west of the Mississippi who are to be admitted. It means only that in choosing among thousands of applicants who are not only 'admissible' academically but have other strong qualities, the Committee, with a number of criteria in mind, pays some attention to distribution among many types and categories of students." Brief for Columbia University, Harvard University, Stanford University, and the University of Pennsylvania, as *Amici Curiae*, App. 2, 3.

In such an admissions program,[33] race or ethnic background may be deemed a "plus" in a particular applicant's file, yet it does not insulate the individual from comparison with all other candidates for the available seats. The file of a particular black applicant may be examined for his potential contribution to diversity without the factor of race being decisive when compared, for example, with that of an applicant identified as an Italian-American if the latter is thought to exhibit qualities more likely to promote beneficial educational pluralism. Such qualities could include exceptional personal talents, unique work or service experience, leadership potential, maturity, demonstrated compassion, a history of overcoming disadvantage, ability to communicate with the poor, or other qualifications deemed important. In short, an admissions program operated in this way is flexible enough to consider all pertinent elements of diversity in light of the particular qualifications of each applicant, and to place them on the same footing for consideration, although not necessarily according them the same weight. Indeed, the weight attributed to a particular quality may vary from year to year depending upon the "mix" both of the student body and the applicants for the incoming class.

The kind of program treats each applicant as an individual in the admissions process. The applicant who loses out on the last available seat to another candidate receiving a "plus" on the basis of ethnic background will not have been foreclosed from all consideration for that seat simply because he was not the right color or had the wrong surname. It would mean only that his combined qualifications, which may have included similar nonobjective factors, did not outweigh those of the other appli-

[33] The admissions program at Princeton has been described in similar terms:

"While race is not in and of itself a consideration in determining basic qualifications, and while there are obviously significant differences in background and experience among applicants of every race, in some situations race can be helpful information in enabling the admissions office to understand more fully what a particular candidate has accomplished—and against what odds. Similarly, such factors as family circumstances and previous educational opportunities may be relevant, either in conjunction with race or ethnic background (with which they may be associated) or on their own." Bowen, *supra*, n. 48, at 8–9.

For an illuminating discussion of such flexible admissions systems, see Manning, *supra*, n. 32, at 57–59.

cant. His qualifications would have been weighed fairly and competitively, and he would have no basis to complain of unequal treatment under the Fourteenth Amendment.[34]

It has been suggested that an admissions program which considers race only as one factor is simply a subtle and more sophisticated—but no less effective—means of according racial preference than the Davis program. A facial intent to discriminate, however, is evident in petitioner's preference program and not denied in this case. No such facial infirmity exists in an admissions program where race or ethnic background is simply one element—to be weighed fairly against other elements—in the selection process. "A boundary line," as Mr. Justice Frankfurter remarked in another connection, "is none the worse for being narrow." *McLeod* v. *Dilworth*, 322 U.S. 327, 329 (1944). And a Court would not assume that a university, professing to employ a racially nondiscriminatory admissions policy, would operate it as a cover for the functional equivalent of a quota system. In short, good faith would be presumed in the absence of a showing to the contrary in the manner permitted by our cases. See, *e.g.*, *Arlington Heights* v. *Metropolitan Housing Development Corp.*, 429 U.S. 252 (1977); *Washington* v. *Davis*, 426 U.S. 229 (1976); *Swain* v. *Alabama*, 380 U.S. 202 (1965).[35]

B

In summary, it is evident that the Davis special admission program involves the use of an explicit racial classification never before countenanced by this Court. It tells applicants who are not Negro, Asian, or "Chicano" that they are totally excluded from a specific percentage of the seats in

---

[34] The denial to respondent of this right to individualized consideration without regard to his race is the principal evil of petitioner's special admissions program. Nowhere in the opinion of MR. JUSTICE BRENNAN, MR. JUSTICE WHITE, MR. JUSTICE MARSHALL, and MR. JUSTICE BLACKMUN is this denial even addressed.

[35] Universities, like the prosecutor in *Swain*, may make individualized decisions, in which ethnic background plays a part, under a presumption of legality and legitimate educational purpose. So long as the university proceeds on an individualized, case-by-case basis, there is no warrant for judicial interference in the academic process. If an applicant can establish that the institution does not adhere to a policy of individual comparisons, or can show that a systematic exclusion of certain groups results, the presumption of legality might be overcome, creating the necessity of proving legitimate educational purpose.

There also are strong policy reasons that correspond to the constitutional distinction between petitioner's preference program and one that assures a measure of competition among all applicants. Petitioner's program will be viewed as inherently unfair by the public generally as well as by applicants for admission to state universities. Fairness in individual competition for opportunities, especially those provided by the State, is a widely cherished American ethic. Indeed, in a broader sense, an underlying assumption of the rule of law is the worthiness of a system of justice based on fairness to the individual. As Mr. Justice Frankfurter declared in another connection, "[j]ustice must satisfy the appearance of justice." *Offut* v. *United States*, 348 U.S. 11, 14 (1954).

an entering class. No matter how strong their qualifications, quantitative and extracurricular, including their own potential for contribution to educational diversity, they are never afforded the chance to compete with applicants from the preferred groups for the special admission seats. At the same time, the preferred applicants have the opportunity to compete for every seat in the class.

The fatal flaw in petitioner's preferential program is its disregard of individual rights as guaranteed by the Fourteenth Amendment. *Shelley v. Kraemer,* 334 U.S. 1, 22 (1948). Such rights are not absolute. But when a State's distribution of benefits or imposition of burdens hinges on the color of a person's skin or ancestry, that individual is entitled to a demonstration that the challenged classification is necessary to promote a substantial state interest. Petitioner has failed to carry this burden. For this reason, that portion of the California court's judgment holding petitioner's special admissions program invalid under the Fourteenth Amendment must be affirmed.

C

In enjoining petitioner from ever considering the race of any applicant, however, the courts below failed to recognize that the State has a substantial interest that legitimately may be served by a properly devised admissions program involving the competitive consideration of race and ethnic origin. For this reason, so much of the California court's judgment as enjoins petitioner from any consideration of the race of any applicant must be reversed.

VI

With respect to respondent's entitlement to an injunction directing his admission to the Medical School, petitioner has conceded that it could not carry its burden of proving that, but for the existence of its unlawful special admissions program, respondent still would not have been admitted. Hence, respondent is entitled to the injunction, and that portion of the judgment must be affirmed.

• • •

Opinion of Mr. Justice Brennan, Mr. Justice White, Mr. Justice Marshall, and Mr. Justice Blackmun, concurring in the judgment in part and dissenting.

The Court today, in reversing in part the judgment of the Supreme Court of California, affirms the constitutional power of Federal and State Government to act affirmatively to achieve equal opportunity for all. The difficulty of the issue presented—whether Government may use race-conscious programs to redress the continuing effects of past discrimination

—and the mature consideration which each of our Brethren has brought to it have resulted in many opinions, no single one speaking for the Court. But this should not and must not mask the central meaning of today's opinions: Government may take race into account when it acts not to demean or insult any racial group, but to remedy disadvantages cast on minorities by past racial prejudice, at least when appropriate findings have been made by judicial, legislative, or administrative bodies with competence to act in this area.

The CHIEF JUSTICE and our BROTHERS STEWART, REHNQUIST, and STEVENS have concluded that Title VI of the Civil Rights Act of 1964, 78 Stat. 252, as amended, 42 U. S. C. § 2000d *et seq.* (1970 ed. and Supp. V), prohibits programs such as that at the Davis Medical School. On this statutory theory alone, they would hold that respondent Allan Bakke's rights have been violated and that he must, therefore, be admitted to the Medical School. Our Brother POWELL, reaching the Constitution, concludes that, although race may be taken into account in university admissions, the particular special admissions program used by petitioner, which resulted in the exclusion of respondent Bakke, was not shown to be necessary to achieve petitioner's stated goals. Accordingly, these Members of the Court form a majority of five affirming the judgment of the Supreme Court of California insofar as it holds that respondent Bakke "is entitled to an order that he be admitted to the University." *Bakke* v. *Regents of the University of California*, 18 Cal. 3d 34, 64, 132 Cal. Rptr. 680, 700, 553 P. 2d 1152, 1172 (1976).

We agree with MR. JUSTICE POWELL that, as applied to the case before us, Title VI goes no further in prohibiting the use of race than the Equal Protection Clause of the Fourteenth Amendment itself. We also agree that the effect of the California Supreme Court's affirmance of the judgment of the Superior Court of California would be to prohibit the University from establishing in the future affirmative action programs that take race into account. Since we conclude that the affirmative admissions program at the Davis Medical School is constitutional, we would reverse the judgment below in all respects. MR. JUSTICE POWELL agrees that some uses of race in university admissions are permissible and, therefore, he joins with us to make five votes reversing the judgment below insofar as it prohibits the University from establishing race-conscious programs in the future.[1]

I

Our Nation was founded on the principle that "all men are created equal." Yet candor requires acknowledgment that the Framers of our Constitution,

---

[1] We also agree with MR. JUSTICE POWELL that a plan like the "Harvard" plan is constitutional under our approach, at least so long as the use of race to achieve an integrated student body is necessitated by the lingering effects of past discrimination.

to forge the Thirteen Colonies into one Nation, openly compromised this principle of equality with its antithesis: slavery. The consequences of this compromise are well known and have aptly been called our "American Dilemma." Still, it is well to recount how recent the time has been, if it has yet come, when the promise of our principles has flowered into the actuality of equal opportunity for all regardless of race or color.

The Fourteenth Amendment, the embodiment in the Constitution of our abiding belief in human equality, has been the law of our land for only slightly more than half of its 200 years. And for half of that half, the Equal Protection Clause of the Amendment was largely moribund so that, as late as 1927, Mr. Justice Holmes could sum up the importance of that Clause by remarking that it was "the last resort of constitutional arguments." *Buck v. Bell,* 274 U.S. 200, 208 (1927). Worse than desuetude, the Clause was early turned against those whom it was intended to set free, condemning them to a "separate but equal" status before the law, a status always separate but seldom equal. Not until 1954—only 24 years ago—was this odious doctrine interred by our decision in *Brown* v. *Board of Education,* 347 U.S. 483 (1954) (*Brown I*), and its progeny, which proclaimed that separate schools and public facilities of all sorts were inherently unequal and forbidden under our Constitution. Even then inequality was not eliminated with "all deliberate speed." *Brown* v. *Board of Education,* 349 U.S. 294, 301 (1955). In 1968 and again in 1971, for example, we were forced to remind school boards of their obligation to eliminate racial discrimination root and branch. And a glance at our docket and at those of lower courts will show that even today officially sanctioned discrimination is not a thing of the past.

Against this background, claims that law must be "colorblind" or that the datum of race is no longer relevant to public policy must be seen as aspiration rather than as description of reality. This is not to denigrate aspiration; for reality rebukes us that race has too often been used by those who would stigmatize and oppress minorities. Yet we cannot—and as we shall demonstrate, need not under our Constitution or Title VI, which merely extends the constraints of the Fourteenth Amendment to private parties who receive federal funds—let color blindness become myopia which marks the reality that many "created equal" have been treated within our lifetimes as inferior both by law and by their fellow citizens.

• • •

III

A

The assertion of human equality is closely associated with the proposition that differences in color or creed, birth or status, are neither significant nor relevant to the way in which persons should be treated. Nonetheless, the position that such factors must be "[c]onstitutionally an irrelevance,"

Edwards v. *California,* 314 U.S. 160, 185 (1941) (Jackson, J., concurring), summed up by the shorthand phrase "[o]ur Constitution is color-blind," *Plessy* v. *Ferguson,* 163 U.S. 537, 559 (1896) (Harlan, J., dissenting), has never been adopted by this Court as the proper meaning of the Equal Protection Clause. Indeed, we have expressly rejected this proposition on a number of occasions.

Our cases have always implied that an "overriding statutory purpose," *McLaughlin* v. *Florida,* 379 U.S. 184, 192 (1964), could be found that would justify racial classifications. See, *e.g., ibid.; Loving* v. *Virginia,* 388 U.S. 1, 11 (1967); *Korematsu* v. *United States,* 323 U.S. 214, 216 (1944); *Hirabayashi* v. *United States,* 320 U.S. 81, 100–101 (1943). More recently, in *McDaniel* v. *Barresi,* 402 U.S. 39 (1971), this Court unanimously reversed the Georgia Supreme Court which had held that a desegregation plan voluntarily adopted by a local school board, which assigned students on the basis of race, was *per se* invalid because it was not colorblind. And in *North Carolina State Board of Ed.* v. *Swann,* 402 U.S. 43 (1971), we held, again unanimously, that a statute mandating colorblind school assignment plans could not stand "against the background of segregation," since such a limit on remedies would "render illusory the promise of *Brown* [*I, supra*]." 402 U.S., at 45–46.

We conclude, therefore, that racial classifications are not *per se* invalid under the Fourteenth Amendment. Accordingly, we turn to the problem of articulating what our role should be in reviewing state action that expressly classifies by race.

B

Respondent argues that racial classifications are always suspect and, consequently, that this Court should weigh the importance of the objectives served by Davis' special admissions program to see if they are compelling. In addition, he asserts that this Court must inquire whether, in its judgment, there are alternatives to racial classifications which would suit Davis' purposes. Petitioner, on the other hand, states that our proper role is simply to accept petitioner's determination that the racial classifications used by its program are reasonably related to what it tells us are its benign purposes. We reject petitioner's view, but because our prior cases are in many respects inapposite to that before us now, we find it necessary to define with precision the meaning of that inexact term, "strict scrutiny."

Unquestionably we have held that a government practice or statute which restricts "fundamental rights" or which contains "suspect classifications" is to be subjected to "strict scrutiny" and can be justified only if it furthers a compelling goverment purpose and, even then, only if no less restrictive alternative is available.[2] See, *e.g., San Antonio Indep. School*

---

[2] We do not pause to debate whether our cases establish a "two-tier" analysis, a "sliding scale" analysis, or something else altogether. It is enough for present purposes that strict scrutiny is applied at least in some cases.

Dist. v. *Rodriguez,* 411 U.S. 1, 16–17 (1973); *Dunn* v. *Blumstein,* 405 U.S. 330 (1972). But no fundamental right is involved here. See *San Antonio, supra,* at 29–36. Nor do whites as a class have any of the "traditional indicia of suspectness: the class is not saddled with such disabilities, or subjected to such a history of purposeful unequal treatment, or relegated to such a position of political powerlessness as to command extraordinary protection from the majoritarian political process." *Id.,* at 28; see *United States* v. *Carolene Products Co.,* 304 U.S. 144, 152 n. 4 (1938).[3]

Moreover, if the University's representations are credited, this is not a case where racial classifications are "irrelevant and therefore prohibited." *Hirabayashi,* 320 U.S., at 100. Nor has anyone suggested that the University's purposes contravene the cardinal principle that racial classifications that stigmatize—because they are drawn on the presumption that one race is inferior to another or because they put the weight of government behind racial hatred and separatism—are invalid without more. See *Yick Wo* v. *Hopkins,* 118 U.S. 356, 374 (1886);[4] accord, *Strauder* v. *West Virginia,* 100 U.S. 303, 308 (1879); *Korematsu* v. *United States,* 323 U.S., at 223; *Oyama* v. *California,* 332 U.S. 633, 663 (1948) (Murphy, J., concurring); *Brown I, supra; McLaughlin* v. *Florida,* 379 U.S., at 191–192; *Loving* v. *Virginia,* 388 U.S., at 11–12; *Reitman* v. *Mulkey,* 387 U.S., 375–376 (1967); *United Jewish Organizations of Williamsburgh, Inc.* v. *Carey,* 430 U.S. 144, 165 (1977) (opinion of WHITE, REHNQUIST, and STEVENS, JJ.) (*UJO*); *id., at* 169 (concurring opinion).[5]

On the other hand, the fact that this case does not fit neatly into our prior analytic framework for race cases does not mean that it should be analyzed by applying the very loose rational basis standard of review that is the very least that is always applied in equal protection cases.[6]

[3] Of course, the fact that whites constitute a political majority in our Nation does not necessarily mean that active judicial scrutiny of racial classifications that disadvantage whites is inappropriate. Cf. *Castaneda* v. *Partida,* 430 U.S. 482, 499–500 (1977); *id.,* at 501 (MARSHALL, J., concurring).

[4] "[T]he conclusion cannot be resisted that no reason for [the refusal to issue permits to Chinese] exists except hostility to the race and nationality to which petitioners belong. . . .The discrimination is, therefore, illegal. . . ."

[5] Indeed, even in *Plessy* v. *Ferguson, supra,* the Court recognized that a classification by race that presumed one race to be inferior to another would have to be condemned. See 163 U.S., at 544–551.

[6] Paradoxically, petitioner's argument is supported by the cases generally thought to establish the "strict scrutiny" standard in race cases, *Hirabayashi* v. *United States,* 320 U.S. 81 (1943), and *Korematsu* v. *United States,* 323 U.S. 214 (1944). In *Hirabayashi,* for example, the Court, responding to a claim that a racial classification was rational, sustained a racial classification solely on the basis of a conclusion in the double-negative that it could not say that facts which might have been available "could afford no ground for differentiating citizens of Japanese ancestry from other groups in the United States." *Id.,* at 101. A similar mode of analysis was followed in *Korematsu,* see 323 U.S., at 224, even though the Court stated there that racial classifications were "immediately suspect" and should be subject to "the most rigid scrutiny." *Id.,* at 216.

" '[T]he mere recitation of a benign, compensatory purpose is not an automatic shield which protects against any inquiry into the actual purposes underlying a statutory scheme.' " *Califano* v. *Webster*, 430 U.S. 313, 317 (1977), quoting *Weinberger* v. *Weisenfeld*, 420 U.S. 636, 648 (1975). Instead, a number of considerations—developed in gender discrimination cases but which carry even more force when applied to racial classifications —lead us to conclude that racial classifications designed to further remedial purposes " 'must serve important governmental objectives and must be substantially related to achievement of those objectives.' " *Califano* v. *Webster, supra,* at 316, quoting *Craig* v. *Boren,* 429 U.S. 190, 197 (1976).[7]

First, race, like, "gender-based classifications too often [has] been inexcusably utilized to stereotype and stigmatize politically powerless segments of society." *Kahn* v. *Shevin,* 416 U.S. 351, 357 (1974) (dissenting opinion). While a carefully tailored statute designed to remedy past discrimination could avoid these vices, see *Califano* v. *Webster, supra; Schlesinger* v. *Ballard,* 419 U.S. 498 (1975); *Kahn* v. *Shevin, supra,* we nonetheless have recognized that the line between honest and thoughtful appraisal of the effects of past discrimination and paternalistic stereotyping is not so clear and that a statute based on the latter is patiently capable of stigmatizing all women with a badge of inferiority. Cf. *Schlesinger* v. *Ballard, supra,* at 508; *UJO,* 430 U.S., at 174, and n. 3 (concurring

---

[7] We disagree with our Brother POWELL's suggestion that the presence of "rival groups who can claim that they, too, are entitled to preferential treatment," distinguishes the gender cases or is relevant to the question of scope of judicial review of race classifications. We are not asked to determine whether groups other than those favored by the Davis program should similarly be favored. All we are asked to do is to pronounce the constitutionality of what Davis has done.

But, were we asked to decide whether any given rival group—German-Americans for example—must constitutionally be accorded preferential treatment, we do have a "principled basis," for deciding this question, one that is well-established in our cases: The Davis program expressly sets out four classes which receive preferred status. The program clearly distinguishes whites, but one cannot reason from this to a conclusion that German-Americans, as a national group, are singled out for invidious treatment. And even if the Davis program had a differential impact on German-Americans, they would have no constitutional claim unless they could prove that Davis intended invidiously to discriminate against German-Americans. See *Village of Arlington Heights* v. *Metropolitan Housing Corp.,* 429 U.S. 252, 264–265 (1977); *Washington* v. *Davis,* 426 U.S. 229, 238–241 (1976). If this could not be shown, then "the principle that calls for the closest scrutiny of distinctions in laws denying fundamental rights . . . is inapplicable," *Katzenbach* v. *Morgan,* 384 U.S. 641, 657 (1967), and the only question is whether it was rational for Davis to conclude that the groups it preferred had a greater claim to compensation than the groups it excluded. See *ibid.; San Antonio Indep. School Dist.* v. *Rodriguez,* 411 U.S. 1, 38–39 (1973) (applying *Katzenbach* test to state action intended to remove discrimination in educational opportunity). Thus, claims of rival groups, although they may create thorny political problems, create relatively simple problems for the courts.

opinion); *Califano* v. *Goldfarb,* 430 U.S. 199, 223 (1977) (STEVENS, J., concurring in the judgment). See also *Stanton* v. *Stanton,* 421 U.S. 7, 14–15 (1975). State programs designed ostensibly to ameliorate the effects of past racial discrimination obviously create the same hazard of stigma, since they may promote racial separatism and reinforce the views of those who believe that members of racial minorities are inherently incapable of succeeding on their own. See *UJO,* 430 U.S., at 172 (concurring opinion); *ante,* at 27 (opinion of POWELL, J.).

Second, race, like gender and illegitimacy, see *Weber* v. *Aetna Cas. & Surety Co.,* 406 U.S. 164 (1972), is an immutable characteristic which its possessors are powerless to escape or set aside. While a classification is not *per se* invalid because it divides classes on the basis of an immutable characteristic, see *supra,* pp. 31–32, it is nevertheless true that such divisions are contrary to our deep belief that "legal burdens should bear some relationship to individual responsibility or wrongdoing," *Weber, supra,* at 175; *Frontiero* v. *Richardson,* 411 U.S. 667, 686 (1973) (opinion of BRENNAN, WHITE, and MARSHALL, JJ.), and that advancement sanctioned, sponsored, or approved by the State should ideally be based on individual merit or achievement, or at the least on factors within the control of an individual. See *UJO,* 430 U.S., at 173 (concurring opinion); *Kotch* v. *Board of River Port Pilot Comm'rs,* 330 U.S. 552, 566 (1947) (Rutledge, J., dissenting).

Because this principle is so deeply rooted it might be supposed that it would be considered in the legislative process and weighed against the benefits of programs preferring individuals because of their race. But this is not necessarily so: The "natural consequence of our governing process [may well be] that the most 'discrete and insular' of whites . . . will be called upon to bear the immediate, direct costs of benign discrimination." *UJO,* 430 U.S., at 174 (concurring opinion). Moreover, it is clear from our cases that there are limits beyond which majorities may not go when they classify on the basis of immutable characteristics. See, *e.g., Weber, supra.* Thus, even if the concern for individualism is weighed by the political process, that weighing cannot waive the personal rights of individuals under the Fourteenth Amendment. See *Lucas* v. *Forty-Fourth General Assembly,* 377 U.S. 713, 736 (1964).

In sum, because of the significant risk that racial classifications established for ostensibly benign purposes can be misused, causing effects not unlike those created by invidious classifications, it is inappropriate to inquire only whether there is any conceivable basis that might sustain such a classification. Instead, to justify such a classification an important and articulated purpose for its use must be shown. In addition, any statute must be stricken that stigmatizes any group or that singles out those least well represented in the political process to bear the brunt of a benign program. Thus our review under the Fourteenth Amendment should be strict—not " 'strict' in theory and fatal in fact," [8] because it is stigma that causes fatality—but strict and searching nonetheless.

IV

Davis' articulated purpose of remedying the effects of past societal discrimination is, under our cases, sufficiently important to justify the use of race-conscious admissions programs where there is a sound basis for concluding that minority underrepresentation is substantial and chronic, and that the handicap of past discrimination is impeding access of minorities to the medical school.

A

At least since *Green v. County School Board*, 391 U.S. 430 (1968), it has been clear that a public body which has itself been adjudged to have engaged in racial discrimination cannot bring itself into compliance with the Equal Protection Clause simply by ending its unlawful acts and adopting a neutral stance. Three years later, *Swann v. Charlotte-Mecklenburg Board of Ed.*, 402 U.S. 1 (1971), and its companion cases, *Davis v. Board of School Comm'rs*, 402 U.S. 33 (1971); *McDaniel v. Barresi, supra*; and *North Carolina State Board of Ed. v. Swann, supra*, reiterated that racially neutral remedies for past discrimination were inadequate where consequences of past discriminatory acts influence or control present decisions. See, *e.g., Charlotte-Mecklenburg, supra*, at 28. And the Court further held both that courts could enter desegregation orders which assigned students and faculty by reference to race, *Charlotte-Mecklenburg, supra*; *Davis, supra*; *United States v. Montgomery County Board of Ed.*, 395 U.S. 225 (1969), and that local school boards could *voluntarily* adopt desegregation plans which made express reference to race if this was necessary to remedy the effects of past discrimination. *McDaniel v. Barresi, supra*. Moreover, we stated that school boards, even in the absence of a judicial finding of past discrimination, could voluntarily adopt plans which assigned students with the end of creating racial pluralism by establishing fixed ratios of black and white students in each school. *Charlotte-Mecklenburg, supra*, at 16. In each instance, the creation of unitary school systems, in which the effects of past discrimination had been "eliminated root and branch," *Green, supra*, at 438, was recognized as a compelling social goal justifying the overt use of race.

Finally, the conclusion that state educational institutions may consti-

---

[8] Gunther, The Supreme Court, 1971 Term—Foreword: In Search of Evolving Doctrine on a Changing Court: A Model for a Newer Equal Protection, 86. Harv. L. Rev. 1, 8 (1972).

tutionally adopt admissions programs designed to avoid exclusion of historically disadvantaged minorities, even when such programs explicitly take race into account, finds direct support in our cases construing congressional legislation designed to overcome the present effects of past discrimination. Congress can and has outlawed actions which have a disproportionately adverse and unjustified impact upon members of racial minorities and has required or authorized race-conscious action to put individuals disadvantaged by such impact in the position they otherwise might have enjoyed. See *Franks* v. *Bowman, supra; International Brotherhood of Teamsters* v. *United States,* 431 U.S. 324 (1977). Such relief does not require as a predicate proof that recipients of preferential advancement have been individually discriminated against; it is enough that each recipient is within a general class of persons likely to have been the victims of discrimination. See *id.,* at 357–362. Nor is it an objection to such relief that preference for minorities will upset the settled expectations of nonminorities. See *Franks, supra.* In addition, we have held that Congress, to remove barriers to equal opportunity, can and has required employers to use test criteria that fairly reflect the qualifications of minority applicants vis-à-vis nonminority applicants, even if this means interpreting the qualifications of an applicant in light of his race. See *Albemarle* v. *Moody,* 422 U.S. 405, 435 (1975).[9]

These cases cannot be distinguished simply by the presence of judicial findings of discrimination, for race-conscious remedies have been approved where such findings have not been made. *McDaniel* v. *Barresi, supra; UJO, supra;* see *Califano* v. *Webster, supra; Schlesinger* v. *Ballard, supra; Kahn* v. *Shevin, supra.* See also *Katzenbach* v. *Morgan,* 384 U.S. 641 (1967). Indeed, the requirement of a judicial determination of a constitutional or statutory violation as a predicate for race-conscious remedial actions would be self-defeating. Such a requirement would severely undermine efforts to achieve voluntary compliance with the requirements of law. And, our society and jurisprudence have always stressed the value of voluntary efforts to further the objectives of the law. Judicial intervention is a last resort to achieve cessation of illegal conduct or the remedying of its effects rather than a prerequisite to action.

Nor can our cases be distinguished on the ground that the entity using explicit racial classifications had itself violated § 1 of the Fourteenth

---

[9] In *Albemarle,* we approved "differential validation" of employment tests. See 422 U.S., at 435. That procedure requires that an employer must ensure that a test score of, for example, 50 for a minority job applicant means the same thing as a score of 50 for a nonminority applicant. By implication, were it determined that a test score of 50 for a minority corresponded in "potential for employment" to a 60 for whites, the test could not be used consistent with Title VII unless the employer hired minorities with scores of 50 even though he might not hire nonminority applicants with scores above 50 but below 60. Thus, it is clear that employers, to ensure equal opportunity, may have to adopt race-conscious hiring practices.

Amendment or an antidiscrimination regulation, for again race-conscious remedies have been approved where this is not the case. See *UJO*, 430 U.S., at 157 (opinion of WHITE, BLACKMUN, REHNQUIST, and STEVENS, JJ); (opinion of WHITE, REHNQUIST, and STEVENS, JJ.); cf. *Califano v. Webster*, 430 U.S., at 317; *Kahn v. Shevin, supra*. Moreover, the presence or absence of past discrimination by universities or employers is largely irrelevant to resolving respondent's constitutional claims. The claims of those burdened by the race-conscious actions of a university or employer who has never been adjudged in violation of an antidiscrimination law are not any more or less entitled to deference than the claims of the burdened nonminority workers in *Franks v. Bowman*, 424 U.S. 747 (1976), in which the employer had violated Title VII, for in each case the employees are innocent of past discrimination. And, although it might be argued that, where an employer has violated an antidiscrimination law, the expectations of nonminority workers are themselves products of discrimination and hence "tainted," see *Franks, supra, at* 776, and therefore more easily upset, the same argument can be made with respect to respondent. If it was reasonable to conclude—as we hold that it was—that the failure of minorities to qualify for admission at Davis under regular procedures was due principally to the effects of past discrimination, then there is a reasonable likelihood that, but for pervasive racial discrimination, respondent would have failed to qualify for admission even in the absence of Davis' special admissions program.[10]

Thus, our cases under Title VII of the Civil Rights Act have held that, in order to achieve minority participation in previously segregated areas of public life, Congress may require or authorize preferential treatment for those likely disadvantaged by societal racial discrimination. Such legislation has been sustained even without a requirement of findings of intentional racial discrimination by those required or authorized to accord preferential treatment, or a case-by-case determination that those to be benefited suffered from racial discrimination. These decisions compel the conclusion that States also may adopt race-conscious programs designed to overcome substantial, chronic minority underrepresentation where there is reason to believe that the evil addressed is a product of past racial discrimination.[11]

· · ·

[10] Our cases cannot be distinguished by suggesting, as our Brother POWELL does, that in none of them was anyone deprived of "the relevant benefit." Our school cases have deprived whites of the neighborhood school of their choice; our Title VII cases have deprived nondiscriminating employees of their settled seniority expectations; and *UJO* deprived the Hassidim of bloc voting strength. Each of these injuries was constitutionally cognizable as is respondent's here.

[11] We do not understand MR. JUSTICE POWELL to disagree that providing a remedy for past racial prejudice can constitute a compelling purpose sufficient to meet strict

B

Properly construed, therefore, our prior cases unequivocally show that a state government may adopt race-conscious programs if the purpose of such programs is to remove the disparate racial impact its actions might otherwise have and if there is reason to believe that the disparate impact is itself the product of past discrimination, whether its own or that of society at large. There is no question that Davis' program is valid under this test.

Certainly, on the basis of the undisputed factual submissions before this Court, Davis had a sound basis for believing that the problem of underrepresentation of minorities was substantial and chronic and that the problem was attributable to handicaps imposed on minority applicants by past and present racial discrimination. Until at least 1973, the practice of medicine in this country was, in fact, of not in law, largely the preroga-

---

scrutiny. Yet, because petitioner is a university, he would not allow it to exercise such power in the absence of "judicial, legislative, or administrative findings of constitutional or statutory violations. While we agree that reversal in this case would follow *a fortiori* had Davis been guilty of invidious racial discrimination or if a federal statute mandated that universities refrain from applying any admissions policy that had a disparate and unjustified racial impact, see *e.g.*, Mc-Daniel v. Barresi, 402 U.S. 39 (1971); *Franks* v. *Bowman Transp. Co.*, 424 U.S. 747 (1976), we do not think it of constitutional significance that Davis has not been so adjudged

Generally, the manner in which a State chooses to delegate governmental functions is for it to decide. Cf. *Sweezy* v. *New Hampshire*, 354 U.S. 234, 256 (1957) (Frankfurter, J., concurring). California, by constitutional provision, has chosen to place authority over the operation of the University of California in the Board of Regents. See Cal. Const. Art. IX, § 9 (a) (1978). Control over the University is to be found not in the legislature, but rather in the Regents who have been vested with full legislative (including policymaking), administrative, and adjudicative powers by the citizens of California. See *ibid.*; *Ishmatsu* v. *Regents*, 266 Cal. App. 2d 854, 863–864, 73 Cal. Rptr. 753, 762–763 (1968); *Goldberg* v. *Regents*, 248 Cal. App. 2d 867, 874, 57 Cal. Rptr. 463, 468 (1967); 30 Ops. Atty. Gen. Cal. 162, 166 (1957) ("The Regents, not the legislature, have the general rule-making or policy-making power in regard to the University"). This is certainly a permissible choice, see *Sweezy*, *supra*, and we, unlike our Brother POWELL, find nothing in the Equal Protection Clause that requires us to depart from established principle by limiting the scope of power the Regents may exercise more narrowly than the powers that may constitutionally be wielded by the Assembly.

Because the Regents can exercise plenary legislative and administrative power, it elevates form over substance to insist that Davis could not use race-conscious remedial programs until it had been adjudged in violation of the Constitution or an antidiscrimination statute. For, if the Equal Protection Clause required such a violation as a predicate, the Regents could simply have promulgated a regulation prohibiting disparate treatment not justified by the need to admit only qualified students, and could have declared Davis to have been in violation of such a regulation on the basis of the exclusionary effect of the admissions policy applied during the first two years of its operation.

tive of whites.[12] In 1950, for example, while Negroes comprised 10% of the total population, Negro physicians constituted only 2.2% of the total number of physicians.[13] The overwhelming majority of these, moreover, were educated in two predominantly Negro medical schools, Howard and Meharry.[14] By 1970, the gap between the proportion of Negroes in medicine and their proportion in the population had widened: The number of Negroes employed in medicine remained frozen at 2.2% [15] while the Negro population had increased to 11.1% [16] The number of Negro admittees to predominantly white medical schools, moreover, had declined in absolute numbers during the years 1955 to 1964. Odegaard 19.

Moreover, Davis had very good reason to believe that the national pattern of underrepresentation of minorities in medicine would be perpetuated if it retained a single admissions standard. For example, the entering classes in 1968 and 1969, the years in which such a standard was used, included only one Chicano and two Negroes out of 100 admittees. Nor is there any relief from this pattern of underrepresentation in the statistics for the regular admissions program in later years.

Davis clearly could conclude that the serious and persistent underrepresentation of minorities in medicine depicted by these statistics is the result of handicaps under which minority applicants labor as a consequence of a background of deliberate, purposeful discrimination against minorities in education and in society generally, as well as in the medical profession. From the inception of our national life, Negroes have been subjected to

[12] According to 89 schools responding to a questionnaire sent to 112 medical schools (all of the then-accredited medical schools in the United States except Howard and Meharry), substantial efforts to admit minority students did not begin until 1968. That year was the earliest year of involvement for 34% of the schools; an additional 66% became involved during the years 1969 to 1973. See C. Odegaard, Minorities in Medicine: From Receptive Passivity to Positive Action, 1966–1976, at 19 (1977) (hereinafter Odegaard). These efforts were reflected in a significant increase in the percentage of minority M.D. graduates. The number of American Negro graduates increased from 2.2% in 1970 to 3.3% in 1973 and 5.0% in 1975. Significant percentage increases in the number of Mexican American, American Indian, and Mainland Puerto Rican graduates were also recorded during those years.

   The statistical information cited in this and the following notes was compiled by government officials or medical educators, and has been brought to our attention in many of the briefs. Neither the parties nor the *amici* challenge the validity of the statistics alluded to in our discussion.

[13] D. Reitzes, Negroes and Medicine XXVII, 3 (1958).

[14] Between 1955 and 1964, for example, the percentage of Negro physicians graduated in the United States who were trained at these schools ranged from 69.0% to 75.8%. See Odegaard, at 19.

[15] Minorities and Women in Health Fields, United States Dept. of Health, Education, and Welfare Pub. No. (HRA) 75–22, at 7 (May 1974).

[16] U.S. Bureau of the Census, 1970 Census, Vol. 1, Characteristics of the Population, Pt. 1, United States Summary, sec. 1, General Population Characteristics, 1–293 (Table 60) (1973).

unique legal disabilities impairing access to equal educational opportunity. Under slavery, penal sanctions were imposed upon anyone attempting to educate Negroes.[17] After enactment of the Fourteenth Amendment the States continued to deny Negroes equal educational opportunity, enforcing a strict policy of segregation that itself stamped Negroes as inferior, *Brown, supra,* which relegated minorities to inferior educational institutions,[18] and which denied them intercourse in the mainstream of professional life necessary to advancement. See *Sweatt* v. *Painter,* 339 U.S. 629 (1950). Segregation was not limited to public facilities, moreover, but was enforced by criminal penalties against private action as well. Thus, as late as 1908, this Court enforced a state criminal conviction against a private college for teaching Negroes together with whites. *Berea College* v. *Kentucky,* 211 U.S. 45. See also *Plessy* v. *Ferguson, supra.*

Green v. *County School Board, supra,* gave explicit recognition to the fact that the habit of discrimination and the cultural tradition of race prejudice cultivated by centuries of legal slavery and segregation were not immediately dissipated when *Brown I, supra,* announced the constitutional principle that equal educational opportunity and participation in all aspects of American life could not be denied on the basis of race. Rather, massive official and private resistance prevented, and to a lesser extent still prevents, attainment of equal opportunity in education at all levels and in the professions. The generation of minority students applying to Davis Medical School since it opened in 1968—most of whom were born before or about the time *Brown I* was decided—clearly have been victims of this discrimination. Judicial decrees recognizing discrimination in public education in California testify to the fact of widespread discrimination suffered by California-born minority applicants; [19] many minority group members living in California, moreover, were born and reared in school districts in southern States segregated by law.[20] Since separation of school children by race "generates a feeling of inferiority as to their status in the community that may affect their hearts and minds in a way unlikely ever to be undone," *Brown I,* 347 U.S., at 494, the conclusion is inescapable that

---

[17] See, *e.g.,* R. Wade, Slavery in the Cities 90–91 (1964).

[18] For an example of unequal facilities in California schools, see *Soria* v. *Oxnard School Dist.,* 386 F. Supp. 539, 542 (C. D. Cal. 1974). See also R. Kluger, Simple Justice (1976)

[19] See, *e.g., Crawford* v. *Board of Educ.,* 17 Cal 3d 280, 130 Cal. Rptr. 724, 551 P. 2d 28 (1976); *Soria* v. *Oxnard School District,* 386 F. Supp. 539 (CD Cal. 1974); *Spangler* v. *Pasadena City Board of Educ.,* 311 F. Supp. 501 (CD Cal. 1970); C. Wollenberg, All Deliberate Speed: Segregation and Exclusion in California's Schools, 1855–1975, at 136–177 (1976).

[20] For example, over 40% of American-born Negro males aged 20 to 24 residing in California in 1970 were born in the South, and the same statistic for females was over 48%. These statistics were computed from data contained in Census, *supra,* n. 49, pt. 6, California, sec. 2, Detailed Characteristics, 6–1146 (table 139), 6–1149 (table 140).

applicants to medical school must be few indeed who endured the effects of *de jure* segregation, the resistance to *Brown I*, or the equally debilitating pervasive private discrimination fostered by our long history of official discrimination, cf. *Reitman* v. *Mulkey, supra,* and yet come to the starting line with an education equal to whites.[21]

Moreover, we need not rest solely on our own conclusion that Davis had sound reason to believe that the effects of past discrimination were handicapping minority applicants to the Medical School, because the Department of Health, Education, and Welfare, the expert agency charged by Congress with promulgating regulations enforcing Title VI of the Civil Rights Act of 1964, see *supra,* pp. 18–19, has also reached the conclusion that race may be taken into account in situations where a failure to do so would limit participation by minorities in federally funded programs, and regulations promulgated by the Department expressly contemplate that appropriate race-conscious programs may be adopted by universities to remedy unequal access to university programs caused by their own or by past societal discrimination. It cannot be questioned that, in the absence of the special admissions programs, access of minority students to the Medical School would be severely limited and, accordingly, race-conscious admissions would be deemed an appropriate response under these federal regulations. Moreover, the Department's regulatory policy is not one that has gone unnoticed by Congress. Indeed, although an amendment to an appropriations bill was introduced just last year that would have prevented the Secretary of Health, Education, and Welfare from mandating race-conscious programs in university admissions, proponents of this measure, significantly, did not question the validity of voluntary implementation of race-conscious admissions criteria. In these circumstances, the conclusion implicit in the regulations—that the lingering effects of past discrimination continue to make race-conscious remedial programs appropriate means for ensuring equal educational opportunity in universities—deserves considerable judicial deference. See, *e.g., Katzenbach* v. *Morgan,* 384 U.S. 641 (1966); *UJO,* 430 U.S., at 175–178 (concurring opinion).[22]

C

The second prong of our test—whether the Davis program stigmatizes any discrete group or individual and whether race is reasonably used in light of the program's objectives—is clearly satisfied by the Davis program.

It is not even claimed that Davis' program in any way operates to stigmatize or single out any discrete and insular, or even any identifiable, nonminority group. Nor will harm comparable to that imposed upon racial

---

[21] See, *e.g.,* O'Neil, Preferential Admissions: Equalizing the Access of Minority Groups to Higher Education, 80 Yale L. J. 699, 729–731 (1971).

[22] Congress and the Executive have also adopted a series of race-conscious programs, each predicated on an understanding that equal opportunity cannot be achieved by neutrality because of the effects of past and present discrimination.

minorities by exclusion or separation on grounds of race be the likely result of the program. It does not, for example, establish an exclusive preserve for minority students apart from and exclusive of whites. Rather, its purpose is to overcome the effects of segregation by bringing the races together. True, whites are excluded from participation in the special admissions program, but this fact only operates to reduce the number of whites to be admitted in the regular admissions program in order to permit admission of a reasonable percentage—less than their proportion of the California population [23]—of otherwise underrepresented qualified minority applicants.[24]

Nor was Bakke in any sense stamped as inferior by the Medical School's rejection of him. Indeed, it is conceded by all that he satisfied those criteria regarded by the School as generally relevant to academic performance better than most of the minority members who were admitted. Moreover, there is absolutely no basis for concluding that Bakke's rejection as a result of Davis' use of racial preference will affect him throughout his life in the same way as the segregation of the Negro school children in *Brown I* would have affected them. Unlike discrimination against racial minorities, the use of racial preferences for remedial purposes does not inflict a pervasive injury upon individual whites in the sense that wherever they go or whatever they do there is a significant likelihood that they will be treated as second-class citizens because of their color. This distinction does not mean that the exclusion of a white resulting from the preferential use of race is not sufficiently serious to require justification; but it does mean that the injury inflicted by such a policy is not distinguishable from disadvantages caused by a wide range of government actions, none of which has ever been thought impermissible for that reason alone.

[23] Negroes and Chicanos alone comprise approximately 22% of California's population. This percentage was computed from data contained in Census, *supra*, n. 49, pt. 6, California, sec. 1, 6–4, and *id.*, sec. 2, 6–1146 to 6–1147 (Table 139).

[24] The constitutionality of the special admissions program is buttressed by its restriction to only 16% of the positions in the Medical School, a percentage less than that of the minority population in California, see *id.*, and to those minority applicants deemed qualified for admission and deemed likely to contribute to the medical school and the medical profession. Record 67. This is consistent with the goal of putting minority applicants in the position they would have been in if not for the evil of racial discrimination. Accordingly, the case does not raise the question whether even a remedial use of race would be unconstitutional if it admitted unqualified minority applicants in preference to qualified applicants or admitted, as a result of preferential consideration, racial minorities in numbers significantly in excess of their proportional representation in the relevant population. Such programs might well be inadequately justified by the legitimate remedial objectives. Our allusion to the proportional percentage of minorities in the population of the State administering the program is not intended to establish either that figure or that population universe as a constitutional benchmark. In this case, even respondent, as we understand him, does not argue that, if the special admissions program is otherwise constitutional, the allotment of 16 places in each entering class for special admittees is unconstitutionally high.

In addition, there is simply no evidence that the Davis program discriminates intentionally or unintentionally against any minority group which it purports to benefit. The program does not establish a quota in the invidious sense of a ceiling on the number of minority applicants to be admitted. Nor can the program reasonably be regarded as stigmatizing the program's beneficiaries or their race as inferior. The Davis program does not simply advance less qualified applicants; rather, it compensates applicants, whom it is uncontested are fully qualified to study medicine, for educational disadvantage which it was reasonable to conclude was a product of state-fostered discrimination. Once admitted, these students must satisfy the same degree requirements as regularly admitted students; they are taught by the same faculty in the same classes; and their performance is evaluated by the same standards by which regularly admitted students are judged. Under these circumstances, their performance and degrees must be regarded equally with the regularly admitted students with whom they compete for standing. Since minority graduates cannot justifiably be regarded as less well qualified than nonminority graduates by virtue of the special admissions program, there is no reasonable basis to conclude that minority graduates at schools using such programs would be stigmatized as inferior by the existence of such programs.

D

We disagree with the lower courts' conclusion that the Davis program's use of race was unreasonable in light of its objectives. First, as petitioner argues, there are no practical means by which it could achieve its ends in the foreseeable future without the use of race-conscious measures. With respect to any factor (such as poverty or family educational background) that may be used as a substitute for race as an indicator of past discrimination, whites greatly outnumber racial minorities simply because whites make up a far larger percentage of the total population and therefore far outnumber minorities in absolute terms at every socioeconomic level.[25] For example, of a class of recent medical school applicants from families with less than $10,000 income, at least 71% were white.[26] Of all 1970 families headed by a person *not* a high school graduate which included related children under 18, 80% were white and 20% were racial minorities.[27] Moreover, while race is positively correlated with differences in GPA and MCAT scores, economic disadvantage is not. Thus, it appears

[25] See Census, *supra*, n. 16, Sources and Structure of Family Income, 1–12.
[26] This percentage was computed from data presented in B. Waldman, Economic and Racial Disadvantage as Reflected in Traditional Medical School Selection Factors: A Study of 1976 Applicants to U.S. Medical Schools 34 (Table A–15), 42 (Table A–23) Association of American Medical Colleges.
[27] This figure was computed from data contained in Census, *supra*, 16, pt. 1, United States Summary, sec. 2, 1–666 (Table 209).

that economically disadvantaged whites do not score less well than economically advantaged whites, while economically advantaged blacks score less
well than do disadvantaged whites.[28] These statistics graphically illustrate
that the University's purpose to integrate its classes by compensating for
past discrimination could not be achieved by a general preference for the
economically disadvantaged or the children of parents of limited education
unless such groups were to make up the entire class.

Second, the Davis admissions program does not simply equate
minority status with disadvantage. Rather, Davis considers on an individual
basis each applicant's personal history to determine whether he or she has
likely been disadvantaged by racial discrimination. The record makes clear
that only minority applicants likely to have been isolated from the mainstream of American life are considered in the special program; other
minority applicants are eligible only through the regular admissions program. True, the procedure by which disadvantage is detected is informal,
but we have never insisted that educators conduct their affairs through
adjudicatory proceedings, and such insistence here is misplaced. A case-by-
case inquiry into the extent to which each individual applicant has been
affected, either directly or indirectly, by racial discrimination, would seem
to be, as a practical matter, virtually impossible, despite the fact that there
are excellent reasons for concluding that such effects generally exist. When
individual measurement is impossible or extremely impractical, there is
nothing to prevent a State from using categorical means to achieve its ends,
at least where the category is closely related to the goal. Cf. *Gaston
County* v. *United States*, 395 U.S. 285, 295–296 (1969); *Katzenbach* v.
Morgan, supra. And it is clear from our cases that specific proof that a
person has been victimized by discrimination is not a necessary predicate
to offering him relief where the probability of victimization is great. See
Teamsters, supra.

E

Finally, Davis' special admissions program cannot be said to violate the
Constitution simply because it has set aside a predetermined number of
places for qualified minority applicants rather than using minority status
as a positive factor to be considered in evaluating the applications of disadvantaged minority applicants. For purposes of constitutional adjudication, there is no difference between the two approaches. In any admissions
program which accords special consideration to disadvantaged racial minorities, a determination of the degree of preference to be given is unavoidable,
and any given preference that results in the exclusion of a white candidate
is no more or less constitutionally acceptable than a program such as that
at Davis. Furthermore, the extent of the preference inevitably depends on
how many minority applicants the particular school is seeking to admit

[28] See Waldman, *supra*, n. 60, 10–14 (Figures 1–5).

in any particular year so long as the number of qualified minority applicants exceeds that number. There is no sensible, and certainly no constitutional, distinction between, for example, adding a set number of points
to the admissions rating of disadvantaged minority applicants as an expression of the preference with the expectation that this will result in the
admission of an approximately determined number of qualified minority
applicants and setting a fixed number of places for such applicants as was
done here.[29]

The "Harvard" program, as those employing it readily concede,
openly and successfully employs a racial criterion for the purpose of ensuring that some of the scarce places in institutions of higher education are
allocated to disadvantaged minority students. That the Harvard approach
does not also make public the extent of the preference and the precise
workings of the system while the Davis program employs a specific, openly
stated number, does not condemn the latter plan for purposes of Fourteenth Amendment adjudication. It may be that the Harvard plan is more
acceptable to the public than is the Davis "quota." If it is, any State,
including California, is free to adopt it in preference to a less acceptable
alternative, just as it is generally free, as far as the Constitution is concerned, to abjure granting any racial preferences in its admissions program.
But there is no basis for preferring a particular preference program simply
because in achieving the same goals that the Davis Medical School is
pursuing, it proceeds in a manner that is not immediately apparent to the
public.

IV

Accordingly, we would reverse the judgment of the Supreme Court of
California holding the Medical School's special admissions program unconstitutional and directing respondent's admission, as well as that portion
of the judgment enjoining the Medical School from according any consideration to race in the admissions process.

· · ·

Mr. Justice Marshall.

I agree with the judgment of the Court only insofar as it permits a
university to consider the race of an applicant in making admissions
decisions. I do not agree that petitioner's admissions program violates the
Constitution. For it must be remembered that, during most of the past
200 years, the Constitution as interpreted by this Court did not prohibit

---

[29] The excluded white applicant, despite Mr. Justice Powell's contention to the
contrary, receives no more or less "individualized consideration" under our approach than under his.

the most ingenious and pervasive forms of discrimination against the Negro. Now, when a State acts to remedy the effects of that legacy of discrimination, I cannot believe that this same Constitution stands as a barrier.

I

A

Three hundred and fifty years ago, the Negro was dragged to this country in chains to be sold into slavery. Uprooted from his homeland and thrust into bondage for forced labor, the slave was deprived of all legal rights. It was unlawful to teach him to read; he could be sold away from his family and friends at the whim of his master; and killing or maiming him was not a crime. The system of slavery brutalized and dehumanized both master and slave.[1]

The denial of human rights was etched into the American colonies' first attempts at establishing self-government. When the colonists determined to seek their independence from England, they drafted a unique document cataloguing their grievances against the King and proclaiming as "self-evident" that "all men are created equal" and are endowed "with certain unalienable Rights," including those to "Life, Liberty and the pursuit of Happiness." The self-evident truths and the unalienable rights were intended, however, to apply only to white men. An earlier draft of the Declaration of Independence, submitted by Thomas Jefferson to the Continental Congress, had included among the charges against the King that

> "[h]e has waged cruel war against human nature itself, violating its most sacred rights of life and liberty in the persons of a distant people who never offended him, captivating and carrying them into slavery in another hemisphere, or to incur miserable death in their transportation thither." Franklin 88.

The Southern delegation insisted that the charge be deleted; the colonists themselves were implicated in the slave trade, and inclusion of this claim might have made it more difficult to justify the continuation of slavery once the ties to England were severed. Thus, even as the colonists embarked on a course to secure their own freedom and equality, they ensured perpetuation of the system that deprived a whole race of those rights.

The implicit protection of slavery embodied in the Declaration of

---

[1] The history recounted here is perhaps too well known to require documentation. But I must acknowledge the authorities on which I rely in retelling it. J. H. Franklin, From Slavery to Freedom (4th ed. 1974) (hereinafter Franklin): R. Kluger, Simple Justice (1975) (hereinafter Kluger); C. V. Woodward, The Strange Career of Jim Crow (3rd ed. 1974) (hereinafter Woodward).

Independence was made explicit in the Constitution, which treated a slave as being equivalent to three-fifths of a person for purposes of apportioning representatives and taxes among the States. Art. I, § 2. The Constitution also contained a clause ensuring that the "migration or importation" of slaves into the existing States would be legal until at least 1808, Art. I, § 9, and a fugitive slave clause requiring that when a slave escaped to another State, he must be returned on the claim of the master. Art. IV, § 2. In their declaration of the principles that were to provide the cornerstone of the new Nation, therefore, the Framers made it plain that "we the people," for whose protection the Constitution was designed, did not include those whose skins were the wrong color. As Professor John Hope Franklin has observed, Americans "proudly accepted the challenge and responsibility of their new political freedom by establishing the machinery and safeguards that insured the continued enslavement of blacks." Franklin 100.

The individual States likewise established the machinery to protect the system of slavery through the promulgation of the Slave Codes, which were designed primarily to defend the property interest of the owner in his slave. The position of the Negro slave as mere property was confirmed by this Court in *Dred Scott* v. *Sandford,* 19 How. 393 (1857), holding that the Missouri Compromise—which prohibited slavery in the portion of the Louisiana Purchase Territory north of Missouri—was unconstitutional because it deprived slave owners of their property without due process. The Court declared that under the Constitution a slave was property, and "[t]he right to traffic in it, like an ordinary article of merchandise and property, was guaranteed to the citizens of the United States. . . ." *Id.,* at 451. The Court further concluded that Negroes were not intended to be included as citizens under the Constitution but were "regarded as beings of an inferior order . . . altogether unfit to associate with the white race, either in social or political relations; and so far inferior, that they had no rights which the white man was bound to respect . . . ." *Id.,* at 407.

B

The status of the Negro as property was officially erased by his emancipation at the end of the Civil War. But the long awaited emancipation, while freeing the Negro from slavery, did not bring him citizenship or equality in any meaningful way. Slavery was replaced by a system of "laws which imposed upon the colored race onerous disabilities and burdens, and curtailed their rights in the pursuit of life, liberty, and property to such an extent that their freedom was of little value." *Slaughter-House Cases,* 16 Wall. 36, 70 (1873). Despite the passage of the Thirteenth, Fourteenth, and Fifteenth Amendments, the Negro was systematically denied the rights those amendments were supposed to secure. The combined actions and inactions of the State and Federal Government maintained Negroes in a position of legal inferiority for another century after the Civil War.

The Southern States took the first steps to re-enslave the Negroes. Immediately following the end of the Civil War, many of the provisional legislatures passed Black Codes, similar to the Slave Codes, which among other things, limited the rights of Negroes to own or rent property and permitted imprisonment for breach of employment contracts. Over the next several decades, the South managed to disenfranchise the Negroes in spite of the Fifteenth Amendment by various techniques, including poll taxes, deliberately complicated balloting processes, property and literacy qualifications, and finally the white primary.

Congress responded to the legal disabilities being imposed in the Southern States by passing the Reconstruction Acts and the Civil Rights Acts. Congress also responded to the needs of the Negroes at the end of the Civil War by establishing the Bureau of Refugees, Freedmen, and Abandoned Lands, better known as the Freedmen's Bureau, to supply food, hospitals, land and education to the newly freed slaves. Thus for a time it seemed as if the Negro might be protected from the continued denial of his civil rights and might be relieved of the disabilities that prevented him from taking his place as a free and equal citizen.

That time, however, was short-lived. Reconstruction came to a close, and, with the assistance of this Court, the Negro was rapidly stripped of his new civil rights. In the words of C. Vann Woodward: "By narrow and ingenious interpretation [the Supreme Court's] decisions over a period of years had whittled away a great part of the authority presumably given the government for protection of civil rights." Woodward 139.

The Court began by interpreting the Civil War Amendments in a manner that sharply curtailed their substantive protections. See, e.g., *Slaughter-House Cases, supra; United States* v. *Reese,* 92 U.S. 214 (1876); *United States* v. *Cruikshank,* 92 U.S. 542 (1876). Then in the notorious *Civil Rights Cases,* 109 U.S. 3 (1883), the Court strangled Congress' efforts to use its power to promote racial equality. In those cases the Court invalidated sections of the Civil Rights Act of 1875 that made it a crime to deny equal access to "inns, public conveyances . . . , theatres, and other places of public amusement." According to the Court, the Fourteenth Amendment gave Congress the power to proscribe only discriminatory action by the State. The Court ruled that the Negroes who were excluded from public places suffered only an invasion of their social rights at the hands of private individuals, and Congress had no power to remedy that. *Id.,* at 24–25. "When a man has emerged from slavery, and by the aid of beneficient legislation has shaken off the inseparable concomitants of that state," the Court concluded, "there must be some stage in the progress of his elevation when he takes the rank of a mere citizen, and ceases to be the special favorite of the laws . . . ." *Id.,* at 25. As Justice Harlan noted in dissent, however, the Civil War Amendments and Civil Rights Acts did not make the Negroes the "special favorite" of the laws but instead "sought to accomplish in reference to that race . . .—what had already been done in every State of the Union for the White race—to secure and protect rights belonging to them as freemen and citizens; nothing more." *Id.*, at 61.

The Court's ultimate blow to the Civil War Amendments and to the equality of Negroes came in *Plessy* v. *Ferguson*, 163 U.S. 537 (1896). In upholding a Louisiana law that required railway companies to provide "equal but separate" accommodations for whites and Negroes, the Court held that the Fourteenth Amendment was not intended "to abolish distinctions based upon color, or to enforce social, as distinguished from political equality, or a commingling of the two races upon terms unsatisfactory to either." *Id.*, at 544. Ignoring totally the realities of the positions of the two races, the Court remarked:

> "We consider the underlying fallacy of the plaintiff's argument to consist in the assumption that the enforced separation of the two races stamps the colored race with a badge of inferiority. If this be so, it is not by reason of anything found in the act, but solely because the colored race chooses to put that construction upon it." *Id.*, at 551.

Mr. Justice Harlan's dissenting opinion recognized the bankruptcy of the Court's reasoning. He noted that the "real meaning" of the legislation was "that colored citizens are so inferior and degraded that they cannot be allowed to sit in public coaches occupied by white citizens." *Id.*, at 560. He expressed his fear that if like laws were enacted in other States, "the effect would be in the highest degree mischievous." *Id.*, at 563. Although slavery would have disappeared, the States would retain the power "to interfere with the full enjoyment of the blessings of freedom; to regulate civil rights, common to all citizens, upon the basis of race; and to place in a condition of legal inferiority a large body of American citizens . . . ." *Id.*, at 563.

The fears of Mr. Justice Harlan were soon to be realized. In the wake of *Plessy*, many States expanded their Jim Crow laws, which had up until that time been limited primarily to passenger trains and schools. The segregation of the races was extended to residential areas, parks, hospitals, theaters, waiting rooms and bathrooms. There were even statutes and ordinances which authorized separate phone booths for Negroes and whites, which required that textbooks used by children of one race be kept separate from those used by the other, and which required that Negro and white prostitutes be kept in separate districts. In 1898, after *Plessy*, the Charlestown News and Courier printed a parody of Jim Crow laws:

> "If there must be Jim Crow cars on the railroads, there should be Jim Crow cars on the street railways. Also on all passenger boats. . . . If there are to be Jim Crow cars, moreover, there should be Jim Crow waiting

saloons at all stations, and Jim Crow eating houses. . . . There should be Jim Crow sections of the jury box, and a separate Jim Crow dock and witness stand in every court—and a Jim Crow Bible for colored witnesses to kiss." Woodward 68.

The irony is that before many years had passed, with the exception of the Jim Crow witness stand, "all the improbable applications of the principle suggested by the editor in derision had been put into practice—down to and including the Jim Crow Bible." Woodward 69.

Nor were the laws restricting the rights of Negroes limited solely to the Southern States. In many of the Northern States, the Negro was denied the right to vote, prevented from serving on juries and excluded from theaters, restaurants, hotels, and inns. Under President Wilson, the Federal Government began to require segregation in Government buildings; desks of Negro employees were curtained off; separate bathrooms and separate tables in the cafeteria were provided; and even the galleries of the Congress were segregated. When his segregationist policies were attacked, President Wilson responded that segregation was "not humiliating but a benefit" and that he was "rendering [the Negroes] more safe in their possession of office and less likely to be discriminated against." Kluger 91.

The enforced segregation of the races continued into the middle of the 20th century. In both World Wars, Negroes were for the most part confined to separate military units; it was not until 1948 that an end to segregation in the military was ordered by President Truman. And the history of the exclusion of Negro children from white public schools is too well known and recent to require repeating here. That Negroes were deliberately excluded from public graduate and professional schools—and thereby denied the opportunity to become doctors, lawyers, engineers, and the like—is also well established. It is of course true that some of the Jim Crow laws (which the decisions of this Court had helped to foster) were struck down by this Court in a series of decisions leading up to *Brown* v. *Board of Education of Topeka*, 347 U.S. 483 (1954). See, *e.g., Morgan* v. *Virginia*, 328 U.S. 373 (1946); *Sweatt* v. *Painter*, 339 U.S. 629 (1950); *McLaurin* v. *Oklahoma State Regents*, 339 U.S. 637 (1950). Those decisions, however, did not automatically end segregation, nor did they move Negroes from a position of legal inferiority to one of equality. The legacy of years of slavery and of years of second-class citizenship in the wake of emancipation could not be so easily eliminated.

II

The position of the Negro today in America is the tragic but inevitable consequence of centuries of unequal treatment. Measured by any benchmark of comfort or achievement, meaningful equality remains a distant dream for the Negro.

A Negro child today has a life-expectancy which is shorter by more than five years than that of a white child.[2] The Negro child's mother is over three times more likely to die of complications in childbirth,[3] and the infant mortality rate for Negroes is nearly twice that for whites.[4] The median income of the Negro family is only 60% that of the median of a white family,[5] and the percentage of Negroes who live in families with incomes below the poverty line is nearly four times greater than that of whites.[6]

When the Negro child reaches working age, he finds that America offers him significantly less than it offers for his white counterpart. For Negro adults, the unemployment rate is twice that of whites,[7] and the unemployment rate for Negro teenagers is nearly three times that of white teenagers.[8] A Negro male who completes four years of college can expect a median annual income of merely $110 more than a white male who has only a high school diploma.[9] Although Negroes represent 11.5% of the population,[10] they are only 1.2% of the lawyers and judges, 2% of the physicians, 2.3% of the dentists, 1.1% of the engineers and 2.6% of the college and university professors.[11]

The relationship between those figures and the history of unequal treatment afforded to the Negro cannot be denied. At every point from birth to death the impact of the past is reflected in the still disfavored position of the Negro.

In light of the sorry history of discrimination and its devastating impact on the lives of Negroes, bringing the Negro into the mainstream of American life should be a state interest of the highest order. To fail to do so is to ensure that America will forever remain a divided society.

III

I do not believe that the Fourteenth Amendment requires us to accept that fate. Neither its history nor our past cases lend any support to the

2 U.S. Dept. of Commerce, Bureau of the Census, Statistical Abstract of the United States 65 (1977) (table 94).

3 *Id.*, at 70 (table 102).

4 *Ibid.*

5 U.S. Dept. of Commerce, Bureau of the Census, Current Population Reports, Series P-60. No. 107, at 7 (1977) (table 1).

6 *Id.*, at 20 (table 14).

7 U.S. Dept. of Labor, Bureau of Labor Statistics, Employment and Earnings, January 1978, at 170 (table 44).

8 *Ibid.*

9 U.S. Dept. of Commerce, Bureau of the Census, Current Population Reports, Series P-60. No. 105, at 198 (1977) (table 47).

10 U.S. Dept. of Commerce, Bureau of the Census, Statistical Abstract of the United States 25 (table 24).

11 *Id.*, at 407–408 (table 662) (based on 1970 census).

conclusion that a University may not remedy the cumulative effects of society's discrimination by giving consideration to race in an effort to increase the number and percentage of Negro doctors.

A

This Court long ago remarked that

> "in any fair and just construction of any section or phrase of these [Civil War] amendments, it is necessary to look to the purpose which we have said was the pervading spirit of them all, the evil which they were designed to remedy. . . ." *Slaughter-House Cases,* 16 Wall., at 72.

It is plain that the Fourteenth Amendment was not intended to prohibit measures designed to remedy the effects of the Nation's past treatment of Negroes. The Congress that passed the Fourteenth Amendment is the same Congress that passed the 1866 Freedman's Bureau Act, an act that provided many of its benefits only to Negroes. Act of July 16, 1866, ch. 200, 14 Stat. 173; see p. 4. *supra.* Although the Freedmen's Bureau legislation provided aid for refugees, thereby including white persons within some of the relief measures, 14 Stat., at 174; see also Act of Mar. 3, 1865, ch. 90, 13 Stat. 507, the bill was regarded, to the dismay of many Congressmen, as "solely and entirely for the freedmen, and to the exclusion of all other persons . . . ." Cong. Globe, 39th Cong., 1st Sess., 544 (1866) (remarks of Rep. Taylor). See also *id.,* at 634–635 (remarks of Rep. Ritter); *id.,* at App. 78, 80–81 (remarks of Rep. Chanler). Indeed, the bill was bitterly opposed on the ground that it "undertakes to make the negro in some respects . . . superior . . . and gives them favors that the poor white boy in the North cannot get." *Id.,* at 401, (remarks of Sen. McDougall). See also *id.,* at 319 (remarks of Sen. Hendricks); *id.,* at 362 (remarks of Sen. Saulsbury); *id.,* at 397 (remarks of Sen. Willey); *id.,* at 544 (remarks of Rep. Taylor). The bill's supporters defended it—not by rebutting the claim of special treatment—but by pointing to the need for such treatment:

> "The very discrimination it makes between 'destitute and suffering' negroes and destitute and suffering white paupers, proceeds upon the distinction that, in the omitted case, civil rights and immunities are already sufficiently protected by the possession of political power, the absence of which in the case provided for necessitates governmental protection." *Id.,* at 75 (remarks of Rep. Phelps).

Despite the objection to the special treatment the bill would provide for Negroes, it was passed by Congress. *Id.,* at 421, 688. President Johnson vetoed this bill and also a subsequent bill that contained some modifications; one of his principal objections to both bills was that they gave special benefits to Negroes. VIII Messages and Papers of the Presidents

3596, 3599, 3620, 3623 (1866). Rejecting the concerns of the President and the bill's opponents, Congress overrode the President's second veto. Cong. Globe, at 3842, 3850.

Since the Congress that considered and rejected the objections to the 1866 Freedman's Bureau Act concerning special relief to Negroes also proposed the Fourteenth Amendment, it is inconceivable that the Fourteenth Amendment was intended to prohibit all race-conscious relief measures. It "would be a distortion of the policy manifested in that amendment, which was adopted to prevent state legislation designed to perpetuate discrimination on the basis of race or color," *Railway Mail Association* v. *Corsi*, 326 U.S. 88, 94 (1945), to hold that it barred state action to remedy the effects of that discrimination. Such a result would pervert the intent of the framers by substituting abstract equality for the genuine equality the amendment was intended to achieve.

B

As has been demonstrated in our joint opinion, this Court's past cases establish the constitutionality of race-conscious remedial measures. Beginning with the school desegregation cases, we recognized that even absent a judicial or legislative finding of constitutional violation, a school board constitutionally could consider the race of students in making school assignment decisions. See *Swann* v. *Charlotte-Mecklenberg Board of Education*, 402 U.S. 1, 16 (1971); *McDaniel* v. *Barresi*, 402 U.S. 39, 41 (1971). We noted, moreover, that a

> "flat prohibition against assignment of students for the purpose of creating a racial balance must inevitably conflict with the duty of school authorities to disestablish dual school systems. As we have held in *Swann*, the Constitution does not compel any particular degree of racial balance or mixing, but when past and continuing constitutional violations are found, some ratios are likely to be useful as starting points in shaping a remedy. An absolute prohibition against use of such a device—even as a starting point—contravenes the implicit command of *Green* v. *County School Board*, 391 U.S. 430 (1968), that all reasonable methods be available to formulate an effective remedy." *Board of Education* v. *Swann*, 402 U.S. 43, 46 (1971).

As we have observed, "[a]ny other approach would freeze the status quo that is the very target of all desegregation processes." *McDaniel* v. *Barresi, supra*, at 41.

Only last Term, in *United Jewish Organizations* v. *Carey*, 430 U.S. 144 (1977), we upheld a New York reapportionment plan that was deliberately drawn on the basis of race to enhance the electoral power of Negroes and Puerto Ricans; the plan had the effect of diluting the electoral strength of the Hasidic Jewish Community. We were willing in *UJO* to sanction the remedial use of a racial classification even though it disadvantaged otherwise "innocent" individuals. In another case last Term, *Califano* v. *Webster*, 430 U.S. 313 (1977), the Court upheld a provision in the Social Security laws that discriminated against men because its purpose was " 'the permissible one of redressing our society's long standing disparate treatment of women.' " *Id.*, at 317, quoting *Califano* v. *Goldfarb*, 430 U.S. 199, 209 n. 8 (1977) (plurality opinion). We thus recognized the permissibility of remedying past societal discrimination through the use of otherwise disfavored classifications.

Nothing in those cases suggests that a university cannot similarly act to remedy past discrimination.[12] It is true that in both *UJO* and *Webster* the use of the disfavored classification was predicated on legislative or administrative action, but in neither case had those bodies made findings that there had been constitutional violations or that the specific individuals to be benefited had actually been the victims of discrimination. Rather, the classification in each of those cases was based on a determination that the group was in need of the remedy because of some type of past discrimination. There is thus ample support for the conclusion that a university can employ race-conscious measures to remedy past societal discrimination, without the need for a finding that those benefited were actually victims of that discrimination.

IV

While I applaud the judgment of the Court that a university may consider race in its admissions process, it is more than a little ironic that, after several hundred years of class-based discrimination against Negroes, the Court is unwilling to hold that a class-based remedy for that discrimination is permissible. In declining to so hold, today's judgment ignores the fact that for several hundred years Negroes have been discriminated against, not as individuals, but rather solely because of the color of their skins. It is unnecessary in 20th century America to have individual Negroes demonstrate that they have been victims of racial discrimination; the racism of our society has been so pervasive that none, regardless of wealth or position, has managed to escape its impact. The experience of Negroes in America has been different in kind, not just in degree, from that of other ethnic groups. It is not merely the history of slavery alone but also that a whole people were marked as inferior by the law. And that mark has endured. The dream of America as the great melting pot has not been realized for the Negro; because of his skin color he never even made it into the pot.

---

[12] Indeed, the action of the University finds support in the regulations promulgated under Title VI by the Department of Health, Education, and Welfare and approved by the President, which authorize a federally funded institution to take affirmative steps to overcome past discrimination against groups even where the institution was not guilty of prior discrimination. 45 CFR § 80.3 (b) (6) (ii).

These differences in the experience of the Negro make it difficult for me to accept that Negroes cannot be afforded greater protection under the Fourteenth Amendment where it is necessary to remedy the effects of past discrimination. In the *Civil Rights Cases, supra,* the Court wrote that the Negro emerging from slavery must cease "to be the special favorite of the laws." 109 U.S., at 25; see p. 5, *supra.* We cannot in light of the history of the last century yield to that view. Had the Court in that case and others been willing to "do for human liberty and the fundamental rights of American citizenship, what it did . . . for the protection of slavery and the rights of the masters of fugitive slaves," *id.,* at 53 (Harlan J., dissenting), we would not need now to permit the recognition of any "special wards."

Most importantly, had the Court been willing in 1896, in *Plessy* v. *Ferguson,* to hold that the Equal Protection Clause forbids differences in treatment based on race, we would not be faced with this dilemma in 1978. We must remember, however, that the principle that the "Constitution is colorblind" appeared only in the opinion of the lone dissenter. 163 U.S., at 559. The majority of the Court rejected the principle of color blindness, and for the next 60 years, from *Plessy* to *Brown* v. *Board of Education,* ours was a Nation where, *by law,* an individual could be given "special" treatment based on the color of his skin.

It is because of a legacy of unequal treatment that we now must permit the institutions of this society to give consideration to race in making decisions about who will hold the positions of influence, affluence and prestige in America. For far too long, the doors to those positions have been shut to Negroes. If we are ever to become a fully integrated society, one in which the color of a person's skin will not determine the opportunities available to him or her, we must be willing to take steps to open those doors. I do not believe that anyone can truly look into America's past and still find that a remedy for the effects of that past is impermissible.

It has been said that this case involves only the individual, Bakke, and this University. I doubt, however, that there is a computer capable of determining the number of persons and institutions that may be affected by the decision in this case. For example, we are told by the Attorney General of the United States that at least 27 federal agencies have adopted regulations requiring recipients of federal funds to take "*affirmative action* to overcome the effects of conditions which resulted in limiting participation . . . by persons of a particular race, color, or national origin." Supplemental Brief for the United States as *Amicus Curiae* 16 (emphasis added). I cannot even guess the number of state and local governments that have set up affirmative action programs, which may be affected by today's decision.

I fear that we have come full circle. After the Civil War our government started several "affirmative action" programs. This Court in the *Civil Rights Cases* and *Plessy* v. *Ferguson* destroyed the movement toward complete equality. For almost a century no action was taken, and this nonaction was with the tacit approval of the courts. Then we had *Brown v. Board of Education* and the Civil Rights Acts of Congress, followed by numerous affirmative action programs. *Now*, we have this Court again stepping in, this time to stop affirmative action programs of the type used by the University of California.

Mr. Justice Blackmun.

I participate fully, of course, in the opinion that bears the names of my Brothers Brennan, White, Marshall, and myself. I add only some general observations that hold particular significance for me, and then a few comments on equal protection.

I

At least until the early 1970's, apparently only a very small number, less than 2%, of the physicians, attorneys, and medical and law students in the United States were members of what we now refer to as minority groups. In addition, approximately three-fourths of our Negro physicians were trained at only two medical schools. If ways are not found to remedy that situation, the country can never achieve its professed goal of a society that is not race conscious.

I yield to no one in my earnest hope that the time will come when an "affirmative action" program is unnecessary and is, in truth, only a relic of the past. I would hope that we could reach this stage within a decade at the most. But the story of *Brown v. Board of Education,* 347 U.S. 483 (1954), decided almost a quarter of a century ago, suggests that that hope is a slim one. At some time, however, beyond any period of what some would claim is only transitional inequality, the United States must and will reach a stage of maturity where action along this line is no longer necessary. Then persons will be regarded as persons, and discrimination of the type we address today will be an ugly feature of history that is instructive but that is behind us.

The number of qualified, indeed highly qualified, applicants for admission to existing medical schools in the United States far exceeds the number of places available. Wholly apart from racial and ethnic considerations, therefore, the selection process inevitably results in the denial of admission to many *qualified* persons, indeed, to far more than the number of those who are granted admission. Obviously, it is a denial to the deserving. This inescapable fact is brought into sharp focus here because Allan Bakke is not himself charged with discrimination and yet is the one who is disadvantaged, and because the Medical School of the University of California at Davis itself is not charged with historical discrimination.

One theoretical solution to the need for more minority members in higher education would be to enlarge our graduate schools. Then all who desired and were qualified could enter, and talk of discrimination would vanish. Unfortunately, this is neither feasible nor realistic. The vast resources that apparently would be required simply are not available. And the need for more professional graduates, in the strict numerical sense, perhaps has not been demonstrated at all.

There is no particular or real significance in the 84–16 division at Davis. The same theoretical, philosophical, social, legal, and constitutional considerations would necessarily apply to the case if Davis' special admissions program had focused on any lesser number, that is, on 12 or 8 or 4 places or, indeed, on only 1.

It is somewhat ironic to have us so deeply disturbed over a program where race is an element of consciousness, and yet to be aware of the fact, as we are, that institutions of higher learning, albeit more on the undergraduate than the graduate level, have given conceded preferences up to a point to those possessed of athletic skills, to the children of alumni, to the affluent who may bestow their largess on the institutions, and to those having connections with celebrities, the famous, and the powerful.

Programs of admission to institutions of higher learning are basically a responsibility for academicians and for administrators and the specialists they employ. The judiciary, in contrast, is ill-equipped and poorly trained for this. The administration and management of educational institutions are beyond the competence of judges and are within the special competence of educators, provided always that the educators perform within legal and constitutional bounds. For me, therefore, interference by the judiciary must be the rare exception and not the rule.

II

I, of course, accept the propositions that (a) Fourteenth Amendment rights are personal; (b) racial and ethnic distinctions where they are stereotypes are inherently suspect and call for exacting judicial scrutiny; (c) academic freedom is a special concern of the First Amendment; and (d) the Fourteenth Amendment has expanded beyond its original 1868 conception and now is recognized to have reached a point where as MR. JUSTICE POWELL states, quoting from the Court's opinion in *McDonald v. Santa Fe Trail Transp. Co.*, 427 U.S. 273, 296 (1976), it embraces a "broader principle."

This enlargement does not mean for me, however, that the Fourteenth Amendment has broken away from its moorings and its original intended purposes. Those original aims persist. And that, in a distinct sense, is what "affirmative action," in the face of proper facts, is all about. If this conflicts with idealistic equality, that tension is original Fourteenth Amendment tension, constitutionally conceived and constitutionally imposed, and it is part of the Amendment's very nature until complete equality is achieved in the area. In this sense, constitutional equal protection is a shield.

I emphasize in particular that the decided cases are not easily to be brushed aside. Many, of course, are not precisely on point, but neither are they off point. Racial factors have been given consideration in the school desegregation cases, in the employment cases, in *Lau* v. *Nichols,* 414 U.S. 563 (1974), and in *United Jewish Organizations* v. *Carey,* 430 U.S. 144 (1977). To be sure, some of these may be "distinguished" on the ground that victimization was directly present. But who is to say that victimization is not present for some members of today's minority groups, although it is of a lesser and perhaps different degree. The petitioners in *United Jewish Organizations* certainly complained bitterly of their reapportionment treatment, and I rather doubt that they regard the "remedy" there imposed as one that was "to improve" the group's ability to participate, as MR. JUSTICE POWELL describes it. And surely in *Lau* v. *Nichols* we looked to ethnicity.

I am not convinced, as MR. JUSTICE POWELL seems to be, that the difference between the Davis program and the one employed by Harvard is very profound or constitutionally significant. The line between the two is a thin and indistinct one. In each, subjective application is at work. Because of my conviction that admission programs are primarily for the educators, I am willing to accept the representation that the Harvard program is one where good faith in its administration is practiced as well as professed. I agree that such a program, where race or ethnic background is only one of many factors, is a program better formulated than Davis' two-track system. The cynical, of course, may say that under a program such as Harvard's one may accomplish covertly what Davis concedes it does openly. I need not go that far, for despite its two-track aspect, the Davis program, for me, is within constitutional bounds, though perhaps barely so. It is surely free of stigma, and, as in *United Jewish Organizations,* I am not willing to infer a constitutional violation.

It is worth noting, perhaps, that governmental preference has not been a stranger to our legal life. We see it in veterans' preferences. We see it in the aid-to-the-handicapped programs. We see it in the progressive income tax. We see it in the Indian programs. We may excuse some of these on the ground that they have specific constitutional protection or, as with Indians, that those benefited are wards of the Government. Nevertheless, these preferences exist and may not be ignored. And in the admissions field, as I have indicated, educational institutions have always used geography, athletic ability, anticipated financial largess, alumni pressure, and other factors of that kind.

I add these only as additional components on the edges of the central question as to which I join my Brothers BRENNAN, WHITE, and MARSHALL in our more general approach. It is gratifying to know that the Court at least finds it constitutional for an academic institution to take race and ethnic background into consideration as one factor, among many, in the administration of its admissions program. I presume that that factor always has been there, though perhaps not conceded or even admitted. It is a fact of life, however, and a part of the real world of which we are all a part. The sooner we get down the road toward accepting and being a part of the real world, and not shutting it out and away from us, the sooner will these difficulties vanish from the scene.

I suspect that it would be impossible to arrange an affirmative action program in a racially neutral way and have it successful. To ask that this be so is to demand the impossible. In order to get beyond racism, we must first take account of race. There is no other way. And in order to treat some persons equally, we must treat them differently. We cannot—we dare not—let the Equal Protection Clause perpetuate racial supremacy.

So the ultimate question, as it was at the beginning of this litigation, is: Among the qualified, how does one choose?

A long time ago, as time is measured for this Nation, a Chief Justice, both wise and far-sighted, said:

> "In considering this question, then, we must never forget, that it is *a constitution* we are expounding" (emphasis in original). *M'Culloch* v. *Maryland*, 4 Wheat. 316, 407 (1819).

In the same opinion, the Great Chief Justice further observed:

> "Let the end be legitimate, let it be within the scope of the constitution, and all means which are appropriate, which are plainly adapted to that end, which are not prohibited but consist with the letter and spirit of the constitution, are constitutional." *Id.*, at 421.

More recently, one destined to become a Justice of this Court observed:

> "The great generalities of the constitution have a content and a significance that vary from age to age." B. Cardozo, The Nature of the Judicial Process 17 (1921).

And an educator who became a President of the United States said:

> "But the Constitution of the United States is not a mere lawyers' document: it is a vehicle of life, and its spirit is always the spirit of the age." W. Wilson, Constitutional Government in the United States 69 (1911).

These precepts of breadth and flexibility and ever-present modernity are basic to our constitutional law. Today, again, we are expounding a *Constitution*. The same principles that governed M'Culloch's case in 1819 govern Bakke's case in 1978. There can be no other answer.

CARL COHEN

Race and the Constitution

The equal protection of the laws seems the plainest, most comprehensive requirement of justice. That equals must be treated equally by the law, all will allow. But who are equals before the law? Distinctions based upon employment, office, wealth and a host of other considerations certainly do (and should) justify differential treatment. But what about race? Religion? National origin? Sex? Do these also sometimes justify differential treatment?

The common conviction that such categories have no bearing upon the just application of law is dramatized by the blindfold that the Goddess of Justice wears while balancing her scales. In this country that conviction reached its apogee with *Brown* v. *Board of Education* in 1954, becoming thereafter almost liberal dogma. It is freshly applied in recent guidelines of the Department of Health, Education, and Welfare to eliminate sex discrimination in colleges and universities. Recipients of federal funds, those rules announce, shall not "administer or operate any test or other criterion for admission which adversely affects any person on the basis of sex, unless use of such test is shown to predict validly successful completion of the education program or activity in question." Splendid. Or is it? That depends upon whose ox is gored.

The ideal of blindfolded equal treatment, as applied to racial groups, encounters competing principles of compensatory justice. It is all very well to laud equality before the law; but when generations, or centuries, of discrimination and outright oppression based on race or ethnic origins have left minority groups in conditions of distressingly marked disadvantage, even-handed treatment cannot yield equal results. Affirmative action in pursuit of just outcomes, deliberate and concrete efforts to compensate for past wrongs, must be undertaken.

Affirmative action, not much in dispute as a generic notion, has many species. The arguments—moral, legal, sociological—for and against one or another of these species are many and tangled. My aim in what follows is to explore a single slice of these controversies: the preferential admission of members of minority groups to programs in higher education. The issues raised in it are delicate and important; they will certainly recur. When the U.S. Supreme Court held moot the case of *DeFunis* v. *Odegaard* (in

Reprinted from *The Nation*, February 8, 1975, 135–145 and reproduced with the permission of the author and the publisher.
Editor's Note: Footnotes have been numbered.

April 1974), the unsigned majority opinion included this unmistakable invitation: "If the admissions procedures of the Law School remain unchanged, there is no reason to suppose that a subsequent case attacking those procedures will not come with relative speed to this Court, now that the Supreme Court of Washington has spoken." [40 L Ed 2d 170.] In a host of similar cases that invitation is being vigorously accepted.

Using the *DeFunis* case, I propose to explicate and evaluate the central arguments upon which resolution of these issues will probably depend. It is to be expected that such resolution will come through judicial interpretation of constitutional principle. In giving concrete meaning to venerable principles the courts—ultimately the Supreme Court—decide not simply what our Constitution requires but what it ought to be understood to require. In many matters, courts give clear moral guidance; judicial reasoning functions as moral reasoning.

Several related issues must be shorn from that of preferential admissions. Preferential employment practices raise like, but often differing, questions; affirmative action is equally essential in the sphere of housing, but assumes very different forms; quotas, strictly considered, are one variety of preferential treatment (whether applied to admissions or employment), but introduce additional questions about the propriety of numerical instruments; discrimination against women differs sufficiently from that against racial minorities to justify its separate treatment. I focus upon the deliberately preferential treatment of minority groups in admission to professional schools. *DeFunis* v. *Odegaard* is archetypal.

In March 1973, the state Supreme Court of Washington decided in favor of the University of Washington (Charles Odegaard then president) against Marco DeFunis, a white, male applicant to the university's Law School, who claimed that the system of admissions applied by that school, incorporating deliberate preference for members of minority groups, and resulting in his rejection, had denied him the equal protection of the laws. A lower court that had supported DeFunis was reversed; but its order obliging the university to admit him had remained in effect during the three years of ensuing litigation. It was DeFunis' impending graduation from that Law School in the spring of 1974 that gave grounds for the ultimate holding by the U.S. Supreme Court that the case was moot.

DeFunis' central contention was that the admitting procedures of the University of Washington Law School (hereafter, the Law School) applied a double standard—one measure for minority group members, another for the rest—in such a way as to violate that clause of the Fourteenth Amendment of the U.S. Constitution which guarantees to all persons "the equal protection of the laws." It was reasonable, he argued, for the Law School to make admissions judgments among competing applicants based upon evidence of many different sorts—academic and non-academic, numerical and nonnumerical—so long as that evidence was in some way relevant to the program of study to which admission was sought. It was not reasonable or lawful, he claimed, for the measures used, whatever they were, to be applied in a systematically differential way to certain sets of persons for no other reason than that such persons were (or were not) members of racial or ethnic minority groups. The University of Washington did not dispute the fact that it gave preferential treatment to such groups in the fierce competition for the relatively few law school slots available each year. But such preference, based on race or national origin, DeFunis contended, is precisely what the equal protection of the laws precludes absolutely.

DeFunis lost, in a decision of the Supreme Court of Washington that stands as the most cogent and persuasive defense of preferential admissions extant. I propose to reconstruct the argument of that decision, to construct the most solid and plausible counterarguments, and to explain why one side of the argument fails.

The factual circumstances of DeFunis' complaint must first be set before us. The facts will differ in coming cases, perhaps critically; but the analysis of principles must have some empirical anchorage, and the procedures of the Washington Law School are in fact so much like those of many sister institutions as to warrant the belief that a just application of constitutional principles to this set of facts will provide useful precedent in judging others.

Marco DeFunis first applied to the Law School for the fall of 1970. Although a Washington resident with a very good undergraduate record (junior-senior grade point average of 3.71 of a possible 4.0), he was refused admission, but advised to apply again the following year. He enrolled in graduate school for that year and, while working full time for the Seattle Park Department, completed twenty-one credit hours of all A work. By the time of his second application in 1971, he had taken the Law School Admissions Test (LSAT) three times, with an average score of 582—his last score of 668 being in the top 7 per cent nationally. After being put on a waiting list, he was again denied admission. Knowing that many applicants with academic credentials inferior to his had been admitted, he concluded that the admissions process had discriminated against him because he did not belong to a minority group. To appraise that conclusion we must look very carefully, as did the Washington Supreme Court, at the actual admitting practice in that Law School. What was done?

The Committee on Admissions and Readmissions, consisting then of five faculty members and two students, faced the awesome task, in the spring of 1971, of selecting from the 1,601 applications received the persons to fill but 150 available seats. Knowing from experience that a good many of those admitted would in fact accept admission elsewhere, the committee sent out 275 letters of admittance; the freshman class eventually enrolled for the fall of 1971 contained 155 students.

The chief sorting instrument of the Admissions Committee was a mathematically determined Predicted First Year Average (PFYA), derived for each applicant by a formula in which both the junior-senior grade point average and the LSAT score were given appropriate weight. The numerical results were used, in general, as follows: applicants with PFYAs above 77 were summarily accepted; those with PFYAs under 74.5 were summarily rejected; applicants with PFYAs between 74.5 and 77.0 were re-examined, some being accepted, some not. However, this system was not applied to everyone. All minority applicants (Philippine-Americans, Chicano-Americans, black Americans and American Indians, by careful university definition) were considered separately. PFYA was also used for minority group students, but they were not judged on the same standards as the rest; they competed only against one another. For how many slots? That was not fixed in advance, but the university reported its objective as "proportionate representation" of minority groups in the entering class. The numerical outcome was this: of the 275 applicants sent letters of admittance, forty-four were minority group members—exactly 16 per cent. Of the forty-four minority admissions, thirty-six had PFYA scores lower than that of DeFunis. Some twenty-nine other unsuccessful applicants were roughly in his case, having PFYA scores higher than most minority admissions. All of those admitted, whether of minority group or not, were deemed qualified by the committee. Among the minority admissions, as one of the judges later wrote (and all parties agreed), "were some whose college grades and aptitude scores were so low that, had they not been minority students, their applications would have been summarily denied." [Wash. 507 P2d 1191.]

Now DeFunis had a PFYA of 76.23. It is not certain, but it is probable, that had there been no system of preferential admission, he would have been admitted. It is certain that, had there been no such system, some of the rejected white applicants with PFYA scores in the high-middle range would have been admitted. DeFunis was a young man with superior abilities and a fine academic record. Some of the minority admissions were, all agree, of uncertain ability and mediocre academic record. There is the nub of the complaint: DeFunis was not accepted by the Law School chiefly, and probably only, because of a preference accorded to others simply on the basis of their race or ethnic origin.[1]

[1] Closely similar systems of preferential admission are widespread. The Stanford University Law School, according to its former Dean, Bayliss Manning, grants admission "substantially automatically" to any minority applicant (1) whose grade point average (GPA) is not below the lowest GPA of regular nonminority students in the previous year's entering class; (2) whose Law School Admissions Test (LSAT) score is not more than 50 points lower than the lowest LSAT of regular non-minority students in the previous entering class; and (3) whose Law Quotient Index (LQI) is not more than 50 points below the lowest LQI of

This complaint is plausible upon its face; required now is an appraisal in depth. This is obviously not a case of racial discrimination in the standard, exploitative mold. If there is racial discrimination here its evident and honorable objective is not to maintain inequality but to overcome an inequality that has been deeply rooted. The Law School had devised a deliberately compensatory instrument, honestly aimed at justice over the long run. Of course, long-term justice was sought with equal fervor by DeFunis and his defenders, who did not deny the historical facts of racial oppression or contest the need for some compensatory action. The two sides concurred in calling for affirmative action, deliberate conduct aimed at uprooting a long-ensconced pattern of racial injustice.

In pursuit of this objective what instruments are constitutionally permissible? That is the key question here. This controversy is not between good guys and bad guys, but between very sophisticated parties who differ about what, in the effort to achieve a very pressing and very difficult end, we may rightly use as means.

The Supreme Court of Washington (hereafter, the Court) dealt sensitively and deeply with this question. Its argument went to the heart of the matter and developed, in three steps, a powerful defense of the Law School. These steps take the form of answers to the following three questions:

(1) Are classifications on the basis of race, for purposes of school admission and the like, *per se* unconstitutional? Does "the equal protection of the laws" require that an admissions committee be "color blind"? If the answer were yes the matter would be settled. But if race can, under some circumstances, be considered as one factor in an admissions policy, there are further questions to resolve.

(2) Suppose that consideration of race is under some circumstances permissible. What standard must then be applied to actual cases to determine whether, in a particular instance, the racial classification used is constitutional?

(3) Suppose that consideration of race is under some circumstances permissible, and that the standard of its constitutional application is known. Has the Law School in the *DeFunis* case (and any school in any similar case) met that standard in its policy and practice?

To the first of these questions the Court's answer, carefully argued, was negative. Consideration of race is not, always and in itself, unconsti-

---

regular non-minority students in the previous year. (The LQI combines GPA, LSAT and a factor based on the law school records of previous students from the same undergraduate institution.) This policy, says Dean Manning, is "strongly preferential in favor of minority applicants, since it will lead to admission of many minority students whose formal academic credentials are below those of hundreds, even thousands, of non-minority applicants to Stanford who will be rejected."

tutional. It is well established, to be sure, that the equal protection clause
of the Fourteenth Amendment prohibits the operation of racially segregated public schools. Racial segregation in schools, the Supreme Court
held in the landmark *Brown* decision of 1954, stigmatizes the minority
group and injures its members in ways not easily (if ever) undone. It is
not constitutionally permissible. But, said the Washington Court in 1973,
the *Brown* decision did not warrant the conclusion that all racial classifications are, *per se*, unconstitutional. The leading principle of that decision
was that racial classifications are unconstitutional when they are invidious,
when they stigmatize a racial group with a stamp of inferiority. But a
preferential admissions policy, like that of the Law School, does not stigmatize the minority and is not invidious because its aim is not to separate
the races but to bring them together.

The principles of the *Brown* case do not settle the matter. Even if,
by that decision, only invidious racial classifications are ruled out, it remains
to ask whether there are any contexts in which non-invidious racial classifications are ruled in. In fact there are, said the Court. The U.S. Supreme
Court has held that there are circumstances in which doing justice demands not that we ignore race, but that we carefully attend to it. When,
for example, a school board, charged with the responsibilities of designing
and implementing policy, proposes to eliminate a long-standing pattern of
racial discrimination with a "freedom-of-choice" enrollment plan that
does not work, that board will be compelled to come forward with a better
scheme that does take steps adequate to abolish its past racially segregated
system. "The burden on a school board today is to come forward with a
plan that promises realistically to work, and promises realistically to work
now." [*Green* v. *County School Board*, 391 U.S. 437 (1968).]

To fulfill such responsibilities, said the Supreme Court in a subsequent case, school authorities need not be "color blind" when the consideration of race is essential to produce an appropriately mixed student
body. "Awareness of the racial composition of the whole school system
is likely to be a useful starting point in shaping a remedy to correct past
constitutional violations. . . . Just as the race of students must be considered in determining whether a constitutional violation has occurred, so
also must race be considered in formulating a remedy." [*Swann* v. *Charlotte-Mecklenburg Board of Education*, 402 U.S.45 (1971).]

Such decisions led the Washington Court to conclude, in the
DeFunis case, that the preferential admissions policy of the Law School,
aimed at insuring a "reasonable representation" of minority persons in
the student body, was not invidious. The Constitution, said the Court,
"is color conscious to prevent the perpetuation of discrimination and to
undo the effects of past segregation." [Wash. 507 P2d 1180.]

The first great hurdle then is jumped: in *some* cases, the Court concludes, racial classification is constitutionally permissible.

The second question concerns the standard to be applied in such cases. Racial classifications are manifestly suspect. What is the test for their proper use, where it is alleged that they have a proper use? The normal test of a questionable classification, one alleged to violate the equal protection clause, is whether that classification "is reasonably related to a legitimate public purpose." But where race is the basis of the classification the Court concluded that a much heavier burden of justification must be imposed. The U.S. Supreme Court, in 1967, was very firm on this point: ". . . at the very least, the Equal Protection Clause demands that racial classifications . . . be subjected to 'the most rigid scrutiny.' " [*Loving* v. *Virginia* 388 U.S. 10.] The Washington Court, seeking to obey that injunction with care, set this standard for the constitutionality of racial classifications: "The burden is upon the Law School to show that its consideration of race in admitting students is necessary to the accomplishment of a compelling state interest."

The third question is whether the Law School, in the *DeFunis* case, had met this standard. This, in turn, raised two subordinate questions:

(1) Are the interests of the state here compelling? The Court's answer: Yes. The underrepresentation of minorities in law schools, and hence in the legal profession, is gross. Considering this imbalance—and in view of the tax support of this Law School by all, including minority groups, on an equal basis—the Court held that the elimination of racial imbalance in public legal education is indeed compelling.

One possible objection to this conclusion is the claim that the need could be compelling only where the pattern of discrimination was *de jure*, the deliberate result of institutional practice—but that in the instant case the pattern was no more than *de facto*, the product of historical circumstances. This objection is ruled out by the Court, reasoning that, whatever the cause of past racial discrimination in this sphere, the state has an "overriding interest" in eradicating its continuing effects. That interest is not reduced an iota because, in the past, a particular institution may have been neutral in the matter. We look to the remedy of social evil, said the Court in effect, not to the apportionment of blame. Had the admissions policy in question been ordered by some court, the past behavior of the institution would be relevant in determining what plan of desegregation is justifiably enforced. But the Washington plan was not the outcome of such an order; it was developed voluntarily by the Law School as part of its autonomous effort to correct a historic injustice. At issue here, the Court emphasized, is not whether the preferential admissions policy under examination is required, but only whether it is permissible.

"Finally," the Court concludes, "the shortage of minority attorneys —and, consequently, of minority prosecutors, judges and public officials— constitutes an undeniably compelling state interest."

(2) Is the consideration of race, in admitting students, necessary for the accomplishment of this end? The Court's answer: Yes. The evil to be corrected is the racial imbalance in the Law School student body.

That imbalance can be put right only, the Court affirms, by actually providing legal education to the minority groups previously denied it.

It is commonly argued that the proper way to do this is to improve elementary and secondary education for minority students to the point that equal representation of minorities in professional schools may be secured through direct competition with non-minority students, on the basis of the same criteria. But, at least to date, this simply has not worked. It is two decades since the *Brown* decision; the time for racial balance is now. Since the Court concludes that the preferential admissions policy is the only one that "promises realistically to work *now*," no policy that is less restrictive will adequately serve the compelling governmental interest at stake.

The core argument of the Washington Supreme Court is thus complete: "We conclude that defendants have shown the necessity of the racial classification herein to the accomplishment of an overriding state interest, and have thus sustained the heavy burden imposed upon them under the equal protection provision of the Fourteenth Amendment."

Two other matters discussed by the Court, tangential to the main issue, I touch upon very briefly. First, in defining minority group applicants, did the Law School's exclusion of some important minorities (e.g., Asian-Americans) render its classification improper because invalidly drawn? The Court's answer: No. Since a significant number of Asian-Americans, and other minorities, could be admitted on the same basis as general applicants, it was held that they need not be treated as minority applicants here—the purpose of this category being the identification of the groups most in need of help. A classification is validly drawn if it includes all and only those persons who are similarly situated with respect to the purpose of the law. The purpose of this classification was "to give special consideration to those racial minority groups which are underrepresented in the law schools and legal profession, and which cannot secure proportionate representation if strictly subjected" to the standard criteria for admission. It did that, said the Court, and was therefore validly drawn.

Second. Much controversy in the *DeFunis* case arose over the operating procedures of this particular Law School, the qualifications of the student members of its Admissions Committee, and so on. DeFunis claimed (and some justices strongly agreed) that the entire process in the Law School, apart from the matter of racial classification, was arbitrary and capricious. He was not sustained in this. The issue, although a fascinating sidelight on university practice, was not central to the main thrust of the decision.

That decision could have gone the other way. A minority of the Washington Supreme Court, led by its Chief Justice, expressed dissenting judgment firmly. Justice William Douglas of the U.S. Supreme Court (concurring with Justices Brennan, Marshall and White that the case was not moot), separately attacked the Law School's efforts to effect proportional representation based on race or ethnicity. But a full response to the Washington Court, developed with careful attention to the logic of its argument, has been missing. I try now to supply that want.

Each of the three steps of that argument must be questioned. Preferential treatment for some racial or ethnic groups is what the words of the U.S. Constitution, given their plainest meaning, seem to prohibit. A great burden clearly falls upon those who defend such preference. If the chain constructed by the Court to carry that burden breaks at any link, the case falls. In fact, upon careful scrutiny—and in spite of the most laudable aims of the Law School and the Court—not one, but all three of the links in their argument crumble.

FIRST. Are classifications on the basis of race, for purposes of law school admission and the like, *per se* unconstitutional? The correct answer is yes. Indeed, the Fourteenth Amendment was deliberately formulated to prohibit precisely such classifications. The Constitution is and always must be, in that sense, color blind. It cannot be, from time to time and at the discretion of certain agencies or administrators, color conscious in order to become color blind at some future date. The principle that a person's race is simply not relevant in the application of the laws is a treasured one. If we are prepared to sacrifice that principle now and then, in an attempt to achieve some very pressing and very honorable objective, we will have given up its force as constitutional principle. No doubt intentions here are of the best, but so, often, are the intentions of those who would from time to time sacrifice other constitutional principles for the attainment of other very worthy ends. The enforcement of justice, the redistribution of wealth, the very protection of the nation, might all be more conveniently, more efficiently, even more effectively accomplished if, from time to time, we winked at the Constitution and did what, as we will be told with honest fervor, is of absolutely overriding importance. In this way is the Congressional authority to declare war conveniently ignored; in this way is the constitutional protection of our persons, houses, papers and effects from unreasonable search and seizure effectively (of course only temporarily) by-passed. In this way, in sum, constitutional government, fragile network of principles that it is, comes apart.

But, some will reply, those other objectives—national security, protection against crime, etc.—are only claimed to be compelling; racial injustice, so long deliberately denied, really is so. Of course. And every person and every group has, at some time, objectives that are, to its complete and profound conviction, so utterly compelling that nothing must be allowed to stand in the way of their accomplishment.[2] But every such

---

[2] Justice Douglas, in his dissenting opinion in *DeFunis* writes: "The argument is that a 'compelling' state interest can justify the racial discrimination that is practiced here. . . . If discrimination based on race is constitutionally permissible when

party must yield in turn to the restrictions of constitutional government; if those in authority do not enforce these restrictions, the Constitution is but paper. A constitution, ideally, is not an expression of particular social ends; rather, it identifies very general common purposes and lays down principles according to which the many specific ends of the body politic may be decided upon and pursued. Its most critical provisions will be those which absolutely preclude certain means. Thus to say that a protection afforded citizens is "constitutional" is at least to affirm that it will be respected, come what may. The specific constitutional provision that each citizen is entitled to equal protection of the laws is assurance that, no matter how vital the government alleges its interest to be, or how laudable the objective of those who would temporarily suspend that principle, it will stand. The highest obligation to respect it is owed by public institutions and government agencies.[3]

Preferential admission systems present instances of this sometimes agonizing tension between important ends and impermissible means. Hence the persuasiveness of the argument on both sides. In facing dilemmas of this kind long experience has taught the supremacy of the procedural principle. With societies, as with individuals, the use of means in themselves corrupt tends to corrupt the user, and to infect the result. So it is with wiretapping, with censorship, with torture. So it is with discriminatory preference by racial grouping for racial balance.

But this is racial classification, the Court insisted, not racial discrimination. The latter is indeed ruled out, said they, but the former is not; Brown and other powerful precedents forbid invidious racial classification, not all racial classification. This argument misses the central point—the sharpest bite of Brown and like cases—that in the distribution of benefits under the laws all racial classifications are necessarily invidious. Invidious distinctions are those tending to excite ill will, or envy, those likely to be viewed as unfair—and that is what racial classifications are likely to do and be when used as instrument for the apportionment of goods or opportunities.

Perhaps the Court would respond: Some such invidiousness is difficult to deny, but our main point is that the racial classifications condemned by Brown and succeeding cases are those that stigmatize one of the groups distinguished, stamping it with inferiority. But the change of

---

those who hold the reins can come up with 'compelling' reasons to justify it, then constitutional guarantees acquire an accordionlike quality." [40 L Ed 2d 184.]

[3] The only previous suspension of this constitutional protection was a national moral disaster. To meet the alleged danger of sabotage and espionage during the Second World War, American citizens of Japanese descent were peremptorily rounded up, moved, and excluded from large sections of our West Coast. The Supreme Court was pained, but found this roundup and detention justified by "pressing public necessity." (Korematsu v. United States, 323 U.S. 216, 1944.) Never before or since has the use of race in applying constitutional protection been expressly approved by our highest Court.

phrase provides no rescue. To stigmatize is to brand, or label, generally with disgrace—and that is exactly what is done by racial classification in this context. Indeed, put to the service of preferential admissions such classification is doubly stigmatizing. It marks one racial group as formally to be handicapped, its members burdened specifically by virtue of race; for the majority applicant (as formerly for the minority) earned personal qualifications will not be enough. Persons in the other racial category are to be officially treated as though unable to compete for the good in question on an equal basis; by physical characteristic the minority applicant is marked as in need of special help. On both sides morale is subverted, accomplishments clouded. On the one side all carry the handicap, regardless of their past deeds or capacity to bear it; on the other, all are received with the supposition of inferiority, regardless of their personal attainments or hatred of condescension. For all, the stigmata are visually prominent and permanent.[4]

I conclude that the first and fundamental step of the Court's argument in defense of preferential admissions cannot be justly taken. Racial classifications, in the application of the laws, or in the distribution of benefits under the laws, are always invidious, always stigmatizing. That is why they are, *per se*, unconstitutional.

How account, then, for the recent school desegregation cases, *Green* and *Swann*, in which the U.S. Supreme Court recognized the need to attend to race for the sake of justice? That the Washington Court was most uncomfortable with its first premise, and troubled by the self-imposed obligation to defend it, is evident in its discussion of these cases. Badly needing some illustration of the reasonable use of race, but having only these as possible analogies, the Court made much of them, while carefully avoiding all mention of the fundamental difference between the remedies approved in them, and the policy at issue in *DeFunis*. It is true that in these school cases the courts attend to race and racial mix. But it is not true that such attention involves, or permits, the classification by race to determine the apportionment of benefits, which is what preferential admission entails. The very reverse, in fact: the desegregation cases have as their main thrust absolute equality of treatment, equality of benefit under the law. Clearly, if that equality has been systematically denied by a school board or other agency through the segregation of races, effective remedy must look to the desegregation of races, and that was done. But no racial classification for the application of laws is there even entertained. Indeed, it is just the use of such classification that, through such cases,

[4] Justice Douglas writes in his dissenting opinion: "A segregated admission process creates suggestions of stigma and caste no less than a segregated classroom, and in the end it may produce that result despite its contrary intentions. . . . [T]hat Blacks or Browns cannot make it on their individual merit . . . is a stamp of inferiority that a state is not permitted to place on any lawyer." [40 L Ed 2d 184.]

we are having now to undo. To use the need of that sort of remedy as a justification for the introduction of another disorder of the very kind that remedy was designed to cure is reasoning both convoluted and dangerous.[5]

Those who say, with the first Justice Harlan, "Our Constitution is color blind, and neither knows nor tolerates classes among citizens" do not suppose that the courts may not attend to the special character of past wrongs done. Rather, the principle they are emphasizing is cautionary: in all circumstances courts must scrupulously avoid and prohibit the use of a person's race as, in itself, a qualification (or a disqualification) for anything that persons of another race are, for that racial reason disqualified (or qualified) for. The critical distinction between attention to race in the enforcement of equal treatment, and the use of race in the fashioning of unequal treatment, was blurred by the Washington Court, but only by straining.

Furthermore, even in the school desegregation cases in which a deliberate racial injustice is identified for which specific remedy is sought, the attention to racial mix in providing that remedy is very delicately supervised by the courts. There is all the difference in the world between a specific remedy thus controlled (as in the *Swann* case) and a general license to professional schools, or universities, or other institutions to ignore the constitutional prohibition of racial discrimination, and to engage in "reasonable" discriminatory activity to correct the effects of past social injustice as they consider such measures needful or convenient. To permit such practice is to abandon constitutional principle entirely.

Preferential admission procedures certainly do result in the discriminatory apportionment of benefits on the basis of race or ethnicity. When any resource is in short supply, and some by virtue of their race are given more of it, others by virtue of their race get less. If that resource be seats in a law school, procedures that assure preference to certain racial groups in allotting those seats necessarily produce a correlative denial of access to those not in the preferred categories. This plain consequence should not be overlooked. Whether the numbers be fixed or flexible; whether "quotas" be established and called "benign"; whether they be measured by percentages or absolute quantities; whether the objective be "reasonable proportionality" or "appropriate representation"—the setting of bene-

---

[5] Congress, especially through Title VII of the Civil Rights Act of 1964, has also sought to undo some of the results of racial categorizing. When, under this title, discriminatory preference for minority races was attempted and tested in court, a unanimous Supreme Court laid down the principle that job qualification standards must be performance-related, and that that may cut against certain types of irrelevant testing, just as it cuts against certain types of irrelevant grouping. "Discriminatory preference for any group, minority or majority, is precisely and only what Congress has proscribed. What is required by Congress is the removal of artificial, arbitrary, and unnecessary barriers to employment when the barriers operate invidiously to discriminate on the basis of racial or other impermissible classification." [*Griggs* v. *Duke Power Co.*, 401 U.S. 430 (1971).]

fit floors for some groups in this context inescapably entails benefit ceilings for other groups.

By fuzzing the numbers and softening the names some manage to hide this conclusion from themselves. The majority of the Washington Court, to their credit, did not do that. Although eager to minimize the discriminatory character of the instrument, they recognized candidly its inevitable result. They wrote: "The minority admissions policy is certainly not benign with respect to non-minority students who are displaced by it." Preference by race is malign; its malignity has no clearer or more fitting name than racism. Widespread in American universities, this well-meant racism will indeed be found, upon reflection, to deny the equal protection of the laws.

SECOND. Suppose (what I do not grant) that the Court was correct in its first step; suppose that racial classifications are in some cases constitutional, and that the school desegregation cases are illustrations of the exceptional cases. Still, to determine whether in any other specific instance (such as that of DeFunis) racial classification is constitutional, some standard for judgment is required. Recognizing that racial categories are intrinsically suspect, the Washington Court concluded that any user of a racial classification in admissions is under an obligation to show "that its consideration of race in admitting students is necessary to the accomplishment of a compelling state interest."

Would this be the correct test? My answer is no. Although rightly higher than the normal standard (that of being reasonably related to a legitimate public purpose), the Court's standard is far from high enough. In addition to the need for the classification, and the compelling character of the interests served by it, "the individual interests affected by the classification," in the words of the U.S. Supreme Court, must be considered. Where the basis for the classification is known to be "inherently suspect," and the individual interest affected is a fundamental constitutional right, the standard for review must be, said the highest Court, "exacting." [*Dunn v. Blumstein*, 405 U.S. 338 (1972).] Now it will be a critical part of any exacting test that that classification not have the consequence of penalizing any person simply by virtue of his race. The importance of this restriction cannot be overemphasized. If it be argued that racial categories are in some contexts relevant to the application of the laws; if the school desegregation cases discussed above are viewed (incorrectly, I submit) as examples in which the just distribution of benefit relies upon racial classification, it is at least certain that such classification is not used in those cases to the prejudice of anyone. No person, under those decisions, gets less than another because of his race. That, we rightly sense, is a critical factor in any consideration here of race. Whenever individuals are penalized solely because they manifest some adventitious characteristic wholly out of their control—their skin color, their national origin, or the like—

the unfairness arouses strong indignation. Our viscera do not mislead us in this; any reasonable standard would certainly exclude such uses of racial classification.

If racial classifications are ever to be used, I conclude, they must pass a far more protective test than that invoked by the Court. The user of any racial classification must show that consideration of race is necessary to the accomplishment of a compelling state interest, *and* that such consideration does not result in adverse consequence to any person simply because of that person's race or ethnic membership. Now it has been demonstrated that one result of preferential policies is to deny to some persons, simply because of their race, what they in every other respect deserve and would receive, were they of the preferred skin color. It is therefore manifest that on this more protective standard no policy of preferential admission by race is acceptable.

THIRD. Suppose the first and second steps of the Court's argument allowed—that racial classifications are sometimes permissible, and that when they are it need be shown only that they are necessary for the accomplishment of a compelling state interest. Would a preferential admissions policy on the Washington Law School model pass that test? No, it would not.

What are the interests to be served by the policy, and which are compelling? Three large, separate interests are involved here, and they are of differing values.

The first is a general interest in the integration of law schools and the legal profession. Unless and until minorities have a fair and genuinely equal opportunity to prepare for the bar, they cannot function properly in many critical roles—that of judge, prosecutor, et al., as well as attorney— to which the law schools give the only entry. And it is obviously unjust for any racial group to be denied opportunity to serve in those roles. Moreover, as the Court pointed out, in this society lawyers have a specially important role in policy making as a consequence of their relatively high level of service in legislatures and other public bodies. The public policy that is molded in these bodies needs the input of the minorities universally concerned—for the sake of minorities and majorities alike. The social role of attorneys is such that their understanding of the needs and views of all slices of society is an important general concern.

Racial integration is indeed a deep and powerful interest. It is not, however, an interest compelling in the sense that, to serve it, any steps are justified. Integration does not, as an objective, justify racial discrimination believed useful in its achievement. Lawyers, judges and prosecutors of all colors and ethnic identities we do need; but we cannot afford to pay for improvement on that front by basing professional qualifications partly on skin color. A community is not justified in advancing its own general health by denying to some of its members constitutional protections that apply to all. It is because the classification of persons by irrelevant, physical properties is so generally odious that the courts are explicit in demanding that the interests served by such classification be literally compelling, over-riding. Grave though the need for integration is, overriding in the sense required by the judicial test proposed it is not.

A second general interest urged by the advocates of preferential ad-missions policies is the achievement of numerical proportionality among the races in the legal (and other) professions. Much different from inte-gration, this is a conception of racial balance which not only measures justice by counting numbers of minority group members in the professions or professional schools, but also finds any result unsatisfactory that does not manifest "reasonable proportionality" or "appropriate representation."

Much that needs to be said on this aspect of compensatory justice cannot be said here. On two levels, however, it quickly becomes clear that racial proportionality is not a compelling need. Numerical proportionality of races in the professions is most commonly defended on the ground that without it the interests of minority groups cannot be properly served. Surely this belief is mistaken if it incorporates the conviction that only black lawyers can serve black clients adequately, that Indians, when sick, are treated properly only by Indian physicians, or that white defendants cannot be fairly tried before black judges. The insistence that proper and consci-entious fulfillment of professional function is dependent upon harmony of race or heritage between client and practitioner is not only destructive but incorrect. The record of professional services completely transcending dif-ferences of race, religion and national origin is long and honorable.

We agree (the rejoinder might begin) that much professional service crosses racial lines; but as a practical matter it cannot be denied that, with-out racial balance in the professional corps, it has proved impossible for racial minorities to obtain professional services in the quantity and quality needed. There is a confusion here. It is true that the legal and health needs of minority groups have not been fairly or adequately met, but it is far from clear that the remedy for that lies in racial proportionality. Differ-ences in professional services are most closely tied to economic considera-tions, within as well as between races; proportionality does not even speak to that fundamental problem. Moreover, to defend forced proportionality on the basis of the professional needs of the minority is to assume, tacitly, that minority group lawyers will, in fact, devote themselves to ethnically exclusive practice. No doubt this will be true for many, but to expect that black professionals will practice only in the black community, or Mexican-Americans only in the Mexican-American community, is quite wrong. The parochialism implicit in that expectation exerts heavy and unfair pressure upon minority professionals.

Well then (the rejoinder might continue) is there not a residual need felt by minority group members for lawyers (and doctors, et al.) of the same race or cultural heritage who are sensitive to their special attitudes and circumstances, share their ethnic spirit, and who alone can make them comfortable? See where this argument takes us. If comfort, in this sense, really is good ground for official preference on the basis of race, it would be entirely appropriate for firms with chiefly minority clientele to discriminate openly against applicants from the ethnic majority in their hiring practices. "Our clients cannot be comfortable with white attorneys," they may say, "and good professional service to our clients requires this psychological confidence. That confidence is possible only with community of heritage." But racism is a two-way street. Depend upon it, that argument, so long used to justify racial discrimination against minority professionals, will be accepted with satisfaction by bigots on all sides.

Arguments of this kind for racial proportionality—some advanced even by the Washington Court—mistakenly suppose a unity and distinctness of interest shared by all and only the members of a racial category. They assume that the diversity among whites, or among blacks, or among Philippine-Americans, or whatever, is wholly submerged, outweighed by racial identification, and that therefore the professional needs of persons of a given race will be fully met only by one of the same race. With decent purpose we are urged to think with our blood.

More deeply, the call for proportionality is inspired by a strange vision of ideal society—one that is pervaded by ethnic identification. According to that ideal the numerical proportionality of races is a principal measure of distributive justice in virtually every sphere of social life. In schools, courts, professions, in business and in recreation, in all public and in much private activity attention to race is encouraged, even obliged. For some this ideal offers a promise of homogeneity that proves captivating; inferences now commonly drawn from it verge upon the absurd. It has been suggested, for example, that a legislature or a jury that does not manifest proportionality of race (or sex, or age) is without legitimate authority. Calls for appropriate numerical representation in various ethnic groups—Italian-Americans, black Americans, Catholic Americans—have already been heard. It is realistic to expect many more, because once this principle for the distribution of benefit appears operative each group is under some pressure to stake an early claim. The pressure is greater when it cannot be known in what fraction(s) the cake will be cut, so that restraint by any group may result in an ethnic apportionment on some continuum taking no account of that group whatever. There is practically no limit to the variety of categories (racial, national, sexual, etc.) from which such demands may come forth. Nor is there limit to the variety of public contexts to which such demands may be applied. All this is no longer speculation.

How seriously are such claims to be taken? That depends upon how seriously the premise of ethnic proportionality as ideal is received.[6] Its

---

[6] Preliminary judgment on the premise of proportionality has been passed by the U.S. Supreme Court. It decided that the state of California has the right to ban

universal applicability will hardly be allowed. Yet it will be difficult to accept the ideal in some contexts while denying it in others that are strictly analogous. It will be difficult to defend the ideal in support of the claims of some ethnic groups while rejecting the coordinate claims of other groups.

The ideal of thorough ethnic proportionality, although impractical and tortuous, may be honestly pursued by some. Others, however inconsistently, may invoke it for some groups or some spheres, but not for other groups or spheres. Still others will reject the ideal. It is at least certain, I conclude, that the realization of such an ideal is not a compelling social need.[7]

There is a third general interest that the advocates of racially preferential policies aim to advance: *compensation*. That wrongful injuries earlier done be compensated for now, to the extent possible, is part of the demands of justice. How they should be compensated for no general principles can determine. Much depends upon the nature and gravity of the injury, upon the wants of the injured, and upon the circumstances at the time compensation is undertaken. To say that compensation for a past injury is required now is to call for an immediate process of tangible redress, suitable in form and substance. But that cannot tell us what precisely is to be done. Compensation is not a particular, describable end, like integration; it is at once more pressing and less measurable, an aim of justice having no certain form.

This compensatory interest is compelling, but no scheme of racial or ethnic preference can be necessary to serve it. Compensation being a form of redress, it is justifiable only as a response to specific wrongs done to specific persons. Preferential admissions policies, by giving favor to all members of certain racial or ethnic groups, cannot be appropriate remedies for the wrongs in question.

---

picketing whose purpose—to compel the hiring of Negroes in proportion to Negro customers—was unlawful. "To deny to California the right to ban picketing in the circumstances of this case would mean that there could be no prohibition of the pressure of picketing to secure proportional employment on ancestral grounds of Hungarians in Cleveland, of Poles in Buffalo, of Germans in Milwaukee, of Portuguese in New Bedford, of Mexicans in San Antonio, of the numerous minority groups in New York, and so on through the whole gamut of racial and religious concentrations in various cities." [*Hughes v. Superior Court of California* 339 U.S. 464 (1950).] In effect, the Supreme Court here declared the unlawfulness of enforced racial proportionality.

[7] Justice Douglas writes in his dissent: "The state, however, may not proceed by racial classification to force strict population equivalencies for every group in every occupation, overriding individual preferences. The equal protection clause commands the elimination of racial barriers, not their creation in order to satisfy our theory as to how society ought to be organized. The purpose of the University of Washington cannot be to produce Black lawyers for Blacks, Polish lawyers for Poles, Jewish lawyers for Jews, Irish lawyers for the Irish. It should be to produce good lawyers for Americans. . . ." [40 L Ed 2d 183.]

Specific past injuries may justify specific present efforts to make up for what was wrongly done. In that spirit it is fair that those who have suffered wrongful economic disadvantage, or wrongful denial of opportunity, now be assisted with affirmative action to help redress those wrongs. Thus in deciding upon admissions to professional schools it may be quite reasonable to take into consideration some past injuries—e.g., whether schooling appropriate to ability had been denied a particular applicant, whether the economic need to work while in school had resulted in another applicant's lessened performance there, etc. Concrete assistance to those so disadvantaged, special efforts to recruit such applicants for professional courses and to retain such students by supplying special needs having root in that earlier maltreatment, offend no reasonable sense of justice.

Responses in this compensatory spirit, however, cannot be tied to race or ethnicity; their being compensatory supposes that they will be devised with a view to the injuries suffered by particular applicants, whatever their surname or color. Of each individually it may be asked: Is there, in this case, a history of wrongfully imposed disadvantage so grave as to justify special treatment now?

At this point advocates of preferential systems may contend that I have missed the point. For the injury suffered by many (say they) is inextricably bound up with race, and hence the remedy must be so as well. That point, powerful in some contexts, is misapplied here. In the public schools of North Carolina, where the task was that of desegregating large numbers of equally qualified students, already enrolled in the system, who had long been sorted by race, a racially attentive remedy was in order. But this consideration cannot justify a remedy that is, as in *DeFunis*, intrinsically prejudicial. However ugly past uses of race have been, constitutional rights are now enjoyed by citizens entirely without regard to race. Hence no deprivation of such individual rights, based on race alone, may be tolerated. The equal protection clause is a safeguard not for categories of persons but for every citizen singly.

On this point the language of the U.S. Supreme Court is definitive: "The rights created by the first section of the Fourteenth Amendment are, by its terms, guaranteed to the individual. The rights established are personal rights. It is, therefore, no answer to these petitioners to say that the Court may also be induced to deny white persons rights of ownership and occupancy on grounds of race or color. Equal protection of the laws is not achieved through indiscriminate imposition of inequalities." [*Shelly* v. *Kraemer*, 344 U.S. 22.]

The tacit supposition that rights are possessed by racial groups has caused much confusion here. But the formulation of the Fourteenth Amendment, recognizing rights as pertaining only to individuals, is exact on this matter. No state shall "deny to any person within its jurisdiction the equal protection of the laws." Any single individual, denied some benefit to which he is otherwise entitled, on the ground of his classification by race or ethnic origin, will have had his rights under that clause infringed. The social interest in compensating other persons who are members of other groups which have, in general, been very cruelly treated in the past, gives no justification for deliberate discrimination against this individual now.[8]

Many among our ethnic minorities have suffered grievous disadvantage simply because they were black or brown or yellow. But the degree of disadvantage suffered, and even the fact of it, varies from case to case. Some have suffered no more than non-minority persons who have unjustly experienced severe economic hardship or family catastrophe. Since every early adversity cannot be weighed in the school admissions process, it is usually thought right to consider the great majority of applicants on an equal footing, without analysis of past disadvantage, when reviewing admission qualifications.

Some past injuries may be thought so cruel and damaging as to justify special consideration for professional school admission. But whether a particular person has been so injured is a question of fact, to be answered in each case separately. If special consideration is in order for those whose early lives were cramped by extreme poverty, the penurious Appalachian white, the oppressed Oriental-American from a Western state, the impoverished Finn from upper Michigan—these and all others who similarly qualify are entitled to that consideration.

This becomes complicated. If the complications grow excessive we may think it well to avoid the artificial inequities likely to flow from inadequate data, or flaws in the compensatory calculations, by refraining altogether from those calculations and again treating all applicants on the same footing. That would oblige reliance chiefly upon some roughly objective credentials—past academic records, examinations and the like—which we know, of course, yield results imperfect in other ways. Or we may think ourselves obliged, whatever the burden, to enter the thicket of compensatory calculations. But if we do so, it is clear that we must make these calculations for all applicants. What we weigh in the case of one we must weigh for all; whatever redress in the sphere of admissions is in order because of past injury is in order for every person who has suffered like injury, without regard to race or national origin.

What we may not do, constitutionally or morally, is announce: "You are black, you get plus points; you are yellow, you don't." An admissions committee must not classify by race or ethnicity and assume, for special

[8] Justice Douglas, in his *DeFunis* dissent, is forceful on this point: "There is no constitutional right for any race to be preferred. . . . A DeFunis who is white is entitled to no advantage by reason of that fact; nor is he subject to any disability, no matter his race or color. Whatever his race, he had a constitutional right to have his application considered on its individual merits in a racially neutral manner." [40 L Ed 2d 180.]

consideration, cultural and/or economic deprivation for all of one category and for none of another. Nor may it do what amounts to the same thing—attend to the deprivations and injuries experienced by members of one ethnic group, but not to those experienced by members of others. Many small, foreign-language subgroups in our country have been humiliated, ostracized, oppressed; some religious groups have been scandalously treated; many in the white, Christian majority have suffered the terrible blight of family disorder and penury. Compensatory affirmative action, if undertaken at all, must be undertaken for every person who qualifies on some reasonably objective standard, a standard free of racial orientation.

Just here the system of the Washington Law School (and all others on that pattern) fails badly. By grouping races separately, and applying different standards to the different racial groups, an admissions office not only *does what is not necessary* to meet the compensatory need but *fails to do what is necessary* to meet that need. The instrument is intolerably blunt. Preference based upon race necessarily fails to respect the principle that all persons are entitled equally to the benefits and protections of the laws.

Distinct from questions concerning compensation for past injury are questions about applicants which bear upon their ability or promise to fulfill the larger social duties of the profession they seek to enter. If participation in community affairs be one of these, an admissions committee may reasonably look to the applicant's record in school or community on that front; if leadership, or industry, or self-discipline be qualities essential in that profession, the applicant may be examined, quite apart from his numerical scores, on those matters; if social service be a critical factor, the applicant's past concern for his fellows, manifested in volunteer work of different sorts, might be weighed. All these and like factors may be considered by an admissions committee, and many of these commonly are considered, both as guides in the interpretation of numerical records, and as qualities which serve as predictors of success in the school, in the profession, and in the role of citizen.

Here again, however, the weighing of such matters cannot rightly depend upon the race of the applicant. Whatever is pertinent in considering applicants of one race is pertinent in considering applicants of all races, and should be given its due weight. Racial classifications by themselves are, as the Supreme Court said in another context, "obviously irrelevant and invidious." [*Goss v. Board of Education*, 373 U.S. 687 (1963).]

The third step of the Washington Court's argument, I conclude, collapses upon scrutiny. For the test proposed by the Court itself—that the racial classification employed be necessary for the accomplishment of a compelling state purpose, though not stiff enough in fact, is too stiff to be met by the Law School's system of preferential admissions. Some of the interests served by that preferential system are not compelling in the required sense, some are not compelling in any sense, and of the one that is compelling it cannot be said that the system proposed is necessary for its accomplishment.

Of those who would defend preferential admissions by race, the Washington Supreme Court has been the most cogent. Yet the argument of that Court, I submit, proves unsuccessful at every critical point.

Some final notes on the counterproductivity of racial preference:

(1) Systems of preferential admission do not integrate, they *disinte-grate* the races. However much the advocates of such systems may hope for ultimate integration (though some may not share the integrationist ideal), the consequence of such systems in practice is ever greater attention to race, agitation about race. The invidious consideration of ethnicity in inappropriate contexts results in rewards and penalties generally thought to be unfair, undeserved. And all with focus on race. No prescription for long-term disharmony among races could be surer of success.

(2) Achieving racial proportionality in the professions through the consideration of race in professional school admissions, even where intellectual and other pertinent considerations are counterindicative, must result in the tendency, at least statistical, to yield minority group professionals less well qualified, less respected, less trusted than their counterparts in the majority. That is a great disservice to minority groups, stigmatizing their members in a most unfortunate way. "I wouldn't hit a dog with some of the minority students I've seen," says Dr. Charles DeLeon, a black psychiatrist at Case Western Reserve University Hospital, "and I have an idea that you honkies are taking in these dummies so that eight years from now you'll be able to turn around and say, 'Look how bad they all turned out.'" [*The New York Times*, April 7, 1974.]

Results on bar examinations have been painful. In Michigan, for example, in the summer of 1971, results showed a passing rate of 71 per cent for white candidates, 17 per cent for black candidates. Some contend that such discrepancies, also encountered elsewhere, are due to the hidden racial bias of the bar exams. The measures may indeed be faulty; but it is unlikely that their flaws fully explain so large a discrepancy. Bar exams are given after three years of law school, the examination papers identified and graded by number, not name. It is probable that poorly prepared minority students, admitted preferentially to law schools, receive a sympathetic consideration in classes that is not possible in the grading of bar examination papers. The general suitability of bar examinations is now much discussed. Justice Douglas joins the National Bar Association (composed of black lawyers) in proposing their abolition. Whatever is necessary to evaluate candidates for the bar in a racially neutral way must be done, of course. But if, on such reasonable measures of performance as there are, preferential admission has distinctly invidious results, it is likely to do much damage to the minority it aims to assist.

(3) One consequence of preferential admissions programs is certain: fully qualified minority group professionals come to be viewed by many, of all races, as having gained their professional positions through favor by virtue of their race. No matter their excellence; it will be suspected that their credentials were received on a double, lower standard. It is a cruel result.

The cruelty comes clear in this statement by Prof. Thomas Sowell, educated in Harlem, now associate professor of economics at UCLA:

> the actual harm done by quotas is far greater than having a few incompetent people here and there—and the harm that will actually be done will be harm primarily to the *black* population. What all the arguments and campaigns for quotas are really saying, loud and clear, is that *black people just don't have it*, and that they will have to be *given* something in order to have something. The devastating impact of this message on black people—particularly black young people—will outweight any few extra jobs that may result from this strategy. Those black people who are already competent, and who could be instrumental in producing more competence among the rising generation, will be completely undermined, as black becomes synonymous—in the minds of black and white alike— with incompetence, and black achievement becomes synonymous with charity or payoffs.
>
> *Black Education, Myths and Tragedies*

The counterproductivity of racial preference should not be surprising. The health of the body politic depends upon a widely shared confidence by its members that public process will be governed by a few very basic principles—among them, that the laws, however imperfect, will apply to all persons equally. Any device that seeks to remedy a sickness in that body by tinkering with its basal metabolism may be expected to do damage that far outweighs its good effects.

JAMES W. NICKEL

Preferential Policies in Hiring and Admissions: A Jurisprudential Approach

This Article discusses some of the troublesome policy issues [1] that arise in connection with preferential policies that are designed to assist blacks and other victims of hardship and discrimination. In dismissing the case of Marco DeFunis Jr. on mootness grounds,[2] the Supreme Court disappointed those who had hoped for a definitive ruling on these matters and insured that the issues involved would be discussed for a while longer. There is still much to be said.

Preferential hiring [3] and admissions policies give an advantage in competitions for jobs or places in educational institutions to members of particular groups. The most common use of preferential policies in the United States has been to provide special educational and employment opportunities for veterans,[4] but the recent controversy over preferential policies has to do with their use in recent years to provide special opportunities to blacks and members of other disadvantaged groups. The advantage conferred on the preferred group may be very small (as it is when

Reprinted from *Columbia Law Review*, Vol. 75 (1975), 534–558 and reprinted with the permission of the author and the publisher.

Work on this paper was supported by a grant from the National Endowment for the Humanities. I am grateful to Charles Frankel, Kent Greenawalt, Virginia Held and Steve Munzer for their contributions to the improvement of this paper.

[1] This Article deals primarily with the policy justifications for, and objections to, preferential policies. Statutory and constitutional constraints may be adverted to, but will not be developed in the discussion below. For an example of a statutory barrier to the use of preferential policies, see Title VII of the Civil Rights Act of 1964, 42 U.S.C. § 2000e–2 (1970).

[2] DeFunis v. Odegaard, 416 U.S. 312 (1974).

[3] For linguistic economy I will take "hiring" to include matters of promotion and retention, although I recognize that preference in promotion and retention may involve different issues from preference in original appointment.

[4] For a history of preferential policies for veterans in public employment, see LIBRARY OF CONGRESS REPORT FOR HOUSE COMM. ON VETERANS' AFFAIRS, 84TH CONG., 1ST SESS., THE PROVISION OF FEDERAL BENEFITS FOR VETERANS 258–65 (Comm. Print No. 171, 1955). The Veterans' Preference Act of 1944, ch. 287, 58 Stat. 387, codified as 5 U.S.C. §§ 2108, 3309 (1972), gives a ten percent bonus on federal civil service examinations to disabled veterans and a five percent bonus to other veterans.

the policy is to give preference to a member of the group only when he or she is as well qualified as any other candidate), or it may be very large (as it is when persons who are not members of the group are not even considered for the position).[5] To hire or admit a person on a preferential basis is to do more than to use special investigative measures to determine, in a case where an applicant has an unusual history or culture, how well his qualifications and potential measure up to that of other applicants.[6] It is rather to use a lower standard in his case which will make it easier for him to succeed.

The use of preferential policies is sometimes accompanied by the use of quotas, and what I have to say about preferential policies will apply in part to quotas as well. A quota, in this context, is a numerical goal or requirement for the hiring or admission of members of specified groups within a certain time or until a certain percentage is reached. Quotas can be used independently of preferential policies in order to provide stimulus for and evidence of nondiscrimination—for example, if the only action required to meet the quota is to stop discriminating and hire the best candidates. Although quotas are sometimes used in these ways, they are more typically used in connection with preferential policies, and this is one of the main reasons why many find quotas objectionable. Hence, if one succeeded in providing a defense of preferential policies, one would thereby succeed in eliminating one of the main objections to quotas. Insofar as quotas involve additional problems such as inflexibility or a threat to institutional autonomy, the following discussion will not provide a defense of their use.

It is important to recognize that preferential policies need not be used in combination with racial or other classifications based on inherent characteristics. One might apply them, for example, to all persons who are on welfare or who have an income below a certain level. Hence, after discussing some justifications for using preferential policies, I will divide my discussion of objections to preferential policies into two parts. The first

[5] The Veterans' Preference Act of 1944, 5 U.S.C. § 3310 (1972), specified that for certain jobs (for example, building guard, elevator operator), no nonveteran was to be considered unless no veterans were available. This is sometimes referred to as "super-preference."

[6] Justice Douglas, in his dissent in DeFunis v. Odegaard, 416 U.S. 312, 335 (1974), claims that preferential policies using racial classifications are unconstitutional, but he is quite prepared to allow law schools to use special tests and procedures to evaluate the potential and qualifications of black, Indian and other minority applicants. The point of these special tests and procedures in his view is not to give an advantage to these applicants, but simply to ensure that they are not disadvantaged by standardized evaluation procedures that do not take into account their unusual backgrounds. In practice, however, it may be difficult to determine whether the school's purpose in using racial or ethnic classifications is to correct for the bias of standardized tests or to implement preferential policies; and it was this difficulty in the case of the University of Washington Law School that led Justice Douglas to urge a remand for a new trial. *Id.* at 344.

part will discussion objections to preferential policies that have nothing to
do with the use of racial or ethnic classifications to define the preferred
group, and the second part will discuss objections that focus on the use
of racial (and ethnic) classifications. My approach, put broadly, is that
of a defender of preferential policies, but I hope that my analysis of the
issues involved will be helpful even to those who disagree. By making
needed distinctions, by exposing important premises and inferences to
scrutiny, and by illustrating how important policy considerations conflict
in this area, it may be possible to make discussions of these matters more
rational.

I. Justifications and Conceptions

It is a commonplace of political life that people often support social programs for different reasons and consequently have varying conceptions of
the proper purposes of a program. Programs which use preferential policies to increase the educational and employment opportunities available
to the poor or to disadvantaged minorities are no exception to this. Although such programs are often called *compensatory*, they are not necessarily designed to meet the requirements of compensatory justice by
providing compensation for past wrongs. To compensate is merely to
counterbalance, and the counterbalancing of disadvantages can be done for
reasons other than those of compensatory justice. One may advocate the
counterbalancing of disadvantages with special opportunities because doing this would eliminate inequities in the distribution of income—a justification in terms of distributive justice—or because it would promote the
public welfare by reducing poverty and its attendant evils, bringing about
a better utilization of our human resources, or providing personnel who
will provide needed services to the poor—justifications in terms of utility
or public welfare. The fact that programs which use preferential policies
can be conceived as means to these different ends, and hence be advocated
on different grounds, complicates discussion of the merits of such programs. Although some people may be willing to accept more than one of
these justifications, others may be bitterly opposed to any conception of
the purposes of these programs other than their own. A person who favors
the use of preferential policies on grounds of utility to provide special
educational and employment opportunities to members of disadvantaged
minorities may be strongly opposed to doing this in the name of compensatory justice, perhaps because he thinks that this would involve some
admission of guilt that he is unwilling to make, even though the actual
operation of the program is amenable to either conception. This is not to
say, of course, that the exact character of such programs is never affected
by which conception is dominant—and I will try to trace out some of

these differences—but in practice many "compensatory" programs admit of all these interpretations.

The situation is further complicated by the fact that two people who would be able to agree in most cases on which particular individuals ought to receive special opportunities may nevertheless disagree hotly over whether racial classifications can be used in dispensing these special opportunities. As a means of clarifying these matters, I will discuss the different sorts of justifications that might be offered for programs that use preferential policies, and the difficulties with each. Depending on the justification used, different groups will benefit by preferential policies, and racial, ethnic, or sexual classifications will be used with greater or lesser defensibility.

A. Compensatory Justice

To argue that programs which use preferential policies to provide greater opportunities to members of disadvantaged minorities are justifiable on grounds of compensatory justice is to argue that either the *actual* recipients or the persons that one thinks *ought* to be the recipients deserve compensation for wrongs they have suffered. Compensatory justice requires that counterbalancing benefits be provided to those individuals who have been wrongfully injured which will serve to bring them up to the level of wealth and welfare that they would now have if they had not been disadvantaged. Compensatory programs differ from redistributive programs mainly in regard to their concern with the past. Redistribution is concerned with eliminating present inequities, while compensatory justice is concerned not only with this but with providing compensation for unfair burdens borne in the past. Considerations of compensatory justice can justify a person's getting more in the present than would be fair if his past losses were not considered. For a person who has been unable to get any decent job because of discrimination, it may be feasible to make up for his past losses by using preferential policies to provide special employment opportunities. Similarly, persons denied adequate educational opportunities by racist school systems can perhaps be brought up to the level they would otherwise have reached if special educational opportunities are provided. Similar steps have often been taken to compensate veterans for opportunities lost, injuries suffered and services rendered during wartime.[7]

There are a number of difficulties involved in using considerations of

---

[7] A distinction should be drawn between compensation for services and compensation for injuries, for the concept of compensatory justice is concerned only with the latter. The special benefits provided to veterans are often compensatory in both ways; they provide compensation for services and they also provide compensation for deprivation of liberty, for being required to take great risks, and for wounds suffered, although, unlike cases of racial discrimination, injuries received in wartime are not seen as having been unfairly imposed by society upon the veteran.

compensatory justice to justify programs that use preferential policies to assist the disadvantaged. These include: (1) questions about whether compensatory benefits are owed only to those particular individuals who have been harmed substantially by discrimination and hardship or to all members of those groups that have been frequent targets of discrimination; (2) questions about whether a person who was once harmed by discrimination but who has overcome his losses through his own efforts still deserves compensation now; (3) questions about whether governments, companies, institutions and individuals have obligations to compensate losses they did not cause; and (4) questions about how far back into the past the view of compensatory justice should extend. Although I cannot undertake here the extended discussion that would be needed for an adequate exploration of these questions, the first one must be given some attention since it is crucial to how justifications in terms of compensatory justice are conceived.

It is sometimes maintained that in addition to compensatory principles that apply to individuals there are compensatory principles that create obligations between groups when one group injures another group or is unjustly enriched at the other group's expense. Paul W. Taylor, for example, argues that there is a principle of compensatory justice which requires that "[w]hen an injustice has been committed to a group of persons, some form of compensation or reparation must be made to that group." [8] In Taylor's view, a group's right to compensation does not derive from the right to compensation of individuals in that group and cannot be satisfied by only compensating those within the group who as individuals deserve compensation.[9] Furthermore, a member of a wronged group who has not personally been wronged may have a right to compensation as a member of the group.[10] Taylor's approach offers a basis for giving preference to all members of wronged groups without regard to their personal histories. Group rights to compensation are not rights against particular wrongdoers but are against society as a whole: "The obligation to offer such benefits to the group as a whole is an obligation that falls on society in general, not on any particular person. For it is society in general that through its established social practice brought upon itself the obligation." [11] Finally, Taylor thinks that "affirmative action" programs are an appropriate way for a government to discharge society's obligation to wronged groups.[12]

Although compensatory principles that apply directly to groups are frequently advocated, I personally do not find them appealing. Although

---

[8] Taylor, *Reverse Discrimination and Compensatory Justice*, 33 ANALYSIS 17 (1973). For another example of this approach, *see* Bayles, *Compensatory Reverse Discrimination in Hiring*, 2 SOCIAL THEORY AND PRACTICE 301 (1973).
[9] Taylor, *supra* note 8, at 181.
[10] *Id.* at 179.
[11] *Id.* at 180.
[12] *Id.*

there may well be moral principles that apply directly to groups, I find the principle that Taylor advocates implausible because it would unnecessarily duplicate many of the rights and obligations created by compensatory principles that apply to individuals, and would provide compensatory benefits to persons who personally have sustained no injury and therefore need not be made whole.[13] It may be desirable to offer special opportunities to, say, all young blacks, whether or not they have personally been significantly harmed by discrimination, but the justification would have to be based on considerations of redistribution, utility, or administrative convenience, not on the claim that all blacks whatever their situation, have a *right* to such benefits on grounds of compensatory justice. Another reason to avoid reliance on compensatory principles for groups in attempting to justify the use of preferential policies is that invoking such principles is likely to be question begging. Since such principles do not have established noncontroversial applications in other areas, a person who is not already committed to the desirability of compensatory programs and who is told that such programs are desirable because they satisfy the requirements of such a principle is likely to find the principle as much in need of justification as the programs it supposedly supports.

Any approach in terms of compensatory justice is likely to be controversial and problematic, but it seems to me that the least problematic approach along these lines is to suggest that the ones who have a right to compensation are those who have personally been injured by discrimination, and who have not yet been able to overcome this injury.

B. Distributive Justice

Programs using preferential policies are also conceived as a means of promoting the redistribution of income and other important benefits. This approach would claim that the justification for such programs lies in the reduction of distributive inequities that they bring about. Since good educations lead to good jobs, and good jobs provide income, security, and status, altering the ways in which educations and jobs are distributed so as to give a bigger share to the previously deprived is one way of bringing about redistribution. A concern with distributive justice is a concern with whether people have fair shares of benefits and burdens. Distributive justice does not require that all people have the same income or equally good jobs, the requirement is rather that benefits and burdens be distributed in accordance with relevant considerations such as the rights, deserts, merits, contributions and needs of the recipients. Thus, if both Jones and Smith have had adequate opportunities for self-development, and if Jones is qualified for a desirable and prestigious job as a director of an art museum, while Smith is only qualified for janitorial positions, then there

---

[13] For an elaboration of this argument, *see* Nickel, *Should Reparations be to Individuals or to Groups?*, 34 ANALYSIS 154, 160 (1974).

will be no injustice in hiring Jones as the director and Smith as the jani-
tor.[14] One who advocates redistribution on grounds of distributive justice
must argue that in spite of the fact that it is possible to justify many inequalities in terms of relevant differences, there are nonetheless many
inequalities in our society that cannot be justified. Although it is often
difficult to pinpoint these inequalities and to discern the extent to which
they reveal discrimination rather than reflect relevant distinctions, it is
clear that many distributive injustices exist in our society and that it
would be desirable to eliminate them. Many people will allow that some
persons are undeservedly poor, others undeservedly rich, and that it would
be a good thing—both on grounds of justice and of utility—to reduce
poverty. But advocates of preferential policies may not be content to
merely increase the opportunities available to those now in poverty. A
person may be getting an unjustly small amount of income even though
he is above the poverty line, and hence one might advocate the use of
preferential policies to help groups that contain many persons who are not
justly rewarded for their contributions.

Those who take this approach are likely to point to large statistical
differences between the incomes of blacks and whites or men and women
as evidence of unjustifiable inequalities.[15] It is beyond doubt that there
has been and still is discrimination in employment against blacks and
women, and that blacks and women have had fewer opportunities to develop qualifications. The difficulty, however, in arguing from such statistics
is in distinguishing the extent to which the differences derive from
discrimination rather than from other factors which may vary in strength
between sexes and among groups. When there are groups which have
different histories and cultures and emphasize different personal goals, it
is unlikely that their members will uniformly utilize the same opportunities, go into the same areas of employment, and have the same attitudes
towards vocational achievement. The ideal of having all groups represented at all levels of income and achievement in proportion to their
numbers in the country's population may therefore be unrealistic, and

---

[14] Whether it would be just for a large difference in income to accompany the difference in jobs is another matter.

[15] The kinds of statistical differences that are likely to be cited are exemplified by the
following: the median income of black families in the United States in 1972 was
59 percent of the median for white families (up from 55 percent in 1960, down
from 61 percent in 1970); the median black *college* graduate had an income in
1970 that was $160 less than that of the median white *high-school* graduate;
full-time female workers in 1970 had a median income that was nearly $4000
less than that of full-time male workers; and white women between 35 and 54
who have worked steadily since leaving school earn nearly $3000 less per year
than white men with parallel careers. E. J. KAHN, JR., THE AMERICAN PEOPLE:
THE FINDINGS OF THE 1970 CENSUS 143–45, 222 (1974). *See also* Wattenberg
& Scammon, *Black Progress and Liberal Rhetoric*, 55 COMMENTARY 35, 36
(April, 1973).

perhaps even unappealing. This ideal, which might be called the ideal of proportional equality, has been criticized by many of those who are opposed to preferential policies for women or blacks, but the case for the use of preferential policies does not stand or fall with its acceptance or rejection.[16]

C. Utility

Redistribution of important benefits may also be advocated because it is believed that the public welfare, on the whole and over the long term, can be promoted by reducing poverty and inequality. On this approach a program using preferential policies to increase educational and employment opportunities would be seen as one means of promoting the public welfare by eliminating poverty and its attendant evils and by eliminating the sort of economic inequality that leads to resentment and strife. Extreme poverty is objectionable to one who is concerned with utility because of what it involves, namely unmet needs and suffering, and because of what it leads to, namely crime, family strife, lack of self-respect and social discontent. Economic inequality of the sort that we currently have, with wide extremes of income and wealth and with some groups largely concentrated at the bottom of the economic ladder is objectionable under this view because it perpetuates stereotypes, deprives people in low-income groups of role models, fosters lack of self-respect, and makes understanding and cooperation between groups more difficult.[17] As long as there are, for example, few black doctors, lawyers, or executives, it will be easy for people, blacks included, to believe that blacks generally lack the abilities to fill these positions, and the maintenance of such belief can only perpetuate inequality with its untoward consequences.

Considerations about unmet needs and suffering may only require

---

[16] Thomas Nagel, in an important recent essay on preferential policies, *Equal Treatment and Compensatory Discrimination*, 2 PHILOSOPHY AND PUBLIC AFFAIRS 348 (1973) suggests that preferential policies for members of disadvantaged groups cannot be justified on grounds of distributive justice but only on grounds of utility because in order to show that differences in income between groups involve injustices one would need "the aid of premises about the source of unequal qualifications between members of different groups. The more speculative the premises, the weaker the argument." *Id.* at 359. Professor Nagel thus confines his arguments about justice to an attempt to show that justice permits the use of preferential policies even if it does not require it. I agree that it is impossible to show that every statistical difference between groups reveals an injustice, but I doubt that it is really very speculative to suggest that many of the differences in income between blacks and whites or between women and men are unjust and derive from the discrimination that keeps many blacks and women from fully developing their abilities and from fully benefiting from the abilities they have. We do not know what statistical difference there would be, if any, between groups within a just distribution, but it seems certain that the differences would be much smaller than they now are.

[17] *See* H. GANS, MORE EQUALITY 20–24 (1973).

the elimination of extreme poverty, but considerations about the bad effects of economic inequality—especially the sort that sees some groups concentrated at the lower levels—suggest stronger measures to facilitate upward mobility for those at lower levels. Hence, moving towards proportional representation might be desirable on grounds of utility even if it is not required by distributive justice.

A much-emphasized connection between utility and the use of preferential policies is found in the need of disadvantaged minorities for persons who can and will provide them with legal and medical services. Thomas Nagel puts this as follows:

> Suppose for example that there is a need for a great increase in the number of black doctors, because the health needs of the black community are unlikely to be met otherwise. And suppose that at the present average level of premedical qualifications among black applicants, it would require a huge expansion of total medical school enrollment to supply the desirable absolute number of black doctors without adopting differential admissions standards. Such an expansion would be unacceptable either because of its cost or because it would produce a total supply of doctors, black and white, much greater than the society requires. This is a strong argument for accepting reverse discrimination, not on grounds of justice but on grounds of social utility. (In addition, there is the salutary effect on the aspirations and expectations of other blacks, from the visibility of exemplars in formerly inaccessible positions.) [18]

This kind of argument is sometimes attacked on the grounds that it falsely supposes that only black doctors or lawyers can serve blacks effectively, that only Chicano doctors or lawyers can serve Chicanos effectively, and so forth. But one who uses this argument does not need to make this strong supposition; all he need assume is that blacks who become doctors or lawyers are *more likely* to help meet the medical needs of the black community than whites who become doctors or lawyers. It is clear, for example, that there would be no impassioned outcry if a state medical school in Nebraska gave preference to natives because they are more likely to stay in the state to practice, or to persons who promise to practice in an area with a shortage of doctors. The objection to increasing the availability of needed medical and legal services through preferential policies ends up simply being an objection to giving such preferences on the basis of race; it would not work against preferences given on the basis of where one was from, on the basis of an agreement to serve in a particular area, or on the basis of particular skills such as an ability to speak Spanish fluently.

I have discussed some of the utilitarian benefits which are thought to follow from the use of preferential policies to increase the educational and employment opportunities available to disadvantaged minorities, but on any utilitarian approach these benefits must be balanced against the

[18] Nagel, *supra* note 16, at 361.

accompanying costs. Taking money or other benefits away from those who have much in order to promote the public good by giving these benefits to the disadvantaged is not without its costs. The rich person now has some of his money taken to finance job programs, or the young person who finds it difficult or impossible to get into professional school because of programs designed to increase the number of economically disadvantaged persons applying or accepted will not normally be made happier or better off as a result. There may also be attendant social costs, for the rich person may have invested the appropriated money in a way that would have benefited more people, or the young professional school applicant may have been more qualified. These costs cannot be ignored; utilitarian advocates of preferential policies must claim that they are outweighed by greater benefits. This is probably true in many cases, but judgments about this depend on particular facts and must be made in particular cases.

D. Comparisons

In practice, at least, the differences between programs which take compensation for past wrongs as their goal and programs which take creation of a more equitable distribution or promotion of utility as their goal are not likely to be very apparent. The point at which differences are most likely to appear is in the criteria that are used to determine which applicants are eligible for preference. If the criteria pertain to the discrimination and wrongful treatment that the applicant suffered, the inequitable position that he presently is in, or the good that would be done by increasing his opportunities, then the program could be seen to be, respectively, compensatory, redistributive, or utilitarian. But preferential programs typically select recipients on the basis of gross criteria such as having a low income or membership in a disadvantaged group.[19] Since the groups selected by these gross criteria overlap substantially, but not completely, with those who have been harmed by discrimination, or who are in an inequitable position, or whose betterment would promote utilitarian objectives, the primary goal of programs based on preferential policies is often not apparent from the selection criteria they use.

    One useful way of comparing the different conceptions of the goals of preferential programs is in terms of whether they can justify, and if so, how they justify, giving preference to *all* applicants who are members of specified disadvantaged groups. If one accepted a compensatory principle that applied directly to wronged groups then one would probably be willing to advocate, for example, preferences for all black applicants regardless of their personal histories. If, however, one held that compensatory principles applied only to individuals then one would advocate pref-

---

[19] At the University of Washington Law School, preference was given to those who were black, Chicano, American Indian, or Filipino. 416 U.S. at 323.

erence only for those black applicants who had personally been harmed by discrimination. On this latter approach, preference for all black applicants would be harder to justify, and could only be done on the basis of a claim that *nearly all* black applicants have been harmed by discrimination and that it is therefore administratively efficient and not intolerably unfair simply to prefer all black applicants.

A similar contrast can be drawn between an approach which holds that the ideal of proportional representation expresses the requirements of distributive justice—and which correspondingly requires that *any* member of an underrepresented group should be preferred, whether or not he personally is in an inequitable position—and an approach which holds that inequities should be recognized and dealt with only in individual cases. The latter approach in terms of distributive justice would find it more difficult to justify preferring *all* female applicants, for example, and could do this only on the basis of a claim that the vast majority of female applicants have been subject to distributive injustices and that it is therefore administratively efficient and not intolerably unfair to prefer all female applicants.

If one is not inclined to accept compensatory principles that apply directly to groups or to believe that proportional equality is required by distributive justice, one will then have to justify preferences for all members of disadvantaged groups in terms of the administrative advantages of doing so. It may be somewhat easier, however, to justify preference for all members of disadvantaged groups on the utilitarian approach. If progress toward proportional equality is desirable on utilitarian grounds, even if not required by distributive justice, the conferral of a preference to all applicants (or all promising applicants) from groups that are substantially underrepresented at higher levels of income and achievement may be justifiable. If the utilitarian approach, however, concentrated on poverty, unmet needs and serving the needs of the poor rather than on inequality per se, then to qualify for preference one would have to be poor. Approaches which emphasize proportional representation (whether they do so on grounds of distributive justice or utility) will sometimes conflict with approaches that emphasize the elimination of poverty and unmet needs. In law school admissions, for example, those who are concerned with proportional representation for blacks in the legal profession may want to admit middle class black applicants on a preferential basis because they often have better educational backgrounds and hence may have a better chance of succeeding in law school and as lawyers. Those who are concerned with poverty and unmet needs, however, may be opposed to extending preferences to these applicants and want to restrict preferences to low-income blacks or to low-income applicants generally.

An interesting difference between the approaches in terms of justice and the approach in terms of utility is in the nature of the recipient's claim to preference. Viewed as a matter of justice, the preference is claimed as something that satisfies the recipient's right to compensation or his right to a fair share. Viewed as a matter of utility, the claim is not that the recipient personally has a right to preference; it is rather that the public good can be promoted by preferring him in awarding opportunities.

II. General Objections to Preferential Policies

In this section and the next I discuss two quite different sorts of objections to preferential policies. The objections discussed in this section apply to any sort of preferential policy for anyone—whether it be for blacks and other minority group members, veterans, or persons with physical handicaps. The objections discussed in the next section go to preferential policies that define the target group in racial, ethnic, or sexual terms.

A. Problems of Incompetency

The use of preferential policies to achieve important social goals rests on the recognition that the distributive effects of hiring and admissions practices are very important in determining the character of the overall distribution of benefits and burdens, and on the recognition that these practices can be altered slightly in order to bring about more desirable results. Preferential policies utilize and alter the distributive practices and effects of existing institutions. In a similar way, special home loan programs altered the distributive effects of the housing market in favor of veterans, and special scholarship programs altered the distributive effects of the educational system in favor of veterans. But preferential hiring and admissions policies do more than provide the money needed to enter the competition; they alter the rules of the competition so that veterans have a better chance of success. And that is why they are more controversial.

Insofar as the use of preferential policies led to the admission or hiring of unqualified persons, significant reductions in the efficiency and productivity of companies and institutions would be likely to follow. Those who are opposed to preferential policies often raise the specter of illiterate students, highway patrolmen who do not know how to drive, teachers who cannot handle children and surgeons who remove tonsils by cutting throats. Although these dangers are easily exaggerated, the importance of competent personnel to institutional efficiency must be recognized, and it can be readily conceded that preferential policies should be restricted to those who are adequately qualified, or who, with the training provided, can become adequately qualified for the position sought. This will mean that if a person is unable to perform the task adequately, then preferential policies will not apply to him with respect to the position. Although there will be cases in which it will be difficult to decide the degree of competence that is adequate, I think that the criterion of adequate competence can serve as a useful general limit for preferential treatment.[20] A narrower limit may be required with regard to jobs where small differences in competence within the range of adequate competence can make a great deal of difference in the level of performance, and hence in the level of institutional efficiency. For gardeners, postal clarks, X-ray technicians and sales personnel, adequate competence may be sufficient; but in the case of surgeons, professional athletes and airline pilots, small differences in competence can make a great difference, respectively, in lives saved, games won, or crashes averted, and hence the scope allowed to preferential policies should be more restricted. One advantage of the minimal preferential policy—hire the preferred person only when he or she is as well qualified as any other candidate (a policy that only serves when a tiebreaker is needed)—is that it does not lead to the selection of a less qualified candidate.

B. Problems of Unfair Burdens

A second objection is that preferential policies unfairly place the burden of helping those who are preferred on those who are thereby excluded. Thus, it might be argued that putting the burden of helping to compensate and meet the needs of veterans on those who are excluded from government jobs by policies which prefer veterans is an unfair way of distributing the cost of a legitimate goal. A well-qualified nonveteran who had hoped to get a government job but who was denied it because of a policy which gives veterans an advantage may feel that too much of the cost of helping veterans was placed on him. This person may feel that providing benefits from taxes—where the cost can be spread among many taxpayers—is preferable as a means of helping veterans to programs which impose the burden on a few people whose opportunities are reduced by preferential policies.[21]

The problem here is one of justice in the spreading of burdens rather than one of total costs. A policy which prefers veterans does not result in any more persons being excluded than a normal policy; the only difference is in who is excluded. The complaint of those excluded will have to be that it is somehow worse to exclude them and to reduce their opportunities than to do the same to the veterans who would not have gotten the job were it not for the preferential policy.

If we assume that preference is only given to adequately qualified candidates, and hence that both preferential and non-preferential policies

[20] The courts have read such a limitation into veterans' preference legislation as constitutionally mandated. See, e.g., Opinion of the Justices, 324 Mass. 736, 85 N.E.2d 238 (1949); Commonwealth ex rel. Graham v. Schmid, 333 Pa. 568, 3 A.2d 701 (1938).

[21] This kind of complaint was made with respect to preference for veterans in promotions in McNamara v. Director of Civil Service, 330 Mass. 22, 25–26, 110 N.E.2d 840, 842–43 (1952).

are compatible with the requirements of efficiency, what is it that makes it worse when those excluded are persons who are better qualified than some of those hired? An answer to this question will obviously refer to the better qualifications of the persons excluded by the preferential policy, but why is it worse to exclude better qualified persons than to deprive less qualified candidates of preferences indicated by considerations of compensation, distributive justice, or utility? One possibility is to say that better qualifications confer upon their holders a prima facie right to be chosen in preference to anyone who is less qualified. This claim is plausible because, other things being equal, the best way of distributing jobs is to give them to the best qualified candidate. Although this is normally the best way, it does not seem to be the only permissible way. If in a case where small differences in competence had little impact on institutional efficiency, a company chose to save money and effort by hiring the first adequately qualified person who applied or to select among the adequately qualified candidates by lot, no one would have good grounds for complaint.[22] It is unclear whether these cases show that there is no right to be hired in preference to less qualified candidates, or simply that this right is one that can be overridden by considerations of efficiency in some cases, but these cases do at least show that the policy of selecting in accordance with the best qualifications is not sacrosanct.

Suppose, however, that one recognized a prima facie right to be hired in preference to all less qualified candidates. To recognize such a right would be to recognize an obligation on the part of hiring officers to award, other things being equal, jobs to the best qualified candidates. The question then arises whether things *are* equal in the case of veterans—that is, whether there are other considerations that can override this obligation. If there are such considerations, they would pertain to the special needs that veterans have, to the utility of a smooth reintegration of veterans into the economy, and to the fact that many veterans deserve compensation for their services and sacrifices. These are considerations which personnel officers do not normally consider, but the question is whether they should be considered.

A proper judgment on this issue depends, I think, on the recognition that when one awards a good job, more is usually at stake than finding a capable employee. One is also awarding or denying a strategic benefit that often has great consequences for a person's long-term levels of income, security and status. Since the decisions of personnel officers often have this effect, it may be appropriate for them to consider matters that are relevant

---

[22] Interestingly, Justice Douglas suggests in DeFunis that law schools might select by lot among well qualified applicants so as to insure that all groups were represented without using racial classifications. DeFunis v. Odegaard, 416 U.S. 312, 344 (1974). This approach might be especially appealing in highly competitive situations where insignificant differences in text scores can, under normal admissions procedures, make great differences in one's chances of being accepted.

to the proper distribution of income, security, and status. When two or more benefits tend to go together—for example, a job and a good and secure income—to consider only those matters that are relevant to whether a person should get one of these is to award or deny one of the benefits on the basis of an incomplete consideration of all the relevant factors.[23] When a society succeeds in providing many paths to good and secure incomes, then personnel officers may be justified in generally ignoring the distributive effects that their decisions have and concentrating on job qualifications. But in cases where a denial of a job, or a pattern of denying jobs, is likely to have very bad consequences for the individual or for society, it may be desirable for personnel officers to take these broader consequences into account.

My presupposition here is that hiring officers, and those who create the policies that guide them, are morally obligated to promote desirable social goals when this can be done at slight institutional cost. I think that this applies to both private and public institutions, but one who disagrees with this can still allow that there is such an obligation for public institutions and for those private institutions that are committed to serving the public good—and this will cover most of the institutions where questions about the desirability of preferential policies have arisen. It is not uncommon in any institution for considerations other than those of qualifications to be taken into account in awarding jobs. Such considerations come into play when it must be decided whether to retain an older employee who has ceased to be very useful to the company but who would find it very difficult or impossible to find another source of income. These considerations also come into play when it must be decided whether to give a job to a qualified handicapped person or to an equally qualified applicant who is not handicapped. Knowing that the scarcity of such jobs may make denying the job to the handicapped person tantamount to denying him a good income and a basis for self-respect, personnel officers are likely to take this into account. In public employment, legislation has dictated that this be done with regard to disabled veterans. The Veterans Preference Act of 1944 gave disabled veterans a ten point advantage in competition for some jobs, and superpreference in others.[24]

Similar considerations apply with regard to nondisabled veterans, but with somewhat less force. In a postwar period, jobs are likely to be scarce because of production cutbacks in war affected industries in the face of an oversupply of labor due to the many returning veterans and the workers who have been laid-off in those industries. In these circumstances,

[23] This point is made by Nagel, *supra* note 16, at 357, in regard to the connection between allocating professional education to the intelligent and awarding the high incomes that go along with being a professional. Although a high intelligence may be a good reason for getting the education, it does not seem to be a good reason for getting the high income.

[24] *See* notes 4–5 *supra*.

a veteran who spent several years as a soldier when he might otherwise have been getting an education or job experience may have special difficulties in getting a good job and the good income that goes with it. Denying such a person a job may be tantamount to denying him a decent income for a period. Not only are veterans likely to have difficulty in getting decent jobs and decent incomes in the period after a war, they are also likely to have a special claim to such benefits because of their services and sacrifices. These are considerations which hiring policies and hiring officers may appropriately take into account.

Even if it is allowed that it is sometimes appropriate for personnel officers to take the special needs and claims of veterans into account, one may continue to hold the view that to place the burden of helping veterans on the nonveterans whose opportunities are reduced by a preferential policy is to place the cost of a legitimate objective on too small a group. Because jobs are such strategic benefits, unfairness in the allocation of job opportunities must be taken seriously. Although one might argue that the excluded nonveterans owe something to veterans because of the services and sacrifices of the veterans, or because of the opportunities that nonveterans had and which veterans missed, this is also true of other nonveterans—not just those who happen to be now competing for jobs—and hence it provides no justification for putting a burden on only some of the nonveterans.

One way to reduce the force of this charge of unfairness would be to combine preferential policies with measures that will increase the total number of jobs available, thereby increasing job opportunities and reducing the loss of opportunities that nonveterans suffer because of preferential policies for veterans. This could be done, for example, by using tax money to create more government jobs, to increase jobs in the private sector, and to provide retirement benefits that will encourage early retirement. Preferential policies might also be restricted to a certain percentage of the jobs or promotions in a given department or bureau so as to insure that nonveterans will not be at a disadvantage with regard to all opportunities within that agency.

Even if all these policies were followed there would probably still be some unfairness in the allocation of the cost of helping veterans. Rather than trying to deny this, it is probably more plausible to argue that the fact that there is some unfairness in the distribution of this burden does not settle the question of whether using preferential policies is acceptable or wise. In order to meet its obligation to veterans, society imposes a greater part of the cost of doing this on some individuals than on others. It is not that these nonveterans owe more than other nonveterans; it is rather that society requires them to live with reduced opportunities in order to meet its obligations.[25] Many wise and acceptable policies involve

[25] This point is made by Thomson, *Preferential Hiring*, 2 PHILOSOPHY AND PUBLIC AFFAIRS 369 (1973).

placing burdens on individuals where similar burdens are not placed on all individuals or even on all individuals who are similar in relevant ways. Fighting a war, building a dam or highway and protecting public access to a beach through zoning restrictions are all activities that inevitably place heavier burdens on some individuals than others. Weaker but more equitable means are preferable if they will do the same job in the same time, but this is seldom the case. The advantage of preferential policies is that they are fast and effective as a means of shifting patterns of distribution, and this, no doubt, is the key to their appeal in the instant context of the use of such policies for blacks and other disadvantaged groups.[26]

III. Objections to Preferential Policies That Use Racial, Ethnic, or Sexual Classifications

Much of the discrimination that blacks have suffered in this country can be viewed as the result of preferential policies that prefer whites, and hence many people are likely to hold the view that using preferential policies in combination with racial classifications is a very dangerous business. The focus of this section is on the objections that are likely to be made by people who feel that racial, ethnic and sexual preferences are dangerous. In order to make the discussion concrete and to avoid the repeated use of lists such as "blacks, women, Chicanos and Indians," I will take as my example preferential policies for blacks.

A. Race as an Irrelevant Characteristic

When a black person is preferentially awarded a job, and a nonblack person is thereby denied it, both the award and the denial seem to be on the basis of an irrelevant characteristic, namely the race of the candidates. Awarding and denying benefits on the basis of such an irrelevant characteristic seems to be no different in principle—even though the motives may be more defensible—from traditional sorts of discrimination against blacks and in favor of whites. Preferential hiring or admissions policies for blacks are therefore likely to be charged with being discriminatory, even though they are done in the name of rectifying discrimination and other evils. If one condemns the original discrimination against blacks because it was based on an irrelevant characteristic, and hence was unreasonable, one is likely to be charged with inconsistency if one now advocates policies that award and deny benefits on the basis of the same characteristic.

---

[26] One's willingness to use preferential policies to remedy problems of injustice, poverty and inequality will probably depend in large measure on one's beliefs about how bad the problems are and on how fast they should be remedied. For a discussion of these matters, see Held, *Reasonable Progress and Self-Respect*, 57 MONIST 12 (1973).

The defect in this charge is that it mistakenly assumes that race is the justification for preferential treatment. This is only apparently so. If preference is given to blacks because of past discrimination and present poverty, the basis for this preference is not that these people are black but rather that they are likely to have been victimized by discrimination, to have fewer benefits and more burdens than is fair, to be members of an underrepresented group, or to be the sorts of persons that can help public institutions meet the needs of those who are now poorly served. Being black does not itself have any relevancy to these goals, but the facts which are associated with being black often do in the present context.[27]

B. Administrative Convenience as Inadequate Justification

When this defect is pointed out, the person arguing that racially based preferential policies are discriminatory may formulate a new version of his objection. This version recognizes that the *justifying basis* for preferential policies is discrimination, injustice, unmet needs, and so forth, but it notes that being black is often a necessary condition for receiving preference and therefore forms the *administrative basis* for preferential programs. Those who defend the use of race as part of the administrative basis allow that race in itself is irrelevant, but they assert that the use of racial classifications in administering preferential policies is justified by the high correlation between being black and having the characteristics that form the justifying basis. Having noted this, the critic of preferential policies using racial classifications is likely to point out that a similar claim was and is made by racists.[28] Racists claim that they do not treat blacks worse than whites simply because they are black, but rather because blacks are lazy or untrustworthy or have some other characteristic that makes them undeserving of good treatment. Like the advocates of preferential policies for blacks, racists deny that they base differential treatment on an irrelevant characteristic such as race. They claim that the justifying basis for their differential treatment of blacks is something relevant such as being lazy or untrustworthy, not something irrelevant such as race. Race only forms, the racist might say, the administrative basis for his policy of treating blacks worse than whites. The critic of preference on the basis of racial classifications will argue, therefore, that an approach to the justifications of preferential policies which distinguishes between the justifying basis—for example, having been harmed by discrimination—and the ad-

---

[27] This argument was advanced in Nickel, *Discrimination and Morally Relevant Characteristics*, 32 ANALYSIS 113 (1972). A somewhat similar argument was recently offered by Karst and Horowitz in *Affirmative Action and Equal Protection*, 60 VA. L. REV. 955 (1974). They claim that what should count as "merit" is a function of social needs, and that in a context where there is a need for rapid and substantial integration one's race can be part of one's "merit."

[28] This criticism was made by Bayles, *Reparations to Wronged Groups*, 33 ANALYSIS 182 (1973).

ministrative basis—for example, being a low-income black—makes the same mistake as the racist since the form of reasoning is exactly the same. Thus, the objection continues, if the advocate of preferential policies can use this distinction between the justifying and the administrative bases to show that he is not practicing invidious discrimination, then so can the racist. But since this defense will not work for the racist, neither will it work for the defender of preferential policies.

But there is a way of distinguishing these cases, and it can be seen by comparing the premises that are used to connect being black with having a relevant characteristic. When these premises are compared, it becomes apparent that for the racist to defend his position, he has to make claims which can be proven to be erroneous about the correlation between being black and having some relevant defect such as being lazy or untrustworthy, while the defender of racially administered preferential policies can make a plausible case without using erroneous premises. Hence, one important way of distinguishing justifiable from unjustifiable uses of racial classifications is in terms of the soundness of the alleged correlation between race and a relevant characteristic.

It is possible, however, that there are cases in which a racist can find genuine correlations between race and a relevant deficiency that will serve his exclusionary purposes. He might claim that blacks are more likely than whites to have a criminal record, no high school diploma, or chronic health problems.[29] But a higher percentage of some relevant deficiency in a particular group does not ordinarily justify excluding all members of that group without considering whether a member personally has that deficiency. Excluding all members of a group on the basis of a correlation between membership and having a relevant deficiency would be justifiable only if (1) the correlation between membership and having the deficiency was very high, and (2) it was so difficult to check for the relevant deficiency itself in individual cases that it would be unacceptably wasteful and inefficient to do so.[30] These conditions are seldom met, and they are

---

[29] There is another reason to avoid using correlations such as these to exclude blacks—namely that these correlations may themselves be the result of racist practices and institutions.

[30] "It is conceivable, for example, that individual examination could have been employed to segregate out those Japanese-Americans who presented a real danger of espionage and sabotage during World War II. But in light of the presumed threat of an imminent invasion, such a time-consuming process might well have been viewed as self-defeating. Hence, this procedure, though avoiding the racial classification, did not appear to be a viable alternative to the exclusion of all Japanese from the West Coast military zones.

"The decision whether a particular alternative is truly feasible cannot be made by resort to a general formula. One can, of course, point to such factors as manpower requirements, financial costs, and time demands as relevant considerations. Furthermore, as the distinction becomes more invidious and the hardship imposed becomes more severe, one can expect the courts to demand greater sac-

certainly not met with regard to correlations between race and characteristics such as having a criminal record, no high school diploma, or chronic health problems—both because the correlations are not high enough and because the relevant deficiencies themselves are not difficult to identify.[31]

Suppose, however, that a racist was able to show that his policy of excluding all blacks was in fact based on a genuine correlation between race and a difficult-to-identify relevant deficiency. Would we then say that his practice of excluding all blacks on that basis was justifiable? To make this even clearer (and even less likely to occur), suppose that there was no question about whether the correlation was high enough or about whether having the relevant deficiency was always sufficient to disqualify one for the position. The question, then, would be whether it would be permissible to exclude all blacks because of a deficiency that statistical sampling revealed, say, 90 percent of them to have.

One might reply that the exclusion of all blacks would not be permissible because it would not be unacceptably wasteful and inefficient to use the difficult-to-identify characteristic itself as the criterion. In *DeFunis*, Justice Douglas dismissed the objection to the administrative inconvenience of the individualized admissions procedures he prefers: "Such a program might be less convenient administratively than simply sorting students by race, but we have never held administrative convenience to justify racial discrimination."[32] Were the racist to use individual tests or investigations to exclude only the 90 percent that had the relevant deficiency, then he would exclude all unqualified blacks without unneces-

---

rifices on the part of the state. But the resolution of this balance in any one decision cannot be given any greater objective precision."
Developments in the Law—Equal Protection, 82 Harv. L. Rev. 1065, 1102 (1969) (citations omitted).

[31] It is likely that the modern day racist will use correlations between race and a relevant deficiency in a different way. Instead of using them to justify a policy of exclusion by race (which is now legally dangerous), the racist is likely to fasten upon a correlation between race and a relevant deficiency, overemphasize the importance of that deficiency, and hereby exclude a disproportionate number of blacks. This method of excluding most black applicants will require the racist to exclude some whites, but he may be willing to pay this price. One does not need to use racial classifications in order to discriminate against blacks. For an interesting discussion of such "facially innocent criteria," see Fiss, A *Theory of Fair Employment Laws*, 38 U. Chi. L. Rev. 235 (1970). *See also* Blumrosen, *Strangers in Paradise: Griggs v. Duke Power Co. and the Concept of Employment Discrimination*, 71 Mich. L. Rev. 59 (1972).

[32] 416 U.S. at 341 (Douglas, J., dissenting). *See also* Justice Brennan's dissenting opinion in Kahn v. Shevin, 416 U.S. 351, 360 (1974). While granting that the state has a compelling interest in providing remedial measures to ameliorate the poor economic positions of many widows, Justice Brennan would find unconstitutional a Florida statute granting a tax exemption to *all* widows since less overinclusive measures were readily available. The state, in his view, could permissibly exempt those widows who earn incomes or possess assets up to specified amounts indicating actual victimization by past economic discrimination.

sarily excluding the qualified 10 percent. In the same way, the objection runs, the advocate of preferential policies could achieve all of his desired results if he were to predicate preference in education and employment directly on relevant characteristics such as having been harmed by discrimination, being unjustly poor, or having unmet needs. By doing this he would give preference to only those persons who had these characteristics. This practice would have the advantage not only of excluding blacks without these characteristics, but also of including nonblacks who had them.[33]

The question, then, is whether the price of excluding that ten percent of the blacks who are qualified for the job that the racist is awarding, and of excluding those nonblacks who also sought to get preference is too high a price to pay for administrative efficiency. Efficiency in administering large-scale programs requires that detailed investigations of individual cases be kept to a minimum, and this means that many allocative decisions will have to be made on the basis of gross but easily discernible characteristics. By giving preferences to all applicants who are members of certain disadvantaged groups, administrative costs can be kept to a minimum. The alternative is to investigate on an individual basis. The expense of such investigations might be reduced by inviting applicants to provide information about their personal history as part of their application materials if they think they deserve special consideration because of past discrimination, hardships, injustice, or present need. But this would merely reduce, not eliminate, the costs of investigation because some check on the authenticity of these claims would be needed. An approach of this sort might be workable and desirable in some circumstances, but it would be expensive both for the applicant and for the institution processing the applications. For this reason, there are considerable advantages in using gross indicators, including racial, ethnic and sexual ones, as indicators of the presence of the characteristics that provide the justifying basis.

C. Problems of Stigmatization and Loss of Self-Respect

One might argue that it is permissible to use gross indicators such as being an honorably-discharged veteran, but not ones such as being black. This, no doubt, is Justice Douglas' position, since he has often expressed his willingness to allow legislatures considerable latitude, outside of the racial and First Amendment areas, in designing classifications for dealing with complex problems.[34] Given our history of evil uses of racial classifi-

---

[33] This position is advocated by Cowan, *Inverse Discrimination*, 33 ANALYSIS 10 (1972).

[34] *See, e.g.*, Williamson v. Lee Optical of Okla., Inc., 348 U.S. 483 (1955); Railway Express Agency v. New York, 336 U.S. 106 (1949). Justice Douglas' defense of underinclusive classifications in *Williamson* is especially interesting: "Evils in the same field may be of different dimensions and proportions, requiring different remedies. . . . Or the reform may take one step at a time, addressing itself to

cations, there are good reasons, both moral and constitutional, for being very cautious in their use, even for good ends. Hence, we should be reluctant to use them to effect a small gain in administrative efficiency. But the consequences of using racial classifications are not always the same as when they were used to stigmatize and exclude blacks, and their likely nonpejorative impact in the present context ought to be taken into account in balancing their use against less efficient procedures. Using racial classifications which place a burden on whites is probably less dangerous than using classifications that put a burden on blacks, since there is little likelihood that whites will ever be an isolated and mistreated minority in this country. The kind of self-hatred and belief in one's own inferiority that sometimes resulted from discrimination against blacks is not likely to result among white applicants who have their opportunities reduced by preferential programs, since such programs carry no implication of white inferiority.

It may be the case, however, that the use of racial classifications in preferential programs favoring blacks may confirm a sense of inferiority among black recipients, since the presupposition of such programs is that blacks deserve or are in need of such assistance. Justice Douglas offered an argument of just this sort:

> A segregrated admissions process creates suggestions of stigma and caste no less than a segregated classroom, and in the end it may produce that result despite its contrary intentions. One other assumption must be clearly disapproved, that Blacks or Browns cannot make it on their individual merit. That is a stamp of inferiority that a State is not permitted to place on any lawyer.[35]

Although special admissions procedures for blacks may, if misunderstood, be taken to imply black inferiority and thereby to stigmatize blacks, it seems to be an exaggeration to say, as Justice Douglas does, that programs designed to remedy injustices and overcome handicaps nevertheless stigmatize blacks no less than policies that required blacks to attend segregated schools. Indeed, if the stigmatizing effect of preferential programs were as great as that of segregated schools; one would expect to find blacks avoiding such programs, black organizations opposing them, and black leaders denouncing them. In practice, however, one finds nothing of the sort and indeed finds the opposite.[36]

Making predictions about the consequences of using racial classifications is a risky and difficult business, but it seems to me that the use of such classifications in remedial programs is not likely to have the bad

---

the phase of the problem which seems most acute to the legislative mind." 348 U.S. at 489.

[35] 416 U.S. at 343 (Douglas, J., dissenting).

[36] On the "problematical benignity" of programs using racial classifications in attempting to help blacks, see Developments in the Law—Equal Protection, 82 HARV. L. REV. 1065, 1113 (1969).

consequences that resulted from using them to exclude and segregate blacks.[37] Condemnations of discrimination, it seems to me, should not go so far as to prohibit all uses of racial classifications; they should rather condemn those that are based on false beliefs of high correlations between race and relevant characteristics, that can be avoided without great loss of efficiency through the use of nonracial classifications, or that result in a group's being stigmatized and subject to loss of self-respect.

IV. A Framework for Analyzing Preferential Policies That Use Racial, Ethnic, or Sexual Classifications: Modifying the Correlation Between Classification and Relevant Characteristic

It will be helpful to begin by introducing some general considerations about the use of gross criteria—characteristics which, although irrelevant in themselves, are useful as statistical indicators of relevant characteristics. For a gross criterion C to be perfectly correlated with a relevant characteristic R, it must be the case that *all* and *only* C's are R's. Thus, for ". . . is black" to be perfectly correlated with ". . . has been harmed by discrimination," it would have to be the case that all and only blacks have been harmed by discrimination. If it is not the case that all American blacks have been harmed by discrimination, then the gross indicator would be overinclusive since it would select some individuals who do not have the relevant characteristic. And if it is not the case that only blacks have been harmed by discrimination—as it clearly is not—then the gross indicator would be underinclusive since it would not select some individuals who have the relevant characteristic.[38] Most classifications used in legislation are both over- and underinclusive to some extent, and the importance of having clear boundaries that are administratively workable requires that some looseness be tolerated. Hence, the requirement cannot be perfect correlation but must rather be something like high correlation (in a case where one is distributing something as important as educational and employment opportunities, and where one is using racial classifications to do so, one would probably want to say that there must be a *very* high correlation). When a gross criterion is overinclusive, one way to remedy

[37] For additional and divergent discussions of this matter, *see* Alexander & Alexander, *The New Racism*, 9 SAN DIEGO L. REV. 190 (1972); O'Neil, *Preferential Admissions: Equalizing the Access of Minority Groups to Higher Education*, 80 YALE L. J. 699 (1971); Vieira, *Racial Imbalance, Black Separatism, and Permissible Classification by Race*, 67 MICH L. REV. 1553 (1969); Kaplan, *Equal Justice in an Unequal World: Equality for the Negro—The Problem of Special Treatment*, 61 Nw. U.L. REV. 363 (1966).

[38] *See generally* Tussman & tenBroek, *The Equal Protection of the Laws*, 37 CALIF. L. REV. 341 (1949); *Developments in the Law—Equal Protection*, 82 HARV. L. REV. 1065, 1084, 1119 (1969).

this is to add additional characteristics to the indicator until one includes only the desired smaller group. Thus, if the gross criterion ". . . is black" is overinclusive because most blacks with a personal income of over $20,000 a year do not have the relevant characteristics of having been harmed by discrimination, then the overinclusiveness could be reduced by adding "with an income of less than $20,000 a year" to the gross criterion. The cost of adding characteristics to the gross criterion is the loss of efficiency that may result from having to verify the presence of more characteristics. When a gross criterion is underinclusive, this can be remedied either by substituting another that has wider scope (for example, substituting ". . . is a member of a disadvantaged minority group" for ". . . is black"), or by using a disjunctive clause to include another gross criterion (for example, substituting ". . . is black *or Chicano*" for ". . . is black"). In the former case, the cost of remedying underinclusiveness would be a loss in efficiency because a vague general classification is likely to be difficult to verify in individual cases, while in the later case, there is ordinarily no significant additional cost.

The extent to which the criteria used by a preferential program are over- or underinclusive will depend on which relevant characteristics one selects as the justification for awarding preference. It is clear, for example, that there are now more blacks who are not in poverty than there are blacks who have not suffered from discrimination, and hence a program which attempted to reduce poverty by giving money to all blacks would be more overinclusive than one which compensated victims of discrimination by giving money to all blacks. If cases of overinclusion are frequent, serious objections can be made on grounds of justice and efficiency. If, for example, a black was hired in preference to a better qualified white, and if this particular black person had not been harmed by discrimination, was not unjustly poor, did not have unmet needs, was not likely to be upwardly mobile if given special opportunities, could not serve as a role model, and could not help to provide needed services to blacks, then a less qualified person was hired, and a better qualified person excluded, without achieving any counterbalancing goal. Although it may be possible to reduce overinclusiveness by adding characteristics to the gross criterion which restrict its scope, it would be pointless to do this if it would reintroduce the need for individual investigations that the use of racial classifications was designed to avoid. Since family income can be checked without too much difficulty, restricting preference to group members with a family income below a certain level may be an effective means of reducing overinclusiveness with regard to some conceptions of the proper goals of preferential programs.

Underinclusiveness is probably a greater problem, since one of the most divisive aspects of preferential programs has been the nonpreferential treatment of disadvantaged persons who are not members of groups that are now deemed to be disadvantaged. Assuming that there is sufficient similarity between the situations of the latter persons and that of blacks to justify similar treatment,[39] these programs are clearly underinclusive. Although some latitude must be allowed those who create such programs in experimenting with small groups, in meeting different problems with different means, and in beginning with programs for those with the greatest needs, none of these considerations can justify a long-term policy of using administrative classifications which provide benefits to some while ignoring others with similar claims for preferential treatment. Although underinclusiveness can sometimes be remedied by adding disjunctive clauses, and hence one could offer benefits to anyone who is black *or* Chicano *or* Puerto Rican *or* Filipino *or* American Indian, this solution will result in groups being either entirely included or excluded and therefore generate intense political pressures on behalf of excluded groups who have some members with the relevant characteristics and perhaps many others who are borderline cases. Justice Douglas accurately sensed this problem:

> The reservation of a proportion of the law school class for members of selected minority groups is fraught with similar dangers, for one must immediately determine which groups are to receive such favored treatment and which are to be excluded. . . . There is no assurance that a common agreement can be reached, and first the schools, and then the courts, will be buffeted with the competing claims. The University of Washington included Filipinos, but excluded Chinese and Japanese; another school may limit its program to Blacks, or to Blacks and Chicanos.[40]

The prospect of controversies of this sort is one reason for switching to a general, nonracial criterion, but the appeal of this alternative will depend on the justification for preferential programs. If one is trying to compensate victims of discrimination or to provide legal and medical personnel for poorly served groups, such a general criterion will be less appealing than if one is trying to reduce poverty and inequality. Since there are many poor persons who are poor for reasons other than that of having been harmed by discrimination, selecting persons for a program designed to help victims of discrimination on the basis of a low income would involve much overinclusion. If no nonracial criteria were found suitable, one might reduce the underinclusiveness of preferential programs that use lists of groups as selection criteria by allowing persons who do not belong to any of the listed groups but who think they have the characteristics that justify preference to apply for preference by presenting a

[39] For a discussion of the exaggerations that these claims of similarity to the hardships borne by blacks sometimes involve, *see* Thalberg, *Justifications of Institutional Racism*, 3 PHILOSOPHICAL FORUM 243, 247–48 (1972).

[40] 416 U.S. at 338 (Douglas, J., dissenting). For an account of one problem of this kind encountered by India in its use of preferential policies, *see* D. E. SMITH, INDIA AS A SECULAR STATE 316–22 (1963).

documented claim. This would still require individual investigations in these cases, but not in the cases of persons who qualified on the basis of membership in one of the listed groups. If one utilized this approach, one could construct a criterion for awarding preference that would be acceptable in regard to over- and underinclusiveness and which would retain considerable administrative efficiency. It would have the following form:

> Preference will be awarded to persons who have a family income of less than _____(specify amount)_____ dollars per year, *and* who are members of any of the following groups __(list groups)__ . Persons who do not qualify in accordance with the above criterion but who believe that they have the characteristics which justify preferences such as ____(list relevant characteristics)____ may apply for preference by presenting evidence for their claim on forms available from the admissions (or personnel) officer.

This kind of scheme, even though it employs racial, ethnic and sexual classifications, is not underinclusive with regard to entire groups, and hence relatively well-off groups who have some disadvantaged members would not need to fight to get on the list. This kind of criterion would be overinclusive only to the extent that having a low income and being a member of one of the listed groups was insufficient to exclude persons who lacked the characteristics that can justify preference.

BERNARD R. BOXILL

The Morality of Reparation

In "Black Reparations—Two Views," [1] Michael Harrington rejected and Arnold Kaufman endorsed James Forman's demand for $500 million in reparation from Christian churches and Jewish Synagogues for their part in the exploitation of black people. Harrington's position involves two different points; he argues that reparation is irrelevant and unwarranted because even if it were made, it would do little to "even up incomes"; and he maintains that the *demand* for reparation will be counterproductive, since it will "divert precious political energies from the actual strug-

Reprinted from *Social Theory and Practice*, Vol. 2, No. 1 (1972), 113–122, with the permission of the author and the publisher.

I am deeply indebted to Professor Thomas Hill, Jr., for helpful criticisms of earlier drafts of this paper.

[1] Michael Harrington and Arnold Kaufman, "Black Reparations—Two Views," *Dissent* 16 (July–Aug. 1969), 317–320.

gle" to even up incomes. Now, though Kaufman seemed to show good reason that, contra Harrington, the demand for reparation could be productive, I shall in the ensuing, completely disregard that issue. Whether the demand for reparation is counterproductive or not is a question the answer to which depends on the assessment of a large number of consequences which cannot be answered by philosophy alone.

In this paper I shall take issue with what I have distinguished as the first of Harrington's points, viz. that reparation is unwarranted and irrelevant because it would do little to even up incomes. I assume that, by implication, Harrington is not averse to special compensatory programs which will effectively raise the incomes of the poor; what he specifically opposes is reparation. By a discussion of the justification and aims of reparation and compensation, I shall now try to show that, though both are parts of justice, they have different aims, and hence compensation cannot replace reparation.

Let me begin with a discussion of how compensation may be justified. Because of the scarcity of positions and resources relative to aspiring individuals, every society that refuses to resort to paternalism or a strict regimentation of aspirations must incorporate competition among its members for scarce positions and resources. Given that freedom of choice necessitates at least the possibility of competition, I believe that justice requires that appropriate compensatory programs be instituted both to ensure that the competition is fair, and that the losers be protected.

If the minimum formal requirement of justice is that persons be given equal consideration, then it is clear that justice requires that compensatory programs be implemented in order to ensure that none of the participants suffers from a removable handicap. The same reasoning supports the contention that the losers in the competition be given, if necessary, sufficient compensation to enable them to reenter the competition on equal terms with the others. In other words, the losers can demand equal opportunity as well as can the beginners.

In addition to providing compensation in the above cases, the community has the duty to provide compensation to the victims of accident where no one was in the wrong, and to the victims of "acts of God" such as floods, hurricanes, and earthquakes. Here again, the justification is that such compensation is required if it is necessary to ensure equality of opportunity.

Now, it should be noted that, in all the cases I have stated as requiring compensation, no prior injustice need have occurred. This is clear, of course, in the case of accidents and "acts of God"; but it is also the case that in a competition, even if everyone abides by the rules and acts fairly and justly, some will necessarily be losers. In such a case, I maintain, if the losers are rendered so destitute as to be unable to compete equally, they can demand compensation from the community. Such a right to compensation does not render the competition nugatory; the losers cannot demand success—they can demand only the minimum necessary to reenter the competition. Neither is it the case that every failure has rights of compensation against the community. As we shall see, the right to compensation depends partly on the conviction that every individual has an equal right to pursue what he considers valuable; the wastrel or indolent man has signified what he values by what he has freely chosen to be. Thus, even if he seems a failure and considers himself a failure, he does not need or have a right of compensation. Finally, the case for compensation sketched is not necessarily paternalistic. It is not argued that society or government can decide what valuable things individuals should have and implement programs to see to it that they have them. Society must see to it that its members can pursue those things they consider valuable.

The justification of compensation rests on two premises: first, each individual is equal in dignity and worth to every other individual, and hence has a right, equal to that of any other, to arrange his life as he sees fit, and to pursue and acquire what he considers valuable; and second, the individuals involved must be members of a community. Both premises are necessary in order to show that compensation is both good and, in addition, mandatory or required by justice. One may, for example, concede that a man who is handicapped by some infirmity should receive compensation; but if the man is a member of no community, and if his infirmity is due to no injustice, then one would be hard put to find the party who could be legitimately forced to bear the cost of such compensation. Since persons can be legitimately compelled to do what justice dictates, then it would seem that in the absence of a community, and if the individual has suffered his handicap because of no injustice, that compensation cannot be part of justice. But given that the individual is a member of a community, then I maintain that he can legitimately demand compensation from that community. The members of a community are, in essential respects, members of a joint undertaking; the activities of the members of a community are interdependent and the community benefits from the efforts of its members even when such efforts do not bring the members what they individually aim at. It is legitimate to expect persons to follow the spirit and letter of rules and regulations, to work hard and honestly, to take calculated risks with their lives and fortunes, all of which helps society generally, only if such persons can demand compensation from society as a whole when necessary.

The case for rights of compensation depends, as I have argued above, on the fact that the individuals involved are members of a single community the very existence of which should imply a tacit agreement on the part of the whole to bear the costs of compensation. The case for reparation I shall try to show is more primitive in the sense that it depends only on the premise that every person has an equal right to pursue and acquire what he values. Recall that the crucial difference between compensation and reparation is that whereas the latter is due only after injustice, the former may be due when no one has acted unjustly to anyone else. It is this relative innocence of all the parties concerned which made it illegitimate, in the absence of prior commitments, to compel anyone to bear the cost of compensation.

In the case of reparation, however, this difficulty does not exist. When reparation is due, it is not the case that one is at fault, or that everyone is innocent; in such a case, necessarily, someone has infringed unjustly on another's right to pursue what he values. This could happen in several different ways, dispossession being perhaps the most obvious. When someone possesses something, he has signified by his choice that he values it. By taking it away from him one infringes on his equal right to pursue and possess what he values. On the other hand, if I thwart, unfairly, another's legitimate attempt to do or possess something, I have also acted unjustly; finally, an injustice has occurred when someone makes it impossible for others to pursue a legitimate goal, even if these others never actually attempt to achieve that goal. These examples of injustice differ in detail, but what they all have in common is that no supposition of prior commitment is necessary in order to be able to identify the parties who must bear the cost of reparation; it is simply and clearly the party who has acted unjustly.

The argument may, perhaps, be clarified by the ideas of a state of nature and a social contract. In the state of nature, as John Locke remarks, every man has the right to claim reparation from his injurer because of his right of self-preservation; if each man has a duty not to interfere in the rights of others, he has a duty to repair the results of his interference.[2] No social contract is required to legitimize compelling him to do so. But when compensation is due, i.e. when everyone has acted justly, and has done his duty, then a social contract or a prior agreement to help must be appealed to in order to legitimately compel an individual to help another.

The case for reparation thus requires for its justification less in the way of assumptions than the case for compensation. Examination of the justifications of reparation and compensation also reveals the difference in their aims.

The characteristic of compensatory programs is that they are essentially "forward looking"; by that I mean that such programs are intended to alleviate disabilities which stand in the way of some *future* good, *however* these disabilities may have come about. Thus, the history of injustices suffered by black and colonial people is quite irrelevant to their right to compensatory treatment. What is strictly relevant to this is that such compensatory treatment is necessary if some future goods such as increased happiness, equality of incomes, and so on, are to be secured. To put it another way, given the contingency of causal connections, the present condition of black and colonial people could have been produced in any one of a very large set of different causal sequences. Compensation

[2] John Locke, *Treatise of Civil Government and A Letter Concerning Toleration*, ed. Charles L. Sherman (New York: Appleton-Century Company, Inc., 1937), 9.

is concerned with the remedying of the present situation however it may have been produced; and to know the present situation, and how to remedy it, it is not, strictly speaking, necessary to know just how it was brought about, or whether it was brought about by injustice.

On the other hand, the justification of reparation is essentially "backward looking"; reparation is due only when a breach of justice *has* occurred. Thus, as opposed to the case of compensation, the case for reparation to black and colonial people depends precisely on the fact that such people have been reduced to their present condition by a history of injustice. In sum, while the aim of compensation is to procure some future good, that of reparation is to rectify past injustices; and rectifying past injustices may not insure equality of opportunity.

The fact that reparation aims precisely at correcting a prior injustice suggests one further important difference between reparation and compensation. Part of what is involved in rectifying an injustice is an acknowledgment on the part of the transgressor that what he is doing is required of him because of his prior error. This concession of error seems required by the premise that every person is equal in worth and dignity. Without the acknowledgment of error, the injurer implies that the injured has been treated in a manner that befits him; hence, he cannot feel that the injured party is his equal. In such a case, even if the unjust party repairs the damage he has caused, justice does not yet obtain between himself and his victim. For, if it is true that when someone has done his duty nothing can be demanded of him, it follows that if, in my estimation, I have acted dutifully even when someone is injured as a result, then I must feel that nothing can be demanded of me and that any repairs I may make are gratuitous. If justice can be demanded, it follows that I cannot think that what I am doing is part of justice.

It will be objected, of course, that I have not shown in this situation that, justice cannot obtain between injurer and victim, but only that the injurer does not *feel* that justice can hold between himself and the one he injures. The objection depends on the distinction between the objective transactions between the individuals and their subjective attitudes, and assumes that justice requires only the objective transactions. The model of justice presupposed by this objection is, no doubt, that justice requires equal treatment of equals, whereas the view I take is that justice requires equal consideration between equals; that is to say, justice requires not only that we *treat* people in a certain way, for whatever reason we please, but that we treat them as equals precisely because we believe they are our equals. In particular, justice requires that we acknowledge that our treatment of others can be required of us; thus, where an unjust injury has occurred, the injurer reaffirms his belief in the other's equality by conceding that repair can be demanded of him, and the injured rejects the allegation of his inferiority contained in the other's behavior by demanding reparation.

Consequently, when injustice has reduced a people to indigency, compensatory programs alone cannot be all that justice requires. Since the avowed aim of compensatory programs is forward looking, such programs *necessarily* cannot affirm that the help they give is required because of a prior injustice. This must be the case even if it is the unjustly injuring party who makes compensation. Thus, since the acknowledgment of error is required by justice as part of what it means to give equal consideration, compensatory programs cannot take the place of reparation.

In sum, *compensation* cannot be substituted for *reparation* where reparation is due, because they satisfy two differing requirements of justice. In addition, practically speaking, since it is by demanding and giving justice where it is due that the members of a community continually reaffirm their belief in each other's equality, a stable and equitable society is not possible without reparation being given and demanded when it is due.

Consider now the assertion that the present generation of white Americans owe the present generation of black Americans reparation for the injustices of slavery inflicted on the ancestors of the black population by the ancestors of the white population. To begin, consider the very simplest instance of a case where reparation may be said to be due: Tom has an indisputable moral right to possession of a certain item, say a bicycle, and Dick steals the bicycle from Tom. Here, clearly, Dick owes Tom, at least the bicycle and a concession of error, in reparation. Now complicate the case slightly; Dick steals the bicycle from Tom and "gives" it to Harry. Here again, even if he is innocent of complicity in the theft, and does not know that his "gift" was stolen, Harry must return the bicycle to Tom with the acknowledgment that, though innocent or blameless, he did not rightfully possess the bicycle. Consider a final complication; Dick steals the bicycle from Tom and gives it to Harry; in the meantime Tom dies, but leaves a will clearly conferring his right to ownership of the bicycle to his son, Jim. Here again we should have little hesitation in saying that Harry must return the bicycle to Jim.

Now, though it involves complications, the case for reparation under consideration is essentially the same as the one last mentioned: the slaves had an indisputable moral right to the products of their labour; these products were stolen from them by the slave masters who ultimately passed them on to their descendants; the slaves presumably have conferred their rights of ownership to the products of their labour to their descendants; thus, the descendants of slave masters are in possession of wealth to which the descendants of slaves have rights; hence, the descendants of slave masters must return this wealth to the descendants of slaves with a concession that they were not rightfully in possession of it.

It is not being claimed that the descendants of slaves must seek reparation from those among the white population who happen to be descendants of slave owners. This perhaps would be the case if slavery had produced for the slave owners merely specific hoards of gold, silver or diamonds, which could be passed on in a very concrete way from father to son. As a matter of fact, slavery produced not merely specific hoards, but wealth which has been passed down mainly to descendants of the white community to the relative exclusion of the descendants of slaves. Thus, it is the white community as a whole that prevents the descendants of slaves from exercising their rights of ownership, and the white community as a whole that must bear the cost of reparation.

The above statement contains two distinguishable arguments. In the first argument the assertion is that each white person, individually, owes reparation to the black community because membership in the white community serves to identify an individual as a recipient of benefits to which the black community has a rightful claim. In the second argument, the conclusion is that the white community as a whole, considered as a kind of corporation or company, owes reparation to the black community.

In the first of the arguments sketched above, individuals are held liable to make reparation even if they have been merely passive recipients of benefits; that is, even if they have not deliberately chosen to accept the benefits in question. This argument invites the objection that, for the most part, white people are simply not in a position to choose to receive or refuse benefits belonging to the descendants of slaves and are, therefore, not culpable or blameable and hence not liable to make reparation. But this objection misses the point. The argument under consideration simply does not depend on or imply the claim that white people are culpable or blameable; the argument is that merely by being white, an individual receives benefits to which others have at least partial rights. In such cases, whatever one's choice or moral culpability, reparation must be made. Consider an extreme case: Harry has an unexpected heart attack and is taken unconscious to the hospital. In the same hospital Dick has recently died. A heart surgeon transplants the heart from Dick's dead body to Harry without permission from Dick's family. If Harry recovers, he must make suitable reparation to Dick's family, conceding that he is not in rightful possession of Dick's heart even if he had no part in choosing to receive it.

The second of the arguments distinguished above concluded that for the purpose in question, the white community can be regarded as a corporation or company which, as a whole, owes reparation to the sons of slaves. Certainly the white community resembles a corporation or company in some striking ways; like such companies, the white community has interests distinct from, and opposed to, other groups in the same society, and joint action is often taken by the members of the white community to protect and enhance their interests. Of course, there are differences; people are generally born into the white community and do not deliberately choose their membership in it; on the other hand, deliberate choice is often the standard procedure for gaining membership in a company. But this difference is unimportant; European immigrants often deliberately choose to become part of the white community in the United States for the obvious benefits this brings, and people often inherit shares and so, without deliberate choice, become members of a company. What is important here is not how deliberately one chooses to become part of a community or a company; what is relevant is that one chooses to continue to accept the benefits which circulate exclusively within the community, sees such benefits as belonging exclusively to the members of the community, identifies one's interests with those of the community, viewing them as opposed to those of others outside the community, and finally, takes joint action with other members of the community to protect such interests. In such a case, it seems not unfair to consider the present white population as members of a company that incurred debts before they were members of the company, and thus to ask them justly to bear the cost of such debts.

It may be objected that the case for reparation depends on the validity of inheritance; for, only if the sons of slaves inherit the rights of their ancestors can it be asserted that they have rights against the present white community. If the validity of inheritance is rejected, a somewhat different, but perhaps even stronger, argument for reparation can still be formulated. For if inheritance is rejected with the stipulation that the wealth of individuals be returned to the whole society at their deaths, then it is even clearer that the white community owes reparation to the black community. For the white community has appropriated, almost exclusively, the wealth from slavery in addition to the wealth from other sources; but such wealth belongs jointly to all members of the society, white as well as black; hence, it owes them reparation. The above formulation of the argument is entirely independent of the fact of slavery and extends the rights of the black community to its just portion of the total wealth of the society.

ROBERT K. FULLINWIDER

Preferential Hiring and Compensation

> If a man shall steal an ox, or a sheep, and kill it, or sell it; he shall restore five oxen for an ox, and four sheep for a sheep.
>
> *Exodus 22*

Persons have rights; but sometimes a right may justifiably be overridden. Can we concede to all job applicants a right to equal consideration, and

Reprinted from *Social Theory and Practice*, Vol. 3, No. 3 (Spring 1975), 307–320, with the permission of the author and the publisher.

yet support a policy of preferentially hiring female over white male applicants?

Judith Thomson, in her article "Preferential Hiring," [1] appeals to the principle of compensation as a ground which justifies us in sometimes overriding a person's rights. She applies this principle to a case of preferential hiring of a woman in order to defend the claim that such preferential hiring is not unjust. Her defense rests upon the contention that a debt of compensation is owed to women, and that the existence of this debt provides us with a justification of preferential hiring of women in certain cases even though this involves setting aside or overriding certain rights of white male applicants.

Although she is correct in believing that the right to compensation sometimes allows us or requires us to override or limit other rights, I shall argue that Thomson has failed to show that the principle of compensation justifies preferential hiring in the case she constructs. Thus, by implication, I argue that she has failed to show that preferential hiring of women in such cases is not unjust. I proceed by setting out Thomson's argument, by identifying the crucial premise. I then show that Thomson fails to defend the premise, and that, given her statement of the principle of compensation, the premise is implausible.

1. Thomson's Case

Thomson asks us to imagine the following case. Suppose for some academic job a while male applicant (WMA) and a female applicant (FA) are under final consideration.[2] Suppose further that we grant that WMA and FA each have a *right to equal consideration* by the university's hiring officer. This means that each has a right to be evaluated for the job solely in terms of his or her possession of job related qualifications. Suppose, finally, that the hiring officer hires FA because she is a woman. How can the hiring officer's choice avoid being unjust?

Since being a woman is, by hypothesis, not a job related qualification in this instance, the hiring officer's act of choosing FA because she is a

[1] Judith Thompson, "Preferential Hiring," *Philosophy and Public Affairs*, 2 (Summer 1973): 364–84.

[2] Thomson asks us to imagine two such applicants *tied* in their qualifications. Presumably, preferring a less qualified teacher would violate students' rights to the best available instruction. If the applicants are equally qualified, then the students' rights are satisfied whichever one is picked. In cases where third party rights are not involved, there would seem to be no need to include the tie stipulation, for if the principle of compensation is strong enough to justify preferring a woman over a man, it is strong enough whether the woman is equally qualified or not, so long as she is minimally qualified. (Imagine hiring a librarian instead of a teacher.) Thus, I leave out the requirement that the applicants be tied in their qualifications. Nothing in my argument turns on whether the applicants are equally qualified. The reader may, if he wishes, mentally reinstate this feature of Thomson's example.

woman seems to violate WMA's right to equal consideration. The hiring officer's act would not be unjust only if in this situation there is some sufficient moral ground for setting aside or overriding WMA's right.

Consider, Thomson asks us, ". . . those debts which are incurred by one who wrongs another. *It is here that we find what seems to me the most powerful argument for the conclusion that preferential hiring of women is not unjust"* (emphasis added).[3] We are promised that the basis for justly overriding WMA's acknowledged right is to be found in the principle of compensation. But, at this crucial point in her paper, Thomson stops short of setting out the actual derivation of her conclusion from the application of the principle of compensation to her imagined case. The reader is left to construct the various steps in the argument. From remarks Thomson makes in dealing with some objections to preferential hiring, I offer the following as a fair construction of the argument she intends.

Women, as a group, are owed a debt of compensation. Historically women, because they were women, have been subject to extensive and damaging discrimination, socially approved and legally supported. The discriminatory practices have served to limit the opportunities for fulfillment open to women and have disadvantaged them in the competition for many social benefits. Since women have been the victims of injustice, they have a moral right to be compensated for the wrongs done to them.

The compensation is owed by the community. The community as a whole is responsible, since the discriminatory practices against women have not been limited to isolated, private actions. These practices have been widespread, and public as well as private. Nowhere does Thomson argue that the case for preferring FA over WMA lies in a debt to FA directly incurred by WMA. In fact, Thomson never makes an effort to show any direct connection between FA and WMA. The moral relationship upon which Thomson's argument must rely exists between women and the community. The sacrifice on WMA's part is exacted from him by the community so it may pay its debt to women. This is a crucial feature of Thomson's case, and creates the need for the next premise: The right to compensation on the part of women justifies the community in overriding WMA's right to equal consideration. This premise is necessary to the argument. If the setting aside of WMA's right is to be justified by appeal to the principle of compensation, and the debt of compensation exists between the community and women, then something like the fourth premise is required to gain the application of the principle of compensation to WMA. This premise grounds the justness of WMA's sacrifice in the community's debt.

In short, Thomson's argument contains the following premises:

1. Women, as a group, are owed a debt of compensation.
2. The compensation is owed to women by the community.

[3] Thomson, 380.

3. The community exacts a sacrifice from WMA (i.e., sets aside his right to equal consideration) in order to pay its debt.[4]

4. The right to compensation on the part of women against the community justifies the community in setting aside WMA's right.

If we assume that the community may legitimately discharge its debt to women by making payments to *individual women,* then from premises 1–4 the conclusion may be drawn that WMA's right to equal consideration may be overridden in order to prefer FA, and, hence, that it is not unjust for the hiring officer to choose FA because she is a woman.

I shall not quarrel with premises 1–3, nor with the assumption that *groups* can be wronged and have rights.[5] My quarrel here is with premise 4. I shall show that Thomson offers no support for 4, and that it does not involve a correct application of the principle of compensation as used by Thomson. I will examine the case for premise 4 in section 4. In the next section I pause to look at Thomson's statement of the principle of compensation.

2. The Principle of Compensation

In the passage quoted earlier, Thomson speaks of those debts incurred by one who wrongs another. These are the debts of compensation. Using Thomson's own language, we may formulate the principle of compensation as the declaration that *he who wrongs another owes the other.*[6] The principle of compensation tells us that, for some person B, B's act of wronging some person A creates a special moral relationship between A and B. The relationship is a species of the relationship of *being indebted to.* In the case of compensation, the indebtedness arises as a result of a wrongdoing, and involves the wrongdoer owing the wronged. To say that B owes something to A is to say that B's liberty of action with respect to what is owed is limited. B is under an obligation to yield to A what he owes him, and A has a right to it.[7] *What* B must yield will be a matter of the kind

---

[4] The comments from which propositions 1–3 are distilled occur on pages 381–82.

[5] For a discussion of these issues, see Robert Simon, "Preferential Hiring: A Reply to Judith Jarvis Thomson," *Philosophy and Public Affairs,* 3 (Spring 1974): 312–20.

[6] There are broader notions of compensation, where it means making up for any deficiency or distortion, and where it means recompense for work. Neither of these notions plays a role in Thomson's argument.

[7] On page 378, Thomson says: "Now it is, I think, widely believed that we may, without injustice, refuse to grant a man what he has a right to only if *either* someone else has a conflicting and more stringent right, *or* there is some very great benefit to be obtained by doing so—perhaps that a disaster of some kind is thereby averted . . . But in fact there are other ways in which a right may be overridden." The "other way" which Thomson mentions derives from the force of debts. A debt consists of rights and obligations, and the force of debts can perhaps be accounted for in terms of superior rights. Then, debts would not be a third ground, independent of the first listed by Thomson, for overriding a right.

of wrong he has done A, and the optional means of compensation open to him. Thus, it is clearly the case that debts of compensation are grounds for limiting or overriding rights. But our being owed compensation by someone, though giving us some purchase on his liberty, does not give us carte blanche in limiting his rights. The debt is limited to what makes good our loss (restores our right), and is limited to us, his victims.

It might be that, for some reason, WMA directly owes FA compensation. If so, it would immediately follow that FA has a moral claim against WMA which limits WMA's liberty with respect to what he owes her. Furthermore, the nature of WMA's wrong may be such as to require a form of compensation interfering with the particular right we are focusing on—his right to equal consideration. Suppose the wrong done by WMA involved his depriving FA of fair opportunities for employment. Such a wrong might be the basis for requiring WMA, in compensation, to forego his right to equal consideration if he and FA were in direct competition for some job. This case would conform precisely to the model of Thomson's stated principle of compensation.

Thomson makes no effort to show that WMA has interfered with FA's chances of employment, or done her any other harm. She claims that it is "wrongheaded" to dwell upon the question of whether WMA has wronged FA or any other woman.[8] As we have already seen, Thomson maintains that the relevant moral relationship exists between *women* and the *community*. Consequently, the full weight of her argument rests on premise 4, and I now turn to it.

3. Applying the Principle of Compensation to Groups

Thomson asserts that there is a relationship of indebtedness between the community and women. Yet it is the overriding of WMA's right which is purportedly justified by this fact. The sacrifice imposed upon WMA is not due to his directly owing FA. The community owes FA (as a woman), and exacts the sacrifice from WMA in order that *it* may pay its debt. This is supposed to be justified by premise 4.

May the community take *any* act it sees fit in order to pay its debts?[9] This question goes to the heart of Thomson's case: what support is there for her premise 4? What is the connection between the community's liability to women (or FA), and WMA's membership in the community? Can we find in the fact that the community owes something to women a moral justification for overriding WMA's right? In this section I explore

[8] Thomson, 380–81.

[9] The U.S. Government owes Japanese companies compensation for losses they incurred when the President imposed an illegal import surtax. May the Government justly discharge its debt by taxing only Japanese-Americans in order to pay the Japanese companies?

two attempts to provide a positive answer to this last question. These are not Thomson's attempts; I consider her own words in the next section.

First, one might attempt to justify the imposition of a sacrifice on WMA by appeal to distributive liability. It might be urged that since the community owes FA, then every member of the community owes FA and thus WMA owes FA. This defense of premise 4 is unconvincing. While it is true that if the community owes FA then its members collectively owe FA, it does not follow that they distributively owe FA. It is not the case that, as a general rule, distributive liability holds between organized groups and their members.[10] What reason is there to suppose it does in this case?

Though this attempt to defend premise 4 is unsatisfactory, it is easy to see why it would be very appealing. Even though the indebtedness is established, in the first instance, between the community and FA, if distributive liability obtained we could derive a debt WMA owed to FA, a debt that arose as a result of the application of the principle of compensation to the community. In imposing a sacrifice on WMA, the community would be enforcing *his* (derived) obligation to FA.

Second, imagine a 36 hole, 2 round, golf tournament among FA, WMA, and a third party, sanctioned and governed by a tournament organizing committee. In previous years FA switched to a new model club, which improved her game. Before the match the third player surreptitiously substitutes for FA's clubs a set of the old type. This is discovered after 18 holes have been played. If we suppose that the match cannot be restarted or cancelled, then the committee is faced with the problem of compensating FA for the unfair disadvantage caused her by the substitution. By calculating her score averages over the years, the committee determines that the new clubs have yielded FA an average two-stroke improvement per 18 holes over the old clubs. The committee decides to compensate FA by penalizing the third player by two strokes in the final 18 holes.

But the committee must also penalize WMA two strokes. If FA has been put at a disadvantage by the wrongful substitution, she has been put at a disadvantage with respect to every player in the game. She is in competition with all the players; what the third player's substitution has done is to deprive her of a fair opportunity to defeat all the other players. That opportunity is not restored by penalizing the third player alone. If the committee is to rectify in mid-match the wrong done to FA, it must penalize WMA as well, though WMA had no part in the wrong done to FA.

Now, if it is right for the committee to choose this course of action, then this example seems promising for Thomson's argument. Perhaps in

---

[10] See Joel Feinberg, "Collective Responsibility," *Journal of Philosophy*, 65 (7 November 1968); and Virginia Held, "Can a Random Collection of Individuals Be Morally Responsible?" *Journal of Philosophy*, 67 (13 July 1970).

it can be found a basis for defending premise 4. This example seems appropriately similar to Thomson's case: in it an organization penalizes WMA to compensate FA, though WMA is innocent of any wrong against FA. If the two situations are sufficiently alike and in the golfing example it is not unjust for the committee to penalize WMA, then by parity of reasoning it would seem that the community is not injust in setting aside WMA's right.

Are the committee's action and the community's action to be seen in the same light? Does the committee's action involve setting aside any player's rights? The committee constantly monitors the game, and intervenes to balance off losses or gains due to infractions or violations. Unfair gains are nullified by penalties; unfair losses are offset by awards. In the end no player has a complaint because the interventions ensure that the outcome has not been influenced by illegitimate moves or illegal actions. Whatever a player's position at the end of the game, it is solely the result of his own unhindered efforts. In penalizing WMA two strokes (along with the third player), the committee does him no injustice nor overrides any of his rights.

The community, or its government, is responsible for preserving fair employment practices for its members. It can penalize those who engage in unfair discrimination; it can vigorously enforce fair employment rules; and, if FA has suffered under unfair practices, it may consider some form of compensation for FA. However, compensating FA by imposing a burden on WMA, when he is not culpable, is *not* like penalizing WMA in the golf match. The loss imposed by the community upon WMA is not part of a game-like scheme, carefully regulated and continuously monitored by the community, wherein it intervenes continually to offset unfair losses and gains by distributing penalties and advantages, ensuring that over their lifetimes WMA's and FA's chances at employment have been truly equal. WMA's loss may endure; and there is no reason to believe that his employment position at the end of his career reflects only his unhindered effort. If the community exacts a sacrifice from WMA to pay FA, *it merely redistributes losses and gains without balancing them.*

Even though the golfing example looked promising as a source of clues for a defense of premise 4, on examination it seems not to offer any support for that premise. Indeed, in seeing how the golfing case is different from the hiring case, we may become even more dubious that Thomson's principle of compensation can justify the community in overriding WMA's right to equal consideration in the absence of his culpability.[11]

---

[11] George Sher, in "Justifying Reverse Discrimination in Employment," *Philosophy and Public Affairs*, 4 (Winter 1975), defends reverse discriminations to "neutralize competitive disadvantages caused by past privations" (165). He seems to view the matter along the lines of my golfing example. Thus, my comments here against the sufficiency of that model apply to Sher's argument. Also, see below,

4. Thomson's Words

Since Thomson never explicitly expresses premise 4 in her paper, she never directly addresses the problem of its defense. In the one place where she seems to take up the problem raised by premise 4, she says:

> Still, the community does impose a burden upon him (WMA): it is able to make amends for its wrongs only by taking something away from him, something which, after all, we are supposing he has a right to. And why should *he* pay the cost of the community's amends-making?
>
> If there were some appropriate way in which the community could make amends to its . . . women, some way which did not require depriving anyone of anything he has a right to, then that would be the best course of action to take. Or if there were anyway some way in which the costs could be shared by everyone, and not imposed entirely on the young white male applicants, then that would be, if not the best, then anyway better than opting for a policy of preferential hiring. But in fact *the nature of the wrongs done is such as to make jobs the best and most suitable form of compensation (emphasis added).*[12]

How does this provide an answer to our question? Is this passage to be read as suggesting, in support of premise 4, the principle that a group may override the rights of its (nonculpable) members in order to pay the "best" form of compensation?[13] If WMA's right to equal consideration stood in the way of the community's paying best compensation to FA, then this principle would entail premise 4. This principle, however, will not withstand scrutiny.

Consider an example: Suppose that you have stolen a rare and elaborately engraved hunting rifle from me. Before you can be made to return it, the gun is destroyed in a fire. By coincidence, however, your brother possesses one of the few other such rifles in existence; perhaps it is the only other model in existence apart from the one you stole from me and which was destroyed. From my point of view, having my gun back, or having one exactly like it, is the best form of compensation I can have from you. No other gun will be a suitable replacement, nor will money serve satisfactorily to compensate me for my loss. I prized the rifle for its rare and unique qualities, not for its monetary value. You can pay me the best form of compensation by giving me your brother's gun. However,

---

section 6, for arguments that bear on Sher's contention that the justification for discriminating against white male applicants is not that they are most responsible for injustice, but benefit the most from it.

[12] Thomson, 383.

[13] In the passage quoted, Thomson is attempting to morally justify the community's imposing a sacrifice on WMA. Thus, her reference to "best" compensation cannot be construed to mean "morally best," since morally best means morally justified. By best compensation Thomson means that compensation which will best make up the loss suffered by the victim. This is how I understand the idea of best compensation in the succeeding example and argument.

this is clearly not a morally justifiable option. I have no moral title to your brother's gun, nor are you (solely in virtue of your debt to me) required or permitted to take your brother's gun to give to me. The gun is not yours to give; and nothing about the fact that you owe me justifies you in taking it.

In this example it is clear that establishing what is the best compensation (best makes up the wrongful loss) does not determine what is the morally appropriate form of compensation. Thus, as a defense of premise 4, telling us that preferential hiring is the best compensation begs the question.

The question of the best form of compensation may properly arise only after we have determined who owes whom, and what are the morally permissible means of payment open to the debtor. The question of the best form of compensation arises, in other words, only after we have settled the moral justifiability of exacting something from someone, and settled the issue of what it is that the debtor has that he can pay.

The case of preferential hiring seems to me more like the case of the stolen rifle than like the case of the golfing match. If WMA has a right to equal consideration, then he, not the community, owns the right. In abridging his right in order to pay FA, the community is paying in stolen coin, just as you would be were you to expropriate your brother's rifle to compensate me. The community is paying with something that does not belong to it. WMA has not been shown by Thomson to owe anybody anything. Nor has Thomson defended or made plausible premise 4, which on its face ill fits her own expression of the principle of compensation. If we reject the premise, then Thomson has not shown what she claimed—that it is not unjust to engage in preferential hiring of women. I fully agree with her that it would be appropriate, if not obligatory, for the community to adopt measures of compensation to women.[14] I cannot agree, on the basis of her argument, that it may do so by adopting a policy of preferential hiring.

5. Benefit and Innocence

Thomson seems vaguely to recognize that her case is unconvincing without a demonstration of culpability on the part of WMA. At the end of her paper, after having made her argument without assuming WMA's

---

[14] And there are many possible modes of compensation open to the community which are free from any moral taint. At the worst, monetary compensation is always an alternative. This may be second- or third-best compensation for the wrongs done, but when the best is not available, second-best has to do. For the loss of my gun, I am going to have to accept cash from you (assuming you have it), and use it to buy a less satisfactory substitute.

guilt, she assures us that after all WMA is not so innocent, and it is not unfitting that he should bear the sacrifice required in preferring FA.

> . . . it is not entirely inappropriate that those applicants (like WMA) should pay the cost. No doubt few, if any, have themselves, individually, done any wrongs to . . . women. But they have profited from the wrongs the community did. Many may actually have been direct beneficiaries of policies which excluded or downgraded . . . women—perhaps in school admissions, perhaps in access to financial aid, perhaps elsewhere; and even those who did not directly benefit in this way had, at any rate, the advantage in the competition which comes of confidence in one's full membership, and of one's rights being recognized as a matter of course.[15]

Does this passage make a plausible case for WMA's diminished "innocence," and the appropriateness of imposing the costs of compensation on him? The principle implied in the passage is, "He who benefits from a wrong shall pay for the wrong." Perhaps Thomson confuses this principle with the principle of compensation itself ("He who wrongs another shall pay for the wrong"). At any rate, the principle, "He who benefits from a wrong shall pay for the wrong," is surely suspect as an acceptable moral principle.

Consider the following example. While I am away on vacation, my neighbor contracts with a construction company to repave his driveway. He instructs the workers to come to his address, where they will find a note describing the driveway to be repaired. An enemy of my neighbor, aware somehow of this arrangement, substitutes for my neighbor's instructions a note describing *my* driveway. The construction crew, having been paid in advance, shows up on the appointed day while my neighbor is at work, finds the letter, and faithfully following its instructions paves my driveway. In this example my neighbor has been wronged and damaged. He is out a sum of money, and his driveway is unimproved. I benefited from the wrong, for my driveway is considerably improved. Yet, am I morally required to compensate my neighbor for the wrong done him? Is it appropriate that the costs of compensating my neighbor fall on me? I cannot see why. My paying the neighbor the cost he incurred in hiring the construction company would be an act of supererogation on my part, not a discharge of an obligation to him. If I could afford it, it would be a decent thing to do; but it is not something I *owe* my neighbor. I am not less than innocent in this affair because I benefited from my neighbor's misfortune; and no one is justified in exacting compensation from me.

The very obvious feature of the situation just described which bears on the fittingness of compensation is the fact of *involuntariness*. Indeed I benefited from the wrong done my neighbor, but the benefit was in-

15 Thomson, 383–84.

voluntary and undesired. If I knowingly and voluntarily benefit from wrongs done to others, though I do not commit the wrongs myself, then perhaps it is true to say that I am less than innocent of these wrongs, and perhaps it is morally fitting that I bear some of the costs of compensation. But it is not like this with involuntary benefits.

Though young white males like WMA have undeniably benefited in many ways from the sexist social arrangements under which they were reared, to a large extent, if not entirely, these benefits are involuntary. From an early age the male's training and education inculcate in him the attitudes and dispositions, the knowledge and skills, which give him an advantage over women in later life. Such benefits are unavoidable (by him) and ineradicable. Most especially is this true of "that advantage . . . which comes of confidence in one's full membership [in the community] and of one's rights being recognized as a matter of course."

The principle, "He who *willingly* benefits from wrong must pay for the wrong," may have merit as a moral principle. To show a person's uncoerced and knowledgeable complicity in wrongdoing is to show him less than innocent, even if his role amounts to no more than ready acceptance of the fruits of wrong. Thomson makes no effort to show such complicity on WMA's part. The principle that she relies upon, "He who benefits from a wrong must pay for the wrong," is without merit. So, too, is her belief that "it is not entirely inappropriate" that WMA (and those like him) should bear the burden of a program of compensation to women. What Thomson ignores is the moral implication of the fact that the benefits of sexism received by WMA may be involuntary and unavoidable. This implication cannot be blinked, and it ruins Thomson's final pitch to gain our approval of a program which violates the rights of some persons.[16]

Selected Bibliography

BAYLES, MICHAEL. "Compensatory Reverse Discrimination in Hiring," *Social Theory and Practice*, Vol. 2, no. 3 (1973), 301.

BLACK, VIRGINIA. "The Erosion of Legal Principles in the Creation of Legal Policies," *Ethics*, Vol. 84, no. 2 (1974), 93.

BLACKSTONE, WILLIAM T., and ROBERT D. HESLEP (eds.). *Social Justice and Preferential Treatment*. Athens, Ga.: The University of Georgia Press, 1977.

[16] But, if FA is *not* given preferential treatment in hiring (the best compensation), are *her* rights violated? In having a right to compensation, FA does not have a right to anything at all that will compensate her. She has a right to the best of the morally available options open to her debtor. Only if the community refuses to pay her this is her right violated. We have seen no reason to believe that setting aside the right of white male applicants to equal consideration is an option morally available to the community.

GROSS, BARRY (ed.). *Reverse Discrimination*. Buffalo, N.Y.: Prometheus Press, 1977.

NAGEL, THOMAS. "Equal Treatment and Compensatory Justice," *Philosophy and Public Affairs*, Vol. 2, no. 4 (1973), 349.

NEWTON, LISA H. "Reverse Discrimination As Unjustified," *Ethics*, Vol. 83, no. 4 (1973), 308.

SHER, GEORGE. "Justifying Reverse Discrimination in Employment," *Philosophy and Public Affairs*, Vol. 4, no. 2 (1975), 159.

SIMON, ROBERT. "Preferential Treatment," *Philosophy and Public Affairs*, Vol. 3, no. 3 (1974), 312.

THALBERG, IRVING. "Reverse Discrimination and the Future," *Philosophical Forum*, Vol. 5, nos. 1–2 (1973–74), 263.

THOMSON, JUDITH JARVIS. "Preferential Hiring," *Philosophy and Public Affairs*, Vol. 2, no. 4 (1973), 364.

VETTERLING-BRAGGIN, MARY, FREDRICK A. ELLISTON, and JANE ENGLISH (eds.). *Feminism and Philosophy*. Totowa, N.J.: Littlefield, Adams & Co., 1977.

four

SEXUAL MORALITY

Pettit v. State Board of Education
10 C.3d 29; 109 Cal.Rptr.665, 513
P.2d 889 (1973)

BURKE, J. In this case we are asked to review a judgment denying plaintiff mandate to vacate an order of the State Board of Education revoking her elementary school life diploma on the ground that she engaged in certain acts of sexual misconduct evidencing her unfitness to teach. We have concluded that the conduct complained of furnished ample ground to support the order of revocation.

Plaintiff is an elementary school teacher, having held a California teaching credential since 1957. According to the record, in November 1967 plaintiff (then 48 years old) and her husband applied for membership in "The Swingers," a private club in Los Angeles evidently devoted primarily to promoting diverse sexual activities between members at club parties. Sergeant Berk, an undercover officer working for the Los Angeles Police Department, investigated the club, was accepted for membership, and, on December 2, 1967, attended a party at a private residence during which he observed the incidents in question. According to Berk, he entered the residence where the party was held and immediately observed a man and woman (not plaintiff) engaged in sexual intercourse in an open bedroom. Throughout the evening Sergeant Berk saw various other couples similarly engaged. Berk estimated that there were 20 persons at the party, some of whom were "walking around the residence observing people engaged in these [sexual] acts." In a one-hour period, Berk observed plaintiff commit three separate acts of oral copulation with three different men at the party. When these acts took place, the participants were undressed, and there were other persons looking on.

Plaintiff was subsequently arrested and charged with violating Penal Code section 288a (oral copulation). Evidently a plea bargain was arranged and plaintiff pleaded guilty to Penal Code section 650½ (outraging public decency), a misdemeanor. Plaintiff was fined and placed on probation; upon payment of the fine probation was terminated and the criminal proceedings dismissed.

Subsequently, in February 1970, the disciplinary proceedings now before us were initiated to revoke plaintiff's teaching credential on the grounds (among others) that her conduct involved moral turpitude and demonstrated her unfitness to teach. At the board hearing, Sergeant Berk testified as summarized above. In addition, three elementary school superintendents testified that in their opinion plaintiff's conduct disclosed her unfitness to teach.[1] Plaintiff did not testify at the hearing. However her husband testified, among other things, that plaintiff realized in advance that sexual activities would occur at the Swingers Club party, and that with her consent he had observed plaintiff engage in sexual intercourse and oral copulation with other men in the past. Mr. Pettit also testified that he and plaintiff had, in 1966, appeared on the Joe Pyne television show and also another similar show a few weeks later, and had on both occasions discussed "nonconventional sexual life styles." Mr. Pettit recalled that the

---

[1] William B. Calton, superintendent of the Cypress School District which employed plaintiff, testified that a person who committed the sexual acts performed by plaintiff would be unfit to teach in an elementary school. In Calton's opinion, a teacher has the responsibility to practice as well as teach moral values; one who failed to practice morality would have difficulty teaching it. Since pupils look to their teacher for moral guidance, plaintiff would lose her effectiveness and ability as a teacher and might even inject her ideas regarding sexual morals into the classroom.

   Sylvester A. Moffett, superintendent of the Huntington Beach City Schools, testified that in his opinion plaintiff was unfit to teach, that every teacher should possess high morals, and that it would be difficult to teach morality without practicing it.

   Archie J. Haskins, assistant superintendent of the Magnolia School District, testified that one who engaged in the sexual conduct performed by plaintiff would be unfit to instruct elementary school children. According to Haskins, a teacher must set a good moral example for her pupils, for she spends much time with them and has a strong influence over them.

subjects of adultery and "wife swapping" were discussed and that "probably" the Pettits expressed a "philosophic" attitude on those subjects since they were not "uptight" about them. Although plaintiff and her husband wore a mask and false beard respectively on these shows, Superintendent Calton testified that one of plaintiff's fellow teachers had discussed plaintiff's televised statements with him and with other teachers.

Dr. William Hartman testified on plaintiff's behalf. Dr. Hartman is a licensed clinical psychologist, a professor of sociology, and a director of a center for marital and sexual studies. He had also known plaintiff socially for several years prior to the hearing. According to Hartman, plaintiff was well-adjusted, and in view of the trauma and emotional turmoil caused by her suspension, was not likely to repeat the prior offenses. Hartman disputed the testimony of the board's witnesses that the nature of the sexual misconduct involved herein would render plaintiff unfit to teach.

Plaintiff introduced an evaluation by her school principal finding her teaching to be satisfactory and commenting upon her classes' progress and improvement. Plaintiff also introduced a contract of employment with her school district offering to rehire her for the 1968–1969 school year. The record is unclear, however, as to when her employer first learned of her Swingers Club activities.

At the conclusion of the hearing, the hearing examiner found that plaintiff has engaged in acts of sexual intercourse and oral copulation with men other than her husband; that plaintiff appeared on television programs while facially disguised and discussed nonconventional sexual behavior, including wife swapping; that although plaintiff's services as a teacher have been "satisfactory," and although she is unlikely to repeat the sexual misconduct, nevertheless she has engaged in immoral and unprofessional conduct, in acts involving moral turpitude, and in acts evidencing her unfitness for service. Accordingly, the hearing examiner concluded that cause exists for the revocation of her life diploma. The board adopted the findings and conclusions of its hearing officer in toto.

Thereafter, plaintiff sought a writ of mandate from the superior court to review and set aside the board's order. (Code Civ. Proc., § 1094.5.) The court, exercising its independent judgment of the evidence,[2] likewise concluded that proper cause existed to revoke plaintiff's teaching credentials and denied mandate.[3] Plaintiff appeals.

[2] See *Morrison* v. *State Board of Education*, 1 Cal.3d 214, 240, and footnote 51 [82 Cal.Rptr. 175, 461 P.2d 375].

[3] The trial court noted that the acts "undeniably committed" by plaintiff were criminal in nature, and were committed in a place where 16 to 20 persons were present. The court also referred to plaintiff's television appearance and the fact that teachers and others on the school staff had learned of them. The court believed that although the opinions of the three school superintendents may not be entitled to great weight, nevertheless they are some evidence of plaintiff's unfitness. In concluding, the court explained the primary basis for its ruling as follows: "The intimate and delicate relationships between teachers and students require

The Education Code contains the provisions governing revocation of a teacher's life diploma or credential. Section 13202 provides in pertinent part that the board "shall revoke or suspend for immoral or unprofessional conduct . . . or for any cause which would have warranted the denial of an application for a certification document or the renewal thereof, or for evident unfitness for service, . . . "Among the various statutory grounds for denial of an application for a credential or life diploma, or renewal thereof, are the commission of an act involving moral turpitude and the failure to furnish reasonable evidence of good moral character. (Former § 13129, subds. (e) and (h), now § 13174, subds. (e) and (h).) Finally, *conviction* of various penal offenses, including Penal Code section 288a, is likewise ground for revocation of a life diploma or credential (§ 13206; see also § 13207 [conviction of sex offenses]; §12912 [definition of sex offenses]; *DiGenova* v. *State Board of Education*, 45 Cal.2d 255 [288 P.2d 862].)

As stated above, plaintiff was not convicted of the offense of oral copulation but of the misdemeanor offense of outraging public decency, an offense not specified in the foregoing sections as sufficient per se to justify revocation. Therefore, revocation of plaintiff's life diploma cannot be upheld solely by reason of the conviction entered against her.[4] On the other

---

that teachers be held to standards of morality in their private lives that may not be required of others. Parents have the right to demand high standards of conduct in the personal lives of the teachers of their children, and should have the right to expect that the teachers' concepts of morals and sexual relationships not be at substantial variance with concepts that are generally accepted and approved in the community, and that they not engage in conduct which is proscribed by the criminal laws of this state. It should not be necessary for such unacceptable conduct to manifest itself in the classroom before the Board may, in the best interests of the educational system and of the students, revoke the teaching credentials of one who has evidenced such a disregard of the accepted standards of moral conduct and of the criminal statutes."

[4] Plaintiff and amici suggest that plaintiff's conviction under Penal Code section 650½ is invalid, because of the vagueness of that statute and its reference to "public decency" (see *In re Davis*, 242 Cal.App.2d 645 [51 Cal.Rptr. 702]), the assertedly "private" nature of the offenses in the instant case, or the "ruse" committed by Sergeant Berk in obtaining admission to the club. However, neither the board nor the trial court relied upon plaintiff's conviction itself as grounds for revocation, but upon her underlying *conduct* apart from the conviction.

Amici also call into question the validity of Penal Code section 288a, asserting that oral copulation is an activity protected by the constitutional rights of association and privacy. (But see *People* v. *Drolet*, 30 Cal.App.3d 207 [105 Cal.Rptr. 824]; *People* v. *Hurd*, 5 Cal.App.3d 865 [85 Cal.Rptr. 718]; *People* v. *Roberts*, 256 Cal.App.2d 488 [64 Cal.Rptr. 70].) Without deciding whether section 288a is valid in all of its various applications, we point out that plaintiff is not here seeking any relief from criminal prosecution for her sexual conduct, and accordingly the validity of section 288a is not before us. Instead, the sole question presented herein is whether the record contains sufficient evidence to sustain the trial court's determination that plaintiff's conduct rendered her unfit to teach.

hand, plaintiff has never denied that the acts of oral copulation took place. Accordingly, we must determine whether the trial court properly concluded that plaintiff's conduct constituted "immoral or unprofessional conduct," "evident unfitness to teach," "acts involving moral turpitude," or acts evidencing a lack of "good moral character" within the meaning of the code sections set forth above.

In *Morrison v. State Board of Education, supra,* 1 Cal.3d 214, this court was faced with the problem whether certain homosexual conduct by a public school teacher justified revocation under the above statutory language. A majority of the court concluded that, in order to save the statute from attack on vagueness grounds, a teacher's actions could not constitute "immoral or unprofessional conduct" or "moral turpitude" unless that conduct indicated an unfitness to teach. In view of the total lack of evidence in the record demonstrating Morrison's unfitness to teach, the court reversed the superior court's judgment denying mandate. We made it clear, however, that in future cases revocation will be upheld if the evidence discloses that the teacher's retention within the school system "poses a significant danger of harm to either students, school employees, or others who might be affected by his actions as a teacher." (P. 235.) The court suggested that a showing of significant "harm" could be based upon adverse inferences drawn from the teacher's past conduct as to his probable future teaching ability, as well as upon the likelihood that the publicity surrounding the past conduct "may in and of itself substantially impair his function as a teacher." (*Id.,* see *Comings v. State Bd. of Education,* 23 Cal.App.3d 94, 104 [100 Cal.Rptr. 73, 47 A.L.R.3d 742]; *Board of Trustees v. Stubblefield,* 16 Cal.App.3d 820, 826–827 [94 Cal.Rptr. 318].)

Plaintiff contends that *Morrison* controls here and that the record contains no substantial evidence of her unfitness to teach. We disagree. Initially, we note several important factors which would distinguish *Morrison* from the instant case. In *Morrison,* the unspecified conduct at issue was noncriminal in nature, and the court was careful to point out that oral copulation was not involved. (1 Cal.3d at p. 218, fn. 4.) We further explained that under the Education Code a distinction was made between certain sex crimes (such as oral copulation) which require automatic revocation, and lesser sex offenses which result in "discipline only if it is 'immoral,' 'unprofessional' or involves 'moral turpitude.'" (*Id.* see *Purifoy v. State Board of Education,* 30 Cal.App.3d 187, 197 [106 Cal.Rptr. 201].)

A second distinguishing feature between *Morrison* and the instant case is, of course, that in *Morrison* the conduct at issue occurred entirely *in private* and involved only two persons, whereas plaintiff's indiscretions involved three different "partners," were witnessed by several strangers, and took place in the semi-public atmosphere of a club party.[5] Plaintiff's

---

[5] Various cases have emphasized the significance of the public nature of a teacher's misconduct, or the notoriety and publicity accorded it. (See *Moser v. State Bd. of Education,* 22 Cal.App.3d 988, 990–991 [101 Cal.Rptr. 86]; *Watson v. State*

performance certainly reflected a total lack of concern for privacy, decorum or preservation of her dignity and reputation. Even without expert testimony, the board was entitled to conclude that plaintiff's flagrant display indicated a serious defect of moral character, normal prudence and good common sense. A further indication that plaintiff lacked that minimum degree of discretion and regard for propriety expected of a public school teacher is disclosed by her television appearances, giving notoriety to her unorthodox views regarding sexual morals. As noted above, apparently plaintiff's disguise was not wholly effective for she was recognized by at least one teacher at plaintiff's school.

Finally, in *Morrison* the board acted without sufficient evidence of unfitness to teach. In the instant case, in addition to the evidence of plaintiff's misconduct itself and its criminal and semi-public nature, the board heard expert testimony asserting plaintiff's unfitness to teach. Unlike *Morrison*, wherein we noted that "The board produced no testimony from school officials or others to indicate whether a man such as petitioner might publicly advocate improper conduct" (1 Cal.3d at p. 236), in the instant case three school administrators gave their opinion that plaintiff is unfit to teach (see fn. 1, *ante*). In general, these witnesses expressed concern that plaintiff might attempt to inject her views regarding sexual morality into the classroom or into her private discussions with her pupils, and that plaintiff would be unable effectively to act as a moral example for the children she taught. Plaintiff attacks this testimony as reflecting only the personal opinions of the witnesses regarding unorthodox sexual mores,[6] yet the testimony goes further and calls into question plaintiff's fitness to teach moral principles. Expert testimony is necessarily based to an extent upon the personal opinion of the witness, supported by his special education and experience. (1) We see no reason for discrediting the opinion of a school superintendent regarding the fitness of teachers to teach merely because that opinion is based in part upon personal moral views. Many courts have recognized that testimony by other teachers or school administrators may furnish the necessary evidence of unfitness to teach required by *Morrison*. (See *Board of Trustees* v. *Metzger*, 8 Cal.3d 206, 210 [104 Cal.Rptr. 452, 501 P.2d 1172]; *Governing Board* v. *Brennan*, 18 Cal.App.3d 396, 402 [95 Cal.Rptr. 712]; *Comings* v. *State Bd. of Education, supra*, 23 Cal.App.3d 94, 105–106.)

As noted above, the board's witnesses testified that in their opinion it was likely that plaintiff would be unable to set a proper example for her pupils or to teach moral principles to them. Yet it is the statutory duty of

---

Bd. of Education, 22 Cal.App.3d 559, 564 [99 Cal.Rptr. 468]; *Comings* v. *State Bd. of Education, supra*, 23 Cal.App.3d 94, 105–106; *Board of Trustees* v. *Stubblefield, supra*, 16 Cal.App.3d 820, 826.)

[6] As noted above (fn. 3), the trial court found that, the superintendents' testimony, although not entitled to "great weight," did constitute some evidence of unfitness to teach.

a teacher to "endeavor to impress upon the minds of the pupils the principles of morality . . . and to instruct them in manners and morals. . . ." (Ed. Code, § 13556.5.) Accordingly, several cases have held that the inability of a teacher to obey the laws of this state or otherwise to act in accordance with traditional moral principles may constitute sufficient ground for revocation or dismissal. (See *Watson v. State Bd. of Education, supra,* 22 Cal.App.3d 559, 564–565 [alcoholic teacher with record of drunken driving]; *Governing Board v. Brennan, supra,* 18 Cal.App.3d 396, 402 [teacher advocated illegal marijuana use]; *Board of Trustees v. Stubblefield, supra,* 16 Cal.App.3d 820, 824–826 [teacher was found in compromising position with student, assaulted police officer and resisted arrest]; *Sarac v. State Bd. of Education,* 249 Cal.App.2d 58, 63–64 [57 Cal.Rptr. 69] [disapproved on other grounds in *Morrison v. State Board of Education, supra,* 1 Cal.3d 214, 238; teacher made homosexual advance toward police officer at public beach]; *Vogulkin v. State Board of Education,* 194 Cal.App.2d 424, 429–430 [15 Cal.Rptr. 335] [teacher convicted of unspecified sex offense].)

As this court stated in *Board of Education v. Swan,* 41 Cal.2d 546, 552 [261 P.2d 261], "A teacher . . . in the public school system is regarded by the public and pupils in the light of an exemplar, whose words and actions are likely to be followed by the children coming under her care and protection." (2) In the instant case, the board and the trial court were entitled to conclude, on the basis of the expert testimony set forth above and the very nature of the misconduct involved, that Mrs. Pettit's illicit and indiscreet actions disclosed her unfitness to teach in public elementary schools.[7]

The judgment is affirmed.

WRIGHT, C. J., McCOMB, J., SULLIVAN, J., and CLARK, J., concurred.

TOBRINER, J.   For the past 13 years plaintiff has taught mentally retarded elementary school children, a task requiring exceptional skill and patience. Throughout her career her competence has been unquestioned; not a scintilla of evidence suggests that she has ever failed properly to perform her professional responsibilities. One can ask for no better proof of fitness to teach than this record of consistent, capable performance.

Yet in the face of this record, the State Board of Education, branding plaintiff "unfit," revokes her elementary school life diploma—a ruling that will not only force her discharge from her present employment, but,

---

[7] Plaintiff points to the finding of the board that she is unlikely to repeat the misconduct which led to her suspension. Yet the "risk of harm" which justied revocation of plaintiff's license in this case is not the likelihood that plaintiff will perform additional sexual offenses but instead that she will be unable to teach moral principles, to act as an exemplar for her pupils, or to offer them suitable moral guidance.

regardless of the need for a teacher of her experience and qualifications, will also bar any school district in California from hiring her. Looking only to the loss of future earnings, we must recognize that the board inflicts a penalty of well over $100,000; the ruling, moreover, entails immeasurably greater psychological damage. Equally immeasurable is the loss to school districts that are denied the right to employ a skilled and dedicated teacher.

One would expect that before inflicting such injury, the board would insist upon solid and credible evidence that clearly established plaintiff's lack of fitness to teach. Instead, as I shall show, the board has acted on the basis of questionable conjecture.[1]

Our analysis of the issues in this case must begin with *Morrison v. State Board of Education* (1969) 1 Cal.3d. 214 [82 Cal.Rptr. 175, 461 P.2d 375], an opinion of this court that defines the showing required for a revocation of teaching credentials. That decision recognized the general proposition that no person may be barred from a profession upon grounds unrelated to his fitness to perform his professional obligations. (See *Board of Trustees v. Metzger* (1972) 8 Cal.3d 206, 210 [104 Cal.Rptr. 452, 501 P.2d 1172]; *Nightingale v. State Personnel Board* (1972) 7 Cal.3d 507, 512 [102 Cal.Rptr. 758, 498 P.2d 1006]; *Monroe v. Trustees of the California State Colleges* (1971) 6 Cal.3d 399, 412 [99 Cal.Rptr. 129, 491 P.2d 1105]; *Perrine v. Municipal Court* (1971) 5 Cal.3d 656, 663 [97 Cal.Rptr. 320, 488 P.2d 648].)

Morrison had engaged in a single incident of homosexual activity involving another teacher. Concluding that this activity constituted "immoral conduct," "unprofessional conduct," and "acts involving moral turpitude" under Education Code section 13202, the State Board of Education revoked his life diploma. On appeal, Morrison contended that the vagueness of the standards for revocation set out in section 13202 would permit the board to discipline a teacher merely because his private, personal conduct affronted the moral views of the board members.

To avoid finding section 13202 unconstitutional, we adopted a limited construction of that statute, holding that its "terms denote immoral or unprofessional conduct or moral turpitude of the teacher which indicates unfitness to teach." (1 Cal.3d at p. 225.) Specifically, we held that "an individual can be removed from the teaching profession only upon a showing that his retention in the profession poses a significant danger of harm to either students, school employees, or others who might be affected by his action as a teacher." (1 Cal.3d at p. 235.)

---

[1] In proceedings for the disbarment of attorneys or for the revocation of real estate licenses, the courts have held that "guilt must be established to a reasonable certainty . . . and cannot be based on surmise or conjecture, suspicion or theoretical conclusions, or uncorroborated hearsay." (*Small v. Smith* (1971) 16 Cal.App.3d 450, 457 [94 Cal.Rptr. 136].) The same degree of proof should be required for the revocation of a teaching certificate.

We then turned to the question whether proof of Morrison's homosexual conduct in itself constituted evidence of unfitness to teach. We stated: "Before the board can conclude that a teacher's continued retention in the profession presents a significant danger of harm to students or fellow teachers, essential factual premises in its reasoning should be supported by evidence or official notice. In this case, despite the quantity and quality of information available about human sexual behavior, the record contains no such evidence as to the significance and implications of the . . . incident. Neither this court nor the superior court is authorized to rectify this failure by uninformed speculation or conjecture as to petitioner's future conduct." (1 Cal.3d at p. 237). Concluding that no competent, credible evidence supported any inference of Morrison's unfitness to teach, we reversed the judgment of the superior court.

The majority opinion maintains that in the present case, unlike *Morrison*, substantial evidence supports the superior court's finding of unfitness to teach. They base this conclusion on three asserted differences between *Morrison* and the present case: that plaintiff's conduct was criminal in nature; that the acts occurred in a "semi-public atmosphere," and that the board presented expert opinion that she was unfit to teach. None of these distinctions will stand analysis.

Although the majority's whole case rests upon the proposition that one who engages in oral copulation commits a criminal act that constitutes "immoral or unprofessional conduct," the record does not show any such conviction for such offense by plaintiff. The majority likewise frankly concede that the "revocation of plaintiff's life diploma cannot be upheld solely by reason of the conviction [of outraging public decency] entered against her." (Majority opn., *ante*, p. 33.) [2] The record of that conviction, moreover, has been cleared from the books; it is no longer extant; those criminal proceedings have been dismissed. (See Pen. Code, § 1203.4.)

The board in the instant case has been driven to exhume an old and admitted indiscretion in order to lay the basis for the revocation of plaintiff's teaching credential. The challenged act was committed on December 2, 1967; the criminal proceedings were thereafter dismissed; subsequently, in February 1970—years later—the disciplinary proceedings were initiated. I am hard-put to understand the motivation of the board in bringing charges on a matter which plaintiff now recognizes as an indiscretion and for which she has paid the penalty—charges brought despite the fact that plaintiff has devoted 13 years to the exemplary and humane teaching of

[2] I note that Penal Code section 650½, which declares the misdemeanor of outraging public decency, was held unconstitutional in *In re Davis* (1966) 242 Cal.App.2d 645 [51 Cal.Rptr. 702]. In any event plaintiff's conduct, which occurred in a private home rather than in "public," and offended no one present, could not fall within the terms of this statute.

retarded elementary school children—charges designed to bar her permanently from teaching.

The kind of wastefulness of needed human resources that this procedure threatens becomes the more dangerous when we examine it in the context of other professions. If a highly proficient attorney commits an unorthodox sex act and thereafter suffers a misdemeanor conviction that is subsequently dismissed, may he then, years later, be disbarred because he admittedly committed the act and hence was guilty of "immoral" and "unprofessional" conduct? Should the skilled surgeon involved in a parallel situation suffer the same tragedy? The university professor? The danger of the majority's doctrine becomes especially onerous when we know that a large proportion of the younger generation do engage in unorthodox sexual activities deemed anathema by some members of the older generation. To what extent will we frustrate highly productive careers of younger persons in order to castigate conduct that is widely practiced by some but regarded by others as abominable? Is the legal standard to be no more definite or precise than that the involved practice is regarded as "immoral" or "unprofessional" or "tasteless" by judges?

The majority opinion does, indeed, proceed on the premise that plaintiff's failure to deny the act of oral copulation suffices to make her a confessed criminal and hence subject to cancellation of her certificate. On this ground the majority would distinguish *Morrison* because there the teacher's conduct infringed no penal statute. Yet in *Morrison* we expressly stated that "[i]n determining whether discipline is authorized and reasonable, a criminal conviction has no talismanic significance." (1 Cal.3d at p. 219, fn. 4.) This principle was recently reaffirmed by the Court of Appeal in *Comings v. State Bd. of Education* (1972) 23 Cal.App.3d 94 [100 Cal.Rptr. 73, 47 A.L.R.3d 742], which held that proof that a teacher had been convicted of possession of marijuana was not evidence of his unfitness to teach, and thus insufficient to sustain the revocation of a credential.

The principle that a criminal conviction is not ipso facto the basis for revocation of a certificate on the grounds of immoral or unprofessional conduct becomes clear when tested against specific acts of unlawful conduct. Obviously the commission of a misdemeanor, such as a traffic offense, could not seriously be urged as an automatic ground for revocation of a certificate. Convictions of other technical and legal offenses common in the society do not intrinsically constitute "immoral" or "unprofessional" conduct. Hence, in order to resolve the issue, we must examine the nature of the conduct and its relation, if any, to the role and functions of the teacher.

In the instant case the conduct involved consensual sexual behavior which deviated from traditional norms. Yet recognized authority tells us the practice pursued here is, indeed, quite common. An estimated "95% of adult American men and a large percentage of American women have experienced orgasm in an illegal manner." (McCary, Human Sexuality (2d ed. 1973) p. 460.) [3] The 1953 Kinsey report, Sexual Behavior in the Human Female, at page 399 indicates that 62 percent of the adult women of plaintiff's educational level and age range engage in oral copulation; more recently, the report's co-authors have stated that newer studies suggest the figure now lies around 75 to 80 percent.[4]

The consensual and, as I shall explain, private act did not affect, and could not have affected, plaintiff's teaching ability. The whole matter would have been forgotten and lost in the limbo of the privacy of its occurrence if it had not been clandestinely observed by means of a surreptitious intrusion which reminds one of the surveillance of restrooms which this court has condemned. (People v. Triggs (1973) 8 Cal.3d 884 [106 Cal.Rptr. 408, 506 P.2d 232].) The commission of a sex act, surreptitiously observed, not disclosed to fellow teachers or to pupils, not remotely adversely affecting plaintiff's teaching ability, must fail to support revocation of the certificate even though the act is labelled "criminal" on the books.

I am at somewhat of a loss to understand the majority's second ground for distinguishing Morrison: that plaintiff's acts in the instant case took place in the "semi-public atmosphere of a club party." (Majority opn., ante, p. 35.) Recognizing that many sexual acts incur no disapprobation when done in private, yet are properly punishable when forced upon an unwilling and disapproving viewer, statutes and decisions distinguish between private acts and those which occur in a public place or are open to public observation. For this purpose, the defining characteristic of a public place (Pen. Code, §647) is "annoyance to or the possibility of annoyance to members of the public present on premises where such acts are committed." (In re Steinke (1969) 2 Cal.App.3d 569, 576–577 [82 Cal. Rptr. 789].)

Plaintiff's acts occurred in the bedroom of a private home. The only persons witnessing the conduct were members of "The Swingers," a private club limited to persons who expressly attested their desire to view or engage in diverse sexual activity. Consequently, I conclude that plaintiff's acts occurred in a private place, not a public one or one open to public view.

By engaging in sexual activity in the presence of other "swingers," plaintiff, the majority assert, demonstrated "a serious defect of moral character, normal prudence and good common sense." (Majority opn., ante, p. 35.)[5] Yet plaintiff took reasonable precautions to assure that she

[3] The Kinsey Reports (Kinsey, Pomeroy & Martin, Sexual Behavior in the Human Male (1948); Kinsey, Pomeroy, Martin & Gebhard, Sexual Behavior in the Human Female (1953)) remain the only large scale studies.
[4] Testimony of Dr. William Hartman, professor of sociology at California State College, Long Beach, before the State Board of Education in the present proceeding.
[5] The majority's argument is analogous to that presented by the school board in Fisher v. Snyder (D.Neb. 1972) 346 F.Supp. 396, in which a teacher who permitted men to stay overnight in her apartment was discharged for "conduct unbecoming

was viewed only by persons who would not be offended by her conduct; many would argue that under such circumstances her behavior was neither imprudent nor immoral. In essence, the majority are saying that even though her fellow "swingers" were not offended, they—the majority—find plaintiff's behavior shocking and embarrassing. Yet this important issue of plaintiff's right to teach should not turn on the personal distaste of judges, the test, as this court has announced in the cases, is the rational one of the effect of the conduct, if any, on the teacher's fitness to teach.

I turn now to an examination of the underlying expert testimony presented to establish plaintiff's unfitness to teach. The first witness, William B. Calton, opined that plaintiff would be unable to teach "moral and spiritual principles." On cross-examination he limited this opinion to asserting that she would be unable to teach principles of sexual morality. But petitioner teaches retarded elementary school children, and, as Calton affirmed, her teaching duties do not encompass instruction on sexual morality. To sum up Calton's testimony: he states that plaintiff is unable to teach principles of sexual morality but that her teaching duties do not include the teaching of sexual morality.[6]

The second expert, Sylvester A. Moffet, testified with a broader brush. He stated that any teacher who ever engaged in sexual relations with anyone other than his lawful spouse was lacking in "clean morals," and thus could not instruct his students in "clean morals." In *Morrison* we stated that "[s]urely incidents of extramarital heterosexual conduct against a background of years of satisfactory teaching would not constitute 'immoral conduct' sufficient to justify revocation of a life diploma without any showing of an adverse effect on fitness to teach." (1 Cal.3d at pp.

---

a teacher." Finding the discharge a violation of the teacher's constitutional right to freedom of association (see 346 F.Supp. at p. 400), the court stated that the evidence supplied "no proof of impropriety in Mrs. Fisher's conduct which affected her classroom performance, . . ." (346 F.Supp. at p. 398.) The court added that the evidence, at most, raised a question of her good judgment in her personal affairs, but that issue was not sufficient to indicate unfitness to teach.

[6] The majority opinion cites Education Code section 13556.5, which requires teachers to "endeavor to impress upon the minds of the pupils the principles of morality," and assumes this statute refers to orthodox sexual practices. The State Board of Education, however, has adopted regulations implementing this statute. Those regulations, which are too lengthy to quote here, make no mention of sexual practices, but define morality in terms of truthfulness, respect for the opinion of others, freedom of conscience, respect for personal and group differences, and appreciation of the contribution of religious heritage. This administrative interpretation of the statute "is entitled to great weight, and courts generally will not depart from such construction unless it is clearly erroneous or unauthorized." (*Coco-Cola Co. v. State Bd. of Equalization* (1945) 25 Cal.2d 918, 921 [156 P.2d 1]; *Meyer v. Board of Trustees* (1961) 195 Cal.App.2d 420, 431 [15 Cal. Rptr. 717].) No evidence appears to suggest that plaintiff is unable to teach principles of honesty and respect for others.

225–226.) Moffet obviously disagrees, and would raise a standard that would furnish grounds for dismissal of innumerable teachers of this state.

The final expert, Archie Haskins, advanced an idiosyncratic definition of a "dishonest marriage"; honesty, to him, is not a matter of truthfulness and open dealing, but of sexual fidelity. Reasoning from this personal premise, he concludes that petitioner's marriage is a dishonest one. On cross-examination Haskins added the interesting note that "possibly sixty or seventy percent of me would feel that she was unfit and thirty percent of me would feel that I would need to give her some latitude personally." Haskins, however, is willing to subordinate his personal doubts to that which he believes would be the desires of his school board; as he testified "I may have private opinions as a school administrator, but I have five people on the Board of Education that I report to, and again, depending on what you know about that board; how they feel . . . I would probably designate her as unfit."

As we said in *People* v. *Bassett* (1968) 69 Cal.2d 122, 141 [70 Cal. Rptr. 193, 443 P.2d 777]: " 'Expert evidence is really an argument of an expert to the court, and is valuable only in regard to the proof of the *facts* and the validity of the *reasons* advanced for the conclusions.' " (Quoting, with added italics, from *People* v. *Martin* (1948) 87 Cal.App.2d 581, 584 [197 P.2d 379].) The only "fact" mentioned by the experts was the incident at the "swingers' " party; this fact was already in the record; we have submitted that in itself, it is not proof of unfitness to teach. The experts present no *reasons* for their conclusions. None of them know plaintiff; none considered her 13-year record of competent teaching; none could point to a single instance of past misconduct with students, nor articulate the nature of any possible future misconduct.

It is not surprising that the trial court concluded that the experts' opinions were not entitled to "great weight." Justice Cobey of the Court of Appeal put it even more accurately, holding that this expert opinion "does not reasonably inspire confidence nor is it of solid value."

The unproven premise of both the expert testimony and the majority opinion is that the fact of plaintiff's sexual acts at the "swingers' " party in itself demonstrates that she would be unable to set a proper example for her pupils or to teach them moral principles; this inability in turn demonstrates her unfitness to teach. This reasoning rests on factual assumptions concerning the relationship of consensual adult sexual behavior to classroom teaching which have absolutely no support in the evidence. If "immoral conduct" ipso facto shows inability to model or teach morals, and this in turn shows unfitness to teach, then we are left with the proposition that proof of "immoral conduct," whatever it may be, will always justify revocation of a teaching credential.

But in traveling this road the majority overlook constitutional predicates. Under the majority's interpretation of Education Code section

13202, the opinion of a superintendent that a teacher has committed an "immoral" act is sufficient to bar that teacher permanently from the profession; so interpreted, section 13202 would be unconstitutionally vague and overbroad. The concept of "immoral" conduct as enunciated by the majority roams without restraint. Undoubtedly some school superintendents believe the drinking of alcohol, the smoking of tobacco, or the playing of cards is immoral; others believe it immoral to serve in the military forces, and still others believe it immoral to refuse to serve. As the present case illustrates, there is a wide divergence of views on sexual morality; plaintiff did not believe her conduct immoral, and many would agree.[7] Since the statute, so interpreted, presents a vortex of vagueness, provides no warning of the kind of conduct that will lead to discipline, and establishes no standard by which the decision of the board can be measured, it is unconstitutionally vague.[8] These are the reasons why this court in *Morrison* concluded that the only viable test was the fitness of the teacher to teach.

In conclusion, I submit that the majority opinion is blind to the reality of sexual behavior. Its view that teachers in their private lives should exemplify Victorian principles of sexual morality, and in the classroom should subliminally indoctrinate the pupils in such principles, is hopelessly unrealistic and atavistic. The children of California are entitled to competent and dedicated teachers; when, as in this case, such a teacher is forced to abandon her lifetime profession, the children are the losers.

MOSK, J.   I dissent for the reasons thoughtfully and persuasively discussed by Justice Tobriner. I am also impressed with the cogent amici curiae argument presented, significantly, by two respected professional organizations: the National Education Association and the California Teachers' Association. And I note that a similar considered conclusion was reached by Justices Cobey and Schweitzer for the Court of Appeal.

In my opinion this court is conclusively bound by two unequivocal factual findings of the State Board of Education: that petitioner's "services as a teacher have been satisfactory and she was invited back to teach by the tender of a contract from her employer for the school year 1968–69" (*subsequent* to the incident involved herein); and that petitioner "is unlikely to repeat" the activities charged in the accusation.

[7] As Justice Sims observed in his concurring opinion in *Oakland Unified Sch. Dist.* v. *Olicker* (1972) 25 Cal.App.3d 1098, 1112 [102 Cal.Rptr. 421]: "[I]n this world there are many cultures and many concepts of what is acceptable sexual conduct, . . . It may be impossible to impose one strict moral code on all of society, and we may have to acquaint ourselves with, and accept, without puritanical prudery, as natural to them, the standards of others."

[8] I note that the United States District Court for the District of Oregon, in a recent decision, held an Oregon statute permitting the dismissal of teachers for "immorality" to be unconstitutionally vague. (*Burton* v. *Cascade School Dist.* (D.Ore. 1973) (353 F.Supp. 254.)

In view of those controlling factual determinations the majority opinion is unsupportable.

RICHARD A. WASSERSTROM

Is Adultery Immoral?

Many discussions of the enforcement of morality by the law take as illustrative of the problem under consideration the regulation of various types of sexual behavior by the criminal law. It was, for example, the Wolfenden Report's recommendations concerning homosexuality and prostitution that led Lord Devlin to compose his now famous lecture, "The Enforcement of Morals." And that lecture in turn provoked important philosophical responses from H. L. A. Hart, Ronald Dworkin, and others.

Much, if not all, of the recent philosophical literature on the enforcement of morals appears to take for granted the immorality of the sexual behavior in question. The focus of discussion, at least, is whether such things as homosexuality, prostitution, and adultery ought to be made illegal even if they are immoral, and not whether they are immoral.

I propose in this paper to think about the latter, more neglected topic, that of sexual morality, and to do so in the following fashion. I shall consider just one kind of behavior that is often taken to be a case of sexual immorality—adultery. I am interested in pursuing at least two questions. First, I want to explore the question of in what respects adulterous behavior falls within the domain of morality at all: For this surely is one of the puzzles one encounters when considering the topic of sexual morality. It is often hard to see on what grounds much of the behavior is deemed to be either moral or immoral, for example, private homosexual behavior between consenting adults. I have purposely selected adultery because it seems a more plausible candidate for moral assessment than many other kinds of sexual behavior.

The second question I want to examine is that of what is to be said about adultery, without being especially concerned to stay within the area of morality. I shall endeavor, in other words, to identify and to assess a number of the major arguments that might be advanced against adultery. I believe that they are the chief arguments that would be given in support of the view that adultery is immoral, but I think they are worth considering even if some of them turn out to be nonmoral arguments and considerations.

A number of the issues involved seem to me to be complicated and difficult. In a number of places I have at best indicated where further philosophical exploration is required without having successfully conducted the exploration myself. The paper may very well be more useful as an illustration of how one might begin to think about the subject of sexual morality than as an elucidation of important truths about the topic.

Before I turn to the arguments themselves there are two preliminary points that require some clarification. Throughout the paper I shall refer to the immorality of such things as breaking a promise, deceiving someone, etc. In a very rough way, I mean by this that there is something morally wrong that is done in doing the action in question. I mean that the action is, in a strong sense, of *"prima facie"* *prima facie* wrong or unjustified. I do not mean that it may never be right or justifiable to do the action; just that the fact that it is an action of this description always does count against the rightness of the action. I leave entirely open the question of what it is that makes actions of this kind immoral in this sense of "immoral."

The second preliminary point concerns what is meant or implied by the concept of adultery. I mean by "adultery" any case of extramarital sex, and I want to explore the arguments for and against extramarital sex, undertaken in a variety of morally relevant situations. Someone might claim that the concept of adultery is conceptually connected with the concept of immorality, and that to characterize behavior as adulterous is already to characterize it as immoral or unjustified in the sense described above. There may be something to this. Hence the importance of making it clear that I want to talk about extramarital sexual relations. If they are always immoral, this is something that must be shown by argument. If the concept of adultery does in some sense entail or imply immorality, I want to ask whether that connection is a rationally based one. If not all cases of extramarital sex are immoral (again, in the sense described above), then the concept of adultery should either be weakened accordingly or restricted to those classes of extramarital sex for which the predication of immorality is warranted.

One argument for the immorality of adultery might go something like this: what makes adultery immoral is that it involves the breaking of a promise, and what makes adultery seriously wrong is that it involves the breaking of an important promise. For, so the argument might continue, one of the things the two parties promise each other when they get married is that they will abstain from sexual relationships with third persons. Because of this promise both spouses quite reasonably entertain the expectation that the other will behave in conformity with it. Hence, when one of the parties has sexual intercourse with a third person he or she breaks that promise about sexual relationships which was made when the marriage was entered into, and defeats the reasonable expectations of exclusivity entertained by the spouse.

In many cases the immorality involved in breaching the promise relating to extramarital sex may be a good deal more serious than that involved in the breach of other promises. This is so because adherence to this promise may be of much greater importance to the parties than is adherence to many of the other promises given or received by them in their lifetime. The breaking of this promise may be much more hurtful and painful than is typically the case.

Why is this so? To begin with, it may have been difficult for the nonadulterous spouse to have kept the promise. Hence that spouse may feel the unfairness of having restrained himself or herself in the absence of reciprocal restraint having been exercised by the adulterous spouse. In addition, the spouse may perceive the breaking of the promise as an indication of a kind of indifference on the part of the adulterous spouse. If you really cared about me and my feelings—the spouse might say—you would not have done this to me. And third, and related to the above, the spouse may see the act of sexual intercourse with another as a sign of affection for the other person and as an additional rejection of the nonadulterous spouse as the one who is loved by the adulterous spouse. It is not just that the adulterous spouse does not take the feelings of the spouse sufficiently into account, the adulterous spouse also indicates through the act of adultery affection for someone other than the spouse. I will return to these points later. For the present, it is sufficient to note that a set of arguments can be developed in support of the proposition that certain kinds of adultery are wrong just because they involve the breach of a serious promise which, among other things, leads to the intentional infliction of substantial pain by one spouse upon the other.

Another argument for the immorality of adultery focuses not on the existence of a promise of sexual exclusivity but on the connection between adultery and deception. According to this argument, adultery involves deception. And because deception is wrong, so is adultery.

Although it is certainly not obviously so, I shall simply assume in this paper that deception is always immoral. Thus the crucial issue for my purposes is the asserted connection between extramarital sex and deception. Is it plausible to maintain, as this argument does, that adultery always does involve deception and is on that basis to be condemned?

The most obvious person on whom deceptions might be practiced is the nonparticipating spouse; and the most obvious thing about which the nonparticipating spouse can be deceived is the existence of the adulterous act. One clear case of deception is that of lying. Instead of saying that the afternoon was spent in bed with A, the adulterous spouse asserts that it was spent in the library with B, or on the golf course with C.

There can also be deception even when no lies are told. Suppose, for instance, that a person has sexual intercourse with someone other than his or her spouse and just does not tell the spouse about it. Is that deception? It may not be a case of lying if, for example, the spouse is never asked by the other about the situation. Still, we might say, it is surely deceptive because of the promises that were exchanged at marriage. As we saw earlier, these promises provide a foundation for the reasonable belief that neither spouse will engage in sexual relationships with any other persons. Hence the failure to bring the fact of extramarital sex to the attention of the other spouse deceives that spouse about the present state of the marital relationship.

Adultery, in other words, can involve both active and passive deception. An adulterous spouse may just keep silent or, as is often the fact, the spouse may engage in an increasingly complex way of life devoted to the concealment of the facts from the nonparticipating spouse. Lies, half-truths, clandestine meetings, and the like may become a central feature of the adulterous spouse's existence. These are things that can and do happen, and when they do they make the case against adultery an easy one. Still, neither active nor passive deception is inevitably a feature of an extramarital relationship.

It is possible, though, that a more subtle but pervasive kind of deceptiveness is a feature of adultery. It comes about because of the connection in our culture between sexual intimacy and certain feelings of love and affection. The point can be made indirectly at first by seeing that one way in which we can, in our culture, mark off our close friends from our mere acquaintances is through the kinds of intimacies that we are prepared to share with them. I may, for instance, be willing to reveal my very private thoughts and emotions to my closest friends or to my wife, but to no one else. My sharing of these intimate facts about myself is from one perspective a way of making a gift to those who mean the most to me. Revealing these things and sharing them with those who mean the most to me is one means by which I create, maintain, and confirm those interpersonal relationships that are of most importance to me.

Now in our culture, it might be claimed, sexual intimacy is one of the chief currencies through which gifts of this sort are exchanged. One way to tell someone—particularly someone of the opposite sex—that you have feelings of affection and love for them is by allowing to them or sharing with them sexual behaviors that one doesn't share with the rest of the world. This way of measuring affection was certainly very much a part of the culture in which I matured. It worked something like this. If you were a girl, you showed how much you liked someone by the degree of sexual intimacy you would allow. If you liked a boy only a little, you never did more than kiss—and even the kiss was not very passionate. If you liked the boy a lot and if your feeling was reciprocated, necking, and possibly petting, was permissible. If the attachment was still stronger and you thought it might even become a permanent relationship, the sexual activity was correspondingly more intense and more intimate, although whether it would ever lead to sexual intercourse depended on whether the parties (and particularly the girl) accepted fully the prohibition on non-marital sex. The situation for the boy was related, but not exactly the same. The assumption was that males did not naturally link sex with affection in the way in which females did. However, since women did, males had to take this into account. That is to say, because a woman would permit sexual intimacies only if she had feelings of affection for the male and only if those feelings were reciprocated, the male had to have and express those feelings, too, before sexual intimacies of any sort would occur.

The result was that the importance of a correlation between sexual intimacy and feelings of love and affection was taught by the culture and assimilated by those growing up in the culture. The scale of possible positive feelings toward persons of the other sex ran from casual liking at the one end to the love that was deemed essential to and characteristic of marriage at the other. The scale of possible sexual behavior ran from brief, passionless kissing or hand-holding at the one end to sexual intercourse at the other. And the correlation between the two scales was quite precise. As a result, any act of sexual intimacy carried substantial meaning with it, and no act of sexual intimacy was simply a pleasurable set of bodily sensations. Many such acts were, of course, more pleasurable to the participants because they were a way of saying what the participants feelings were. And sometimes they were less pleasurable for the same reason. The point is, however, that in any event sexual activity was much more than mere bodily enjoyment. It was not like eating a good meal, listening to good music, lying in the sun, or getting a pleasant back rub. It was behavior that meant a great deal concerning one's feelings for persons of the opposite sex in whom one was most interested and with whom one was most involved. It was among the most authoritative ways in which one could communicate to another the nature and degree of one's affection.

If this sketch is even roughly right, then several things become somewhat clearer. To begin with, a possible rationale for many of the rules of conventional sexual morality can be developed. If, for example, sexual intercourse is associated with the kind of affection and commitment to another that is regarded as characteristic of the marriage relationship, then it is natural that sexual intercourse should be thought properly to take place between persons who are married to each other. And if it is thought that this kind of affection and commitment is only to be found within the marriage relationship, then it is not surprising that sexual intercourse should only be thought to be proper within marriage.

Related to what has just been said is the idea that sexual intercourse ought to be restricted to those who are married to each other as a means by which to confirm the very special feelings that the spouses have for each other. Because the culture teaches that sexual intercourse means that the strongest of all feelings for each other are shared by the lovers, it is natural that persons who are married to each other should be able to say this to each other in this way. Revealing and confirming verbally that these feelings are present is one thing that helps to sustain the relationship; engaging in sexual intercourse is another.

In addition, this account would help to provide a framework within which to make sense of the notion that some sex is better than other sex. As I indicated earlier, the fact that sexual intimacy can be meaningful in the sense described tends to make it also the case that sexual intercourse can sometimes be more enjoyable than at other times. On this view, sexual intercourse will typically be more enjoyable where the strong feelings of affection are present than it will be where it is merely "mechanical." This is so in part because people enjoy being loved, especially by those whom they love. Just as we like to hear words of affection, so we like to receive affectionate behavior. And the meaning enhances the independently pleasurable behavior.

More to the point, moreover, an additional rationale for the prohibition on extramarital sex can now be developed. For given this way of viewing the sexual world, extramarital sex will almost always involve deception of a deeper sort. If the adulterous spouse does not in fact have the appropriate feelings of affection for the extramarital partner, then the adulterous spouse is deceiving that person about the presence of such feelings. If, on the other hand, the adulterous spouse does have the corresponding feelings for the extramarital partner but not toward the nonparticipating spouse, the adulterous spouse is very probably deceiving the nonparticipating spouse about the presence of such feelings toward that spouse. Indeed, it might be argued, whenever there is no longer love between the two persons who are married to each other, there is deception just because being married implies both to the participants and to the world that such a bond exists. Deception is inevitable, the argument might conclude, because the feelings of affection that ought to accompany any act of sexual intercourse can only be held toward one other person at any given time in one's life. And if this is so, then the adulterous spouse always deceives either the partner in adultery or the nonparticipating spouse about the existence of such feelings. Thus extramarital sex involves deception of this sort and is for this reason immoral even if no deception vis-à-vis the occurrence of the act of adultery takes place.

What might be said in response to the foregoing arguments? The first thing that might be said is that the account of the connection between sexual intimacy and feelings of affection is inaccurate. Not inaccurate in the sense that no one thinks of things that way, but in the sense that there is substantially more divergence of opinion than that account suggests. For example, the view I have delineated may describe reasonably accurately the concepts of the sexual world in which I grew up, but it does not capture the sexual *weltanschauung* of today's youth at all. Thus, whether or not adultery implies deception in respect to feelings depends very much on the persons who are involved and the way they look at the "meaning" of sexual intimacy.

Second, the argument leaves to be answered the question of whether it is desirable for sexual intimacy to carry the sorts of messages described above. For those persons for whom sex does have these implications, there are special feelings and sensibilities that must be taken into account. But it is another question entirely whether any valuable end—moral or otherwise—is served by investing sexual behavior with such significance. That is something that must be shown and not just assumed. It might, for instance, be the case that substantially more good than harm would come from a kind of demystification of sexual behavior: one that would encourage the enjoyment of sex more for its own sake and one that would reject the centrality both of the association of sex with love and of love with only one other person.

I regard these as two of the more difficult, unresolved issues that our culture faces today in respect to thinking sensibly about the attitudes toward sex and love that we should try to develop in ourselves and in our children. Much of the contemporary literature that advocates sexual liberation of one sort or another embraces one or the other of two different views about the relationship between sex and love.

One view holds that sex should be separated from love and affection. To be sure sex is probably better when the partners genuinely like and enjoy each other. But sex is basically an intensive, exciting sensuous activity that can be enjoyed in a variety of suitable settings with a variety of suitable partners. The situation in respect to sexual pleasure is no different from that of the person who knows and appreciates fine food and who can have a very satisfying meal in any number of good restaurants with any number of congenial companions. One question that must be settled here is whether sex can be so demystified; another, more important question is whether it would be desirable to do so. What would we gain and what might we lose if we all lived in a world in which an act of sexual intercourse was no more or less significant or enjoyable than having a delicious meal in a nice setting with a good friend? The answer to this question lies beyond the scope of this paper.

The second view seeks to drive the wedge in a different place. It is not the link between sex and love that needs to be broken; rather, on this view, it is the connection between love and exclusivity that ought to be severed. For a number of the reasons already given, it is desirable, so this argument goes, that sexual intimacy continue to be reserved to and shared with only those for whom one has very great affection. The mistake lies in thinking that any "normal" adult will only have those feelings toward one other adult during his or her lifetime—or even at any time in his or her life. It is the concept of adult love, not ideas about sex, that, on this view, needs demystification. What are thought to be both unrealistic and unfortunate are the notions of exclusivity and possessiveness that attach to the dominant conception of love between adults in our and other cultures. Parents of four, five, six, or even ten children can certainly claim and sometimes claim correctly that they love all of their children, that they love them all equally, and that it is simply untrue to their feelings to insist that the numbers involved diminish either the quantity or the quality of their love. If this is an idea that is readily understandable in the case of parents and children, there is no necessary reason why it is an impossible or undesirable ideal in the case of adults. To be sure, there is probably a limit to the number of intimate, "primary" relationships that any person can maintain at any given time without the quality of the relationship being affected. But one adult ought surely be able to love two, three, or even six other adults at any one time without that love being different in kind or degree from that of the traditional, monogomous, lifetime marriage. And as between the individuals in these relationships, whether within a marriage or without, sexual intimacy is fitting and good.

The issues raised by a position such as this one are also surely worth exploring in detail and with care. Is there something to be called "sexual love" which is different from parental love or the nonsexual love of close friends? Is there something about love in general that links it naturally and appropriately with feelings of exclusivity and possession? Or is there something about sexual love, whatever that may be, that makes these feelings especially fitting here? Once again the issues are conceptual, empirical, and normative all at once: What is love? How could it be different? Would it be a good thing or a bad thing if it were different?

Suppose, though, that having delineated these problems we were now to pass them by. Suppose, moreover, we were to be persuaded of the possibility and the desirability of weakening substantially either the links between sex and love or the links between sexual love and exclusivity. Would it not then be the case that adultery could be free from all of the morally objectionable features described so far? To be more specific, let us imagine that a husband and wife have what is today sometimes characterized as an "open marriage." Suppose, that is, that they have agreed in advance that extramarital sex is—under certain circumstances—acceptable behavior for each to engage in. Suppose, that as a result there is no impulse to deceive each other about the occurrence or nature of any such relationships, and that no deception in fact occurs. Suppose, too, that there is no deception in respect to the feelings involved between the adulterous spouse and the extramarital partner. And suppose, finally, that one or the other or both of the spouses then has sexual intercourse in circumstances consistent with these understandings. Under this description, so the agreement might conclude, adultery is simply not immoral. At a minimum, adultery cannot very plausibly be condemned either on the ground that it involves deception or on the ground that it requires the breaking of a promise.

At least two responses are worth considering. One calls attention to the connection between marriage and adultery; the other looks to more instrumental arguments for the immorality of adultery. Both issues deserve further exploration.

One way to deal with the case of the "open marriage" is to question whether the two persons involved are still properly to be described as being married to each other. Part of the meaning of what it is for two persons to be married to each other, so this argument would go, is to have committed oneself to have sexual relationships only with one's spouse. Of course, it would be added, we know that that commitment is not always honored. We know that persons who are married to each other often do commit adultery. But there is a difference between being willing to make a commitment to marital fidelity, even though one may fail to honor that commitment, and not making the commitment at all. Whatever the relationship may be between the two individuals in the case described above, the absence of any commitment to sexual exclusivity requires the conclusion that their relationship is not a marital one. For a commitment to sexual exclusivity is a necessary although not a sufficient condition for the existence of a marriage.

Although there may be something to this suggestion, as it is stated it is too strong to be acceptable. To begin with, I think it is very doubtful that there are many, if any, *necessary* conditions for marriage; but even if there are, a commitment to sexual exclusivity is not such a condition.

To see that this is so, consider what might be taken to be some of the essential characteristics of a marriage. We might be tempted to propose that the concept of marriage requires the following: a formal ceremony of some sort in which mutual obligations are undertaken between two persons of the opposite sex; the capacity on the part of the persons involved to have sexual intercourse with each other; the willingness to have sexual intercourse only with each other; and feelings of love and affection between the two persons. The problem is that we can imagine relationships that are clearly marital and yet lack one or more of these features. For example, in our own society, it is possible for two persons to be married without going through a formal ceremony, as in the common-law marriages recognized in some jurisdictions. It is also possible for two persons to get married even though one or both lacks the capacity to engage in sexual intercourse. Thus, two very elderly persons who have neither the desire nor the ability to have intercourse can, nonetheless, get married, as can persons whose sexual organs have been injured so that intercourse is not possible. And we certainly know of marriages in which love was not present at the time of the marriage, as, for instance, in marriages of state and marriages of convenience.

Counterexamples not satisfying the condition relating to the abstention from extramarital sex are even more easily produced. We certainly know of societies and cultures in which polygamy and polyandry are practiced, and we have no difficulty in recognizing these relationships as cases of marriages. It might be objected, though, that these are not counterexamples because they are plural marriages rather than marriages in which sex is permitted with someone other than with one of the persons to whom one is married. But we also know of societies in which it is permissible for married persons to have sexual relationships with persons to whom they were not married, for example, temple prostitutes, concubines, and homosexual lovers. And even if we knew of no such societies, the conceptual claim would still, I submit, not be well taken. For suppose all of the other indicia of marriage were present: suppose the two persons were of the opposite sex, suppose they had the capacity and desire to have intercourse with each other, suppose they participated in a formal ceremony in which they understood themselves voluntarily to be entering into a relationship with each other in which substantial mutual commitments were assumed. If all these conditions were satisfied, we would not be in any doubt about whether or not the two persons were married even though they had not taken on a commitment of sexual exclusivity and even though they had expressly agreed that extramarital sexual intercourse was a permissible behavior for each to engage in.

A commitment to sexual exclusivity is neither a necessary nor a sufficient condition for the existence of a marriage. It does, nonetheless, have this much to do with the nature of marriage: like the other indicia enumerated above, its presence tends to establish the existence of a marriage. Thus, in the absence of a formal ceremony of any sort, an explicit commitment to sexual exclusivity would count in favor of regarding the two persons as married. The conceptual role of the commitment to sexual exclusivity can, perhaps, be brought out through the following example. Suppose we found a tribe which had a practice in which all the other indicia of marriage were present but in which the two parties were *prohibited* ever from having sexual intercourse with each other. Moreover, suppose that sexual intercourse with others was clearly permitted. In such a case we would, I think, reject the idea that the two were married to each other and we would describe their relationship in other terms, for example, as some kind of formalized, special friendship relation—a kind of heterosexual "blood-brother" bond.

Compare that case with the following. Suppose again that the tribe had a practice in which all of the other indicia of marriage were present, but instead of a prohibition on sexual intercourse between the persons in the relationship there was no rule at all. Sexual intercourse was permissible with the person with whom one had this ceremonial relationship, but it was no more or less permissible than with a number of other persons to whom one was not so related (for instance, all consenting adults of the opposite sex). Although we might be in doubt as to whether we ought to describe the persons as married to each other, we would probably conclude that they were married and that they simply were members of a tribe whose views about sex were quite different from our own.

What all of this shows is that *a prohibition* on sexual intercourse between the two persons involved in a relationship is conceptually incompatible with the claim that the two of them are married. The *permissi-*

bility of intramarital sex is a necessary part of the idea of marriage. But no such incompatibility follows simply from the added permissibility of extramarital sex.

These arguments do not, of course, exhaust the arguments for the prohibition on extramarital sexual relations. The remaining argument that I wish to consider—as I indicated earlier—is a more instrumental one. It seeks to justify the prohibition by virtue of the role that it plays in the development and maintenance of nuclear families. The argument, or set of arguments, might, I believe, go something like this.

Consider first a farfetched nonsexual example. Suppose a society were organized so that after some suitable age—say, 18, 19, or 20—persons were forbidden to eat anything but bread and water with anyone but their spouse. Persons might still choose in such a society not to get married. Good food just might not be very important to them because they have underdeveloped taste buds. Or good food might be bad for them because there is something wrong with their digestive system. Or good food might be important to them, but they might decide that the enjoyment of good food would get in the way of the attainment of other things that were more important. But most persons would, I think, be led to favor marriage in part because they preferred a richer, more varied, diet to one of bread and water. And they might remain married because the family was the only legitimate setting within which good food was obtainable. If it is important to have society organized so that persons will both get married and stay married, such an arrangement would be well suited to the preservation of the family, and the prohibitions relating to food consumption could be understood as fulfilling that function.

It is obvious that one of the more powerful human desires is the desire for sexual gratification. The desire is a natural one, like hunger and thirst, in the sense that it need not be learned in order to be present within us and operative upon us. But there is in addition much that we do learn about what the act of sexual intercourse is like. Once we experience sexual intercourse ourselves—and in particular once we experience orgasm—we discover that it is among the most intensive, short-term pleasures of the body.

Because this is so, it is easy to see how the prohibition upon extramarital sex helps to hold marriage together. At least during that period of life when the enjoyment of sexual intercourse is one of the desirable bodily pleasures, persons will wish to enjoy those pleasures. If one consequence of being married is that one is prohibited from having sexual intercourse with anyone but one's spouse, then the spouses in a marriage are in a position to provide an important source of pleasure for each other that is unavailable to them elsewhere in the society.

The point emerges still more clearly if this rule of sexual morality is seen as of a piece with the other rules of sexual morality. When this prohibition is coupled, for example, with the prohibition on nonmarital sexual intercourse, we are presented with the inducement both to get married and to stay married. For if sexual intercourse is only legitimate within marriage, then persons seeking that gratification which is a feature of sexual intercourse are furnished explicit social directions for its attainment; namely marriage.

Nor, to continue the argument, is it necessary to focus exclusively on the bodily enjoyment that is involved. Orgasm may be a significant part of what there is to sexual intercourse, but it is not the whole of it. We need only recall the earlier discussion of the meaning that sexual intimacy has in our own culture to begin to see some of the more intricate ways in which sexual exclusivity may be connected with the establishment and maintenance of marriage as the primary heterosexual, love relationship. Adultery is wrong, in other words, because a prohibition on extramarital sex is a way to help maintain the institutions of marriage and the nuclear family.

Now I am frankly not sure what we are to say about an argument such as this one. What I am convinced of is that, like the arguments discussed earlier, this one also reveals something of the difficulty and complexity of the issues that are involved. So, what I want now to do—in the brief and final portion of this paper—is to try to delineate with reasonable precision what I take several of the fundamental, unresolved issues to be.

The first is whether this last argument is an argument for the *immorality* of extramarital sexual intercourse. What does seem clear is that there are differences between this argument and the ones considered earlier. The earlier arguments condemned adulterous behavior because it was behavior that involved breaking of a promise, taking unfair advantage, or deceiving another. To the degree to which the prohibition on extramarital sex can be supported by arguments which invoke considerations such as these, there is little question but that violations of the prohibition are properly regarded as immoral. And such a claim could be defended on one or both of two distinct grounds. The first is that things like promise-breaking and deception are just wrong. The second is that adultery involving promise-breaking or deception is wrong because it involves the straightforward infliction of harm on another human being—typically the nonadulterous spouse—who has a strong claim not to have that harm so inflicted.

The argument that connects the prohibition on extramarital sex with the maintenance and preservation of the institution of marriage is an argument for the instrumental value of the prohibition. To some degree this counts, I think, against regarding all violations of the prohibition as obvious cases of immorality. This is so partly because hypothetical imperatives are less clearly within the domain of morality than are categorical ones, and even more because instrumental prohibitions are within the domain of morality only if the end they serve or the way they serve it is itself within the domain of morality.

What this should help us see, I think, is the fact that the argument that connects the prohibition on adultery with the preservation of marriage is at best seriously incomplete. Before we ought to be convinced by it, we ought to have reasons for believing that marriage is a morally desirable and just social institution. And this is not quite as easy or obvious a task as it may seem to be. For the concept of marriage is, as we have seen, both a loosely structured and a complicated one. There may be all sorts of intimate, interpersonal relationships which will resemble but not be identical with the typical marriage relationship presupposed by the traditional sexual morality. There may be a number of distinguishable sexual and loving arrangements which can all legitimately claim to be called *marriages*. The prohibitions of the traditional sexual morality may be effective ways to maintain some marriages and ineffective ways to promote and preserve others. The prohibitions of the traditional sexual morality may make good psychological sense if certain psychological theories are true, and they may be purveyors of immense psychological mischief if other psychological theories are true. The prohibitions of the traditional sexual morality may seem obviously correct if sexual intimacy carries the meaning that the dominant culture has often ascribed to it, and they may seem equally bizarre when sex is viewed through the perspective of the counterculture. Irrespective of whether instrumental arguments of this sort are properly deemed moral arguments, they ought not to fully convince anyone until questions like these are answered.

JEROME NEU

What Is Wrong with Incest?

Incest taboos should be seen as involving non-sexual objections to sexual relations, that is, objections based on who people are in relation to each other, rather than their activities. What is at stake is brought out by considering certain objections to father–daughter incest and certain features of taboos. The objections that matter do not depend on social ties and distinctions having a biological basis, but there is nonetheless a biological element in incest taboos. To see it, one must look to the nature of the Oedipus complex, and to the conditions for the development of the individual and of society. There may be prohibitions which are necessary (to morality, to society, to humanity) even though they may not be justifiable within a narrower

Reprinted from *Inquiry*, Vol. 19, No. 1 (1976), 27–39, with the permission of the author and the publisher, Universitetsforlaget, Oslo.

conception (e.g. utilitarian) of morality and justification. And so taboos which are universal (occur, in one form or another, in every society), and absolute (allow no questioning), and impose strict liability (allow no excuse), may not be irrational: they may mark the boundaries that shape a way of life.

A friend wanted to have an affair with her cousin. She asked me if I could think of any reason why she should not. I could not (on just that basis) think of any. But then, are there any grounds other than affection that are admissible in limiting the choice of sexual objects (especially in those cases where affection is presumably most natural)? Are all possible relations open? Are taboos silly? Is everything (in the sphere of sexuality) permissible? If we cannot think of good reasons for existing institutions or practices, does that mean that the institutions or practices are dismissible? What is a 'good reason'? . . . I thought some more:

I

What is 'incest'? I shall take it to cover prohibited sexual relations where it is the identity of the persons involved rather than the nature of their acts that is essential, and where the relevant features of the parties are defined in terms of social roles or positions. Social roles or positions may or may not in turn be defined (within a particular society) in terms of biological relationships. This notion is broad enough to include prohibited sexual activities other than male–female genital intercourse (e.g. homosexual relations between fathers and sons), so long as the objection depends on the persons rather than the activity. The notion is narrow enough to exclude sexual prohibitions, say against homosexuality or particular perversions (e.g. shoe fetishism or bestiality), which do not include essential reference to particular parties (specified by social position) to whom the activities are prohibited. If an activity is prohibited to all in relation to all, the prohibition is not an 'incest taboo.' Thus, 'incest' is meant to pick out a particular type of objection to sexual activities: objection based on *who* people are in relation to each other, on social position, that is, on nonsexual relationships.

What is wrong with incest? As I am using the term, incestuous relations are by nature objectionable, and the problem is what in their nature makes them so. Posed in this way, I doubt that the question admits of an informative general answer. The answer will vary from society to society, with the types of social relationships leading to prohibitions, and the basis for drawing distinctions among social positions and relationships. Some more general insight may perhaps be obtained if we narrow our conception of incest to objections to sexual relations on the basis of social closeness rather than distance. So rules of exogamy (where these cover sexual relations—whatever else may or may not be included in 'marriage' relations) would be included, but rules of endogamy would not. (Of course there are restrictions on sexual relations within endogamous societies, the question is whether it is helpful to treat the restrictions on sexual relations with outsiders, the rules of endogamy, as themselves cases of 'incest' prohibitions.) And the fact that a woman may be prohibited in a certain society from marrying a man of lesser wealth does not necessarily reveal much about that society's view of the interdependence of class and sexuality. Such a prohibition might serve a vast range of functions and be based on a wide variety of beliefs. The same would be true were the prohibition to make reference to the man being of equal or greater wealth or even being 'too close' in wealth. This suggests a further narrowing of the conception of incestuous relationships so that specifications of social role having to do only with 'family,' and not (say) 'class,' would be relevant. But this sort of distinction is very difficult and would require elaborate discussion, and we would risk losing the generality I had hoped to obtain by not taking 'incest' as simply sexual relations between blood relatives. So I will try to take some first steps towards the problem by discussing a particular conception of incest, ours, and a particular incestuous relationship, father–daughter, bearing in mind their connection with the broader concept we started with.

II

What is wrong with father–daughter incest in the eyes of the West? Or rather, what reasons might there be for prohibiting father–daughter incest in our society if a prohibition did not already exist?

1. An easy, but inadequate, answer is that it leads to genetic disaster. That discovery (if the claim is true) may well have come long after the prohibitions it is meant to explain, and in relation to the present, modern contraceptive technology makes it irrelevant. And the truth is that under certain conditions, as animal breeders can tell us, inbreeding can actually help maintain desirable traits. In any case, since sexual relations need no longer carry with them the danger of procreation, one need neither calculate nor fear the genetic consequences of incest.

2. The next answer is far more significant: mother will not like it. This difficulty is real and serious. A person who has a right to consideration and affection is sure to be hurt. The Oedipal triangle exists (and conceived broadly enough may exist in every society),[1] and so the suffering comes inevitably (though allowing special exceptions) with the incest. This difficulty is structural and rather different from (say) the problem

[1] This point is elaborated in my 'Genetic Explanation in *Totem and Taboo*,' in Richard Wollheim (Ed.), *Freud: A Collection of Critical Essays*, Anchor Modern Studies in Philosophy, Doubleday & Co., Garden City, New York 1974, pp. 366–93.

that daughters may not happen to find their fathers sexually attractive: lack of physical attraction may arise as an objection to any sexual partner, but the suffering of an important third party, while not peculiar to incestuous relationships, is inherent in them. Other affairs in other circumstances may, it is true, leave third parties unhappy (the usual case with adultery). But, outside of incestuous situations, there is nothing to guarantee that any third parties who might be involved will be significant to *both* participants in an affair. Mothers are bound to their daughters as well as to their husbands. Societal structure ensures that they are significant figures to both, and entitled to the concern of both. And the impact may be reciprocal: from harm to the mother's feelings there may follow danger to the daughter's developmental needs. That is, if the mother has even the fantasy that she is raising her daughter to be a sexual object for the father (and it is significant that humans can have such fantasies and that there is no reason to believe that animals can), she may be less willing and able to provide the needed mothering. The taboo is a barrier to certain thoughts (including fantasies) as well as to action.

3. A third answer is one that attracted Freud's interest in *Civilization and Its Discontents*: it is difficult enough to break out of the family as it is, with the addition of sexual relations and dependence it becomes virtually impossible. Incest is (literally) anti-social. Dependence comes with the relations. Sexual urges (in the context of incest prohibitions) are among the leading forces for breaking out of the family and forming complex social structures and relationships; necessary conditions for civilization. It may also be true, as Freud suggests, that sex (even non-incestuous sex) is by its nature anti-social. The parties may become sufficient unto themselves. But where they are part of the same family, society is more likely to break up into little divided family enclaves, perhaps cooperating where they must but never forming a community.[2] If we add a further assumption about limited psychic energy, so that what is given over to sexuality is not available for social purposes, the difficulties for society are obvious. (We should note, of course, that this added assumption makes matters no worse in the case of incestuous sexual relations than for other kinds.) From the point of view of the individual, in addition to the loss of the advantages of larger society and civilization, if the family encroaches on sexual as well as all other needs, she becomes so much the more the prisoner of the family. And, of course, should the affair fail she may have to go on living in the midst of a ruined prison. (And even if she need not stay, the family may be ruined—though that involves a different sort of loss.)

4. This relation of dependence brings us to a fourth objectionable

---

[2] Lévi-Strauss develops this idea (though perhaps confusing sex and marriage—incest and exogamy—in the process) in terms of women as tokens for exchange in his *The Elementary Structures of Kinship*. See Edmund Leach, *Lévi-Strauss*, Fontana Modern Masters, Collins Publishers, Glasgow and London 1970, Ch. VI.

feature of incestuous relations, or at least the form we have been focussing on. And it is perhaps the feature that contributes most to making incest seem worse than merely odd or disagreeable. The power structure, the structure of dependency, is such that the propositioned daughter is put in an unfair position. (This way of putting it assumes that the father makes the initial overt move, even if in response to a seductively active daughter. But the point holds in any case.) Too much is at stake. The situation may be compared to that of the boss who insists on sexual relations with his secretary. She may fear for her job. Her refusal is not a simple refusal of sexual relations, for she remains involved and dependent in other ways. The situation is even more extreme in the case of the father who propositions his daughter. Even if there is no direct threat of breaking the many other ties, a refusal of sexual relations may be experienced (by both parties) as a rejection on more levels than that of the original approach. Society's disapproval takes the burden off the daughter (and father) by helping ensure that the question does not arise. Teacher–student affairs may also provide an analogy, perhaps a better one than bosses and secretaries, for here the age-gap, custodial obligations, and societal disapproval are clearer. Some taboos are irrational. Some, when understood, have a variety of virtues.

III

Now, where do these points take us? Some way, to be sure; but, unfortunately, not terribly far nor terribly deep. If we were a daughter wondering whether to have an affair with our father (or vice versa), we would now have some general reasons not to. These reasons are independent of whether or not a taboo against this form of incest happens to exist in our society. But precisely because the reasons are independent reasons for a prohibition, they do not explain why the prohibition should take the form of a taboo (we have only 'rationalized' the taboo). Taboos allow no questioning. Reasons, precisely because they are reasons, leave room for questioning. The reasons we have brought forward depend on features (admittedly, broad structural features) of our society; and so, in a given case, may not apply. What if (looking to our second point) mother does not mind, or, what if she is dead? The inevitable suffering of a significant third party may no longer seem so inevitable. And who would be the aggrieved third party in brother–sister incest? To explain the taboo here one might have to consider that a father who cannot have his daughter may nonetheless be jealous of her and so place her off limits for his son as well. (Of course, he might wish to stop all rivals, but he can most readily enforce his jealousy against the rival who is in his home. In any case, there is a question about whether the jealousy is justifiable.) Clearly, not all of the four factors we have brought out underlie all incest taboos in all cultures, nor are they the only factors even in our own. And certainly more must be done to distinguish factors connected with incest from factors that may apply to more general sexual prohibitions. For example, what makes father–daughter incest more than just a special case of prohibitions on adult–child sexual relations? For one thing, incest taboos, as we have said, are a matter of closeness and adult–child (as opposed to parent–child) prohibitions are a matter of distance. For another thing, objections to father–daughter incest presumably hold even when the daughter has become an adult. But (thinking back) are the objections to incest really the same or as strong when the child has become an adult as when she (or he) is an adolescent or pre-pubescent? (In this connection, it might be useful to consider the different applications and consequences of laws against statutory rape and incest laws.) So far we have only a beginning or a fragment of an analysis; a hint at the character of some of the non-sexual objections to sexual relations involved in 'incest' (understood in the broad sense we started with). It should be noted, however, that the points made already extend beyond a narrowly biological conception of incest: we rejected the objection to father–daughter incest that depended on genealogy and genetics, and the other points made would all (in our society) be as applicable to step-fathers as to fathers. (Lawyers speak of 'consanguinity' and 'affinity'.)

Though the points we have so far brought forward may justify certain incest prohibitions, they neither justify nor explain incest taboos— even within our society and even restricting our view to father–daughter incest. They may provide reasons for obeying an incest prohibition for someone who does not accept the prohibition as a taboo. But there may be good reasons why the prohibition takes the form of a taboo—a form which puts the demand for reasons out of place, and which imposes strict liability and so puts the offering of excuses out of place as well. Moreover, every society, every way of life, has its taboos, and these taboos always include (so the anthropologists tell us) incest taboos. No society allows all forms of sexual activity among all of its members. Every society prohibits absolutely (that is, unconditionally) certain sexual relations between certain persons on the basis of their social closeness. Why should this be so?

IV

Let us look at a famous case of parent–child incest. What is the tragedy of Oedipus? Why is Oedipus so upset? As far as is in his power he does no wrong, at every point he makes what (in his culture) would be the right choice, and yet, despite his best intentions and efforts, he kills his father and sleeps with his mother. In reality, he has no choice. When he comes to know of what he has done, he recognizes that his actions, though they fulfill his fate and are not his fault (he did not know what he was doing, indeed he did what he did precisely in order to avoid his predicted fate—and so, by the standards of post-Kantian morality and perhaps by those of Sophocles' own later play, *Oedipus at Colonus,* he is not responsible), nevertheless constitute a misfortune. As far as the four factors brought out in relation to father–daughter incest go, it is not even clear what the misfortune in his case is. Ignorance, and the other circumstances in his case, would seem to make his actions unobjectionable. But surely something is wrong. We may wish Oedipus had not blinded himself— the punishment may seem extreme—but what would we think if he had merely chuckled and said 'Oh well, too bad, I tried to avoid it but fate seems to have won through'? Part of the point of tragedy, like the point of taboo, is that it allows no excuse. It was *his* fate and *his* misfortune. Despite circumstances, certain losses cannot be cancelled and certain hands cannot be made clean. Ancient morality leaves important room for the actual, for what in fact happens (detached from one's will and intentions), and it may still have a place in modern morality marked, perhaps, by taboo, by strict prohibitions.

What stands on the surface of ancient morality may perhaps be understood with the help of the depth vision of modern psychology. Though Oedipus knew not what he did at the time he did it, he nonetheless *meant* to do it. It was his unconscious wish. And that it was his unconscious wish, that it included a sexual desire, that that desire was the object of an incest taboo, that incest taboos (of one form or another) are universal, and that the particular form of incest taboos is patterned on features of a given society's social structure—none of these things are accidents. I mentioned earlier that the Oedipal triangle, if conceived broadly enough, may exist in every society. Let me sketch briefly what I mean and why it is a consequence of the conditions (biological and social) for human development that such a constellation of desires and emotions should exist, and be the object of prohibitions.

Born a helpless mammal into the world, if the human infant is to survive there must be a supporting figure (or figures)—typically, in our society and in most (here consider the facts of lactation), the mother. A dependency relation is formed, and this early attachment is a primary form of love. But with the supporting figure there always comes a rival. And it is not a mere accident that there is a rival, that there is another party that takes the child's 'mother' as a love object. That there was at one point, at least, a third party is a biological necessity, a matter of the conditions for procreation. That there continues to be a third party (or parties) after the child's birth—though it need not be the child's biological father—also has a biological basis. The mother is herself a mammal with needs and desires of her own, needs and desires that cannot be met by her infant, and that impel her to establish and maintain relations with other adult mammals. And these others come to be seen, by the child, as rivals for the love, affection, time and concern of the mother. Hence the

Oedipal triangle is complete, and the essential emotional constellation established on the basis of the biologically prolonged dependency of the mammalian child and the biological needs and relations of the supporting mammalian adults. Breaking out of the triangle of dependent love and concomitant jealousy involves a long and complex process of growth. The conflicts themselves become most acute at a particular stage in the child's growth and development, a stage determined by biological conditions and the conditions for socialization. The shape of a particular society will help determine who the loved supporting figures and who the hated rivals and socializing authority figures will be. In the end, according to psychoanalytic theory, a superego is formed as the result of identification and introjection of the figures who restrain one's Oedipal wishes: moral prohibitions arise out of fear of punishment by or fear of the loss of love of an authority figure on whom one is dependent. In telling his complex story (and the story is doubtless more complex for women), Freud employs (in *Totem and Taboo*) the myth of the brothers who band together and slay and eat (and so literally incorporate) the primal father. The incest taboo emerges because their (ambivalent) love for the father comes to the fore after his slaying. The sons then identify with his prohibitions (incorporated in their superegos). What is prohibited is what father would not have liked. The taboo emerges also because the liberated brothers might otherwise renew among themselves the conflict over the women that led to their revolt against their father in the first place—without the taboo they might all continue their strife for their father's role. (Note that these two points have important connections with the second and third points in our discussion of father–daughter incest, points about mother not liking it and breaking out of the family for social cooperation.) It may be a condition for the maintenance of each society that it be true to its origins. The superego and its requirements, the strict liability that it imposes on us all, may be conditions for the formation of mature object relations and societal order. That every society must feel those prohibitions (in one form or another) may follow (perhaps not simply, but nonetheless may follow) from the conditions for its existence as a society.[3]

V

More has to be done, I think, to show how taboos may connect with the conditions of a moral consciousness and how, in the light of their universality, they connect with the conditions for any society. Taboos, particularly incest taboos, may be essential to the development of character,

---

[3] What the role of the performance of plays such as *Oedipus Rex* and related rituals (e.g. the tetomic feasts discussed by Freud) may be raises interesting questions. It may be that they provide occasions both for violating the taboo and for reaffirming its force (by repeating the feelings that led to its original institution).

to the development of the superego and to full object relations, to the shape of a way of life. Unless we were able to feel guilt at incest, perhaps we could not feel guilt at anything, or be fit for social relations. A person undisturbed by incest might be undisturable by any social prohibition. In my too brief sketch, it can be seen that we get our superego from precisely those whose love we fear to lose. Granted that we do not want their disapproval, however, why should they disapprove incest in particular? I hope that discussion of the nature of incest, of the nature of incest prohibitions, and of the place of drives towards incest in the development of individuals and societies may help us to see how the pieces fit together.

I cannot carry that discussion much further here, but perhaps I can at least suggest that the (or a) key may be in the notions of identity and identification. Each generation must win its identity, partly through struggle with the older generation and partly through something like mourning for its loss. The 'something like mourning' amounts to identification. But the identification makes sense only through difference, as a culmination of the effort to overcome infantile dependence and achieve autonomy. Incest destroys difference: categories collapse, people cease to have clear and distinct sexual and social places (consider the scene in the film *Chinatown* where the confusion bursts out in the anguished 'sister/daughter, sister/daughter . . .' confrontation); and with the destructoin of difference people cease to have the possibility of shifting from one place to another as they develop. Perhaps that might make incest seem attractive to some. But I suspect that violation of incest taboos would not itself be an effective revolutionary act. While destroying difference and confusing roles and perhaps undermining authority, it would not overcome dependence—which, as I have said, I think is a biological and social necessity. Violation of incest taboos or their abolition would not, I think, allow the establishment of a stable, mature, independent identity.

If one turns to the clinical literature to confirm one's suspicions about the effects of incest on development, one encounters a number of problems. First, there is not much data. Secondly, the paucity is apparently systematic, i.e. in our society father–daughter incest is the form most commonly reported, but there is reason to believe sibling incest is the most common in occurrence. Mother–son incest is extremely rare in published accounts and homosexual incest is hardly ever even mentioned. Perhaps sibling incest is not usually reported precisely because its effects are not particularly deleterious, or perhaps precisely because it is so common. There are also questions about *who* would report it—is there a victim? an aggrieved third party?—and what exactly is the line between childish or adolescent sex play and incest? (If we understand sexuality in the broad way suggested by Freud in his *Three Essays on the Theory of Sexuality* then incestuous desires and acts need not involve genital intercourse.) Thirdly, the data are clinical (or even less helpful, criminal) and therefore of course reveal (if they reveal anything) severe psychological disruption. It is extremely difficult to get data on cases where consummated incest is not harmful. (Louis Malle's film, *Souffle au Coeur*, plays on the assumption, or wish, that such cases are possible.) Fourthly and finally, it is difficult to distinguish, in those cases where there is harm, how much of it is attributable to the existence of the prohibition rather than the incest itself. That is, is the harm a product of the prohibition or an independent reason for having a prohibition? The prohibition itself may cause problems, or given the prohibition perhaps only people who are already otherwise disturbed engage in incest. All this makes it difficult to isolate its consequences.

VI

But perhaps this sort of calculation of consequences is wrongheaded (or really only illuminates one special aspect of our question). For the prohibition is a taboo. It is unconditional. That is, in one sense of unconditional, it is not a means to an independently valued end, but a necessary part of a way of life and ideal of human relationship. And these notions of a 'way of life' and an 'ideal of relationship' may be more central than the conditions for development of the superego in understanding the role of fixed boundaries or prohibitions in morality. The simple calculation of psychological consequences may miss the importance of 'identity,' where the identity of the individual is intimately connected with the coherence of a way of life distinguished by the characteristic virtues and vices and patterns of relationship recognized within it. When one says taboos are absolute and unconditional but may not be irrational one should compare them with something like ideals of justice which are also not simply assimilable to utilitarian calculations. There are in fact a number of ideals in various spheres which make for absolute prohibitions. One must not betray friends, not simply because they might become angry, but because they would no longer be 'friends,' indeed, the betrayal might reveal that they never were. Certain sorts of loyalty may be necessary to certain sorts of friendship. And those sorts of friendship are valuable. One must beware too narrow notions of what counts as a reason here. Certain sorts of love demand certain sorts of trust. And certain sorts of trust may rule out certain sorts of reasons. To trust because one has weighed the evidence (where one is willing to waver if the evidence does) may be as bad as not trusting at all. One's love may then be of the wrong kind. A certain ideal of love lies behind unquestioning trust. And the value of that ideal, its place in a way of life, may count as a reason for valuing that sort of trust and excluding certain sorts of doubts. Unquestioning attitudes are needed for certain kinds or qualities of relationship. The role of faith in religion might provide another way to get a handle on this difficult set of issues. (We should remember that 'taboo' is itself originally a religious notion.)

I am inclined to think that these sorts of cases, and especially the restrictions placed on action by ideals of justice (which make certain actions
'unthinkable' or 'unconscionable'), provide the most useful parallels for
understanding the restrictions that incest taboos place on sexual relations.

There may be prohibitions which are necessary (to morality, to society, to humanity) even though they may not be justifiable within a
narrower conception (e.g. utilitarian) of morality and justification.[4] It is
not an accident that every society has incest taboos, that every society
prohibits some sexual relations on grounds independent of the intrinsic
character of the activity involved (which is, in other circumstances, approved) but based rather on social relations. It may be that it is a condition of social relations that members of a society be able to feel the force
of (if not obey) such prohibitions. The pattern of the prohibitions may
vary from society to society and with the structure of social relations, but
there could be no society without some such prohibitions and the possibility of respect for them. And the fact that the prohibitions are sexual
may have to do with the conditions for psychosocial development of the
individual, and so have a biological basis. (Restrictions on impulses to
murder, on aggression, may similarly be universal, and necessary, and
absolute, and also have a biological basis.) Prohibitions which are absolute
within a particular society (even if they are different in different societies)
even though they cannot be fully understood or justified (in a narrow
sense) may be essential to morality (in a broader sense) and to society
and so to humanity (insofar as man is a social animal). The key to understanding taboos, as opposed to other sorts of social prohibitions (legal,
utilitarian, etc.), may lie in those very features of taboos that are most
puzzling to modern moral consciousness: taboos are universal (every society has some, including, in particular, taboos on murder and incest), and
absolute (are unconditional and allow no questioning), and impose strict
liability (allow no excuse). These features may not be irrational. But
while we must consider this possibility, we should also be aware of how
paradoxical it is to reach this sort of conclusion, which calls a halt to
questioning, after the sort of questioning or as the result of the sort of
questioning we have just ourselves engaged in. The taboo is, of course,
meant to extend to thought and not just action. Some things (incest,
betrayal of a friend . . .) are supposed to be unthinkable. Is there a line
between 'thinking' and 'thinking about'?

VII

In summary: Incest taboos should be seen as involving non-sexual objections to sexual relations, that is, objections based on who people are in

---

[4] On the place of absolute prohibitions in morality and ways of life, see Stuart Hampshire, 'Morality and Pessimism,' *New York Review of Books*, Vol. XIX, Nos.
11–12 (January 25, 1973), pp. 26–33.

relation to each other, rather than their activities. What is at stake is brought out by considering certain objections to father–daughter incest and certain features of taboos. The objections that matter do not depend on social ties and distinctions having a biological basis, but there is nonetheless a biological element in incest taboos. To see it, one must look to the nature of the Oedipus complex, and to the conditions for the development of the individual and of society. There may be prohibitions which are necessary (to morality, to society, to humanity) even though they may not be justifiable within a narrower conception (e.g. utilitarian) of morality and justification. And so taboos which are universal (occur, in one form or another, in every society), and absolute (allow no questioning), and impose strict liability (allow no excuse), may not be irrational: they may mark the boundaries that shape a way of life.[5]

RONALD ATKINSON

The Morality of Homosexual Behavior

The Wolfenden Committee did not spend much time on the question of morality of homosexual behaviour. Possibly they felt that in any way to question its immorality would only arouse opposition to their recommendation concerning the attitude to be taken to it by the law. They are emphatic that, in staking a claim for a sphere of private morality and immorality beyond the reach of the law, they do not wish to be understood as condoning private immorality. Moreover, in so far as the concern is with *positive* morality, the received code of behaviour such as it is, there is no doubt at all that homosexual activity is immoral. But can one avoid asking the question whether positive morality is right on this matter? Suppose, as the Wolfenden Committee thought, that there may be homosexual acts which do no harm to non-consenting non-adults, and which, being private, are no affront to public decency—on what grounds could they be held to be morally wrong?

Reprinted from Ronald Atkinson, *Sexual Morality*, copyright © 1965 by Ronald Atkinson. Reprinted by permission of the author, Harcourt Brace Jovanovich, Inc., and Hutchinson & Co., London.

[5] A version of this paper was presented at the Pacific Division Meeting of the American Philosophical Association in March 1975. It has benefited from the comments of a number of people, but I am especially indebted to Robert Meister for criticism of an earlier draft. What is best in the paper is due to him.

Not on utilitarian grounds, obviously; nor, leaving out of account the present state of the law and public opinion, on prudential grounds either. People do not choose to become homosexuals, they rather find that they are: and even if they should then want to change the direction of their sexual inclinations, which they may not, there would at present seem to be no certainty that this can be successfully accomplished. To deny one's sexual nature all physical expression, still ignoring the consequences homosexuals may suffer from law and public opinion, goes beyond, if not contrary to, the demands of prudence.

It may be that, in fact, many homosexual relationships present morally objectionable features: they may involve seduction, and exploitation of the young. But the evidence noticed above suggests that most do not, and that the risk of a homosexual who practices with fellow adults turning to boys is comparatively small. It is, moreover, relevant to the assessment of the moral importance of such risk as there is to point out that the harm done by seduction, or even assault, to young boys can easily be exaggerated—as can the damage done by heterosexual interference with small girls. In both cases the extreme reactions of parents, understandable though they may be, tend to increase the harm. And the likelihood of a boy being turned into a homosexual by seduction would not seem to be very great, as home influences are more important than outside encounters in determining one's sexual orientation. Most men who engage in homosexual activity in special circumstances—school, prison, the army—appear to abandon it when heterosexual opportunities become available. Some, much, even most homosexual activity may be morally exceptionable: so too is a good deal of heterosexual activity. In neither case is this necessarily so. Nor does it appear that homosexual relationships in themselves are necessarily more objectionable than heterosexual ones. I can see no good reason to doubt that it is possible for a homosexual to conduct his sexual life with prudence, beneficence, fairness and responsibility. If he does, there is no ground for moral complaint.

Another claim that is often made is that homosexual relationships are apt to be morally worthless or of little worth, to fall very far short of the ideal form of human relationship. (It is important to distinguish this complaint from the previous one. *That* was to the effect that they offended against, so to say, 'basic morality': *this* is to the effect that they are not ideal. . . .) Homosexual relations seem normally to be of brief duration, and homosexual promiscuity to be common. They seem, that is to say, to resemble those heterosexual relationships which are held to be least worth while. This sort of contention has great rhetorical force. It purports to make a lavish concession, to allow, as, of course, many people do not, that homosexual relationships are to be judged on the *same footing* as heterosexual ones, and yet still contrives to find them objectionable. How far must we go along with it?

Two comments are in place. The first, and less important one, is that the unworthwhile features manifested by some homosexual relationships may largely be the result of the public attitude to them. The result of, and hence not the justification for, that attitude. Stable relationships are hardly possible when all homosexual associations are condemned out of hand The more important point is that, low though casual sexual encounters may be on the heterosexual's scale of preference, they may still be the best or only form of sexual association available to the homosexuals involved. The basic morality of avoiding harm and unfairness to others we may reasonably demand of everybody: our ideals in so far as they go beyond this are for the guidance of our own, not other people's, conduct. In general we do not blame people, or hold them to be wicked or immoral, for not sharing our ideals; at worst we may hold them misguided or mistaken, or that they are 'missing something'. It is doubtful, in fact, whether even such mild criticisms or commiserations fit the case of the homosexual, who has not chosen his condition and probably cannot change it.

It may further be noted that from the point of view of the morality of personal relationships, which was considered in a different connexion above . . . , homosexual associations as such cannot be held to be immoral. The authors of the Quaker pamphlet recognize this with characteristic candour:

> . . . we see no reason why the physical nature of a sexual act should be the criterion by which the question whether it is moral should be decided. An act which (for example) expresses true affection between two individuals and gives pleasure to them both, does not seem to us to be sinful by reason *alone* of the fact that it is homosexual. The same criteria seems to us to apply whether a relationship is heterosexual or homosexual [p. 36].

I expressed some doubt above about the responsibility of viewing heterosexual associations exclusively from the agent-centred ethic of personal relationships. This seemed to me to take insufficient account of the possibility of children being conceived. This consideration does not arise where homosexual associations are concerned.

It is true, of course, that many people find the thought of homosexual practice deeply disgusting. It is sometimes suggested that this is the result of over-compensation for their own latent homosexuality, but whatever the explanation of it, the fact remains. One cannot, however, allow any simple inference from the disgusting to the immoral. In fact, surely, in this case the movement of thought is the other way. Homosexual practices are felt to be peculiarly disgusting because they are held to be exceptionally sinful or immoral. They disgust because they are 'unnatural'.

No one who thinks like this will be induced to improve his view of homosexual activity by such claims as that made by Chesser (*Live and Let Live*, pp. 30–31) that the most abominated homosexual act, anal intercourse, is probably commoner among married than homosexual couples.

The act is felt to be abominable whenever and between whomsoever it occurs. What puts homosexuals utterly beyond the pale is that *all* their physical sexual activities are necessarily unnatural in some degree, even if not in the very highest.

It is, as already suggested . . . , a matter of great difficulty to grasp the rationale of this way of thinking, to make sense of the notions of *nature* and *the natural* involved. As a beginning one has to suppose that the purpose or function of sex is mainly procreation. It would seem to follow that heterosexual intercourse which is intended to be fertile is the ideally natural sexual act. This is not, however, exactly the conclusion usually desired, for such intercourse clearly could take place outside marriage or even a loving relationship. Consequently sex has to be allowed a second, non-procreative, 'relational' or companionate purpose, which may then be held to be achievable only within marriage. Provided not too much is made of the relational purpose, provided that it is kept firmly subordinate to the procreational one, homosexual activity is still bound to come out as unnatural—it cannot fulfil procreational purposes at all. But, as we shall see in connexion with contraception in the next chapter, there are snags in emphasising the importance of the procreational purpose. Suppose we want to allow deliberately infertile heterosexual intercourse within marriage. Even in this case it is still possible to pay some regard to the claims of procreation by insisting that couples should not refuse to have children altogether, even though they may use contraceptives for a large proportion of their married life. This is a typically Anglican attitude, expressed for instance by Dr. D. S. Bailey in his 'Homosexuality and Christian Morals' (in Rees & Usill). From this point of view homosexual activity can still consistently be held to be unnatural. I do not, however, see how it can be by anyone prepared to allow permanently childless marriages, or intentionally infertile heterosexual relationships outside marriage.

It is, in my opinion, *possible* consistently to hold homosexual activity to be unnatural. Much care and ingenuity are, however, required, and I suspect that many people who do regard it as unnatural are, in fact, inconsistent at one point or another. Nor, rare though it is, is consistency enough. The *truth* of the premises concerning the purposes of sex, and the relative importance of the purposes assigned, is crucial too. And yet, as observed above, it is very difficult to see how it is to be ascertained. They are not empirical premises, of which the truth could be assessed by some sort of morally neutral scientific enquiry—biological, psychological, sociological, or whatever it might be. The relevant form of enquiry is, perhaps, theological—but whether there is a subject-matter for theology is itself a controversial question. There is no ground, even in principle, for expecting reasonable men to agree on matters of theology, as there is on matters of biology, psychology and sociology. The credentials of theology as a subject are in dispute. And the propositions of natural theology are just as uncertain as those of revealed.

Accordingly, to the unbeliever, arguing to moral conclusions from theologically based premises about the nature or purpose of sex seems to be little more than a matter of arbitrarily selecting those premises which yield the moral conclusions desired. If you want to condemn contraception and homosexuality you have to emphasise the procreational purpose. If you want to permit contraception you must give greater weight to non-procreational purposes. To the believer, on the other hand, it does not seem like this at all. He must believe that questions about the nature and purpose of sex relate to matters of (non-empirical) fact. He will not see himself as arbitrarily choosing answers that are in line with moral judgments he has reached on other grounds, but rather, when he differs from his predecessors in moral theology, as correcting their mistakes of emphasis. These mistakes he may see as the result of prejudices resulting from local and temporary features of his predecessors' situation. If they attributed undue importance to procreation this will be because they did not write from the vantage point of a potentially over-populated world. The truth will never change, but our view of it does, perhaps getting nearer to it all the time.

I have myself no enthusiasm at all for appraising human conduct as natural or unnatural. I have, however, tried to draw attention to the *complexity* of the notion of the natural employed by moral theologians, mainly in order to show how different it is from that implicit in the popular condemnation of homosexual behaviour as unnatural. In the popular view the unnatural and the disgusting are closely connected, and judging something to be unnatural is felt to be the simple, direct, inevitable reaction of the 'healthy' mind to it. But there can be nothing simple in any notion of the natural which will admit of application over the whole range of sexual behaviour, which will serve as the key idea in a comprehensive sexual morality. Nor will there by any necessary connexion between the correcsponding notion of the *un*natural and the disgusting.

J. M. CAMERON

The Prison of Sexual Liberation

"Revolution," like "tragedy," is a bit overused; but there can't be any doubt that we are in the course of, perhaps at the end of, a revolution in

Reprinted from *The New York Review of Books*, Vol. 23, No. 8, May 13, 1976, 19–20, 24–25, 27–28 with the permission of the author. Reprinted with permission from *The New York Review of Books*. Copyright © 1976 Nyrev, Inc. *Editor's Note:* Footnotes have been renumbered.

sexual mores. From Sweden there has just come a report that a government committee has recommended that children be legally free to make their hetero- or homosexual debuts at fourteen, that all legal prohibitions of incest be lifted, and that the word "homosexual" be dropped from the terminology of the law. As to what goes on, it is easy to say what has happened in our society, and I will attempt a short account presently, but it isn't and can't be clear how far behavior that is in one sense characteristic represents how most people conduct their lives.

Other questions even harder to answer are: how far the revolution has added to human happiness or misery, and if to both how the proportions are distributed; what the effects on civilization and culture will be; what the connections are between the revolution and other things that go on in the opulent societies of the West, things both good and bad. Finally, we must surely ask what we are now to think of what has been, in the matter of sexual morality, the central tradition of our culture; this comes from Deuteronomy and was given a circulation outside the Jewish tradition by the first Christians. It forbids fornication, adultery, incest, homosexuality, sexual connection with the brutes, and sacred prostitution (in our own day this last could perhaps be understood as sex as theater).

The content of the sexual revolution seems as follows:

1. In sexual practice virtually everything is interesting and nothing is grave. It is still thought wrong to force people, especially the young, to engage in sexual practices against their will, though there is sometimes to be heard a Pecksniffian voice claiming that rape is really a protest against a repressive social order. Apart from this, pretty well anything goes so long as it doesn't *harm* other people. What is to count as harm isn't easy to determine, for sadism and masochism are interesting too. It is supposed, strangely, that what is harmful is immediately evident. Whatever gives sexual pleasure is all right; the burden of proving that it isn't rests upon the objector.

2. Masturbation is the prototype of all sexual activity, the most harmless, even the "best." Proficiency in masturbation was a necessary condition of fitness for taking part in the Masters and Johnson experiments. Paul Robinson observes in *The Modernization of Sex* [1] that "from its pathogenic status among the Victorians, masturbation has risen to the position of final sexual arbiter"; its rewards are held by some to be superior to those of any other sexual activity. In particular, female masturbation is the badge of sexual independence. Virtually all the sexual fantasies in Nancy Friday's compilation [2] are used in masturbation as well as in other activities. It is now commonly known that the nineteenth-century belief that (male) masturbation causes a variety of physical and mental ills is groundless. There isn't absolute unanimity that masturbation is without

---

[1] Paul Robinson, *The Modernization of Sex: Havelock Ellis, Alfred Kinsey, William Masters and Virginia Johnson* (Harper and Row, 1976).
[2] Nancy Friday, *My Secret Garden: Women's Sexual Fantasies* (Trident Press, 1973).

bad emotional consequences, but most students of sex think it at least harmless, like chewing gum or backscratching.

3. Oral sex—fallatio and cunnilingus—is now a very big activity. Morton Hunt [3] finds there is a great increase of these practices among the married. Such practices, once called perversions, live in a legal twilight in many countries. Even more noteworthy is the fairly wide acceptance of buggery between heterosexual partners. (It is curious that "buggery" is seldom used, though the vernacular terms for other acts and for the male and female genitals are often used and their use is taken to be a mark of emancipation; but for "buggery" is commonly substituted the prim "anal penetration.") The acceptance by so many of the practice of buggery makes very plain one of the messages of the sexual revolution: that there are now in sexual matters no common principles of decorum.

4. Homosexuality, male and female, is now thought to be a native sexual orientation, not a genetic endowment but in most cases as firm and as unalterable as though it were genetic. Homosexual men and women are often pictured as members of an oppressed third sex in need of emancipation.

5. In many cities of the Western world there are openly advertised emporia that stock curious "objects." These are such things as vibrators (Morton Hunt has a sad and hilarious story about a lady whose Acapulco holiday was ruined because she had forgotten to pack her vibrator), dildos, boots, chains, underclothes of unusual cut, books, photographs, even (though these are perhaps more often procured by mail order) life-size plastic dolls in female shapes with which the shy and lonely may cohabit. These emporia correspond in their own field to gourmet shops for lovers of rare foods, and it is characteristic of our time that the publication of gourmet books on sexual techniques reinforces the analogy.

6. Such periodicals as *Playboy* and *Penthouse* and their proliferating imitations should be mentioned. Their appearance both satisfies and stimulates demand. They represent big money and their proprietors have a strong interest in persuading readers to accept the picture of the sexually liberated human being they offer. Such periodicals are beginning to achieve a kind of respectability and are not too slowly moving into the picture of the normal American home, along with the *Reader's Digest*, cola beverages, contraceptive pills, laxatives, instant coffee, and stuff to make the floor shine.

No doubt these six "notes" of the sexual revolution could be added to and subdivided in various ways; but as they stand they provide enough material for discussion. It is also clear that the revolution as I have described it is confined to Western, free, middle-class, capitalist societies of some degree of opulence. The governments of even the more prosperous socialist societies proscribe most of its manifestations as signs of a bourgeois corruption against which they wish to protect their citizens.

[3] Morton Hunt, *Sexual Behavior in the Seventies* (Playboy Press, 1974).

As for the poor societies, of whatever political complexion, these are delights they can't afford. In them the much derided (in the West) *machismo* of the males keeps an uncomplicated heterosexuality as the predominant pattern; and even where, as in some of the Arab countries, male homosexuality is traditional, the business of procreation is well attended to. Here homosexuality seems not so much a way of life as a kind of gentlemanly relaxation. This is how it must have seemed to Maynard Keynes, who, before the First World War, wrote to Lytton Strachey to recommend Tunis as a place where "bed and boy" were not dear.[4] (It is curious that in none of the books under review is Bloomsbury given even the modest place it deserves in the prehistory of the sexual revolution.)

In 1948 Lionel Trilling published in *Partisan Review* a comment on the first Kinsey Report. It is a classic statement, calm, judicious, prescient. Trilling was the first to remark on the bland assurance implied in the chosen title of the Report: *Sexual Behavior in the Human Male*. A cross-section, not even complete, of North American males was to serve as material for generalizing about all human males. The article is still worth reading: indeed, it may be said to have gathered weight in the almost thirty years since it appeared. I wish to mention two of its points. First, there is what might be called the vulgar democratic (on the analogy of "vulgar Marxist") view of social research.

We might say that those who most explicitly assert and wish to practice the democratic virtues have taken it as their assumption that all social facts—with the exception of exclusion and economic hardship—must be *accepted*, not merely in the scientific sense but also in the social sense, in the sense, that is, that no judgment must be passed on them, that any conclusion drawn from them which perceives values and consequences will turn out to be "undemocratic."[5]

· · ·

Then Trilling spoke of "the large permissive effect the Report is likely to have." It was, in fact, as he saw, a powerful agent of revolution; it changed the sexual mores of the time. Its scientism, its half-concealed complacency toward mechanical models of the life of feeling and action, the bad faith which presented as a purely technical work what it was foreknown would be widely read by an audience quite unable to weigh its claims, all these gave it a unique authority wherever it was read. Without Kinsey's work other writings about sexual matters would have taken a different form.

· · ·

[4] Michael Holroyd, *Lytton Strachey* (Holt Rinehart & Winston, 1968), Vol. II, p. 80.
[5] Lionel Trilling, *The Liberal Imagination* (Doubleday Anchor, 1957), p. 234.

Aristotle (*Nicomachean Ethics* v.7) remarks that "of political [here "political" has a greater breadth than in its modern use] justice part is natural, part legal—natural, that which everywhere has the same force and does not exist by people thinking this or that; legal, that which is originally indifferent, e.g. . . . that a goat and not two sheep shall be sacrificed." [6] Aristotle doesn't think it is easy to distinguish one kind of justice from another. He is claiming that we are compelled to make a distinction between what is required or forbidden simply in virtue of the culture we live in and what is required or forbidden in a more stringent sense. An ability to make this distinction may even be a mark of sanity. One who thought how we are to pick our teeth in public a grave matter would be deranged; so would one who thought the requirements of the Nuremberg Laws under Hitler were brute features of the national culture about which further questions couldn't be raised. No decent or sane man, we should be inclined to say without formality, could have accepted such requirements as morally binding. It is also plain that what is in itself indifferent, e.g., whether to drive on the right or the left, may become a stringent requirement through agreement.

That is, there are three things: what is required or forbidden by a culture where falling in with the culture or not doesn't seem greatly to matter; what is required or forbidden belongs to the culture but its being agreed upon makes it morally obligatory—I must keep to the right, I must keep poisons in *blue* bottles; what has prescriptive or interdictory force "but does not exist by people thinking this or that." It is interesting that Aristotle, on the whole not very interested in absolutes, should have bruised himself against this problem. In the Biblical tradition there are three things a man may not do, even to save the city or his own life: he must not worship false gods, he must not spill innocent blood, he must not commit any of the sexual sins forbidden by the Law. Leon Roth remarks that these prohibitions "are specifically distinguished from ritual and social commandments," that is, their force "does not exist by people thinking this or that." [7]

It is very common now for people to find such a discussion boring and stupid. They are confident there is a hedonistic calculus that will get them out of their moral difficulties and they have a strong impression that somehow or other it has been shown, to all except a few religious freaks, that *all* moral requirements "exist by people thinking this or that." To argue that there must be such a thing as being in the right if it is possible for a man to think he is in the right seems to them mere logic-chopping. [8] It isn't then surprising that in the works so far discussed there is no serious consideration of the moral problems that may be raised by changes in

[6] *The Nicomachean Ethics*, translated by Sir David Ross (London: World's Classics, 1969), p. 124.
[7] Cf. Leon Roth, *Judaism: A Portrait* (London, 1960), p. 68.
[8] I think I got this argument from Professor G. E. M. Anscombe, in conversation.

the sexual mores of our society; still less is the notion ever canvassed of the possibility of there being in this field absolute interdictions. Very occasionally, perhaps, this is discussed, but with derision, as modern chemists would talk about phlogiston.

It is as though somewhere in life there must be a happy corner where menacing authorities, sad consequences, agonizing choices, tragic blunders don't exist or don't count. Elsewhere in modern society everything is harsh, acrid, dark, and no one can wish away what is disagreeable. Once there were those who offered mescaline or LSD or other magical substances as the ultimates in happy corners. The dark and the acrid turned up there, too. Free sexual activity seems at first glance to offer a happy corner where all is sweetness and light. A second or a third glance leaves one a bit unsure. It may occur to us that the makers of the how-to and gourmet books, and the prophets upon whom they rely, are absurdly trying to make the erotic tractable and domestic. The student of the Song of Songs or of the *Symposium* isn't likely to make this mistake, even if he offers no cure for our disquiets.

• • •

Courtly love was one aspect of medieval asceticism, and yet it tempered it, deepening and complicating sexual feeling. The two most influential books on the matter are C. S. Lewis's *The Allegory of Love* and Denis de Rougemont's *L'Amour et l'Occident* (published here as *Love in the Western World*). The origins of the cult are obscure and the features of its development matters of controversy; what there can be no doubt about are the large consequences of the cult as, through poetry and, later, the novel, the romantic sensibility came to be shared by more and more people. Mr. Owen has given us a useful popular history and a pleasant picture book.[9] He sees that the really interesting problem about courtly love is its legacy rather than its origin. The most obvious facts of the legacy's history no one could dispute over: Ronsard, Shakespeare, Cervantes, the novel from *Clarissa* to *A Farewell to Arms* or *The Heart of the Matter*, all these and much ephemeral stuff enlivened European culture.

The complex picture of male and female sensibility we find in the tradition isn't easily judged. What is certain is that without the tradition we shouldn't have had the heroic woman. As I think about Rosalind (*As You Like It*), Beatrice (*Much Ado About Nothing*), about Elizabeth Bennet and Lucy Snowe and even Trollope's Lily Dale, I become more and more dissatisfied with our stereotypes of female exploitation and oppression, and with such repeated general statements as that sexual feeling was not, in the Victorian age, supposed to exist in respectable women. Trollope was a popular novelist who depicted and even shaped *les moeurs*

[9] D. D. R. Owen, *Noble Lovers* (N.Y.U. Press, 1975).

de province, and he is therefore good evidence for what people thought and felt in the mid-Victorian period. Now, it is plain that most of his heroines glow with sexual feeling. The liberationists judge the past badly and this coarsens their judgment of the present.

It is impossible to say whether or not there is in the Western world a growing synthesis of ideas on sexual behavior. There is evidence that the loosely associated ideas held by sexual liberationists are deeply affecting groups that have traditionally accepted the Biblical prohibitions of fornication, adultery, and the rest. Father Grinder's book [10] and *From Machismo to Mutuality* [11] may represent what is going on in the minds of some religious believers in our society. How far such changes speak of a collapse before current fashion we need not determine. We must assume that there is a felt logical compulsion in any line of thought that ends with the acceptance of modes of sexual activity that have always been thought forbidden among orthodox Jews, most Protestants, and almost all Roman Catholics. Bianchi and Ruether stress as a premise of their argument a special view of the marriage relation and would, I think, argue that their view is a legitimate development of what is implicit in the Christian view of sexuality. Bianchi writes:

> Mutuality for us men points towards a threefold acceptance that is denied in contemporary society. It means that we cultivate the feminine dimensions of our male selves, that we respect the diversity of homosexuality and that we come to live with women as diverse but equal others who do not exist for our aggrandizement but for our mutual growth as persons.

This rests upon a belief strongly resembling early Gnosticism. The belief is that in a union of love between two people, personal, nonsexual relations are fundamental and that to these relations, between males and females, males and males, females and females, there may be added sexual relations, as relaxation, play, signs of affection, on occasion as means to procreation. In the Biblical tradition, by contrast, it is the sexual relation between man and woman that constitutes the relation of marriage, and the love of friendship—this can exist outside marriage and without sexual relations—is an added grace that belongs to the perfection of marriage but isn't constitutive of it. The sexual relation of marriage lies within the protection of covenant: the communally ratified exchange of promises establishing mutual and exclusive rights to sexual activity between the parties. Thus, for the partners in marriage conceived in this way, adultery resembles self-contradiction.

---

[10] Richard Grinder, *Binding with Briars: Sex and Sin in the Catholic Church* (Prentice-Hall, 1975).

[11] Eugene C. Bianchi and Rosemary Radford Ruether, *From Machismo to Mutuality: Essays on Sexism and Woman–Man Liberation* (Paulist Press, 1976).

If Jewish-Christian prescriptions about marriage and sexuality are in retreat, this is in part a consequence of the secularization of social life. *Pietas* toward natural processes and established institutions is rare in our society and not often counted as a virtue. The absence of *pietas* toward some natural processes is beginning to disturb us; this is evident in the growth of movements to protect and purify the natural environment. *Pietas* toward sexuality, so strong a feature of the entire human past, seems much diminished. If there is sense in Freud, if anything of what Lawrence says in "Apropos of *Lady Chatterley*" and *Fantasia of the Unconscious* is to the point, too easy and familiar an approach to sex risks more than we can understand. The taboos of the past, the touch of hysteria men of today discover in past religious pronouncements on the topic, speak of the uncannily powerful in sexuality; and it seems an implication of what Freud thought that the ending of sexual repression could unravel the web of culture. This may be what the Marxist regimes obscurely understand. No high culture without guilt, as Philip Rieff would say.

A culture without guilt, in which all conceivable sexual practices are innocent, such is the happy arrangement many believe to be already practicable. There may be guilt over one's inadequacies as a sexual performer (this is what Robinson has in mind when he remarks that the Masters and Johnson programs tends to transform sexual activity into labor); but the great guilt and the dread that went with the violation of the taboos will have gone.

In such a culture it would come to be thought that all sexual mores essentially resemble those other things that are in themselves indifferent. (Of course, *some* sexual mores are plainly of this kind: the male-superior position in coitus would be an example of a local and temporal peculiarity.) But it may be that other things (the prohibition of incest, for example) can't be settled "by people thinking this or that." If everything is interesting and nothing is grave, satire cannot bite and tragedy gives way to the social illness of maladjustment. For many, human life under such conditions would lose its music. It may be that life can't in any case be like this and that the hurt of guilt and the pity and terror of tragedy are ineluctably with us, as much in our sexual relations as in all other dealings between members of the family of man.

Paris Adult Theatre I v. Slaton, 413 U.S. 49, 93 S.Ct. 2628 (1973)

The State of Georgia brought a civil action to enjoin the showing of two motion pictures, "It All Comes Out in the End" and "Magic Mirror," being shown at the Paris Adult Theatres I and II in Atlanta, Georgia. The State claimed that the films were obscene under the standards set forth in Georgia Code § 26–2101 (b) which defined obscene material as follows:

Material is obscene if considered as a whole, applying community standards, its predominant appeal is to prurient interest, that is, a shameful or morbid interest in nudity, sex or excretion, and utterly without redeeming social value and if, in addition, it goes substantially beyond customary limits of candor in describing or representing such matters. Undeveloped photographs, molds, printing plates and the like shall be deemed obscene notwithstanding that processing or other acts may be required to make the obscenity patent or to disseminate it.

The trial court denied injunctive relief, holding that even if the films were obscene, this commercial presentation could not be prohibited in the absence of proof that they were shown to minors or unconsenting adults.

The Supreme Court of Georgia reversed, holding that the films were obscene and that it was constitutionally irrelevant whether care was taken to avoid showing the movies to minors or unconsenting adults. What follows is Part II of the majority opinion by Chief Justice Burger of the Supreme Court of the United States together with Parts V and VI of the dissenting opinion of Mr. Justice Brennan.

Many of the case citations have been omitted, and the footnotes have been renumbered.

The Opinion of Mr. Chief Justice Burger

We categorically disapprove the theory, apparently adopted by the trial judge, that obscene, pornographic films acquire constitutional immunity from state regulation simply because' they are exhibited for consenting adults only. This holding was properly rejected by the Georgia Supreme Court. Although we have often pointedly recognized the high importance of the state interest in regulating the exposure of obscene materials to juveniles and unconsenting adults, . . . this Court has never declared these to be the only legitimate state interests permitting regulation of obscene material. The States have a long-recognized legitimate interest in regulating the use of obscene material in local commerce and in all places of public accommodation, as long as these regulations do not run afoul of specific constitutional prohibitions. . . . "In an unbroken series of cases extending over a long stretch of this Court's history, it has been accepted as a postulate that 'the primary requirements of decency may be enforced against obscene publications.' *Id.* [Near v. Minnesota ex rel. Olson, 283 U.S. 697 (1931)], at 716 [51 S.Ct. 625 at 631, 15 L.Ed. 1357]." Kingsley Books, Inc. v. Brown, *supra,* 354 U.S., at 440, 77 S.Ct., at 1327 (1957).

In particular, we hold that there are legitimate state interests at stake in stemming the tide of commercialized obscenity, even assuming it is feasible to enforce effective safeguards against exposure to juveniles and to the passerby.[1] Rights and interests "other than those of the advocates are involved." Cf. Breard v. Alexandria, 341 U.S. 622, 642, 71 S.Ct. 920, 932, 95 L.Ed. 1233 (1951). These include the interest of the public in the quality of life and the total community environment, the tone of commerce in the great city centers, and, possibly, the public safety itself. The Hill-Link Minority Report of the Commission on Obscenity and Pornography indicates that there is at least an arguable correlation between obscene material and crime.[2] Quite apart from sex crimes, however, there

---

[1] It is conceivable that an "adult" theatre can—if it really insists—prevent the exposure of its obscene wares to juveniles. An "adult" bookstore, dealing in obscene books, magazines, and pictures, cannot realistically make this claim. The Hill-Link Minority Report of the Commission on Obscenity and Pornography emphasizes evidence (the Abelson National Survey of Youth and Adults) that, although most pornography may be bought by elders, "the heavy users and most highly exposed people to pornography are adolescent females (among women) and adolescent and young males (among men)." The Report of the Commission on Obscenity (1970 ed.), 401. The legitimate interest in preventing exposure of juveniles to obscene materials cannot be fully served by simply barring juveniles from the immediate physical premises of "adult" book stores, when there is a flourishing "outside business" in these materials.

[2] The Report of the Commission on Obscenity and Pornography (1970 ed.), 390–412 (Hill-Link Minority Report). For a discussion of earlier studies indicating "a division of thought [among behavioral scientists] on the correlation between obscenity and socially deleterious behavior" and references to expert opinions that obscene material may induce crime and antisocial conduct, see Memoirs v. Massachusetts, *supra,* 383 U.S., at 451–453, 86 S.Ct., at 993–995 (1966) (Clark, J., dissenting). As Mr. Justice Clark emphasized:

"While erotic stimulation caused by pornography may be legally insignificant in itself, there are medical experts who believe that such stimulation frequently manifests itself in criminal sexual behavior or other antisocial conduct. For example, Dr. George W. Henry of Cornell University has expressed the opinion that obscenity, with its exaggerated and morbid emphasis on sex, particularly abnormal and perverted practices, and its unrealistic presentation of sexual be-

remains one problem of large proportions aptly described by Professor Bickel:

> It concerns the tone of the society, the mode, or to use terms that have perhaps greater currency, the style and quality of life, now and in the future. A man may be entitled to read an obscene book in his room, or expose himself indecently there. . . . We should protect his privacy. But if he demands a right to obtain the books and pictures he wants in the market and to foregather in public places—discreet, if you will, but accessible to all—with others who share his tastes, *then to grant him his right is to affect the world about the rest of us, and to impinge on other privacies.* Even supposing that each of us can, if he wishes, effectively avert the eye and stop the ear (which, in truth, we cannot), what is commonly read and seen and heard and done intrudes upon us all, want it or not.
>
> 22 *The Public Interest* 25, 25–26 (*Winter, 1971*).[3] (*Emphasis supplied.*)

As Chief Justice Warren stated there is a "right of the Nation and of the States to maintain a decent society . . . ," Jacobellis v. Ohio, 378 U.S. 184, 199, 84 S.Ct. 1676, 1684, 12 L.Ed. 793 (1964) (Warren, C. J., dissenting).[4] . . .

But, it is argued, there is no scientific data which conclusively demonstrates that exposure to obscene materials adversely affects men and women or their society. It is urged on behalf of the petitioner that, absent such a demonstration, any kind of state regulation is "impermissible." We reject this argument. It is not for us to resolve empirical uncertainties underlying state legislation, save in the exceptional case where that legislation plainly impinges upon rights protected by the Constitution itself, Mr. Justice Brennan, speaking for the Court in Ginsberg v. New York, 390 U.S. 629, 642, 88 S.Ct. 1274, 1282, 20 L.Ed.2d 195 (1968), said "We

---

havior and attitudes, may induce antisocial conduct by the average person. A number of sociologists think that this material may have adverse effects upon individual mental health, with potentially disruptive consequences for the community.
        ". . .
    "Congress and the legislatures of every State have enacted measures to restrict the distribution of erotic and pornographic material, justify these controls by reference to evidence that antisocial behavior may result in part from reading obscenity." [Footnotes omitted.] *Id.*, 383 U.S., at 452–453, 86 S.Ct., at 994–995.

[3] See also Berns, Pornography v. Democracy: The Case for Censorship, in 22 The Public Interest 3 (Winter, 1971); Van der Haag, Censorship: For and Against (H. H. Hart ed., 1971), 156–157.

[4] "In this and other cases in this area of law, which are coming to us in ever-increasing numbers, we are faced with the resolution of rights basic both to individuals and to society as a whole. Specifically, we are called upon to reconcile the right of the Nation and of the States to maintain a decent society and, on the other hand, the right of individuals to express themselves freely in accordance with the guarantees of the First and Fourteenth Amendments." Jacobellis v. Ohio, *supra*, 378 U.S., at 199, 84 S.Ct., at 1684 (1964) (Warren, C. J., dissenting).

do not demand of legislatures 'scientifically certain criteria of legislation.' Noble State Bank v. Haskell, 219 U.S. 104, 110 [31 S.Ct. 186, 187] 55 L.Ed. 112." Although there is no conclusive proof of a connection between antisocial behavior and obscene material, the legislature of Georgia could quite reasonably determine that such a connection does or might exist. In deciding *Roth*, this Court implicitly accepted that a legislature could legitimately act on such a conclusion to protect *"the social interest in order and morality."* Roth v. United States, *supra*, 354 U.S., at 485, 77 S.Ct., at 1309 (1957), quoting Chaplinsky v. New Hampshire, 315 U.S. 568, 572, 62 S.Ct. 766, 769, 86 L.Ed. 1031 (1942) (emphasis added in *Roth*).[5]

From the beginning of civilized societies, legislators and judges have acted on various unprovable assumptions. Such assumptions underlie much lawful state regulation of commercial and business affairs. . . . The same is true of the federal securities, antitrust laws and a host of other federal regulations. . . . On the basis of these assumptions both Congress and state legislatures have, for example, drastically restricted associational rights by adopting antitrust laws, and have strictly regulated public expression by issues of and dealers in securities, profit sharing "coupons," and "trading stamps," commanding what they must and may not publish and announce. . . . Understandably those who entertain an absolutist view of the First Amendment find it uncomfortable to explain why rights of association, speech, and press should be severely restrained in the marketplace of goods and money, but not in the marketplace of pornography.

Likewise, when legislatures and administrators act to protect the physical environment from pollution and to preserve our resources of forests, streams and parks, they must act on such imponderables as the impact of a new highway near or through an existing park or wilderness area. . . . Thus the Federal-Aid Highway Act of 1968, 82 Stat. 823, 23 U.S.C. § 138, and the Department of Transportation Act of 1966, 82 Stat. 824, 49 U.S.C. § 1653 (f), have been described by Mr. Justice Black as "a solemn determination of the highest law-making body of this Nation that beauty and health-giving facilities of our parks are not to be taken away for public roads without hearings, fact-findings, and policy determinations under the supervision of a Cabinet officer. . . ." *Citizens to Preserve Overton Park, supra*, 401 U.S., at 421, 91 S.Ct., at 826 (separate opinion joined by Brennan, J.) (1971). The fact that a congressional directive reflects unprovable assumptions about what is good for the people, including imponderable aesthetic assumptions, is not a sufficient reason to find that statute unconstitutional.

[5] "It has been well observed that such [lewd and obscene] utterances are no essential part of any exposition of ideas, and are of such slight social value as a step to truth that any benefit that may be derived from them is clearly outweighed by the social interest in order and morality." Roth v. United States, *supra*, 354 U.S., at 485, 77 S.Ct., at 1309 (1957), quoting Chaplinsky v. New Hampshire, 315 U.S., *supra*, at 572, 62 S.Ct., at 769 (1942) (emphasis added in *Roth*).

If we accept the unprovable assumption that a complete education requires certain books, . . . and the well nigh universal belief that good books, plays, and art uplift the spirit, improve the mind, enrich the human personality and develop character, can we then say that a state legislature may not act on the corollary assumption that commerce in obscene books, or public exhibitions focused on obscene conduct, have a tendency to exert a corrupting and debasing impact leading to antisocial behavior? "Many of these effects may be intangible and indistinct, but they are nonetheless real." *American Power & Light Co., supra,* 329 U.S., at 103, 67 S.Ct., at 141 (1946). Mr. Justice Cardozo said that all laws in Western civilization are "guided by a robust common sense. . . ." *Steward Machine Co. v. Davis,* 301 U.S. 548, 590, 57 S.Ct. 883, 892, 81 L.Ed 1279 (1937). The sum of experience, including that of the past two decades, affords an ample basis for legislatures to conclude that a sensitive, key relationship of human existence, central to family life, community welfare, and the development of human personality, can be debased and distorted by crass commercial exploitation of sex. Nothing in the Constitution prohibits a State from reaching such a conclusion and acting on it legislatively simply because there is no conclusive evidence or empirical data.

It is argued that individual "free will" must govern, even in activities beyond the protection of the First Amendment and other constitutional guarantees of privacy, and that Government cannot legitimately impede an individual's desire to see or acquire obscene plays, movies, and books. We do indeed base our society on certain assumptions that people have the capacity for free choice. Most exercises of individual free choice —those in politics, religion, and expression of ideas—are explicitly protected by the Constitution. Totally unlimited play for free will, however, is not allowed in ours or any other society. We have just noted, for example, that neither the First Amendment nor "free will" precludes States from having "blue sky" laws to regulate what sellers of securities may write or publish about their wares. . . . Such laws are to protect the weak, the uninformed, the unsuspecting, and the gullible from the exercise of their own volition. Nor do modern societies leave disposal of garbage and sewage up to the individual "free will," but impose regulation to protect both public health and the appearance of public places. States are told by some that they must await a "laissez faire" market solution to the obscenity-pornography problem, paradoxically "by people who have never otherwise had a kind word to say for laissez-faire," particularly in solving urban, commercial, and environmental pollution problems. See Kristol, On the Democratic Idea in America (1972 ed.) 37.

The States, of course, may follow such a "laissez faire" policy and drop all controls on commercialized obscenity, if that is what they prefer, just as they can ignore consumer protection in the market place, but nothing in the Constitution *compels* the States to do so with regard to matters falling within state jurisdiction. . . . "We do not sit as a superlegislature to determine the wisdom, need, and propriety of laws that touch economic problems, business affairs, or social conditions." Griswold v. Connecticut, 381 U.S. 479, 482, 85 S.Ct. 1678, 1680, 14 L.Ed.2d 510 (1965). . . .

It is asserted, however, that standards for evaluating state commercial regulations are inapposite in the present context, as state regulation of access by consenting adults to obscene material violates the constitutionally protected right to privacy enjoyed by petitioners' customers. Even assuming that petitioners have vicarious standing to assert potential customers' rights, it is unavailing to compare a theatre, open to the public for a fee, with the private home of Stanley v. Georgia, 394 U.S. 557, 568, 89 S.Ct. 1243, 1249, 22 L.Ed.2d 542 (1969), and the marital bedroom of Griswold v. Connecticut, 381 U.S. 479, 485–486, 85 S.Ct. 1678, 1682–1683, 14 L.Ed.2d 510 (1965). This Court, has, on numerous occasions, refused to hold that commercial ventures such as a motion-picture house are "private" for the purpose of civil rights litigation and civil rights statutes. . . . The Civil Rights Act of 1964 specifically defines motion-picture houses and theatres as places of "public accommodation" covered by the Act as operations affecting commerce. 42 U.S.C. § 2000a(b)(3), (c).

Our prior decisions recognizing a right to privacy guaranteed by the Fourteenth Amendment included "only those personal rights that can be deemed 'fundamental' or 'implicit in the concept of ordered liberty.' Palko v. Connecticut, 302 U.S. 319, 325, [58 S.Ct. 149, 152] 82 L.Ed. 288." Roe v. Wade, 410 U.S. 113, 152, 93 S.Ct. 705, 726, 35 L.Ed.2d 147 (1973). This privacy right encompasses and protects the personal intimacies of the home, the family, marriage, motherhood, procreation, and child rearing. . . . Nothing, however, in this Court's decisions intimates that there is any "fundamental" privacy right "implicit in the concept of ordered liberty" to watch obscene movies in places of public accommodation.

If obscene material unprotected by the First Amendment in itself carried with it a "penumbra" of constitutionally protected privacy, this Court would not have found it necessary to decide *Stanley* on the narrow basis of the "privacy of the home," which was hardly more than a reaffirmation that "a man's home is his castle." Stanley v. Georgia, *supra*, 394 U.S. 557, at 564, 89 S.Ct. 1243, at 1247, 22 L.Ed.2d 542 (1969).[6] Moreover, we have declined to equate the privacy of the home relied on in

---

[6] The protection afforded by Stanley v. Georgia, *supra*, is restricted to a place, the home. In contrast, the constitutionally protected privacy of family, marriage, motherhood, procreation, and child rearing is not just concerned with a particular place, but with a protected intimate relationship. Such protected privacy extends to the doctor's office, the hospital, the hotel room, or as otherwise required to safeguard the right to intimacy involved. Cf. Roe v. Wade, *supra*, 410 U.S., at 152–154, 93 S.Ct., at 726–727 (1973); Griswold v. Connecticut, *supra*, 381 U.S., at 485–486, 85 S.Ct., at 1682–1683. Obviously, there is no necessary or legitimate expectation of privacy which would extend to marital intercourse on a street corner or a theatre stage.

Stanley with a "zone" of "privacy" that follows a distributor or a consumer of obscene materials wherever he goes. . . . The idea of a "privacy" right and a place of public accommodation are, in this context, mutually exclusive. Conduct or depictions of conduct that the state police power can prohibit on a public street does not become automatically protected by the Constitution merely because the conduct is moved to a bar or a "live" theatre stage, any more than a "live" performance of a man and woman locked in a sexual embrace at high noon in Times Square is protected by the Constitution because they simultaneously engage in a valid political dialogue.

It is also argued that the State has no legitimate interest in "control [of] the moral content of a person's thoughts," Stanley v. Georgia, *supra,* 394 U.S., at 565, 89 S.Ct., at 1248 (1969), and we need not quarrel with this. But we reject the claim that the State of Georgia is here attempting to control the minds or thoughts of those who patronize theatres. Preventing unlimited display or distribution of obscene material, which by definition lacks any serious literary, artistic, political, or scientific value as communication,. . . is distinct from a control of reason and the intellect. . . . Where communication of ideas, protected by the First Amendment, is not involved, nor the particular privacy of the home protected by *Stanley,* nor any of the other "areas or zones" of constitutionally protected privacy, the mere fact that, as a consequence, some human "utterances" or "thoughts" may be incidentally affected does not bar the State from acting to protect legitimate state interests. . . . The fantasies of a drug addict are his own and beyond the reach of government, but government regulation of drug sales is not prohibited by the Constitution. . . .

Finally, petitioners argue that conduct which directly involves "consenting adults" only has, for that sole reason, a special claim to constitutional protection. Our Constitution establishes a broad range of conditions on the exercise of power by the States, but for us to say that our Constitution incorporates the proposition that conduct involving consenting adults only is always beyond state regulation,[7] that is a step we are unable to take.[8] Commercial exploitation of depictions, descriptions, or exhibitions of obscene conduct on commercial premises open to the adult public

---

[7] Cf. Mill, On Liberty (1955 ed.), 13.

[8] The state statute books are replete with constitutionally unchallenged laws against prostitution, suicide, voluntary self-mutilation, brutalizing "bare fist" prize fights, and duels, although these crimes may only directly involve "consenting adults." Statutes making bigamy a crime surely cut into an individual's freedom to associate, but few today seriously claim such statutes violate the First Amendment or any other constitutional provision. . . . Consider also the language of this Court in McLaughlin v. Florida, 379 U.S. 184, 196, 85 S.Ct. 283, 290, 13 L.Ed. 2d 222 (1964), as to adultery, Southern Surety Co. v. Oklahoma, 241 U.S. 582, 586, 36 S.Ct. 692, 694, 60 L.Ed. 1187 (1916), as to fornication; Hoke v. United States, 227 U.S. 308, 320–322, 33 S.Ct. 281, 283–284, 57 L.Ed. 523 (1913), and Caminetti v. United States, 242 U.S. 470, 484–487, 491–492, 37 S.Ct. 192, 194–195, 196–197, 61 L.Ed. 442 (1917), as to "white slavery"; Murphy v.

falls within a State's broad power to regulate commerce and protect the public environment. The issue in this context goes beyond whether someone, or even the majority, considers the conduct depicted as "wrong" or "sinful." The States have the power to make a morally neutral judgment that public exhibition of obscene material, or commerce in such material, has a tendency to injure the community as a whole, to endanger the public safety, or to jeopardize in Chief Justice Warren's words, the States' "right . . . to maintain a decent society." Jacobellis v. Ohio, *supra*, 378 U.S., at 199, 84 S.Ct., at 1684 (1964) (dissenting opinion).

To summarize, we have today reaffirmed the basic holding of United States v. Roth, *supra*, that obscene material has no protection under the First Amendment. . . . We have directed our holdings, not at thoughts or speech, but at depiction and description of specifically defined sexual conduct that States may regulate within limits designed to prevent infringement of First Amendment rights. We have also reaffirmed the holdings of United States v. Reidel, *supra*, and United States v. Thirty-Seven Photographs, *supra*, that commerce in obscene material is unprotected by any constitutional doctrine of privacy. . . . In this case we hold that the States have a legitimate interest in regulating commerce in obscene material and in regulating exhibition of obscene material in places of public accommodation, including so-called "adult" theatres from which minors are excluded. In light of these holdings, nothing precludes the State of Georgia from the regulation of the allegedly obscene materials exhibited in Paris Adult Theatre I or II, provided that the applicable Georgia law, as written or authoritatively interpreted by the Georgia courts, meets the First Amendment standards set forth in Miller v. California, *supra*, . . .

Vacated and remanded for further proceedings.

The Dissenting Opinion of Mr. Justice Brennan

Our experience since *Roth* requires us not only to abandon the effort to pick out obscene materials on a case-by-case basis, but also to reconsider a fundamental postulate of *Roth*: that there exists a definable class of sexually oriented expression that may be totally suppressed by the Federal

California, 225 U.S. 623, 629, 32 S.Ct. 697, 698, 56 L.Ed. 1229 (1912), as to billiard halls; and The Lottery Case, 188 U.S. 321, 355–356, 23 S.Ct. 321, 326–327, 47 L.Ed. 492 (1903), as to gambling. See also the summary of state statutes prohibiting bear baiting, cock-fighting, and other brutalizing animal "sports," in Stevens, Fighting and Baiting, Animals and Their Legal Rights (Leavitt ed., 1970 ed.), 112–127. As Professor Kristol has observed "Bearbaiting and cockfighting are prohibited only in part out of compassion for the suffering animals; the main reason they were abolished was because it was felt that they debased and brutalized the citizenry who flocked to witness such spectacles." On the Democratic Idea in America, *supra*, 33.

and State Governments. Assuming that such a class of expression does in fact exist, I am forced to conclude that the concept of "obscenity" cannot be defined with sufficient specificity and clarity to provide fair notice to persons who create and distribute sexually oriented materials, to prevent substantial erosion of protected speech as a by-product of the attempt to suppress unprotected speech, and to avoid very costly institutional harms. Given these inevitable side-effects of state efforts to suppress what is assumed to be *unprotected* speech, we must scrutinize with care the state interest that is asserted to justify the suppression. For in the absence of some very substantial interest in suppressing such speech, we can hardly condone the ill-effects that seem to flow inevitably from the effort.[9]

. . .

Obscenity laws have a long history in this country. Most of the States that had ratified the Constitution by 1792 punished the related crime of blasphemy or profanity despite the guarantees of free expression in their constitutions, and Massachusetts expressly prohibited the "composing, writing, printing or publishing of any filthy, obscene or profane song, pamphlet, libel or mock-sermon, in imitation of preaching, or any other part of divine worship." Province Laws, 1711–1712, ch. 6, § 19. In 1815 the first reported obscenity conviction was obtained under the common law of Pennsylvania. See Commonwealth v. Sharpless, 2 S. & R. 91. A conviction in Massachusetts under its common law and colonial statute followed six years later. See Commonwealth v. Holmes, 17 Mass. 336 (1821). In 1821 Vermont passed the first state law proscribing the publication or sale of "lewd or obscene" material, Laws of Vermont, 1824, ch. XXIII, No. 1, § 23, and federal legislation barring the importation of similar matter appeared in 1842. See Customs Law of 1842, § 28, 5 Stat. 566. Although the number of early obscenity laws was small and their enforcement exceedingly lax, the situation significantly changed after about 1870 when Federal and State Governments, mainly as a result of

[9] Cf. United States v. O'Brien, 391 U.S. 367, 376–377, 88 S.Ct. 1673, 1678–1679, 20 L.Ed.2d 672 (1968):
"This Court has held that when 'speech' and 'nonspeech' elements are combined in the same course of conduct, a sufficiently important governmental interest in regulating the nonspeech element can justify incidental limitations on First Amendment freedoms. To characterize the quality of the governmental interest which must appear, the Court has employed a variety of descriptive terms: compelling; substantial; subordinating; paramount; cogent; strong. Whatever imprecision inheres in these terms, we think it clear that a government regulation is sufficiently justified if it is within the constitutional power of the Government; if it furthers an important or substantial government interest; if the governmental interest is unrelated to the suppression of free expression; and if the incidental restriction on alleged First Amendment freedoms is no greater than is essential to the furtherance of that interest." (Footnotes omitted.) See also Speiser v. Randall, 357 U.S. 513, 78 S.Ct. 1332, 2 L.Ed.2d 1460 (1958).

the efforts of Anthony Comstock, took an active interest in the suppression of obscenity. By the end of the 19th Century at least 30 States had some type of general prohibition on the dissemination of obscene materials, and by the time of our decision in *Roth* no State was without some provision on the subject. The Federal Government meanwhile had enacted no fewer than 20 obscenity laws between 1842 and 1956. . . .

This history caused us to conclude in *Roth* "that the unconditional phrasing of the First Amendment [that "Congress shall make no law . . . abridging the freedom of speech, or of the press . . ."] was not intended to protect every utterance." 354 U.S., at 483, 77 S.Ct., at 1308. It also caused us to hold, as numerous prior decisions of this Court had assumed, see *id.*, at 481, 77 S.Ct., at 1306, that obscenity could be denied the protection of the First Amendment and hence suppressed because it is a form of expression "utterly without redeeming social importance," *id.*, at 484, 77 S.Ct., at 1309, as "mirrored in the universal judgment that [it] should be restrained. . . ." *Id.*, at 485, 77 S.Ct., at 1309.

Because we assumed—incorrectly, as experience has proven—that obscenity could be separated from other sexually oriented expression without significant costs either to the First Amendment or to the judicial machinery charged with the task of safeguarding First Amendment freedoms, we had no occasion in *Roth* to probe the asserted state interest in curtailing unprotected, sexually oriented speech. Yet as we have increasingly come to appreciate the vagueness of the concept of obscenity, we have begun to recognize and articulate the state interests at stake. Significantly, in Redrup v. New York, *supra*, where we set aside findings of obscenity with regard to three sets of material, we pointed out that

> [i]n none of the cases was there a claim that the statute in question reflected a specific and limited state concern for juveniles. See Prince v. Massachusetts, 321 U.S. 158 [64 S.Ct. 438] 88 L.Ed. 645; cf. Butler v. Michigan, 352 U.S. 380 [77 S.Ct. 524] 1 L.Ed.2d 412. In none was there any suggestion of an assault upon individual privacy by publication in a manner so obtrusive as to make it impossible for an unwilling individual to avoid exposure to it. Cf. Breard v. Alexandria, 341 U.S. 622 [71 S.Ct. 920] 95 L.Ed. 1233; Public Utilities Comm'n v. Pollak, 343 U.S. 451 [72 S.Ct. 813] 96 L.Ed. 1068. And in none was there evidence of the sort of 'pandering' which the Court found significant in Ginzburg v. United States, 383 U.S. 463 [86 S.Ct. 942] 16 L.Ed.2nd 31." 386 U.S., at 769, 87 S.Ct., at 1415.

· · ·

The opinions in *Redrup* and Stanley v. Georgia reflected our emerging view that the state interests in protecting children and in protecting unconsenting adults may stand on a different footing from the other asserted state interests. It may well be, as one commentator has argued, that "exposure to [erotic material] is for some persons an intense emotional experience. A communication of this nature, imposed upon a person contrary to his wishes, has all the characteristics of a physical assault. . . . [And it] constitutes an invasion of his privacy. . . .[10]" Similarly, if children are "not possessed of that full capacity for individual choice which is the presupposition of the First Amendment guarantees," Ginsberg v. New York, 390 U.S., at 649–650, 88 S.Ct., at 1286 (Stewart, J., concurring), then the State may have a substantial interest in precluding the flow of obscene materials even to consenting juveniles. . . .

But whatever the strength of the state interests in protecting juveniles and unconsenting adults from exposure to sexually oriented materials, those interests cannot be asserted in defense of the holding of the Georgia Supreme Court in this case. That court assumed for the purposes of its decision that the films in issue were exhibited only to persons over the age of 21 who viewed them willingly and with prior knowledge of the nature of their contents. And on that assumption the state court held that the films could still be suppressed. The justification for the suppression must be found, therefore, in some independent interest in regulating the reading and viewing habits of consenting adults.

At the outset it should be noted that virtually all of the interests that might be asserted in defense of suppression, laying aside the special interests associated with distribution to juveniles and unconsenting adults, were also posited in Stanley v. Georgia, *supra,* where we held that the State could not make the "mere private possession of obscene material a crime." *Id.,* 394 U.S., at 568, 89 S.Ct., at 1249. That decision presages the conclusions I reach here today.

In *Stanley* we pointed out that "[t]here appears to be little empirical basis for" the assertion that "exposure to obscene materials may lead to deviant sexual behavior or crimes of sexual violence." *Id.,* at 566 and n. 9, 89 S.Ct., at 1249.[11] In any event, we added that "if the State is only concerned about printed or filmed materials inducing antisocial conduct, we believe that in the context of private consumption of ideas and information we should adhere to the view that '[a]mong free men, the deterrents

---

10 T. Emerson, The System of Freedom of Expression 496 (1970).

11 Indeed, since *Stanley* was decided, the President's Commission on Obscenity and Pornography has concluded:

"In sum, empirical research designed to clarify the question has found no evidence to date that exposure to sexual materials plays a significant role in the causation of delinquent or criminal behavior among youth or adults. The Commission cannot conclude that exposure to erotic materials is a factor in the causation of sex crime or sex delinquency." Report of the Commission on Obscenity and Pornography 27 (1970) (footnote omitted).

To the contrary, the Commission found that "[o]n the positive side, explicit sexual materials are sought as a source of entertainment and information by substantial numbers of American adults. At times, these materials also appear to serve to increase and facilitate constructive communication about sexual matters within marriage." *Id.,* at 53.

ordinarily to be applied to prevent crime are education and punishment for violations of the law. . . .' Whitney v. California, 274 U.S. 357, 378 . . . (1927) (Brandeis, J., concurring)." *Id.*, at 566–567, 89 S.Ct., at 1249.

Moreover, in *Stanley* we rejected as "wholly inconsistent with the philosophy of the First Amendment," *id.*, at 566, 89 S.Ct., at 1248, the notion that there is a legitimate state concern in the "control [of] the moral content of a person's thoughts," *id.*, at 565, 89 S.Ct., at 1248, and we held that a State "cannot constitutionally premise legislation on the desirability of controlling a person's private thoughts." *Id.*, at 566, 89 S.Ct., at 1249. That is not to say, of course, that a State must remain utterly indifferent to—and take no action bearing on—the morality of the community. The traditional description of state police power does embrace the regulation of morals as well as the health, safety, and general welfare of the citizenry. . . . And much legislation— compulsory public education laws, civil rights laws, even the abolition of capital punishment—are grounded at least in part on a concern with the morality of the community. But the State's interest in regulating morality by suppressing obscenity, while often asserted, remains essentially unfocused and ill-defined. And, since the attempt to curtail unprotected speech necessarily spills over into the area of protected speech, the effort to serve this speculative interest through the suppression of obscene material must tread heavily on rights protected by the First Amendment.

In Roe v. Wade, 410 U.S. 113, 93 S.Ct. 705, 35 L.Ed.2d 147 (1973), we held constitutionally invalid a state abortion law, even though we were aware of

> the sensitive and emotional nature of the abortion controversy, of the vigorous opposing views, even among physicians, and of the deep and seemingly absolute convictions that the subject inspires. One's philosophy, one's experiences, one's exposure to the raw edges of human existence, one's religious training, one's attitudes toward life and family and their values, and the moral standards one establishes and seeks to observe, are all likely to influence and to color one's thinking and conclusions about abortion. 410 U.S., at 116, 93 S.Ct., at 708.

Like the proscription of abortions, the effort to suppress obscenity is predicated on unprovable, although strongly held, assumptions about human behavior, morality, sex, and religion.[12] The existence of these assumptions cannot validate a statute that substantially undermines the guarantees of the First Amendment, any more than the existence of similar assumptions on the issue of abortion can validate a statute that infringes the constitutionally protected privacy interests of a pregnant woman.

If, as the Court today assumes, "a state legislature may . . . act on the . . . assumption that . . . commerce in obscene books, or public ex-

---

[12] See Henkin, Morals and the Constitution; The Sin of Obscenity, 63 Col.L.Rev. 391, 395 (1963).

hibitions focused on obscene conduct, have a tendency to exert a corrupting and debasing impact leading to antisocial behavior," Paris Adult Theatre I v. Slaton, *ante*, at 2638, then it is hard to see how state-ordered regimentation of our minds can ever be forestalled. For if a State may, in an effort to maintain or create a particular moral tone, prescribe what its citizens cannot read or cannot see, then it would seem to follow that in pursuit of that same objective a State could decree that its citizens must read certain books or must view certain films. . . . However laudable its goal—and that is obviously a question on which reasonable minds may differ—the State cannot proceed by means that violate the Constitution. The precise point was established a half century ago in Meyer v. Nebraska, 262 U.S. 390, 43 S.Ct. 625, 67 L.Ed. 1042 (1923).

"That the State may do much, go very far, indeed, in order to improve the quality of its citizens, physically, mentally and morally, is clear; but the individual has certain fundamental rights which must be respected. The protection of the Constitution extends to all, to those who speak other languages as well as to those born with English on the tongue. Perhaps it would be highly advantageous if all had ready understanding of our ordinary speech, but this cannot be coerced by methods which conflict with the Constitution—a desirable end cannot be promoted by prohibited means.

"For the welfare of his Ideal Commonwealth, Plato suggested a law which should provide: "That the wives of our guardians are to be common, and their children are to be common, and no parent is to know his own child, nor any child his parent. . . . The proper officers will take the offspring of the good parents to the pen or fold, and there they will deposit them with certain nurses who dwell in a separate quarter; but the offspring of the inferior, or of the better when they chance to be deformed, will be put away in some mysterious, unknown place, as they should be.' In order to submerge the individual and develop ideal citizens, Sparta assembled the males at seven into barracks and intrusted their subsequent education and training to official guardians. Although such measures have been deliberately approved by men of great genius, their ideas touching the relation between individual and State were wholly different from those upon which our institutions rest; and it hardly will be affirmed that any legislature could impose such restrictions upon the people of a State without doing violence to both letter and spirit of the Constitution." *Id.*, at 401–402, 43 S.Ct., at 627–628.

Recognizing these principles, we have held that so-called thematic obscenity—obscenity which might persuade the viewer or reader to engage in "obscene" conduct—is not outside the protection of the First Amendment:

It is contended that the State's action was justified because the motion picture attractively portrays a relationship which is contrary to the moral standards, the religious precepts, and the legal code of its citizenry. This argument misconceives what it is that the Constitution protects. Its guarantee is not confined to the expression of ideas that are conventional or shared by a majority. It protects advocacy of the opinion that adultery may sometimes be proper, no less than advocacy of socialism or the single tax. And in the realm of ideas it protects expression which is eloquent no less than that which is unconvincing. Kingsley Int'l Pictures Corp. v. Regents, 360 U.S. 684, 688–689, 79 S.Ct. 1362, 1365, 3 L.Ed.2d 1512 (1959).

Even a legitimate, sharply focused state concern for the morality of the community cannot, in other words, justify an assault on the protections of the First Amendment. . . . Where the state interest in regulation of morality is vague and ill-defined, interference with the guarantees of the First Amendment is even more difficult to justify.[13]

In short, while I cannot say that the interests of the State—apart from the question of juveniles and unconsenting adults—are trivial or nonexistent, I am compelled to conclude that these interests cannot justify the substantial damage to constitutional rights and to this Nation's judicial machinery that inevitably results from state efforts to bar the distribution even of unprotected material to consenting adults. . . . I would hold, therefore, that at least in the absence of distribution to juveniles or obtrusive exposure to unconsenting adults, the First and Fourteenth Amendments prohibit the state and federal governments from attempting wholly to suppress sexually oriented materials on the basis of their allegedly "obscene" contents. Nothing in this approach precludes those governments from taking action to serve what may be strong and legitimate interests through regulation of the manner of distribution of sexually oriented material.

---

[13] "[I]n our system, undifferentiated fear or apprehension of disturbance is not enough to overcome the right to freedom of expression. Any departure from absolute regimentation may cause trouble. Any variation from the majority's opinion may inspire fear. Any word spoken, in class, in the lunchroom, or on the campus, that deviates from the views of another person may start an argument or cause a disturbance. But our Constitution says we must take this risk, Terminiello v. Chicago, 337 U.S. 1 [69 S.Ct. 894], 93 L.Ed. 1131 (1949); and our history says that it is this sort of hazardous freedom—this kind of openness—that is the basis of our national strength and of the independence and vigor of Americans who grow up and live in this relatively permissive, often disputatious, society." Tinker v. Des Moines Indep. Commun. School Dist., 393 U.S. 503, 508–509, 89 S.Ct. 733, 737–738, 21 L.Ed.2d 731 (1969). See also Cohen v. California, 403 U.S. 15, 23, 91 S.Ct. 1780, 1787, 29 L.Ed. 2d 284 (1971).

FRED R. BERGER

Pornography, Sex, and Censorship

An observer of American attitudes toward pornography faces a bewildering duality: on the one hand, we buy and read and view more of it than just about anyone else, while, on the other hand, we seek to suppress it as hard as anybody else. I presume that these facts do not merely reflect a judgment of social utilities, namely, that the best balance of goods is achieved by having it available, but under conditions of prohibition![1] I believe, in fact, that this state of things reflects aspects of our attitudes toward sex, and much of the current controversy has tended to obscure this fact, and to ignore important issues concerning sex and freedom to which the pornography issue points.

There is an important reason why the pornography controversy in the American context has tended to be narrowly focused. Our First Amendment prohibits government from abridging freedom of speech and press. Whatever interpretation is to be given that amendment, it is, in fact, stated in absolutist terms, and carries no mention or definition of obscenity or pornography. This difficulty is exacerbated by the fact that in the common-law background of our legal system, there is very little litigation which established clear legal definitions and doctrines. Obscenity convictions in the form we know them seem very much an invention of the 1800s, and the late 1800s at that.[2] Moreover, in our experience with

Reprinted from *Social Theory and Practice*, Vol. 4, No. 2, (Spring 1977) with the permission of the author and publisher.

A somewhat shorter version of this paper was presented at the meeting of the Society for Philosophy and Public Affairs, held in conjunction with the Pacific Division meetings of the American Philosophical Association, March 28, 1975, in San Diego. Professor Ann Garry delivered a commentary on the paper, for which I am grateful; in several places I have utilized points she made. I also wish to thank Susan Denning for her extremely diligent and helpful research assistance.

[1] This proposition is argued for by one advocate of censorship. See Irving Kristol, "Pornography, Obscenity, and the Case for Censorship," *New York Times Magazine* (March 28, 1971): 23.

[2] There are a number of brief summaries available of the development of the common-law approach to obscenity. See *The Report of the Commission on Obscenity and Pornography* (New York: Bantam, 1970), 348–54; Michael J. Goldstein and Harold S. Kant, *Pornography and Sexual Deviance* (Berkeley: University of

obscenity litigation, we have discovered that an enormous array of serious, even important, literature and art has fallen to the censor's axe. Thus, liberals and conservatives alike have feared that the removal of pornography from the protections of the First Amendment can endanger materials the Constitution surely ought to protect. This has given the constitutional issue great urgency.

The upshot has been that much of the debate has centered on the question of definition, and, moreover, that question has been pursued with legal needs in mind.

In this paper, I want to put aside the First Amendment to ask if there are any justifiable grounds for rejecting the arguments offered for the censorship of pornography independent of First Amendment considerations. Moreover, I shall be concerned with the *censorship* of pornography, not its *regulation*. The regulation of speech often has the same effect as censorship, and that is an important danger; nevertheless, censorship and regulation differ radically in intention, and that is an important difference.[3] I should also indicate that I shall suppose that those who favor censorship (I shall refer to them as "the censors") are not *generally* in favor of censorship, and would not prohibit what they regard as "true" art or literature.

Moreover, to lend further clarity to my discussion I shall propose a definition which is useful for the purposes of this paper, and which picks out most of what is usually regarded as pornographic, and that is all I claim for it. I define pornography as art or literature which explicitly depicts sexual activity or arousal in a manner having little or no artistic or literary value.[4] (I am assuming that scientific and medical texts are a kind of literature, with appropriate criteria of acceptability.)

California Press, 1973), 154–56; and an untitled essay by Charles Rembar in *Censorship: For and Against*, ed. Harold H. Hart (New York: Hart Publishing Co., 1971), 198–227. Apparently, the leading case prior to the 18th century involved Sir Charles Sedley, who, with some friends, had become drunk in a tavern, appeared naked on a balcony overlooking Covent Garden, and shouted profanities at the crowd which gathered below; then he urinated upon, and threw bottles of urine on, the bystanders.

[3] Regulation of speech is one of the most pressing problems for free speech in our contemporary, mass society, in which the control of the media is in relatively few hands, primarily concerned with the use of that media to produce profits. Moreover, the spectre of nonlegal controls, which Mill feared, is very much with us. It is surprising that so little attention has been given to the issue of the principles properly governing regulation. An indication of various forms of control utilized by government for the suppression of pornography is found by studying the development of censorship in the United States. See James C. N. Paul and Murray L. Schwartz, *Federal Censorship: Obscenity in the Mail* (New York: The Free Press, 1961).

[4] I regard it as a serious drawback of the definition that it rules out by *fiat*, the claim that pornography *can* be, in and of itself, significant literature. This claim is convincingly argued for by Susan Sontag in her essay "The Pornographic Imagination," reprinted in *Perspectives on Pornography*, ed. Douglas A. Hughes (New

The definition does, I believe, make pornography a relatively objective classification, insofar as there are clear cases on both sides of the divide, and there are relatively standard literary and artistic criteria by which to judge disputed cases.[5] In this respect, I am somewhat sympathetic to the conservatives who chide those liberals who claim they are not able to recognize standard cases of pornography as such.[6]

1. Objections to Pornography: Conflicting Views on Sex

Generally speaking, there are three forms of argument employed by the conservatives in favor of censorship. First, they simply hold that pornography itself is immoral or evil, irrespective of illconsequences which may flow from it.[7] Second, they sometimes assert that, irrespective of its morality, a practice which most people in a community find abhorrent and disgusting may be rightfully suppressed. Finally, they sometimes contend that pornography promotes or leads to certain kinds of socially harmful attitudes and/or behavior.

In this paper, I wish to concentrate on this last form of argument. The proponents of the first kind of claim cannot, for the most part, meet Ronald Dworkin's challenge to specify some recognizable sense of morality according to which their claims are true.[8] Though I am aware of one form

---

York: St. Martin's Press, 1970), 131–69; also in her book *Styles of Radical Will* (New York: Farrar, Straus & Giroux, 1966). The argument for a broader, more inclusive definition is made convincingly by Morse Peckham in *Art and Pornography* (New York: Basic Books, 1969), chapter 1. Anyone with a serious interest in the subject of pornography will find this a most important work.

[5] It is also clear that the definition would be a disaster in the legal context, since there is so great an area òf *disagreement*. Moreover, there is a tremendous danger of a secondary form of censorship, in which literary critics come to watch closely how they criticize a work lest the critique be used by the censors. That this in fact has happened is testified to in an eye-opening note by the English critic Horace Judson, in *Encounter* 30 (March 1968): 57–60. To his dismay, a critical review he wrote of Selby's *Last Exit to Brooklyn* was read into the record and used in banning that book in England.

[6] See, for example, Ernest van den Haag, writing in *Censorship: For and Against*, 158. Also, in "Is Pornography a Cause of Crime?" *Encounter* 29 (December 1967): 54.

[7] I believe that the minority report of the Presidential Commission on Obscenity and Pornography reduces to such a view, when it is not concerned specifically with possible harms. See, for example, the rationale given on 498–500 of the report, for their legislative recommendations. Sense can be made of these passages *only* on the assumption the commissioners believe pornography is itself immoral. I might also note that if one looks up "pornography" in the *Readers' Guide*, he is advised "See immoral literature and pictures."

[8] Ronald Dworkin, "Lord Devlin and the Enforcement of Morals," *Yale Law Journal* 75 (1966): 986–1005; reprinted in *Morality and the Law*, ed. Richard Wasserstrom (Belmont, Calif.: Wadsworth, 1971), 55–72.

of this argument which I think *can* meet that challenge, it is dealt with obliquely in my responses to the other claims. The second form of argument has been widely debated in the literature, and I have little to add to that debate.[9] The arguments do not turn on the nature of pornography as such, and, moreover, it is fairly clear that in contemporary America there is not an overwhelming abhorrence of pornography as such.[10] The last form of argument has been given new life, however, by claims based on analyses of pornographic materials as such. These new conservative arguments differ in important ways from the traditional views of the censors, and their arguments have been extremely influential. Each of the articles I shall discuss has been widely referred to; each has been reprinted a number of times, and all but one are cited in support of recent decisions in the courts.[11]

The traditional form of the claim can be labeled the "incitement to rape" theory. It holds that pornography arouses sexual desire, which seeks an outlet, often in antisocial forms such as rape. It is this version of the claim we are most familiar with, and the evidence which is available tends to refute it.[12] I shall have more to say about it later.

The conservative views I want to take up hold that the harms from pornography are somewhat long-range. These commentators maintain that the modes of sex depicted in pornography, and the manner of depiction, will result in altering our basic attitudes toward sex and to one another, so that in the end a climate of antisocial behavior will result. I have isolated four instances of such arguments in the literature of pornography.

The first claim I shall take up is put forth in an essay by George Steiner, entitled "Night Words," which has provoked considerable comment.[13] Though Steiner expressed disapproval of censorship because it is "stupid" and cannot work, his views have been taken as an argument supporting censorship. Steiner holds that pornography constitutes an invasion of privacy:

> Sexual relations are, or should be, one of the citadels of privacy, the night place where we must be allowed to gather the splintered, harried elements of our consciousness to some kind of inviolate order and repose. It is in sexual experience that a human being alone, and two human beings in that attempt at total communication which is also communion, can discover the unique bent of their identity. There we may find our-

---

[9] For starters, one might review the essays in Wasserstrom, *Morality and the Law.*

[10] In surveys done for the Presidential Commission, it was found that a (slim) majority of adults would not object to the availability of pornography if it could be shown it is not harmful. While hardly a declaration of adoration for pornography, this is not a demonstration of utter, overwhelming intolerance for it, either.

[11] See, for example, Paris Adult Theatre I v. Slaton, 413 U.S. 49 (1973).

[12] Report of the Commission on Obscenity, 26–32, in which the effects are summarized. Also, Goldstein and Kant, *Pornography and Sexual Deviance,* 139–53.

[13] George Steiner, "Night Words: High Pornography and Human Privacy," in *Perspectives on Pornography,* 96–108.

selves through imperfect striving and repeated failure, the words, the gestures, the mental images which set the blood to racing. In that dark and wonder ever renewed both the fumblings and the light must be our own.

The new pornographers subvert this last, vital privacy; they do our imagining for us. They take away the words that were of the night and shout them over the rooftops, making them hollow. The images of our love-making, the stammerings we resort to in intimacy come prepackaged. . . . Natural selection tells of limbs and functions which atrophy through lack of use; the power to feel, to experience and realize the precarious uniqueness of each other's being, can also wither in a society.[14]

The second claim against pornography is made by Irving Kristol, in an article arguing for censorship. Kristol claims that pornography depersonalizes sex, reducing it to animal activity and thus debases it; that it essentially involves only the readers' or viewers' sexual arousal, and thus promotes an infantile sexuality which is dangerous to society:

The basic psychological fact about pornography and obscenity is that it appeals to and provokes a kind of sexual regression. The sexual pleasure one gets from pornography and obscenity is autoerotic and infantile; put bluntly, it is a masturbatory exercise of the imagination, when it is not masturbation pure and simple. . . . Infantile sexuality is not only a permanent temptation for the adolescent or even the adult—it can quite easily become a permanent, self-reinforcing neurosis. It is because of an awareness of this possibility of regression toward the infantile condition, a regression which is always open to us, that all the codes of sexual conduct ever devised by the human race take such a dim view of autoerotic activities and try to discourage autoerotic fantasies. Masturbation is indeed a perfectly natural autoerotic activity. . . . And it is precisely because it is so perfectly natural that it can be so dangerous to the mature or maturing person, if it is not controlled or sublimated in some way.[15]

The danger is borne out, he thinks in *Portnoy's Complaint.* Portnoy's sexuality is fixed in an infantile mode (he is a prolific and inventive masturbator), and he is incapable of an adult sexual relationship with a woman. The final consequences are quite dire, as Kristol concludes: "What is at stake is civilization and humanity, nothing less. The idea that 'everything is permitted,' as Nietzsche put it, rests on the premise of nihilism and has nihilistic implications." [16]

Professor Walter Berns, writing in the magazine *The Public Interest*, maintains that pornography breaks down the feelings of shame we associate with sex. This shame, he holds, is not merely a dictate of our society, it is natural in that it protects love, and promotes the self-restraint which is requisite for a democratic polity:

[14] Ibid., 106–07.
[15] Kristol, "Pornography, Obscenity and the Case for Censorship," 113.
[16] Ibid.

> Whereas sexual attraction brings man and woman together seeking a unity that culminates in the living being they together create, the voyeur maintains a distance; and because he maintains a distance he looks at, he does not communicate; and because he looks at he objectifies, he makes an object of that which it is natural to join; objectifying, he is incapable of uniting and is therefore incapable of love. The need to conceal voyeurism—the concealing shame—is corollary of the peotective shame, the shame that impels lovers to search for privacy and for an experience protected from the profane and the eyes of the stranger. . . . Shame, both concealing and protective, protects lovers and therefore love.[17]

The upshot, as we might have suspected, is catastrophic. Under the banner of "the forgotten argument," Berns writes:

> To live together requires rules and a governing of the passions, and those who are without shame will be unruly and unreliable; having lost the ability to restrain themselves by observing the rules they collectively give themselves, they will have to be ruled by others. Tyranny is the natural and inevitable mode of government for the shameless and the self-indulgent who have carried liberty beyond any restraint, natural and conventional.[18]

Finally, Professor Ernest van den Haag, in a series of articles, has argued for censorship on the grounds that pornography encourages "the pure libidinal principle," which leads to loss of empathy with others, and encourages violence and antisocial acts:

> By de-individualizing and dehumanizing sexual acts, which thus become impersonal, pornography reduces or removes the empathy and the mutual identification which restrain us from treating each other merely as objects or means. This empathy is an individual barrier to nonconsensual acts, such as rape, torture, and assaultive crimes in general. . . .
> By reducing life to varieties of sex, pornography invites us to regress to a premoral world, to return to, and to spin out, preadolescent fantasies—fantasies which reject reality and the burdens of individuation, of restraint, of tension, of conflict, of regarding others as more than objects of commitment, of thought, of consideration, and of love. These are the burdens which become heavy and hard to avoid in adolescence. By rejecting them, at least in fantasy, a return to the pure libidinal pleasure principle is achieved. And once launched by pornography, fantasy may regress to ever more infantile fears and wishes: people, altogether dehumanized, may be tortured, mutilated, and literally devoured.[19]

[17] Walter Berns, "Pornography vs. Democracy: The Case for Censorship," *The Public Interest* 22 (Winter 1971): 12.

[18] Ibid., 13. Berns cites Washington, Jefferson, and Lincoln as holding that democracy requires citizens of good character and self-restraint, and he seems to think that somehow this is a "forgotten argument" against pornography.

[19] Van den Haag, in *Censorship: For and Against*, 146–48.

My response to these claims has two parts. First, I shall try to show that they reflect certain attitudes toward sex that are rejected by many, and that pornography will be judged differently by people with different attitudes toward sex. Second, I shall try to show why the gruesome results these writers foresee as the consequences of the state's failure to suppress dirty books and art are *not* likely consequences. Pornographic materials, *by their nature,* I shall contend, are an unlikely source or means of altering and influencing our basic attitudes toward one another.

Let us begin by noting certain features of pornography on which the conservative claims seem to hinge. First of all, by virtue of its lack of finesse, pornography is stark; it tends to remove those nuances of warmth and feeling which a more delicate approach is more apt to preserve. Second, there is some tendency of much pornography to assault our sensibilities and sense of the private, to estrange us somewhat. This is not difficult to understand, and it is not simply a result of our culture's attitudes toward sex. Sex, quite naturally, is associated with the notion of privacy because in sex we are in a vulnerable state, both emotionally and physically—we are very much in the control of our feelings and sensations, less aware of environmental factors, very much involved in and attending to our state of feeling and present activity.[20] Such vulnerability is the mark of private states—states on which we do not want others to intrude. This is reflected also in our attitudes toward grief and dying. Moreover, because we *want* to be totally taken with the activity itself, we do not usually want others present. So, we can concede that there is some truth to the conservative analyses of the nature of pornography.

These conservative arguments, however, involve and presuppose views on sex that many people reject. I think it is important to make these more explicit. Steiner, as we have seen, regards sex as a source of "inviolate order and repose," in which a sense of our identity is achieved by virtue of the private words, gestures, mental images which are shared with loved ones. (I envisage a hushed atmosphere.) For Van den Haag, sex, or mature sex, properly involves the burdens of "conflict, commitment, thought, consideration and love." And Kristol has distinguished mere "animal coupling" from making love, labeling the former "debased." Professor Berns's views about the nature of sex are, perhaps, clarified in a footnote:

> It is easy to prove that shamefulness is not the only principle governing the question of what may properly be presented on the stage; shameful-

---

20 The extent to which feelings of vulnerability can be involved in sex is testified to by the kinds of fears which can inhibit orgasmic response. In her book reporting on techniques she has used with non or preorgasmic women, Dr. Lonnie Garfield Barbach reports that among the factors which inhibit these women from having orgasms is the fear of appearing ugly, of their partners being repulsed by them, of losing control, fainting, or screaming. See Lonnie Garfield Barbach, *For Yourself: The Fulfillment of Female Sexuality* (Garden City, N.Y.: Doubleday, 1975), 11–12.

ness would not, for example, govern the case of a scene showing the copulating of a married couple who love each other very much. That is not intrinsically shameful—on the contrary—yet it ought not to be shown. The principle here is, I think, an aesthetic one; such a scene is dramatically weak because the response of the audience would be characterized by prurience and not by a sympathy with what the scene is intended to portray, a beautiful love.[21]

The trouble with these views is that they see sex as normal or proper only within the context of deep commitment, shared responsibility, loving concern, and as involving restraint and repression of pure pleasure. Indeed, Professor Berns's footnote not only carries the suggestion that anything but married love is shameful, but also could be uncharitably interpreted as holding that "a beautiful love" is something which holds between disembodied souls, and in no way involves sexual communion, or the sharing of physical joy and pleasure. It seems to him that if we got some sense of the pleasure the couple take in one another physically, some hint of the physical forms of their communication and sense of mutuality, that this would somehow detract from our sympathy with their "beautiful love."

Now, many in our society reject these analyses of sex, either totally or partially. I want to sketch two possible views so that we might have a sense of the wider context of attitudes within which the pornography problem should be discussed. As many liberals share the conservative attitudes toward sex and many political conservatives do not, I shall label the views I discuss as "radical" and "radical-liberal," with no further political significance to be attached to them.

The radical maintains that the entire facade of sexual attitudes in contemporary society represents sham, hypocrisy, and unnecessary forms of social control. Sexual relations are governed by the notions of duty, shame, guilt. As such, there can be no honest sexuality, since mediating all sexual relations are feelings and associations which have nothing to do with our feelings *for* one another, and, often, little to do really with our sexual natures. The conservative picture of shared communication, in an aura of intimate connection, expressive of tender love, concern, commitment which are involved in mature (preferably married) sex, is an idealized, romanticized, unreal (perhaps even infantile) depiction of what really happens in sex. The fact is that most sex is routinized, dull, unfulfilling, a source of neurosis, precisely because its practice is governed by the restraints the conservatives insist on. Those constraints dictate with *whom* one has sex, *when* one has sex, how *often* one has sex, *where* one has sex, and so on. Moreover, the web of shame and guilt which is spun around sex tends to destroy its enjoyment, and thus to stunt our sexual natures—our capacity for joy and pleasure through sex. The result is a society which is highly neurotic in its attitudes toward and practice of sex —all of which interferes with honest communication and self-realization.

[21] Berns, "Pornography vs. Democracy," 12.

The radical solution to this perceived situation is to treat sex *as* a physical act, unencumbered with romanticized notions of love. Human sex just *is* a form of animal coupling, and to make more of it is to invite dishonesty and neurosis.

It seems to me that it is *this* sort of attitude which the conservative most fears. Though the conservative claims that such an attitude will result in devaluing humans, it is not clear why. He seems to infer that because the radical is willing to treat others as sources of pleasure, without the necessity of emotional commitment, he therefore perceives them as mere *instruments* of pleasure. This, of course, does not follow, either logically or as a matter of probability. Nor have I ever met a conservative who thought that correspondingly, if people are permitted to make profits from others in business dealings, they will come to view them as mere sources of profits. The point is that it is absurd to suppose that one who no longer thinks of *sex* in terms of shame and guilt must lose the sense of shame and guilt at harming others, either through sex, or in other ways.

I do not wish to dwell on the radical position, however, because there is a more widespread view which I have labeled the "radical-liberal" view which I wish to consider. This conception accepts a large part of the radical critique, in particular the notion that guilt and shame, duty and commitment, are not necessary to fully human sex. The radical-liberal agrees that much of our ordinary sexual relations are marred by the inhibitions these impose. He or she need not, however, reject sex as an element in loving relationships, and he or she may well insist that love does engender special commitments and concern with which sex is properly entangled. But, the radical-liberal does not reject physical sex for its own sake as something debased or wicked, or shorn of human qualities. Indeed, he or she may insist that greater concern with the physical aspects of sexuality is needed to break down those emotional connections with sex which stand as barriers to its enjoyment, and as barriers to free open communication with others, and to one's development of a sense of one's sexual identity—a development in terms of one's own needs, desires, and life-style.

The intensity of such needs on the part of many people is, I believe, well-depicted in Erica Jong's contemporary novel, *Fear of Flying*. In the book, her heroine expresses her reaction to the attitude that a woman's identity is to be found in her relationship with a man. Female solitude is perceived as un-American and selfish. Thus, women live waiting to be half of something else, rather than being simply themselves. These American attitudes are perceived as inhibitions to the woman's self-discovery. The heroine describes her reaction:

> My response to all this was not (not yet) to have an affair and not (not yet) to hit the open road, but to evolve my fantasy of the Zipless Fuck. The zipless fuck was more than a fuck. It was a platonic ideal. Zipless because when you came together zippers fell away like rose petals, under-

wear blew off in one breath like dandelion fluff. Tongues intertwined and turned liquid. Your whole soul flowed out through your tongue and into the mouth of your lover.

For the true, ultimate zipless A-1 fuck, it was necessary that you never get to know the man very well. I had noticed, for example, how all my infatuations dissolved as soon as I really became friends with a man, became sympathetic to his problems, listened to him *kvetch* about his wife, or ex-wives, his mother, his children. After that I would like him, perhaps even love him—but without passion. And it was passion that I wanted.[22]

She thus concludes that brevity and anonymity are requisite to the perfect zipless fuck. Finally, after describing a sample fantasy, she says:

The incident has all the swift compression of a dream and is seemingly free of all remorse and guilt; because there is no talk of her late husband or of his fiancee; because there is no rationalizing; because there is no talk at *all*. The zipless fuck is absolutely pure. It is free of ulterior motives. There is no power game. The man is not "taking" and the woman is not "giving." No one is attempting to cuckold a husband or humiliate a wife. No one is trying to prove anything or get anything out of anyone. The zipless fuck is the purest thing there is. And it is rarer than the unicorn.[23]

Whatever one may interpret as the book's final evaluation of the Zipless Fuck, it is clear that the fantasy is a response to the need for a different attitude toward sex.

The point is that to many people, the conservative's picture of sex, and the sorts of social relations in which he imbeds it, has served to starve them of the unique development of their personalities, or an aspect of it. The antidote they see is a freer, more open attitude toward sex, removed from what they regard as a mystique of duty and guilt and shame.

People with the attitudes of the radical-liberal, or who see themselves as impeded in their full self-realization by the traditional views on sex, may well find pornography something of no consequence, or may even find it beneficial—a means of removing from their own psyches the associations which inhibit their sexual natures. The plain fact is that pornography is used for this effect by various therapists, who have thereby aided people to more fulfilled lives for themselves, and happier, healthier relations with loved ones.[24]

---

[22] Erica Jong, *Fear of Flying* (New York: Signet, 1973), 11.

[23] Ibid., 14.

[24] In *For Yourself*, Dr. Lonnie Garfield Barbach recommends the use of pornography for preorgasmic women seeking increased sexual responsiveness and fulfillment. See *For Yourself*, 75, 77, 85, 86. Dr. Wardell B. Pomeroy, one of Kinsey's collaborators, wrote *Playboy*, in reaction to a 1973 Supreme Court ruling on pornography:

"As a psychotherapist and marriage counselor, I sometimes recommend various erotic films, books and pictures to my patients. Many of them report that

Will such a concern with physical pleasure result in nonattachment, in antihuman feelings, in the loss of loving relationships? It is at least as plausible that just the opposite is the probable result, that by virtue of lessened anxiety and guilt over sex, an important source of human communion will be enhanced. In a Kinsey-type sex survey sponsored by *Playboy*, there was demonstrated a greatly heightened freedom in sex in America, and a greater emphasis on physical enjoyment, but this has not resulted in a significant lessening of the importance accorded to emotional ties.[25] Greater concern with pleasure has been used to *enhance* those relationships. Thus, it is no accident that among the millions who have lined up to see *Deep Throat, Behind the Green Door,* and *The Devil in Miss Jones,* have been a great many loving, married couples. Indeed, that there has come to be a body of "popular pornography"—porno for the millions—holds out some small hope that our culture will eventually develop a truly erotic artistic tradition, as explicitness becomes more natural, and tastes demand more of the productions.

We have seen that the conservative position presupposes attitudes toward sex which many reject, and that the alternative attitudes are consistent both with the acceptance of pornography and the values of care and concern for others. Let us turn now to the specific points the conservatives make concerning alleged harms.

2. The Response to Conservative Objections

I want to consider first the argument concerning privacy. It was Steiner's claim that pornography takes the "words of the night," and "by shouting them over the rooftops," robs us of the ability to use them or find them in private—sex becomes a matter in the public domain. Moreover, by dehumanizing the individual, people are treated as in concentration camps. As Steiner expressed it subsequent to the original publication of his essay: "Both pornography and totalitarianism seem to me to set up power relations which must necessarily violate privacy." [26]

If there is any plausibility to the first part of these claims, it must

---

erotica helps them to free them of their inhibitions and, thus, helps them function better with their spouses. Now they will have more difficulty in seeing and reading such seriously valuable material, and I am afraid I must enlarge my own library for their perusal. " *Playboy* 20 (October 1973): 57.

[25] This point is made at length in the report. One example: "Despite the extensive changes that the liberation has made in the feelings that most Americans have about their own bodies, about the legitimacy of maximizing sexual pleasure and about the acceptability and normality of a wide variety of techniques of foreplay and coitus, sexual liberation has not replaced the liberal-romantic concept of sex with the recreational one. The latter attitude toward sex now coexists with the former in our society, and in many a person's feeling, but the former remains the dominant ideal." *Playboy* 20 (October 1973): 204.

[26] Steiner, "Night Words," in *Perspectives*, 97.

derive entirely from the metaphor of shouting the sacred night words over the rooftops. Were anyone to do such a thing with night words, day words, winter words, and so on, we would have a legitimate gripe concerning our privacy. But in what *way* is the voluntary perusal or viewing of pornography an invasion of privacy? His point *seems* to be that the constant consumption by the public of explicit sexual materials will come to make sex something "pre-packaged" for us, so that we will not discover how to do it ourselves, in our own ways. This is extraordinarily implausible, and if it were true, would constitute a reason for banning all literature dealing with human feelings and emotions, and ways of relating to one another. The evidence is that greater sexual explicitness is utilized as a means for people to have greater awareness of their sexuality and its possibilities, and to assimilate the experiences of others into their own lifestyles. The capacity to do this is *part* of what is involved in our being the unique individuals we are. At any rate, people who *want* the stimulation of erotic materials, who feel freer in expressing themselves through the influence of sexy art, who do not *want* an environment in which sex cannot be appreciated through explicit literature and art, will hardly be impressed with the manner in which the censor protects *their* privacy.

I want now to turn to Kristol's view that pornography is autoerotic, hence, infantile, and thus promotes a sexual regression which is a danger to civilization itself. The danger which this supposed form of infantilism poses is that it would destroy the capacity for an integral feature of mature relations (and ultimately civilized relations) if "not controlled or sublimated in some way."

Now the ultimate ground for censorship which the argument poses really has only secondary connections with the charges of autoeroticism and infantilism. Lots of things are "self-pleasuring" without being thought infantile or dangerous on that account. Consider the pleasures of the gourmet, or wine afficionado, or devotees of Turkish baths.

Kristol believes that masturbation, and pornography which is its mental form, has an appeal to us as adults, and this is dangerous. Because it *is so* attractive, it is liable to draw us away from real love, and this is why it must be headed off at the pass. The charge of infantilism, then, is only Kristol's way of making us feel bad about masturbating. By virtue of his claiming to know the rationale underlying "all the codes of sexual conduct ever devised by the human race," we are made to feel beyond the pale of civilized adult society. The argument turns, really, on the supposed dangers of an *overly* autoeroticized society, which he thinks the legalization of pornography will help produce.

In criticizing pornography on these grounds, Kristol has surely overshot his mark; for, there is nothing more masturbatory than masturbation itself. If Kristol is right, then his concern with pornography is too tepid a treatment of the danger. What the argument would show is that we must stamp out masturbation itself!

Moreover, Kristol is mistaken if he thinks that censorship of por-

nography will make one whit of difference to the incidence of masturbation. This is because the masturbatory imagination is perfectly limitless;
it does not *need* explicit sexual stimuli. Deprived of that, it can make do
with virtually anything—the impassioned kisses of film lovers, a well-filled
female's sweater, or male's crotch,[27] even, we are told, a neatly displayed
ankle or bare shoulder. The enormity of the problem Kristol faces is
shown in the revelation of the *Playboy* survey that: "a large majority of
men and women in every age group say that while they masturbate, they
fantasize about having intercourse with persons they love." [28] The implications for the censor are staggering!

There are two further reasons why reasonable people will not take
Kristol's view seriously. First, he underestimates the human capacity to
assimilate varieties of sexual experience. People can enjoy pornography
and intercourse without giving up one or the other.[29] Second, his entire
argument grossly undervalues the appeal and attraction to us of the very
thing he wants to preserve—mature sexual love which is fulfilling, rewarding, and integrated into the course of a loving relationship. Pornography
may be in some sense autoerotic; it can be pleasant to be sexually stimu-
lated. But it is rarely its own source of ultimate satisfaction; it usually
stimulates to acquire further satisfactions. Indeed, this is presupposed by
some of the conservative arguments. But there is no reason to assume that
such satisfaction will be sought exclusively through masturbation, when a
healthy sex relation is available with a loved one. I have *never* heard anyone, male or female, complain that their love life had been ruined by their
partner's turn to masturbation as a result of an excess of pornography. On
the other hand, I have heard couples rave about sex had after viewing
pornographic films.

Still, there does seem to be a lingering problem which the conservatives will regard as not adequately dealt with in anything said thus far.
They think that literature and art *can* influence people's attitudes and
beliefs, and also their behavior, and they cannot understand why the
liberal, who believes this to be true in other cases, is unwilling to admit
this with respect to pornography. Now, I believe the liberal *can* admit
the possibility of a causal role for pornography with respect to people's
attitudes and behavior. Such an admission does not, however, establish a
case for censorship.

It would be quite extraordinary if literary and visual materials which
are capable of arousing normal men and women did not also have some
tendency to arouse people already predisposed to harmful conduct, and

---

[27] That women look at, and are excited by, the bulges in men's trousers is given ample
testimony in Nancy Friday's book on women's sexual fantasies. See *My Secret
Garden* (New York: Pocket Book, 1974), the section entitled "Women Do
Look," 214–22.

[28] *Playboy*, 202.

[29] See, for example, *Report of the Commission on Obscenity*, 28–29; also, Goldstein
and Kant, *Pornography and Sexual Deviance*, 30.

especially people with an unstable psychological makeup. It is believable, even apart from any evidence, that such people might act from the fantasies such stimuli generate.

When the conservative is reasonable, however, he recognizes that the stimulation and consequent influence of pornography is a function not merely of the nature of the stimulus, but also of the person's background, upbringing, cultural environment, and his own genetic and personality structure and predispositions.[30] Put *this* way, the conservative has a somewhat plausible claim that pornography can sometimes be implicated as having some causal role in the etiology of social harms.

Put in its most reasonable form, however, the claim makes quite *unreasonable* the censorship of pornography. There are two primary reasons for this: (1) Pornography is not distinguishable from other materials in producing *direct* harms of this kind; it may, in fact, exert a counter-influence to other materials which are more likely to have these effects. (2) The *indirect* harms—those produced through the influence of altered attitudes and beliefs, are highly unlikely, and not of a kind a society which values freedom will allow to become the basis of suppression without strong evidence of probable causal connections. It will seek to counter such remote influences with noncoercive means.

Let us turn to the first point—that other materials which no one would dream of suppressing are as likely to produce harms. Earl Finbar Murphy, writing in the *Wayne Law Review*, has given some graphic illustrations. He begins by pointing out that "everything, every idea, is capable of being obscene if the personality perceiving it so apprehends it." He continues:

> It is for this reason that books, pictures, charades, ritual, the spoken word, *can* and *do* lead directly to conduct harmful to the self indulging in it and to others. Heinrich Pommerenke, who was a rapist, abuser, and mass slayer of women in Germany, was prompted to his series of ghastly deeds by Cecil B. DeMille's *The Ten Commandments*. During the scene of the Jewish women dancing about the Golden Calf, all the doubts of his life came clear: women were the source of the world's trouble and it was his mission to both punish them for this and to execute them. Leaving the theater, he slew his first victim in a park nearby. John George Haigh, the British vampire who sucked his victims' blood through soda straws and dissolved their drained bodies in acid baths, first had his murder-inciting dreams and vampire-longings from watching the "voluptuous" procedure of—an Anglican High Church Service!
>
> The prohibition and effective suppression of what the average consensus would regard as pornographic would not have reached these two. Haigh, who drank his own urine as well as others' blood, was educated to regard "all forms of pleasure as sinful, and the reading of newspapers undesirable." Pommerenke found any reference to sex in a film, however oblique, made him feel so tense inside that, "I had to do

[30] Van den Haag seems to recognize this point. See "Is Pornography a Cause of Crime?" in *Encounter*, 53.

something to a woman." Albert Fish, who has been called the most perverse case known to psychiatry, decided he had a mission to castrate small boys and offer them as human sacrifices to God as a result of reading the Old Testament. Each of these had the common quality of being beyond the reach of the conventionally pornographic. They had altered the range of the erotically stimulating, and each illustrates how impossible it is to predict what will precipitate or form psycho-neurotic conduct. . . . The scope of pornography, so far from being in any way uniform, is as wide as the peculiarities of the human psyche.[31]

These are extreme cases, but they do represent a pattern on the part of people disposed to deviant behavior, as is borne out by studies of the personalities and backgrounds of sex offenders. In their book, *Pornography and Sexual Deviance*, Michael J. Goldstein and Harold S. Kant report:

A problem that arises in studying reactions to pornography among sex offenders is that they appear to generate their own pornography from nonsexual stimuli. . . . The sex offenders deduced a significantly greater number of sexual activities from the drawings (children playing near a tree, figure petting a dog, and three people standing unrelated to each other) than did the nonsex offenders. They also were more prone to incorporate recently viewed sexual pictures into a series of gradually more explicit drawings. These results imply that the sex offender is highly receptive to sexual stimuli, and reads sexual meanings into images that would be devoid of erotic connotations for the normal person. Certainly, this finding was borne out by our study of institutional pedophiles (child molesters), who found the familiar suntan lotion ad showing a young child, with buttocks exposed to reveal his sunburn as a dog pulls at his bathing suit, to be one of the most erotic stimuli they had encountered.[32]

Indeed, their studies seem to yield the conclusion that pornography itself does not tend to produce antisocial behavior, and that, at least in the case of rapists, other materials are more likely to do so:

We must consider that sex offenders are highly receptive to suggestions of sexual behavior congruent with their previously formed desires and will interpret the material at hand to fit their needs. It is true, however, that while few, if any, sex offenders suggest that erotica played a role in the commission of sex crimes, stimuli expressing brutality, with or without concomitant sexual behavior, were often mentioned as disturbing, by rapists in particular. This raises the question of whether the stimulus most likely to release antisocial behavior is one representing sexuality, or one representing aggression.[33]

In summarizing the evidence they gathered, and which is supported by other studies, they conclude that pornography does not seem to be a

---

[31] Earl Finbar Murphy, "The Value of Pornography," *Wayne Law Review* (1964): 668–69.

[32] Goldstein and Kant, *Pornography and Sexual Deviance*, 31.

[33] Ibid., 108–09.

significant factor in the behavior of sex offenders. Moreover, there is some evidence that "for rapists, exposure to erotica portraying 'normal' heterosexual relations can serve to ward off antisocial sexual impulses." [34]

The point is that if we take the conservative's "harm" claim in its most plausible form, we must conclude that while pornography *can* play a causal role of this type, the evidence is that many other ordinary visual and literary depictions are more likely to do so. If we take seriously the claim that having this kind of causal role is sufficient for a case for censorship, then we must do a much greater housecleaning of our media offerings than we had imagined. The problem is that while we know where to begin—with unalloyed portrayals of violence, we can hardly know where to end.

A further serious difficulty for the conservative "harm" argument arises when we ask just what *kinds* of backgrounds and attitudes *do* predispose to the unwanted behavior. The studies of Kant and Goldstein are of help here, especially with respect to rapists:

> The rapists, who found it very difficult to talk about sex, said there was little nudity in their homes while they were growing up and that sex was never discussed. Only 18 percent of the rapists said their parents had caught them with erotic materials; in those instances the parents had become angry and had punished them. (In the control group, 37 percent reported that their parents knew they read erotic materials, but only 7 percent reported being punished. Most said their parents had been indifferent, and some said their parents had explained the materials to them —an occurrence not reported by any other group.) [35]
>
> For the *rapists*, the data suggest very repressive family backgrounds regarding sexuality.[36]

Moreover: "It appears that all our noncontrol groups, no matter what their ages, education, or occupations, share one common characteristic: they had little exposure to erotica when they were adolescents." [37]

These results at the very least carry the suggestion that the very attitudes toward sex which motivate the censor are part of the background and psychological formation of the personality patterns of sex offenders— backgrounds which include the repression of sexual feelings, repression of exposure to explicit sexual stimuli, an overly developed sense of shame and guilt related to sex. As we have seen, some of the censors advocate *just* this sort of model for all of society, wherein suppression of pornography is just *one* way of safeguarding society. It may well be that they are in the paradoxical position of isolating a possible evil of great extent, and

[34] Ibid., 152.
[35] Ibid., 143.
[36] Ibid., 145.
[37] Ibid., 147.

then recommending and fostering a response which will help produce that very evil.[38]

There is, however, a more profound reason why the admission of a possible causal role for pornography in affecting attitudes and behavior need not support the conservative view, and why the traditional liberal may well have been right in not taking pornography seriously.

To begin with, I believe we have granted the conservatives too much in admitting that pornography depersonalizes sex. While there is a measure of truth in this claim, it is not literally true. By concentrating on physical aspects of sex, pornography does, somewhat, abstract from the web of feelings, emotions, and needs which are usually attendant on sexual experience in ordinary life. Nonetheless, people are not depicted as mere machines or animals. Indeed, where there is explicit pornographic purpose—the arousal of the reader or viewer—the end could not be accomplished were it not real fleshy people depicted. In addition, pornography almost always does have *some* human context within which sex takes place—a meeting in a bar, the bridegroom carrying his bride over the threshold, the window washer observing the inhabitant of an apartment. A study of pornography will reveal certain set patterns of such contexts; there is, indeed, a sort of orthodoxy among pornographers. And, there is an obvious reason: pornography springs from and caters to sexual fantasies. This also explains why so little context is needed; the observer quickly identifies with the scene, and is able to elaborate it in his or her own mind to whatever extent he or she wishes or feels the need. That pornography is intimately tied to fantasy—*peopled* fantasy—also accounts for one of its worst features—its tendency to treat women in conventional male chauvinist ways. Pornography, as a matter of sociological fact, has been produced by and for men with such sexual attitudes.

There are further grounds for holding that pornography does not, by its nature, dehumanize sex in the feared ways. It usually depicts people as enjoying physical activity, that is, as mutually experiencing *pleasure*. Typical pornography displays sex as something people take fun in and enjoy. There is usually little doubt the persons involved are *liking* it. All of the censors we have discussed treat *Fanny Hill* as pornographic, but it is obvious to anyone who has read the book that it absolutely resists the claim that the characters are not portrayed as real people with the usual hopes and fears, who desire not to be harmed, and desire a measure of respect as persons. The book concentrates on sex and sexual enjoyment, and *that* is why it is taken as pornographic.[39] Even sadistic pornography, it should be noted, depicts people as having enjoyment; and, it is usually sado-*masochistic* pleasures which are portrayed, with a resultant equaliz-

[38] To compound the paradox, if being a remote cause of harms is a prima facie ground for censoring literature, then we have some evidence that the conservative arguments ought to be censored. This is *not* a view I advocate.

[39] I do not appeal to its conventional format—girl meets boy, girl loses boy, girl reunites with boy in marriage.

ing of the distribution of pleasure (if not of pain). In this respect, most pornography does not portray humans as *mere* instruments of whatever ends we have. And, in this respect, pornography does not express or evoke the genuinely immoral attitudes which a great deal of our movie, television, and literary materials cater to and reinforce.[40]

Indeed, much of what is found in the media *is* immoral in that it is expressive of, caters to, and fosters attitudes which *are* morally objectionable. People are treated as expendable units by international spies for whom *anything* is permitted in the name of national security; the typical laundry soap commercial treats women as idiotic house slaves; situation comedy typically portrays fathers as moronic bunglers who, nonetheless, rightfully rule their homes as dictators (albeit, benevolent ones); the various detective programs cater to the aggressive, dominating, *macho* image of male sexuality which is endemic within large portions of American society. Pornography cannot get off the hook merely by pointing out that it depicts *people*. On the other hand, most of it does not reflect or cater to attitudes as objectionable as one now finds dominating the output of television alone. And, where it does, it is not a result of the fact it is pornographic, but, rather, that it reflects conventional views widely expressed in other forms.[41]

There remains a final point to be made about the influence of pornography on attitudes. Pornography, when it does attract us, affect us, appeal to us, has a limited, narrowly focused appeal—to our sexual appetite. Such appeal tends toward short-lived enjoyments, rather than any far-reaching effects on the personality.[42] This is why pornography has essentially entertainment and recreational use and attraction; it is taken

---

[40] Professor Van den Haag holds that pornography "nearly always leads to sadistic pornography." It is not clear what this means; moreover, his argument is that this results *because* pornography dehumanizes sex. Since we have grounds for doubting this, we have grounds for doubting the alleged result. Also, since I am denying that pornography significantly dehumanizes sex, I am implicitly rejecting a further conservative argument I have not taken up, namely, that pornography is itself expressive of immoral attitudes irrespective of any further harmful effects. Since some liberals seem to be willing to silence Nazis or racists on such grounds, some conservatives think this argument will appeal to such liberals. I believe that both Kristol and Van den Haag maintain this view. See also Richard Kuh, *Foolish Figleaves?* (New York: Macmillan, 1967), 280ff. A position of this sort is maintained by Susan Brownmiller in her book *Against Our Will: Men, Women and Rape* (New York: Simon and Schuster, 1975), 201. Brownmiller regards pornography as an invention designed to humiliate women. I have not responded to her arguments as she gives none. Moreover, she employs a curious "double standard." She gives great weight to law enforcement officials' opinions about pornography, but would hardly be willing to take these same persons' views on rape at face value.

[41] In this paragraph I have attempted to bring to bear on the argument some points made by Professor Ann Garry, in her commentary on the paper at the meeting of the Society for Philosophy and Public Affairs in San Diego, March 18, 1975.

[42] *Report of the Commission on Obscenity*, 28; and Goldstein and Kant, *Pornography and Sexual Deviance*, 151.

seriously by almost no one but the censors. It shows us people having sex, and that is it; we must do the rest. Serious literature and art, however, appeal to the whole person—to the entire range of his sensibilities, desires, needs, attitude patterns and beliefs and is thus far more likely to affect our ultimate behavior patterns. Even the limited reaction of sexual arousal is often better achieved through artistic technique. The conservatives deny this, but it is difficult to see on what grounds. Both in the essays of Van den Haag and of Walter Berns, there is the claim that aesthetic value would detract from the purely sexual appeal of a work.[43] I can only suppose that they think all people are possessed with, and exercise, the aesthetic sensibilities of literary and art critics, and thus readily separate out and analyze devices of technique in the experiencing of a work. This assuredly is not the case. Moreover, it is hardly plausible that artistic technique should enhance and further every *other* objective of an artist, and *not* be an accessory to the end of evoking sexual arousal. Real artistic value is unobtrusive in this respect.

Of course, television pap may well influence attitudes without having significant artistic value, merely by its sheer preponderance on the airwaves. But it is not *this* sort of role we need envisage for pornography liberated from censorship. Moreover, it is not clear its influence would be worse than that of other materials which now hog the channels.

It seems to me, however, that we have yet to make the most important response to the conservative's claims. For, up to now, we have treated the issue as if it were merely a matter of weighing up possible harms from pornography against possible benefits, and the likelihood of the occurrence of the harms. Unfortunately, this is the form the debate usually takes, when it is not strictly concerned with the First Amendment. But, something important is lost if we think the issue resolves into these questions. The more important issue turns on the fact that a great many people *like* and *enjoy* pornography, and *want* it as part of their lives, either for its enjoyment, or for more serious psychological purposes. This fact means that censorship is an interference with the freedom and self-determination of a great many people, and it is on this ground that the conservative harm argument must ultimately be rejected. For a society which accepts freedom and self-determination as centrally significant values cannot allow interferences with freedom on such grounds as these.

To give a satisfactory argument for these claims would require another paper. Moreover, I believe (with certain reservations) this has been adequately done in Mill's *On Liberty*. As the conservatives do not regard *that* as enunciating a clear, defensible body of doctrine,[44] I cannot hope to present an entirely convincing argument here. I want at the very least,

---

[43] Berns, in *The Public Interest*, 12 footnote, and Van den Haag, in *Perspectives*, 129.

[44] See, for example, Gertrude Himmelfarb's recent critical account of Mill, *On Liberty and Liberalism: The Case of John Stuart Mill* (New York: Alfred A. Knopf, 1974). It appears to me that she has not really understood Mill. Ronald Dworkin has picked out some of the most glaring of her errors in his review in *The New York Review of Books* 21 (October 31, 1974): 21.

however, to outline a minimal set of claims which I think bear on the issue, and which can provide ground for further debate.

The idea of a self-determining individual involves a person developing his or her own mode of life according to the person's own needs, desires, personality, and perceptions of reality. This conception has at least three features: (1) the person's desires are (so far as possible) expressions of his or her own nature—not imposed from without; (2) the manner of the development of his or her character and the pattern of the person's life, are, in large measure, a resultant of his or her own judgment, choice, and personal experience; and (3) the person's unique capacities and potentialities have been developed, or at least tried out.[45] Now, *if* one regards this as a valuable manner of living, and freedom as of value, *both* because it is intrinsic to treating others *as* self-determining agents, *and* because it is requisite for the realization of self-determination, then I think one will accept the following propositions concerning freedom:

1. The burden of producing convincing reasons and evidence is always on the person who would interfere with people's freedom and life-styles.
2. The person who would interfere with freedom must show that the activity interfered with is likely to harm others or interfere with their rights as individuals.[46]

---

[45] I believe this is Mill's conception. See also Sharon [Bishop] Hill's essay, "Self-Determination and Autonomy," in *Today's Moral Problems*, ed. Richard Wasserstrom (New York: Macmillan, 1975), 171–86. [See pp. 118–33 in this edition.]

[46] I want to note three points here. First, this view of freedom permits interferences for *moral* reasons; it does *not* insist on the moral neutrality of the law. It does, however, focus on the *kinds* of moral reasons allowed to count as grounds for the denial of freedom. Second, it does not rule out special legal recognition of modes of living which are central to the culture, for example, monogamous marriage. This will have indirect effects on freedom which a liberal theory would have to recognize and deal with, but it need not rule out such recognition out of hand. In addition, the notion of "harm" could be taken to include conduct or practices which are both intrusive on public consciousness, and offensive. This could provide a basis for *regulating* the sale and distribution of pornography, even if *prohibition* is not justified. Important discussion of the principles underlying the treatment of offensiveness in the law is to be found in an article by Joel Feinberg, "Harmless Immoralities and Offensive Nuisances," in *Issues in Law and Morality*, ed. Norman Care and Thomas Trelogan (Cleveland: Case Western Reserve University, 1973). Michael Bayles's commentary on that paper, also found in the same volume, is very useful. Third, valuing self-determination may entail a limited paternalism in circumstances where noninterference cannot possibly further autonomy. That it is at least possible for noninterference to promote self-determination seems to have been conceived by Mill as a presupposition for applications of his principle of liberty. This helps explain some of his "applications" at the end of the essay. Just how to incorporate limited paternalism in a liberal theory is a thorny issue. The pornography issue, however, does not appear to significantly involve that issue. A useful treatment of paternalism is in Gerald Dworkin, "Paternalism," in *Morality and the Law*, 107–26.

3. Those who would deny freedom must show that the harm or interference threatened is one from which others have a superior right to protection.

Though these propositions are subject to considerable interpretation, it seems to me that one who accepts them will, at the least, recognize that the burden of proof is not symmetric either in structure or degree. The person who would deny freedom shoulders the burden, and, moreover, he or she does not succeed merely by showing *some* harms are likely to result. Accepting freedom and self-determination as central values entails accepting some risks, in order to *be* free. We do *not* presuppose that freedom will always produce good. And, insofar as the alleged harms are indirect and remote, we are committed to employing noncoercive means to combat them. Of course, we need not interpret this in a suicidal way—allowing interference only when the harm is inevitably upon us. But, at the least, we should require a strong showing of likely harms which are far from remote, and this is a burden which the censors of pornography *cannot* meet. Indeed, on this score, the conservative arguments are *many* times weaker than ones which can be made concerning many other kinds of communications, and such activities as hunting for sport, automobile racing, boxing, and so on.[47] If anyone wants a display of the extent to which our society allows recreation to instigate socially harmful attitudes and feelings, all he or she need do is sit in the stands during a hotly contested high school football or basketball game. And, of course these feelings quite often spill over into antisocial behavior.

Though I have defended pornography from criticisms based on its content or nature, I have certainly not shown that it is always unobjectionable. Insofar as it arises in a social context entirely infused with male sexism, much of it reflects the worst aspects of our society's approved conceptions of sexual relations. Too often, the scenes depicted involve male violence and aggression toward women, male dominance over women, and females as sexual servants. Moreover, there are aspects of the commercial institutions which purvey it in the market which are quite

---

[47] So far as I can judge, the most telling "evidence" the conservatives have thus far come up with is: (a) *some* reasonable criticisms of the studies which have been done, and the interpretations which have been given them; and (b) a few, isolated, contrary studies (which are, coincidentally, open to similar or stronger objections). See especially the criticisms of Victor B. Cline in the minority report of the Presidential Commission on Obscenity and Pornography, 463–89. While I do not think the conservatives need produce ironclad scientific data demonstrating their claims, we surely cannot allow the suppression of freedom when the reasons offered are poor, and the weight of available evidence is heavily *against* those claims. The minority report (it may be Dr. Cline writing in this instance—it is unclear) asserts that the "burden of proof" is on the one who would change current law. This is an indefensible imprimatur of existing law as such; and it is absolutely inconsistent with the recognition of freedom and self-determination as important moral values. The mere *existence* of law cannot be allowed as a ground for its continued existence, if freedom is to have anything but secondary importance.

objectionable. My argument has been that this is not necessary to pornography as such; where it is true, this reflects social and sexual attitudes already fostered by other social forces. Moreover, I have maintained that by virtue of a feature which does seem to characterize pornography—its break with certain inhibiting conceptions of sexuality, pornography may well play a role in people determining for themselves the life-style which most suits them. A society which values self-determination will interfere with it only under circumstances which the censors of pornography cannot show to hold.

Of course, I have said almost nothing about the nature of the specific freedoms we incorporate in our notion of freedom of speech. It may well be that that set of rights imposes even stricter obligations on those who would suppress forms of its exercise.

Selected Bibliography

BAKER, ROBERT, and FREDERICK ELLISTON (eds.). *Philosophy and Sex.* Buffalo, N.Y.: Prometheus Books, 1975.

BERTOCCI, PETER A. *Sex, Love, and the Person.* New York: Sheed and Ward, Inc., 1967.

GOLDMAN, ALAN H. "Plain Sex," *Philosophy and Public Affairs*, Vol. 6, no. 3 (1977), 267.

JAGGAR, ALISON M., and PAULA ROTHENBERG STRUHL (eds.). *Feminist Frameworks.* New York: McGraw-Hill Book Company, 1978.

LEISER, BURTON. *Liberty, Justice and Morals.* New York: Macmillan Publishing Co., Inc., 1973, chaps. 1, 2, 3, 4, and 6.

MORRISON, ELEANOR S., and VERA BOROSAGE (eds.). *Human Sexuality: Contemporary Perspectives* (2d ed.). Palo Alto, Calif.: Mayfield Publishing Co., 1977.

NAGEL, THOMAS. "Sexual Perversion," *The Journal of Philosophy*, Vol. 66 (1969), 5.

RUDDICK, SARA. "On Sexual Morality," in James Rachel (ed.), *Moral Problems.* New York: Harper and Row Publishers, 1971, p. 85.

RUSSELL, BERTRAND. *Marriage and Morals.* New York: Liveright, 1929.

SOLOMON, ROBERT. "Sexual Paradigms," *The Journal of Philosophy*, Vol. 71, no. 11 (1974), 336.

TRIPP, C. A. *The Homosexual Matrix.* New York: McGraw-Hill Book Company, 1975.

VETTERLING-BRAGGIN, MARY, FREDERICK A. ELLISTON, and JANE ENGLISH (eds.). *Feminism and Philosophy.* Totowa, N.J.: Littlfield, Adams & Co., 1977.

WASSERSTROM, RICHARD (ed.). *Morality and the Law.* Belmont, Calif.: Wadsworth Publishing Co., Inc., 1970.

WHITELY, C. H., and W. M. WHITELY. *Sex and Morals.* London: Batsford, 1967.

WILSON, JOHN. *Logic and Sexual Morality.* Harmondsworth, England: Penguin Books, 1965.

PRIVACY

Katz v. United States 389 U.S. 349, 88 S.Ct. 507 (1967)

Mr. Justice Stewart delivered the opinion of the Court.

The petitioner was convicted in the District Court for the Southern District of California under an eight-count indictment charging him with transmitting wagering information by telephone from Los Angeles to Miami and Boston in violation of a federal statute.[1] At trial the Govern-

Editor's Note: Reprinted with some footnotes omitted; footnotes remaining have been renumbered.

[1] 18 U.S.C. § 1084. That statute provides in pertinent part:
"(a) Whoever being engaged in the business of betting or wagering knowingly uses a wire communication facility for the transmission in interstate or foreign commerce of bets or wagers or information assisting in the placing of bets or wagers on any sporting event or contest, or for the transmission of a wire communication which entitles the recipient to receive money or credit as a result of bets or wagers, or for information assisting in the placing of bets or

ment was permitted, over the petitioner's objection, to introduce evidence of the petitioner's end of telephone conversations, overheard by FBI agents who had attached an electronic listening and recording device to the outside of the public telephone booth from which he had placed his calls. In affirming his conviction, the Court of Appeals rejected the contention that the recordings had been obtained in violation of the Fourth Amendment, because "[t]here was no physical entrance into the area occupied by, [the petitioner]." [2] We granted certiorari in order to consider the constitutional questions thus presented.

The petitioner has phrased those questions as follows:

"A. Whether a public telephone booth is a constitutionally protected area so that evidence obtained by attaching an electronic listening recording device to the top of such a booth is obtained in violation of the right to privacy of the user of the booth.

"B. Whether physical penetration of a constitutionally protected area is necessary before a search and seizure can be said to be violative of the Fourth Amendment to the United States Constitution."

We decline to adopt this formulation of the issues. In the first place the correct solution of Fourth Amendment problems is not necessarily promoted by incantation of the phrase "constitutionally protected area." Secondly, the Fourth Amendment cannot be translated into a general constitutional "right to privacy." That Amendment protects individual privacy against certain kinds of governmental intrusion, but its protections go further, and often have nothing to do with privacy at all.[3] Other provisions of the Constitution protect personal privacy from other forms of governmental invasion. But the protection of a person's *general* right to privacy—his right to be let alone by other people [4]—is, like the protection of his property and of his very life, left largely to the law of the individual States.

---

wagers, shall be fined not more than $10,000 or imprisoned not more than two years, or both.

"(b) Nothing in this section shall be construed to prevent the transmission in interstate or foreign commerce of information for use in news reporting of sporting events or contests, or for the transmission of information assisting in the placing of bets or wagers on a sporting event or contest from a State where betting on that sporting event or contest is legal into a State in which such betting is legal."

[2] 9 Cir., 369 F.2d 130, 134.

[3] "The average man would very likely not have his feelings soothed any more by having his property seized openly than by having it seized privately and by stealth. . . . And a person can be just as much, if not more, irritated, annoyed and injured by an unceremonious public arrest by a policeman as he is by a seizure in the privacy of his office or home." Griswold v. State of Connecticut, 381 U.S. 479, 509, 85 S.Ct. 1678, 1695, 14 L.Ed.2d 510 (dissenting opinion of MR. JUSTICE BLACK).

[4] See Warren & Brandeis, The Right to Privacy, 4 Harv.L.Rev. 193 (1890).

Because of the misleading way the issues have been formulated, the parties have attached great significance to the characterization of the telephone booth from which the petitioner placed his calls. The petitioner has strenuously argued that the booth was a "constitutionally protected area." The Government has maintained with equal vigor that it was not.[5] But this effort to decide whether or not a given "area," viewed in the abstract, is "constitutionally protected" deflects attention from the problem presented by this case. For the Fourth Amendment protects people, not places. What a person knowingly exposes to the public, even in his own home or office, is not a subject of Fourth Amendment protection. But what he seeks to preserve as private, even in an area accessible to the public, may be constitutionally protected. . . .

The Government stresses the fact that the telephone booth from which the petitioner made his calls was constructed partly of glass, so that he was as visible after he entered it as he would have been if he had remained outside. But what he sought to exclude when he entered the booth was not the intruding eye—it was the uninvited ear. He did not shed his right to do so simply because he made his calls from a place where he might be seen. No less than an individual in a business office, in a friend's apartment, or in a taxicab, a person in a telephone booth may rely upon the protection of the Fourth Amendment. One who occupies it, shuts the door behind him, and pays the toll that permits him to place a call is surely entitled to assume that the words he utters into the mouthpiece will not be broadcast to the world. To read the Constitution more narrowly is to ignore the vital role that the public telephone has come to play in private communication.

The Government contends, however, that the activities of its agents in this case should not be tested by Fourth Amendment requirements, for the surveillance technique they employed involved no physical penetration of the telephone booth from which the petitioner placed his calls. It is true that the absence of such penetration was at one time thought to foreclose Fourth Amendment inquiry, . . . for that Amendment was thought to limit only searches and seizures of tangible property.[6] But "[t]he premise that property interests control the right of the Government to search and seize has been discredited." Warden, Md. Penitentiary

[5] In support of their respective claims, the parties have compiled competing lists of "protected areas" for our consideration. It appears to be common ground that a private home is such an area, . . . but that an open field is not. . . . Defending the inclusion of a telephone booth in his list the petitioner cites United States v. Stone, D.C., 232 F.Supp. 396, and United States v. Madison, 32 L.W. 2243 (D.C.Ct.Gen.Sess.). Urging that the telephone booth should be excluded, the Government finds support in United States v. Borgese, D.C., 235 F.Supp. 286.

[6] See Olmstead v. United States, 277 U.S. 438, 464–466, 48 S.Ct. 564, 567–569, 72 L.Ed. 944. We do not deal in this case with the law of detention or arrest under the Fourth Amendment.

v. Hayden, 387 U.S. 294, 304, 87 St.Ct. 1642, 1648, 18 L.Ed.2d 782. Thus, although a closely divided Court supposed in *Olmstead* that surveillance without any trespass and without the seizure of any material object fell outside the ambit of the Constitution, we have since departed from the narrow view on which that decision rested. Indeed, we have expressly held that the Fourth Amendment governs not only the seizure of tangible items, but extends as well to the recording of oral statements overheard without any "technical trespass under * * * local property law." Silverman v. United States, 365 U.S. 505, 511, 81 S.Ct. 679, 682, 5 L.Ed.2d 734. Once this much is acknowledged, and once it is recognized that the Fourth Amendment protects people—and not simply "areas"—against unreasonable searches and seizures it becomes clear that the reach of that Amendment cannot turn upon the presence or absence of a physical intrusion into any given enclosure.

We conclude that the underpinnings of *Olmstead* and *Goldman* have been so eroded by our subsequent decisions that the "trespass" doctrine there enunciated can no longer be regarded as controlling. The Government's activities in electronically listening to and recording the petitioner's words violated the privacy upon which he justifiably relied while using the telephone booth and thus constituted a "search and seizure" within the meaning of the Fourth Amendment. The fact that the electronic device employed to achieve that end did not happen to penetrate the wall of the booth can have no constitutional significance.

The question remaining for decision, then, is whether the search and seizure conducted in this case complied with constitutional standards. In that regard, the Government's position is that its agents acted in an entirely defensible manner: They did not begin their electronic surveillance until investigation of the petitioner's activities had established a strong probability that he was using the telephone in question to transmit gambling information to persons in other States, in violation of federal law. Moreover, the surveillance was limited, both in scope and in duration, to the specific purpose of establishing the contents of the petitioner's unlawful telephonic communications. The agents confined their surveillance to the brief periods during which he used the telephone booth,[7] and they took great care to overhear only the conversations of the petitioner himself.[8]

Accepting this account of the Government's actions as accurate, it is

[7] Based upon their previous visual observations of the petitioner, the agents correctly predicted that he would use the telephone booth for several minutes at approximately the same time each morning. The petitioner was subjected to electronic surveillance only during this predetermined period. Six recordings, averaging some three minutes each, were obtained and admitted in evidence. They preserved the petitioner's end of conversations concerning the placing of bets and the receipt of wagering information.

[8] On the single occasion when the statements of another person were inadvertently intercepted, the agents refrained from listening to them.

clear that this surveillance was so narrowly circumscribed that a duly authorized magistrate, properly notified of the need for such investigation, specifically informed of the basis on which it was to proceed, and clearly apprised of the precise intrusion it would entail, could constitutionally have authorized, with appropriate safeguards, the very limited search and seizure that the Government asserts in fact took place. Only last Term we sustained the validity of such an authorization, holding that, under sufficiently "precise and discriminate circumstances," a federal court may empower government agents to employ a concealed electronic device "for the narrow and particularized purpose of ascertaining the truth of the * * * allegations" of a "detailed factual affidavit alleging the commission of a specific criminal offense." Osborn v. United States, 385 U.S. 323, 329–330, 87 S.Ct. 429, 433, 17 L.Ed.2d 394. Discussing that holding, the Court in Berger v. State of New York, 388 U.S. 41, 87 S.Ct. 1873, 18 L.Ed.2d 1040, said that "the order authorizing the use of the electronic device" in Osborn "afforded similar protections to those * * * of conventional warrants authorizing the seizure of tangible evidence." Through those protections, "no greater invasion of privacy was permitted than was necessary under the circumstances." Id., at 57, 87 S.Ct. at 1882. Here, too, a similar judicial order could have accommodated "the legitimate needs of law enforcement" by authorizing the carefully limited use of electronic surveillance.

The Government urges that, because its agents relied upon the decisions in Olmstead and Goldman, and because they did no more here than they might properly have done with prior judicial sanction, we should retroactively validate their conduct. That we cannot do. It is apparent that the agents in this case acted with restraint. Yet the inescapable fact is that this restraint was imposed by the agents themselves, not by a judicial officer. They were not required, before commencing the search, to present their estimate of probable cause for detached scrutiny by a neutral magistrate. They were not compelled, during the conduct of the search itself, to observe precise limits established in advance by a specific court order. Nor were they directed, after the search had been completed, to notify the authorizing magistrate in detail of all that had been seized. In the absence of such safeguards, this Court has never sustained a search upon the sole ground that officers reasonably expected to find evidence of a particular crime and voluntarily confined their activities to the least intrusive means consistent with that end. Searches conducted without warrants have been held unlawful "notwithstanding facts unquestionably showing probable cause," Agnello v. United States, 269 U.S. 20, 33, 46 S.Ct. 4, 6, 70 L.Ed. 145, for the Constitution requires "that the deliberate, impartial judgment of a judicial officer * * * be interposed between the citizen and the police * * *." Wong Sun v. United States, 371 U.S. 471, 481–482, 83 S.Ct. 407, 414, 9 L.Ed.2d 441. "Over and again this Court has emphasized that the mandate of the [Fourth] Amendment requires adherence to judicial processes," United States v. Jeffers, 342 U.S. 48, 51, 72 S.Ct. 93, 95, 96 L.Ed. 59, and that searches conducted outside the judicial process, without prior approval by judge or magistrate, are *per se* unreasonable under the Fourth Amendment—subject only to a few specifically established and well-delineated exceptions.

It is difficult to imagine how any of those exceptions could ever apply to the sort of search and seizure involved in this case. Even electronic surveillance substantially contemporaneous with an individual's arrest could hardly be deemed an "incident" of that arrest. Nor could the use of electronic surveillance without prior authorization be justified on grounds of "hot pursuit." [9] And, of course, the very nature of electronic surveillance precludes its use pursuant to the suspect's consent.

The Government does not question these basic principles. Rather, it urges the creation of a new exception to cover this case.[10] It argues that surveillance of a telephone booth should be exempted from the usual requirement of advance authorization by a magistrate upon a showing of probable cause. We cannot agree. Omission of such authorization

> bypasses the safeguards provided by an objective predetermination of probable cause, and substitutes instead the far less reliable procedure of an after-the-event justification for the * * * search, too likely to be subtly influenced by the familiar shortcomings of hindsight judgment. Beck v. State of Ohio, 379 U.S. 89, 96, 85 S.Ct. 223, 228, 13 L.Ed.2d 142.

And bypassing a neutral predetermination of the *scope* of a search leaves individuals secure from Fourth Amendment violations "only in the discretion of the police." Id., at 97, 85 S.Ct. at 229.

These considerations do not vanish when the search in question is transferred from the setting of a home, an office, or a hotel room to that of a telephone booth. Wherever a man may be, he is entitled to know that he will remain free from unreasonable searches and seizures. The government agents here ignored "the procedure of antecedent justification * * * that is central to the Fourth Amendment," [11] a procedure that we hold to be a constitutional precondition of the kind of electronic surveillance involved in this case. Because the surveillance here failed to meet

[9] Although "[t]he Fourth Amendment does not require police officers to delay in the course of an investigation if to do so would gravely endanger their lives or the lives of others," Warden Md. Penitentiary v. Hayden, 387 U.S. 294, 298–299, 87 S.Ct. 1642, 1646, 18 L.Ed.2d 782, there seems little likelihood that electronic surveillance would be a realistic possibility in a situation so fraught with urgency.

[10] Whether safeguards other than prior authorization by a magistrate would satisfy the Fourth Amendment in a situation involving the national security is a question not presented by this case.

[11] See Osborn v. United States, 385 U.S. 323, 330, 87 S.Ct. 429, 433, 17 L.Ed.2d 394.

that condition, and because it led to the petitioner's conviction, the judgment must be reversed.

It is so ordered.

Judgment reversed.

CHARLES FRIED

Privacy: A Rational Context

In this chapter I analyze the concept of privacy and attempt to show why it assumes such high significance in our system of values. There is a puzzle here, since we do not feel comfortable about asserting that privacy is intrinsically valuable, an end in itself—privacy is always for or in relation to something or someone. On the other hand, to view privacy as simply instrumental, as one way of getting other goods, seems unsatisfactory, too. For we feel that there is a necessary quality, after all, to the importance we ascribe to privacy. This perplexity is displayed when we ask how privacy might be traded off against other values. We wish to ascribe to privacy more than an ordinary priority. My analysis attempts to show why we value privacy highly and why also we do not treat it as an end in itself. Briefly, my argument is that privacy provides the rational context for a number of our most significant ends, such as love, trust and friendship, respect, and self-respect. Since it is a necessary element of those ends, it draws its significance from them. And yet since privacy is only an element of those ends, not the whole, we have not felt inclined to attribute to privacy ultimate significance. In general this analysis of privacy illustrates how the concepts in this essay can provide a rational account for deeply held moral values.

An Immodest Proposal: Electronic Monitoring

There are available today electronic devices to be worn on one's person which emit signals permitting one's exact location to be determined by a monitor some distance away. These devices are so small as to be entirely unobtrusive: other persons cannot tell that a subject is "wired," and even the subject himself—if he could forget the initial installation—need be no more aware of the device than of a small bandage. Moreover, existing technology can produce devices capable of monitoring not only a person's location, but other significant facts about him: his temperature, pulse rate, blood pressure, the alcoholic content of his blood, the sounds in his immediate environment—for example, what he says and what is said to him —and perhaps in the not too distant future even the pattern of his brain waves. The suggestion has been made, and is being actively investigated, that such devices might be employed in the surveillance of persons on probation or parole.

Probation leaves an offender at large in the community as an alternative to imprisonment, and parole is the release of an imprisoned person prior to the time that all justification for supervising him and limiting his liberty has expired. Typically, both probation and parole are granted subject to various restrictions. Most usually the probationer or parolee is not allowed to leave a prescribed area. Also common are restrictions on the kinds of places he may visit—bars, pool halls, brothels, and the like may be forbidden—the persons he may associate with, and the activities he may engage in. The most common restriction on activities is a prohibition on drinking, but sometimes probation and parole have been revoked for "immorality"—that is, intercourse with a person other than a spouse. There are also affirmative conditions, such as a requirement that the subject work regularly in an approved employment, maintain an approved residence, report regularly to correctional, social, or psychiatric personnel. Failure to abide by such conditions is thought to endanger the rehabilitation of the subject and to identify him as a poor risk.

Now the application of personal monitoring to probation and parole is obvious. Violations of any one of the conditions and restrictions could be uncovered immediately by devices using present technology or developments of it; by the same token, a wired subject assured of detection would be much more likely to obey. Although monitoring is admitted to be unusually intrusive, it is argued that this particular use of monitoring is entirely proper, since it justifies the release of persons who would otherwise remain in prison, and since surely there is little that is more intrusive and unprivate than a prison regime. Moreover, no one is obliged to submit to monitoring: an offender may decline and wait in prison until his sentence has expired or until he is judged a proper risk for parole even without monitoring. Proponents of monitoring suggest that seen in this way monitoring of offenders subject to supervision is no more offensive than the monitoring on an entirely voluntary basis of epileptics, diabetics, cardiac patients, and the like.

Much of the discussion about this and similar (though perhaps less futuristic) measures has proceeded in a fragmentary way to catalog the disadvantages they entail: the danger of the information falling into the wrong hands, the opportunity presented for harassment, the inevitable involvement of persons as to whom no basis for supervision exists, the use of the material monitored by the government for unauthorized purposes, the danger to political expression and association, and so on.

Such arguments are often sufficiently compelling, but situations may be envisaged where they are overridden. The monitoring case in some of its aspects is such a situation. And yet one often wants to say the invasion of privacy is wrong, intolerable, although each discrete objection can be met. The reason for this, I submit, is that privacy is much more than just a possible social technique for assuring this or that substantive interest. Such analyses of the value of privacy often lead to the conclusion that the various substantive interests may after all be protected as well by some other means, or that if they cannot be protected quite as well, still those other means will do, given the importance of our reasons for violating privacy. It is just because this instrumental analysis makes privacy so vulnerable that we feel impelled to assign to privacy some intrinsic significance. But to translate privacy to the level of an intrinsic value might seem more a way of cutting off analysis than of carrying it forward.

It is my thesis that privacy is not just one possible means among others to insure some other value, but that it is necessarily related to ends and relations of the most fundamental sort: respect, love, friendship, and trust. Privacy is not merely a good technique for furthering these fundamental relations; rather without privacy they are simply inconceivable. They require a context of privacy or the possibility of privacy for their existence. To make clear the necessity of privacy as a context for respect, love, friendship, and trust is to bring out also why a threat to privacy seems to threaten our very integrity as persons. To respect, love, trust, or feel affection for others and to regard ourselves as the objects of love, trust, and affection is at the heart of our notion of ourselves as persons among persons, and privacy is the necessary atmosphere for these attitudes and actions, as oxygen is for combustion.

Privacy and Personal Relations

Before going further, it is necessary to sharpen the intuitive concept of privacy. As a first approximation, privacy seems to be related to secrecy, to limiting the knowledge of others about oneself. This notion must be refined. It is not true, for instance, that the less that is known about us the more privacy we have. Privacy is not simply an absence of information about us in the minds of others; rather it is the control we have over information about ourselves.

To refer, for instance, to the privacy of a lonely man on a desert island would be to engage in irony. The person who enjoys privacy is able to grant or deny access to others. Even when one considers private situations into which outsiders could not possibly intrude, the context implies some alternative situation where the intrusion is possible. A man's house may be private, for instance, but that is because it is constructed—with doors, windows, window shades—to allow it to be made private, and because the law entitles a man to exclude unauthorized persons. And even the remote vacation hideaway is private just because one resorts to it in order—in part—to preclude access to unauthorized persons.

Privacy, thus, is control over knowledge about oneself. But it is not simply control over the quality of information abroad; there are modulations in the quality of the knowledge as well. We may not mind that a person knows a general fact about us, and yet feel our privacy invaded if he knows the details. For instance, a casual acquaintance may comfortably know that I am sick, but it would violate my privacy if he knew the nature of the illness. Or a good friend may know what particular illness I am suffering from, but it would violate my privacy if he were actually to witness my suffering from some symptom which he must know is associated with the disease.

Privacy in its dimension of control over information is an aspect of personal liberty. Acts derive their meaning partly from their social context—from how many people know about them and what the knowledge consists of. For instance, a reproof administered out of the hearing of third persons may be an act of kindness, but if administered in public it becomes cruel and degrading. Thus if a man cannot be sure that third persons are not listening—if his privacy is not secure—he is denied the freedom to do what he regards as an act of kindness.

Besides giving us control over the context in which we act, privacy has a more defensive role in protecting our liberty. We may wish to do or say things not forbidden by the restraints of morality but nevertheless unpopular or unconventional. If we thought that our every word and deed were public, fear of disapproval or more tangible retaliation might keep us from doing or saying things which we would do or say if we could be sure of keeping them to ourselves or within a circle of those who we know approve or tolerate our tastes.

These reasons support the familiar arguments for the right of privacy. Yet they leave privacy with less security than we feel it deserves; they leave it vulnerable to arguments that a particular invasion of privacy will secure to us other kinds of liberty which more than compensate for what is lost. To present privacy, then, only as an aspect of or an aid to general liberty is to miss some of its most significant differentiating features. The value of control over information about ourselves is more nearly absolute than that. For privacy is the necessary context for relationships which we would hardly be human if we had to do without—the relationships of love, friendship, and trust.

Love and friendship . . . involve the initial respect for the rights of others which morality requires of everyone. They further involve the voluntary and spontaneous relinquishment of something between friend and friend, lover and lover. The title to information about oneself conferred by privacy provides the necessary something. To be friends or lovers persons must be intimate to some degree with each other. Intimacy is the sharing of information about one's actions, beliefs or emotions which one does not share with all, and which one has the right not to share with anyone. By conferring this right, privacy creates the moral capital which we spend in friendship and love.

The entitlements of privacy are not just one kind of entitlement among many which a lover can surrender to show his love. Love or friendship can be partially expressed by the gift of other rights—gifts of property or of service. But these gifts, without the intimacy of shared private information, cannot alone constitute love or friendship. The man who is generous with his possessions, but not with himself, can hardly be a friend, nor—and this more clearly shows the necessity of privacy for love —can the man who, voluntarily or involuntarily, shares everything about himself with the world indiscriminately.

Privacy is essential to friendship and love in another respect besides providing what I call moral capital. The rights of privacy are among those basic entitlements which men must respect in each other; and mutual respect is the minimal precondition for love and friendship.

Privacy also provides the means for modulating those degrees of friendship which fall short of love. Few persons have the emotional resources to be on the most intimate terms with all their friends. Privacy grants the control over information which enables us to maintain degrees of intimacy. Thus even between friends the restraints of privacy apply; since friendship implies a voluntary relinquishment of private information, one will not wish to know what his friend or lover has not chosen to share with him. The rupture of this balance by a third party—the state perhaps—thrusting information concerning one friend upon another might well destroy the limited degree of intimacy the two have achieved.

Finally, there is a more extreme case where privacy serves not to save something which will be "spent" on a friend, but to keep it from all the world. There are thoughts whose expression to a friend or lover would be a hostile act, though the entertaining of them is completely consistent with friendship or love. That is because these thoughts, prior to being given expression, are mere unratified possibilities for action. Only by expressing them do we adopt them, choose them as part of ourselves, and draw them into our relations with others. Now a sophisticated person knows that a friend or lover must entertain thoughts which if expressed would be wounding, and so—it might be objected—why should he attach any significance to their actual expression? In a sense the objection is well taken. If it were possible to give expression to these thoughts and yet make clear to ourselves and to others that we do not thereby ratify them, adopt them as our own, it might be that in some relations, at least, another could be allowed complete access to us. But this possibility is not a very likely one. Thus the most complete form of privacy is perhaps also the most basic, since it is necessary not only to our freedom to define our relations with others but also to our freedom to define ourselves. To be deprived of this control over what we do and who we are is the ultimate assault on liberty, personality, and self-respect.

Trust is the attitude of expectation that another will behave according to the constraints of morality. Insofar as trust is only instrumental to the more convenient conduct of life, its purposes could be as well served by cheap and efficient surveillance of the person upon whom one depends. One does not trust machines or animals; one takes the fullest economically feasible precautions against their going wrong. Often, however, we choose to trust people where it would be safer to take precautions—to watch them or require a bond from them. This must be because, as I have already argued, we value the relation of trust for its own sake. It is one of those relations, less inspiring than love or friendship but also less tiring, through which we express our humanity.

There can be no trust where there is no possibility of error. More specifically, man cannot know that he is trusted unless he has a right to act without constant surveillance so that he knows he can betray the trust. Privacy confers that essential right. And since, as I have argued, trust in its fullest sense is reciprocal, the man who cannot be trusted cannot himself trust or learn to trust. Without privacy and the possibility of error which it protects that aspect of his humanity is denied to him.

The Concrete Recognition of Privacy

In concrete situations and actual societies, control over information about oneself, like control over one's bodily security or property, can only be relative and qualified. As is true for property or bodily security, the control over privacy must be limited by the rights of others. And as in the cases of property and bodily security, so too with privacy, the more one ventures into the outside, the more one pursues one's other interests with the aid of, in competition with, or even in the presence of others, the more one must risk invasions. As with property and personal security, it is the business of legal and social institutions to define and protect the right of privacy which emerges intact from the hurly-burly of social interactions. Now it would be absurd to argue that these concrete definitions and protections, differing as they do from society to society, are or should be strict derivations from general principles, the only legitimate variables being differing empirical circumstances (such as differing technologies or climatic conditions). The delineation of standards must be left to a political and social process the results of which will accord with justice if two conditions are met: (1) the process itself is just, that is, the interests of all are fairly represented; and (2) the outcome of the process protects basic dignity and provides moral capital for personal relations in the form of absolute title to at least some information about oneself.

The particular areas of life which are protected by privacy will be conventional at least in part, not only because they are the products of political processes, but also because of one of the reasons we value privacy. Insofar as privacy is regarded as moral capital for relations of love, friendship, and trust, there are situations where what kinds of information one is entitled to keep to oneself is not of the first importance. The important thing is that there be *some* information which is protected. Convention may quite properly rule in determining the particular areas which are private.

Convention plays another more important role in fostering privacy and the respect and esteem which it protects; it designates certain areas, intrinsically no more private than other areas, as symbolic of the whole institution of privacy, and thus deserving of protection beyond their particular importance. This apparently exaggerated respect for conventionally protected areas compensates for the inevitable fact that privacy is gravely compromised in any concrete social system: it is compromised by the inevitably and utterly just exercise of rights by others, it is compromised by the questionable but politically sanctioned exercise of rights by others, it is compromised by conduct which society does not condone but which it is unable or unwilling to forbid, and it is compromised by plainly wrongful invasions and aggressions. In all this there is a real danger that privacy might be crushed altogether, or, what would be as bad, that any venture outside the most limited area of activity would mean risking an almost total compromise of privacy.

Given those threats to privacy in general, social systems have given symbolic importance to certain conventionally designated areas of privacy. Thus in our culture the excretory functions are so shielded that situations in which this privacy is violated are experienced as extremely distressing, as detracting from one's dignity and self-esteem. Yet there does not seem to be any reason connected with the principles of respect, esteem, and the like why this would have to be so, and one can imagine other cultures in which it was not so, but where the same symbolic privacy was attached to, say, eating and drinking. There are other more subtly modulated symbolic areas of privacy, some of which merge into what I call substantive privacy (that is, areas where privacy does protect substantial interests). The very complex norms of privacy about matters of sex and health are good examples.

An excellent, very different sort of example of a contingent, symbolic recognition of an area of privacy as an expression of respect for personal integrity is the privilege against self-incrimination and the associated doctrines denying officials the power to compel other kinds of information without some explicit warrant. By according the privilege as fully as it does, our society affirms the extreme value of the individual's control over information about himself. To be sure, prying into a man's personal affairs by asking questions of others or by observing him is not prevented. Rather it is the point of the privilege that a man cannot be forced to make public information about himself. Thereby his sense of control over what others know of him is significantly enhanced, even if other sources of the same information exist. Without his cooperation, the other sources are necessarily incomplete, since he himself is the only ineluctable witness to his own present life, public or private, internal or manifest. And information about himself which others have to give out is in one sense information over which he has already relinquished control.

The privilege is contingent and symbolic. It is part of a whole structure of rules by which there is created an institution of privacy sufficient to the sense of respect, trust, and intimacy. It is contingent in that it cannot, I believe, be shown that some particular set of rules is necessary to the existence of such an institution of privacy. It is symbolic because the exercise of the privilege provides a striking expression of society's willingness to accept constraints on the pursuit of valid, perhaps vital, interests in order to recognize the right of privacy and the respect for the individual that privacy entails. Conversely, a proceeding in which compulsion is brought to bear on an individual to force him to make revelations about himself provides a striking and dramatic instance of a denial of title to control information about oneself, to control the picture we would have others have of us. In this sense such a procedure quite rightly seems profoundly humiliating. Nevertheless it is not clear to me that a system is unjust which sometimes allows such an imposition.

In calling attention to the symbolic aspect of some areas of privacy I do not mean to minimize their importance. On the contrary, they are highly significant as expressions of respect for others in a general situation where much of what we do to each other may signify a lack of respect or at least presents no occasion for expressing respect. That this is so is shown not so much on the occasions where these symbolic constraints are observed, for they are part of our system of expectations, but where they are violated. Not only does a person feel his standing is gravely compromised by such symbolic violations, but also those who wish to degrade and humiliate others often choose just such symbolic aggressions and invasions on the assumed though conventional area of privacy.

The Concept of Privacy Applied to the
Problem of Monitoring

Let us return now to the concrete problem of electronic monitoring to see whether the foregoing elucidation of the concept of privacy will help to establish on firmer ground the intuitive objection that monitoring is an

intolerable violation of privacy. Let us consider the more intrusive forms
of monitoring where not only location but conversations and perhaps other
data are monitored.

Obviously such a system of monitoring drastically curtails or elim-
inates altogether the power to control information about oneself. But, it
might be said, this is not a significant objection if we assumed the monitored data will go only to authorized persons—probation or parole officers
—and cannot be prejudicial so long as the subject of the monitoring is
not violating the conditions under which he is allowed to be at liberty.
This retort misses the importance of privacy as a context for all kinds of
relations, from the most intense to the most casual. For all of these may
require a context of some degree of intimacy, and intimacy is made impossible by monitoring.

It is worth being more precise about this notion of intimacy. Monitoring obviously presents vast opportunities for malice and misunderstanding on the part of authorized personnel. For that reason the subject has
reason to be constantly apprehensive and inhibited in what he does.. There
is always an unseen audience, which is the more threatening because of
the possibility that one may forget about it and let down his guard, as one
would not with a visible audience. Even assuming the benevolence and
understanding of the official audience, there are serious consequences to
the fact that no degree of true intimacy is possible for the subject. Privacy
is not, as we have seen, just a defensive right. It forms the necessary
context for the intimate relations of love and friendship which give our
lives much of whatever affirmative value they have. In the role of citizen
or fellow worker, one need reveal himself to no greater extent than is
necessary to display the attributes of competence and morality appropriate
to those roles. In order to be a friend or lover one must reveal far more
of himself. Yet where any intimate revelation may be heard by monitoring officials, it loses the quality of exclusive intimacy required of a gesture
of love or friendship. Thus monitoring, in depriving one of privacy, destroys the possibility of bestowing the gift of intimacy, and makes impossible the essential dimension of love and friendship.

Monitoring similarly undermines the subject's capacity to enter into
relations of trust. As I analyzed trust, it required the possibility of error
on the part of the person trusted. The negation of trust is constant surveillance—such as monitoring—which minimizes the possibility of unde-
tected default. The monitored parolee is denied the sense of self-respect
inherent in being trusted by the government which has released him. More
important, monitoring prevents the parolee from entering into true *relations* of trust with persons in the outside world. An employer, unaware
of the monitoring, who entrusts a sum of money to the parolee cannot
thereby grant him the sense of responsibility and autonomy which an
unmonitored person in the same position would have. The parolee in a
real—if special and ironical—sense, cannot be trusted.

Now let us consider the argument that however intrusive monitoring may seem, surely prison life is more so. In part, of course, this will be a matter of fact. It may be that a reasonably secure and well-run prison will allow prisoners occasions for conversation among themselves, with guards, or with visitors, which are quite private. Such a prison regime would in this respect be less intrusive than monitoring. Often prison regimes do not allow even this, and go far toward depriving a prisoner of any sense of privacy: if the cells have doors, they may be equipped with peepholes. But there is still an important difference between this kind of prison and monitoring: the prison environment is overtly, even punitively unprivate. The contexts for relations to others are obviously and drastically different from what they are on the "outside." This itself, it seems to me, protects the prisoner's human orientation where monitoring only assails it. If the prisoner has a reasonably developed capacity for love, trust, and friendship and has in fact experienced ties of this sort, he is likely to be strongly aware (at least for a time) that prison life is a drastically different context from the one in which he enjoyed those relations, and this awareness will militate against his confusing the kinds of relations that can obtain in a "total institution" like a prison with those of freer social settings on the outside.

Monitoring, by contrast, alters only in a subtle and unobtrusive way —though a significant one—the context for relations. The subject appears free to perform the same actions as others and to enter the same relations, but in fact an important element of autonomy, of control over one's environment, is missing: he cannot be private. A prisoner can adopt a stance of withdrawal, of hibernation as it were, and thus preserve his sense of privacy intact to a degree. A person subject to monitoring by virtue of being in a free environment, dealing with people who expect him to have certain responses, capacities, and dispositions, is forced to make at least a show of intimacy to the persons he works closely with, those who would be his friends, and so on. They expect these things of him, because he is assumed to have the capacity and disposition to enter into ordinary relations with them. Yet if he does—if, for instance, he enters into light banter with slight sexual overtones with the waitress at the diner where he eats regularly—he has been forced to violate his own integrity by revealing to his official monitors even so small an aspect of his private personality, the personality he wishes to reserve for persons toward whom he will make some gestures of intimacy and friendship. Theoretically, of course, a monitored parolee might adopt the same attitude of withdrawal that a prisoner does, but in fact that too would be a costly and degrading experience. He would be tempted, as in prison he would not be, to "give himself away" and to act like everyone else, since in every outward respect he seems like everyone else. Moreover, by withdrawing, the person subject to monitoring would risk seeming cold, unnatural, odd, inhuman, to the very people whose esteem and affection he craves. In prison the circumstances dictating a reserved and tentative facade are so apparent to all that adopting such a facade is no reflection on the prisoner's humanity.

The insidiousness of a technique which forces a man to betray himself in this humiliating way or else seem inhuman is compounded when one considers that the subject is also forced to betray others who may become intimate with him. Even persons in the overt oppressiveness of a prison do not labor under the burden of this double betrayal.

As against all of these considerations, there remains the argument that so long as monitoring depends on the consent of the subject, who feels it is preferable to prison, to close off this alternative in the name of a morality so intimately concerned with liberty is absurd. This argument may be decisive; I am not at all confident that the alternative of monitored release should be closed off. My analysis does show, I think, that it involves costs to the prisoner which are easily overlooked, that on inspection it is a less desirable alternative than might at first appear. Moreover, monitoring presents systematic dangers to potential subjects as a class. Its availability as a compromise between conditional release and continued imprisonment may lead officials who are in any doubt whether or not to trust a man on parole or probation to assuage their doubts by resorting to monitoring.

The seductions of monitored release disguise not only a cost to the subject but to society as well. The discussion of trust should make clear that unmonitored release is a very different experience from monitored release, and so the educational and rehabilitative effect of unmonitored release is also different. Unmonitored release affirms in a far more significant way the relations of trust between the convicted criminal and the society which he violated by his crime and which he should now be seeking to re-establish. But trust can only arise, as any parent knows, through the experience of being trusted.

Finally, it must be recognized that more limited monitoring—for instance where only the approximate location of the subject is revealed—lacks the offensive features of total monitoring, and is obviously preferable to prison.

The Role of Law

This evaluation of the proposal for electronic monitoring has depended on the general theoretical framework of this whole essay. It is worth noting the kind of evaluation that framework has permitted. Rather than inviting a fragmentation of the proposal into various pleasant and unpleasant elements and comparing the "net utility" of the proposal with its alternatives, we have been able to evaluate the total situation created by the proposal in another way. We have been able to see it as a system in which certain actions and relations, the pursuit of certain ends, are possible or impossible. Certain systems of actions, ends, and relations are possible or impossible in different social contexts. Moreover, the social context itself is a system of actions and relations. The social contexts created by monitoring and its alternatives, liberty or imprisonment, are thus evaluated by their conformity to a model system in which are instantiated the principles of morality, justice, friendship, and love. Such a model, which is used as a standard, is of course partially unspecified in that there is perhaps an infinite number of specific systems which conform to those principles. Now actual systems, as we have seen, may vary in respect to how other ends—for example, beauty, knowledge—may be pursued in them, and they may be extremely deficient in allowing for the pursuit of such ends. But those who design, propose, and administer social systems are first of all bound to make them conform to the model of morality and justice, for in so doing they express respect and even friendship—what might be called civic friendship—toward those implicated in the system. If designers and administrators fail to conform to this model, they fail to express that aspect of their humanity which makes them in turn fit subjects for the respect, friendship, and love of others.

Finally, a point should be noted about the relation between legal structures and other social structures in establishing a rational context such as privacy. This context is established in part by rules which guarantee to a person the claim to control certain areas, his home, perhaps his telephone communications, and so forth, and back this guarantee with enforceable sanctions. These norms are, of course, legal norms. Now these legal norms are incomprehensible without some understanding of what kind of a situation one seeks to establish with their aid. Without this understanding we cannot grasp their importance, the vector of development from them in changing circumstances (such as new technology), the consequences of abandoning them, and so on.[1] What is less obvious is that law is not just an instrument for bringing about a separately identifiable and significant social result: it is a part of the very situation that it helps to bring about. The concept of privacy requires, as we have seen, a sense of control and a justified, acknowledged power to control aspects of one's environment. In most developed societies the only way to give a person the full measure of both the sense and the fact of control is to give him a legal title to control. A legal right to control is control which is the least open to question and argument, it is the kind of control we are most serious about. Consider the analogy of the power of testamentary disposition. A testator is subject to all sorts of obligations, pressures, and argu-

[1] It is a tenet of some forms of positivism that this statement is wrong insofar as it suggests that without appreciation of the context we have no understanding of the meaning of legal norms. This tenet seems wrong for a number of reasons. Legal norms are necessarily phrased in open-ended language, and their specification in actual circumstances needs the aid of the context—that is, the reason for the norm—to determine the appropriate application. This is obviously so when there are changed circumstances and recourse must be had to the principle of the norm. It is less obvious in so-called "central" or "paradigm" cases, but I suggest this is less obvious only because the context is so unproblematic as to require no explicit attention.

ments: certain things are so outrageous that he would scarcely dare to do them. Yet, within very broad limits, in the last analysis he is after all free to do the outrageous. And both the fact that certain dispositions are outrageous, immoral, wrong, and the fact that the testator is nevertheless free to make them are *together* important to define the autonomy and personality of a person in the particular situation. In the same way the public and ultimate character of law is part of the definition of the rational context of privacy.

—————————————————————————— **JEFFREY H. REIMAN**

Privacy, Intimacy, and Personhood

The Summer 1975 issue of *Philosophy & Public Affairs* featured three articles on privacy, one by Judith Jarvis Thomson, one by Thomas Scanlon in response to Thomson, and one by James Rachels in response to them both.[1] Thomson starts from the observation that "the most striking thing about the right to privacy is that nobody seems to have any very clear idea what it is" (p. 295) and goes on to argue that nobody should have one —a very clear idea, that is. Her argument is essentially that all the various protections to which we feel the right to privacy entitles us are already included under other rights, such as "the cluster of rights which the right over the person consists in and also . . . the cluster of rights which owning property consists in" (p. 306). After a romp through some exquisitely fanciful examples, she poses and answers some questions about some of the kinds of "invasions" we would likely think of as violations of the right to privacy:

> Someone looks at your pornographic picture in your wall-safe? He violates your right that your belongings not be looked at, and you have

Reprinted from *Philosophy and Public Affairs*, Vol. 6, No. 1 (1976), 26–44. Copyright © 1976 by Princeton University Press. Reprinted by permission of the author and Princeton University Press.

I am grateful to the editors of *Philosophy & Public Affairs* for many helpful comments and suggestions which have aided me in clarifying and communicating the views presented here.

[1] Judith Jarvis Thomson, "The Right to Privacy," Thomas Scanlon, "Thomson on Privacy," and James Rachels, "Why Privacy is Important," *Philosophy & Public Affairs* 4, no. 4 (Summer 1975): 295–333. Unless otherwise indicated, page numbers in the text refer to this issue.

that right because you have ownership rights—and it is because you have them that what he does is wrong. Someone uses an X-ray device to look at you through the walls of your house? He violates your right not to be looked at, and you have that right because you have rights over your person analogous to the rights you have over your property—and it is because you have these rights that what he does is wrong [p. 313].

From this she concludes that the right to privacy is "derivative," and therefore that "there is no need to find the that-which-is-in-common to all rights in the right to privacy cluster and no need to settle disputes about its boundaries" (p. 313). In other words, we are right not to have any very clear idea about what the right is, and we ought not spin our wheels trying to locate some unique "something" that is protected by the right to privacy. Now I think Thomson is wrong about this—and, incidentally, so do Scanlon and Rachels, although I am inclined to believe they think so for the wrong reasons.

Thomson's argument is a large non sequitur balanced on a small one. She holds that the right to privacy is "derivative" in the sense that each right in the cluster of rights to privacy can be explained by reference to another right and thus without recourse to the right to privacy. This is the little non sequitur. The easiest way to see this is to recognize that it is quite consistent with the notion that the other rights (that is, the rights over one's person and one's property) are—in whole or in part—expressions of the right to privacy, and thus *they* are "derivative" from *it*. If all the protections we include under the right to privacy were specified in the Fourth and Fifth Amendments, this would hardly prove that the right to privacy is "derivative" from the right to be secure against unreasonable search or seizure and the privilege against self-incrimination. It would be just as plausible to assert that this is evidence that the Fourth and Fifth Amendment protections are "derivative" from the right to privacy.[2]

Now all of this would amount to mere semantics, and Professor Thomson could define "derivative" however she pleased, if she didn't use this as an argument against finding (indeed, against even looking for) the "that-which-is-in-common" to the cluster of rights in the right to privacy. This is the large non sequitur. Even if the right were deriva-

---

[2] This reversibility of "derivative"-ness is to be found in Justice Douglas' historic opinion on the right to privacy in Griswold v. State of Connecticut. He states there that "specific guarantees in the Bill of Rights have penumbras, formed by emanations from those guarantees that help give them life and substance." The right of privacy, he goes on to say, is contained in the penumbras of the First, Third, Fourth, Fifth, and Ninth Amendment guarantees. Surely the imagery of penumbral emanations suggests that the right to privacy is "derivative" from the rights protected in these amendments. But later Douglas states that the Court is dealing "with a right of privacy older than the Bill of Rights," which along with other language he uses, suggests that the rights in the Bill of Rights are meant to give reality to an even more fundamental right, the right to privacy. 381 U.S. 479, 85 S.Ct. 1678 (1965).

tive in the sense urged by Thomson, it would not follow that there is nothing in common to all the protections in the right-to-privacy cluster, or that it would be silly to try to find what they have in common. Criminology is probably derivative from sociology and psychology and law and political science in just the way that Thomson holds privacy rights to be derivative from rights to person and property. This hardly amounts to a reason for not trying to define the unifying theme of criminological studies —at least a large number of criminologists do not think so.[3] In other words, even if privacy rights were a grab-bag of property and personal rights, it might still be revealing, as well as helpful, in the resolution of difficult moral conflicts to determine whether there is anything unique that this grab-bag protects that makes it worthy of distinction from the full field of property and personal rights.

I shall argue that there is indeed something unique protected by the right to privacy. And we are likely to miss it if we suppose that what is protected is just a subspecies of the things generally safeguarded by property rights and personal rights. And if we miss it, there may come a time when we think we are merely limiting some personal or property right in favor of some greater good, when in fact we are really sacrificing something of much greater value.

At this point, I shall leave behind all comments on Thomson's paper, since if I am able to prove that there is something unique and uniquely valuable protected by the right to privacy, I shall take this as refutation of her view. It will serve to clarify my own position, however, to indicate briefly what I take to be the shortcomings of the responses of Scanlon and Rachels to Thomson.

Scanlon feels he has refuted Thomson by finding the "special interests" which are the "common foundation" for the right(s) to privacy. He says:

> I agree with Thomson that the rights whose violation strikes us as invasion of privacy are many and diverse, and that these rights do not derive from any single overarching right to privacy. I hold, however, that these rights have a common foundation in the special interests that we have in being able to be free from certain kinds of intrusions. The most obvious examples of such offensive intrusions involve observation of our bodies, our behavior or our interactions with other people (or overhearings of the last two), but while these are central they do not exhaust the field [p. 315].

Now on first glance, it is certainly hard to dispute this claim. But it is nonetheless misleading. Scanlon's position is arresting and appears true because it rests on a tautology, not unlike the classic "explanation" of the

---

[3] See for instance, Herman and Julia Schwendinger, "Defenders of Order or Guardians of Human Rights?" *Issues in Criminology* 5, no. 2 (Summer 1970): 123–157, especially the section entitled "The Thirty-Year-Old Controversy," pp. 123–129.

capacity of sedatives to induce sleep by virtue of their "dormative powers." The right to privacy *is* the right "to be free from certain kinds of (offensive) intrusions." Scanlon's position is equivalent to holding that the common foundation of our right to privacy lies in our "privatistic interests."

In sum, Scanlon announces that he has found the common element in rights to privacy: rights to privacy protect our special interest in privacy! Thomson could hardly deny this, although I doubt she would find it adequate to answer the questions she raised in her essay. What Scanlon has not told us is *why* we have a special interest in privacy, that is, a special interest in being free from certain kinds of intrusions; and *why* it is a legitimate interest, that is, an interest of sufficient importance to warrant protection by our fellow citizens.[4] I suspect that this is the least that would be necessary to convince Thomson that there is a common foundation to privacy rights.

James Rachels tries to provide it. He tries to answer precisely the questions Scanlon leaves unanswered. He asks, "Why, exactly, is privacy important to us?" (p. 323). He starts his answer by categorizing some of the interests we might have in privacy and finds that they basically have to do with protecting our reputations or the secrecy of our plans or the like. Rachels recognizes, however, that

> reflection on these cases gives us little help in understanding the value which privacy has in *normal* or *ordinary* situations. By this I mean situations in which there is nothing embarrassing or shameful or unpopular in what we are doing, and nothing ominous or threatening connected with its possible disclosure. For example, even married couples whose sex-lives are normal (whatever that is), and so who have nothing to be ashamed of, by even the most conventional standards, and certainly nothing to be blackmailed about, do not want their bedrooms bugged [p. 325].

In other words, Rachels recognizes that if there is a unique interest to be protected by the right(s) to privacy, it must be an interest simply in being able to limit other people's observation of us or access to information about us—even if we have certain knowledge that the observation or information would not be used to our detriment or used at all. Rachels tries to identify such an interest and to point out why it is important.

His argument is this. Different human relationships are marked—indeed, in part, constituted—by different degrees of sharing personal information. One shares more of himself with a friend than with an employer, more with a life-long friend than with a casual friend, more with a lover than an acquaintance. He writes that "*however* one conceives one's relations with other people, there is inseperable from that conception an idea

---

[4] I think it is fair to say that Scanlon makes no claim to answer these questions in his essay.

of how it is appropriate to behave with and around them, and what information about oneself it is appropriate for them to have" (pp. 328–329). It is "an important part of what it means to have a friend that we welcome his company, that we confide in him, *that we tell him things about ourselves, and that we show him sides of our personalities which we would not tell or show to just anyone*" (pp. 327–328, my emphasis). And therefore, Rachels concludes, "because our ability to control who has access to us, and who knows what about us, allows us to maintain the variety of relationships with other people that we want to have, it is, I think, one of the most important reasons why we value privacy" (p. 329).

Rachels acknowledges that his view is similar to that put forth by Charles Fried in *An Anatomy of Values*. Since, for our purposes, we can regard these views as substantially the same, and since they amount to an extremely compelling argument about the basis of our interest in privacy, it will serve us well to sample Fried's version of the doctrine. He writes that

> privacy is the necessary context for relationships which we would hardly be human if we had to do without—the relationships of love, friendship, and trust.
>
> Love and friendship . . . involve the voluntary and spontaneous relinquishment of something between friend and friend, lover and lover. The title to information about oneself conferred by privacy provides the necessary something. To be friends or lovers persons must be intimate to some degree with each other. Intimacy is the sharing of information about one's actions, beliefs or emotions, which one does not share with all, and which one has the right not to share with anyone. By conferring this right, privacy creates the moral capital which we spend in friendship and love.[5]

The Rachels–Fried theory is this. Only because we are able to withhold personal information about—and forbid intimate observation of—ourselves from the rest of the world, can we give out the personal information—and allow the intimate observations—to friends and/or lovers, that constitute intimate relationships. On this view, intimacy is both

---

[5] Charles Fried, *An Anatomy of Values: Problems of Personal and Social Choice* (Cambridge, Mass., 1970), p. 142. It might be thought that in lifting Fried's analysis of privacy out of his book, I have lifted it out of context and thus done violence to his theory. Extra weight is added to this objection by the recognition that when Fried speaks about love in his book (though not in the chapter relating privacy to love), he speaks of something very like the caring that I present as a basis for refuting his view. For instance Fried writes that, "There is rather a creation of love, a middle term, which is a new pattern or system of interests which both share and both value, in part at least just because it is shared" (ibid., p. 79). What is in conflict between us then is not recognition of this or something like this as an essential component of the love relationship. The conflict rather lies in the fact that I argue that recognition of this factor undermines Fried's claim that *privacy* is *necessary* for the very existence of love relationships.

signaled and constituted by the sharing of information and allowing of observation *not shared with or allowed to the rest of the world*. If there were nothing about myself that the rest of the world did not have access to, I simply would not have anything to give that would mark off a relationship as intimate. As Fried says,

> The man who is generous with his possessions, but not with himself, can hardly be a friend, nor—and this more clearly shows the necessity of privacy for love—can the man who, voluntarily or involuntarily, shares everything about himself with the world indiscriminately.[6]

Presumably such a person cannot enter into a friendship or a love because he has literally squandered the "moral capital" which is necessary for intimate emotional investment in another.

Now I find this analysis both compelling and hauntingly distasteful. It is compelling first of all because it fits much that we ordinarily experience. For example, it makes jealously understandable. If the value—indeed, the very reality—of my intimate relation with you lies in your sharing with me what you don't share with others, then if you do share it with another, what I have is literally decreased in value and adulterated in substance. This view is also compelling because it meets the basic requirement for identifying a compelling interest at the heart of privacy. That basic requirement is, as I have already stated, an important interest in simply being able to restrict information about, and observation of, myself regardless of what may be done with that information or the results of that observation.

The view is distasteful, however, because it suggests a market conception of personal intimacy. The value and substance of intimacy—like the value and substance of my income—lies not merely in what I have but essentially in what others do *not* have. The reality of my intimacy with you is constituted not simply by the quality and intensity of what we share, but by its unavailability to others—in other words, by its scarcity. It may be that our personal relations are valuable to us because of their exclusiveness rather than because of their own depth or breadth or beauty. But it is not clear that this is necessary. It may be a function of the historical limits of our capacity for empathy and feeling for others. It may be a function of centuries of acculturation to the nuclear family with its narrow intensities. The Rachels-Fried thesis, however, makes it into a logical necessity by asserting that friendship and love *logically* imply exclusiveness and narrowness of focus.

As compelling as the Rachels–Fried view is then, there is reason to believe it is an example of the high art of ideology: the rendering of aspects of our present possessive market-oriented world into the eternal forms of logical necessity. Perhaps the tip-off lies precisely in the fact that, on their theory, jealousy—the most possessive of emotions—is ren-

[6] Ibid., p. 142.

dered rational. All of this is not itself an argument against the Rachels–Fried view, but rather an argument for suspicion. However, it does suggest an argument against that view.

I think the fallacy in the Rachels–Fried view of intimacy is that it overlooks the fact that what constitutes intimacy is not merely the sharing of otherwise withheld information, but the context of caring which makes the sharing of personal information significant. One ordinarily reveals information to one's psychoanalyst that one might hesitate to reveal to a friend or lover. That hardly means one has an intimate relationship with the analyst. And this is not simply because of the asymmetry. If two analysts decided to psychoanalyze one another alternately—the evident unwisdom of this arrangement aside—there is no reason to believe that their relationship would necessarily be the most intimate one in their lives, even if they revealed to each other information they withheld from everyone else, lifelong friends and lovers included. And this wouldn't be changed if they cared about each other's well-being. What is missing is that particular kind of caring that makes a relationship not just personal but intimate.

The kind of caring I have in mind is not easily put in words, and so I shall claim no more than to offer an approximation. Necessary to an intimate relationship such as friendship or love is a reciprocal desire to share present and future intense and important experiences together, not merely to swap information. Mutual psychoanalysis is not love or even friendship so long as it is not animated by this kind of caring. This is why it remains localized in the office rather than tending to spread into other shared activities, as do love and friendship. Were mutual psychoanalysis animated by such caring it might indeed be part of a love or friendship—but then the "prime mover" of the relationship would not be the exchange of personal information. It would be the caring itself.

In the context of a reciprocal desire to share present and future intense and important experiences, the revealing of personal information takes on significance. The more one knows about the other, the more one is able to understand how the other experiences things, what they mean to him, how they feel to him. In other words the more each knows about the other, the more they are able to really share an intense experience instead of merely having an intense experience alongside one another. The revealing of personal information then is not what constitutes or powers the intimacy. Rather it deepens and fills out, invites and nurtures, the caring that powers the intimacy.

On this view—in contrast to the Rachels–Fried view—it is of little importance who has access to personal information about me. What matters is who cares about it and to whom I care to reveal it. Even if all those to whom I am indifferent and who return the compliment were to know the intimate details of my personal history, my capacity to enter into an intimate relationship would remain unhindered. So long as I could find someone who did not just want to collect data about me, but who cared to know about me in order to share my experience with me and to whom I cared to reveal information about myself so that person could share my experience with me, and vice versa, I could enter into a meaningful friendship or love relationship.

On the Rachels–Fried view, it follows that the significance of sexual intimacy lies in the fact that we signal the uniqueness of our love relationships by allowing our bodies to be seen and touched by the loved one in ways that are forbidden to others. But here too, the context of caring that turns physical contact into intimacy is overlooked. A pair of urologists who examine each other are no more lovers than our reciprocating psychoanalysts. What is missing is the desire to share intense and important experiences. And to say this is to see immediately the appropriateness of sexual intimacy to love: in sexual intimacy one is literally and symbolically stripped of the ordinary masks that obstruct true sharing of experience. This happens not merely in the nakedness of lovers but even more so in the giving of themselves over to the physical forces in their bodies. In surrendering the ordinary restraints, lovers allow themselves to be what they truly are—at least as bodies—intensely and together. (Recall Sartre's marvelous description of the *caress*.) [7] If this takes place in the context of caring—in other words if people are making love and not just fucking—their physical intimacy is an expression and a consummation of that caring. It is one form of the authentic speech of loving.

Finally, on this view—in contrast to the Rachels–Fried view—the unsavory market notion of intimacy is avoided. Since the content of intimacy is caring, rather than the revealing of information or the granting of access to the body usually withheld from others, there is no necessary limit to the number of persons one can be intimate with, no logical necessity that friendship or love be exclusive. The limits rather lie in the limits of our capacity to care deeply for others, and of course in the limits of time and energy. In other words it may be a fact—for us at this point in history, or even for all people at all points in history—that we can only enter into a few true friendships and loves in a lifetime. But this is not an inescapable logical necessity. It is only an empirical fact of our capacity, one that might change and might be worth trying to change. It might be a fact that we are unable to disentangle love from jealousy. But this, too, is not an a priori truth. It is rather an empirical fact, one that

[7] "The Other's flesh did not exist explicitly for me since I grasped the Other's body in situation; neither did it exist for her since she transcended it toward her possibilities and toward the object. The caress causes the Other to be born as flesh for me and for herself. . . , the caress reveals the flesh by stripping the body of its action, by cutting it off from the possibilities which surround it; the caress is designed to uncover the web of inertia beneath the action—i.e., the pure 'being-there'—which sustains it. . . . The caress is designed to cause the Other's body to be born, through pleasure, for the Other—and for myself. . . ." Jean-Paul Sartre, *Being and Nothingness*, trans. Hazel E. Barnes (New York, 1956), p. 390.

might change if fortune brought us into a less possessive, less exclusive, less invidious society.

This much is enough, I think, to cast doubt on the relationship between privacy and friendship or love asserted by Rachels and Fried. It should also be enough to refute their theory of the grounds on which the right to privacy rests. For if intimacy *may* be a function of caring and not of the yielding of otherwise withheld information, their claim to have established the *necessity* of privacy for important human relationships must fall. I think, however, that there is another equally fundamental ground for rejecting their position: it makes the right to individual privacy "derivative" from the right to social (that is, interpersonal) relationships. And I mean "derivative" in a much more irreversible way than Thomson does.

On the Rachels–Fried view, my right to parade around naked alone in my house free from observation by human or electronic peeping toms, is not a fundamental right. It is derived from the fact that without this right, I could not meaningfully reveal my body to the loved one in that exclusive way that is necessary to intimacy on the Rachels–Fried view. This strikes me as bizarre. It would imply that a person who had no chance of entering into social relations with others, say a catatonic or a perfectly normal person legitimately sentenced to life imprisonment in solitary confinement, would thereby have no ground for a right to privacy. This must be false, because it seems that if there is a right to privacy it belongs to individuals regardless of whether they are likely to have friends or lovers, regardless of whether they have reason to amass "the moral capital which we spend in friendship and love." What this suggests is that even if the Rachels–Fried theory of the relationship of privacy and intimacy were true, it would not give us a fundamental interest that can provide the foundation for a right to privacy for all human individuals. I believe, however, that such a fundamental interest can be unearthed. Stanley I. Benn's theory of the foundation of privacy comes closer to the view which I think is ultimately defensible.

Benn attempts to base the right to privacy on the principle of respect for persons. He too is aware that utilitarian considerations—for example, prevention of harm that may result from misuse of personal information—while important, are not adequate to ground the right to privacy.

> The underpinning of a claim not to be watched without leave will be more general if it can be grounded in this way on the principle of respect for persons than on a utilitarian duty to avoid inflicting suffering. That duty may, of course, reinforce the claim in particular instances. But respect for persons will sustain an objection even to secret watching, which may do no actual harm at all. Covert observation— spying—is objectionable because it deliberately deceives a person about his world [that is, it transforms the situation he thinks is unobserved into one which is observed], thwarting, for reasons that *cannot* be his

reasons, his attempts to make a rational choice. One cannot be said to respect a man as engaged on an enterprise worthy of consideration if one knowingly and deliberately alters his conditions of action, concealing the fact from him. The offense is different in this instance, of course, from A's open intrusion on C's conversation. In that case, A's attentions were liable to affect C's enterprise by changing C's perception of it; he may have felt differently about his conversation with D, even to the extent of not being able to see it as any longer the same activity, knowing that A was now listening.[8]

Benn's view is that the right to privacy rests on the principle of respect for persons as choosers. Covert observation or unwanted overt observation deny this respect because they transform the actual conditions in which the person chooses and acts, and thus make it impossible for him to act in the way he set out to act, or to choose in the way he thinks he is choosing.

This too is a compelling analysis. I shall myself argue that the right to privacy is fundamentally connected to personhood. However, as it stands, Benn's theory gives us too much—and though he appears to know it, his way of trimming the theory to manageable scale is not very helpful. Benn's theory gives us too much because it appears to establish a person's right never to be observed when he thought he wasn't being observed, and never to be overtly observed when he didn't wish it. This would give us a right not to have people look at us from their front windows as we absent-mindedly stroll along, as well as a right not to be stared in the face. To deal with this, Benn writes,

> it cannot be sufficient that I do not *want* you to observe something; for the principle of respect to be relevant, it must be something about my own person that is in question, otherwise the principle would be so wide that a mere wish of mine would be a prima facie reason for everyone to refrain from observing and reporting on anything at all. I do not make something a part of me merely by having feelings about it. The principle of privacy proposed here is, rather, that any man who desires that he *himself* should not be an object of scrutiny has a reasonable claim to immunity.[9]

Benn goes on to say that what is rightly covered by this immunity are one's body and those things, like possessions, which the conventions of a culture may cause one to think of as part of one's identity.

But this begs the question. Benn has moved from the principle that respect for me as a person dictates that I am entitled not to have the conditions in which I choose altered by unknown or unwanted observation, to the principle that I am entitled to have those things (conventionally) bound up with my identity exempt from unknown or unwanted

---

[8] Stanley I. Benn, "Privacy, Freedom, and Respect for Persons," in J. Roland Pennock and John Chapman, eds., *Privacy* (New York, 1971) pp. 10–11.
[9] Ibid., p. 12.

observation. But the first principle does not entail the second, because the second principle is not merely a practical limitation on the first; it is a moral limitation. It asserts that it is wrong (or at least, significantly worse) to have the conditions in which I choose altered, when things closely bound up with my identity are concerned. But this follows only if the first principle is conjoined with another that holds that the closer something is to my identity, the worse it is for others to tamper with it. But this is after all just an abstract version of the right to privacy itself. And since Benn has not shown that it follows from the principle of respect for persons as choosers, his argument presupposes what he seeks to establish. It is quite strictly a *petitio principii*.

In sum then, though we have moved quite a bit further in the direction of the foundation of privacy, we have still not reached our destination. What we are looking for is a fundamental interest, connected to personhood, which provides a basis for a right to privacy to which all human beings are entitled (even those in solitary confinement) and which does not go so far as to claim a right never to be observed (even on crowded streets). I proceed now to the consideration of a candidate for such a fundamental interest.

Privacy is a social practice. It involves a complex of behaviors that stretches from refraining from asking questions about what is none of one's business to refraining from looking into open windows one passes on the street, from refraining from entering a closed door without knocking to refraining from knocking down a locked door without a warrant.

Privacy can in this sense be looked at as a very complicated social ritual. But what is its point? In response I want to defend the following thesis. *Privacy is a social ritual by means of which an individual's moral title to his existence is conferred.* Privacy is an essential part of the complex social practice by means of which the social group recognizes—and communicates to the individual—that his existence is his own. And this is a precondition of personhood. To be a person, an individual must recognize not just his actual capacity to shape his destiny by his choices. He must also recognize that he has an exclusive moral right to shape his destiny. And this in turn presupposes that he believes that the concrete reality which he is, and through which his destiny is realized, belongs to him in a moral sense.

And if one takes—as I am inclined to—the symbolic interactionist perspective which teaches that "selves" are created in social interaction rather than flowering innately from inborn seeds, to this claim is added an even stronger one: privacy is necessary to the creation of *selves* [10] out

---

[10] For purposes of this discussion, we can take "self" and "person" as equivalent. I use them both insofar as they refer to an individual who recognizes that he *owns* his physical and mental reality in the sense that he is morally entitled to realize his destiny through it, and thus that he has at least a strong presumptive moral right not to have others interfere with his self-determination.

of human beings, since a self is at least in part a human being who regards his existence—his thoughts, his body, his actions—as his *own*.

Thus the relationship between privacy and personhood is a twofold one. First, the social ritual of privacy seems to be an essential ingredient in the process by which "persons" are created out of prepersonal infants. It conveys to the developing child the recognition that this body to which he is uniquely "connected" is a body over which he has some exclusive moral rights. Secondly, the social ritual of privacy confirms, and demonstrates respect for, the personhood of already developed persons. I take the notion of "conferring title to one's existence" to cover both dimensions of the relationship of privacy to personhood: the original bestowal of title and the ongoing confirmation. And of course, to the extent that we believe that the creation of "selves" or "persons" is an ongoing social process—not just something which occurs once and for all during childhood—the two dimensions become one: privacy is a condition of the original and continuing creation of "selves" or "persons."

To understand the meaning of this claim, it will be helpful to turn to Erving Goffman's classic study, "On the Characteristics of Total Institutions." [11] Goffman says of total institutions that "each is a natural experiment on what can be done to the self." [12] The goal of these experiment is *mortification of the self*, and in each case total deprivation of privacy is an essential ingredient in the regimen. I have taken the liberty of quoting Goffman at length, since I think his analysis provides poignant testimony to the role that elimination of privacy plays in destruction of the self. And thus conversely, he shows the degree to which the self *requires* the social rituals of privacy to exist.

> There is another form of mortification in total institutions; beginning with admission a kind of contaminative exposure occurs. On the outside, the individual can hold objects of self-feeling—such as his body, his immediate actions, his thoughts, and some of his possessions—clear of contact with alien and contaminating things. But in total institutions *these territories of the self are violated.* . . .
>
> There is, first, a violation of one's informational preserve regarding self. During admission, facts about the inmate's social statuses and past behavior—especially discreditable facts—are collected and recorded in a dossier available to staff. . . .
>
> New audiences not only learn discreditable facts about oneself that are ordinarily concealed but are also in a position to perceive some of these facts directly. Prisoners and mental patients cannot prevent their visitors from seeing them in humiliating circumstances. Another example is the shoulder-patch of ethnic identification worn by concentration-camp inmates. Medical and security examinations often expose the inmate physically, sometimes to persons of both sexes; a similar exposure follows

---

[11] Erving Goffman, *Asylums* (New York, 1961), pp. 1–124.
[12] Ibid, p. 12.

from collective sleeping arrangements and doorless toilets. . . . In general, of course, the inmate is never fully alone; he is always within sight and often earshot of someone, if only his fellow inmates. Prison cages with bars for walls fully realize such exposure.[13]

That social practices which penetrate "the private reserve of the individual" [14] are effective means to mortify the inmate's self—that is, literally, to kill it off—suggests (though it doesn't prove) that privacy is essential to the creation and maintenance of selves. My argument for this will admittedly be speculative. However, in view of the fact that it escapes the shortcomings of the views we have already analyzed, fits Goffman's evidence on the effects of deprivation of privacy, fulfills the requirement that it be a fundamental human interest worthy of protection, provides the basis for a right to privacy to which all human beings are entitled, and yet does not claim a right never to be observed, I think it is convincing.

If I am sitting with other people, how do I know this body which is connected to the thoughts I am having is *mine* in the moral sense? That is, how do I know that I have a unique moral right to this body? It is not enough to say that it is connected to my consciousness, since that simply repeats the question or begs the question of what makes these thoughts *my* consciousness. In any event, connection to my consciousness is a factual link, not a moral one. In itself it accounts for why I am not likely to confuse the events in this body (mine) with events in that body (yours). It does not account for the moral title which gives me a unique right to control the events in this body which I don't have in respect to the events in that body.

Ownership in the moral sense presupposes a social institution. It is based upon a complex social practice. A social order in which bodies were held to belong to others or to the collectivity, and in which individuals grew up believing that their bodies were not theirs from a moral point of view, is conceivable. To imagine such an order does not require that we deny that for each body only one individual is able to feel or move it. Such a social order is precisely what Goffman portrays in his description of total institutions and it might be thought of as displaying the ultimate logic of totalitarianism. Totalitarianism is the political condition that obtains when a state takes on the characteristics of a total institution. For a society to exist in which individuals do not own their bodies, what is necessary is that people not be treated as if entitled to control what the bodies they can feel and move do, or what is done by those bodies— in particular that they not be treated as if entitled to determine when and by whom that body is experienced. [15]

---

[13] Ibid., pp. 23–25; my emphasis.

[14] Ibid., p. 29.

[15] Macabre as it may sound, a world in which the body that I can feel and move *is distinct from* the body that I own *is* conceivable. Imagine, for example, a world

This suggests that there are two essential conditions of moral ownership of one's body. The right to do with my body what I wish, and the
right to control when and by whom my body is experienced. This in turn
reflects the fact that things can be appropriated in two ways: roughly
speaking, actively and cognitively. That is, something is "mine" to the
extent that I have the power to use it, to dispose of it as I see fit. But
additionally there is a way in which something becomes "mine" to the
extent that I know it. What I know is "my" knowledge; what I experience
is "my" experience. Thus, it follows that if an individual were granted the
right to control his bodily movements although always under observation,
he might develop some sense of moral ownership of his physical existence.[16] However, that ownership would surely be an impoverished and
partial one compared to what we take to be contained in an individual's
title to his existence. This is because it would be ownership only in one
of the two dimensions of appropriation, the active. Ownership, in the
sense we know it, requires control over cognitive appropriation as well.
It requires that the individual have control over whether or not his physical existence becomes part of someone else's experience. That is, it requires that the individual be treated as entitled to determine when and
by whom his concrete reality is experienced. Moral ownership in the full
sense requires the social ritual of privacy.

As I sit among my friends, I know this body is mine because first of
all, unlike any other body present, I believe—and my friends have acted
and continue to act as if they believe—that I am entitled to do with this
body what I wish. Secondly, but also essential, I know this body is mine
because unlike any other body present, I have in the past taken it outside
of the range of anyone's experience but my own, I can do so now, and I
expect to be able to do so in the future. What's more, I believe—and my
friends have acted and continue to act as if they believe—that it would
be wrong for anyone to interfere with my capacity to do this. In other
words, they have and continue to treat me according to the social ritual
of privacy. And since my view of myself is, in important ways, a reflection
of how others treat me, I come to view myself as the kind of entity that
is entitled to the social ritual of privacy. That is, I come to believe that
this body is mine in the moral sense.

I think the same thing can be said about the thoughts of which I
am aware. That there are thoughts, images, reveries and memories of
which only I am conscious does not make them mine in the moral sense
—any more than the cylinders in a car belong to it just because they are
in it. This is why ascribing ownership of my body to the mere connection
with my consciousness begs the question. Ownership of my thoughts

---

of 365 people each born on a different day of the year, in which each person has
complete access to the body of the person whose birthday is the day after his.
[16] I am indebted to Professor Phillip H. Scribner for pointing this out to me.

requires a social practice as well. It has to do with learning that I can control when, and by whom, the thoughts in my head will be experienced by someone other than myself and learning that I am entitled to such control—that I will not be forced to reveal the contents of my consciousness, even when I put those contents on paper. The contents of my consciousness become mine because they are treated according to the ritual of privacy.

It may seem that this is to return full circle to Thomson's view that the right to privacy is just a species of the rights over person and property. I would argue that it is more fundamental. The right to privacy is the right to the existence of a social practice which makes it possible for me to think of this existence as *mine*. This means that it is the right to conditions necessary for me to think of myself as the kind of entity for whom it would be meaningful and important to claim personal and property rights. It should also be clear that the ownership of which I am speaking is surely more fundamental than property rights. Indeed, it is only when I can call this physical existence mine that I can call objects somehow connected to this physical existence mine. That is, the transformation of physical possession into ownership presupposes ownership of the physical being I am. Thus the right to privacy protects something that is presupposed by both personal and property rights. Thomson's recognition that there is overlap should come as no surprise. The conclusion she draws from the existence of this overlap is, however, unwarranted. Personal and property rights presuppose an individual with title to his existence—and privacy is the social ritual by which that title is conferred.

The right to privacy, then, protects the individual's interest in becoming, being, and remaining a person. It is thus a right which *all* human individuals possess—even those in solitary confinement. It does not assert a right never to be seen even on a crowded street. It is sufficient that I can control whether and by whom my body is experienced in some significant places and that I have the real possibility of repairing to those places. It is a right which protects my capacity to enter into intimate relations, not because it protects my reserve of generally withheld information, but because it enables me to make the commitment that underlies caring as *my* commitment uniquely conveyed by *my* thoughts and witnessed by *my* actions.

RICHARD A. WASSERSTROM

Privacy

I

One thing that is true of privacy is that there are several different phenomena that have been and that can be discussed under the heading of "privacy." Almost all of the discussion are of comparatively recent vintage. In legal scholarship, the classic reference to a right of privacy is the article by Brandeis and Warren entitled, "The Right of Privacy," which appeared in *The Harvard Law Review* in 1890.[1] The first enunciation by the United States Supreme Court of an explicit constitutional right of privacy occurred in 1965 in the case of *Griswold v. Connecticut.*[2] And almost all philosophical and public policy examinations of privacy have appeared within the past fifteen years. However, while the topic of privacy is very much in the air and in the news, part of the problem in thinking about privacy is, that the same thing is not always meant at all by the term, "privacy." More specifically, there are at least three distinct kinds of interests or claims that may be involved when commentators, the courts, legislatures, and ordinary citizens talk about privacy and its importance.

The kind of thing that Brandeis and Warren were concerned with was the unconsented to use by an individual of another's identity in order to secure some special advantage. The central focus here, is upon the improper use of a person's name or likeness for commercial purposes, as, for example, when a person's name and picture are included in the advertising for a product in order to enhance the sale of the product. But included within this category are cases in which true facts of a certain sort about an individual are made public, as for instance when there is an unconsented-to public showing of a film of a woman giving birth to a child.

The United States Supreme Court was concerned with a rather different sense of "privacy" in the Griswold case. That case involved the constitutionality of a Connecticut statute, which made it a crime for any person to use any drug, medicinal article, or instrument for the purpose

---

[1] Brandeis, Louis D. and Warren, Charles. "The Right to Privacy," 4 *Harvard Law Review* 193 (1890).

[2] *Griswold v. State of Connecticut*, 381 U.S. 479, 85 S.Ct. 1678 (1965).

of preventing conception. One reason some of the members of the Court gave for holding the statute unconstitutional was that the statute intruded improperly into a constitutionally protected zone of privacy. That zone of privacy existed, apparently, in virtue of the fact that the behavior covered by the statute included that of married persons in respect to their own sexual relationship. This idea—that certain relationships and certain behaviors were immune from governmental regulation—was also utilized by the Court in the abortion decision [3] and in a case involving an individual's right to possess and read pornographic literature in his home.[4]

The third sense of "privacy" is reflected in the concern over the wrong, if any, that was done by the members of the "Plumber's Squad" who broke into the office of Daniel Ellsberg's psychiatrist to see what they could learn about Ellsberg from the notes of his psychiatrist. It is reflected, as well, in the worry many persons have over the development and use of sophisticated spying devices that make it possible surreptitiously to overhear another's conversations or observe another's behavior. And it is reflected, too, in the concern expressed by many over the large-scale accumulation of data that now exists about each one of us and which is capable of being stored in and retrieved from large-scale data banks. Here, the root issue captured by this idea of privacy is that of the kind and degree of control that an individual will be able to maintain over information about himself or herself.

It is this third sense of "privacy" that I concentrate upon in this essay. The question I want to consider is that of the type of control a person ought to be able to exercise in respect to knowledge of or the disclosure of information about himself or herself. In this essay I attempt to do three things. First, I consider what this kind of privacy is. More specifically, I examine the different types of information and situations that might be thought to be private. Second, I consider the arguments that might be given for the value of certain types of informational privacy, and the reasons why persons might worry about various types of information gathering practices and procedures. And finally, I examine fairly briefly some of the assumptions of these arguments in an endeavor to raise more explicitly the question of how important or essential this concern for privacy is.

II

As I have indicated, there are a number of different claims that can be and are made in the name of privacy. What a number of them, but by no means all, have in common is that they involve the question of the kind and degree of control that a person ought to be able to exercise in

---

[3] *Roe v. Wade*, 410 U.S. 113, 93 S.Ct. 705 (1973).
[4] *Stanley v. Georgia*, 394 U.S. 557, 89 S.Ct. 1243 (1969).

respect to the access by others to information about himself or herself. But even when the focus is upon information, it is evident that information about oneself is not all of the same type; control over some kinds may be thought to be of more importance than control over others. For this reason, the first thing that must be done is to identify some of the different types of information about themselves over which persons might desire to retain substantial access and control, and to describe the situations in which this information comes into being. One way to do this is to consider three situations and look at the ways they resemble each other and differ from one another.

There is first of all the fact that one can, if one wishes to, look "inward" and become aware of the ideas that are running through one's mind, the various emotions one is experiencing, and the variety of bodily sensations one is having—an itch on one's scalp or a pain in one's side. One thing that is significant about one's mental states—about one's dreams, conscious thoughts, hopes, fears and desires is that the most direct, the best, and often the only evidence for another of what they are consists in the individual deliberately revealing them to another. The only way to obtain very detailed and accurate information about what a person is thinking, fearing, imagining, desiring, or hating and how he or she is experiencing it is for that person to tell or show another. If one does not, the ideas and feeling remain within the person and in some sense, at least, known only to him or her. To be sure, nonverbal behavior may give an observer a clue as to what is going on in another's mind. If, for example, a person has a faraway look in her eyes another may infer that she is daydreaming about something and not paying very much attention. In addition there is, perhaps, a more intimate and even conceptual connection, between observable behavior and certain states of feeling. If someone is blushing that may mean that he is embarrassed. If she is talking very fast that may lead another to infer correctly that she is excited or nervous. It is even sometimes the case that one will not know very clearly one's own thoughts and feelings, and that by saying what one thinks they are a skilled observer can, by listening and watching, tell better than can the speaker what is really being thought or felt.

Nonetheless, even taking all of the qualifications into account, it still remains the case that the only way to obtain much detailed and accurate information about what an individual is thinking, fearing, imagining, desiring, or hating and how it is being experienced is for the person to disclose it to another. Because people cannot read other people's minds, many of these things about a person are known only to him or her in a way in which other things are not, unless there is a deliberate decision to disclose them. They occupy, for the most part, a unique place in respect to the possibility of knowledge by others.

In some ways the situation in respect to what is going on within one's body is similar to that of mental events and in some respects different. There are things that are going on in one's body that are like one's thoughts, fear and fantasies. If, for example, a person has a slight twinge of pain in his toe, there is no way for anyone else to know that unless the person having the pain chooses to disclose it. There are, however, other things about one's body concerning which this privileged position does not obtain. Even though they are one's ribs, one cannot tell very well what they look like; even though it is one's semen, one cannot tell in virtue of that fact also whether it contains sperm. These kinds of facts about a person's body can be known at least as well by another as by the individual.

So there are some facts about one's body that can be known in a way others logically cannot know them, that can be known to others only if they are deliberately disclosed. And there are other kinds of facts about one's body that a person does not know in this special way and that can be learned quite as well by someone or something outside of the individual.

In the second place, there is some information that is private only in virtue of the *setting* in which the information is disclosed or communicated. For example, suppose that a person has broken an arm and that the person is in a room with the door closed, alone with the doctor while he or she sets the break. Here it is the setting that makes the behavior distinctive and relevant. If no one is in a position to see the patient and the doctor then no one is in a position at that time to know about the broken arm. This kind of case can usefully be described as a case of things being done in private—meaning by that only that they are done in a setting in which there did not appear to be anyone other than the person to whom one was talking, etc., who was in a position to hear what was being said or to see what was being done. This is, of course, an extremely weak sense of privacy, and for at least two reasons. To begin with, the information is less within the individual's control than is information about his or her mental states, not yet revealed to anyone, because the other person can if he or she chooses reveal what he or she has learned. And in addition, there is nothing about *the character* of the information which seems to make further revelation a source of concern.

It is this last point which leads to the third kind of case. Suppose that instead of having a broken arm set by a doctor, a person consults a therapist in the therapist's office, where the doors are closed, etc., in order to discuss what the patient regards as a very loathsome sexual fantasy. Such a conversation takes place in private in the same sense in which the treatment of the broken arm was private, i.e., no one else could see or hear. But this also has an additional quality not possessed by the other example. When a person such as this one consults a therapist he or she typically expects that what is said will not be overheard by anyone else and will be kept in confidence by the recipient of the information. It is what might be called a private *kind* of communication. And that is not the case with other information about oneself. Absent a further specification of the circumstances, there is no way to tell to what degree individuals have a particular interest in retaining control over the disclosure of facts about themselves.

All of what has been said so far is reasonably obvious. What is also rather apparent is that the most important connection between the idea of doing something in private and doing a private kind of thing is that persons typically do private things only in situations where they reasonably believe that they are doing them in private, i.e., in situations where they believe confidentiality or its equivalent obtains in respect to what is being disclosed. That they believe they are doing something in private in this sense is, often, a condition that has to be satisfied before they are willing to disclose an intimate fact about themselves or to engage in the doing of an intimate act.

It should be evident, too, that there are important similarities, as well as some differences, between the first and third cases—between knowledge of one's own mental states and the disclosure of intimate information to those to whom one chooses to disclose it. A thought-experiment can illuminate much of what is involved in the special concerns persons have that information of certain sorts not become known, without their consent, to others.

Suppose existing technology made it possible for an outsider in some way to look into or monitor another's mind. What, if anything, would be especially disturbing or objectionable about that?

To begin with, there is a real sense in which persons have far less control over when they shall have certain thoughts and what their content will be, than they have over, for example, to whom they shall reveal them and to what degree. Because one's inner thoughts, feelings and bodily sensations are so largely beyond one's control, persons would, no doubt, feel appreciably more insecure in their social environment than they do at present were it possible for others to "look in" without consent to see what was going on in their heads.

This is so at least in part because many, although by no means all, of one's uncommunicated thoughts and feelings are about very intimate matters. One's fantasies and one's fears often concern just those matters that in our culture we would least choose to reveal to anyone else. At a minimum persons might suffer great anxiety and feelings of shame were the decisions as to where, when and to whom to disclose, not to be wholly theirs. Were access to thoughts possible in this way persons would see themselves as creatures who are far more vulnerable at the hands of other persons than they are now.

In addition, there is always the more straightforward worry about accountability for one's thoughts and feelings. As has been mentioned, they are often not within one's control. For all of the reasons that it is wrong to hold people accountable for behavior not within their control, individuals would not want the possibility of accountability to extend to uncommunicated thoughts and feelings.

A third reason why control over intimate facts and behaviors might be of appreciable importance to individuals is this. Our *social* universe would be altered in fundamental and deleterious ways were that control to be surrendered or lost. And this is so because one way in which we mark off and distinguish our most important interpersonal relationships from other ones is in terms of the kind of intimate information and behavior that we are willing to share with other persons. One way in which we make someone a close friend rather than an acquaintance is by revealing things about ourselves to that person that we do not reveal to the world at large. One way in which persons often enter into a special relationship with another is by engaging in sexual behavior not engaged in with the world at large. Knowledge about ourselves is what has been called "moral capital" which is exchanged and otherwise used to create and maintain relationships of intimacy and closeness. On this view privacy is a logically necessary condition for the existence of many of our most meaningful social relationships.[5]

Finally, one rather plausible conception of what it is to be a person carried with it the idea of the existence of a core of thoughts and feelings that are the person's alone. If anyone else could know all that one was thinking or perceive all that one was feeling except in the form one chose to filter and reveal what one was and how one saw oneself—if anyone could, so to speak, be aware of all this at will, individuals might cease to have as complete a sense of themselves as distinct and separate persons as they have now. For a significant, if not fundamental, part of what it is to be an individual person is to be an entity that is capable of being exclusively aware of at least some of its own thoughts and feelings.

Considerations such as these—and particularly the last one—may help to unravel some of the puzzles concerning the privilege against self-incrimination, as well as some of the worries about coercive therapies. Because of the significance of exclusive control over a person's own thoughts and feelings, the privilege against self-incrimination could be seen to rest, at least in part, upon a concern that confessions not be coerced or required by the state. On this view, the point of the privilege is not primarily that the privilege should exist as the means by which to induce the state not to torture individuals in order to extract information from them. Nor is the point even essentially that the topics of confession will necessarily (or even typically) be of the type that persons would be most unwilling to disclose because of the unfavorable nature of what this would reveal about them. Rather, the fundamental point would be that

---

[5] This argument is advanced by Charles Fried in "Privacy," 77 *Yale Law Journal* 475 (1968) and in *An Anatomy of Values: Problems of Personal and Social Choice* (Cambridge, Mass.: Harvard University Press, 1970) Chapter IX.

required disclosure of one's thoughts by itself diminishes the significance or role of the concept of individual personhood within the society.[6]

Similarly, non-consensual drug therapies which reduce if not destroy the patient's resistance to disclosing the things that he or she is thinking are subject to the same kind of criticism. The objection to such therapies is not merely that the individuals involved will be led to say things which they would have not otherwise said, because they regarded such disclosures as shameful or otherwise reflecting badly on themselves (although this is certainly a substantial if not decisive consideration against this kind of a practice). The additional objection to such therapies is that they take away from the individual control over that one area which is for others exclusively within their control and by which they are helped to maintain a clear sense of their own selfhood and individuality.

The more prominent worry today does not, however, concern intrusion into the domain of one's uncommunicated thoughts and feelings, but rather concerns the degree to which communications between persons about intimate things should remain exclusively within their control. What, for example, would be the wrong that was done to a patient were another to have eavesdropped upon a conversation between the patient

---

[6] A somewhat similar analysis is presented by Robert Gerstein in "Privacy and Self-Incrimination," *Ethics*, Vol. 80 (1970) 87. Gerstein observes that historically the privilege against self-incrimination was viewed as especially important in respect to offenses related to religious belief and freedom. He goes on to argue that a contemporary justification for the privilege—on grounds of privacy—can be developed through an account of what might be especially objectionable about requiring an individual to admit and confess to his or her own serious wrongdoing. "It is not the disclosure of the facts of the crime, but the '*mea culpa*,' the public admission of the private judgment of self-condemnation, that seems to be of real concern." (Gerstein, "Privacy and Self-Incrimination," *Ethics*, Vol. 80 (1970) p. 91.)

Both Gerstein's analysis and my own have implications for the way in which the privilege against self-incrimination should be interpreted. Thus, in *Schmerber v. California*, 384 U.S. 757, 86 St.Ct. 1826 (1966), the Supreme Court held that it did not violate the privilege to extract a blood sample from a defendant without his consent. On my analysis, this makes sense because an individual is in no special position in respect to knowledge about the composition of his or her blood. In Gerstein's view, this makes sense because the extraction of the blood sample in no way involves the individual in a public confession of any sort.

On the other hand, immunity statutes may be more troublesome than the Supreme Court has supposed. The Supreme Court has thought that as long as immunity from the use of that testimony by the prosecution is given to an individual there can be no serious worry about the privilege. See, e.g., *Kastigar v. United States*, 406 U.S. 441, 92 S.Ct. 1653 (1972). However, since at least some of the privacy arguments for the privilege do not depend upon the possibility of subsequent prosecution of the person who is required to give evidence as to his or her own wrongdoing, these arguments are left unmet by a grant of immunity from prosecution, no matter how extensive the grant of immunity may be.

and a therapist, or if the therapist had told other persons what had been told to her by the patient? Or what would have been the injury that would have been done to a couple if, unknown to them, they had been observed engaged in sexual intercourse by others?

What comes first to mind is that because of social attitudes toward the disclosure of intimate facts and behavior, most persons would be extremely pained were they to learn that these had become known to persons other than those to whom they chose to disclose them. It is important to see that the pain can come about in several different ways. If one does something private with another and they believe that they are doing it in private, they may very well be hurt or embarrassed if they learn subsequently that they were observed but did not know it. Thus if they learn after the fact that they were observed while they were having intercouse, the knowledge that they were observed will cause them distress both because their expectations of privacy were incorrect and because they do not like the idea that there was an observer present during this kind of intimate act. People have the right, perhaps, simply to have the world be what it appears to be precisely in those cases in which they regard privacy as essential to the diminution of their own vulnerability.

Reasoning such as this lies behind, I think, a case that arose some years ago in California. A department store had complained to the police that homosexuals were using its men's room as a meeting place. The police responded by drilling a small hole in the ceiling over the enclosed stalls. A policeman then stationed himself on the floor above and peered down through the hole observing the persons using the stall for eliminatory purposes. Eventually the policeman discovered and apprehended two homosexuals who used the stall as a place to engage in forbidden sexual behavior. The California Supreme Court held the observations of the policeman to have been the result of an illegal search and ordered the conviction reversed. What made the search objectionably illegal, I believe, was that it occurred in the course of this practice which deceived all of the persons who used the stall and who believed that they were doing in private something that was socially regarded as a private kind of thing. They were entitled, especially for this kind of activity, both to be free from observation and to have their expectations of privacy honored by the state.[7]

There is an additional reason why the observation or disclosure of certain sorts of activity is objectionable. That is because the kind of spontaneity and openness that is essential to them disappears with the presence of an observer or the lack of a guarantee of confidentiality. To see that this is so, consider a different case. Suppose people know in advance that they will be observed during intercourse. Here there is no problem of defeated reasonable expectations. But there may be injury

---

[7] The case is *Bielicki v. Superior Court*, 57 Cal. 2d 600, 371 P.2d 288 (1962).

nonetheless. For one thing, they may be unwilling or unable to communicate an intimate fact or engage in intimate behavior in the presence of an observer. In this sense they will be quite directly prevented from going forward. For another thing, even if they do go ahead the character of the experience may very well be altered. Knowing that someone is watching or listening may render what would have been an enjoyable experience unenjoyable. Or, having someone watch or listen may so alter the character of the activity that it is simply not the same kind of activity it was before. The presence of the observer may make spontaneity impossible. Aware of the observer, individuals will be engaged in part in viewing or imagining what is going on from his or her perspective. They thus cannot "lose" themselves as completely in the activity. And for some kinds of activities—for example, sexual intercourse—that may be an essential feature.

Nor is this the only problem presented by a nondeceptive absence of privacy. Suppose that one is in a setting in which one can be certain that there will never be privacy, that virtually everything one does and virtually everything that happens to one will be recorded and known to others. Even if nothing particularly embarrassing, incriminating, or intimate goes on (or is apt to go on) there is, perhaps, something else that is troublesome and objectionable about such an environment. To see whether this would be so, it is necessary to consider a different kind of case, that of data banks. Is there anything to worry about if a society possesses and utilizes its technological capacity to store an enormous amount of information about each of the individual members of the society in such a way that the information can be retrieved in a rapid, efficient, and relatively inexpensive fashion?

Consider a society in which the kinds of data collected about an individual are not very different from the kinds and quantity already collected in some fashion or other in our own society. It is surprising what a large number of interactions are deemed sufficiently important to record in some way. Thus, there are, for example, records of the traffic accidents one has been in, the applications one has made for life insurance, the purchases that one has made with a Mastercharge Card, the C.O.D. packages that have been signed for, the schools one's children are enrolled in, the telephone numbers that have been called from one's telephone, and so on. Now suppose all of that information, which is presently recorded in some written fashion, were to be stored in some way so that all of it that concerns a person could be extracted on demand. What would result?

It is apparent that at least two different kinds of pictures of the individual would emerge. First, some sort of a qualitative picture of the person would emerge. A number of nontemporal facts would be made available—what kind of driver the person is, how many children the person has, what sorts of purchases have been made, how often the telephone is used, how many times the person has been arrested and for what offenses, what diseases the person has had, how much life insurance, and so on.

Second, it would also be possible to reconstruct a rough, temporal picture of how an individual had been living his or her life and what the person had been doing with his or her time. Thus, there might for any given day be evidence that two or three stores were visited and purchases made, that a check had been cashed at the bank, that lunch had been eaten at a particular restaurant, and so on. There might well, however, be whole days for which there were no entries and there might be many days for which the entries would give a very sketchy and incomplete picture of how one had been spending one's time. Still, it would be a picture that is much more detailed, accurate, and complete than the one most persons could supply from their own memory, or from their own memory as it was augmented by that of their friends. One would have to spend a substantial amount of time each day writing in a diary in order to begin to produce as complete and accurate a picture as the one that might be rendered by the storage and retrieval system envisaged—and even then it is doubtful that the diary would be as accurate or as complete, unless one made it a major life task to keep accurate and detailed records of everything that was done.

If we ask would there be anything troublesome about living in such a society, the first thing to recognize is that there are several different things that might be objectionable.

In the first place, such a scheme might make less confidential communications that were about intimate kinds of things. In order to receive welfare, life insurance, or psychiatric counseling, persons may be required to supply information of a personal or confidential nature. If so, they might reasonably expect that the material revealed will be known only to the recipient. If, however, the information is stored in a data bank, it now becomes possible for the information to be disclosed to persons other than those to whom disclosure was intended. Even if access to the data is controlled in all sorts of ways so as to avoid the risks of improper access, storage of the confidential information in the data bank necessarily makes the information less confidential than it was before it was so stored.

In the second place information that does not concern intimate things can get distorted in one way or another through storage. The clearest contemporary case of this kind of information is a person's arrest record. Now the fact that someone has been arrested is probably not the kind of fact that the arrestee can insist ought to be kept secret. But he or she can legitimately make two other demands about it. The person can insist that incorrect inferences not be drawn from the information. The person can, that is, legitimately point out that many individuals who are arrested are never prosecuted for the alleged offense nor are they in any sense guilty of the offense for which they were arrested. He or she can, therefore, quite appropriately complain about any practice which, for instance, routinely and without more being known denies employment to persons with arrest records. And if such a practice exists, then a person can legitimately complain about the increased dissemination and availability of arrest records just because of the systematic misuse of that information. The storage of arrest records in a data bank becomes objectionable not because the arrest record is intrinsically private but because the information is so regularly misused that the unavailability of the information is less of an evil than its general availability.

This does not, however, end the matter, although this is where the discussion of data banks often ends. Suppose that the information is appropriately derogatory in respect to the individual. Suppose that it is, for instance, a record of arrest and conviction in circumstances, moreover, that in no way suggest that the conviction was unfairly or improperly obtained. Does the individual have any sort of a claim that information of this sort not be put into the data bank? One might, of course, complain on the grounds that there was a practice of putting too much weight on the conviction. Here the argument would be similar to that just discussed. In addition, though, it might also be maintained that there are important gains that come from living in a society in which certain kinds of derogatory information about an individual are permitted to disappear from view after a certain amount of time. What is involved is the creation of a kind of social environment that holds out to the members of the society the possibility of self-renewal and change, which is often dependent upon the individual's belief that a fresh start is in fact an option that is still open. A society that is concerned to encourage persons to believe in the possibility of genuine individual redemption and that is concerned not to make the process of redemption unduly onerous or interminable, might, therefore, actively discourage the development of institutions that impose *permanent* marks of disapprobation upon any of the individuals in the society.

In addition, and related to some of the things already mentioned, there are independent worries about the storage of vast quantities of ostensibly innocuous material about the individual in the data bank. Suppose nothing intrinsically private is stored in the data bank; suppose nothing potentially or improperly derogatory is included; and suppose what does get stored is an enormous quantity of information about the individual—information about the person and the public, largely commercial, transactions which were entered into. One can imagine lots of useful, efficient uses to which such a data bank might be put. Can there be any serious objections?

One thing is apparent. With such a data bank it would be possible to reconstruct a person's movements and activities more accurately and completely than could the individual—or any group of individuals—do simply from memory. As has been indicated, there would, of course, still be gaps in the picture; no one would be able to tell in detail what the individual had been doing a lot of the time. But still, as has been suggested, it would be a surprisingly rich and comprehensive sketch that is exceeded in detail in our society only by the keeping of a careful, thorough personal diary, or by having someone under the surveillance of a corps of private detectives.

What distinguishes this scheme is the fact that it would make it possible to render an account of the movements and habits of every member of the society and in so doing it might transform the society in several notable respects.

In part what is involved is the fact that every transaction in which one engages would now take on additional significance. In such a society one would be both buying a tank of gas and leaving part of a systematic record of where one was on that particular date. One would not just be applying for life insurance; one would also be recording in a permanent way one's health on that date and a variety of other facts about oneself. No matter how innocent one's intentions and actions at any given moment, a likely if not inevitable consequence of such a practice of data collection would be that persons would think more carefully before they did things that would become part of the record. Life would to this degree become less spontaneous and more measured than it is today.

More significant are the consequences of such a practice upon attitudes toward privacy in the society. If it became routine to record and have readily accessible vast quantities of information about every individual we might come to hold the belief that the detailed inspection of any individual's behavior is a perfectly appropriate societal undertaking. We might tend to take less seriously than we do at present the idea that there are ever occasions upon which an individual can plausibly claim to be left alone and unobserved. We might in addition become so used to being objects of public scrutiny that we would cease to deem important privacy in any of our social relationships. Thus as observers we might become insensitive to the legitimate claims of an individual to a sphere of life in which the individual is at present autonomous and around which he or she can erect whatever shield is wished. And as the subjects of continual observation we might become forgetful of the degree to which many of the most important relationships within which we now enter depend for their existence upon the possibility of privacy.

On the other hand, if we do continue to have a high regard for privacy both because of what it permits us to be as individuals and because of the kinds of relationships and activities it makes possible and promotes, the maintenance of a scheme of systematic data collection would necessarily get in the way. This is so for the same reason discussed earlier. Much of the value and significance of being able to do intimate things in private is impaired whenever there is a serious lack of confidence about the privacy of the situation. No one could rationally believe that the establishment of data banks—no matter how pure the motives of those who maintain and have access to them—is calculated to enhance the confidentiality of much that is now known about each one of us. And even if only apparently innocuous material is to be stored, we could never be sure that it all was innocuous as it seemed at the time. It is very likely, therefore, that we would go through life alert to these new, indelible consequences of everyday interactions and transactions. Just as our lives would be different from what they are now if we believed that every telephone conversation was being overheard, so our lives would be similarly affected if we believed that every transaction and application was being stored. In both cases we would almost surely go through life encumbered by a wariness and deliberateness that would make it less easy to live a kind of life often associated with that of a free person.

III

Many of the arguments presented in Part II may not be arguments for, one might say, the intrinsic desirability of privacy and confidentiality in respect to matters of intimate behavior and belief. For most of the arguments already discussed may turn only on the true but contingent fact that persons in our (and most cultures) are socialized in certain ways in respect to intimate matters of different sorts. As I have tried to indicate, given this socialization, an array of arguments and considerations can then be advanced to show why privacy and confidentiality in respect to these matters will be of great importance to individuals and how they may be specially injured and threatened by any loss of control over who, if anyone, will have access to any information concerning their intimate behavior or their thoughts, attitudes and beliefs. And, as has been suggested, in some cases the character of the experience may itself be altered when others are permitted to enter into the participant's ideational and experiential world.

Conceding all of this, however, it is also worth asking whether it would be desirable were individuals to be socialized differently. It might be that different attitudes and practices would be more desirable than those which happen to exist in our society. An alternative view is possible, and it is worth taking seriously. One problem is that it is seldom made explicit or argued for very extensively. But a reconstruction of such a view is possible. It is one which depends at least in part, upon a less individualistic, more collectivist conception of social life and social relationships. The alternative view to that which has been assumed so far might go something like this.

We have made ourselves vulnerable—or at least far more vulnerable than we need be—by accepting the notion that there are thoughts and actions concerning which we ought to feel ashamed or embarrassed. When we realize that everyone has fantasies, desires, worries about all sorts of supposedly terrible, wicked, and shameful things, we ought to see that they really are not things to be ashamed of at all. We regard ourselves as vulnerable because in part we think we are different, if not unique. We have sexual feelings toward our parents and no one else has ever had such wicked feelings. But if everyone does, then the fact that others know of this fantasy is less threatening—one is less vulnerable to their disapproval and contempt.

We have made ourselves excessively vulnerable, so this alternative point of view might continue, because we have accepted the idea that many things are shameful unless done in private. And there is no reason to accept that convention. Of course we are embarrassed if others watch us having sexual intercourse—just as we are embarrassed if others see us unclothed. But that is because the culture has taught us to have these attitudes and not because they are intrinsically fitting. Indeed, our culture would be a healthier, happier culture if we diminished substantially the kinds of actions that we now feel comfortable only doing in private, or the kind of thoughts we now feel comfortable disclosing only to those with whom we have special relationships. This is so for at least three reasons. In the first place, there is simply no good reason why privacy is essential to these things. Sexual intercourse could be just as pleasurable in public (if we grew up unashamed) as is eating a good dinner in a good restaurant. Sexual intercourse is better in private only because society has told us so.

In the second place, it is clear that a change in our attitudes will make us more secure and at ease in the world. If we would be as indifferent to whether we are being watched when we have intercourse as we are to when we eat a meal then we cannot be injured by the fact that we know others are watching us, and we cannot be injured nearly as much by even unknown observations.

In the third place, it might be argued, interpersonal relationships will in fact be better if there is less of a concern for privacy. After all, forthrightness, honesty, and candor are, for the most part virtues, while hypocrisy and deceit are not. Yet this emphasis upon the maintenance of a private side to life tends to encourage hypocritical and deceitful ways of behavior. Individuals see themselves as leading dual lives—public ones and private ones. They present one view of themselves to the public—to casual friends, acquaintances and strangers; and a different view of themselves to themselves and a few intimate associates. This way of living is hypocritical because it is, in essence, a life devoted to camouflaging the real, private self from public scrutiny. It is a dualistic, unintegrated life which renders the individuals who live it needlessly vulnerable, shame-ridden and lacking in a clear sense of self. It is to be contrasted with the more open, less guarded life of the person who has so little to fear from disclosures of self because he or she has nothing that requires hiding.

This is a start toward an alternative view that deserves to be taken seriously. Any attempt to do so, moreover, should begin by considering more precisely the respects in which it departs from the more conventional view of the role of privacy maintained in the body of this essay and the respects in which it does not. In particular, there are at least three issues which must be examined in detail before an intelligent decision can be made. The first is the question of the value that this alternative view attaches to those characteristics of spontaneity and individuality that play such an important role in the more traditional view —as I have described it. On at least one interpretation both views prize spontaneity and individuality equally highly, with this alternative account seeing openness in interpersonal relationships as a better way of achieving just those ends. On another interpretation, however, autonomy, spontaneity and individuality are replaced as values by the satisfactions that attend the recognition of the likeness of all human experience and the sameness that characterizes all interpersonal relationships. Which way of living gives one more options concerning the kind of life that one will fashion for oneself is one of the central issues to be settled.

Still another issue that would have to be explored is the question of what would be gained and what would be lost in respect to the character of interpersonal relationship. For one of the important arguments for the view put forward earlier is that the sharing of one's intimate thoughts and behaviors is one of the primary media through which close, meaningful interpersonal relationships are created, nourished and confirmed. One thing that goes to define a relationship of close friendship is that the friends are willing to share truths about themselves with each other that they are unprepared to reveal to the world at large. One thing that helps to define and sustain a sexual, love relationship is the willingness of the parties to share sexual intimacies with each other that they are unprepared to share with the world at large. If this makes sense, either as a conceptual or as an empirical truth, then perhaps acceptance of this alternative view would mean that these kinds of relationships were either no longer possible or less likely. Or perhaps the conventional view is equally unsatisfactory here, too. Perhaps friendship and love both can and ought to depend upon some other, less proprietary, commercial conception of the exchange of commodities. Perhaps this view of intimate interpersonal relationships is as badly in need of alteration as is the attendant conception of the self.

Finally, related to what has just been said, one would want, I think, to examine more closely some other features of the other view. For example, even if it was no longer thought important to mark off and distinguish one's close friends from strangers (or even if it could still be done, but in some other way) perhaps the alternative conception of openness and honesty in all interpersonal relationships would make ordinary social interactions vastly more complex and time-consuming than they are now. So much so, in fact, that these interactions, rather than the other tasks of living, would become the focus of one's waking hours.

Still another example concerns the character of sexuality and sexual relationships. For most persons in our culture, matters relating to sex are paradigmatically private in all of the sense described in Part II. This is probably so for a variety of reasons. To begin with, during sexual behavior with another one is extremely vulnerable in two, quite straightforward, physical senses. The participants are vulnerable in the sense that they are fully engaged in the activity. They are vulnerable to attack in the same primitive respect in which persons who are asleep are vulnerable. And the participants are also vulnerable vis-a-vis one another. Sexual behavior brings persons in close, physical contact with each other. Trust in the security of the physical environment and in each other may, therefore, be a simple dictate of prudence.

In addition, sex and vulnerability are linked psychically in the culture. The culture appears, for instance, to teach individuals to attach great significance to their sexual competency—to their ability to achieve and bestow sexual satisfaction. Hence, many persons come to see their success or failure as individuals bound up in all sorts of ways with their sexual abilities or problems. Hence, they plausibly regard information about their sexual behavior as relating directly to an area of great vulnerability and as potentially very damaging.

The culture also teaches many individuals that all matters pertaining to sex are shameful. One strain of the culture teaches that it is wrong to have any interest in sex for its own sake or for the pleasure it provides. Another strain of the culture teaches that there is a sharp and important difference between sexual activity that is normal and appropriate, e.g., heterosexual intercourse between persons who are married to each other, and other sexual activity that is abnormal, unnatural, or perverse. Although there will be disagreement as to where and how to draw the line precisely between these two kinds of sexual activity, it will be thought wrong to have the sorts of sexual fantasies, desires, etc.—or to engage in the kinds of sexual conduct—falling outside of the bounds of the normal and appropriate. As a result, individuals who have been socialized in these ways will regard virtually all disclosure about their own sexual beliefs and life as reflecting discreditably upon them. And finally, of course, the culture also teaches almost everyone that matters pertaining to sexual thoughts and behavior should be done in private—even if there is nothing wrong or shameful about the content of the thoughts or behavior in question. For this reason persons will be rendered uncomfortable, caused pain and discomfort, whenever the environment is altered so as to contain observers to acts of sexual intimacy or after-the-fact confidants to whom are disclosed descriptions of past sexual behavior.

What requires development and examination are theories of sexuality and eroticism so that it is possible to disentangle the distinguishable biological, psychological, social and normative components of these phenomena in order to assess the roles they can and should play in human sexual activity. For only then would one be in a position to have a well-founded opinion concerning the connection that ought to obtain between privacy and sexual behavior and attitudes. Perhaps, for instance, less privacy in respect to sexual matters would reduce the sense of vulnerability individuals now feel, but that a weakening of the connection between sex and privacy would also produce a diminished sense of the erotic.

These are some, but by no means all, of the central issues that require continued exploration. They are certainly among the issues that the fully developed theory of privacy, its value and its place within society must confront and examine, and not settle by way of assumption or presupposition.

Griswold v. State of Connecticut
381 U.S. 479, 85 S.Ct. 1678 (1965)

Mr. Justice Douglas delivered the opinion of the Court.

Appellant Griswold is Executive Director of the Planned Parenthood League of Connecticut. Appellant Buxton is a licensed physician and a professor at the Yale Medical School who served as Medical Director for the League at its Center in New Haven—a center open and operating from November 1 to November 10, 1961, when appellants were arrested.

They gave information, instruction, and medical advice to *married persons* as to the means of preventing conception. They examined the wife and prescribed the best contraceptive device or material for her use. Fees were usually charged, although some couples were serviced free.

The statutes whose constitutionality is involved in this appeal are §§ 53–32 and 54–196 of the General Statutes of Connecticut (1958 rev.). The former provides:

Any person who uses any drug, medicinal article or instrument for the purpose of preventing conception shall be fined not less than fifty dollars or imprisoned not less than sixty days nor more than one year or be both fined and imprisoned.

Editor's Note: The opinions have been edited. In addition the concurring opinions of Justices Goldberg and Harlan, the dissenting opinion of Justice Black, and a number of case citations and footnotes have been omitted.

Section 54–196 provides:

Any person who assists, abets, counsels, causes, hires or commands another to commit any offense may be prosecuted and punished as if he were the principal offender.

The appellants were found guilty as accessories and fined $100 each, against the claim that the accessory statute as so applied violated the Fourteenth Amendment. The Appellate Division of the Circuit Court affirmed. The Supreme Court of Errors affirmed that judgment. 151 Conn. 544, 200 A. 2d 479. We noted probable jurisdiction. 379 U.S. 926.

. . .

Coming to the merits, we are met with a wide range of questions that implicate the Due Process Clause of the Fourteenth Amendment. . . .
The association of people is not mentioned in the Constitution nor in the Bill of Rights. The right to educate a child in a school of the parents' choice—whether public or private or parochial—is also not mentioned. Nor is the right to study any particular subject or any foreign language. Yet the First Amendment has been construed to include certain of those rights.
By Pierce v. Society of Sisters, . . . , the right to educate one's children as one chooses is made applicable to the States by the force of the First and Fourteenth Amendments. By Meyer v. State of Nebraska, . . . , the same dignity is given the right to study the German language in a private school. In other words, the State may not, consistently with the spirit of the First Amendment, contract the spectrum of available knowledge. The right of freedom of speech and press includes not only the right to utter or to print, but the right to distribute, the right to receive, the right to read . . . and freedom of inquiry, freedom of thought, and freedom to teach . . . indeed the freedom of the entire university community. . . . Without those peripheral rights the specific rights would be less secure. And so we reaffirm the principle of the Pierce and the Meyer cases.
In NAACP v. State of Alabama, 357 U.S. 449, 462, 78 S.Ct. 1163, 1172, we protected the "freedom to associate and privacy in one's associations," noting that freedom of association was a peripheral First Amendment right. Disclosure of membership lists of a constitutionally valid association, we held, was invalid "as entailing the likelihood of a substantial restraint upon the exercise by petitioner's members of their right to freedom of association." Ibid. In other words, the First Amendment has a penumbra where privacy is protected from governmental intrusion. In like context, we have protected forms of "association" that are not political in the customary sense but pertain to the social, legal, and eco-

nomic benefit of the members. NAACP v. Button, 371 U.S. 415, 430–431, 83 S.Ct. 328, 336–337. In Schware v. Board of Bar Examiners, 353 U.S. 232, 77 S.Ct. 752, 1 L.Ed.2d 796, we held it not permissible to bar a lawyer from practice, because he had once been a member of the Communist Party. The man's "association with that Party" was not shown to be "anything more than a political faith in a political party" (id., at 244, 77 S.Ct. at 759) and was not action of a kind proving bad moral character. Id., at 245–246, 77 S.Ct. at 759–760.

Those cases involved more than the "right of assembly"—a right that extends to all irrespective of their race or ideology. . . . The right of "association," like the right of belief . . . is more than the right to attend a meeting; it includes the right to express one's attitudes or philosophies by membership in a group or by affiliation with it or by other lawful means. Association in that context is a form of expression of opinion; and while it is not expressly included in the First Amendment its existence is necessary in making the express guarantees fully meaningful.

The foregoing cases suggest that specific guarantees in the Bill of Rights have penumbras, formed by emanations from those guarantees that help give them life and substance. See Poe v. Ullman, 367 U.S. 497, 516–522, 81 S.Ct. 1752, 6 L.Ed.2d 989 (dissenting opinion). Various guarantees create zones of privacy. The right of association contained in the penumbra of the First Amendment is one, as we have seen. The Third Amendment in its prohibition against the quartering of soldiers "in any house" in time of peace without the consent of the owner is another facet of that privacy. The Fourth Amendment explicitly affirms the "right of the people to be secure in their persons, houses, papers, and effects, against unreasonable searches and seizures." The Fifth Amendment in its Self-Incrimination Clause enables the citizen to create a zone of privacy which government may not force him to surrender to his detriment. The Ninth Amendment provides: "The enumeration in the Constitution, of certain rights, shall not be construed to deny or disparage others retained by the people."

The Fourth and Fifth Amendments were described in Boyd v. United States, 161 U.S. 616, 630, 6 S.Ct. 524, 532, 29 L.Ed. 746, as protection against all governmental invasions "of the sanctity of a man's home and the privacies of life." [1] We recently referred in Mapp v. Ohio, 367

---

[1] The Court said in full about this right of privacy:

"The principles laid down in this opinion [by Lord Camden in Entick v. Carrington, 19 How.St.Tr. 1029] affect the very essence of constitutional liberty and security. They reach further than the concrete form of the case then before the court, with its adventitious circumstances; they apply to all invasions on the part of the government and its employees of the sanctity of a man's home and the privacies of life. It is not the breaking of his doors, and the rummaging of his drawers, that constitutes the essence of the offense; but it is the invasion of his indefeasible right of personal security, personal liberty and private property, where that right has never been forfeited by his conviction of some public of-

U.S. 643, 656, 81 S.Ct. 1684, 1692, 6 L.Ed.2d 1081, to the Fourth Amendment as creating a "right to privacy, no less important than any other right carefully and particularly reserved to the people." See Beaney, The Constitutional Right to Privacy, 1962 Sup.Ct.Rev. 212; Griswold, The Right to be Let Alone, 55 Nw.U.L.Rev. 216 (1960).

. . .

The present case, then, concerns a relationship lying within the zone of privacy created by several fundamental constitutional guarantees. And it concerns a law which, in forbidding the *use* of contraceptives rather than regulating their manufacture or sale, seeks to achieve its goals by means having a maximum destructive impact upon that relationship. Such a law cannot stand in light of the familiar principle, so often applied by this Court, that a "governmental purpose to control or prevent activities constitutionally subject to state regulation may not be achieved by means which sweep unnecessarily broadly and thereby invade the area of protected freedoms." NAACP v. Alabama, 377 U.S. 288, 307, 84 S.Ct. 1302, 1314, 12 L.Ed.2d 325. Would we allow the police to search the sacred precincts of marital bedrooms for telltale signs of the use of contraceptives? The very idea is repulsive to the notions of privacy surrounding the marriage relationship.

We deal with a right of privacy older than the Bill of Rights—older than our political parties, older than our school system. Marriage is a coming together for better or for worse, hopefully enduring, and intimate to the degree of being sacred. It is an association that promotes a way of life, not causes; a harmony in living, not political faiths; a bilateral loyalty, not commercial or social projects. Yet it is an association for as noble a purpose as any involved in our prior decisions.

Reversed.

. . .

MR. JUSTICE WHITE, concurring in the judgment.

In my view this Connecticut law as applied to married couples deprives them of "liberty" without due process of law, as that concept is used in the Fourteenth Amendment. I therefore concur in the judgment

---

fense,—it is the invasion of this sacred right which underlies and constitutes the essence of Lord Camden's judgment. Breaking into a house and opening boxes and drawers are circumstances of aggravation; but any forcible and compulsory extortion of a man's own testimony, or of his private papers to be used as evidence to convict him of crime, or to forfeit his goods, is within the condemnation of that judgment. In this regard the fourth and fifth amendments run almost into each other." 116 U.S., at 630, 6 S.Ct., at 532.

of the Court reversing these convictions under Connecticut's aiding and abetting statute.

It would be unduly repetitious, and belaboring the obvious, to expound on the impact of this statute on the liberty guaranteed by the Fourteenth Amendment against arbitrary or capricious denials or on the nature of this liberty. Suffice it to say that this is not the first time this Court has had occasion to articulate that the liberty entitled to protection under the Fourteenth Amendment includes the right "to marry, establish a home and bring up children," Meyer v. State of Nebraska, 262 U.S. 390, 399, 43 S.Ct. 625, 626, 67 L.Ed.2d 1042 and "the liberty * * * to direct the upbringing and education of children," Pierce v. Society of Sisters, 268 U.S. 510, 534–535, 45 S.Ct. 571, 573, 69 L.Ed. 1070, and that these are among "the basic civil rights of man." Skinner v. State of Oklahoma, 316 U.S. 535, 541, 62 S.Ct. 1110, 1113, 86 L.Ed. 1655. These decisions affirm that there is a "realm of family life which the state cannot enter" without substantial justification. Prince v. Com. of Massachusetts, 321 U.S. 158, 166, 64 S.Ct. 438, 442, 88 L.Ed. 645.

Surely the right invoked in this case, to be free of regulation of the intimacies of the marriage relationship, "come[s] to this Court with a momentum for respect lacking when appeal is made to liberties which derive merely from shifting economic arrangements." Kovacs v. Cooper, 336 U.S. 77, 95, 69 S.Ct. 448, 458, 93 L.Ed. 513 (opinion of Frankfurter, J.).

The Connecticut anti-contraceptive statute deals rather substantially with this relationship. For it forbids all married persons the right to use birth-control devices, regardless of whether their use is dictated by considerations of family planning, . . . health, or indeed even of life itself. . . . The anti-use statute, together with the general aiding and abetting statute, prohibits doctors from affording advice to married persons on proper and effective methods of birth control. . . . And the clear effect of these statutes, as enforced, is to deny disadvantaged citizens of Connecticut, those without either adequate knowledge or resources to obtain private counseling, access to medical assistance and up-to-date information in respect to proper methods of birth control. . . . In my view, a statute with these effects bears a substantial burden of justification when attacked under the Fourteenth Amendment. . . .

An examination of the justification offered, however, cannot be avoided by saying that the Connecticut anti-use statute invades a protected area of privacy and association or that it demeans the marriage relationship. The nature of the right invaded is pertinent, to be sure, for statutes regulating sensitive areas of liberty do, under the cases of this Court, require "strict scrutiny," Skinner v. State of Oklahoma, 316 U.S. 535, 541, 62 S.Ct. 1110, and "must be viewed in the light of less drastic means for achieving the same basic purpose." Shelton v. Tucker,

364 U.S. 479, 488, 81 S.Ct. 247, 252, 5 L.Ed.2d 231. "Where there is a significant encroachment upon personal liberty, the State may prevail only upon showing a subordinating interest which is compelling." Bates v. City of Little Rock, 361 U.S. 516, 524, 80 S.Ct. 412, 417. See also McLaughlin v. State of Florida, 379 U.S. 184, 85 S.Ct. 283. But such statutes, if reasonably necessary for the effectuation of a legitimate and substantial state interest, and not arbitrary or capricious in application, are not invalid under the Due Process Clause. . . .

As I read the opinions of the Connecticut courts and the argument of Connecticut in this Court, the State claims but one justification for its anti-use statute. . . . There is no serious contention that Connecticut thinks the use of artificial or external methods of contraception immoral or unwise in itself, or that the anti-use statute is founded upon any policy of promoting population expansion. Rather, the statute is said to serve the State's policy against all forms of promiscuous or illicit sexual relationships, be they premarital or extramarital, concededly a permissible and legitimate legislative goal.

Without taking issue with the premise that the fear of conception operates as a deterrent to such relationships in addition to the criminal proscriptions Connecticut has against such conduct, I wholly fail to see how the ban on the use of contraceptives by married couples in any way reinforces the State's ban on illicit sexual relationships. . . . Connecticut does not bar the importation or possession of contraceptive devices; they are not considered contraband material under state law, . . and their availability in that State is not seriously disputed. The only way Connecticut seeks to limit or control the availability of such devices is through its general aiding and abetting statute whose operation in this context has been quite obviously ineffective and whose most serious use has been against birth-control clinics rendering advice to married, rather than unmarried, persons. . . . Indeed, after over 80 years of the State's proscription of use, the legality of the sale of such devices to prevent disease has never been expressly passed upon, although it appears that sales have long occurred and have only infrequently been challenged. This "undeviating policy * * * throughout all the long years * * * bespeaks more than prosecutorial paralysis." Poe v. Ullman, 367 U.S. 497, 502, 81 S.Ct. 1752, 1755. Moreover, it would appear that the sale of contraceptives to prevent disease is plainly legal under Connecticut law.

In these circumstances one is rather hard pressed to explain how the ban on use by married persons in any way prevents use of such devices by persons engaged in illicit sexual relations and thereby contributes to the State's policy against such relationships. Neither the state courts nor the State before the bar of this Court has tendered such an explanation. It is purely fanciful to believe that the broad proscription on use facilitates discovery of use by persons engaging in a prohibited relationship or for some other reason makes such use more unlikely and thus can be supported by any sort of administrative consideration. Perhaps the theory is that a flat ban on use prevents married people from possessing contraceptives and without the ready availability of such devices for use in the marital relationship, there will be no or less temptation to use them in extramarital ones. This reasoning rests on the premise that married people will comply with the ban in regard to their marital relationship, notwithstanding total enforcement in this context and apparent nonenforcibility, but will not comply with criminal statutes prohibiting extramarital affairs and the anti-use statute in respect to illicit sexual relationships, a premise whose validity has not been demonstrated and whose intrinsic validity is not very evident. At most the broad ban is of marginal utility to the declared objective. A statute limiting its prohibition on use to persons engaging in the prohibited relationship would serve the end posited by Connecticut in the same way, and with the same effectiveness, or ineffectiveness, as the broad anti-use statute under attack in this case. I find nothing in this record justifying the sweeping scope of this statute, with its telling effect on the freedoms of married persons, and therefore conclude that it deprives such persons of liberty without due process of law.

• • •

MR. JUSTICE STEWART, whom MR. JUSTICE BLACK joins, dissenting.

Since 1879 Connecticut has had on its books a law which forbids the use of contraceptives by anyone. I think this is an uncommonly silly law. As a practical matter, the law is obviously unenforceable, except in the oblique context of the present case. As a philosophical matter, I believe the use of contraceptives in the relationship of marriage should be left to personal and private choice, based upon each individual's moral, ethical, and religious beliefs. As a matter of social policy, I think professional counsel about methods of birth control should be available to all, so that each individual's choice can be meaningfully made. But we are not asked in this case to say whether we think this law is unwise, or even asinine. We are asked to hold that it violates the United States Constitution. And that I cannot do.

In the course of its opinion the Court refers to no less than six Amendments to the Constitution: the First, the Third, the Fourth, the Fifth, the Ninth, and the Fourteenth.

But the Court does not say which of these Amendments, if any, it thinks is infringed by this Connecticut law.

We *are* told that the Due Process Clause of the Fourteenth Amendment is not, as such, the "guide" in this case. With that much I agree. There is no claim that this law, duly enacted by the Connecticut Legislature, is unconstitutionally vague. There is no claim that the appellants were denied any of the elements of procedural due process at their trial, so as to make their convictions constitutionally invalid. And, as the Court says, the day has long passed since the Due Process Clause was regarded as a proper instrument for determining "the wisdom, need, and propriety" of state laws. . . . My Brothers HARLAN and WHITE to the contrary, "[w]e have returned to the original constitutional proposition that courts do not substitute their social and economic beliefs for the judgment of legislative bodies, who are elected to pass laws." Ferguson v. Skrupa, supra, 372 U.S. at 730, 83 S.Ct. at 1031.

As to the First, Third, Fourth, and Fifth Amendments, I can find nothing in any of them to invalidate this Connecticut law, even assuming that all those Amendments are fully applicable against the States.[2] It has not even been argued that this is a law "respecting an establishment of religion, or prohibiting the free exercise thereof." [3]And surely, unless the solemn process of constitutional adjudication is to descend to the level of a play on words, there is not involved here any abridgment of "the freedom of speech, or of the press; or the right of the people peaceably to assemble, and to petition the Government for a redress of grievances." [4] No soldier has been quartered in any house.[5] There has been no search, and no seizure.[6] Nobody has been compelled to be a witness against himself.[7]

The Court also quotes the Ninth Amendment, and my Brother GOLDBERG's concurring opinion relies heavily upon it. But to say that the Ninth Amendment has anything to do with this case is to turn somersaults with history. The Ninth Amendment, like its companion the Tenth, which this Court held "states but a truism that all is retained which has not been surrendered," United States v. Darby, 312 U.S. 100, 124, 61 S.Ct.

---

[2] The Amendments in question were, as everyone knows, originally adopted as limitations upon the power of the newly created Federal Government, not as limitations upon the powers of the individual States. But the Court has held that many of the provisions of the first eight amendments are fully embraced by the Fourteenth Amendment as limitations upon state action, and some members of the Court have held the view that the adoption of the Fourteenth Amendment made every provision of the first eight amendments fully applicable against the States. See Adamson v. People of State of California, 332 U.S. 46, 68, 67 S.Ct. 1672, 1684 (dissenting opinion of Mr. Justice Black).

[3] U.S. Constitution, Amendment I. To be sure, the injunction contained in the Connecticut statute coincides with the doctrine of certain religious faiths. But if that were enough to invalidate a law under the provisions of the First Amendment relating to religion, then most criminal laws would be invalidated. See, e.g., the Ten Commandments, The Bible, Exodus 20:2–17 (King James).

[4] U.S. Constitution, Amendment I. If all the appellants had done was to advise people that they thought the use of contraceptives was desirable, or even to counsel their use, the appellants would, of course, have a substantial First Amendment claim. But their activities went far beyond mere advocacy. They prescribed specific contraceptive devices and furnished patients with the prescribed contraceptive materials.

[5] U.S. Constitution, Amendment III.

[6] U.S. Constitution, Amendment IV.

[7] U.S. Constitution, Amendment V.

451, 462, 85 L.Ed. 609, was framed by James Madison and adopted by the States simply to make clear that the adoption of the Bill of Rights did not alter the plan that the *Federal Government* was to be a government of express and limited powers, and that all rights and powers not delegated to it were retained by the people and the individual States. Until today no member of this Court has ever suggested that the Ninth Amendment meant anything else, and the idea that a federal court could ever use the Ninth Amendment to annul a law passed by the elected representatives of the people of the State of Connecticut would have caused James Madison no little wonder.

What provision of the Constitution, then, does make this state law invalid? The Court says it is the right of privacy "created by several fundamental constitutional guarantees." With all deference, I can find no such general right of privacy in the Bill of Rights, in any other part of the Constitution, or in any case ever decided by this Court.[8]

At the oral argument in this case we were told that the Connecticut law does not "conform to current community standards. " But it is not the function of this Court to decide cases on the basis of community standards. We are here to decide cases "agreeably to the Constitution and laws of the United States." It is the essence of judicial duty to subordinate our own personal views, our own ideas of what legislation is wise and what is not. If, as I should surely hope, the law before us does not reflect the standards of the people of Connecticut, the people of Connecticut can freely exercise their true Ninth and Tenth Amendment rights to persuade their elected representatives to repeal it. That is the constitutional way to take this law off the books.

LORD PATRICK DEVLIN

Morals and the Criminal Law

The Report of the Committee on Homosexual Offences and Prostitution, generally known as the Wolfenden Report, is recognized to be an excellent study of two very difficult legal and social problems. But it has also

From *The Enforcement of Morals* by Patrick Devlin © Oxford University Press 1965. Reprinted by permission of Oxford University Press.
Editor's Note: Footnotes have been renumbered.

[8] . . . The Court does not say how far the new constitutional right of privacy announced today extends. See, e.g., Mueller, Legal Regulation of Sexual Conduct, at 127; Ploscowe, Sex and the Law, at 189. I suppose, however, that even after today a State can constitutionally still punish at least some offenses which are not committed in public.

a particular claim to the respect of those interested in jurisprudence; it does what law reformers so rarely do; it sets out clearly and carefully what in relation to its subjects it considers the function of the law to be.[1] Statutory additions to the criminal law are too often made on the simple principle that 'there ought to be a law against it.' The greater part of the law relating to sexual offences is the creation of statute and it is difficult to ascertain any logical relationship between it and the moral ideas which most of us uphold. Adultery, fornication, and prostitution are not, as the Report[2] points out, criminal offences: homosexuality between males is a criminal offence, but between females it is not. Incest was not an offence until it was declared so by statute only fifty years ago. Does the legislature select these offences haphazardly, or are there some principles which can be used to determine what part of the moral law should be embodied in the criminal? There is, for example, being now considered a proposal to make A.I.D., that is, the practice of artificial insemination of a woman with the seed of a man who is not her husband, a criminal offence; if, as is usually the case, the woman is married, this is in substance, if not in form, adultery. Ought it to be made punishable when adultery is not? This sort of question is of practical importance, for a law that appears to be arbitrary and illogical, in the end and after the wave of moral indignation that has put it on the statute book subsides, forfeits respect. As a practical question it arises more frequently in the field of sexual morals than in any other, but there is no special answer to be found in that field. The inquiry must be general and fundamental. What is the connexion between crime and sin and to what extent, if at all, should the criminal law of England concern itself with the enforcement of morals and punish sin or immorality as such?

. . .

Early in the Report[3] the Committee put forward:

Our own formulation of the function of the criminal law so far as it concerns the subject of this enquiry. In this field, its function, as we see it, is to preserve public order and decency, to protect the citizen from what is offensive or injurious, and to provide sufficient safeguards against exploitation and corruption of others, particularly those who are specially

---

[1] The Committee's 'statement of juristic philosophy' (to quote Lord Pakenham) was considered by him in a debate in the House of Lords on 4 December 1957, reported in *Handsard Lords Debates*, vol. ccvi at 738; and also in the same debate by the Archbishop of Canterbury at 753 and Lord Denning at 806. The subject has also been considered by Mr. J. E. Hall Williams in the *Law Quarterly Review*, January 1958, vol. lxxiv, p. 76.

[2] Para. 14.

[3] Para. 13.

vulnerable because they are young, weak in body or mind, inexperienced, or in a state of special physical, official or economic dependence.

It is not, in our view, the function of the law to intervene in the private lives of citizens, or to seek to enforce any particular pattern of behaviour, further than is necessary to carry out the purposes we have outlined.

The Committee preface their most important recommendation [4]

that homosexual behaviour between consenting adults in private should no longer be a criminal offence, [by stating the argument [5]] which we believe to be decisive, namely, the importance which society and the law ought to give to individual freedom of choice and action in matters of private morality. Unless a deliberate attempt is to be made by society, acting through the agency of the law, to equate the sphere of crime with that of sin, there must remain a realm of private morality and immorality which is, in brief and crude terms, not the law's business. To say this is not to condone or encourage private immorality.

Similar statements of principle are set out in the chapters of the Report which deal with prostitution. No case can be sustained, the Report says, for attempting to make prostitution itself illegal.[6] The Committee refer to the general reasons already given and add: 'We are agreed that private immorality should not be the concern of the criminal law except in the special circumstances therein mentioned.' They quote [7] with approval the report of the Street Offences Committee,[8] which says: 'As a general proposition it will be universally accepted that the law is not concerned with private morals or with ethical sanctions.' It will be observed that the emphasis is on *private* immorality. By this is meant immorality which is not offensive or injurious to the public in the ways defined or described in the first passage which I quoted. In other words, no act of immorality should be made a criminal offence unless it is accompanied by some other feature such as indecency, corruption, or exploitation. This is clearly brought out in relation to prostitution: 'It is not the duty of the law to concern itself with immorality as such . . . it should confine itself to those activities which offend against public order and decency or expose the ordinary citizen to what is offensive or injurious.' [9]

These statements of principle are naturally restricted to the subject-matter of the Report. But they are made in general terms and there seems to be no reason why, if they are valid, they should not be applied to the criminal law in general. They separate very decisively crime from sin, the divine law from the secular, and the moral from the criminal. They do

[4] Para. 62.
[5] Para. 61.
[6] Para. 224.
[7] Para. 227.
[8] Cmd. 3231 (1928).
[9] Para. 257.

not signify any lack of support for the law, moral or criminal, and they do not represent an attitude that can be called either religious or irreligious. There are many schools of thought among those who may think that morals are not the law's business. There is first of all the agnostic or free-thinker. He does not of course disbelieve in morals, nor in sin if it be given the wider of the two meanings assigned to it in the *Oxford English Dictionary* where it is defined as 'transgression against divine law or the principles of morality.' He cannot accept the divine law; that does not mean that he might not view with suspicion any departure from moral principles that have for generations been accepted by the society in which he lives; but in the end he judges for himself. Then there is the deeply religious person who feels that the criminal law is sometimes more of a hindrance than a help in the sphere of morality, and that the reform of the sinner—at any rate when he injures only himself—should be a spiritual rather than a temporal work. Then there is the man who without any strong feeling cannot see why, where there is freedom in religious belief, there should not logically be freedom in morality as well. All these are powerfully allied against the equating of crime with sin.

. . .

    Morals and religion are inextricably joined—the moral standards generally accepted in Western civilization being those belonging to Christianity. Outside Christendom other standards derive from other religions. None of these moral codes can claim any validity except by virtue of the religion on which it is based. Old Testament morals differ in some respects from New Testament morals. Even within Christianity there are differences. Some hold that contraception is an immoral practice and that a man who has carnal knowledge of another woman while his wife is alive is in all circumstances a fornicator; others, including most of the English-speaking world, deny both these propositions. Between the great religions of the world, of which Christianity is only one, there are much wider differences. It may or may not be right for the State to adopt one of these religions as the truth, to found itself upon its doctrines, and to deny to any of its citizens the liberty to practise any other. If it does, it is logical that it should use the secular law wherever it thinks it necessary to enforce the divine. If it does not, it is illogical that it should concern itself with morals as such. But if it leaves matters of religion to private judgement, it should logically leave matters of morals also. A State which refuses to enforce Christian beliefs has lost the right to enforce Christian morals.

    If this view is sound, it means that the criminal law cannot justify any of its provisions by reference to the moral law. It cannot say, for example, that murder and theft are prohibited because they are immoral or sinful. The State must justify in some other way the punishments which it imposes on wrongdoers and a function for the criminal law independent of morals must be found. This is not difficult to do. The smooth functioning of society and the preservation of order require that a number of activities should be regulated. The rules that are made for that purpose and are enforced by the criminal law are often designed simply to achieve uniformity and convenience and rarely involve any choice between good and evil. Rules that impose a speed limit or prevent obstruction on the highway have nothing to do with morals. Since so much of the criminal law is composed of rules of this sort, why bring morals into it at all? Why not define the function of the criminal law in simple terms as the preservation of order and decency and the protection of the lives and property of citizens, and elaborate those terms in relation to any particular subject in the way in which it is done in the Wolfenden Report? The criminal law in carrying out these objects will undoubtedly overlap the moral law. Crimes of violence are morally wrong and they are also offences against good order; therefore they offend against both laws. But this is simply because the two laws in pursuit of different objectives happen to cover the same area. Such is the argument.

. . .

In jurisprudence, as I have said, everything is thrown open to discussion and, in the belief that they cover the whole field, I have framed three interrogatories addressed to myself to answer:

1. Has society the right to pass judgement at all on matters of morals? Ought there, in other words, to be a public morality, or are morals always a matter for private judgement?
2. If society has the right to pass judgement, has it also the right to use the weapon of the law to enforce it?
3. If so, ought it to use that weapon in all cases or only in some; and if only in some, on what principles should it distinguish?

I shall begin with the first interrogatory and consider what is meant by the right of society to pass a moral judgement, that is, a judgement about what is good and what is evil. The fact that a majority of people may disapprove of a practice does not of itself make it a matter for society as a whole. Nine men out of ten may disapprove of what the tenth man is doing and still say that it is not their business. There is a case for a collective judgement (as distinct from a large number of individual opinions which sensible people may even refrain from pronouncing at all if it is upon somebody else's private affairs) only if society is affected. Without a collective judgement there can be no case at all for intervention. Let me take as an illustration the Englishman's attitude to religion as it is now and as it has been in the past. His attitude now is that a man's religion is his private affair; he may think of another man's religion that it is right or wrong, true or untrue, but not that it is good or bad. In earlier times that was not so; a man was denied the right to practise what was thought of as heresy, and heresy was thought of as destructive of society.

The language used in the passages I have quoted from the Wolfenden Report suggests the view that there ought not to be a collective judgement about immorality *per se*. Is this what is meant by 'private morality' and 'individual freedom of choice and action'? Some people sincerely believe that homosexuality is neither immoral nor unnatural. Is the 'freedom of choice and action' that is offered to the individual, freedom to decide for himself what is moral or immoral, society remaining neutral; or is it freedom to be immoral if he wants to be? The language of the Report may be open to question, but the conclusions at which the Committee arrive answer this question unambiguously. If society is not prepared to say that homosexuality is morally wrong, there would be no basis for a law protecting youth from 'corruption' or punishing a man for living on the 'immoral' earnings of a homosexual prostitute, as the Report recommends. [10] This attitude the Committee make even clearer when they come to deal with prostitution. In truth, the Report takes it for granted that there is in existence a public morality which condemns homosexuality and prostitution. What the Report seems to mean by private morality might perhaps be better described as private behaviour in matters of morals.

This view—that there is such a thing as public morality—can also be justified by *a priori* argument. What makes a society of any sort is community of ideas, not only political ideas but also ideas about the way its members should behave and govern their lives; these latter ideas are its morals. Every society has a moral structure as well as a political one: or rather, since that might suggest two independent systems, I should say that the structure of every society is made up both of politics and morals. Take, for example, the institution of marriage. Whether a man should be allowed to take more than one wife is something about which every society has to make up its mind one way or the other. In England we believe in the Christian idea of marriage and therefore adopt monogamy as a moral principle. Consequently the Christian institution of marriage has become the basis of family life and so part of the structure of our society. It is there not because it is Christian. It has got there because it is Christian, but it remains there because it is built into the house in which we live and could not be removed without bringing it down. The great majority of those who live in this country accept it because it is the Christian idea of marriage and for them the only true one. But a non-Christian is bound by it, not because it is part of Christianity but because, rightly or wrongly, it has been adopted by the society

10 Para. 76.

in which he lives. It would be useless for him to stage a debate designed to prove that polygamy was theologically more correct and socially preferable; if he wants to live in the house, he must accept it as built in the way in which it is.

We see this more clearly if we think of ideas or institutions that are purely political. Society cannot tolerate rebellion; it will not allow argument about the rightness of the cause. Historians a century later may say that the rebels were right and the Government was wrong and a percipient and conscientious subject of the State may think so at the time. But it is not a matter which can be left to individual judgement.

The institution of marriage is a good example for my purpose because it bridges the division, if there is one, between politics and morals. Marriage is part of the structure of our society and it is also the basis of a moral code which condemns fornication and adultery. The institution of marriage would be gravely threatened if individual judgements were permitted about the morality of adultery; on these points there must be a public morality. But public morality is not to be confined to those moral principles which support institutions such as marriage. People do not think of monogamy as something which has to be supported because our society has chosen to organize itself upon it; they think of it as something that is good in itself and offering a good way of life and that it is for that reason that our society has adopted it. I return to the statement that I have already made, that society means a community of ideas; without shared ideas on politics, morals, and ethics no society can exist. Each one of us has ideas about what is good and what is evil; they cannot be kept private from the society in which we live. If men and women try to create a society in which there is no fundamental agreement about good and evil they will fail; if, having based it on common agreement, the agreement goes, the society will disintegrate. For society is not something that is kept together physically; it is held by the invisible bonds of common thought. If the bonds were too far relaxed the members would drift apart. A common morality is part of the bondage. The bondage is part of the price of society; and mankind, which needs society, must pay its price.

.   .   .

You may think that I have taken far too long in contending that there is such a thing as public morality, a proposition which most people would readily accept, and may have left myself too little time to discuss the next question which to many minds may cause greater difficulty: to what extent should society use the law to enforce its moral judgements? But I believe that the answer to the first question determines the way in which the second should be approached and may indeed very nearly dictate the answer to the second question. If society has no right to make judgements on morals, the law must find some special justification for entering the field of morality: if homosexuality and prostitution are not in themselves wrong, then the onus is very clearly on the lawgiver who wants to frame a law against certain aspects of them to justify the exceptional treatment. But if society has the right to make a judgement and has it on the basis that a recognized morality is as necessary to society as, say, a recognized government, then society may use the law to preserve morality in the same way as it uses it to safeguard anything else that is essential to its existence. If therefore the first proposition is securely established with all its implications, society has a prima facie right to legislate against immorality as such.

The Wolfenden Report, notwithstanding that it seems to admit the right of society to condemn homosexuality and prostitution as immoral, requires special circumstances to be shown to justify the intervention of the law. I think that this is wrong in principle and that any attempt to approach my second interrogatory on these lines is bound to break down. I think that the attempt by the Committee does break down and that this is shown by the fact that it has to define or describe its special circumstances so widely that they can be supported only if it is accepted that the law *is* concerned with immorality as such.

The widest of the special circumstances are described as the provision of 'sufficient safeguards against exploitation and corruption of others, particularly those who are specially vulnerable because they are young, weak in body or mind, inexperienced, or in a state of special physical, official or economic dependence.' [11] The corruption of youth is a well-recognized ground for intervention by the State and for the purpose of any legislation the young can easily be defined. But if similar protection were to be extended to every other citizen, there would be no limit to the reach of the law. The 'corruption and exploitation of others' is so wide that it could be used to cover any sort of immorality which involves, as most do, the co-operation of another person. Even if the phrase is taken as limited to the categories that are particularized as 'specially vulnerable,' it is so elastic as to be practically no restriction. This is not merely a matter of words. For if the words used are stretched almost beyond breaking-point, they still are not wide enough to cover the recommendations which the Committee make about prostitution.

Prostitution is not in itself illegal and the Committee do not think that it ought to be made so.[12] If prostitution is private immorality and not the law's business, what concern has the law with the ponce or the brothel-keeper or the householder who permits habitual prostitution? The Report recommends that the laws which make these activities criminal offences should be maintained or strengthened and brings them (so far as it goes into principle; with regard to brothels it says simply that the law

[11] Para. 13.
[12] Paras. 224, 285, and 318.

rightly frowns on them) under the head of exploitation.[13] There may be cases of exploitation in this trade, as there are or used to be in many others, but in general a ponce exploits a prostitute no more than an impresario exploits an actress. The Report finds that 'the great majority of prostitutes are women whose psychological makeup is such that they choose this life because they find in it a style of living which is to them easier, freer and more profitable than would be provided by any other occupation. . . . In the main the association between prostitute and ponce is voluntary and operates to mutual advantage.'[14] The Committee would agree that this could not be called exploitation in the ordinary sense. They say: 'It is in our view an over-simplification to think that those who live on the earnings of prostitution are exploiting the prostitute as such. What they are really exploiting is the whole complex of the relationship between prostitute and customer; they are, in effect, exploiting the human weaknesses which cause the customer to seek the prostitute and the prostitute to meet the demand.[15]

All sexual immorality involves the exploitation of human weaknesses. The prostitute exploits the lust of her customers and the customer the moral weakness of the prostitute. If the exploitation of human weaknesses is considered to create a special circumstance, there is virtually no field of morality which can be defined in such a way as to exclude the law.

I think, therefore, that it is not possible to set theoretical limits to the power of the State to legislate against immorality. It is not possible to settle in advance exceptions to the general rule or to define inflexibly areas of morality into which the law is in no circumstances to be allowed to enter. Society is entitled by means of its laws to protect itself from dangers, whether from within or without. Here again I think that the political parallel is legitimate. The law of treason is directed against aiding the king's enemies and against sedition from within. The justification for this is that established government is necessary for the existence of society and therefore its safety against violent overthrow must be secured. But an established morality is as necessary as good government to the welfare of society. Societies disintegrate from within more frequently than they are broken up by external pressures. There is disintegration when no common morality is observed and history shows that the loosening of moral bonds is often the first stage of disintegration, so that society is justified in taking the same steps to preserve its moral code as it does to preserve its government and other essential institutions.[16] The suppression of vice is

[13] Para. 223.
[14] Paras. 302 and 320.
[15] Para. 306.
[16] It is somewhere about this point in the argument that Professor Hart in *Law, Liberty and Morality* discerns a proposition which he describes as central to my thought. He states the proposition and his objection to it as follows (p. 51). 'He appears to move from the acceptable proposition that *some* shared morality is essential

as much the law's business as the suppression of subversive activities; it is no more possible to define a sphere of private morality than it is to define one of private subversive activity. It is wrong to talk of private morality or of the law not being concerned with immorality as such or to try to set rigid bounds to the part which the law may play in the suppression of vice. There are no theoretical limits to the power of the State to

---

to the existence of any society [this I take to be the proposition on p. 12] to the unacceptable proposition that a society is identical with its morality as that is at any given moment of its history, so that a change in its morality is tantamount to the destruction of a society. The former proposition might be even accepted as a necessary rather than an empirical truth depending on a quite plausible definition of society as a body of men who hold certain moral views in common. But the latter proposition is absurd. Taken strictly, it would prevent us saying that the morality of a given society had changed, and would compel us instead to say that one society had disappeared and another one taken its place. But it is only on this absurd criterion of what it is for the same society to continue to exist that it could be asserted without evidence that any deviation from a society's shared morality threatens its existence.' In conclusion (p. 82) Professor Hart condemns the whole thesis in the lecture as based on 'a confused definition of what a society is.'

I do not assert that *any* deviation from a society's shared morality threatens its existence any more than I assert that *any* subversive activity threatens its existence. I assert that they are both activities which are capable in their nature of threatening the existence of society so that neither can be put beyond the law.

For the rest, the objection appears to me to be all a matter of words. I would venture to assert, for example, that you cannot have a game without rules and that if there were no rules there would be no game. If I am asked whether that means that the game is 'identical' with the rules, I would be willing for the question to be answered either way in the belief that the answer would lead to nowhere. If I am asked whether a change in the rules means that one game has disappeared and another has taken its place, I would reply probably not, but that it would depend on the extent of the change.

Likewise I should venture to assert that there cannot be a contract without terms. Does this mean that an 'amended' contract is a 'new' contract in the eyes of the law? I once listened to an argument by an ingenious counsel that a contract, because of the substitution of one clause for another, had 'ceased to have effect' within the meaning of a statutory provision. The judge did not accept the argument; but if most of the fundamental terms had been changed, I daresay he would have done.

The proposition that I make in the text is that if (as I understand Professor Hart to agree, at any rate for the purposes of the argument) you cannot have a society without morality, the law can be used to enforce morality as something that is essential to a society. I cannot see why this proposition (whether it is right or wrong) should mean that morality can never be changed without the destruction of society. If morality is changed, the law can be changed. Professor Hart refers (p. 72) to the proposition as 'the use of legal punishment to freeze into immobility the morality dominant at a particular time in a society's existence.' One might as well say that the inclusion of a penal section into a statute prohibiting certain acts freezes the whole statute into immobility and prevent the prohibitions from ever being modified.

These points are elaborated in the sixth lecture at pp. 115–16.

legislate against treason and sedition, and likewise I think there can be no theoretical limits to legislation against immorality. You may argue that if a man's sins affect only himself it cannot be the concern of society. If he chooses to get drunk every night in the privacy of his own home, is any one except himself the worse for it? But suppose a quarter or a half of the population got drunk every night, what sort of society would it be? You cannot set a theoretical limit to the number of people who can get drunk before society is entitled to legislate against drunkenness. The same may be said of gambling. The Royal Commission on Betting, Lotteries, and Gaming took as their test the character of the citizen as a member of society. They said: 'Our concern with the ethical significance of gambling is confined to the effect which it may have on the character of the gambler as a member of society. If we were convinced that whatever the degree of gambling this effect must be harmful we should be inclined to think that it was the duty of the state to restrict gambling to the greatest extent practicable.' [17]

. . .

I do not think that one can talk sensibly of a public and private morality any more than one can of a public or private highway. Morality is a sphere in which there is a public interest and a private interest, often in conflict, and the problem is to reconcile the two. This does not mean that it is impossible to put forward any general statements about how in our society the balance ought to be struck. Such statements cannot of their nature be rigid or precise; they would not be designed to circumscribe the operation of the law-making power but to guide those who have to apply it. While every decision which a court of law makes when it balances the public against the private interest is an *ad hoc* decision, the cases contain statements of principle to which the court should have regard when it reaches its decision. In the same way it is possible to make general statements of principle which it may be thought the legislature should bear in mind when it is considering the enactment of laws enforcing morals.

I believe that most people would agree upon the chief of these elastic principles. There must be toleration of the maximum individual freedom that is consistent with the integrity of society. . . . The principle appears to me to be peculiarly appropriate to all questions of morals. Nothing should be punished by the law that does not lie beyond the limits of tolerance. It is not nearly enough to say that a majority dislike a practice; there must be a real feeling of reprobation. Those who are dissatisfied with the present law on homosexuality often say that the opponents of reform are swayed simply by disgust. If that were so it would be wrong, but I do not think one can ignore disgust if it is deeply felt and

[17] (1951) Cmd. 8190, para. 159.

not manufactured. Its presence is a good indication that the bounds of toleration are being reached. Not everything is to be tolerated. No society can do without intolerance, indignation, and disgust; [18] they are the forces behind the moral law, and indeed it can be argued that if they or something like them are not present, the feelings of society cannot be weighty enough to deprive the individual of freedom of choice. I suppose that there is hardly anyone nowadays who would not be disgusted by the thought of deliberate cruelty to animals. No one proposes to relegate that or any other form of sadism to the realm of private morality or to allow it to be practised in public or in private. It would be possible no doubt to point out that until a comparatively short while ago nobody thought very much of cruelty to animals and also that pity and kindliness and the unwillingness to inflict pain are virtues more generally esteemed now than they have ever been in the past. But matters of this sort are not determined by rational argument. Every moral judgement, unless it claims a divine source, is simply a feeling that no right-minded man could behave in any other way without admitting that he was doing wrong. It is the power of a common sense and not the power of reason that is behind the judgements of society. But before a society can put a practice beyond the limits of tolerance there must be a deliberate judgement that the practice is injurious to society. There is, for example, a general abhorrence of homosexuality. We should ask ourselves in the first instance whether, looking at it calmly and dispassionately, we regard it as a vice so abominable that its mere presence is an offence. If that is the genuine feeling of the society in which we live, I do not see how society can be denied the right to eradicate it. Our feeling may not be so intense as that. We may feel about it that, if confined, it is tolerable, but that if it spread it might be gravely injurious; it is in this way that most societies look upon fornication, seeing it as a natural weakness which must be kept within bounds but which cannot be rooted out. It becomes than a question of balance, the danger to society in one scale and the extent of the restriction in the other. On this sort of point the value of an investigation by such a body as the Wolfenden Committee and of its conclusions is manifest.

. . .

A third elastic principle must be advanced more tentatively. It is that as far as possible privacy should be respected. This is not an idea that has ever been made explicit in the criminal law. Acts or words done or said in public or in private are all brought within its scope without distinction in principle. But there goes with this a strong reluctance on the part of judges and legislators to sanction invasions of privacy in the de-

---

[18] These words which have been much criticized, are considered again in the Preface at p. viii.

tection of crime. The police have no more right to trepass than the ordinary citizen has; there is no general right of search; to this extent an
Englishman's home is still his castle. The Government is extremely careful in the exercise even of those powers which it claims to be undisputed.
Telephone tapping and interference with the mails afford a good illustration of this. A Committee of three Privy Councillors who recently in-
quired [19] into these activities found that the Home Secretary and his predecessors had already formulated strict rules governing the exercise of these
powers and the Committee were able to recommend that they should be
continued to be exercised substantially on the same terms. But they reported that the power was 'regarded with general disfavour'.

This indicates a general sentiment that the right to privacy is something to be put in the balance against the enforcement of the law. Ought
the same sort of consideration to play any part in the formation of the
law? Clearly only in a very limited number of cases. When the help of
the law is invoked by an injured citizen, privacy must be irrelevant; the
individual cannot ask that his right to privacy should be measured against
injury criminally done to another. But when all who are involved in the
deed are consenting parties and the injury is done to morals, the public
interest in the moral order can be balanced against the claims of privacy.
The restriction on police powers of investigation goes further than the
affording of a parallel; it means that the detection of crime committed in
private and when there is no complaint is bound to be rather haphazard
and this is an additional reason for moderation. These considerations do
not justify the exclusion of all private immorality from the scope of the
law. I think that, as I have already suggested, the test of 'private behaviour' should be substituted for 'private morality' and the influence of
the factor should be reduced from that of a definite limitation to that of
a matter to be taken into account. Since the gravity of the crime is also a
proper consideration, a distinction might well be made in the case of
homosexuality between the lesser acts of indecency and the full offence,
which on the principles of the Wolfenden Report it would be illogical
to do.

The last and the biggest thing to be remembered is that the law is
concerned with the minimum and not with the maximum; there is much
in the Sermon on the Mount that would be out of place in the Ten
Commandments. We all recognize the gap between the moral law and the
law of the land. No man is worth much who regulates his conduct with
the sole object of escaping punishment, and every worthy society sets for
its members standards which are above those of the law. We recognize the
existence of such higher standards when we use expressions such as 'moral
obligation' and 'morally bound'. The distinction was well put in the
judgment of African elders in a family dispute: 'We have power to make

[19] (1957) Cmd. 283.

you divide the crops, for this is our law, and we will see this is done. But we have not power to make you behave like an upright man.' [20]

It can only be because this point is so obvious that it is so frequently ignored. Discussion among law-makers, both professional and amateur, is too often limited to what is right or wrong and good or bad for society. There is a failure to keep separate the two questions I have earlier posed—the question of society's right to pass a moral judgement and the question of whether the arm of the law should be used to enforce the judgement. The criminal law is not a statement of how people ought to behave; it is a statement of what will happen to them if they do not behave; good citizens are not expected to come within reach of it or to set their sights by it, and every enactment should be framed accordingly.

H. L. A. HART

Immorality and Treason

The most remarkable feature of Sir Patrick's lecture is his view of the nature of morality—the morality which the criminal law may enforce. Most previous thinkers who have repudiated the liberal point of view have done so because they thought that morality consisted either of divine commands or of rational principles of human conduct discoverable by human reason. Since morality for them had this elevated divine or rational status as the law of God or reason, it seemed obvious that the state should enforce it, and that the function of human law should not be merely to provide men with the opportunity for leading a good life, but actually to see that they lead it. Sir Patrick does not rest his repudiation of the liberal point of view on these religious or rationalist conceptions. Indeed much that he writes reads like an abjuration of the notion that reasoning or thinking has much to do with morality. English popular morality has no doubt its historical connexion with the Christian religion: 'That,' says Sir Patrick, 'is how it got there.' But it does not owe its present status or social significance to religion any more than to reason.

What, then, is it? According to Sir Patrick it is primarily a matter of feeling. 'Every moral judgment,' he says, 'is a feeling that no right-minded man could act in any other way without admitting that he was

"Immorality and Treason" originally appeared in *The Listener* (July 30, 1959), pp. 162–163, and it is reprinted here by permission of the author.

[20] A case in the Saa-Katengo Kuta at Lialiu, August 1942, quoted in *The Judicial Process among the Barotse of Northern Rhodesia* by Max Gluckman, Manchester University Press, 1955, p. 172.

doing wrong.' Who then must feel this way if we are to have what Sir Patrick calls a public morality? He tells us that it is 'the man in the street,' 'the man in the jury box,' or (to use the phrase so familiar to English lawyers) 'the man on the Clapham omnibus.' For the moral judgments of society so far as the law is concerned are to be ascertained by the standards of the reasonable man, and he is not to be confused with the rational man. Indeed, Sir Patrick says 'he is not expected to reason about anything and his judgment may be largely a matter of feeling.'

Intolerance, Indignation, and Disgust

But what precisely are the relevant feelings, the feelings which may justify use of the criminal law? Here the argument becomes a little complex. Widespread dislike of a practice is not enough. There must, says Sir Patrick, be 'a real feeling of reprobation.' Disgust is not enough either. What is crucial is a combination of intolerance, indignation, and disgust. These three are the forces behind the moral law, without which it is not 'weighty enough to deprive the individual of freedom of choice.' Hence there is, in Sir Patrick's outlook, a crucial difference between the mere adverse moral judgment of society and one which is inspired by feeling raised to the concert pitch of intolerance, indignation, and disgust.

This distinction is novel and also very important. For on it depends the weight to be given to the fact that when morality is enforced individual liberty is necessarily cut down. Though Sir Patrick's abstract formulation of his views on this point is hard to follow, his examples make his position fairly clear. We can see it best in the contrasting things he says about fornication and homosexuality. In regard to fornication, public feeling in most societies is not now of the concert-pitch intensity. We may feel that it is tolerable if confined: only its spread might be gravely injurious. In such cases the question whether individual liberty should be restricted is for Sir Patrick a question of balance between the danger to society in the one scale, and the restriction of the individual in the other. But if, as may be the case with homosexuality, public feeling is up to concert pitch, if it expresses a 'deliberate judgment' that a practice as such is injurious to society, if there is 'a genuine feeling that it is a vice so abominable that its mere presence is an offence,' then it is beyond the limits of tolerance, and society may eradicate it. In this case, it seems, no further balancing of the claims of individual liberty is to be done, though as a matter of prudence the legislator should remember that the popular limits of tolerance may shift: the concert pitch feeling may subside. This may produce a dilemma for the law; for the law may then be left without the full moral backing that it needs, yet it cannot be altered without giving the impression that the moral judgment is being weakened.

A Shared Morality

If this is what morality is—a compound of indignation, intolerance, and disgust—we may well ask what justification there is for taking it, and turning it as such, into criminal law with all the misery which criminal punishment entails. Here Sir Patrick's answer is very clear and simple. A collection of individuals is not a society; what makes them into a society is among other things a shared or public morality. This is as necessary to its existence as an organized government. So society may use the law to preserve its morality like anything else essential to it. 'The suppression of vice is as much the law's business as the suppression of subversive activities.' The liberal point of view which denies this is guilty of 'an error in jurisprudence': for it is no more possible to define an area of private morality than an area of private subversive activity. There can be no 'theoretical limits' to legislation against immorality just as there are no such limits to the power of the state to legislate against treason and sedition.

    Surely all this, ingenious as it is, is misleading. Mill's formulation of the liberal point of view may well be too simple. The grounds for interfering with human liberty are more various than the single criterion of 'harm to others' suggests: cruelty to animals or organizing prostitution for gain do not, as Mill himself saw, fall easily under the description of harm to others. Conversely, even where there is harm to others in the most literal sense, there may well be other principles limiting the extent to which harmful activities should be repressed by law. So there are multiple criteria, not a single criterion, determining when human liberty may be restricted. Perhaps this is what Sir Patrick means by a curious distinction which he often stresses between theoretical and practical limits. But with all its simplicities the liberal point of view is a better guide than Sir Patrick to clear thought on the proper relation of morality to the criminal law: for it stresses what he obscures—namely, the points at which thought is needed before we turn popular morality into criminal law.

Society and Moral Opinion

No doubt we would all agree that a consensus of moral opinion on certain matters is essential if society is to be worth living in. Laws against murder, theft, and much else would be of little use if they were not supported by a widely diffused conviction that what these laws forbid is also immoral. So much is obvious. But it does not follow that everything to which the moral vetoes of accepted morality attach is of equal importance to society; nor is there the slightest reason for thinking of morality as a seamless web: one which will fall to pieces carrying society with it, unless all its emphatic vetoes are enforced by law. Surely even in the face of the moral feeling that is up to concert pitch—the trio of intolerance, indignation, and disgust—we must pause to think. We must ask a question at two different levels which Sir Patrick never clearly enough identifies or separates. First, we must ask whether a practice which offends moral feeling is harmful, independently of its repercussion on the general moral code. Secondly, what about repercussion on the moral code? Is it really true that failure to translate this item of general morality into criminal law will jeopardize the whole fabric of morality and so of society?

We cannot escape thinking about these two different questions merely by repeating to ourselves the vague nostrum: 'This is part of public morality and public morality must be preserved if society is to exist.' Sometimes Sir Patrick seems to admit this, for he says in words which both Mill and the Wolfenden Report might have used, that there must be the maximum respect for individual liberty consistent with the integrity of society. Yet this, as his contrasting examples of fornication and homosexuality show, turns out to mean only that the immorality which the law may punish must be generally felt to be intolerable. This plainly is no adequate substitute for a reasoned estimate of the damage to the fabric of society likely to ensue if it is not suppressed.

Nothing perhaps shows more clearly the inadequacy of Sir Patrick's approach to this problem than his comparison between the suppression of sexual immorality and the suppression of treason or subversive activity. Private subversive activity is, of course, a contradiction in terms because 'subversion' means overthrowing government, which is a public thing. But it is grotesque, even where moral feeling against homosexuality is up to concert pitch, to think of the homosexual behavior of two adults in private as in any way like treason or sedition either in intention or effect. We can make it *seem* like treason only if we assume that deviation from a general moral code is bound to affect that code, and to lead not merely to its modification but to its destruction. The analogy could begin to be plausible only if it was clear that offending against this item of morality was likely to jeopardize the whole structure. But we have ample evidence for believing that people will not abandon morality, will not think any better of murder, cruelty, and dishonesty, merely because some private sexual practice which they abominate is not punished by the law.

Because this is so the analogy with treason is absurd. Of course 'No man is an island': what one man does in private, if it is known, may affect others in many different ways. Indeed it may be that deviation from general sexual morality by those whose lives, like the lives of many homosexuals, are noble ones and in all other ways exemplary will lead to what Sir Patrick calls the shifting of the limits of tolerance. But if this has any analogy in the sphere of government it is not the overthrow of ordered government, but a peaceful change in its form. So we may listen to the promptings of common sense and of logic, and say that though there could not logically be a sphere of private treason there is a sphere of private morality and immorality.

Sir Patrick's doctrine is also open to a wider, perhaps a deeper, criticism. In his reaction against a rationalist morality and his stress on feeling, he has I think thrown out the baby and kept the bath water; and the bath water may turn out to be very dirty indeed. When Sir Patrick's lecture was first delivered *The Times* greeted it with these words: 'There is a moving and welcome humility in the conception that society should not be asked to give its reason for refusing to tolerate what in its heart it feels intolerable.' This drew from a correspondent in Cambridge the retort: 'I am afraid that we are less humble than we used to be. We once burnt old women because, without giving our reasons, we felt in our hearts that witchcraft was intolerable.'

This retort is a bitter one, yet its bitterness is salutary. We are not, I suppose, likely, in England, to take again to the burning of old women for witchcraft or to punishing people for associating with those of a different race or colour, or to punishing people again for adultery. Yet if these things were viewed with intolerance, indignation, and disgust, as the second of them still is in some countries, it seems that on Sir Patrick's principles no rational criticism could be opposed to the claim that they should be punished by law. We could only pray, in his words, that the limits of tolerance might shift.

Curious Logic

It is impossible to see what curious logic has led Sir Patrick to this result. For him a practice is immoral if the thought of it makes the man on the Clapham omnibus sick. So be it. Still, why should we not summon all the resources of our reason, sympathetic understanding, as well as critical intelligence, and insist that before general moral feeling is turned into criminal law it is submitted to scrutiny of a different kind from Sir Patrick's? Surely, the legislator should ask whether the general morality is based on ignorance, superstition, or misunderstanding; whether there is a false conception that those who practise what is condemns are in other ways dangerous or hostile to society; and whether the misery to many parties, the blackmail and the other evil consequences of criminal punishment, especially for sexual offences, are well understood. It is surely extraordinary that among the things which Sir Patrick says are to be considered before we legislate against immorality these appear nowhere; not even as 'practical considerations,' let alone 'theoretical limits.' To any theory which, like this one, asserts that the criminal law may be used on the vague ground that the preservation of morality is essential to society and yet omits to stress the need for critical scrutiny, our reply should be: 'Morality, what crimes may be committed in thy name!'

As Mill saw, and de Tocqueville showed in detail long ago in his critical but sympathetic study of democracy, it is fatally easy to confuse the democratic principle that power should be in the hands of the majority with the utterly different claim that the majority, with power in their hands, need respect no limits. Certainly there is a special risk in a democracy that the majority may dictate how all should live. This is the risk we run, and should gladly run; for it is the price of all that is so good in democratic rule. But loyalty to democratic principles does not require us to maximize this risk: yet this is what we shall do if we mount the man in the street on the top of the Clapham omnibus and tell him that if only he feels sick enough about what other people do in private to demand its suppression by law no theoretical criticism can be made of his demand.

JOEL FEINBERG

Legal Paternalism

The principle of legal paternalism justifies state coercion to protect individuals from self-inflicted harm, or in its extreme version, to guide them, whether they like it or not, toward their own good. Parents can be expected to justify their interference in the lives of their children (e.g., telling them what they must eat and when they must sleep) on the ground that "daddy knows best." Legal paternalism seems to imply that since the state often can know the interests of individual citizens better than the citizens know them themselves, it stands as a permanent guardian of those interests *in loco parentis*. Put in this blunt way, paternalism seems a preposterous doctrine. If adults are treated as children they will come in time to be like children. Deprived of the right to choose for themselves, they will soon lose the power of rational judgment and decision. Even children, after a certain point, had better not be "treated as children," else they will never acquire the outlook and capability of responsible adults.

Yet if we reject paternalism entirely, and deny that a person's own good is *ever* a valid ground for coercing him, we seem to fly in the face both of common sense and our long established customs and laws. In the criminal law, for example, a prospective victim's freely granted consent is no defense to the charge of mayhem or homicide. The state simply refuses

This material is here reprinted from Volume 1, Number 1 of the *Canadian Journal of Philosophy* (1971), 105–124, by permission of the author and the Canadian Association for Publishing in Philosophy.

to permit anyone to agree to his own disablement or killing. The law of contracts, similarly, refuses to recognize as valid, contracts to sell oneself into slavery, or to become a mistress, or a second wife. Any ordinary citizen is legally justified in using reasonable force to prevent another from mutilating himself or committing suicide. No one is allowed to purchase certain drugs even for therapeutic purposes without a physician's prescription (Doctor knows best). The use of other drugs, such as heroin, for pleasure merely, is permitted under no circumstances whatever. It is hard to find any plausible rationale for all such restrictions apart from the argument that beatings, mutilations, and death, concubinage, slavery, and bigamy are always bad for a person whether he or she knows it or not, and that antibiotics are too dangerous for any non-expert, and heroin for anyone at all, to take on his own initiative.

The trick is stopping short once we undertake this path, unless we wish to ban whiskey, cigarettes, and fried foods, which tend to be bad for people too, whether they know it or not. The problem is to reconcile somehow our general repugnance for paternalism with the apparent necessity, or at least reasonableness, of some paternalistic regulations. My method of dealing with this problem will not be particularly ideological. Rather, I shall try to organize our elementary intuitions by finding a principle that will render them consistent. Let us begin, then, by rejecting the views both that the protection of a person from himself is *always* a valid ground for interference in his affairs, and that it is *never* a valid ground. It follows that it is a valid ground only under certain conditions, and we must now try to state those conditions.[1]

I

It will be useful to make some preliminary distinctions. The first distinction is between harms or likely harms that are produced directly by a person upon himself and those produced by the actions of another person to which the first party has consented. Committing suicide would be an example of self-inflicted harm; arranging for a person to put one out of one's misery would be an example of a "harm" inflicted by the action of

---

[1] The discussion that follows has two important unstated and undefended presuppositions. The first is that in some societies, at least, and at some times, a line can be drawn (as Mill claimed it could in Victorian England) between other-regarding behaviour and behaviour that is primarily and directly self-regarding and only indirectly and remotely, therefore trivially, other-regarding. If this assumption is false, there is no interesting problem concerning legal paternalism since all "paternalistic" restrictions, in that case, could be defended as necessary to protect persons other than those restricted, and hence would not be (wholly) paternalistic. The second presupposition is that the spontaneous repugnance toward paternalism (which I assume the reader shares with me) is well-grounded and supportable.

another to which one has consented. There is a venerable legal maxim traceable to the Roman Law that "*Volenti non fit inuria*," sometimes translated, misleadingly, as: "To one who consents no harm is done." Now, I suppose that the notion of consent applies, strictly speaking, only to the actions of another person that affect oneself. If so, then, consent to one's *own* actions is a kind of metaphor. Indeed, to say that I consented to my own actions, seems just a colorful way to saying that I acted voluntarily. My involuntary actions, after all, are, from the moral point of view, no different from the actions of someone else to which I have not had an opportunity to consent. In any case, it seems plainly false to say that a person cannot be *harmed* by actions, whether his own or those of another, to which he has consented. People who quite voluntarily eat an amount that is in fact too much cause themselves to suffer from indigestion; and girls who consent to advances sometimes become pregnant.

One way of interpreting the *Volenti* maxim is to take it as a kind of presumptive principle. A person does not generally consent to what he believes will be, on balance, harmful to himself, and by and large, an individual is in a better position to appraise risks to himself than are outsiders. Given these data, and considerations of convenience in the administration of the law, the *Volenti* maxim might be understood to say that for the purposes of the law (whatever the actual facts might be) nothing is to count as harm to a given person that he has freely consented to. If this presumption is held to be conclusive, then the *Volenti* maxim becomes a kind of "legal fiction" when applied to cases of undeniable harm resulting from behavior to which the harmed one freely consented. A much more likely interpretation, however, takes the *Volenti* maxim to say nothing at all, literal or fictional, about *harms*. Rather, it is about what used to be called "injuries," that is, injustices or wrongs. To one who freely consents to a thing no *wrong* is done, no matter how harmful to him the consequences may be. "He cannot waive his right," says Salmond, "and then complain of its infringement." [2] If the *Volenti* maxim is simply an expression of Salmond's insight, it is not a presumptive or fictional principle about harms, but rather an absolute principle about wrongs.

The *Volenti* maxim (or something very like it) plays a key role in the argument for John Stuart Mill's doctrine about liberty. Characteristically, Mill seems to employ the maxim in both of its interpretations, as it suits his purposes, without noticing the distinction between them. On the one hand, Mill's argument purports to be an elaborate application of the calculus of harms and benefits to the problem of political liberty. The state can rightly restrain a man to prevent harm to others. Why then can it not restrain a man to prevent him from harming himself? After all, a harm is a harm whatever its cause, and if our sole concern is to minimize

---

[2] See Glanville Williams (ed.), *Salmond on Jurisprudence*, Eleventh Edition (London: Sweet & Maxwell, 1957), p. 531.

harms all round, why should we distinguish between origins of harm? One way Mill answers this question is to employ the V*olenti* maxim in its first interpretation. For the purposes of his argument, he will presume conclusively that "to one who consents no *harm* is done." Self-inflicted or consented-to harm simply is not to count as harm at all; and the reasons for this are that the coercion required to prevent such harm is itself a harm of such gravity that it is likely in the overwhelming proportion of cases to outweigh any good it can produce for the one coerced; and moreover, individuals themselves, in the overwhelming proportion of cases, can know their own true interests better than any outsiders can, so that outside coercion is almost certain to be self-defeating.

But as Gerald Dworkin has pointed out,[3] arguments of this merely statistical kind at best create a strong but rebuttable presumption against coercion of a man in his own interest. Yet Mill purports to be arguing for an absolute prohibition. Absolute prohibitions are hard to defend on purely utilitarian grounds, so Mill, when his confidence wanes, tends to move to the second interpretation of the V*olenti* maxim. To what a man consents he may be harmed, but he cannot be wronged; and Mill's "harm principle," reinterpreted accordingly, is designed to protect him and others only from wrongful invasions of their interest. Moreover, when the state intervenes on any other ground, its *own* intervention is a wrongful invasion. What justifies the absolute prohibition of interference in primarily self-regarding affairs is *not* that such interference is self-defeating and likely (merely likely) to cause more harm than it prevents, but rather that it would itself be an injustice, a wrong, a violation of the private sanctuary which is every person's self; and this is so whatever the calculus of harms and benefits might show.[4]

The second distinction is between those cases where a person directly

---

[3] See his excellent article, "Paternalism" in *Morality and the Law*, ed. by R. A. Wasserstrom (Belmont, Calif.: Wadsworth Publishing Co., 1971).

[4] Mill's rhetoric often supports this second interpretation of his argument. He is especially fond of such political metaphors as independence, legitimate rule, dominion, and sovereignty. The state must respect the status of the individual as an independent entity whose "*sovereignty* over himself" (in Mill's phrase), like Britain's over its territory, is absolute. In self-regarding affairs, a person's individuality ought to "*reign* uncontrolled from the outside" (another phrase of Mill's). Interference in those affairs, whether successful or self-defeating, is a violation of *legitimate boundaries*, like trespass in law, or aggression between states. Even self-mutilation and suicide are permissible if the individual truly chooses them, and other interests are not directly affected. The individual person has an absolute right to choose for himself, to be wrong, to go to hell on his own, and it is nobody else's proper *business* or *office* to interfere. The individual *owns* (not merely possesses) his life; he has *title* to it. He alone is *arbiter* of his own life and death. See how legalistic and un-utilitarian these terms are! The great wonder is that Mill could claim to have foregone any benefit in argument from the notion of an abstract right. Mill's intentions aside, however, I can not conceal my own preference for this second interpretation of his argument.

produces harm to himself, where the harm is the certain upshot of his conduct and its desired end, on the one hand, and those cases where a person simply creates a *risk* of harm to himself in the course of activities directed toward other ends. The man who knowingly swallows a lethal dose of arsenic will certainly die, and death must be imputed to him as his goal in acting. Another man is offended by the sight of his left hand, so he grasps an ax in his right hand and chops his left hand off. He does not thereby "endanger" his interest in the physical integrity of his limbs or "risk" the loss of his hand. He brings about the loss directly and deliberately. On the other hand, to smoke cigarettes or to drive at excessive speeds is not directly to harm oneself, but rather to increase beyond a normal level the probability that harm to oneself will result.

The third distinction is that between reasonable and unreasonable risks. There is no form of activity (or inactivity either for that matter) that does not involve some risks. On some occasions we have a choice between more and less risky actions and prudence dictates that we take the less dangerous course; but what is called "prudence" is not always reasonable. Sometimes it is more reasonable to assume a great risk for a great gain than to play it safe and forfeit a unique opportunity. Thus it is not necessarily more reasonable for a coronary patient to increase his life expectancy by living a life of quiet inactivity than to continue working hard at his career in the hope of achieving something important even at the risk of a sudden fatal heart attack at any moment. There is no simple mathematical formula to guide one in making such decisions or for judging them "reasonable" or "unreasonable." On the other hand, there are other decisions that are manifestly unreasonable. It is unreasonable to drive at sixty miles an hour through a twenty mile an hour zone in order to arrive at a party on time, but it may be reasonable to drive fifty miles an hour to get a pregnant wife to the maternity ward. It is foolish to resist an armed robber in an effort to protect one's wallet, but it may be worth a desperate lunge to protect one's very life, or the life of a loved one.

In all of these cases a number of district considerations are involved.[5] If there is time to deliberate one should consider: (1) the degree of probability that harm to oneself will result from a given course of action, (2) the seriousness of the harm being risked, i.e., "the value or importance of that which is exposed to the risk," (3) the degree of probability that the goal inclining one to shoulder the risk will in fact result from the course of action, (4) the value or importance of achieving that goal, that is, just how worthwhile it is to one (this is the intimately personal factor, requiring a decision about one's own preferences, that makes the reasonableness of a risk-assessment on the whole so difficult for the *outsider* to make), and (5) the necessity of the risk, that is, the availability or absence of alternative, less risky, means to the desired goal. Certain judgments about the

[5] The distinctions in this paragraph are borrowed from: Henry T. Terry, "Negligence," *Harvard Law Review*, Vol. 29 (1915).

reasonableness of risk-assumptions are quite uncontroversial. We can say, for example, that the greater are considerations (1) the probability of harm to self, and (2) the magnitude of the harm risked, the *less* reasonable the risk; and the greater considerations (3) the probability the desired goal will result, (4) the importance of that goal to the actor, and (5) the necessity of the means, the *more* reasonable the risk. But in a given difficult case, even where questions of "probability" are meaningful and beyond dispute, and where all the relevant facts are known, the risk-decision may defy objective assessment because of its component personal value judgments. In any case, if the state is to be given the right to prevent a person from risking harm to himself (and only himself) this must not be on the ground that the prohibited action is risky, or even that it is extremely risky, but rather on the ground that the risk is extreme and, in respect to its objectively assessable components, manifestly *unreasonable*. There are very good reasons, sometimes, for regarding even a person's judgment of personal worthwhileness (consideration 4) to be "manifestly unreasonable," but it remains to be seen whether (or when) that kind of unreasonableness can be sufficient grounds for interference.

The fourth and final distinction is between fully voluntary and not fully voluntary assumptions of a risk. One assumes a risk in a fully voluntary way when one shoulders it while fully informed of all relevant facts and contingencies, with one's eyes wide open, so to speak, and in the absence of all coercive pressure of compulsion. There must be calmness and deliberateness, no distracting or unsettling emotions, no neurotic compulsion, no misunderstanding. To whatever extent there is compulsion, misinformation, excitement or impetuousness, clouded judgment (as e.g. from alcohol), or immature or defective faculties of reasoning, to that extent the choice falls short of perfect voluntariness. Voluntariness then is a matter of degree. One's "choice" is *completely involuntary* either when it is no choice at all, properly speaking—when one lacks all muscular control of one's movements, or when one is knocked down, or pushed, or sent reeling by a blow, or a wind, or an explosion—or when through ignorance one chooses something other than what one means to choose, as when one thinks the arsenic powder is table salt, and thus chooses to sprinkle it on one's scrambled eggs. Most harmful choices, as most choices generally, fall somewhere in between the extremes of perfect voluntariness and complete involuntariness.

Now, the terms "voluntary" and "involuntary" have a variety of disparate but overlapping uses in philosophy, law, and ordinary life, and some of them are not altogether clear. I should point out here that my usage does not correspond with that of Aristotle, who allowed that infants, animals, drunkards, and men in a towering rage might yet act voluntarily if only they are undeceived and not overwhelmed by external physical force. What I call a voluntary assumption of risk corresponds more closely to what Aristotle called "deliberate choice." Impulsive and emotional actions, and those of animals and infants are voluntary in Aristotle's sense, but they are not *chosen.* Chosen actions are those that are decided upon by *deliberation,* and that is a process that requires time, information, a clear head, and highly developed rational faculties. When I use such phrases then as "voluntary act," "free and genuine consent," and so on, I refer to acts that are more than "voluntary" in the Aristotelian sense, acts that Aristotle himself would call "deliberately chosen." Such acts not only have their origin "in the agent," they also represent him faithfully in some important way: they express his settled values and preferences. In the fullest sense, therefore, they are actions for which he can take responsibility.

II

The central thesis of John Stuart Mill and other individualists about paternalism is that the fully voluntary choice or consent of a mature and rational human being concerning matters that affect only his own interests is such a precious thing that no one else (and certainly not the state) has a right to interfere with it simply for the person's "own good." No doubt this thesis was also meant to apply to almost-but-not-quite fully voluntary choices as well, and probably also even to some substantially non-voluntary ones (e.g. a neurotic person's choice of a wife who will satisfy his neurotic needs but only at the price of great unhappiness, eventual divorce, and exacerbated guilt); but it is not probable that the individualist thesis was meant to apply to choices near the bottom of the scale of voluntariness, and Mill himself left no doubt that he did *not* intend it to apply to completely involuntary "choices." Nor should we *expect* anti-paternalistic individualism to deny protection to a person from his own nonvoluntary choices, for insofar as the choices are not voluntary they are just as alien to him as the choices of someone else.

Thus Mill would permit the state to protect a man from his own ignorance at least in circumstances that create a strong presumption that his uninformed or misinformed choice would not correspond to his eventual one.

> If either a public officer or anyone else saw a person attempting to cross a bridge which had been ascertained to be unsafe, and there were no time to warn him of his danger, they might seize him and turn him back, without any real infringement of his liberty; for liberty consists in doing what one desires, and he does not desire to fall into the river.[6]

Of course, for all the public officer may know, the man on the bridge does desire to fall into the river, or to take the risk of falling for other purposes. If the person is then fully warned of the danger and wishes to proceed anyway, then, Mill argues, that is his business alone; but because most people do *not* wish to run such risks, there was a solid presumption, in

[6] J. S. Mill, *On Liberty* (New York: Liberal Arts Press, 1956), p. 117.

advance of checking, that this person did not wish to run the risk either. Hence the officer was justified, Mill would argue, in his original interference.

On other occasions a person may need to be protected not from his ignorance but from some other condition that may render his informed choice substantially less than voluntary. He may be "a child, or delirious, or in some state of excitement or absorption incompatible with the full use of the reflecting faculty." [7] Mill would not permit any such person to cross an objectively unsafe bridge. On the other hand, there is no reason why a child, or an excited person, or a drunkard, or a mentally ill person should not be allowed to proceed on his way home across a perfectly safe thoroughfare. Even substantially nonvoluntary choices deserve protection unless there is good reason to judge them dangerous.

Now it may be the case, for all we can know, that the behaviour of a drunk or an emotionally upset person would be exactly the same even if he were sober and calm; but when the behaviour seems patently self-damaging and is of a sort that most calm and normal persons would not engage in, then there are strong grounds, if only a statistical sort, for inferring the opposite; and these grounds, on Mill's principle, would justify interference. It may be that there is no kind of action of which it can be said "No mentally competent adult in a calm, attentive mood, fully informed, etc. would *ever* choose (or consent to) *that*." Nevertheless, there are actions of a kind that create a powerful *presumption* that any given actor, if he were in his right mind, would not choose them. The point of calling this hypothesis a "presumption" is to require that it be completely overridden before legal permission be given to a person, who has already been interfered with, to go on as before. So, for example, if a policeman (or anyone else) sees John Doe about to chop off his hand with an ax, he is perfectly justified in using force to prevent him, because of the presumption that no one could voluntarily choose to do such a thing. The presumption, however, should always be taken as rebuttable in principle; and now it will be up to Doe to prove before an official tribunal that he is calm, competent, and free, and that he still wishes to chop off his hand. Perhaps this is too great a burden to expect Doe himself to "prove," but the tribunal should require that the presumption against voluntariness be overturned by evidence from some source or other. The existence of the presumption should require that an objective determination be made, whether by the usual adversary procedures of law courts, or simply by a collective investigation by the tribunal into the available facts. The greater the presumption to be overridden, the more elaborate and fastidious should be the legal paraphernalia required, and the stricter the standards of evidence. (The law of wills might prove a model for this.) The point of the procedure would not be to evaluate the wisdom or worthiness of a person's choice, but rather to determine whether the choice really is his.

[7] *Loc. cit.*

This seems to lead us to a form of paternalism that is so weak and innocuous that it could be accepted even by Mill, namely, that the state has the right to prevent self-regarding harmful conduct only when it is substantially nonvoluntary or when temporary intervention is necessary to establish whether it is voluntary or not. When there is a strong presumption that no normal person would voluntarily choose or consent to the kind of conduct in question, that should be a proper ground for detaining the person until the voluntary character of his choice can be established. We can use the phrase "the standard of voluntariness" as a label for the considerations that mediate the application of the principle that a person may properly be protected from his own folly. (Still another ground for forcible delay and inquiry that is perfectly compatible with Mill's individualism is the possibility that important third party interests might be involved. Perhaps a man's wife and family should have some say before he is permitted to commit suicide—or even to chop off his hand.)

III

Working out the details of the voluntariness standard is far too difficult to undertake here, but some of the complexities, at least, can be illustrated by a consideration of some typical hard cases. Consider first of all problem of harmful drugs. Suppose Richard Roe requests a prescription of drug X from Dr. Doe, and the following discussion ensues:

DR. DOE: I cannot prescribe drug X to you because it will do you physical harm.

MR. ROE: But you are mistaken. It will not cause me physical harm.

In a case like this, the state, of course, backs the doctor. The state deems medical questions to be technical matters subject to expert opinions. This entails that a non-expert layman is not the best judge of his own medical interests. If a layman disagrees with a physician on a question of medical fact the layman can be presumed wrong, and if nevertheless he chooses to act on his factually mistaken belief, his action will be substantially less than fully voluntary in the sense explained above. That is to say that the action of *ingesting a substance which will in fact harm him* is not the action he voluntarily chooses to do. Hence the state intervenes to protect him not from his own free and voluntary choices, but from his own ignorance.

Suppose however that the exchange goes as follows:

DR. DOE: I cannot prescribe drug X to you because it will do you physical harm.

MR. ROE: Exactly. That's just what I want. I want to harm myself.

In this case Roe *is* properly apprised of the facts. He suffers from no delusions or misconceptions. Yet his choice is so odd that there exists a reasonable presumption that he has been deprived somehow of the "full use of his reflecting faculty." It is because we know that the overwhelming majority of choices to inflict injury for its own sake on oneself are not fully voluntary that we are entitled to presume that the present choice too is not fully voluntary. If no further evidence of derangement, or illness, or severe depression, or unsettling excitation can be discovered, however, and the patient can convince an objective panel that his choice is voluntary (unlikely event!) and further if there are no third party interests, for example those of wife or family, that require protection, then our "voluntariness standard" would permit no further state constraint.

Now consider the third possibility:

DR. DOE: I cannot prescribe drug X to you because it is very likely to do you physical harm.

MR. ROE: I don't care if it causes me physical harm. I'll get a lot of pleasure first, so much pleasure in fact, that it is well worth running the risk of physical harm. If I must pay a price for my pleasure I am willing to do so.

This is perhaps the most troublesome case. Roe's choice is not patently irrational on its face. He may have a well thought-out philosophical hedonism as one of his profoundest convictions. He may have made a fundamental decision of principle committing himself to the intensely pleasurable, even if brief life. If no third party interests are directly involved, the state can hardly be permitted to declare his philosophical convictions unsound or "sick" and prevent him from practicing them, without assuming powers that it will inevitably misuse disastrously.

On the other hand, this case may be very little different from the preceding one, depending of course on what the exact facts are. If the drug is known to give only an hour's mild euphoria and then cause an immediate violently painful death, then the risks incurred appear so unreasonable as to create a powerful presumption of nonvoluntariness. The desire to commit suicide must always be presumed to be both nonvoluntary and harmful to others until shown otherwise. (Of course in some cases it *can* be shown otherwise.) On the other hand, drug X may be harmful in the way nicotine is now known to be harmful; twenty or thirty years of heavy use may create a grave risk of lung cancer or heart disease. Using the drug for pleasure merely, when the risks are of this kind, may be to run unreasonable risks, but that is no strong evidence of nonvoluntariness. Many perfectly normal, rational persons voluntarily choose to run precisely these risks for whatever pleasures they find in smoking.[8] The way for the state

---

[8] Perfectly rational men can have "unreasonable desires" as judged by other perfectly rational men, just as perfectly rational men (e.g. great philosophers) can hold "unreasonable beliefs" or doctrines as judged by other perfectly rational men. Particular unreasonableness, then, can hardly be strong evidence of general irrationality.

to assure itself that such practices are truly voluntary is continually to confront smokers with the ugly medical facts so that there is no escaping the knowledge of what the medical risks to health exactly are. Constant reminders of the hazards should be at every hand and with no softening of the gory details. The state might even be justified in using its taxing, regulatory, and persuasive powers to make smoking (and similar drug usage) more difficult or less attractive; but to prohibit it outright for everyone would be to tell the voluntary risk-taker that even his informed judgments of what is worthwhile are less reasonable than those of the state, and that therefore, he may not act on them. This is paternalism of the strong kind, unmediated by the voluntariness standard. As a principle of public policy, it has an acrid moral flavour, and creates serious risks of governmental tyranny.

IV

Another class of hard cases are those involving contracts in which one party agrees to restrict his own liberty in some respect. The most extreme case is that in which one party freely sells himself into slavery to another, perhaps in exchange for some benefit that is to be consumed before the period of slavery begins, perhaps for some reward to be bestowed upon some third party. Our point of departure will be Mill's classic treatment of the subject:

> In this and most other civilized countries . . . an engagement by which a person should sell himself, or allow himself to be sold, as a slave would be null and void, neither enforced by law nor by opinion. The ground for *thus limiting his power of voluntarily disposing of his own lot in life* is apparent, and is very clearly seen in this extreme case. The reason for not interfering, unless for the sake of others, with a person's voluntary acts is consideration for his liberty. His voluntary choice is evidence that what he so chooses is desirable, or at least endurable to him, and his good is on the whole best provided for by allowing him to take his own means of pursuing it. But by selling himself for a slave, he abdicates his liberty; he foregoes any future use of it beyond that single act. He therefore defeats, in his own case, the very purpose which is the justification of allowing him to dispose of himself. He is no longer free, but is thenceforth in a position which has no longer the presumption in its favour that would be afforded by his voluntarily remaining in it. The principle of freedom cannot require that he should be free not to be free.[9] [my italics]

It seems plain to me that Mill, in this one extreme case, has been driven to embrace the principle of paternalism. The "harm-to-others prin-

[9] Mill, *op. cit.*, p. 125.

ciple," as mediated by the *Volenti* maxim [10] would permit a competent, fully informed adult, who is capable of rational reflection and free of undue pressure, to be himself the judge of his own interests, no matter how queer or perverse his judgment may seem to others. There is, of course, always the presumption, and a very strong one indeed, that a person who elects to "sell" himself into slavery is either incompetent, unfree, or misinformed. Hence the state should require very strong evidence of voluntariness—elaborate tests, swearings, psychiatric testifying, waiting periods, public witnessing, and the like—before validating such contracts. Similar forms of official "making sure" are involved in marriages and wills, and slavery is even more serious a thing, not to be rashly undertaken. Undoubtedly, very few slavery contracts would survive such procedures, perhaps even none at all. It may be literally true that "no one in his right mind would sell himself into slavery," but if this is a truth it is not an *a priori* one but rather one that must be tested anew in each case by the application of independent, non-circular criteria of mental illness.

The supposition is at least intelligible, therefore, that every now and then a normal person in full possession of his faculties would voluntarily consent to permanent slavery. We can imagine any number of intelligible (if not attractive) motives for doing such a thing. A person might agree to become a slave in exchange for a million dollars to be delivered in advance to a loved one or to a worthy cause, or out of a religious conviction requiring a life of humility or penitence, or in payment for the prior enjoyment of some supreme benefit, as in the *Faust* legend. Mill, in the passage quoted above, would disallow such a contract no matter how certain it is that the agreement is fully voluntary, apparently on the ground that the permanent and irrevocable loss of freedom is such a great evil, and slavery so harmful a condition, that no one ought ever to be allowed to choose it, even voluntarily. Any person who thinks that he can be a gainer, in the end, from such an agreement, Mill implies, is simply wrong whatever his reasons, and can be known *a priori* to be wrong. Mill's earlier argument, if I understand it correctly, implies that a man should be permitted to mutilate his body, take harmful drugs, or commit suicide, provided only that his decision to do these things is voluntary and no other person will be directly and seriously harmed. But voluntarily acceding to slavery is too much for Mill to stomach. Here is an evil of another order, he seems to say; so the "harm to others" principle and the *Volenti* maxim come to their limiting point here, and paternalism in the strong sense (unmediated by the voluntariness test) must be invoked, if only for this one kind of case.

There are, of course, other ways of justifying the refusal to enforce slavery contracts. Some of these are derived from principles not acknowl-

---

[10] That is, the principle that prevention of harm to others is the sole ground for legal coercion, *and* that what is freely consented to is not to count as harm. These are Mill's primary normative principles in *On Liberty*.

edged in Mill's moral philosophy but which at least have the merit of being non-paternalistic. One might argue that what is odious in "harsh and unconscionable" contracts, even when they are voluntary on both sides, is not that a man should suffer the harm he freely risked, but rather that another party should "exploit" or take advantage of him. What is to be prevented, according to this line of argument, is one man exploiting the weakness, or foolishness, or recklessness of another. If a weak, foolish, or reckless man freely chooses to harm or risk harm to himself, that is all right, but that is no reason why another should be a party to it, or be permitted to benefit himself at the other's expense. (This principle, however, can only apply to extreme cases, else it will ban all competition.) Applied to voluntary slavery, the principle of non-exploitation might say that it isn't aimed at preventing one man from being a slave so much as preventing the other from being a slave-owner. The basic principle of argument here is a form of legal moralism. To own another human being, as one might own a table or a horse, is to be in a relation to him that is inherently immoral, and therefore properly forbidden by law. That, of course, is a line of argument that would be uncongenial to Mill, as would also be the Kantian argument that there is something in every man that is not his to alienate or dispose of, viz., the "humanity" that we are enjoined to "respect, whether in our own person or that of another." (It is worth noting, in passing, that Kant was an uncompromising foe of legal paternalism.)

There are still other ways of arguing against the recognition of slavery contracts, however, that are neither paternalistic (in the strong sense) nor inconsistent with Mill's primary principles. One might argue, for example, that weakening respect for human dignity (which is weak enough to begin with) can lead in the long run to harm of the most serious kind of nonconsenting parties. Or one might use a variant of the "public charge" argument commonly used in the nineteenth century against permitting even those without dependents to assume the risk of penury, illness, and starvation. We could let men gamble recklessly with their own lives, and then adopt inflexibly unsympathetic attitudes toward the losers. "They made their beds," we might say in the manner of some proper Victorians, "now let them sleep in them." But this would be to render the whole national character cold and hard. It would encourage insensitivity generally and impose an unfair economic penalty on those who possess the socially useful virtue of benevolence. Realistically, we just can't let men wither and die right in front our eyes; and if we intervene to help, as we inevitably must, it will cost us a lot of money. There are certain risks then of an *apparently* self-regarding kind that men cannot be permitted to run, if only for the sake of others who must either pay the bill or turn their backs on intolerable misery. This kind of argument, which can be applied equally well to the slavery case, is at least not *very* paternalistic.

Finally, a non-paternalistic opponent of voluntary slavery might argue (and this the argument to which I wish to give the most emphasis) that while exclusively self-regarding and fully voluntary "slavery contracts" are unobjectionable in principle, the legal machinery for testing voluntariness would be so cumbersome and expensive as to be impractical. Such procedures, after all, would have to be paid for out of tax revenues, the payment of which is mandatory for taxpayers. (And psychiatric consultant fees, among other things, are very high.) Even expensive legal machinery might be so highly fallible that there could be no sure way of determining voluntariness, so that some mentally ill people, for example, might become enslaved. Given the uncertain quality of evidence on these matters, and the enormous general presumption of nonvoluntariness, the state might be justified simply in *presuming nonvoluntariness conclusively in every case as the least risky course.* Some rational bargain-makers might be unfairly restrained under this policy, but on the alternative policy, even more people, perhaps, would become unjustly (mistakenly) enslaved, so that the evil prevented by the absolute prohibition would be greater than the occasional evil permitted. The principles involved in this argument are of the following two kinds: (1) It is better (say) that one hundred people be wrongly denied permission to be enslaved than that one be wrongly permitted, and (2) If we allow the institution of "voluntary slavery" at all, then no matter how stringent our tests of voluntariness are, it is likely that a good many persons *will* be wrongly permitted.

V

Mill's argument that leads to a (strong) paternalistic conclusion in this one case (slavery) employs only calculations of harms and benefits and the presumptive interpretation of *Volenti non fit inuria.* The notion of the inviolable sovereignty of the individual person over his own life does not appear in the argument. Liberty, he seems to tell us, is one good or benefit (though an extremely important one) among many, and its loss, one evil or harm (though an extremely serious one) among many types of harm. The aim of the law being to prevent harms of all kinds and from all sources, the law must take a very negative attitude toward forfeitures of liberty. Still, by and large, legal paternalism is an unacceptable policy because in attempting to impose upon a man an external conception of his own good, it is very likely to be self-defeating. "His voluntary choice is *evidence* (emphasis added) that what he so chooses is desirable, or at least endurable to him, and his good is *on the whole* (more emphasis added) best provided for by allowing him to take his own means of pursuing it." On the whole, then, the harm of coercion will outweigh any good it can produce for the person coerced. But when the person chooses slavery, the scales are clearly and necessarily tipped the other way, and the normal case against intervention is defeated. The ultimate appeal in this argument of Mill's is to the prevention of personal harms, so that permitting a person voluntarily to sell all his freedom would be to permit him to be "free not to be free," that is, free to inflict an *undeniable* harm upon himself, and this (Mill would say) is as paradoxical as permitting a legislature to vote by a majority to abolish majority rule. If, on the other hand, our ultimate principle expresses respect for a person's voluntary choice as *such*, even when it is the choice of a loss of freedom, we can remain adamantly opposed to paternalism even in the most extreme cases of self-harm, for we shall be committed to the view that there is something more important (even) than the avoidance of harm. The principle that shuts and locks the door leading to strong paternalism is that every man has a human right to "voluntarily dispose of his own lot in life" whatever the effect on his own net balance of benefits (including "freedom") and harms.

What does Mill say about less extreme cases of contracting away liberty? His next sentence (but one) is revealing: "These reasons, the force of which is so conspicuous in this particular case [slavery], are evidently of far wider application, yet a limit is everywhere set to them by the necessities of life, which continually require, not indeed that we should resign our freedom, but that we should consent to this and the other limitation of it." [11] Mill seems to say here that the same reasons that justify preventing the total and irrevocable relinquishment of freedom also militate against agreements to relinquish lesser amounts for lesser periods, but that unfortunately such agreements are sometimes rendered necessary by practical considerations. I would prefer to argue in the very opposite way, from the obvious permissibility of limited resignations of freedom to the permissibility in principle even of extreme forfeitures, except that in the latter case (slavery) the "necessities of life"—administrative complications in determining voluntariness, high expenses, and so on—forbid it.

Many perfectly reasonable employment contracts involve an agreement by the employee virtually to abandon his liberty to do as he pleases for a daily period, and even to do (within obvious limits) whatever his boss tells him, in exchange for a salary that the employer, in turn, is not at liberty to withhold. Sometimes, of course, the terms of such agreements are quite unfavourable to one of the parties, but when the agreements have been fairly bargained, with no undue pressure or deception (i.e., when they are fully voluntary) the courts enforce them even though lopsided in their distribution of benefits. Employment contracts, of course, are relatively easily broken; so in that respect they are altogether different from "slavery contracts." Perhaps better examples for our purposes, therefore, are contractual forfeitures of some extensive liberty for long periods of time or even forever. Certain contracts "in restraint of trade" are good examples. Consider contracts for the sale of the "good will" of a business:

> Manifestly, the buyer of a shop or of a practice will not be satisfied with what he buys unless he can persuade the seller to contract that he will

[11] *Loc. cit.*

not immediately set up a competing business next door and draw back most of his old clients or customers. Hence the buyer will usually request the seller to agree not to enter into competition with him. . . . Clauses of this kind are [also] often found in written contracts of employment, the employer requiring his employee to agree that he will not work for a competing employer after he leaves his present work.[12]

There are limits, both spatial and temporal, to the amount of liberty the courts will permit to be relinquished in such contracts. In general, it is considered reasonable for a seller to agree not to reopen a business in the same neighborhood or even the same city for several years, but not reasonable to agree not to re-enter the trade in a distant city, or for a period (say) of fifty years. The courts insist that the agreed-to-self-restraint be no wider "than is reasonably necessary to protect the buyer's purchase;" [13] but where the buyer's interests are very large the restraints may cover a great deal of space and time:

> For instance, in the leading case on the subject, a company which bought an armaments business for the colossal sum of £287,000 was held justified in taking a contract from the seller that he would not enter into competition with this business anywhere in the world for a period of twenty-five years. In view of the fact that the business was world-wide in its operations, and that its customers were mainly governments, any attempt by the seller to re-enter the armament business anywhere in the world might easily have affected the value of the buyer's purchase.[14]

The courts then do permit people to contract away extensive liberties for extensive periods of time in exchange for other benefits in reasonable bargains. Persons are even permitted to forfeit their future liberties in exchange for cash. Sometimes such transactions are perfectly reasonable, promoting the interests of both parties. Hence there would appear to be no good reason why they should be prohibited. Selling oneself into slavery is forfeiting *all* one's liberty for the rest of one's life in exchange for some prized benefit, and thus is only the extreme limiting case of contracting away liberty, but not altogether different in principle. Mill's argument that liberty is not the sort of good that by its very nature can properly be traded, then, does not seem a convincing way of arguing against voluntary slavery.

On the other hand, a court does not permit the seller of a business freely to forfeit any more liberty than is reasonable or necessary, and reserves to *itself* the right to determine the question of reasonableness. This restrictive policy *could* be an expression of paternalism designed to protect contracters from their own foolishness; but in fact it is based on an entirely different ground—the public interest in maintaining a competitive system

---

[12] P. S. Atiyah, *An Introduction to the Law of Contracts* (Oxford: Clarendon Press, 1961), p. 176.

[13] *Ibid.*, pp. 176–77.

[14] *Ibid.*, p. 177.

of free trade. The consumer's interests in having prices determined by a competitive marketplace rather than by uncontrolled monopolies requires that the state make it difficult for wealthy businessmen to buy off their competitors. Reasonable contracts "in restraint of trade" are a limited class of exceptions to a general policy designed to protect the economic interests of third parties (consumers) rather than the expression of an independent paternalistic policy of protecting free bargainers from their own mistakes.

There is still a final class of cases that deserve mention. These too are instances of persons voluntarily relinquishing liberties for other benefits; but they occur under such circumstances that prohibitions against them could not plausibly be justified except on paternalistic grounds, and usually not even on those grounds. I have in mind examples of persons who voluntarily "put themselves under the protection of rules" that deprive them and others too of liberties, when those liberties are unrewarding and burdensome. Suppose all upperclass undergraduates are given the option by their college to live either in private apartment buildings entirely unrestricted or else in college dormitories subject to the usual curfew and parietal rules. If one chooses the latter, he or she must be in after a certain hour, be quiet after a certain time, and so on, subject to certain sanctions. In "exchange" for these forfeitures, of course, one is assured that the other students too must be predictable in their habits, orderly, and quiet. The net gain for one's interests as a student over the "freer" private life could be considerable. Moreover, the curfew rule can be a great convenience for a girl who wishes to "date" boys very often, but who also wishes: (a) to get enough sleep for good health, (b) to remain efficient in her work, and (c) to be free of tension and quarrels when on dates over the question of when it is time to return home. If the rule requires a return at a certain time then neither the girl nor the boy has any choice in the matter, and what a boon that can be! To invoke these considerations is *not* to resort to paternalism unless they are employed in support of a prohibition. It is paternalism to *forbid* a student to live in a private apartment "for his own good" or "his own safety." It is not paternalism to *permit* him to live under the governance of coercive rules when he freely chooses to do so, and the other alternative is kept open to him. In fact it would be paternalism to deny a person the liberty of trading liberties for other benefits when he voluntarily chooses to do so.

VI

In summary: There are weak and strong versions of legal paternalism. The weak version is hardly an independent principle and can be entirely acceptable to the philosopher who, like Mill, is committed only to the "harm to others" principle as mediated by the *Volenti* maxim, where the latter is more than a mere presumption derived from generalizations about the causes of harm. According to the strong version of legal paternalism, the state is justified in protecting a person, against his will, from the harmful consequences even of his fully voluntary choices and undertakings. Strong paternalism is a departure from the "harm to others" principle and the strictly interpreted *Volenti* maxim that Mill should not, or need not, have taken in his discussion of contractual forfeitures of liberty. According to the weaker version of legal paternalism, a man can rightly be prevented from harming himself (when other interests are not directly involved) only if his intended action is substantially non-voluntary or can be presumed to be so in the absence of evidence to the contrary. The "harm to others" principle, after all, permits us to protect a man from the choices of other people; weak paternalism would permit us to protect him from "nonvoluntary choices," which, being the choices of no one at all, are no less foreign to him.

Selected Bibliography

BRANDEIS, LOUIS D., and CHARLES WARREN. "The Right to Privacy," *Harvard Law Review*, 4 (1890), 193.

GERETY, TOM. "Dedefining Privacy," *Harvard Civil Rights–Civil Liberties Law Review*, Vol. 12, no. 2 (1977), 233.

GERSTEIN, ROBERT. "Privacy and Self-Incrimination," *Ethics*, Vol. 80 (1970), 87.

GREENAWALT, KENT. "Privacy and Its Legal Protections," *Hastings Center Studies* (September 1974), 45.

PENNOCK, J. ROLAND, and JOHN W. CHAPMAN (eds.). *Privacy* (Nomos, Vol. XIII). New York: Atherton Press, 1971.

RACHELS, JAMES. "Why Privacy Is Important," *Philosophy and Public Affairs*, Vol. 4, no. 4 (1975), 323.

SCANLON, THOMAS. "Thomson on Privacy," *Philosophy and Public Affairs*, Vol. 4, no. 4 (1975), 315.

THOMSON, JUDITH. "The Right to Privacy," *Philosophy and Public Affairs*, Vol. 4, no. 4 (1975), 295.

WASSERSTROM, RICHARD (ed.). *Morality and the Law*. Belmont, Calif.: Wadsworth Publishing Co., Inc., 1970.

WESTIN, ALAN. *Privacy and Freedom*. New York: Atheneum Publishers, 1967.

PUNISHMENT

JOHN RAWLS

Two Concepts of Rules

In this paper I want to show the importance of the distinction between justifying a practice [1] and justifying a particular action falling under it, and I want to explain the logical basis of this distinction and how it is possible to miss its significance. While the distinction has frequently been made,[2]

Reprinted from *The Philosophical Review*, Vol. 6 (1955), 3–13. Reprinted by permission of the author and *The Philosophical Review*.

[1] I use the word "practice" throughout as a sort of technical term meaning any form of activity specified by a system of rules which defines offices, roles, moves, penalties, defenses, and so on, and which gives the activity its structure. As examples one may think of games and rituals, trials and parliaments.

[2] The distinction is central to Hume's discussion of justice in *A Treatise of Human Nature*, bk. III, pt. 11, esp. secs. 2–4. It is clearly stated by John Austin in the second lecture of *Lectures on Jurisprudence* (4th ed.; London, 1873), I, 116ff. (1st ed., 1832). Also it may be argued that J. S. Mill took it for granted in *Utilitarianism*; on this point cf. J. O. Urmson, "The Interpretation of the Moral Philosophy of J. S. Mill," *Philosophical Quarterly*, Vol. III (1953). In addition to the arguments given by Urmson there are several clear statements of the

and is now becoming commonplace, there remains the task of explaining the tendency either to overlook it altogether, or to fail to appreciate its importance.

To show the importance of the distinction I am going to defend utilitarianism against those objections which have traditionally been made against it in connection with punishment and the obligation to keep promises. I hope to show that if one uses the distinction in question then one can state utilitarianism in a way which makes it a much better explication of our considered moral judgments than these traditional objections would seem to admit.[3] Thus the importance of the distinction is shown by the way it strengthens the utilitarian view regardless of whether that view is completely defensible or not.

To explain how the significance of the distinction may be overlooked, I am going to discuss two conceptions of rules. One of these conceptions conceals the importance of distinguishing between the justification of a rule or practice and the justification of a particular action falling under it. The other conception makes it clear why this distinction must be made and what is its logical basis.

I

The subject of punishment, in the sense of attaching legal penalties to the violation of legal rules, has always been a troubling moral question.[4] The trouble about it has not been that people disagree as to whether or not punishment is justifiable. Most people have held that, freed from certain abuses, it is an acceptable institution. Only a few have rejected punishment entirely, which is rather surprising when one considers all that can be said

---

distinction in *A System of Logic* (8th ed.; London, 1872), bk. VI, ch. xii pars. 2, 3, 7. The distinction is fundamental to J. D. Mabbott's important paper, "Punishment," *Mind*, n.s., vol. XLVIII (April, 1939). More recently the distinction has been stated with particular emphasis by S. E. Toulmin in *The Place of Reason in Ethics* (Cambridge, 1950), see esp. ch. xi, where it plays a major part in his account of moral reasoning. Toulmin doesn't explain the basis of the distinction, nor how one might overlook its importance, as I try to in this paper, and in my review of his book (*Philosophical Review*, Vol. LX [October, 1951]), as some of my criticisms show, I failed to understand the force of it. See also H. D. Aiken, "The Levels of Moral Discourse," *Ethics*, vol. LXII (1952), A. M. Quinton, "Punishment," *Analysis*, vol. XIV (June, 1954), and P. H. Nowell-Smith, *Ethics* (London, 1954), pp. 236–239, 271–273.

[3] On the concept of explication see the author's paper *Philosophical Review*, Vol. LX (April, 1951).

[4] While this paper was being revised, Quinton's appeared; footnote 2 supra. There are several respects in which my remarks are similar to his. Yet as I consider some further questions and rely on somewhat different arguments, I have retained the discussion of punishment and promises together as two test cases for utilitarianism.

against it. The difficulty is with the justification of punishment: various arguments for it have been given by moral philosophers, but so far none of them has won any sort of general acceptance; no justification is without those who detest it. I hope to show that the use of the aforementioned distinction enables one to state the utilitarian view in a way which allows for the sound points of its critics.

For our purposes we may say that there are two justifications of punishment. What we may call the retributive view is that punishment is justified on the grounds that wrongdoing merits punishment. It is morally fitting that a person who does wrong should suffer in proportion to his wrongdoing. That a criminal should be punished follows from his guilt, and the severity of the appropriate punishment depends on the depravity of his act. The state of affairs where a wrongdoer suffers punishment is morally better than the state of affairs where he does not; and it is better irrespective of any of the consequences of punishing him.

What we may call the utilitarian view holds that on the principle that bygones are bygones and that only future consequences are material to present decisions, punishment is justifiable only by reference to the probable consequences of maintaining it as one of the devices of the social order. Wrongs committed in the past are, as such, not relevant considerations for deciding what to do. If punishment can be shown to promote effectively the interest of society it is justifiable, otherwise it is not.

I have stated these two competing views very roughly to make one feel the conflict between them: one feels the force of *both* arguments and one wonders how they can be reconciled. From my introductory remarks it is obvious that the resolution which I am going to propose is that in this case one must distinguish between justifying a practice as a system of rules to be applied and enforced, and justifying a particular action which falls under these rules; utilitarian arguments are appropriate with regard to questions about practices, while retributive arguments fit the application of particular rules to particular cases.

We might try to get clear about this distinction by imagining how a father might answer the question of his son. Suppose the son asks, "Why was J put in jail yesterday?" The father answers, "Because he robbed the bank at B. He was duly tried and found guilty. That's why he was put in jail yesterday." But suppose the son had asked a different question, namely, "Why do people put other people in jail?" Then the father might answer, "To protect good people from bad people" or "To stop people from doing things that would make it uneasy for all of us; for otherwise we wouldn't be able to go to bed at night and sleep in peace." There are two very different questions here. One question emphasizes the proper name: it asks why J was punished rather than someone else, or it asks what he was punished for. The other question asks why we have the institution of punishment: why do people punish one another rather than, say, always forgiving one another?

Thus the father says in effect that a particular man is punished, rather than some other man, because he is guilty, and he is guilty because he broke the law (past tense). In his case the law looks back, the judge looks back, the jury looks back, and a penalty is visited upon him for something he did. That a man is to be punished, and what his punishment is to be, is settled by its being shown that he broke the law and that the law assigns that penalty for the violation of it.

On the other hand we have the institution of punishment itself, and recommend and accept various changes in it, because it is thought by the (ideal) legislator and by those to whom the law applies that, as a part of a system of law impartially applied from case to case arising under it, it will have the consequence, in the long run, of furthering the interests of society.

One can say, then, that the judge and the legislator stand in different positions and look in different directions: one to the past, the other to the future. The justification of what the judge does, qua judge, sounds like the retributive view; the justification of what the (ideal) legislator does, qua legislator, sounds like the utilitarian view. Thus both views have a point (this is as it should be since intelligent and sensitive persons have been on both sides of the argument); and one's initial confusion disappears once one sees that these views apply to persons holding different offices with different duties, and situated differently with respect to the system of rules that make up the criminal law.[5]

One might say, however, that the utilitarian view is more fundamental since it applies to a more fundamental office, for the judge carries out the legislator's will so far as he can determine it. Once the legislator decides to have laws and to assign penalties for their violation (as things are there must be both the law and the penalty) an institution is set up which involves a retributive conception of particular cases. It is part of the concept of the criminal law as a system of rules that the application and enforcement of these rules in particular cases should be justifiable by arguments of a retributive character. The decision whether or not to use law rather than some other mechanism of social control, and the decision as to what laws to have and what penalties to assign, may be settled by utilitarian arguments, but if one decides to have laws then one has decided on something whose working in particular cases is retributive in form.[6]

The answer, then, to the confusion engendered by the two views of punishment is quite simple: one distinguishes two offices, that of the judge and that of the legislator, and one distinguishes their different stations with respect to the system of rules which make up the law; and then one notes that the different sorts of considerations which would usually be

[5] Note the fact that different sorts of arguments are suited to different offices. One way of taking the differences between ethical theories is to regard them as accounts of the reasons expected in different offices.

[6] In this connection see Mabbott, op. cit., pp. 163–164.

offered as reasons for what is done under the cover of these offices can be paired off with the competing justifications of punishment. One reconciles the two views by the time-honored device of making them apply to different situations.

But can it really be this simple? Well, this answer allows for the apparent intent of each side. Does a person who advocates the retributive view necessarily advocate, as an *institution*, legal machinery whose essential purpose is to set up and preserve a correspondence between moral turpitude and suffering? Surely not.[7] What retributionists have rightly insisted upon is that no man can be punished unless he is guilty, that is, unless he has broken the law. Their fundamental criticism of the utilitarian account is that, as they interpret it, it sanctions an innocent person's being punished (if one may call it that) for the benefit of society.

On the other hand, utilitarians agree that punishment is to be inflicted only for the violation of law. They regard this much as understood from the concept of punishment itself.[8] The point of the utilitarian account concerns the institution as a system of rules: utilitarianism seeks to limit its use by declaring it justifiable only if it can be shown to foster effectively the good of society. Historically it is a protest against the indiscriminate and ineffective use of the criminal law.[9] It seeks to dissuade us from assigning to penal institutions the improper, if not sacrilegious, task of matching suffering with moral turpitude. Like others, utilitarians want penal institutions designed so that, as far as humanly possible, only those who break the law run afoul of it. They hold that no official should have discretionary power to inflict penalties whenever he thinks it for the benefit of society; for on utilitarian grounds an institution granting such power could not be justified.[10]

[7] On this point see Sir David Ross, *The Right and the Good* (Oxford, 1930), pp. 57–60.

[8] See Hobbes's definition of punishment in *Leviathan*, ch. xxviii; and Bentham's definition in *The Principle of Morals and Legislation*, ch. xii, par. 36, ch. xv, par. 28, and in *The Rationale of Punishment*, (London, 1830), bk. I, ch. i. They could agree with Bradley that: "Punishment is punishment only when it is deserved. We pay the penalty, because we owe it, and for no other reason; and if punishment is inflicted for any other reason whatever than because it is [8] merited by wrong, it is a gross immorality, a crying injustice, an abominable crime, and not what it pretends to be." *Ethical Studies* (2nd ed.; Oxford, 1927), 26–27. Certainly by definition it isn't what it pretends to be. The innocent can only be punished by mistake; deliberate "punishment" of the innocent necessarily involves fraud.

[9] Cf. Leon Radzinowicz, *A History of English Criminal Law: The Movement for Reform 1750–1833* (London, 1948), esp. ch. xi on Bentham.

[10] Bentham discusses how corresponding to a punitory provision of a criminal law there is another provision which stands to it as an antagonist and which needs a name as much as the punitory. He calls it, as one might expect, the *anaetiosostic*, and of it he says: "The punishment of guilt is the object of the former one: the preservation of innocence that of the latter." In the same connection he asserts

The suggested way of reconciling the retributive and the utilitarian justifications of punishment seems to account for what both sides have wanted to say. There are, however, two further questions which arise, and I shall devote the remainder of this section to them.

First, will not a difference of opinion as to the proper criterion of just law make the proposed reconciliation unacceptable to retributionists? Will they not question whether, if the utilitarian principle is used as the criterion, it follows that those who have broken the law are guilty in a way which satisfies their demand that those punished deserve to be punished? To answer this difficulty, suppose that the rules of the criminal law are justified on utilitarian grounds (it is only for laws that meet his criterion that the utilitarian can be held responsible). Then it follows that the actions which the criminal law specifies as offenses are such that, if they were tolerated, terror and alarm would spread in society. Consequently, retributionists can only deny that those who are punished deserve to be punished if they deny that such actions are wrong. This they will not want to do.

The second question is whether utilitarianism doesn't justify too much. One pictures it as an engine of justification which, if consistently adopted, could be used to justify cruel and arbitrary institutions. Retributionists may be supposed to concede that utilitarians *intend* to reform the law and to make it more humane; that utilitarians do not *wish* to justify any such thing as punishment of the innocent; and that utilitarians may appeal to the fact that punishment presupposes guilt in the sense that by punishment one understands an institution attaching penalties to the infraction of legal rules, and therefore that it is logically absurd to suppose that utilitarians in justifying *punishment* might also have justified punishment (if we may call it that) of the innocent. The real question, however, is whether the utilitarian, in justifying punishment, hasn't used arguments which commit him to accepting the infliction of suffering on innocent persons if it is for the good of society (whether or not one calls this punishment). More generally, isn't the utilitarian committed in principle to accepting many practices which he, as a morally sensitive person, wouldn't want to accept? Retributionists are inclined to hold that there is no way to stop the utilitarian principle from justifying too much except by adding to it a principle which distributes certain rights to individuals. Then the amended criterion is not the greatest benefit of society *simpliciter*, but the greatest benefit of society subject to the constraint that no one's rights may be violated. Now while I think that the classical utilitarians proposed a

---

that it is never thought fit to give the judge the option of deciding whether a thief (that is, a person whom he believes to be a thief, for the judge's belief is what the question must always turn upon) should hang or not, and so the law writes the provision: "The judge shall not cause a thief to be hanged unless he have been duly convicted and sentenced in course of law" (*The Limits of Jurisprudence Defined*, ed. C. W. Everett [New York, 1945], pp. 238–239).

criterion of this more complicated sort, I do not want to argue that point here.[11] What I want to show is that there is *another* way of preventing the utilitarian principle from justifying too much, or at least of making it much less likely to do so: namely, by stating utilitarianism in a way which accounts for the distinction between the justification of an institution and the justification of a particular action falling under it.

I begin by defining the institution of punishment as follows: a person is said to suffer punishment whenever he is legally deprived of some of the normal rights of a citizen on the ground that he has violated a rule of law, the violation having been established by trial according to the due process of law, provided that the deprivation is carried out by the recognized legal authorities of the state, that the rule of law clearly specifies both the offense and the attached penalty, that the courts construe statutes strictly, and that the statute was on the books prior to the time of the offense.[12] This definition specifies what I shall understand by punishment. The question is whether utilitarian arguments may be found to justify institutions widely different from this and such as one would find cruel and arbitrary.

This question is best answered, I think, by taking up a particular accusation. Consider the following from Carritt:

> . . . the utilitarian must hold that we are justified in inflicting pain always and only to prevent worse pain or bring about greater happiness. This, then, is all we need to consider in so-called punishment, which must be purely preventive. But if some kind of very cruel crime becomes common, and none of the criminals can be caught, it might be highly expedient, as an example, to hang an innocent man, if a charge against him could be so framed that he were universally thought guilty; indeed this would only fail to be an ideal instance of utilitarian 'punishment' because the victim himself would not have been so likely as a real felon to commit such a crime in the future; in all other respects it would be perfectly deterrent and therefore felicific.[13]

Carritt is trying to show that there are occasions when a utilitarian argument would justify taking an action which would be generally condemned; and thus that utilitarianism justifies too much. But the failure of Carritt's argument lies in the fact that he makes no distinction between the justification of the general system of rules which constitutes penal institutions and the justification of particular applications of these rules to particular cases by the various officials whose job it is to administer them. This becomes perfectly clear when one asks who the "we" are of whom Carritt speaks. Who is this who has a sort of absolute authority on particular occasions to decide that an innocent man shall be "punished" if everyone can be convinced that he is guilty? Is this person the legislator, or the

[11] By the classical utilitarians I understand Hobbes, Hume, Bentham, J. S. Mill, and Sidgwick.
[12] All these features of punishment are mentioned by Hobbes; cf. *Leviathan*, ch. xxviii.
[13] *Ethical and Political Thinking* (Oxford, 1947), p. 65.

judge, or the body of private citizens, or what? It is utterly crucial to know who is to decide such matters, and by what authority, for all of this must be written into the rules of the institution. Until one knows these things one doesn't know what the institution is whose justification is being challenged; and as the utilitarian principle applies to the institution one doesn't know whether it is justifiable on utilitarian grounds or not.

Once this is understood it is clear what the countermove to Carritt's argument is. One must describe more carefully what the *institution* is which his example suggests, and then ask oneself whether or not it is likely that having this institution would be for the benefit of society in the long run. One must not content oneself with the vague thought that, when it's a question of *this* case, it would be a good thing if *somebody* did something even if an innocent person were to suffer.

Try to imagine, then, an institution (which we may call "telishment") which is such that the officials set up by it have authority to arrange a trial for the condemnation of an innocent man whenever they are of the opinion that doing so would be in the best interests of society. The discretion of officials is limited, however, by the rule that they may not condemn an innocent man to undergo such an ordeal unless there is, at the time, a wave of offenses similar to that with which they charge him and telish him for. We may imagine that the officials having the discretionary authority are the judges of the higher courts in consultation with the chief of police, the minister of justice, and a committee of the legislature.

Once one realizes that one is involved in setting up an *institution*, one sees that the hazards are very great. For example, what check is there on the officials? How is one to tell whether or not their actions are authorized? How is one to limit the risks involved in allowing such systematic deception? How is one to avoid giving anything short of complete discretion to the authorities to telish anyone they like? In addition to these considerations, it is obvious that people will come to have a very different attitude towards their penal system when telishment is adjoined to it. They will be uncertain as to whether a convicted man has been punished or telished. They will wonder whether or not they should feel sorry for him. They will wonder whether the same fate won't at any time fall on them. If one pictures how such an institution would actually work, and the enormous risks involved in it, it seems clear that it would serve no useful purpose. A utilitarian justification for this institution is most unlikely.

It happens in general that as one drops off the defining features of punishment one ends up with an institution whose utilitarian justification is highly doubtful. One reason for this is that punishment works like a kind of price system: by altering the prices one has to pay for the performance of actions it supplies a motive for avoiding some actions and doing others. The defining features are essential if punishment is to work in this way; so that an institution which lacks these features, e.g., an institution which is set up to "punish" the innocent, is likely to have about as much point as a price system (if one may call it that) where the prices of things change at random from day to day and one learns the price of something after one has agreed to buy it.[14]

If one is careful to apply the utilitarian principle to the institution which is to authorize particular actions, then there is *less* danger of its justifying too much. Carritt's example gains plausibility by its indefiniteness and by its concentration on the particular case. His argument will only hold if it can be shown that there are utilitarian arguments which justify an institution whose publicly ascertainable offices and powers are such as to permit officials to exercise that kind of discretion in particular cases. But the requirement of having to build the arbitrary features of the particular decision into the institutional practice makes the justification much less likely to go through.

BARBARA WOOTTON

The Problem of the Mentally Abnormal Offender

The problem of the mentally abnormal offender raises in a particularly acute form the question of the primary function of the courts. If that function is conceived as punitive, mental abnormality must be related to guilt;

Reprinted from Barbara Wootton, *Crime and the Criminal Law* (London: Sweet & Maxwell Ltd, 1963), pp. 58–66, 78–84, with the permission of the author and the publisher. Some footnotes omitted; original footnote numbering retained.

[14] The analogy with the price system suggests an answer to the question how utilitarian considerations insure that punishment is proportional to the offense. It is interesting to note that Sir David Ross, after making the distinction between justifying a penal law and justifying a particular application of it, and after stating that utilitarian considerations have a large place in determining the former, still holds back from accepting the utilitarian justification of punishment on the grounds that justice requires that punishment be proportional to the offense, and that utilitarianism is unable to account for this. Cf. *The Right and the Good* (Oxford: Clarendon Press, 1930), pp. 61–62. I do not claim that utilitarianism can account for this requirement as Sir David might wish, but it happens, nevertheless, that if utilitarian considerations are followed penalties will be proportional to offenses in this sense: the order of offenses according to seriousness can be paired off with the order of penalties according to severity. Also the absolute level of penalties will be as low as possible. This follows from the assumption that people are rational (i.e., that they are able to take into account the "prices" the

for a severely subnormal offender must be less blameworthy, and ought therefore to incur a less severe punishment, than one of greater intelligence who has committed an otherwise similar crime, even though he may well be a worse risk for the future. But from the preventive standpoint it is this future risk which matters, and the important question to be asked is not: does his abnormality mitigate or even obliterate his guilt? but, rather, is he a suitable subject for medical, in preference to any other, type of treatment? In short, the punitive and the preventive are respectively concerned the one with culpability and the other with treatability.

In keeping with its traditional obsession with the concept of guilt, English criminal law has, at least until lately, been chiefly concerned with the effect of mental disorder upon culpability. In recent years, however, the idea that an offender's mental state might also have a bearing on his treatability has begun to creep into the picture—with the result that the two concepts now lie somewhat uneasily side by side in what has become a very complex pattern.

Under the present law there are at least six distinct legal formulae under which an accused person's mental state may be put in issue in a criminal case. First, he may be found unfit to plead, in which case of course no trial takes place at all, unless and until he is thought to have sufficiently recovered. Second, on a charge of murder (and theoretically in other cases also) a defendant may be found to be insane within the terms of the M'Naughten Rules, by the illogical verdict of guilty but insane which, to be consistent with the normal use of the term guilt, ought to be revised to read—as it once did—"not guilty on the ground of insanity." Third, a person accused of murder can plead diminished responsibility under section 2 of the Homicide Act, in which case, if this defense succeeds, a verdict of manslaughter will be substituted for one of murder.

Up to this point it is, I think, indisputable that it is the relation between the accused's mental state and his culpability or punishability which is in issue. Obviously a man who cannot be tried cannot be punished. Again, one who is insane may have to be deprived of his liberty in the interests of the public safety, but, since an insane person is not held to be blameworthy in the same way as one who is in full possession of his faculties, the institution to which he is committed must be of a medical not a penal character; and for the same reason, he must not be hung if found guilty on a capital charge. So also under the Homicide Act a defence of diminished responsibility opens the door to milder punishments than the sentences of death and life imprisonment which automatically follow the respective verdicts of capital and non-capital murder; and the fact that diminished responsibility is conceived in terms of reduced culpability, and

---

state puts on actions), the utilitarian rule that a penal system should provide a motive for preferring the less serious offense, and the principle that punishment as such is an evil. All this was carefully worked out by Bentham in *The Principles of Morals and Legislation*, chs. xiii–xv.

not as indicative of the need for medical treatment, is further illustrated by the fact that in less than half the cases in which this defence has succeeded since the courts have had power to make hospital orders under the Mental Health Act, have such orders actually been made.[1] In the great majority of all the successful cases under section 2 of the Homicide Act a sentence of imprisonment has been imposed, the duration of this ranging from life to a matter of not more than a few months. Moreover, the Court of Criminal Appeal has indicated[2] approval of such sentences on the ground that a verdict of manslaughter based on diminished responsibility implies that a "residue of responsibility" rests on the accused person and that this "residue of criminal intent" may be such as to deserve punishment—a judgment which surely presents a sentencing judge with a problem of nice mathematical calculation as to the appropriate measure of punishment.

Under the Mental Health Act of 1959, however, the notion of reduced culpability begins to be complicated by the alternative criterion of treatability. Section 60 of that Act provides the fourth and fifth of my six formulae. Under the first subsection of this section an offender who is convicted at a higher court (or at a magistrates' court if his offence is one which carries liability to imprisonment) may be compulsorily detained in hospital, or made subject to a guardianship order, if the court is satisfied, on the evidence of two doctors (one of whom must have special experience in the diagnosis or treatment of mental disorders) that this is in all the circumstances the most appropriate way of dealing with him. In the making of such orders emphasis is clearly on the future, not on the past: the governing consideration is not whether the offender deserves to be punished, but whether in fact medical treatment is likely to succeed. No sooner have we said this, however, than the old concept of culpability rears its head again. For a hospital order made by a higher court may be accompanied by a restriction order of either specified or indefinite duration, during the currency of which the patient may only be discharged on the order of the Home Secretary; and a magistrates' court also, although it has no similar power itself to make a restriction order, may commit an offender to sessions to be dealt with, if it is of the opinion that, having regard to the nature of the offence, the antecedents of the offender and the risk of his committing further offences if set at liberty, a hospital order should be accompanied by a restriction order.

The restriction order is thus professedly designed as a protection to the public; but a punitive element also, I think, still lingers in it. For if the sole object was the protection of the public against the premature discharge of a mentally disordered dangerous offender, it could hardly be argued that the court's prediction of the safe moment for release, perhaps years ahead, is likely to be more reliable than the judgment at the appro-

[1] House of Lords Debates, May 1, 1963, col. 174.
[2] R. v. *James* [1961] Crim.L.R. 842.

priate time of the hospital authorities who will have had the patient continuously under their surveillance.[3] If their purpose is purely protective all orders ought surely to be of indefinite duration, and the fact that this is not so suggests that they are still tainted with the tariff notion of sentencing —that is to say, with the idea that a given offence "rates" a certain period of loss of liberty. Certainly, on any other interpretation the judges who have imposed restriction orders on offenders to run for ten or more years must credit themselves with truly remarkable powers of medical prognosis. In fairness, however, it should be said that the practice of imposing indefinite rather than fixed term orders now seems to be growing.

So, too, with the fifth of my formulae, which is to be found in a later subsection of section 60 of the same Act. Under this, an offender who is charged before a magistrates' court with an offence for which he could be imprisoned, may be made the subject of a hospital or guardianship order *without being convicted*, provided that the court is satisfied that he did the act or made the omission of which he is accused. This power, however (which is itself an extended version of section 24 of the Criminal Justice Act, 1948, and has indeed a longer statutory history), may only be exercised if the accused is diagnosed as suffering from either mental illness or severe subnormality. It is not available in the case of persons suffering from either of the two other forms of mental disorder recognised by the Act, namely psychopathy, or simple, as distinct from severe, subnormality. And why not? One can only presume that the reason for this restriction is the fear that in cases in which only moderate mental disorder is diagnosed, or in which the diagnosis is particularly difficult and a mistake might easily be made, an offender might escape the punishment that he deserved. Even though no hospital or guardianship order can be made unless the court is of opinion that this is the "most suitable" method of disposing of the case, safeguards against the risk that this method might be used for the offender who really deserved to be punished are still written into the law.

One curious ambiguity in this provision, however, deserves notice at this stage. Before a hospital order is made the court must be satisfied that the accused "did the act, or made the omission with which he is charged." Yet what, one may ask, is the meaning, in this context, of "the act"? Except in the case of crimes of absolute liability, a criminal charge does not relate to a purely physical action. It relates to a physical action accompanied by a guilty mind or malicious intention. If then a person is so mentally disordered as to be incapable of forming such an intention, is he not strictly incapable of performing the act with which he is charged? The

[3] One curious feature of this provision is the fact that a hospital order can apparently be made on a diagnosis of mental disorder, even if the disorder has no connection with the offence. See the Court of Criminal Appeal's judgment in the unsuccessful appeal of R. v. *Hatt* [1962] Crim.L.R. 647) in which the appellant claimed that his predilection for unnecessary surgical operations had no connection with his no less fervent passion for making off with other people's cars.

point seems to have been raised when the 1948 Criminal Justice Bill was in Committee in the House of Commons, but it was not pursued.[4] Such an interpretation would, of course, make nonsense of the section, and one must presume, therefore, that the words "the act" must be construed to refer solely to the prohibited physical action, irrespective of the actor's state of mind. But in that case the effect of this subsection would seem to be to transfer every type of crime, in the case of persons of severely disordered mentality, to the category of offences of absolute liability. In practice little use appears to be made of this provision (and in my experience few magistrates are aware of its existence); but there would seem to be an important principle here, potentially capable, as I hope to suggest later, of wider application.

The last of my six formulae, which, however, antedates all the others, stands in a category by itself. It is to be found in section 4 of the Criminal Justice Act of 1948, under which a court may make mental treatment (residential or non-residential) a condition of a probation order, provided that the offender's mental condition is "such as requires and as may be susceptible to treatment," but is not such as to justify his being in the language of that day certified as "of unsound mind" or "mentally defective." Such a provision represents a very whole-hearted step in the direction of accepting the criterion of treatability. For, although those to whom this section may be applied must be deemed to be guilty—in the sense that they have been convicted of offences involving *mens rea*—the only question to be decided is that of their likely response to medical or other treatment. Moreover, apart from the exclusion of insanity or mental defect, no restriction is placed on the range of diagnostic categories who may be required to submit to mental treatment under this section, although as always in the case of a probation order imposed on adults, the order cannot be made without the probationer's own consent. Nor is any reference anywhere made or even implied as to the effect of their mental condition upon their culpability. It is of interest, too, that, in practice, the use of these provisions has not been confined to what are often regarded as "pathological" crimes. Dr. Grünhut who made a study of cases to which the section was applied in 1953 [5] found that out of a total of 636 probationers, 275 had committed offences against property, 216 sexual offences, ninety-seven offences of violence (other than sexual) and forty-eight other types of offence. Some of the property crimes had, it is true, "an apparently pathological background," but no less than 48 per cent were classified as "normal" acquisitive thefts.

All these modifications in the criminal process in the case of the mentally abnormal offender thus tend (with the possible exception of the 1948 Act) to treat such abnormality as in greater or less degree exculpatory.

[4] House of Commons Standing Committee A, February 12, 1948, col. 1054.
[5] Grünhut, M., *Probation and Mental Treatment* (to be published in the Library of Criminology).

Their purpose is not just to secure that medical treatment should be provided for any offender likely to benefit from this, but rather to guard against the risk that the mentally disordered will be unjustly punished. Their concern with treatability, where it occurs, is in effect consequential rather than primary: the question—can the doctors help him? follows, if at all, upon a negative answer to the question: is he really to blame?

Nowhere is this more conspicuous than in section 2 of the Homicide Act; and it was indeed from a study of the operation of that section that I was led nearly four years ago to the conclusion that this was the wrong approach; that any attempt to distinguish between wickedness and mental abnormality was doomed to failure; and that the only solution for the future was to allow the concept of responsibility to "wither away" and to concentrate instead on the problem of the choice of treatment, without attempting to assess the effect of mental peculiarities or degrees of culpability. That opinion was based on a study of the files of some seventy-three cases in which a defence of diminished responsibility had been raised,[6] which were kindly made available by the Home Office. To these have since been added the records of another 126 cases, the two series together covering the five and a half years from the time that the Act came into force down to mid-September 1962.

. . .

I have dealt at some length with our experience of diminished responsibility cases under the Homicide Act because taken together, the three facts, first, that under this Act questions of responsibility have to be decided before and not after conviction; second, that these questions fall to be decided by juries; and, third, that the charges involved are of the utmost gravity, have caused the relationship of responsibility to culpability to be explored with exceptional thoroughness in this particular context. But the principles involved are by no means restricted to the narrow field of charges of homicide. They have a far wider applicability, and are indeed implicit also in section 60 of the Mental Health Act. Unfortunately, up till now, and pending completion of the researches upon which I understand that Mr. Nigel Walker and his colleagues at Oxford are engaged, little is known of the working of this section. But it seems inevitable that if in any case a convicted person wished (as might well happen) to challenge the diagnosis of mental disorder which must precede the making of a hospital order, he would quickly be plunged into arguments about subnormality and psychopathy closely parallel to those which occupy so many hours of diminished responsibility trials.

At the same time the proposal that we should bypass, or disregard, the concept of responsibility is only too easily misunderstood; and I pro-

---

[6] Wootton, Barbara, "Diminished Responsibility: A Layman's View" (1960) 76 *Law Quarterly Review* 224.

pose, therefore, to devote the remainder of this lecture to an attempt to meet some of the criticisms which have been brought against this proposal, to clarify just what it does or does not mean in the present context and to examine its likely implications.

First, it is to be observed that the term "responsibility" is here used in a restricted sense, much narrower than that which it often carries in ordinary speech. The measure of a person's responsibility for his actions is perhaps best defined in the words that I used earlier in terms of his capacity to act otherwise than as he did. A person may be described as totally irresponsible if he is wholly incapable of controlling his actions, and as being in a state of diminished responsibility if it is abnormally difficult for him to control them. Responsibility in this restricted sense is not to be confused with the sense in which a man is often said to be responsible for an action if he has in fact committed it. The questions: who broke the window? and could the man who broke the window have prevented himself from doing so? are obviously quite distinct. To dismiss the second as unanswerable in no way diminishes the importance of finding an answer to the first. Hence the primary job of the courts in determining by whom a forbidden act has actually been committed is wholly unaffected by any proposal to disregard the question of responsibility in the narrower sense. Indeed the only problem that arises here is linguistic, inasmuch as one is accustomed to say that X was "responsible" for breaking the window when the intention is to convey no more than that he did actually break it. Another word is needed here (and I must confess that I have not succeeded in finding one) to describe "responsibility" for doing an action as distinct from the capacity to refrain from doing it. "Accountable" has sometimes been suggested, but its usage in this sense is often awkward. "Instrumental" is perhaps better, though one could still wish for an adjective such perhaps as "agential" derived from the word "agent." However, all that matters is to keep firmly in mind that responsibility in the present context has nothing to do with the authorship of an act, only with the state of mind of its author.

In the second place, to discard the notion of responsibility does not mean that the mental condition of an offender ceases to have any importance, or that psychiatric considerations become irrelevant. The difference is that they become relevant, not to the question of determining the measure of his culpability, but to the choice of the treatment most likely to be effective in discouraging him from offending again; and even if these two aspects of the matter may be related, this is not to be dismissed as a distinction without a difference. The psychiatrist to whom it falls to advise as to the probable response of an offender to medical treatment no doubt has his own opinion as to the man's responsibility or capacity for self-control; and doubtless also those opinions are a factor in his judgment as to the outlook for medical treatment, or as to the probability that the offence will be repeated. But these are, and must remain, matters of opinion, "incapable," in Lord Parker's words, "of scientific proof." Opinions as to treatability, on the other hand, as well as predictions as to the likelihood of further offences can be put to the test of experience and so proved right or wrong. And by systematic observation of that experience, it is reasonable to expect that a body of knowledge will in time be built up, upon which it will be possible to draw, in the attempt to choose the most promising treatment in future cases.

Next, it must be emphasised that nothing in what has been said involves acceptance of a deterministic view of human behavior. It is an indisputable fact of experience that human beings do respond predictably to various stimuli—whether because they choose to or because they can do no other it is not necessary to inquire. There are cases in which medical treatment works: there are cases in which it fails. Equally there are cases in which deterrent penalties appear to deter those upon whom they are imposed from committing further offences; and there are cases in which they do not. Once the criminal law is conceived as an instrument of crime prevention, it is these facts which demand attention, and from which we can learn to improve the efficiency of that instrument; and the question whether on any occasion a man could or could not have acted otherwise than as he did can be left on one side or answered either way, as may be preferred. It is no longer relevant.

Failure to appreciate this has, I think, led to conflicts between psychiatry and the law being often fought on the wrong ground. Even so radical a criminologist as Dr. Sheldon Glueck seems to see the issue as one between "those who stress the prime social need of blameworthiness and retributive punishment as the core-concept in crime and justice and those who, under the impact of psychiatric, psycho-analytic, sociological, and anthropological views insist that man's choices are the product of forces largely beyond his conscious control . . ." [14] Indeed Dr. Glueck's discussion of the relation of psychiatry to law is chiefly devoted to an analysis of the exculpatory effect of psychiatric knowledge, and to the changes that have been, or should be, made in the assessment of guilt as the result of the growth of this knowledge. In consequence much intellectual ingenuity is wasted in refining the criteria by which the wicked may be distinguished from the weak-minded. For surely to argue thus is to argue from the wrong premises: the real difference between the psychiatric and the legal approach has nothing to do with free will and determinism. It has to do with their conceptions of the objectives of the criminal process, with the question whether the aim of that process is punitive or preventive, whether what matters is to punish the wrongdoer or to set him on the road to virtue; and, in order to take a stand on that issue, neither party need be a determinist.

So much for what disregard of responsibility does not mean. What,

[14] Glueck, Sheldon, *Law and Psychiatry* (Tavistock Publications) 1962, p. 6.

in a more positive sense, is it likely to involve? Here, I think, one of the most important consequences must be to obscure the present rigid distinction between the penal and the medical institution. As things are, the supposedly fully responsible are consigned to the former: only the wholly or partially irresponsible are eligible for the latter. Once it is admitted that we have no reliable criterion by which to distinguish between those two categories, strict segregation of each into a distinct set of institutions becomes absurd and impracticable. For purposes of convenience offenders for whom medical treatment is indicated will doubtless tend to be allocated to one building, and those for whom medicine has nothing to offer to another; but the formal distinction between prison and hospital will become blurred, and, one may reasonably expect, eventually obliterated altogether. Both will be simply "places of safety" in which offenders receive the treatment which experience suggests is most likely to evoke the desired response.

Does this mean that the distinction between doctors and prison officers must also become blurred? Up to a point it clearly does. At the very least it would seem that some fundamental implications for the medical profession must be involved when the doctor becomes part of the machinery of law enforcement. Not only is the normal doctor-patient relationship profoundly disturbed, but far-reaching questions also arise as to the nature of the condition which the doctor is called upon to treat. If a tendency to break the law is not in itself to be classified as a disease, which does he seek to cure—the criminality or the illness? To the medical profession these questions, which I have discussed at length elsewhere,[15] must be of primary concern. But for present purposes it may be more relevant to notice how, as so often happens in this country, changes not yet officially recognised in theory are already creeping in by the back door. Already the long-awaited institution at Grendon Underwood is administered as an integral part of the prison system; yet the régime is frankly medical. Its purpose has been described by the Prison Commission's Director of Medical Services as the investigation and treatment of mental disorder generally recognised as calling for a psychiatric approach; the investigation of the mental condition of offenders whose offences in themselves suggest mental instability; and an exploration of the problem of the treatment of the psychopath. Recommendations for admission are to come from prison medical officers, and the prison itself is under the charge of a medical superintendent with wide experience in psychiatry.[16]

Grendon Underwood is (unless one should include Broadmoor which has, of course, a much narrower scope) the first genuinely hybrid institution. Interchange between medical and penal institutions is, however,

[15] Wootton, Barbara, "The Law, The Doctor and The Deviant," British Medical Journal, July 27, 1963.
[16] Snell, H. K. (Director of Medical Services, Prison Commission), "H.M. Prison Grendon," British Medical Journal, September 22, 1962.

further facilitated by the power of the Home Secretary to transfer to hospital persons whom, on appropriate medical evidence, he finds to be suffering from mental disorder of a nature or degree to warrant their detention in a hospital for medical treatment. Such transfers have the same effect as does a hospital order, and they may be (and usually are) also accompanied by an order restricting discharge. It is, moreover, of some interest that transfers are sometimes made quite soon after the court has passed sentence. Out of six cases convicted under section 2 of the Homicide Act in which transfers under section 72 were effected, three were removed to hospital less than three months after sentence. Although it is, of course, always possible that the prisoner had been mentally normal at the time of his offence and had only suffered a mental breakdown later, transfer after a relatively short period does indicate at least a possibility that in the judgment of the Home Secretary some mental abnormality may have been already present either at the time of sentence or even when the crime was committed.

The courts, however, seem to be somewhat jealous of the exercise of this power, which virtually allows the Home Secretary to treat as sick persons whom they have sentenced to imprisonment and presumably regard as wicked. Indeed it seems that, if a diagnosis of mental disorder is to be made, the courts hold that it is, generally speaking, their business, and not the Home Secretary's, to make it. So at least it would appear from the judgments of the Court of Criminal Appeal in the cases of Constance Ann James [17] and Philip Morris,[18] both of whom had been found guilty of manslaughter on grounds of diminished responsibility and had been sentenced to imprisonment. In the former case, in which the evidence as to the accused's mental condition was unchallenged, the trial judge apparently had misgivings about the public safety and in particular the safety of the convicted woman's younger child whose brother she had killed. He therefore passed a sentence of three years' imprisonment, leaving it, as he said, to the appropriate authorities to make further inquiries so that the Secretary of State might, if he thought fit, transfer the prisoner to hospital under section 72 of the Mental Health Act. The appeal was allowed, on the ground that there was obviously no need for punishment, and that there were reasonable hopes that the disorder from which the woman suffered would prove curable. In the circumstances, though reluctant to interfere with the discretion of the sentencing court, the Court of Criminal Appeal substituted a hospital order accompanied by an indefinite restriction.

In Philip Morris' case, in which, however, the appellant was unsuccessful, the matter was put even more clearly. Again the trial judge had refused to make a hospital order on grounds of the public safety and, failing any vacancy in a secure hospital, had passed a sentence of life

---

[17] R. v. *James* [1961] Crim.L.R. 842.
[18] R. v. *Morris* (1961) 45 Cr.App.R. 233.

imprisonment. But on this the Court of Criminal Appeal commented as follows: "Although the discretion . . . is very wide indeed, the basic principle must be that in the ordinary case where punishment as such is not intended, and where the sole object of the sentence is that a man should receive mental treatment, and be at large as soon as he can safely be discharged, a proper exercise of the discretion demands that steps should be taken to exercise the powers under section 60 and that the matter should not be left to be dealt with by the Secretary of State under section 72."

These difficulties are, one may hope, of a transitional nature. They would certainly not arise if all sentences involving loss of liberty were indeterminate in respect of the type of institution in which the offender is to be detained: still less if rigid distinctions between medical and penal institutions were no longer maintained. The elimination of those distinctions, moreover, though unthinkable in a primarily punitive system which must at all times segregate the blameworthy from the blameless, is wholly in keeping with a criminal law which is preventive rather than punitive in intention.

In this lecture and in that which preceded it I have tried to signpost the road towards such a conception of the law, and to indicate certain landmarks which suggest that this is the road along which we are, if hesitantly, already treading. At first blush it might seem that strict liability and mental abnormality have not much in common; but both present a challenge to traditional views as to the point at which, and the purpose for which, considerations of guilty intent become relevant; and both illustrate the contemporary tendency to use the criminal law to protect the community against damage, no matter what might be the state of mind of those by whom that damage is done. In this context, perhaps, the little-noticed provisions of section 60 (2) of the Mental Health Act, with its distinction between the forbidden act and the conviction, along with the liberal implications of section 4 of the Criminal Justice Act with its emphasis on treatability rather than culpability, are to be seen as the writing on the wall. And perhaps, too, it is significant that Dr. Glueck, notwithstanding his immediate preoccupation with definitions of responsibility, lets fall, almost as if with a sigh, the forecast that some day it may be possible "to limit criminal law to matters of behavior alone," and that in his concluding lecture he foresees the "twilight of futile blameworthiness." [19] That day may be still a long way off: but at least it seems to be nearer than it was.

[19] Glueck, Sheldon, *Law and Psychiatry* (Tavistock Publications) 1962, pp. 33, 147.

-- **HERBERT MORRIS**

Persons and Punishment

> They acted and looked . . . at us, and around in our house, in a way
> that had about it the feeling—at least for me—that we were not people.
> In their eyesight we were just things, that was all.
>
> *[Malcolm X]*

> We have no right to treat a man like a dog.
>
> *[Governor Maddox of Georgia]*

Alfredo Traps in Durrenmatt's tale discovers that he has brought off, all
by himself, a murder involving considerable ingenuity. The mock prosecutor in the tale demands the death penalty "as reward for a crime that merits
admiration, astonishment, and respect." Traps is deeply moved; indeed, he
is exhilarated, and the whole of his life becomes more heroic, and, ironically, more precious. His defense attorney proceeds to argue that Traps
was not only innocent but incapable of guilt, "a victim of the age." This
defense Traps disavows with indignation and anger. He makes claim to the
murder as his and demands the prescribed punishment—death.

The themes to be found in this macabre tale do not often find their
way into philosophical discussions of punishment. These discussions deal
with large and significant questions of whether or not we ever have the
right to punish, and if we do, under what conditions, to what degree, and
in what manner. There is a tradition, of course, not notable for its present
vitality, that is closely linked with motifs in Durrenmatt's tale of crime and
punishment. Its adherents have urged that justice requires a person be
punished if he is guilty. Sometimes—though rarely—these philosophers
have expressed themselves in terms of the criminal's *right to be punished*.
Reaction to the claim that there is such a right has been astonishment
combined, perhaps, with a touch of contempt for the perversity of the
suggestion. A strange right that no one would ever wish to claim! With
that flourish the subject is buried and the right disposed of. In this paper
the subject is resurrected.

My aim is to argue for four propositions concerning rights that will
certainly strike some as not only false but preposterous: first, that we have
a right to punishment; second, that this right derives from a fundamental
human right to be treated as a person; third, that this fundamental right

Reprinted from *The Monist*, Vol. 52, No. 4 (October 1968), 475–501, La Salle,
Illinois, with the permission of the publisher and the author.

is a natural, inalienable, and absolute right; and, fourth, that the denial of this right implies the denial of all moral rights and duties. Showing the truth of one, let alone all, of these large and questionable claims, is a tall order. The attempt or, more properly speaking, the first steps in an attempt, follow.

1. When someone claims that there is a right to be free, we can easily imagine situations in which the right is infringed and easily imagine situations in which there is a point to asserting or claiming the right. With the right to be punished, matters are otherwise. The immediate reaction to the claim that there is such a right is puzzlement. And the reasons for this are apparent. People do not normally value pain and suffering. Punishment is associated with pain and suffering. When we think about punishment we naturally think of the strong desire most persons have to avoid it, to accept, for example, acquittal of a criminal charge with relief and eagerly, if convicted, to hope for pardon or probation. Adding, of course, to the paradoxical character of the claim of such a right is difficulty in imagining circumstances in which it would be denied one. When would one rightly demand punishment and meet with any threat of the claim being denied?

So our first task is to see when the claim of such a right would have a point. I want to approach this task by setting out two complex types of institutions both of which are designed to maintain some degree of social control. In the one a central concept is punishment for wrongdoing and in the other the central concepts are control of dangerous individuals and treatment of disease.

Let us first turn attention to the institutions in which punishment is involved. The institutions I describe will resemble those we ordinarily think of as institutions of punishment; they will have, however, additional features we associate with a system of just punishment.

Let us suppose that men are constituted roughly as they now are, with a rough equivalence in strength and abilities, a capacity to be injured by each other and to make judgments that such injury is undesirable, a limited strength of will, and a capacity to reason and to conform conduct to rules. Applying to the conduct of these men are a group of rules, ones I shall label 'primary', which closely resemble the core rules of our criminal law, rules that prohibit violence and deception and compliance with which provides benefits for all persons. These benefits consist in noninterference by others with what each person values, such matters as continuance of life and bodily security. The rules define a sphere for each person, then, which is immune from interference by others. Making possible this mutual benefit is the assumption by individuals of a burden. The burden consists in the exercise of self-restraint by individuals over inclinations that would, if satisfied, directly interfere or create a substantial risk of interference with others in proscribed ways. If a person fails to exercise self-restraint even though he might have and gives in to such inclinations, he renounces a burden which others have voluntarily assumed and thus gains an advantage which others, who have restrained themselves, do not possess. This system, then, is one in which the rules establish a mutuality of benefit and burden and in which the benefits of noninterference are conditional upon the assumption of burdens.

Connecting punishment with the violation of these primary rules, and making public the provision for punishment, is both reasonable and just. First, it is only reasonable that those who voluntarily comply with the rules be provided some assurance that they will not be assuming burdens which others are unprepared to assume. Their disposition to comply voluntarily will diminish as they learn that others are with impunity renouncing burdens they are assuming. Second, fairness dictates that a system in which benefits and burdens are equally distributed have a mechanism designed to prevent a maldistribution in the benefits and burdens. Thus, sanctions are atttached to noncompliance with the primary rules so as to induce compliance with the primary rules among those who may be disinclined to obey. In this way the likelihood of an unfair distribution is diminished.

Third, it is just to punish those who have violated the rules and caused the unfair distribution of benefits and burdens. A person who violates the rules has something others have—the benefits of the system— but by renouncing what others have assumed, the burdens of self-restraint, he has acquired an unfair advantage. Matters are not even until this advantage is in some way erased. Another way of putting it is that he owes something to others, for he has something that does not rightfully belong to him. Justice—that is punishing such individuals—restores the equilibrium of benefits and burdens by taking from the individual what he owes, that is, exacting the debt. It is important to see that the equilibrium may be restored in another way. Forgiveness—with its legal analogue of a pardon —while not the righting of an unfair distribution by making one pay his debt is, nevertheless, a restoring of the equilibrium by forgiving the debt. Forgiveness may be viewed, at least in some types of cases, as a gift after the fact, erasing a debt, which had the gift been given before the fact, would not have created a debt. But the practice of pardoning has to proceed sensitively, for it may endanger in a way the practice of justice does not, the maintenance of an equilibrium of benefits and burdens. If all are indiscriminately pardoned less incentive is provided individuals to restrain their inclinations, thus increasing the incidence of persons taking what they do not deserve.

There are also in this system we are considering a variety of operative principles compliance with which provides some guarantee that the system of punishment does not itself promote an unfair distribution of benefits and burdens. For one thing, provision is made for a variety of defenses, each one of which can be said to have as its object diminishing the chances of forcibly depriving a person of benefits others have if that person has not derived an unfair advantage. A person has not derived an unfair advantage if he could not have restrained himself or if it is unreasonable to expect him to behave otherwise than he did. Sometimes the rules preclude punishment of classes of persons such as children. Sometimes they provide a defense if on a particular occasion a person lacked the capacity to conform his conduct to the rules. Thus, someone who in an epileptic seizure strikes another is excused. Punishment in these cases would be punishment of the innocent, punishment of those who do not voluntarily renounce a burden others have assumed. Punishment in such cases, then, would not equalize but rather cause an unfair distribution in benefits and burdens.

Along with principles providing defenses there are requirements that the rules be prospective and relatively clear so that persons have a fair opportunity to comply with the rules. There are, also, rules governing, among other matters, the burden of proof, who shall bear it and what it shall be, the prohibition on double jeopardy, and the privilege against self-incrimination. Justice requires conviction of the guilty, and requires their punishment, but in setting out to fulfill the demands of justice we may, of course, because we are not omniscient, cause injustice by convicting and punishing the innocent. The resolution arrived at in the system I am describing consists in weighing as the greater evil the punishment of the innocent. The primary function of the system of rules was to provide individuals with a sphere of interest immune from interference. Given this goal, it is determined to be a greater evil for society to interfere unjustifiably with an individual by depriving him of good than for the society to fail to punish those that have unjustifiably interfered.

Finally, because the primary rules are designed to benefit all and because the punishments prescribed for their violation are publicized and the defenses respected, there is some plausibility in the exaggerated claim that in choosing to do an act violative of the rules an individual has chosen to be punished. This way of putting matters brings to our attention the extent to which, when the system is as I have described it, the criminal "has brought the punishment upon himself" in contrast to those cases where it would be misleading to say "he has brought it upon himself," cases, for example, where one does not know the rules or is punished in the absence of fault.

To summarize, then: first, there is a group of rules guiding the behavior of individuals in the community which establish spheres of interest immune from interference by others; second, provision is made for what is generally regarded as a deprivation of some thing of value if the rules are violated; third, the deprivations visited upon any person are justified by that person's having violated the rules; fourth, the deprivation, in this just system of punishment, is linked to rules that fairly distribute benefits and burdens and to procedures that strike some balance between not punishing the guilty and punishing the innocent, a class defined as those who have not voluntarily done acts violative of the law, in which it is evident that the evil of punishing the innocent is regarded as greater than the non-punishment of the guilty.

At the core of many actual legal systems one finds, of course, rules and procedures of the kind I have sketched. It is obvious, though, that any ongoing legal system differs in significant respects from what I have presented here, containing 'pockets of injustice'.

I want now to sketch an extreme version of a set of institutions of a fundamentally different kind, institutions proceeding on a conception of man which appears to be basically at odds with that operative within a system of punishment.

Rules are promulgated in this system that prohibit certain types of injuries and harms.

In this world we are now to imagine when an individual harms another his conduct is to be regarded as a symptom of some pathological condition in the way a running nose is a symptom of a cold. Actions diverging from some conception of the normal are viewed as manifestations of a disease in the way in which we might today regard the arm and leg movements of an epileptic during a seizure. Actions conforming to what is normal are assimilated to the normal and healthy functioning of bodily organs. What a person does, then, is assimilated, on this conception, to what we believe today, or at least most of us believe today, a person undergoes. We draw a distinction between the operation of the kidney and raising an arm on request. This distinction between mere events or happenings and human actions is erased in our imagined system.[1]

---

[1] "When a man is suffering from an infectious disease, he is a danger to the community, and it is necessary to restrict his liberty of movement. But no one associates any idea of guilt with such a situation. On the contrary, he is an object of commiseration to his friends. Such steps as science recommends are taken to cure him of his disease, and he submits as a rule without reluctance to the curtailment of liberty involved meanwhile. The same method in spirit ought to be shown in the treatment of what is called 'crime.'"

Bertrand Russell, *Roads to Freedom* (London: George Allen and Unwin Ltd., 1918), p. 135.

"We do not hold people responsible for their reflexes—for example, for coughing in church. We hold them responsible for their operant behavior—for example, for whispering in church or remaining in church while coughing. But there are variables which are responsible for whispering as well as coughing, and these may be just as inexorable. When we recognize this, we are likely to drop the notion of responsibility altogether and with it the doctrine of free will as an inner causal agent."

B. F. Skinner, *Science and Human Behavior* (1953), pp. 115–6.

"Basically, criminality is but a symptom of insanity, using the term in its widest generic sense to express unacceptable social behavior based on unconscious motivation flowing from a disturbed instinctive and emotional life, whether this appears in frank psychoses, or in less obvious form in neuroses and unrecognized psychoses. . . . If criminals are products of early environmental influences in

There is, however, bound to be something strange in this erasing of a recognized distinction, for, as with metaphysical suggestions generally, and I take this to be one, the distinction may be reintroduced but given a different description, for example, 'happenings with X type of causes' and 'happenings with Y type of causes'. Responses of different kinds, today legitimated by our distinction between happenings and actions may be legitimated by this new manner of description. And so there may be isomorphism between a system recognizing the distinction and one erasing it. Still, when this distinction is erased certain tendencies of thought and responses might naturally arise that would tend to affect unfavorably values respected by a system of punishment.

Let us elaborate on this assimilation of conduct of a certain kind to symptoms of a disease. First, there is something abnormal in both the case of conduct, such as killing another, and a symptom of a disease such as an irregular heart beat. Second, there are causes for this abnormality in action such that once we know of them we can explain the abnormality as we now can explain the symptoms of many physical diseases. The abnormality is looked upon as a happening with a causal explanation rather than an action for which there were reasons. Third, the causes that account for the abnormality interfere with the normal functioning of the body, or, in the case of killing with what is regarded as a normal functioning of an individual. Fourth, the abnormality is in some way a part of the individual, necessarily involving his body. A well going dry might satisfy our three foregoing conditions of disease symptoms, but it is hardly a disease or the symptom of one. Finally, and most obscure, the abnormality arises in some way from within the individual. If Jones is hit with a mallet by Smith, Jones may reel about and fall on James who may be injured. But this abnormal conduct of Jones is not regarded as a symptom of disease. Smith, not Jones, is suffering from some pathological condition.

With this view of man the institutions of social control respond, not with punishment, but with either preventive detention, in case of 'carriers', or therapy in the case of those manifesting pathological symptoms. The

---

the same sense that psychotics and neurotics are, then it should be possible to reach them psychotherapeutically."

Benjamin Karpman, "Criminal Psychodynamics," *Journal of Criminal Law and Criminology*, 47 (1956), p. 9.

"We, the agents of society, must move to end the game of tit-for-tat and blow-for-blow in which the offender has foolishly and futilely engaged himself and us. We are not driven, as he is, to wild and impulsive actions. With knowledge comes power, and with power there is no need for the frightened vengeance of the old penology. In its place should go a quiet, dignified, therapeutic program for the rehabilitation of the disorganized one, if possible, the protection of society during the treatment period, and his guided return to useful citizenship, as soon as this can be effected."

Karl Menninger, "Therapy, Not Punishment," *Harper's Magazine* (August 1959), pp. 63–64.

logic of sickness implies the logic of therapy. And therapy and punishment differ widely in their implications. In bringing out some of these differences I want again to draw attention to the important fact that while the distinctions we now draw are erased in the therapy world, they may, in fact, be reintroduced but under different descriptions. To the extent they are, we really have a punishment system combined with a therapy system. I am concerned now, however, with what the implications would be were the world indeed one of therapy and not a disguised world of punishment and therapy, for I want to suggest tendencies of thought that arise when one is immersed in the ideology of disease and therapy.

First, punishment is the imposition upon a person who is believed to be at fault of something commonly believed to be a deprivation where that deprivation is justified by the person's guilty behavior. It is associated with resentment, for the guilty are those who have done what they had no right to do by failing to exercise restraint when they might have and where others have. Therapy is not a response to a person who is at fault. We respond to an individual, not because of what he has done, but because of some condition from which he is suffering. If he is no longer suffering from the condition, treatment no longer has a point. Punishment, then, focuses on the past; therapy on the present. Therapy is normally associated with compassion for what one undergoes, not resentment for what one has illegitimately done.

Second, with therapy, unlike punishment, we do not seek to deprive the person of something acknowledged as a good, but seek rather to help and to benefit the individual who is suffering by ministering to his illness in the hope that the person can be cured. The good we attempt to do is not a reward for desert. The individual suffering has not merited by his disease the good we seek to bestow upon him but has, because he is a creature that has the capacity to feel pain, a claim upon our sympathies and help.

Third, we saw with punishment that its justification was related to maintaining and restoring a fair distribution of benefits and burdens. Infliction of the prescribed punishment carries the implication, then, that one has 'paid one's debt' to society, for the punishment is the taking from the person of something commonly recognized as valuable. It is this conception of 'a debt owed' that may permit, as I suggested earlier, under certain conditions, the nonpunishment of the guilty, for operative within a system of punishment may be a concept analogous to forgiveness, namely pardoning. Who it is that we may pardon and under what conditions—contrition with its elements of self-punishment no doubt plays a role—I shall not go into though it is clearly a matter of the greatest practical and theoretical interest. What is clear is that the conceptions of 'paying a debt' or 'having a debt forgiven' or pardoning have no place in a system of therapy.

Fourth, with punishment there is an attempt at some equivalence between the advantage gained by the wrongdoer—partly based upon the seriousness of the interest invaded, partly on the state of mind with which the wrongful act was performed—and the punishment meted out. Thus, we can understand a prohibition on 'cruel and unusual punishments' so that disproportionate pain and suffering are avoided. With therapy attempts at proportionality make no sense. It is perfectly plausible giving someone who kills a pill and treating for a lifetime within an institution one who has broken a dish and manifested accident proneness. We have the concept of 'painful treatment'. We do not have the concept of 'cruel treatment'. Because treatment is regarded as a benefit, though it may involve pain, it is natural that less restraint is exercised in bestowing it, than in inflicting punishment. Further, protests with respect to treatment are likely to be assimilated to the complaints of one whose leg must be amputated in order for him to live, and, thus, largely disregarded. To be sure, there is operative in the therapy world some conception of the "cure being worse than the disease," but if the disease is manifested in conduct harmful to others, and if being a normal operating human being is valued highly, there will naturally be considerable pressure to find the cure acceptable.

Fifth, the rules in our system of punishment governing conduct of individuals were rules violation of which involved either direct interference with others or the creation of a substantial risk of such interference. One could imagine adding to this system of primary rules other rules proscribing preparation to do acts violative of the primary rules and even rules proscribing thoughts. Objection to such suggestions would have many sources but a principal one would consist in its involving the infliction of punishment on too great a number of persons who would not, because of a change of mind, have violated the primary rules. Though we are interested in diminishing violations of the primary rules, we are not prepared to punish too many individuals who would never have violated the rules in order to achieve this aim. In a system motivated solely by a preventive and curative ideology there would be less reason to wait until symptoms manifest themselves in socially harmful conduct. It is understandable that we should wish at the earliest possible stage to arrest the development of the disease. In the punishment system, because we are dealing with deprivations, it is understandable that we should forbear from imposing them until we are quite sure of guilt. In the therapy system, dealing as it does with benefits, there is less reason for forbearance from treatment at an early stage.

Sixth, a variety of procedural safeguards we associate with punishment have less significance in a therapy system. To the degree objections to double jeopardy and self-incrimination are based on a wish to decrease the chances of the innocent being convicted and punished, a therapy system, unconcerned with this problem, would disregard such safeguards. When one is out to help people there is also little sense in urging that the burden of proof be on those providing the help. And there is less point to imposing the burden of proving that the conduct was pathological beyond a reasonable doubt. Further, a jury system which, within a system of justice, serves to make accommodations to the individual situation and to introduce a human element, would play no role or a minor one in a world where expertise is required in making determinations of disease and treatment.

In our system of punishment an attempt was made to maximize each individual's freedom of choice by first of all delimiting by rules certain spheres of conduct immune from interference by others. The punishment associated with these primary rules paid deference to an individual's free choice by connecting punishment to a freely chosen act violative of the rules, thus giving some plausibility to the claim, as we saw, that what a person received by way of punishment he himself had chosen. With the world of disease and therapy all this changes and the individual's free choice ceases to be a determinative factor in how others respond to him. All those principles of our own legal system that minimize the chances of punishment of those who have not chosen to do acts violative of the rules tend to lose their point in the therapy system, for how we respond in a therapy system to a person is not conditioned upon what he has chosen but rather on what symptoms he has manifested or may manifest and what the best therapy for the disease is that is suggested by the symptoms.

Now, it is clear I think, that were we confronted with the alternatives I have sketched, between a system of just punishment and a thoroughgoing system of treatment, a system, that is, that did not reintroduce concepts appropriate to punishment, we could see the point in claiming that a person has a right to be punished, meaning by this that a person had a right to all those institutions and practices linked to punishment. For these would provide him with, among other things, a far greater ability to predict what would happen to him on the occurrence of certain events than the therapy system. There is the inestimable value to each of us of having the responses of others to us determined over a wide range of our lives by what we choose rather than what they choose. A person has a right to institutions that respect his choices. Our punishment system does; our therapy system does not.

Apart from those aspects of our therapy model which would relate to serious limitations on personal liberty, there are clearly objections of a more profound kind to the mode of thinking I have associated with the therapy model.

First, human beings pride themselves in having capacities that animals do not. A common way, for example, of arousing shame in a child is to compare the child's conduct to that of an animal. In a system where all actions are assimilated to happenings we are assimilated to creatures—indeed, it is more extreme than this—whom we have always thought possessed of less than we. Fundamental to our practice of praise and order of attainment is that one who can do more—one who is capable of more and one who does more is more worthy of respect and admiration. And we have thought of ourselves as capable where animals are not of making, of creating, among other things, ourselves. The conception of man I have outlined would provide us with a status that today, when our conduct is assimilated to it in moral criticism, we consider properly evocative of shame.

Second, if all human conduct is viewed as something men undergo, thrown into question would be the appropriateness of that extensive range of peculiarly human satisfactions that derive from a sense of achievement. For these satisfactions we shall have to substitute those mild satisfactions attendant upon a healthy well-functioning body. Contentment is our lot if we are fortunate; intense satisfaction at achievement is entirely inappropriate.

Third, in the therapy world nothing is earned and what we receive comes to us through compassion, or through a desire to control us. Resentment is out of place. We can take credit for nothing but must always regard ourselves—if there are selves left to regard once actions disappear —as fortunate recipients of benefits or unfortunate carriers of disease who must be controlled. We know that within our own world human beings who have been so regarded and who come to accept this view of themselves come to look upon themselves as worthless. When what we do is met with resentment, we are indirectly paid something of a compliment.

Fourth, attention should also be drawn to a peculiar evil that may be attendant upon regarding a man's actions as symptoms of disease. The logic of cure will push us toward forms of therapy that inevitably involve changes in the person made against his will. The evil in this would be most apparent in those cases where the agent, whose action is determined to be a manifestation of some disease, does not regard his action in this way. He believes that what he has done is, in fact, 'right' but his conception of 'normality' is not the therapeutically accepted one. When we treat an illness we normally treat a condition that the person is not responsible for. He is 'suffering' from some disease and we treat the condition, relieving the person of something preventing his normal functioning. When we begin treating persons for actions that have been chosen, we do not lift from the person something that is interfering with his normal functioning but we change the person so that he functions in a way regarded as normal by the current therapeutic community. We have to change him and his judgments of value. In doing this we display a lack of respect for the moral status of individuals, that is, a lack of respect for the reasoning and choices of individuals. They are but animals who must be conditioned. I think we can understand and, indeed, sympathize with a man's preferring death to being forcibly turned into what he is not.

Finally, perhaps most frightening of all would be the derogation in status of all protests to treatment. If someone believes that he has done something right, and if he protests being treated and changed, the protest will itself be regarded as a sign of some pathological condition, for who would not wish to be cured of an affliction? What this leads to are questions of an important kind about the effect of this conception of man upon what we now understand by reasoning. Here what a person takes to be a reasoned defense of an act is treated, as the action was, on the model of a happening of a pathological kind. Not just a person's acts are taken from him but also his attempt at a reasoned justification for the acts. In a system of punishment a person who has committed a crime may argue that what he did was right. We make him pay the price and we respect his right to retain the judgment he has made. A conception of pathology precludes this form of respect.

It might be objected to the foregoing that all I have shown—if that—is that if the only alternatives open to us are a *just* system of punishment or the mad world of being treated like sick or healthy animals, we do in fact have a right to a system of punishment of this kind. But this hardly shows that we have a right *simpliciter* to punishment as we do, say, to be free. Indeed, it does not even show a right to a just system of punishment, for surely we can, without too much difficulty, imagine situations in which the alternatives to punishment are not this mad world but a world in which we are still treated as persons and there is, for example, not the pain and suffering attendant upon punishment. One such world is one in which there are rules but responses to their violation is not the deprivation of some good but forgiveness. Still another type of world would be one in which violation of the rules were responded to by merely comparing the conduct of the person to something commonly regarded as low or filthy, and thus, producing by this mode of moral criticism, feelings of shame rather than feelings of guilt.

I am prepared to allow that these objections have a point. While granting force to the above objections I want to offer a few additional comments with respect to each of them. First, any existent legal system permits the punishment of individuals under circumstances where the conditions I have set forth for a just system have not been satisfied. A glaring example of this would be criminal strict liability which is to be found in our own legal system. Nevertheless, I think it would be difficult to present any system we should regard as a system of punishment that would not still have a great advantage over our imagined therapy system. The system of punishment we imagine may more and more approximate a system of sheer terror in which human beings are treated as animals to be intimidated and prodded. To the degree that the system is of this character it is, in my judgment, not simply an unjust system but one that diverges from what we normally understand by a system of punishment. At least some deference to the choice of individuals is built into the idea of punishment. So there would be some truth in saying we have a right to any system of punishment if the only alternative to it was therapy.

Second, people may imagine systems in which there are rules and in which the response to their violation is not punishment but pardoning, the legal analogue of forgiveness. Surely this is a system to which we would claim a right as against one in which we are made to suffer for violating the rules. There are several comments that need to be made about this. It may be, of course, that a high incidence of pardoning would increase the incidence of rule violations. Further, the difficulty with suggesting pardoning as a general response is that pardoning presupposes the very responses that it is suggested it supplant. A system of deprivations, or a practice of deprivations on the happening of certain actions, underlies the practice of pardoning and forgiving, for it is only where we possess the idea of a wrong to be made up or of a debt owed to others, ideas we acquire within a world in which there have been deprivations for wrong acts, that we have the idea of pardoning for the wrong or forgiving the debt.

Finally, if we look at the responses I suggested would give rise to feelings of shame, we may rightly be troubled with the appropriateness of this response in any community in which each person assumes burdens so that each may derive benefits. In such situations might it not be that individuals have a right to a system of punishment so that each person could be assured that inequities in the distribution of benefits and burdens are unlikely to occur and if they do, procedures exist for correcting them? Further, it may well be that, everything considered, we should prefer the pain and suffering of a system of punishment to a world in which we only experience shame on the doing of wrong acts, for with guilt there are relatively simple ways of ridding ourselves of the feeling we have, that is, gaining forgiveness or taking the punishment, but with shame we have to bear it until we no longer are the person who has behaved in the shameful way. Thus, I suggest that we have, wherever there is a distribution of benefits and burdens of the kind I have described, a right to a system of punishment.

I want also to make clear in concluding this section that I have argued, though very indirectly, not just for a right to a system of punishment, but for a right to be punished once there is in existence such a system. Thus, a man has the right to be punished rather than treated if he is guilty of some offense. And, indeed, one can imagine a case in which, even in the face of an offer of a pardon, a man claims and ought to have acknowledged his right to be punished.

2. The primary reason for preferring the system of punishment as against the system of therapy might have been expressed in terms of the one system treating one as a person and the other not. In invoking the right to be punished, one justifies one's claim by reference to a more fundamental right. I want now to turn attention to this fundamental right and attempt to shed light—it will have to be little, for the topic is immense—on what is meant by 'treating an individual as a person'.

When we talk of not treating a human being as a person or 'showing no respect for one as a person' what we imply by our words is a contrast between the manner in which one acceptably responds to human beings and the manner in which one acceptably responds to animals and inanimate objects. When we treat a human being merely as an animal or some inanimate object our responses to the human being are determined, not by his choices, but ours in disregard of or with indifference to his. And when we 'look upon' a person as less than a person or not a person, we consider the person as incapable of rational choice. In cases of not treating a human being as a person we interfere with a person in such a way that what is done, even if the person is involved in the doing, is done not by the person but by the user of the person. In extreme cases there may even be an elision of a causal chain so that we might say that X killed Z even though Y's hand was the hand that held the weapon, for Y's hand may have been entirely in X's control. The one agent is in some way treating the other as a mere link in a causal chain. There is, of course, a wide range of cases in which a person is used to accomplish the aim of another and in which the person used is less than fully free. A person may be grabbed against his will and used as a shield. A person may be drugged or hypnotized and then employed for certain ends. A person may be deceived into doing other than he intends doing. A person may be ordered to do something and threatened with harm if he does not and coerced into doing what he does not want to. There is still another range of cases in which individuals are not used, but in which decisions by others are made that affect them in circumstances where they have the capacity for choice and where they are not being treated as persons.

But it is particularly important to look at coercion, for I have claimed that a just system of punishment treats human beings as persons; and it is not immediately apparent how ordering someone to do something and threatening harm differs essentially from having rules supported by threats of harm in case of noncompliance.

There are affinities between coercion and other cases of not treating someone as a person, for it is not the coerced person's choices but the coercer's that are responsible for what is done. But unlike other indisputable cases of not treating one as a person, for example using someone as a shield, there is some choice involved in coercion. And if this is so, why does the coercer stand in any different relation to the coerced person than the criminal law stands to individuals in society?

Suppose the person who is threatened disregards the order and gets the threatened harm. Now suppose he is told, "Well, you did after all bring it upon yourself." There is clearly something strange in this. It is the person doing the threatening and not the person threatened who is responsible. But our reaction to punishment, at least in a system that resembles the one I have described, is precisely that the person violating the rules brought it upon himself. What lies behind these different reactions?

There exist situations in the law, of course, which resemble coercion situations. There are occasions when in the law a person might justifiably say "I am not being treated as a person but being used" and where he might properly react to the punishment as something "he was hardly responsible for." But it is possible to have a system in which it would be misleading to say, over a wide range of cases of punishment for noncompliance, that we are using persons. The clearest case in which it would be inappropriate to so regard punishment would be one in which there were explicit agreement in advance that punishment should follow on the voluntary doing of certain acts. Even if one does not have such conditions satisfied, and obviously such explicit agreements are not characteristic, one can see significant differences between our system of just punishment and a coercion situation.

First, unlike the case with one person coercing another 'to do his will', the rules in our system apply to all, with the benefits and burdens equally distributed. About such a system it cannot be said that some are being subordinated to others or are being used by others or gotten to do things by others. To the extent that the rules are thought to be to the advantage of only some or to the extent there is a maldistribution of benefits and burdens, the difference between coercion and law disappears.

Second, it might be argued that at least any person inclined to act in a manner violative of the rules stands to all others as the person coerced stands to his coercer, and that he, at least, is a person disadvantaged as others are not. It is important here, I think, that he is part of a system in which it is commonly agreed that forbearance from the acts proscribed by the rules provides advantages for all. This system is the accepted setting; it is the norm. Thus, in any coercive situation, it is the coercer who deviates from the norm, with the responsibility of the person he is attempting to coerce, defeated. In a just punishment situation, it is the person deviating from the norm, indeed he might be a coercer, who is responsible, for it is the norm to restrain oneself from acts of that kind. A voluntary agent diverging in his conduct from what is expected or what is the norm, on general causal principles, regarded as the cause of what results from his conduct.

There is, then, some plausibility in the claim that, in a system of punishment of the kind I have sketched, a person chooses the punishment that is meted out to him. If, then, we can say in such a system that the rules provide none with advantages that others do not have, and further, that what happens to a person is conditioned by that person's choice and not that of others, then we can say that it is a system responding to one as a person.

We treat a human being as a person provided: first, we permit the person to make the choices that will determine what happens to him and second, when our responses to the person are responses respecting the person's choices. When we respond to a person's illness by treating the illness it is neither a case of treating or not treating the individual as a person. When we give a person a gift we are neither treating or not treating him as a person, unless, of course, he does not wish it, chooses not to have it, but we compel him to accept it.

3. This right to be treated as a person is a fundamental human right belonging to all human beings by virtue of their being human. It is also a natural, inalienable, and absolute right. I want now to defend these claims so reminiscent of an era of philosophical thinking about rights that many consider to have been seriously confused.

If the right is one that we possess by virtue of being human beings, we are immediately confronted with an apparent dilemma. If, to treat another as a person requires that we provide him with reasons for acting and avoid force or deception, how can we justify the force and deception we exercise with respect to children and the mentally ill? If they, too, have a right to be treated as persons are we not constantly infringing their rights? One way out of this is simply to restrict the right to those who satisfy the conditions of being a person. Infants and the insane, it might be argued, do not meet these conditions, and they would not then have the right. Another approach would be to describe the right they possess as a prima facie right to be treated as a person. This right might then be outweighed by other considerations. This approach generally seems to me, as I shall later argue, inadequate.

I prefer this tack. Children possess the right to be treated as persons but they possess this right as an individual might be said in the law of property to possess a future interest. There are advantages in talking of individuals as having a right though complete enjoyment of it is postponed. Brought to our attention, if we ascribe to them the right, is the legitimacy of their complaint if they are not provided with opportunities and conditions assuring their full enjoyment of the right when they acquire the characteristics of persons. More than this, all persons are charged with the sensitive task of not denying them the right to be a person and to be treated as a person by failing to provide the conditions for their becoming individuals who are able freely and in an informed way to choose and who are prepared themselves to assume responsibility for their choices. There is an obligation imposed upon us all, unlike that we have with respect to animals, to respond to children in such a way as to maximize the chances of their becoming persons. This may well impose upon us the obligation to treat them as persons from a very early age, that is, to respect their choices and to place upon them the responsibility for the choices to be made. There is no need to say that there is a close connection between how we respond to them and what they become. It also imposes upon us all the duty to display constantly the qualities of a person, for what they become they will largely become because of what they learn from us is acceptable behavior.

In claiming that the right is a right that human beings have by virtue of being human, there are several other features of the right, that should be noted, perhaps better conveyed by labelling them 'natural'. First, it is a right we have apart from any voluntary agreement into which we have entered. Second, it is not a right that derives from some defined position or status. Third, it is equally apparent that one has the right regardless of the society or community of which one is a member. Finally, it is a right linked to certain features of a class of beings. Were we fundamentally different than we now are, we would not have it. But it is more than that, for the right is linked to a feature of human beings which, were that feature absent—the capacity to reason and to choose on the basis of reasons—, profound conceptual changes would be involved in the thought about human beings. It is a right, then, connected with a feature of men that sets men apart from other natural phenomena.

The right to be treated as a person is inalienable. To say of a right that it is inalienable draws attention not to limitations placed on what others may do with respect to the possessor of the right but rather to limitations placed on the dispositive capacities of the possessor of the right. Something is to be gained in keeping the issues of alienability and absoluteness separate.

There are a variety of locutions qualifying what possessors of rights may and may not do. For example, on this issue of alienability, it would be worthwhile to look at, among other things, what is involved in abandoning, abdicating, conveying, giving up, granting, relinquishing, surrendering, transferring, and waiving one's rights. And with respect to each of these concepts we should also have to be sensitive to the variety of uses of the term 'rights'. What it is, for example, to waive a Hohfeldian 'right' in his strict sense will differ from what it is to waive a right in his 'privilege' sense.

Let us look at only two concepts very briefly, those of transferring and waiving rights. The clearest case of transferring rights is that of transferring rights with respect to specific objects. I own a watch and owning it I have a complicated relationship, captured in this area rather well I think by Hohfeld's four basic legal relationships, to all persons in the world with respect to the watch. We crudely capture these complex relationships by talking of my 'property rights' in or with respect to the watch. If I sell the watch, thus exercising a capacity provided by the rules of property, I have transferred rights in or with respect to the watch to someone else, the buyer, and the buyer now stands, as I formerly did, to all persons in the world in a series of complex relationships with respect to the watch.

While still the owner, I may have given to another permission to use it for several days. Had there not been the permission and had the person taken the watch, we should have spoken of interfering with or violating or, possibly, infringing my property rights. Or, to take a situation in which transferring rights is inappropriate, I may say to another "go ahead and slap me—you have my permission." In these types of situations philosophers and others have spoken of 'surrendering' rights or, alternatively and, I believe, less strangely, of 'waiving one's rights'. And recently, of course, the whole topic of 'waiving one's rights to remain silent' in the context of police interrogation of suspects has been a subject of extensive litigation and discussion.

I confess to feeling that matters are not entirely perspicuous with respect to what is involved in 'waiving' or 'surrendering' rights. In conveying to another permission to take a watch or slap one, one makes legally permissible what otherwise would not have been. But in saying those words that constitute permission to take one's watch one is, of course, exercising precisely one of those capacities that leads us to say he has, while others have not, property rights with respect to the watch. Has one then waived his right in Hohfeld's strict sense in which the correlative is the duty to forbear on the part of others?

We may wish to distinguish here waiving the right to have others forbear to which there is a corresponding duty on their part to forbear, from placing oneself in a position where one has no legitimate right to complain. If I say the magic words "take the watch for a couple of days" or "go ahead and slap me," have I waived my right not to have my property taken or a right not to be struck or have I, rather, in saying what I have, simply stepped into a relation in which the rights no longer apply with respect to a specified other person? These observations find support in the following considerations. The right is that which gives rise, when infringed, to a legitimate claim against another person. What this suggests is that the right is that sphere interference with which entitles us to complain or gives us a right to complain. From this it seems to follow that a right to bodily security should be more precisely described as 'a right that others not interfere without permission.' And there is the corresponding duty not to interfere unless provided permission. Thus when we talk of waiving our rights or 'giving up our rights' in such cases we are not waiving or giving up our right to property nor our right to bodily security, for we still, of course, possess the right not to have our watch taken without permission. We have rather placed ourselves in a position where we do not possess the capacity, sometimes called a right, to complain if the person takes the watch or slaps us.

There is another type of situation in which we may speak of waiving our rights. If someone without permission slaps me, there is an infringement of my right to bodily security. If I now acquiesce or go further and say "forget it" or "you are forgiven," we might say that I had waived my right to complain. But here, too, I feel uncomfortable about what is involved. For I do have the right to complain (a right without a corresponding duty) in the event I am slapped and I have that right whether I wish it or not. If I say to another after the slap, "you are forgiven" what I do is not waive the right to complain but rather make illegitimate my subsequent exercise of that right.

Now, if we turn to the right to be treated as a person, the claim that I made was that it was inalienable, and what I meant to convey by that word of respectable age is that (a) it is a right that cannot be transferred to another in the way one's right with respect to objects can be transferred and (b) that it cannot be waived in the ways in which people talk of waiving rights to property or waiving, within certain limitations, one's right to bodily security.

While the rules of the law of property are such that persons may, satisfying certain procedures, transfer rights, the right to be treated as a person logically cannot be transferred anymore than one person can transfer to another his right to life or privacy. What, indeed, would it be like for another to have our right to be treated as a person? We can understand transferring a right with respect to certain objects. The new owner stands where the old owner stood. But with a right to be treated as a person what could this mean? My having the right meant that my choices were respected. Now if I transfer it to another this will mean that he will possess the right that my choices be respected? This is nonsense. It is only each person himself that can have his choices respected. It is no more possible to transfer this right than it is to transfer one's right to life.

Nor can the right be waived. It cannot be waived because any agreement to being treated as an animal or an instrument does not provide others with the moral permission to so treat us. One can volunteer to be a shield, but then it is one's choice on a particular occasion to be a shield. If without our permission, without our choosing it, someone used us as a shield, we may, I should suppose, forgive the person for treating us as an object. But we do not thereby waive our right to be treated as a person, for that is a right that has been infringed and what we have at most done is put ourselves in a position where it is inappropriate any longer to exercise the right to complain.

This is the right, then, such that the moral rules defining relationships among persons preclude anyone from morally giving others legitimate permissions or rights with respect to one by doing or saying certain things. One stands, then, with respect to one's person as the nonowner of goods stands to those goods. The nonowner cannot, given the rule-defined relationships, convey to others rights and privileges that only the owner possesses. Just as there are agreements nonenforceable because void as contrary to public policy, so there are permissions our moral outlook regards as without moral force. With respect to being treated as a person, one is 'disabled' from modifying relations of others to one.

The right is absolute. This claim is bound to raise eyebrows. I have an innocuous point in mind in making this claim.

In discussing alienability we focused on incapacities with respect to disposing of rights. Here what I want to bring out is a sense in which a right exists despite considerations for refusing to accord the person his rights. As with the topic of alienability there are a host of concepts that deserve a close look in this area. Among them are according, acknowledging, annulling, asserting, claiming, denying, destroying, exercising, infringing, insisting upon, interfering with, possessing, recognizing and violating.

The claim that rights are absolute has been construed to mean that 'assertions of rights cannot, for any reason under any circumstances be denied'. When there are considerations which warrant refusing to accord persons their rights, there are two prevalent views as to how this should be described: there is, first, the view that the person does not have the right, and second, the view that he has rights but of a prima facie kind and that these have been outweighed or overcome by the other considerations. "We can conceive times when such rights must give away, and, therefore, they are only prima facie and not absolute rights." (Brandt)

Perhaps there are cases in which a person claims a right to do a certain thing, say with his property, and argues that his property rights are absolute, meaning by this he has a right to do whatever he wishes with his property. Here, no doubt, it has to be explained to the person that the right he claims he has, he does not in fact possess. In such a case the person does not have and never did have, given a certain description of the right, a right that was prima facie or otherwise, to do what he claimed he had the right to do. If the assertion that a right is absolute implies that we have a right to do whatever we wish to do, it is an absurd claim and as such should not really ever have been attributed to political theorists arguing for absolute rights. But, of course, the claim that we have a prima facie right to do whatever we wish to do is equally absurd. The right is not prima facie either, for who would claim, thinking of the right to be free, that one has a prima facie right to kill others, if one wishes, unless there are moral considerations weighing against it?

There are, however, other situations in which it is accepted by all that a person possesses rights of a certain kind, and the difficulty we face is that of according the person the right he is claiming when this will promote more evil than good. The just act is to give the man his due and giving a man what it is his right to have is giving him his due. But it is a mistake to suppose that justice is the only dimension of morality. It may be justifiable not to accord to a man his rights. But it is no less a wrong to him, no less an infringement. It is seriously misleading to turn all justifiable infringements into noninfringements by saying that the right is only prima facie, as if we have, in concluding that we should not accord a man his rights, made out a case that he had none. To use the language of 'prima facie rights' misleads, for it suggests that a presumption of the existence of a right has been overcome in these cases where all that can be said is that the presumption in favor of according a man his rights has been overcome. If we begin to think the right itself is prima facie, we shall, in cases in which we are justified in not according it, fail sufficiently to bring out that we have interfered where justice says we should not. Our moral framework is unnecessarily and undesirably impoverished by the theory that there are such rights.

When I claim, then, that the right to be treated as a person is absolute what I claim is that given that one is a person, one always has the right so to be treated, and that while there may possibly be occasions morally requiring not according a person this right, this fact makes it no less true that the right exists and would be infringed if the person were not accorded it.

4. Having said something about the nature of this fundamental right I want now, in conclusion, to suggest that the denial of this right entails the denial of all moral rights and duties. This requires bringing out what is surely intuitively clear that any framework of rights and duties presupposes individuals that have the capacity to choose on the basis of reasons presented to them, and that what makes legitimate actions within such a system are the free choices of individuals. There is, in other words, a distribution of benefits and burdens in accord with a respect for the freedom of choice and freedom of action of all. I think that the best way to make this point may be to sketch some of the features of a world in which rights and duties are possessed.

First, rights exist only when there is some conception of some things valued and others not. Secondly, and implied in the first point, is the fact that there are dispositions to defend the valued commodities. Third, the valued commodities may be interfered with by others in this world. A group of animals might be said to satisfy these first three conditions. Fourth, rights exist when there are recognized rules establishing the legitimacy of some acts and ruling out others. Mistakes in the claim of right are possible. Rights imply the concepts of interference and infringement, concepts the elucidation of which requires the concept of a rule applying to the conduct of persons. Fifth, to possess a right is to possess something that constitutes a legitimate restraint on the freedom of action of others. It is clear, for example, that if individuals were incapable of controlling their actions we would have no notion of a legitimate claim that they do so. If, for example, we were all disposed to object or disposed to complain, as the elephant seal is disposed to object when his territory is invaded, then the objection would operate in a causal way, or approximating a causal way, in getting the behavior of noninterference. In a system of rights, on the other hand, there is a point to appealing to the rules in legitimating one's complaint. Implied, then, in any conception of rights are the existence of individuals capable of choosing and capable of choosing on the basis of considerations with respect to rules. The distribution of freedom throughout such a system is determined by the free choice of individuals. Thus any denial of the right to be treated as a person would be a denial undercutting the whole system, for the system rests on the assumption that spheres of legitimate and illegitimate conducts are to be delimited with regard to the choices made by persons.

This conclusion stimulates one final reflection on the therapy world we imagined.

The denial of this fundamental right will also carry with it, ironically, the denial of the right to treatment to those who are ill. In the world as

we now understand it, there are those who do wrong and who have a right
to be responded to as persons who have done wrong. And there are those
who have not done wrong but who are suffering from illnesses that in a
variety of ways interfere with their capacity to live their lives as complete
persons. These persons who are ill have a claim upon our compassion. But
more than this they have, as animals do not, a right to be treated as persons.
When an individual is ill he is entitled to that assistance which will make
it possible for him to resume his functioning as a person. If it is an injustice
to punish an innocent person, it is no less an injustice, and a far more
significant one in our day, to fail to promote as best we can through adequate facilities and medical care the treatment of those who are ill. Those
human beings who fill our mental institutions are entitled to more than
they do in fact receive; they should be viewed as possessing the right to be
treated as a person so that our responses to them may increase the likelihood that they will enjoy fully the right to be so treated. Like the child
the mentally ill person has a future interest we cannot rightly deny him.
Society is today sensitive to the infringement of justice in punishing the
innocent; elaborate rules exist to avoid this evil. Society should be no less
sensitive to the injustice of failing to bring back to the community of
persons those whom it is possible to bring back.

JEFFRIE G. MURPHY

Marxism and Retribution

Punishment in general has been defended as a means either of ameliorating or of intimidating. Now what right have you to punish me for
the amelioration or intimidation of others? And besides there is history
—there is such a thing as statistics—which prove with the most complete evidence that since Cain the world has been neither intimidated
nor ameliorated by punishment. Quite the contrary. From the point of

Reprinted from *Philosophy and Public Affairs*, Vol. 2, No. 3 (1973), 217–243.
Copyright © 1973 by Princeton University Press. Reprinted by permission of
the author and the publisher.

An earlier version of this essay was delivered to the Third Annual Colloquium in
Philosophy ("The Philosophy of Punishment") at the University of Dayton in
October, 1972. I am grateful to the Department of Philosophy at the University
of Dayton for inviting me to participate and to a number of persons at the
Colloquium for the useful discussion on my paper at the time. I am also grateful
to Anthony D. Woozley of the University of Virginia and to two of my colleagues, Robert M. Harnish and Francis V. Raab, for helping me to clarify the
expression of my views.

view of abstract right, there is only one theory of punishment which recognizes human dignity in the abstract, and that is the theory of Kant, especially in the more rigid formula given to it by Hegel. Hegel says: "Punishment is the *right* of the criminal. It is an act of his own will. The violation of right has been proclaimed by the criminal as his own right. His crime is the negation of right. Punishment is the negation of this negation, and consequently an affirmation of right, solicited and forced upon the criminal by himself."

There is no doubt something specious in this formula, inasmuch as Hegel, instead of looking upon the criminal as the mere object, the slave of justice, elevates him to the position of a free and self-determined being. Looking, however, more closely into the matter, we discover that German idealism here, as in most instances, has but given a transcendental sanction to the rules of existing society. Is it not a delusion to substitute for the individual with his real motives, with multifarious social circumstances pressing upon him, the abstraction of "free will"—one among the many qualities of man for man himself? . . . Is there not a necessity for deeply reflecting upon an alteration of the system that breeds these crimes, instead of glorifying the hangman who executes a lot of criminals to make room only for the supply of new ones?

Karl Marx, "Capital Punishment,"
New York Daily Tribune, *18 February 1853* [1]

Philosophers have written at great length about the moral problems involved in punishing the innocent—particularly as these problems raise obstacles to an acceptance of the moral theory of Utilitarianism. Punishment of an innocent man in order to bring about good social consequences is, at the very least, not always clearly wrong on utilitarian principles. This being so, utilitarian principles are then to be condemned by any

---

[1] In a sense, my paper may be viewed as an elaborate commentary on this one passage, excerpted from a discussion generally concerned with the efficacy of capital punishment in eliminating crime. For in this passage, Marx (to the surprise of many I should think) expresses a certain admiration for the classical retributive theory of punishment. Also (again surprisingly) he expresses this admiration in a kind of language he normally avoids—i.e., the moral language of rights and justice. He then, of course, goes on to reject the applicability of that theory. But the question that initially perplexed me is the following: what is the explanation of Marx's ambivalence concerning the retributive theory; why is he both attracted and repelled by it? (This ambivalence is not shared, for example, by utilitarians—who feel nothing but repulsion when the retributive theory is even mentioned.) Now except for some very brief passages in The Holy Family, Marx himself has nothing more to say on the topic of punishment beyond what is contained in this brief *Daily Tribune* article. Thus my essay is in no sense an exercise in textual scholarship (there are not enough texts) but is rather an attempt to construct an assessment of punishment, Marxist at least in spirit, that might account for the ambivalence found in the quoted passage. My main outside help comes, not from Marx himself, but from the writings of the Marxist criminologist Willem Bonger.

morality that may be called Kantian in character. For punishing an innocent man, in Kantian language, involves using that man as a mere means
or instrument to some social good and is thus not to treat him as an end
in himself, in accord with his dignity or worth as a person.

The Kantian position on the issue of punishing the innocent, and the
many ways in which the utilitarian might try to accommodate that position, constitute extremely well-worn ground in contemporary moral and
legal philosophy.[2] I do not propose to wear the ground further by adding
additional comments on the issue here. What I do want to point out,
however, is something which seems to me quite obvious but which philosophical commentators on punishment have almost universally failed to
see—namely, that problems of the very same kind and seriousness arise
for the utilitarian theory with respect to the punishment of the guilty. For
a utilitarian theory of punishment (Bentham's is a paradigm) must involve justifying punishment in terms of its social results—e.g., deterrence,
incapacitation, and rehabilitation. And thus even a guilty man is, on this
theory, being punished because of the instrumental value the action of
punishment will have in the future. He is being used as a means to some
future good—e.g., the deterrence of others. Thus those of a Kantian persuasion, who see the importance of worrying about the treatment of persons as mere means, must, it would seem, object just as strenuously to the
punishment of the guilty on utilitarian grounds as to the punishment of
the innocent. Indeed the former worry, in some respects, seems more
serious. For a utilitarian can perhaps refine his theory in such a way that
it does not commit him to the punishment of the innocent. However, if
he is to approve of punishment at all, he must approve of punishing the
guilty in at least some cases. This makes the worry about punishing the
guilty formidable indeed, and it is odd that this has gone generally unnoticed.[3] It has generally been assumed that if the utilitarian theory can
just avoid entailing the permissibility of punishing the innocent, then all
objections of a Kantian character to the theory will have been met. This
seems to me simply not to be the case.

What the utilitarian theory really cannot capture, I would suggest, is
the notion of persons having rights. And it is just this notion that is central to any Kantian outlook on morality. Any Kantian can certainly agree
that punishing persons (guilty or innocent) may have either good or bad
or indifferent consequences and that insofar as the consequences (whether
in a particular case or for an institution) are good, this is something in
favor of punishment. But the Kantian will maintain that this consequential
outlook, important as it may be, leaves out of consideration entirely that
which is most morally crucial—namely, the question of rights. Even if

2 Many of the leading articles on this topic have been reprinted in *The Philosophy of Punishment*, ed. H. B. Acton (London, 1969). Those papers not included are cited in Acton's excellent bibliography.
3 One writer who has noticed this is Richard Wasserstrom. See his "Why Punish the Guilty?" *Princeton University Magazine* 20 (1964), pp. 14–19.

punishment of a person would have good consequences, what gives us (i.e., society) the moral right to inflict it? If we have such a right, what is its origin or derivation? What social circumstances must be present for it to be applicable? What does this right to punish tell us about the status of the person to be punished—e.g., how are we to analyze his rights, the sense in which he must deserve to be punished, his obligations in the matter? It is this family of questions which any Kantian must regard as morally central and which the utilitarian cannot easily accommodate into his theory. And it is surely this aspect of Kant's and Hegel's retributivism, this seeing of rights as basic, which appeals to Marx in the quoted passage. As Marx himself puts it: "What right have you to punish me for the amelioration or intimidation of others?" And he further praises Hegel for seeing that punishment, if justified, must involve respecting the rights of the person to be punished. [4] Thus Marx, like Kant, seems prepared to draw the important distinction between (a) what it would be good to do on grounds of utility and (b) what we have a right to do. Since we do not always have the right to do what it would be good to do, this distinction is of the greatest moral importance; and missing the distinction is the Achilles heel of all forms of Utilitarianism. For consider the following example: A Jehovah's Witness needs a blood transfusion in order to live; but, because of his (we can agree absurd) religious belief that such transfusions are against God's commands, he instructs his doctor not to give him one. Here is a case where it would seem to be good or for the best to give the transfusion and yet, at the very least, it is highly doubtful that the doctor has a right to give it. This kind of distinction is elementary, and any theory which misses it is morally degenerate. [5]

To move specifically to the topic of punishment: How exactly does retributivism (of a Kantian or Hegelian variety) respect the rights of per-

---

[4] Marx normally avoids the language of rights and justice because he regards such language to be corrupted by bourgeois ideology. However, if we think very broadly of what an appeal to rights involves—namely, a protest against unjustified coercion—there is no reason why Marx may not legitimately avail himself on occasion of this way of speaking. For there is surely at least some moral overlap between Marx's protests against exploitation and the evils of a division of labor, for example, and the claims that people have a right not to be used solely for the benefit of others and a right to self-determination.

[5] I do not mean to suggest that under no conceivable circumstances would the doctor be justified in giving the transfusion even though, in one clear sense, he had no right to do it. If, for example, the Jehovah's Witness was a key man whose survival was necessary to prevent the outbreak of a destructive war, we might well regard the transfusion as on the whole justified. However, even in such a case, a morally sensitive man would have to regretfully realize that he was sacrificing an important principle. Such a realization would be impossible (because inconsistent) for a utilitarian, for his theory admits only one principle—namely, do that which on the whole maximizes utility. An occupational disease of utilitarians is a blindness to the possibility of genuine moral dilemmas—i.e., a blindness to the possibility that important moral principles can conflict in ways that are not obviously resolvable by a rational decision procedure.

sons? Is Marx really correct on this? I believe that he is. I believe that retributivism can be formulated in such a way that it is the only morally defensible theory of punishment. I also believe that arguments, which may be regarded as Marxist at least in spirit, can be formulated which show that social conditions as they obtain in most societies make this form of retributivism largely inapplicable within those societies. As Marx says, in those societies retributivism functions merely to provide a "transcendental sanction" for the status quo. If this is so, then the only morally defensible theory of punishment is largely inapplicable in modern societies. The consequence: modern societies largely lack the moral right to punish.[6] The upshot is that a Kantian moral theory (which in general seems to me correct) and a Marxist analysis of society (which, if properly qualified, also seems to me correct) produces a radical and not merely reformist attack not merely on the scope and manner of punishment in our society but on the institution of punishment itself. Institutions of punishment constitute what Bernard Harrison has called structural injustices [7] and are, in the absence of a major social change, to be resisted by all who take human rights to be morally serious—i.e., regard them as genuine action guides and not merely as rhetorical devices which allow people to morally sanctify institutions which in fact can only be defended on grounds of social expediency.

Stating all of this is one thing and proving it, of course, is another. Whether I can ever do this is doubtful. That I cannot do it in one brief article is certain. I cannot, for example, here defend in detail my belief that a generally Kantian outlook on moral matters is correct.[8] Thus I shall content myself for the present with attempting to render at least plausible two major claims involved in the view that I have outlined thus far: (1) that a retributive theory, in spite of the bad press that it has received, is a morally credible theory of punishment—that it can be, H. L. A. Hart to the contrary,[9] a reasonable general justifying aim of punishment; and (2) that a Marxist analysis of a society can undercut the practical applicability of that theory.

The Right of the State to Punish

It is strong evidence of the influence of a utilitarian outlook in moral and legal matters that discussions of punishment no longer involve a consid-

---

[6] I qualify my thesis by the word "largely" to show at this point my realization, explored in more detail later, that no single theory can account for all criminal behavior.

[7] Bernard Harrison, "Violence and the Rule of Law," in *Violence*, ed. Jerome A. Shaffer (New York, 1971), pp. 139–176.

[8] I have made a start toward such a defense in my "The Killing of the Innocent," forthcoming in *The Monist* 57, no. 4 (October 1973).

[9] H. L. A. Hart, "Prolegomenon to the Principles of Punishment," from *Punishment and Responsibility* (Oxford, 1968), pp. 1–27.

eration of the right of anyone to inflict it. Yet in the eighteenth and nineteenth centuries, this tended to be regarded as the central aspect of the problem meriting philosophical consideration. Kant, Hegel, Bosanquet, Green—all tended to entitle their chapters on punishment along the lines explicitly used by Green: "The Right of the State to Punish." [10] This is not just a matter of terminology but reflects, I think, something of deeper philosophical substance. These theorists, unlike the utilitarian, did not view man as primarily a maximizer of personal satisfactions—a maximizer of individual utilities. They were inclined, in various ways, to adopt a different model of man—man as a free or spontaneous creator, man as autonomous. (Marx, it may be noted, is much more in line with this tradition than with the utilitarian outlook.) [11] This being so, these theorists were inclined to view punishment (a certain kind of coercion by the state) as not merely a causal contributor to pain and suffering, but rather as presenting at least a prima facie challenge to the values of autonomy and personal dignity and self-realization—the very values which, in their view, the state existed to nurture. The problem as they saw it, therefore, was that of reconciling punishment as state coercion with the value of individual autonomy. (This is an instance of the more general problem which Robert Paul Wolff has called the central problem of political philosophy—namely, how is individual moral autonomy to be reconciled with legitimate political authority?) [12] This kind of problem, which I am inclined to agree is quite basic, cannot even be formulated intelligibly from a utilitarian perspective. Thus the utilitarian cannot even see the relevance of Marx's charge: Even if punishment has wonderful social consequences, what gives anyone the right to inflict it on me?

Now one fairly typical way in which others acquire rights over us is by our own consent. If a neighbor locks up my liquor cabinet to protect me against my tendencies to drink too heavily, I might well regard this as a presumptuous interference with my own freedom, no matter how good the result intended or accomplished. He had no right to do it and indeed violated my rights in doing it. If, on the other hand, I had asked him to do this or had given my free consent to his suggestion that he do it, the same sort of objection on my part would be quite out of order. I had given him the right to do it, and he had the right to do it. In doing it, he violated no rights of mine—even if, at the time of his doing it, I did not desire or want the action to be performed. Here then we seem to have a case where my autonomy may be regarded as intact even though a desire of mine is thwarted. For there is a sense in which the thwarting of the desire can be

[10] Thomas Hill Green, *Lectures on the Principles of Political Obligation* (1885), (Ann Arbor, 1967), pp. 180–205.

[11] For an elaboration of this point, see Steven Lukes, "Alienation and Anomie," in *Philosophy, Politics and Society* (Third Series), ed. Peter Laslett and W. G. Runciman (Oxford, 1967), pp. 134–156.

[12] Robert Paul Wolff, *In Defense of Anarchism* (New York, 1970).

imputed to me (my choice or decision) and not to the arbitrary intervention of another.

How does this apply to our problem? The answer, I think, is obvious.
What is needed, in order to reconcile my undesired suffering of punishment at the hands of the state with my autonomy (and thus with the
state's right to punish me), is a political theory which makes the state's
decision to punish me in some sense my own decision. If I have willed
my own punishment (consented to it, agreed to it) then—even if at the
time I happen not to desire it—it can be said that my autonomy and
dignity remain intact. Theories of the General Will and Social Contract
theories are two such theories which attempt this reconciliation of autonomy with legitimate state authority (including the right or authority of
the state to punish). Since Kant's theory happens to incorporate elements
of both, it will be useful to take it for our sample.

Moral Rights and the Retributive Theory of Punishment

To justify government or the state is necessarily to justify at least some
coercion.[13] This poses a problem for someone, like Kant, who maintains
that human freedom is the ultimate or most sacred moral value. Kant's
own attempt to justify the state, expressed in his doctrine of the *moral
title (Befugnis)*,[14] involves an argument that coercion is justified only in
so far as it is used to prevent invasions against freedom. Freedom itself is
the only value which can be used to limit freedom, for the appeal to any
other value (e.g., utility) would undermine the ultimate status of the value
of freedom. Thus Kant attempts to establish the claim that some forms
of coercion (as opposed to violence) are morally permissible because, contrary to appearance, they are really consistent with rational freedom. The
argument, in broad outline, goes in the following way. Coercion may keep
people from doing what they desire or want to do on a particular occasion and is thus prima facie wrong. However, such coercion can be shown
to be morally justified (and thus not absolutely wrong) if it can be estab-

[13] In this section, I have adapted some of my previously published material: *Kant: The
Philosophy of Right* (London, 1970), pp. 109–112 and 140–144; "Three Mistakes About Retributivism," *Analysis* (April 1971): 166–169; and "Kant's Theory
of Criminal Punishment," in *Proceedings of the Third International Kant Congress*, ed. Lewis White Beck (Dordrecht, 1972), pp. 434–441. I am perfectly
aware that Kant's views on the issues to be considered here are often obscure
and inconsistent—e.g., the analysis of "willing one's own punishment" which I
shall later quote from Kant occurs in a passage the primary purpose of which is
to argue that the idea of "willing one's own punishment" makes no sense! My
present objective, however, is not to attempt accurate Kant scholarship. My goal
is rather to build upon some remarks of Kant's which I find philosophically suggestive.

[14] Immanuel Kant, *The Metaphysical Elements of Justice* (1797), trans. John Ladd
(Indianapolis, 1965), pp. 35ff.

lished that the coercion is such that it could have been rationally willed
even by the person whose desire is interfered with:

> Accordingly, when it is said that a creditor has a right to demand from
> his debtor the payment of a debt, this does not mean that he can *per-
> suade* the debtor that his own reason itself obligates him to this per-
> formance; on the contrary, to say that he has such a right means only
> that the use of coercion to make anyone do this is entirely compatible
> with everyone's freedom, *including the freedom of the debtor*, in accor-
> dance with universal laws.[15]

Like Rousseau, Kant thinks that it is only in a context governed by
social practice (particularly civil government and its Rule of Law) that
this can make sense. Laws may require of a person some action that he
does not desire to perform. This is not a violent invasion of his freedom,
however, if it can be shown that in some antecedent position of choice
(what John Rawls calls "the original position"),[16] he would have been
rational to adopt a Rule of Law (and thus run the risk of having some of
his desires thwarted) rather than some other alternative arrangement like
the classical State of Nature. This is, indeed, the only sense that Kant is
able to make of classical Social Contract theories. Such theories are to be
viewed, not as historical fantasies, but as ideal models of rational decision.
For what these theories actually claim is that the only coercive institutions
that are morally justified are those which a group of rational beings
could agree to adopt in a position of having to pick social institutions to
govern their relations:

> The contract, which is called *contractus originarius*, or *pactum sociale*
> . . . need not be assumed to be a fact, indeed it is not [even possible
> as such. To suppose that would be like insisting] that before anyone
> would be bound to respect such a civic constitution, it be proved first of
> all from history that a people, whose rights and obligations we have
> entered into as their descendants, had *once upon a time* executed such
> an act and had left a reliable document or instrument, either orally or in
> writing, concerning this contract. Instead, this contract is a *mere idea* of
> reason which has undoubted practical reality; namely, to oblige every
> legislator to give us laws in such a manner that the laws *could* have orig-
> inated from the united will of the entire people and to regard every
> subject in so far as he is a citizen as though he had consented to such
> [an expression of the general] will. This is the testing stone of the right-
> ness of every publicly-known law, for if a law were such that it was im-
> possible for an entire people to give consent to it (as for example a law
> that a certain class of subjects, by inheritance, should have the privilege
> of the *status of lords*), then such a law is unjust. On the other hand,
> if there is a mere *possibility* that a people might consent to a (certain)

---

[15] *Ibid.*, p. 37.

[16] John Rawls, "Justice as Fairness," *The Philosophical Review* 67 (1958): 164–194;
and *A Theory of Justice* (Cambridge, Mass., 1971), especially pp. 17–22.

law, then it is a duty to consider that the law is just even though at the moment the people might be in such a position or have a point of view that would result in their refusing to give their consent to it if asked.[17]

The problem of organizing a state, however hard it may seem, can be solved even for a race of devils, if only they are intelligent. The problem is: "Given a multiple of rational beings requiring universal laws for their preservation, but each of whom is secretly inclined to exempt himself from them, to establish a constitution in such a way that, although their private intentions conflict, they check each other, with the result that their public conduct is the same as if they had no such intentions." [18]

Though Kant's doctrine is superficially similar to Mill's later self-protection principle, the substance is really quite different. For though Kant in some general sense argues that coercion is justified only to prevent harm to others, he understands by "harm" only certain invasions of freedom and not simply disutility. Also, his defense of the principle is not grounded, as is Mill's, on its utility. Rather it is to be regarded as a principle of justice, by which Kant means a principle that rational beings could adopt in a situation of mutual choice:

> The concept [of justice] applies only to the relationship of a will to another person's will, not to his wishes or desires (or even just his needs) which are the concern of acts of benevolence and charity. . . . In applying the concept of justice we take into consideration only the form of the relationship between the wills insofar as they are regarded as free, and whether the action of one of them can be conjoined with the freedom of the other in accordance with universal law. Justice is therefore the aggregate of those conditions under which the will of one person can be conjoined with the will of another in accordance with a universal law of freedom.[19]

How does this bear specifically on punishment? Kant, as everyone knows, defends a strong form of a retributive theory of punishment. He holds that guilt merits, and is a sufficient condition for, the infliction of punishment. And this claim has been universally condemned—particularly by utilitarians—as primitive, unenlightened and barbaric.

But why is it so condemned? Typically, the charge is that infliction of punishment on such grounds is nothing but pointless vengeance. But what is meant by the claim that the infliction is "pointless"? If "pointless" is tacitly being analyzed as "disutilitarian," then the whole question is simply being begged. You cannot refute a retributive theory merely by

[17] Immanuel Kant, "Concerning the Common Saying: This May be True in Theory but Does Not Apply in Practice (1793)," in *The Philosophy of Kant*, ed. and trans. Carl J. Friedrich (New York, 1949), pp. 421–422.

[18] Immanuel Kant, *Perpetual Peace* (1795), trans. Lewis White Beck in the Kant anthology *On History* (Indianapolis 1963), p. 112.

[19] Immanuel Kant, *The Metaphysical Elements of Justice*, p. 34.

noting that it is a retributive theory and not a utilitarian theory. This is to confuse redescription with refutation and involves an argument whose circularity is not even complicated enough to be interesting.

Why, then, might someone claim that guilt merits punishment? Such a claim might be made for either of two very different reasons. (1) Someone (e.g., a Moral Sense theorist) might maintain that the claim is a primitive and unanalyzable proposition that is morally ultimate—that we can just intuit the "fittingness" of guilt and punishment. (2) It might be maintained that the retributivist claim is demanded by a general theory of political obligation which is more plausible than any alternative theory. Such a theory will typically provide a technical analysis of such concepts as crime and punishment and will thus not regard the retributivist claim as an indisputable primitive. It will be argued for as a kind of theorem within the system.

Kant's theory is of the second sort. He does not opt for retributivism as a bit of intuitive moral knowledge. Rather he offers a theory of punishment that is based on his general view that political obligation is to be analyzed, quasi-contractually, in terms of reciprocity. If the law is to remain just, it is important to guarantee that those who disobey it will not gain an unfair advantage over those who do obey voluntarily. It is important that no man profit from his own criminal wrongdoing, and a certain kind of "profit" (i.e., not bearing the burden of self-restraint) is intrinsic to criminal wrongdoing. Criminal punishment, then, has as its object the restoration of a proper balance between benefit and obedience. The criminal himself has no complaint, because he has rationally consented to or willed his own punishment. That is, those very rules which he has broken work, when they are obeyed by others, to his own advantage as a citizen. He would have chosen such rules for himself and others in the original position of choice. And, since he derives and voluntarily accepts benefits from their operation, he owes his own obedience as a debt to his fellow-citizens for their sacrifices in maintaining them. If he chooses not to sacrifice by exercising self-restraint and obedience, this is tantamount to his choosing to sacrifice in another way—namely, by paying the prescribed penalty:

> A transgression of the public law that makes him who commits it unfit to be a citizen is called . . . a crime. . . .
>
> What kind of what degree of punishment does public legal justice adopt as its principle and standard? None other than the principle of equality (illustrated by the pointer of the scales of justice), that is, the principle of not treating one side more favorably than the other. Accordingly, any undeserved evil that you inflict on someone else among the people is one you do to yourself. If you vilify him, you vilify yourself; if you steal from him, you steal from yourself; if you kill him, you kill yourself. . . .
>
> To say, "I will to be punished if I murder someone" can mean nothing more than, "I submit myself along with everyone else to those laws

which, if there are any criminals among the people, will naturally include penal laws." [20]

This analysis of punishment regards it as a debt owed to the law-abiding members of one's community; and, once paid, it allows reentry into the community of good citizens on equal status.

Now some of the foregoing no doubt sounds implausible or even obscurantist. Since criminals typically desire not to be punished, what can it really mean to say that they have, as rational men, really willed their own punishment? Or that, as Hegel says, they have a right to it? Perhaps a comparison of the traditional retributivist views with those of a contemporary Kantian—John Rawls—will help to make the points clearer.[21] Rawls (like Kant) does not regard the idea of the social contract as an historical fact. It is rather a model of rational decision. Respecting a man's autonomy, at least on one view, is not respecting what he now happens, however uncritically, to desire; rather it is to respect what he desires (or would desire) as a rational man. (On Rawls's view, for example, rational men are said to be unmoved by feelings of envy; and thus it is not regarded as unjust to a person or a violation of his rights, if he is placed in a situation where he will envy another's advantage or position. A rational man would object, and thus would never consent to, a practice where another might derive a benefit from a position at his expense. He would not, however, envy the position *simpliciter*, would not regard the position as itself a benefit.) Now on Kant's (and also, I think, on Rawls's) view, a man is genuinely free or autonomous only in so far as he is rational. Thus it is man's rational will that is to be respected.

Now this idea of treating people, not as they in fact say that they want to be treated, but rather in terms of how you think they would, if rational, will to be treated, has obviously dangerous (indeed Fascistic) implications. Surely we want to avoid cramming indignities down the throats of people with the offhand observation that, no matter how much they scream, they are really rationally willing every bit of it. It would be particularly ironic for such arbitrary repression to come under the mask of respecting autonomy. And yet, most of us would agree, the general principle (though subject to abuse) also has important applications—for example, preventing the suicide of a person who, in a state of psychotic depression, wants to kill himself. What we need, then, to make the general

20 *Ibid.*, pp. 99, 101, and 105, in the order quoted.

21 In addition to the works on justice by Rawls previously cited, the reader should consult the following for Rawls's application of his general theory to the problem of political obligation: John Rawls, "Legal Obligation and the Duty of Fair Play," in *Law and Philosophy*, ed. Sidney Hook (New York, 1964), pp. 3–18. This has been reprinted in my anthology *Civil Disobedience and Violence* (Belmont, Cal., 1971), pp. 39–52. For a direct application of a similar theory to the problem of punishment, see Herbert Morris, "Persons and Punishment," *The Monist* 52, no. 4 (October 1968): 475–501.

view work, is a check on its arbitrary application; and a start toward providing such a check would be in the formulation of a public, objective theory of rationality and rational willing. It is just this, according to both Kant and Rawls, which the social contract theory can provide. On this theory, a man may be said to rationally will X if, and only if, X is called for by a rule that the man would necessarily have adopted in the original position of choice—i.e., in a position of coming together with others to pick rules for the regulation of their mutual affairs. This avoids arbitrariness because, according to Kant and Rawls at any rate, the question of whether such a rule would be picked in such a position is objectively determinable given certain (in their view) noncontroversial assumptions about human nature and rational calculation. Thus I can be said to will my own punishment if, in an antecedent position of choice, I and my fellows would have chosen institutions of punishment as the most rational means of dealing with those who might break the other generally beneficial social rules that had been adopted.

Let us take an analogous example: I may not, in our actual society, desire to treat a certain person fairly—e.g., I may not desire to honor a contract I have made with him because so doing would adversely affect my own self-interest. However, if I am forced to honor the contract by the state, I cannot charge (1) that the state has no right to do this, or (2) that my rights or dignity are being violated by my being coerced into doing it. Indeed, it can be said that I rationally will it since, in the original position, I would have chosen rules of justice (rather than rules of utility) and the principle, "contracts are to be honored," follows from the rules of justice.

Coercion and autonomy are thus reconciled, at least apparently. To use Marx's language, we may say (as Marx did in the quoted passage) that one virtue of the retributive theory, at least as expounded by Kant and Hegel on lines of the General Will and Social Contract theory, is that it manifests at least a formal or abstract respect for rights, dignity, and autonomy. For it as least recognizes the importance of attempting to construe state coercion in such a way that it is a product of each man's rational will. Utilitarian deterrence theory does not even satisfy this formal demand.

The question of primary interest to Marx, of course, is whether this formal respect also involves a material respect, i.e., does the theory have application in concrete fact in the actual social world in which we live? Marx is confident that it does not, and it is to this sort of consideration that I shall now pass.

Alienation and Punishment

What can the philosopher learn from Marx? This question is a part of a more general question: What can philosophy learn from social science?

Philosophers, it may be thought, are concerned to offer a priori theories, theories about how certain concepts are to be analyzed and their application justified. And what can the mundane facts that are the object of behavioral science have to do with exalted theories of this sort?

The answer, I think, is that philosophical theories, though not themselves empirical, often have such a character that their intelligibility depends upon certain empirical presuppositions. For example, our moral language presupposes, as Hart has argued,[22] that we are vulnerable creatures—creatures who can harm and be harmed by each other. Also, as I have argued elsewhere,[23] our moral language presupposes that we all share certain psychological characteristics—e.g., sympathy, a sense of justice, and the capacity to feel guilt, shame, regret, and remorse. If these facts were radically different (if, as Hart imagines for example, we all developed crustaceanlike exoskeletons and thus could not harm each other), the old moral language, and the moral theories which employ it, would lack application to the world in which we live. To use a crude example, moral prohibitions against killing presuppose that it is in fact possible for us to kill each other.

Now one of Marx's most important contributions to social philosophy, in my judgment, is simply his insight that philosophical theories are in peril if they are constructed in disregard of the nature of the empirical world to which they are supposed to apply.[24] A theory may be formally correct (i.e., coherent, or true for some possible world) but materially incorrect (i.e, inapplicable to the actual world in which we live). This insight, then, establishes the relevance of empirical research to philosophical theory and is a part, I think, of what Marx meant by "the union of theory and practice." Specifically relevant to the argument I want to develop are the following two related points:

(1) The theories of moral, social, political and legal philosophy presuppose certain empirical propositions about man and society. If these propositions are false, then the theory (even if coherent or formally correct) is materially defective and practically inapplicable. (For example, if persons tempted to engage in criminal conduct do not in fact tend to calculate carefully the consequences of their actions, this renders much of deterrence theory suspect.)

---

[22] H. L. A. Hart, *The Concept of Law* (Oxford, 1961), pp. 189–195.

[23] Jeffrie G. Murphy, "Moral Death: A Kantian Essay on Psychopathy," *Ethics* 82, no. 4 (July 1972): 284–298.

[24] Banal as this point may seem, it could be persuasively argued that all Enlightenment political theory (e.g., that of Hobbes, Locke and Kant) is built upon ignoring it. For example, once we have substantial empirical evidence concerning how democracies really work in fact, how sympathetic can we really be to classical theories for the justification of democracy? For more on this, see C. B. Macpherson, "The Maximization of Democracy," in *Philosophy, Politics and Society* (Third Series), ed. Peter Laslett and W. G. Runciman (Oxford, 1967), pp. 83–103. This article is also relevant to the point raised in note 11 above.

(2) Philosophical theories may put forth as a necessary truth that which is in fact merely an historically conditioned contingency. (For example, Hobbes argued that all men are necessarily selfish and competitive. It is possible, as many Marxists have argued, that Hobbes was really doing nothing more than elevating to the status of a necessary truth the contingent fact that the people around him in the capitalistic society in which he lived were in fact selfish and competitive.) [25]

In outline, then, I want to argue the following: that when Marx challenges the material adequacy of the retributive theory of punishment, he is suggesting (a) that it presupposes a certain view of man and society that is false and (b) that key concepts involved in the support of the theory (e.g., the concept of "rationality" in Social Contract theory) are given analyses which, though they purport to be necessary truths, are in fact mere reflections of certain historical circumstances.

In trying to develop this case, I shall draw primarily upon Willem Bonger's *Criminality and Economic Conditions* (1916), one of the few sustained Marxist analyses of crime and punishment.[26] Though I shall not have time here to qualify my support of Bonger in certain necessary ways, let met make clear that I am perfectly aware that his analysis is not the whole story. (No monolithic theory of anything so diverse as criminal behavior could be the whole story.) However, I am convinced that he has discovered part of the story. And my point is simply that insofar as Bonger's Marxist analysis is correct, then to that same degree is the retributive theory of punishment inapplicable in modern societies. (Let me emphasize again exactly how this objection to retributivism differs from those traditionally offered. Traditionally, retributivism has been rejected because it conflicts with the moral theory of its opponent, usually a utilitarian. This is not the kind of objection I want to develop. Indeed, with Marx, I have argued that the retributive theory of punishment grows out of the moral theory— Kantianism—which seems to me generally correct. The objection I want to pursue concerns the empirical falsity of the factual presuppositions of the theory. If the empirical presuppositions of the theory are false, this does indeed render its application immoral. But the immorality consists, not in a conflict with some other moral theory, but immorality in terms

---

[25] This point is well developed in C. B. Macpherson, *The Political Theory of Possessive Individualism* (Oxford, 1962). In a sense, this point affects even the formal correctness of a theory. For it demonstrates an empirical source of corruption in the analyses of the very concepts in the theory.

[26] The writings of Willem Adriaan Bonger (1876–1940), a Dutch criminologist, have fallen into totally unjustified neglect in recent years. Anticipating contemporary sociological theories of crime, he was insisting that criminal behavior is in the province of normal psychology (though abnormal society) at a time when most other writers were viewing criminality as a symptom of psychopathology. His major works are: *Criminality and Economic Conditions* (Boston, 1916); *An Introduction to Criminology* (London, 1936); and *Race and Crime* (New York, 1943).

of a moral theory that is at least close in spirit to the very moral theory which generates retributivism itself—i.e., a theory of justice.) [27]

To return to Bonger. Put bluntly, his theory is as follows. Criminality has two primary sources: (1) need and deprivation on the part of disadvantaged members of society, and (2) motives of greed and selfishness that are generated and reinforced in competitive capitalistic societies. Thus criminality is economically based—either directly in the case of crimes from need, or indirectly in the case of crimes growing out of motives or psychological states that are encouraged and developed in capitalistic society. In Marx's own language, such as economic system alienates men from themselves and from each other. It alienates men from themselves by creating motives and needs that are not "truly human." It alienates men from their fellows by encouraging a kind of competitiveness that forms an obstacle to the development of genuine communities to replace mere social aggregates.[28] And in Bonger's thought, the concept of community is central. He argues that moral relations and moral restraint are possible only in genuine communities characterized by bonds of sympathetic identification and mutual aid resting upon a perception of common humanity. All this he includes under the general rubric of reciprocity.[29] In the absence of reciprocity in this rich sense, moral relations among men will break down and criminality will increase.[30] Within bourgeois society, then, crimes are to be regarded as normal, and not psychopathological,

[27] I say "at least in spirit" to avoid begging the controversial question of whether Marx can be said to embrace a theory of justice. Though (as I suggested in note 4) much of Marx's own evaluative rhetoric seems to overlap more traditional appeals to rights and justice (and a total lack of sympathy with anything like Utilitarianism), it must be admitted that he also frequently ridicules at least the terms "rights" and "justice" because of their apparent entrenchment in bourgeois ethics. For an interesting discussion of this issue, see Allen W. Wood, "The Marxian Critique of Justice," *Philosophy & Public Affairs* 1, no. 3 (Spring 1972): 244–282.

[28] The importance of community is also, I think, recognized in Gabriel de Tarde's notion of "social similarity" as a condition of criminal responsibility. See his *Penal Philosophy* (Boston, 1912). I have drawn on de Tarde's general account in my "Moral Death: A Kantian Essay on Psychopathy."

[29] By "reciprocity" Bonger intends something which includes, but is much richer than, a notion of "fair trading or bargaining" that might initially be read into the term. He also has in mind such things as sympathetic identification with others and tendencies to provide mutual aid. Thus, for Bonger, reciprocity and egoism have a strong tendency to conflict. I mention this lest Bonger's notion of reciprocity be too quickly identified with the more restricted notion found in, for example, Kant and Rawls.

[30] It is interesting how greatly Bonger's analysis differs from classical deterrence theory—e.g., that of Bentham. Bentham, who views men as machines driven by desires to attain pleasure and avoid pain, tends to regard terror as the primary restraint against crime. Bonger believes that, at least in a healthy society, moral motives would function as a major restraint against crime. When an environment that destroys moral motivation is created, even terror (as statistics tend to confirm) will not eradicate crime.

acts. That is, they grow out of need, greed, indifference to others, and sometimes even a sense of indignation—all, alas, perfectly typical human motives.

To appreciate the force of Bonger's analysis, it is necessary to read his books and grasp the richness and detail of the evidence he provides for his claims. Here I can but quote a few passages at random to give the reader a tantalizing sample in the hope that he will be encouraged to read further into Bonger's own text:

> The abnormal element in crime is a social, not a biological, element. With the exception of a few special cases, crime lies within the boundaries of normal psychology and physiology. . . .
>
> We clearly see that [the egoistic tendencies of the present economic system and of its consequences] are very strong. Because of these tendencies the social instinct of man is not greatly developed; they have weakened the moral force in man which combats the inclination towards egoistic acts, and hence toward the crimes which are one form of these acts. . . . Compassion for the misfortunes of others inevitably becomes blunted, and a great part of morality consequently disappears. . . .
>
> As a consequence of the present environment, man has become very egoistic and hence more *capable of crime,* than if the environment had developed the germs of altruism. . . .
>
> There can be no doubt that one of the factors of criminality among the bourgeoisie is bad [moral] education. . . . The children—speaking of course in a general way—are brought up with the idea that they must succeed, no matter how; the aim of life is presented to them as getting money and shining in the world. . . .
>
> Poverty (taken in the sense of absolute want) kills the social sentiments in man, destroys in fact all relations between men. He who is abandoned by all can no longer have any feeling for those who have left him to his fate. . . .
>
> [Upon perception that the system tends to legalize the egoistic actions of the bourgeoisie and to penalize those of the proletariat], the oppressed resort to means which they would otherwise scorn. As we have seen above, the basis of the social feeling is reciprocity. As soon as this is trodden under foot by the ruling class the social sentiments of the oppressed become weak towards them. . . .[31]

[31] *Introduction to Criminology,* pp. 75–76, and *Criminality and Economic Conditions,* pp. 532, 402, 483–484, 436, and 407, in the order quoted. Bonger explicitly attacks Hobbes: "The adherents of [Hobbes's theory] have studied principally men who live under capitalism, or under civilization; their correct conclusion has been that egoism is the predominant characteristic of these men, and they have adopted the simplest explanation of the phenomenon and say that this trait is inborn." If Hobbists can cite Freud for modern support, Bonger can cite Darwin. For, as Darwin had argued in the *Descent of Man,* men would not have survived as a species if they had not initially had considerably greater social sentiments than Hobbes allows them.

The essence of this theory has been summed up by Austin J. Turk. "Criminal behavior," he says, "is almost entirely attributable to the combination of egoism and an environment in which opportunities are not equitably distributed." [32]

No doubt this claim will strike many as extreme and intemperate—a sample of the old-fashioned Marxist rhetoric that sophisticated intellectuals have outgrown. Those who are inclined to react in this way might consider just one sobering fact: of the 1.3 million criminal offenders handled each day by some agency of the United States correctional system, the vast majority (80 percent on some estimates) are members of the lowest 15-percent income level—that percent which is below the "poverty level" as defined by the Social Security Administration.[33] Unless one wants to embrace the belief that all these people are poor because they are bad, it might be well to reconsider Bonger's suggestion that many of them are "bad" because they are poor.[34] At any rate, let us suppose for purposes of discussion that Bonger's picture of the relation between crime and economic conditions is generally accurate. At what points will this challenge the credentials of the contractarian retributive theory as outlined above? I should like to organize my answer to this question around three basic topics:

[32] Austin J. Turk, in the Introduction to his abridged edition of Bonger's *Criminality and Economic Conditions* (Bloomington, 1969), p. 14.

[33] Statistical data on characteristics of offenders in America are drawn primarily from surveys by the Bureau of Census and the National Council on Crime and Delinquency. While there is of course wide disagreement on how such data are to be interpreted, there is no serious disagreement concerning at least the general accuracy of statistics like the one I have cited. Even government publications openly acknowledge a high correlation between crime and socioeconomic disadvantages: "From arrest records, probation reports, and prison statistics a 'portrait' of the offender emerges that progressively highlights the disadvantaged character of his life. The offender at the end of the road in prison is likely to be a member of the lowest social and economic groups in the country, poorly educated and perhaps unemployed. . . . Material failure, then, in a culture firmly oriented toward material success, is the most common denominator of offenders" (*The Challenge of Crime in a Free Society, A Report by the President's Commission on Law Enforcement and Administration of Justice*, U.S. Government Printing Office, Washington, D.C., 1967, pp. 44 and 160). The Marxist implications of this admission have not gone unnoticed by prisoners. See Samuel Jorden, "Prison Reform: In Whose Interest?" *Criminal Law Bulletin* 7, no. 9 (November 1971): 779–787.

[34] There are, of course, other factors which enter into an explanation of this statistic. One of them is the fact that economically disadvantaged guilty persons are more likely to wind up arrested or in prison (and thus be reflected in this statistic) than are economically advantaged guilty persons. Thus economic conditions enter into the explanation, not just of criminal behavior, but of society's response to criminal behavior. For a general discussion on the many ways in which crime and poverty are related, see Patricia M. Wald, "Poverty and Criminal Justice," *Task Force Report: The Courts*, U.S. Government Printing Office, Washington, D.C., 1967, pp. 139–151.

1. RATIONAL CHOICE. The model of rational choice found in Social Contract theory is egoistic—rational institutions are those that would be agreed to by calculating egoists ("devils" in Kant's more colorful terminology). The obvious question that would be raised by any Marxist is: Why give egoism this special status such that it is built, a priori, into the analysis of the concept of rationality? Is this not simply to regard as necessary that which may be only contingently found in the society around us? Starting from such an analysis, a certain result is inevitable—namely, a transcendental sanction for the status quo. Start with a bourgeois model of rationality and you will, of course, wind up defending a bourgeois theory of consent, a bourgeois theory of justice, and a bourgeois theory of punishment.

Though I cannot explore the point in detail here, it seems to me that this Marxist claim may cause some serious problems for Rawls's well-known theory of justice, a theory which I have already used to unpack some of the evaluative support for the retributive theory of punishment. One cannot help suspecting that there is a certain sterility in Rawls's entire project of providing a rational proof for the preferability of a certain conception of justice over all possible alternative evaluative principles, for the description which he gives of the rational contractors in the original position is such as to guarantee that they will come up with his two principles. This would be acceptable if the analysis of rationality presupposed were intuitively obvious or argued for on independent grounds. But it is not. Why, to take just one example, is a desire for wealth a rational trait whereas envy is not? One cannot help feeling that the desired result dictates the premises.[35]

---

[35] The idea that the principles of justice could be proved as a kind of theorem (Rawls's claim in "Justice as Fairness") seems to be absent, if I understand the work correctly, in Rawls's recent A Theory of Justice. In this book, Rawls seems to be content with something less than a decision procedure. He is no longer trying to pull his theory of justice up by its own bootstraps, but now seems concerned simply to *exhibit* a certain elaborate conception of justice in the belief that it will do a good job of systematizing and ordering most of our considered and reflective intuitions about moral matters. To this, of course, the Marxist will want to say something like the following: "The considered and reflective intuitions current in our society are a product of bourgeois culture, and thus any theory based upon them begs the question against us and in favor of the status quo." I am not sure that this charge cannot be answered, but I am sure that it deserves an answer. Someday Rawls may be remembered, to paraphrase Georg Lukács's description of Thomas Mann, as the last and greatest philosopher of bourgeois liberalism. The virtue of this description is that it perceives the limitations of his outlook in a way consistent with acknowledging his indisputable genius. (None of my remarks here, I should point out, are to be interpreted as denying that our civilization derived major moral benefits from the tradition of bourgeois liberalism. Just because the freedoms and procedures we associate with bourgeois liberalism—speech, press, assembly, due process of law, etc.—are not the only important freedoms and procedures, we are not to conclude with some witless radicals that these freedoms are not terribly important and that the victories of bourgeois revolutions are not worth preserving. My point is much more

2. JUSTICE, BENEFITS, AND COMMUNITY. The retributive theory claims to be grounded on justice; but is it just to punish people who act out of those very motives that society encourages and reinforces? If Bonger is correct, much criminality is motivated by greed, selfishness, and indifference to one's fellows; but does not the whole society encourage motives of greed and selfishness ("making it," "getting ahead"), and does not the competitive nature of the society alienate men from each other and thereby encourage indifference—even, perhaps, what psychiatrists call psychopathy? The moral problem here is similar to one that arises with respect to some war crimes. When you have trained a man to believe that the enemy is not a genuine human person (but only a gook, or a chink), it does not seem quite fair to punish the man if, in a war situation, he kills indiscriminately. For the psychological trait you have conditioned him to have, like greed, is not one that invites fine moral and legal distinctions. There is something perverse in applying principles that presuppose a sense of community in a society which is structured to destroy genuine community.[36]

Related to this is the whole allocation of benefits in contemporary society. The retributive theory really presupposes what might be called a "gentlemen's club" picture of the relation between man and society—i.e, men are viewed as being part of a community of shared values and rules. The rules benefit all concerned and, as a kind of debt for the benefits derived, each man owes obedience to the rules. In the absence of such obedience, he deserves punishment in the sense that he owes payment for the benefits. For, as rational man, he can see that the rules benefit everyone (himself included) and that he would have selected them in the original position of choice.

Now this may not be too far off for certain kinds of criminals—e.g., business executives guilty of tax fraud. (Though even here we might regard their motives of greed to be a function of societal reinforcement.) But to think that it applies to the typical criminal, from the poorer classes, is to live in a world of social and political fantasy. Criminals typically are not members of a shared community of values with their jailers; they suffer from what Marx calls alienation. And they certainly would be hard-pressed to name the benefits for which they are supposed to owe obedience. If justice, as both Kant and Rawls suggest, is based on reciprocity, it is hard to see what these persons are supposed to reciprocate for. Bonger addresses this point in a passage quoted earlier (p. 236): "The oppressed

---

modest and noncontroversial—namely, that even bourgeois liberalism requires a critique. It is not self-justifying and, in certain very important respects, is not justified at all.)

[36] Kant has some doubts about punishing bastard infanticide and dueling on similar grounds. Given the stigma that Kant's society attached to illegitimacy and the halo that the same society placed around military honor, it did not seem totally fair to punish those whose criminality in part grew out of such approved motives. See *Metaphysical Elements of Justice*, pp. 106–107.

resort to means which they would otherwise scorn. . . . The basis of social feelings is reciprocity. As soon as this is trodden under foot by the ruling class, the social sentiments of the oppressed become weak towards them."

3. VOLUNTARY ACCEPTANCE. Central to the Social Contract idea is the claim that we owe allegiance to the law because the benefits we have derived have been voluntarily accepted. This is one place where our autonomy is supposed to come it. That is, having benefited from the Rule of Law when it was possible to leave, I have in a sense consented to it and to its consequences—even my own punishment if I violate the rules. To see how silly the factual presuppositions of this account are, we can do no better than quote a famous passage from David Hume's essay "Of the Original Contract":

> Can we seriously say that a poor peasant or artisan has a free choice to leave his country—when he knows no foreign language or manners, and lives from day to day by the small wages which he acquires? We may as well assert that a man, by remaining in a vessel, freely consents to the dominion of the master, though he was carried on board while asleep, and must leap into the ocean and perish the moment he leaves her.

A banal empirical observation, one may say. But it is through ignoring such banalities that philosophers generate theories which allow them to spread iniquity in the ignorant belief that they are spreading righteousness.

It does, then, seem as if there may be some truth in Marx's claim that the retributive theory, though formally correct, is materially inadequate. At root, the retributive theory fails to acknowledge that criminality is, to a large extent, a phenomenon of economic class. To acknowledge this is to challenge the empirical presupposition of the retributive theory —the presupposition that all men, including criminals, are voluntary participants in a reciprocal system of benefits and that the justice of this arrangement can be derived from some eternal and ahistorical concept of rationality.

The upshot of all this seems rather upsetting, as indeed it is. How can it be the case that everything we are ordinarily inclined to say about punishment (in terms of utility and retribution) can be quite beside the point? To anyone with ordinary language sympathies (one who is inclined to maintain that what is correct to say is a function of what we do say), this will seem madness. Marx will agree that there is madness, all right, but in his view the madness will lie in what we do say—what we say only because of our massive (and often self-deceiving and self-serving) factual ignorance or indifference to the circumstances of the social world in which we live. Just as our whole way of talking about mental phenomena hardened before we knew any neurophysiology—and this leads us astray, so Marx would argue that our whole way of talking about moral and political phenomena hardened before we knew any of the relevant empirical facts about man and society—and this, too, leads us astray. We all suffer from what might be called the *embourgeoisment* of language, and thus part of any revolution will be a linguistic or conceptual revolution. We have grown accustomed to modifying our language or conceptual structures under the impact of empirical discoveries in physics. There is no reason why discoveries in sociology, economics, or psychology could not and should not have the same effect on entrenched patterns of thought and speech. It is important to remember, as Russell remarked, that our language sometimes enshrines the metaphysics of the Stone Age.

Consider one example: a man has been convicted of armed robbery. On investigation, we learn that he is an impoverished black whose whole life has been one of frustrating alienation from the prevailing socio-economic structure—no job, no transportation if he could get a job, substandard education for his children, terrible housing and inadequate health care for his whole family, condescending-tardy-inadequate welfare payments, harassment by the police but no real protection by them against the dangers in his community, and near total exclusion from the political process. Learning all this, would we still want to talk—as many do—of his suffering punishment under the rubric of "paying a debt to society"? Surely not. Debt for what? I do not, of course, pretend that all criminals can be so described. But I do think that this is a closer picture of the typical criminal than the picture that is presupposed in the retributive theory —i.e., the picture of an evil person who, of his own free will, intentionally acts against those just rules of society which he knows, as a rational man, benefit everyone including himself.

But what practical help does all this offer, one may ask. How should we design our punitive practices in the society in which we now live? This is the question we want to ask, and it does not seem to help simply to say that our society is built on deception and inequity. How can Marx help us with our real practical problem? The answer, I think, is that he cannot and obviously does not desire to do so. For Marx would say that we have not focused (as all piecemeal reform fails to focus) on what is truly the real problem. And this is changing the basic social relations. Marx is the last person from whom we can expect advice on how to make our intellectual and moral peace with bourgeois society. And this is surely his attraction and his value.

What does Bonger offer? He suggests, near the end of his book, that in a properly designed society all criminality would be a problem "for the physician rather than the judge." But this surely will not do. The therapeutic state, where prisons are called hospitals and jailers are called psychiatrists, simply raises again all the old problems about the justification of coercion and its reconciliation with autonomy that we faced in worrying about punishment. The only difference is that our coercive practices are now surrounded with a benevolent rhetoric which makes it even harder to raise the important issues. Thus the move to therapy, in my judgment, is only an illusory solution—alienation remains and the problem of reconciling coercion with autonomy remains unsolved. Indeed, if the alternative is having our personalities involuntarily restructured by some state psychiatrist, we might well want to claim the "right to be punished" that Hegel spoke of.[37]

Perhaps, then, we may really be forced seriously to consider a radical proposal. If we think that institutions of punishment are necessary and desirable, and if we are morally sensitive enough to want to be sure that we have the moral right to punish before we inflict it, then we had better first make sure that we have restructured society in such a way that criminals genuinely do correspond to the only model that will render punishment permissible—i.e., make sure that they are autonomous and that they do benefit in the requisite sense. Of course, if we did this then—if Marx and Bonger are right—crime itself and the need to punish would radically decrease if not disappear entirely.

Furman v. Georgia, 408 U.S. 238
92 S.Ct. 2726, 33 L. Ed. 2d 346 (1972)

MR. JUSTICE DOUGLAS, concurring.

In these three cases the death penalty was imposed, one of them for murder, and two for rape. In each the determination of whether the penalty should be death or a lighter punishment was left by the State to the discretion of the judge or of the jury. In each of the three cases the trial was to a jury. They are here on petitions for certiorari which we granted limited to the question whether the imposition and execution of the death penalty constitute "cruel and unusual punishment" within the meaning of the

Editor's Note: Each of the nine Justices of the Supreme Court filed an opinion in this case in which the Court, by vote of 5 to 4, reversed the imposition of the death sentence in the three cases on appeal. Reproduced are portions of the opinions of Justices Douglas, Brennan, Powell, and Chief Justice Burger. Footnotes have been renumbered.

[37] This point is pursued in Herbert Morris, "Persons and Punishment." Bonger did not appreciate that "mental illness," like criminality, may also be a phenomenon of social class. On this, see August B. Hollingshead and Frederick C. Redlich, *Social Class and Mental Illness* (New York, 1958). On the general issue of punishment versus therapy, see my *Punishment and Rehabilitation* (Belmont, Cal., 1973).

Eighth Amendment as applied to the States by the Fourteenth.[1] I vote to vacate each judgment, believing that the exaction of the death penalty does violate the Eighth and Fourteenth Amendments.

. . .

It has been assumed in our decisions that punishment by death is not cruel, unless the manner of execution can be said to be inhuman and barbarous. *In re Kemmler,* 136, U. S. 436, 447. It is also said in our opinions that the proscription of cruel and unusual punishments "is not fastened to the obsolete but may acquire meaning as public opinion becomes enlightened by a humane justice." *Weems* v. *United States, supra,* at 378. A like statement was made in *Trop* v. *Dulles,* 356 U.S. 86, 101, that the Eighth Amendment "must draw its meaning from the evolving standards of decency that mark the progress of a maturing society."

The generality of a law inflicting capital punishment is one thing. What may be said of the validity of a law on the books and what may be done with the law in its application do, or may, lead to quite different conclusions.

It would seem to be incontestable that the death penalty inflicted on one defendant is "unusual" if it discriminates against him by reason of his race, religion, wealth, social position, or class, or if it is imposed under a procedure that gives room for the play of such prejudices.

. . .

There is increasing recognition of the fact that the basic theme of equal protection is implicit in "cruel and unusual" punishments. "A penalty . . . should be considered 'unusually' imposed if it is administered arbitrarily or discriminatorily." [2] The same authors add that "[t]he extreme rarity with which applicable death penalty provisions are put to use raises a strong inference of arbitrariness." [3] The President's Commission on Law Enforcement and Administration of Justice recently concluded: [4]

> Finally there is evidence that the imposition of the death sentence and the exercise of dispensing power by the courts and the executive follow discriminatory patterns. The death sentence is disproportionately imposed and carried out on the poor, the Negro, and the members of unpopular groups.

[1] The opinion of the Supreme Court of Georgia affirming Furman's conviction of murder and sentence of death is reported in 225 Ga. 253, 167 S. E. 2d 628, and its opinion affirming Jackson's conviction of rape and sentence of death is reported in 225 Ga. 790, 171 S. E. 2d 501. The conviction of Branch of rape and the sentence of death were affirmed by the Court of Criminal Appeals of Texas and reported in 447 S. W. 2d 932.

[2] Goldberg & Dershowitz, Declaring the Death Penalty Unconstitutional, 83 Harv. L. Rev. 1773, 1790.

[3] *Id.*, at 1792.

[4] The Challenge of Crime in a Free Society 143 (1967).

A study of capital cases in Texas from 1924 to 1968 reached the following conclusions: [5]

> Application of the death penalty is unequal: most of those executed were poor, young, and ignorant.

• • •

> Seventy-five of the 460 cases involved co-defendants, who, under Texas law, were given separate trials. In several instances where a white and a Negro were co-defendants, the white was sentenced to life imprisonment or a term of years, and the Negro was given the death penalty.
> Another ethnic disparity is found in the type of sentence imposed for rape. The Negro convicted of rape is far more likely to get the death penalty than a term sentence, whereas whites and Latins are far more likely to get a term sentence than the death penalty.

Warden Lewis E. Lawes of Sing Sing said: [6]

[5] Koeninger, Capital Punishment in Texas, 1924–1968, 15 Crime & Delin. 132, 141 (1969).

In H. Bedau, The Death Penalty in America 474 (1967 rev. ed.), it is stated:

RACE OF THE OFFENDER BY FINAL DISPOSITION

Final Disposition	Negro		White		Total	
	N	%	N	%	N	%
Executed	130	88.4	210	79.8	340	82.9
Commuted	17	11.6	53	20.2	70	17.1
Total	147	100.0	263	100.0	410	100.0

$X^2 = 4.33$; P less than .05. (For discussion of statistical symbols, see Bedau, *supra*, at 469.)

> "Although there may be a host of factors other than race involved in this frequency distribution, something more than chance has operated over the years to produce this racial difference. On the basis of this study it is not possible to indict the judicial and other public processes prior to the death row as responsible for the association between Negroes and higher frequency of executions; nor is it entirely correct to assume that from the time of their appearance on death row Negroes are discriminated against by the Pardon Board. Too many unknown or presently immeasurable factors prevent our making definitive statements about the relationship. Nevertheless, because the Negro/high-execution association is statistically present, some suspicion of racial discrimination can hardly be avoided. If such a relationship had not appeared, this kind of suspicion could have been allayed; the existence of the relationship, although not 'proving' differential bias by the Pardon Boards over the years since 1914, strongly suggests that such bias has existed."
> The latter was a study in Pennsylvania of people on death row between 1914 and 1958, made by Wolfgang, Kelly, & Nolde and printed in 53 J. Crim. L. C. & P. S. 301 (1962). And see Hartung, Trends in the Use of Capital Punishment, 284 Annals 8, 14–17 (1952).

[6] Life and Death in Sing Sing 155–160 (1928).

Not only does capital punishment fail in its justification, but no punishment could be invented with so many inherent defects. It is an unequal punishment in the way it is applied to the rich and to the poor. The defendant of wealth and position never goes to the electric chair or to the gallows. Juries do not intentionally favour the rich, the law is theoretically impartial, but the defendant with ample means is able to have his case presented with every favourable aspect, while the poor defendant often has a lawyer assigned by the court. Sometimes such assignment is considered part of political patronage; usually the lawyer assigned has had no experience whatever in a capital case.

Former Attorney General Ramsey Clark has said, "It is the poor, the sick, the ignorant, the powerless and the hated who are executed." [7] One searches our chronicles in vain for the execution of any member of the affluent strata of this society. The Leopolds and Loebs are given prison terms, not sentenced to death.

•   •   •

Those who wrote the Eighth Amendment knew what price their forebears had paid for a system based, not on equal justice, but on discrimination. In those days the target was not the blacks or the poor, but the dissenters, those who opposed absolutism in government, who struggled for a parliamentary regime, and who opposed governments' recurring efforts to foist a particular religion on the people. . . . But the tool of capital punishment was used with vengeance against the opposition and those unpopular with the regime. One cannot read this history without realizing that the desire for equality was reflected in the ban against "cruel and unusual punishments" contained in the Eighth Amendment.

In a Nation committed to equal protection of the laws there is no permissible "caste" aspect [8] of law enforcement. Yet we know that the discretion of judges and juries in imposing the death penalty enables the penalty to be selectively applied, feeding prejudices against the accused if he is poor and despised, and lacking political clout, or if he is a member of a suspect or unpopular minority, and saving those who by social position may be in a more protected position. In ancient Hindu law a Brahman was exempt from capital punishment,[9] and under that law, "[g]enerally, in the law books, punishment increased in severity as social status diminished." [10] We have, I fear, taken in practice the same position, partially as a result of making the death penalty discretionary and partially as a result of the ability of the rich to purchase the services of the most respected and most resourceful legal talent in the Nation.

[7] Crime in America 335 (1970).
[8] See Johnson, The Negro and Crime, 217 Annals 93 (1941).
[9] See J. Spellman, Political Theory of Ancient India 112 (1964).
[10] C. Drekmeier, Kingship and Community in Early India 233 (1962).

The high service rendered by the "cruel and unusual" punishment clause of the Eighth Amendment is to require legislatures to write penal laws that are even-handed, nonselective, and nonarbitrary, and to require judges to see to it that general laws are not applied sparsely, selectively, and spottily to unpopular groups.

A law that stated that anyone making more than $50,000 would be exempt from the death penalty would plainly fall, as would a law that in terms said that blacks, those who never went beyond the fifth grade in school, those who made less than $3,000 a year, or those who were unpopular or unstable should be the only people executed. A law which in the overall view reaches that result in practice [11] has no more sanctity than a law which in terms provides the same.

Thus, these discretionary statutes are unconstitutional in their operation. They are pregnant with discrimination and discrimination is an ingredient not compatible with the idea of equal protection of the laws that is implicit in the ban on "cruel and unusual" punishments.

Any law which is nondiscriminatory on its face may be applied in such a way as to violate the Equal Protection Clause of the Fourteenth Amendment. *Yick Wo* v. *Hopkins*, 118 U.S. 356. Such conceivably might be the fate of a mandatory death penalty, where equal or lesser sentences were imposed on the elite, a harsher one on the minorities or members of the lower castes. Whether a mandatory death penalty would otherwise be constitutional is a question I do not reach.

---

[11] Cf. B. Prettyman, Jr., Death and The Supreme Court 296–297 (1961).

"The disparity of representation in capital cases raises doubts about capital punishment itself, which has been abolished in only nine states. If a James Avery [345 U.S. 559] can be saved from electrocution because his attorney made timely objection to the selection of a jury by the use of yellow and white tickets, while an Aubry Williams [349 U.S. 375] can be sent to his death by a jury selected in precisely the same manner, we are imposing our most extreme penalty in an uneven fashion.

"The problem of proper representation is not a problem of money, as some have claimed, but of a lawyer's ability, and it is not true that only the rich have able lawyers. Both the rich and the poor usually are well represented—the poor because more often than not the best attorneys are appointed to defend them. It is the middle-class defendant, who can afford to hire an attorney but not a very good one, who is at a disadvantage. Certainly William Fikes [352 U.S. 191], despite the anomalous position in which he finds himself today, received as effective and intelligent a defense from his court-appointed attorneys as he would have received from an attorney his family had scraped together enough money to hire.

"And it is not only a matter of ability. An attorney must be found who is prepared to spend precious hours—the basic commodity he has to sell—on a case that seldom fully compensates him and often brings him no fee at all. The public has no conception of the time and effort devoted by attorneys to indigent cases. And in a first-degree case, the added responsibility of having a man's life depend upon the outcome exacts a heavy toll."

I concur in the judgments of the Court.

MR. JUSTICE BRENNAN, concurring.

. . .

The primary principle is that a punishment must not be so severe as to be degrading to the dignity of human beings. Pain, certainly, may be a factor in the judgment. The infliction of an extremely severe punishment will often entail physical suffering. See *Weems* v. *United States*, 217 U.S., at 366.[12] Yet the Framers also knew "that there could be exercises of cruelty by laws other than those which inflicted bodily pain or mutilation." *Id.*, at 372. Even though "[t]here may be involved no physical mistreatment, no primitive torture," *Trop* v. *Dulles, supra, at* 101, severe mental pain may be inherent in the infliction of a particular punishment. See *Weems* v. *United States, supra, at* 366.[13] That, indeed, was one of the conclusions underlying the holding of the plurality in *Trop* v. *Dulles* that the punishment of expatriation violates the Clause.[14] And the physical and mental

[12] "It may be that even the cruelty of pain is not omitted. He must bear a chain night and day. He is condemned to painful as well as hard labor. What painful labor may mean we have no exact measure. It must be something more than hard labor. It may be hard labor pressed to the point of pain."

[13] "His prison bars and chains are removed, it is true, after twelve years, but he goes from them to a perpetual limitation of his liberty. He is forever kept under the shadow of his crime, forever kept within voice and view of the criminal magistrate, not being able to change his domicil without giving notice to the 'authority immediately in charge of his surveillance,' and without permission in writing. He may not seek, even in other scenes and among other people, to retrieve his fall from rectitude. Even that hope is taken from him and he is subject to tormenting regulations that, if not so tangible as iron bars and stone walls, oppress as much by their continuity, and deprive of essential liberty."

[14] "This punishment is offensive to cardinal principles for which the Constitution stands. It subjects the individual to a fate of ever-increasing fear and distress. He knows not what discriminations may be established against him, what proscriptions may be directed against him, and when and for what cause his existence in his native land may be terminated. He may be subject to banishment, a fate universally decried by civilized people. He is stateless, a condition deplored in the international community of democracies. It is no answer to suggest that all the disastrous consequences of this fate may not be brought to bear on a stateless person. The threat makes the punishment obnoxious." *Trop* v. *Dulles*, 356 U.S. 86, 102 (1958). Cf. *id.*, at 110–111 (BRENNAN, J., concurring): "[I]t can be supposed that the consequences of greatest weight, in terms of ultimate impact on the petitioner, are unknown and unknowable. Indeed, in truth, he may live out his life with but minor inconvenience. . . . Nevertheless it cannot be denied that the impact of expatriation—especially where statelessness is the upshot—may be severe. Expatriation, in this respect, constitutes an especially demoralizing sanction. The uncertainty, and the consequent psychological hurt, which must accompany one who becomes an outcast in his own land must be reckoned a substantial factor in the ultimate judgment."

suffering inherent in the punishment of *cadena temporal* . . . was an obvious basis for the Court's decision in *Weems* v. *United States* that the punishment was "cruel and unusual." [15]

More than the presence of pain, however, is comprehended in the judgment that the extreme severity of a punishment makes it degrading to the dignity of human beings. The barbaric punishments condemned by history, "punishments which inflict torture, such as the rack, the thumb-screw, the iron boot, the stretching of limbs and the like," are, of course, "attended with acute pain and suffering." *O'Neil* v. *Vermont,* 144 U.S. 323, 339 (1892) (Field, J., dissenting). When we consider why they have been condemned, however, we realize that the pain involved is not the only reason. The true significance of these punishments is that they treat members of the human race as nonhumans, as objects to be toyed with and discarded. They are thus inconsistent with the fundamental premise of the Clause that even the vilest criminal remains a human being possessed of common human dignity.

The infliction of an extremely severe punishment, then, like the one before the Court in *Weems* v. *United States,* from which "[n]o circumstance of degradation [was] omitted," 217 U.S., at 366, may reflect the attitude that the person punished is not entitled to recognition as a fellow human being. That attitude may be apparent apart from the severity of the punishment itself. In *Louisiana ex rel. Francis* v. *Resweber,* 329 U.S. 459, 464 (1947), for example, the unsuccessful electrocution, although it caused "mental anguish and physical pain," was the result of "an unforeseeable accident." Had the failure been intentional, however, the punishment would have been, like torture, so degrading and indecent as to amount to a refusal to accord the criminal human status. Indeed, a punishment may be degrading to human dignity solely because it *is* a punishment. A State may not punish a person for being "mentally ill, or a leper, or . . . afflicted with a venereal disease," or for being addicted to narcotics. *Robinson* v. *California,* 370 U.S. 660, 666 (1962). To inflict punishment for having a disease is to treat the individual as a diseased thing rather than as a sick human being. That the punishment is not severe, "in the abstract," is irrelevant; "[e]ven one day in prison would be a cruel and unusual punishment for the 'crime' of having a common cold." *Id.,* at 667. Finally, of course, a punishment may be degrading simply by reason of its enormity. A prime example is expatriation, a "punishment more primitive than torture," *Trop* v. *Dulles,* 356 U.S., at 101, for it necessarily involves a denial by society of the individual's existence as a member of the human community.[16]

---

[15] "It is cruel in its excess of imprisonment and that which accompanies and follows imprisonment. It is unusual in its character. Its punishments come under the condemnation of the bill of rights, both on account of their degree and kind." *Weems* v. *United States,* 217 U.S., at 377.

[16] "There may be involved no physical mistreatment, no primitive torture. There is instead the total destruction of the individual's status in organized society. It is

In determining whether a punishment comports with human dignity, we are aided also by a second principle inherent in the Clause—that the State must not arbitrarily inflict a severe punishment. This principle derives from the notion that the State does not respect human dignity when, without reason, it inflicts upon some people a severe punishment that it does not inflict upon others. Indeed, the very words "cruel and unusual punishments" imply condemnation of the arbitrary infliction of severe punishments. And, as we now know, the English history of the Clause [17] reveals a particular concern with the establishment of a safeguard against arbitrary punishments.

. . .

A third principle inherent in the Clause is that a severe punishment must not be unacceptable to contemporary society. Rejection by society, of course, is a strong indication that a severe punishment does not comport with human dignity. In applying this principle, however, we must make certain that the judicial determination is as objective as possible. [18] Thus, for example, *Weems* v. *United States*, 217 U.S., at 380, and *Trop* v. *Dulles*, 356 U.S., at 102–103, suggest that one factor that may be considered is the existence of the punishment in jurisdictions other than those before the

---

a form of punishment more primitive than torture, for it destroys for the individual the political existence that was centuries in the development. The punishment strips the citizen of his status in the national and international political community. His very existence is at the sufferance of the country in which he happens to find himself. While any one country may accord him some rights, and presumably as long as he remained in this country he would enjoy the limited rights of an alien, no country need do so because he is stateless. Furthermore, his enjoyment of even the limited rights of an alien might be subject to termination at any time by reason of deportation. In short, the expatriate has lost the right to have rights." *Trop* v. *Dulles*, 356 U.S., at 101–102.

[17] "The phrase in our Constitution was taken directly from the English Declaration of Rights of [1689]. . . ." *Id.*, at 100.

[18] The danger of subjective judgment is acute if the question posed is whether a punishment "shocks the most fundamental instincts of civilized man," *Louisiana ex rel Francis* v. *Resweber, supra,* at 473 (Burton, J., dissenting), or whether "any man of right feeling and heart can refrain from shuddering," *O'Neil* v. *Vermont, supra,* at 340 (Field, J., dissenting), or whether "a cry of horror would rise from every civilized and Christian community of the country," *ibid.* Mr. Justice Frankfurter's concurring opinion in *Louisiana ex rel. Francis* v. *Resweber, supra,* is instructive. He warned "against finding in personal disapproval a reflection of more or less prevailing condemnation" and against "enforcing . . . private view[s] rather than that consensus of society's opinion which, for purposes of due process, is the standard enjoined by the Constitution." *Id.*, at 471. His conclusions were as follows: "I cannot bring myself to believe that [the State's procedure] . . . offends a principle of justice 'rooted in the traditions and conscience of our people.'" *Id.*, at 470. ". . . I cannot say that it would be 'repugnant to the conscience of mankind.'" *Id.*, at 471. Yet nowhere in the opinion is there any explanation of how he arrived at those conclusions.

Court. *Wilkerson* v. *Utah, supra,* suggests that another factor to be considered is the historic usage of the punishment.[19] *Trop* v. *Dulles, supra,* at 99, combined present acceptance with past usage by observing that "the death penalty has been employed throughout our history, and, in a day when it is still widely accepted, it cannot be said to violate the constitutional concept of cruelty." In *Robinson* v. *California,* 370 U.S., at 666, which involved the infliction of punishment for narcotics addiction, the Court went a step further, concluding simply that "in the light of contemporary human knowledge, a law which made a criminal offense of such a disease would doubtless be universally thought to be an infliction of cruel and unusual punishment."

The question under this principle, then, is whether there are objective indicators from which a court can conclude that contemporary society considers a severe punishment unacceptable. Accordingly, the judicial task is to review the history of a challenged punishment and to examine society's present practices with respect to its use. Legislative authorization, of course, does not establish acceptance. The acceptability of a severe punishment is measured, not by its availability, for it might become so offensive to society as never to be inflicted, but by its use.

The final principle inherent in the Clause is that a severe punishment must not be excessive. A punishment is excessive under this principle if it is unnecessary: The infliction of a severe punishment by the State cannot comport with human dignity when it is nothing more than the pointless infliction of suffering. If there is a significantly less severe punishment adequate to achieve the purposes for which the punishment is inflicted; ef. *Robinson* v. *California, supra,* at 666; *id.,* at 677 (DOUGLAS J., concurring); *Trop* v. *Dulles, supra,* at 114 (BRENNAN, J., concurring), the punishment inflicted is unnecessary and therefore excessive.

. . .

There are, then, four principles by which we may determine whether a particular punishment is "cruel and unusual." The primary principle, which I believe supplies the essential predicate for the application of the others, is that a punishment must not by its severity be degrading to human dignity. The paradigm violation of this principle would be the infliction of a torturous punishment of the type that the Clause has always prohibited. Yet "[i]t is unlikely that any State at this moment in history," *Robinson* v. *California,* 370 U.S., at 666, would pass a law providing for the infliction of such a punishment. Indeed, no such punishment has ever been before this Court. The same may be said of the other principles. It is unlikely that this Court will confront a severe punishment that is obviously inflicted in

---

[19] Cf. *Louisiana ex rel. Francis* v. *Resweber, supra,* at 463: "The traditional humanity of modern Anglo-American law forbids the infliction of unnecessary pain in the execution of the death sentence."

wholly arbitrary fashion; no State would engage in a reign of blind terror. Nor is it likely that this Court will be called upon to review a severe punishment that is clearly and totally rejected throughout society; no legislature would be able even to authorize the infliction of such a punishment. Nor, finally, is it likely that this Court will have to consider a severe punishment that is patently unnecessary; no State today would inflict a severe punishment knowing that there was no reason whatever for doing so. In short, we are unlikely to have occasion to determine that a punishment is fatally offensive under any one principle.

Since the Bill of Rights was adopted, this Court has adjudged only three punishments to be within the prohibition of the Clause. See *Weems* v. *United States*, 217 U.S. 349 (1910) (12 years in chains at hard and painful labor); *Trop* v. *Dulles*, 356 U.S. 86 (1958) (expatriation); *Robinson* v. *California*, 370 U.S. 660 (1962) (imprisonment for narcotics addiction). Each punishment, of course, was degrading to human dignity, but of none could it be said conclusively that it was fatally offensive under one or the other of the principles. Rather, these "cruel and unusual punishments" seriously implicated several of the principles, and it was the application of the principles in combination that supported the judgment. That, indeed, is not surprising. The function of these principles, after all, is simply to provide means by which a court can determine whether a challenged punishment comports with human dignity. They are, therefore, interrelated, and in most cases it will be their convergence that will justify the conclusion that a punishment is "cruel and unusual." The test, then, will ordinarily be a cumulative one: If a punishment is unusually severe, if there is a strong probability that it is inflicted arbitrarily, if it is substantially rejected by contemporary society, and if there is no reason to believe that it serves any penal purpose more effectively than some less severe punishment, then the continued infliction of that punishment violates the command of the Clause that the State may not inflict inhuman and uncivilized punishments upon those convicted of crimes.

. . .

The question, then, is whether the deliberate infliction of death is today consistent with the command of the Clause that the State may not inflict punishments that do not comport with human dignity. I will analyze the punishment of death in terms of the principles set out above and the cumulative test to which they lead: It is a denial of human dignity for the State arbitrarily to subject a person to an unusually severe punishment that society has indicated it does not regard as acceptable, and that cannot be shown to serve any penal purpose more effectively than a significantly less drastic punishment. Under these principles and this test, death is today a "cruel and unusual" punishment.

Death is a unique punishment in the United States. In a society that so strongly affirms the sanctity of life, not surprisingly the common view is that death is the ultimate sanction. This natural human feeling appears all about us. There has been no national debate about punishment, in general or by imprisonment, comparable to the debate about the punishment of death. No other punishment has been so continuously restricted . . . nor has the State yet abolished prisons, as some have abolished this punishment. And those States that still inflict death reserve it for the most heinous crimes. Juries, of course, have always treated death cases differently, as have governors exercising their commutation powers. Criminal defendants are of the same view. "As all practicing lawyers know, who have defended persons charged with capital offenses, often the only goal possible is to avoid the death penalty." *Griffin* v. *Illinois*, 351 U.S. 12, 28 (1956) (Burton and Minton, JJ., dissenting). Some legislatures have required particular procedures, such as two-stage trials and automatic appeals, applicable only in death cases. "It is the universal experience in the administration of criminal justice that those charged with capital offenses are granted special considerations." *Ibid.* See *Williams* v. *Florida*, 399 U.S. 78, 103 (1970) (all States require juries of 12 in death cases). This Court, too, almost always treats death cases as a class apart.[20] And the unfortunate effect of this punishment upon the functioning of the judicial process is well known; no other punishment has a similar effect.

The only explanation for the uniqueness of death is its extreme severity. Death is today an unusually severe punishment, unusual in its pain, in its finality, and in its enormity. No other existing punishment is comparable to death in terms of physical and mental suffering. Although our information is not conclusive, it appears that there is no method available that guarantees an immediate and painless death.[21] Since the discontinuance of flogging as a constitutionally permissible punishment, *Jackson* v.

---

[20] "That life is at stake is of course another important factor in creating the extraordinary situation. The difference between capital and non-capital offenses is the basis of differentiation in law in diverse ways in which the distinction becomes relevant." *Williams* v. *Georgia*, 349 U.S. 375, 391 (1955) (Frankfurter, J.). "When the penalty is death, we, like state court judges, are tempted to strain the evidence and even, in close cases, the law in order to give a doubtfully condemned man another chance." *Stein* v. *New York*, 346 U.S. 156, 196 (1953) (Jackson, J.). "In death cases doubts such as those presented here should be resolved in favor of the accused." *Andres* v. *United States*, 333 U.S. 740, 752 (1948) (Reed, J.). Mr. Justice Harlan expressed the point strongly: "I do not concede that whatever process is 'due' an offender faced with a fine or a prison sentence necessarily satisfies the requirements of the Constitution in a capital case. The distinction is by no means novel, . . . nor is it negligible, being literally that between life and death." *Reid* v. *Covert*, 354 U.S. 1, 77 (1957) (concurring in result). And, of course, for many years this Court distinguished death cases from all others for purposes of the constitutional right to counsel. See *Powell* v. *Alabama*, 287 U.S. 45 (1932); *Betts* v. *Brady*, 316 U.S. 455 (1942); *Bute* v. *Illinois*, 333 U.S. 640 (1948).

[21] See Report of Royal Commission on Capital Punishment 1949–1953, §§ 700–789, pp. 246–273 (1953); Hearings on S. 1760 before the Subcommittee on Crim-

Bishop, 404 F. 2d 571 (CA8 1968), death remains as the only punishment that may involve the conscious infliction of physical pain. In addition, we know that mental pain is an inseparable part of our practice of punishing criminals by death, for the prospect of pending execution exacts a frightful toll during the inevitable long wait between the imposition of sentence and the actual infliction of death. Cf. *Ex parte Medley,* 134 U.S. 160, 172 (1890). As the California Supreme Court pointed out, "the process of carrying out a verdict of death is often so degrading and brutalizing to the human spirit as to constitute psychological torture." *People* v. *Anderson,* 6 Cal. 3d 628, 649, 493 P. 2d 880, 894 (1972).[22] Indeed, as Mr. Justice Frankfurter noted, "the onset of insanity while awaiting execution of a death sentence is not a rare phenomenon." *Solesbee* v. *Balkcom,* 339 U.S. 9, 14 (1950) (dissenting opinion). The "fate of ever-increasing fear and distress" to which the expatriate is subjected, *Trop* v. *Dulles,* 356 U.S., at 102, can only exist to a greater degree for a person confined in prison awaiting death.[23]

---

inal Laws and Procedures of the Senate Committee on the Judiciary, 90th Cong., 2d Sess., 19–21 (1968) (testimony of Clinton Duffy); H. Barnes & N. Teeters, New Horizons in Criminology 306–309 (3d ed. 1959); C. Chessman, Trial by Ordeal 195–202 (1955); M. DiSalle, The Power of Life and Death 84–85 (1965); C. Duffy & A. Hirschberg, 88 Men and 2 Women 13–14 (1962); B. Eshelman, Death Row Chaplain 26–29, 101–104, 159–164 (1962); R. Hammer, Between Life and Death 208–212 (1969); K. Lamott, Chronicles of San Quentin 228–231 (1961); L. Lawes, Life and Death in Sing Sing 170–171 (1928); Rubin, The Supreme Court, Cruel and Unusual Punishment, and the Death Penalty, 15 Crime & Delin. 121, 128–129 (1969); Comment, The Death Penalty Cases, 56 Calif. L. Rev. 1268, 1338–1341 (1968); Brief *amici curiae* filed by James V. Bennett, Clinton T. Duffy, Robert G. Sarver, Harry C. Tinsley, and Lawrence E. Wilson 12–14.

[22] See Barnes & Teeters, *supra,* at 309–311 (3d ed. 1959); Camus, Reflections on the Guillotine, in A. Camus, Resistance, Rebellion, and Death 131, 151–156 (1960); C. Duffy & A. Hirschberg, *supra,* at 68–70, 254 (1962); Hammer, *supra,* at 222–235, 244–250, 269–272 (1969); S. Rubin, The Law of Criminal Correction 340 (1963); Bluestone & McGahee, Reaction to Extreme Stress: Impending Death by Execution, 119 Amer. J. Psychiatry 393 (1962); Gottlieb, Capital Punishment, 15 Crime & Delin. 1, 8–10 (1969); West, Medicine and Capital Punishment, in Hearings on S. 1760 before the Subcommittee on Criminal Laws and Procedures of the Senate Committee on the Judiciary, 90th Cong., 2d Sess., 124 (1968); Ziferstein, Crime and Punishment, The Center Magazine 84 (Jan. 1968); Comment, The Death Penalty Cases, 56 Calif. L. Rev. 1268, 1342 (1968); Note, Mental Suffering under Sentence of Death: A Cruel and Unusual Punishment, 57 Iowa L. Rev. 814 (1972).

[23] The State, of course, does not purposely impose the lengthy waiting period in order to inflict further suffering. The impact upon the individual is not the less severe on that account. It is no answer to assert that long delays exist only because condemned criminals avail themselves of their full panoply of legal rights. The right not to be subjected to inhuman treatment cannot, of course, be played off against the right to pursue due process of law, but, apart from that, the plain truth is that it is society that demands, even against the wishes of the criminal, that all legal avenues be explored before the execution is finally carried out.

The unusual severity of death is manifested most clearly in its finality and enormity. Death, in these respects, is in a class by itself. Expatriation, for example, is a punishment that "destroys for the individual the political existence that was centuries in the development," that "strips the citizen of his status in the national and international political community," and that puts "[h]is very existence" in jeopardy. Expatriation thus inherently entails "the total destruction of the individual's status in organized society." *Id.*, at 101. "In short, the expatriate has lost the right to have rights." *Id.*, at 102. Yet, demonstrably, expatriation is not "a fate worse than death." *Id.*, at 125 (Frankfurter, J., dissenting).[24] Although death, like expatriation, destroys the individual's "political existence" and his "status in organized society," it does more, for, unlike expatriation, death also destroys "[h]is very existence." There is, too, at least the possibility that the expatriate will in the future regain "the right to have rights." Death forecloses even that possibility.

Death is truly an awesome punishment. The calculated killing of a human being by the State involves, by its very nature, a denial of the executed person's humanity. The contrast with the plight of a person punished by imprisonment is evident. An individual in prison does not lose "the right to have rights." A prisoner retains, for example, the constitutional rights to the free exercise of religion, to be free of cruel and unusual punishments, and to treatment as a "person" for purposes of due process of law and the equal protection of the laws. A prisoner remains a member of the human family. Moreover, he retains the right of access to the courts. His punishment is not irrevocable. Apart from the common charge, grounded upon the recognition of human fallibility, that the punishment of death must inevitably be inflicted upon innocent men, we know that death has been the lot of men whose convictions were unconstitutionally secured in view of later, retroactively applied, holdings of this Court. The punishment itself may have been unconstitutionally inflicted, see *Witherspoon v. Illinois*, 391 U.S. 510 (1968), yet the finality of death precludes relief. An executed person has indeed "lost the right to have rights." As one 19th century proponent of punishing criminals by death declared, "When a man is hung, there is an end of our relations with him. His execution is a way of saying, 'You are not fit for this world, take your chance elsewhere.'"[25]

In comparison to all other punishments today, then, the deliberate extinguishment of human life by the State is uniquely degrading to human dignity. I would not hesitate to hold, on that ground alone, that death is today a "cruel and unusual" punishment, were it not that death is a punishment of longstanding usage and acceptance in this country. I therefore

[24] It was recognized in *Trop* itself that expatriation is a "punishment short of death." 356 U.S., at 99. Death, however, was distinguished on the ground that it was "still widely accepted." *Ibid.*

[25] Stephen, Capital Punishments, 69 Fraser's Magazine 753, 763 (1864).

turn to the second principle—that the State may not arbitrarily inflict an unusually severe punishment.

The outstanding characteristic of our present practice of punishing criminals by death is the infrequency with which we resort to it. The evidence is conclusive that death is not the ordinary punishment for any crime.

. . .

Thus, although "the death penalty has been employed throughout our history," *Trop* v. *Dulles*, 356 U.S., at 99, in fact the history of this punishment is one of successive restriction. What was once a common punishment has become, in the context of a continuing moral debate, increasingly rare. The evolution of this punishment evidences, not that it is an inevitable part of the American scene, but that it has proved progressively more troublesome to the national conscience. The result of this movement is our current system of administering the punishment, under which death sentences are rarely imposed and death is even more rarely inflicted. It is, of course, "We, the People" who are responsible for the rarity both of the imposition and the carrying out of this punishment. Juries, "express[ing] the conscience of the community on the ultimate question of life or death," *Witherspoon* v. *Illinois*, 391 U.S., at 519, have been able to bring themselves to vote for death in a mere 100 or so cases among the thousands tried each year where the punishment is available. Governors, elected by and acting for us, have regularly commuted a substantial number of those sentences. And it is our society that insists upon due process of law to the end that no person will be unjustly put to death, thus ensuring that many more of those sentences will not be carried out. In sum, we have made death a rare punishment today.

The progressive decline in, and the current rarity of, the infliction of death demonstrate that our society seriously questions the appropriateness of this punishment today. The States point out that many legislatures authorize death as the punishment for certain crimes and that substantial segments of the public, as reflected in opinion polls and referendum votes, continue to support it. Yet the availability of this punishment through statutory authorization, as well as the polls and referenda, which amount simply to approval of that authorization, simply underscores the extent to which our society has in fact rejected this punishment. When an unusually severe punishment is authorized for wide-scale application but not, because of society's refusal, inflicted save in a few instances, the inference is compelling that there is a deep-seated reluctance to inflict it. Indeed, the likelihood is great that the punishment is tolerated only because of its disuse. The objective indicator of society's view of an unusually severe punishment is what society does with it, and today society will inflict death upon only a small sample of the eligible criminals. Rejection could hardly be more complete without becoming absolute. At the very least, I must conclude that contemporary society views this punishment with substantial doubt.

The final principle to be considered is that an unusually severe and degrading punishment may not be excessive in view of the purposes for which it is inflicted. This principle, too, is related to the others. When there is a strong probability that the State is arbitrarily inflicting an unusually severe punishment that is subject to grave societal doubts, it is likely also that the punishment cannot be shown to be serving any penal purpose that could not be served equally well by some less severe punishment.

The States' primary claim is that death is a necessary punishment because it prevents the commission of capital crimes more effectively than any less severe punishment. The first part of this claim is that the infliction of death is necessary to stop the individuals executed from committing further crimes. The sufficient answer to this is that if a criminal convicted of a capital crime poses a danger to society, effective administration of the State's pardon and parole laws can delay or deny his release from prison, and techniques of isolation can eliminate or minimize the danger while he remains confined.

The more significant argument is that the threat of death prevents the commission of capital crimes because it deters potential criminals who would not be deterred by the threat of imprisonment. The argument is not based upon evidence that the threat of death is a superior deterrent. Indeed, as my Brother MARSHALL establishes, the available evidence uniformly indicates, although it does not conclusively prove, that the threat of death has no greater deterrent effect than the threat of imprisonment. The States argue, however, that they are entitled to rely upon common human experience, and that experience, they say, supports the conclusion that death must be a more effective deterrent than any less severe punishment. Because people fear death the most, the argument runs, the threat of death must be the greatest deterrent.

It is important to focus upon the precise import of this argument. It is not denied that many, and probably most, capital crimes cannot be deterred by the threat of punishment. Thus the argument can apply only to those who think rationally about the commission of capital crimes. Particularly is that true when the potential criminal, under this argument, must not only consider the risk of punishment, but also distinguish between two possible punishments. The concern, then, is with a particular type of potential criminal, the rational person who will commit a capital crime knowing that the punishment is long-term imprisonment, which may well be for the rest of his life, but will not commit the crime knowing that the punishment is death. On the face of it, the assumption that such persons exist is implausible.

In any event, this argument cannot be appraised in the abstract. We are not presented with the theoretical question whether under any imaginable circumstances the threat of death might be a greater deterrent to the commission of capital crimes than the threat of imprisonment. We are concerned with the practice of punishing criminals by death as it exists in the United States today. Proponents of this argument necessarily admit that its validity depends upon the existence of a system in which the punishment of death is invariably and swiftly imposed. Our system, of course, satisfies neither condition. A rational person contemplating a murder or rape is confronted, not with the certainty of a speedy death, but with the slightest possibility that he will be executed in the distant future. The risk of death is remote and improbable; in contrast, the risk of long-term imprisonment is near and great. In short, whatever the speculative validity of the assumption that the threat of death is a superior deterrent, there is no reason to believe that as currently administered the punishment of death is necessary to deter the commission of capital crimes. Whatever might be the case were all or substantially all eligible criminals quickly put to death, unverifiable possibilities are an insufficient basis upon which to conclude that the threat of death today has any greater deterrent efficacy than the threat of imprisonment.[26]

There is, however, another aspect to the argument that the punishment of death is necessary for the protection of society. The infliction of death, the States urge, serves to manifest the community's outrage at the commission of the crime. It is, they say, a concrete public expression of moral indignation that inculcates respect for the law and helps assure a more peaceful community. Moreover, we are told, not only does the punishment of death exert this widespread moralizing influence upon community values, it also satisfies the popular demand for grievous condemnation of abhorrent crimes and thus prevents disorder, lynching, and attempts by private citizens to take the law into their own hands.

The question, however, is not whether death serves these supposed purposes of punishment, but whether death serves them more effectively than imprisonment. There is no evidence whatever that utilization of imprisonment rather than death encourages private blood feuds and other disorders. Surely if there were such a danger, the execution of a handful of criminals each year would not prevent it. The assertion that death alone is a sufficiently emphatic denunciation for capital crimes suffers from the

---

26 There is also the more limited argument that death is a necessary punishment when criminals are already serving or subject to a sentence of life imprisonment. If the only punishment available is further imprisonment, it is said, those criminals will have nothing to lose by committing further crimes, and accordingly the threat of death is the sole deterrent. But "life" imprisonment is a misnomer today. Rarely, if ever, do crimes carry a mandatory life sentence without possibility of parole. That possibility ensures that criminals do not reach the point where further crimes are free of consequences. Moreover, if this argument is simply an assertion that the threat of death is a more effective deterrent than the threat of increased imprisonment by denial of release on parole, then, as noted above, there is simply no evidence to support it.

same defect. If capital crimes require the punishment of death in order to provide moral reinforcement for the basic values of the community, those values can only be undermined when death is so rarely inflicted upon the criminals who commit the crimes. Furthermore, it is certainly doubtful that the infliction of death by the State does in fact strengthen the community's moral code; if the deliberate extinguishment of human life has any effect at all, it more likely tends to lower our respect for life and brutalize our values. That, after all, is why we no longer carry out public executions. In any event, this claim simply means that one purpose of punishment is to indicate social disapproval of crime. To serve that purpose our laws distribute punishments according to the gravity of crimes and punish more severely the crimes society regards as more serious. That purpose cannot justify any particular punishment as the upper limit of severity.

There is, then, no substantial reason to believe that the punishment of death, as currently administered, is necessary for the protection of society. The only other purpose suggested, one that is independent of protection for society, is retribution. Shortly stated, retribution in this context means that criminals are put to death because they deserve it.

Although it is difficult to believe that any State today wishes to proclaim adherence to "naked vengeance," *Trop* v. *Dulles*, 356 U.S., at 112 (BRENNAN, J., concurring), the States claim, in reliance upon its statutory authorization, that death is the only fit punishment for capital crimes and that this retributive purpose justifies its infliction. In the past, judged by its statutory authorization, death was considered the only fit punishment for the crime of forgery, for the first federal criminal statute provided a mandatory death penalty for that crime. Act of April 30, 1790, § 14, 1 Stat. 115. Obviously, concepts of justice change; no immutable moral order requires death for murderers and rapists. The claim that death is a just punishment necessarily refers to the existence of certain public beliefs. The claim must be that for capital crimes death alone comports with society's notion of proper punishment. As administered today, however, the punishment of death cannot be justified as a necessary means of exacting retribution from criminals. When the overwhelming number of criminals who commit capital crimes go to prison, it cannot be concluded that death serves the purpose of retribution more effectively than imprisonment. The asserted public belief that murderers and rapists deserve to die is flatly inconsistent with the execution of a random few. As the history of the punishment of death in this country shows, our society wishes to prevent crime; we have no desire to kill criminals simply to get even with them.

In sum, the punishment of death is inconsistent with all four principles: Death is an unusually severe and degrading punishment; there is a strong probability that it is inflicted arbitrarily; its rejection by contemporary society is virtually total; and there is no reason to believe that it serves any penal purpose more effectively than the less severe punishment of imprisonment. The function of these principles is to enable a court to determine whether a punishment comports with human dignity. Death, quite simply, does not.

. . .

Mr. Chief Justice Burger, with whom Mr. Justice Blackmun, Mr. Justice Powell, and Mr. Justice Rehnquist join, dissenting.

At the outset it is important to note that only two members of the Court, Mr. Justice Brennan and Mr. Justice Marshall, have concluded that the Eighth Amendment prohibits capital punishment for all crimes and under all circumstances. Mr. Justice Douglas has also determined that the death penalty contravenes the Eighth Amendment, although I do not read his opinion as necessarily requiring final abolition of the penalty. For the reasons set forth in Parts I-IV of this opinion, I conclude that the constitutional prohibition against "cruel and unusual punishments" cannot be construed to bar the imposition of the punishment of death.

Mr. Justice Stewart and Mr. Justice White have concluded that petitioners' death sentences must be set aside because prevailing sentencing practices do not comply with the Eighth Amendment. For the reasons set forth in Part V of this opinion, I believe this approach fundamentally misconceives the nature of the Eighth Amendment guarantee and flies directly in the face of controlling authority of extremely recent vintage.

I

If we were possessed of legislative power, I would either join with Mr. Justice Brennan *and* Mr. Justice Marshall or, at the very least, restrict the use of capital punishment to a small category of the most heinous crimes. Our constitutional inquiry, however, must be divorced from personal feelings as to the morality and efficacy of the death penalty, and be confined to the meaning and applicability of the uncertain language of the Eighth Amendment. There is no novelty in being called upon to interpret a constitutional provision that is less than self-defining, but, of all our fundamental guarantees, the ban on "cruel and unusual punishments" is one of the most difficult to translate into judicially manageable terms. The widely divergent views of the Amendment expressed in today's opinions reveal the haze that surrounds this constitutional command. Yet it is essential to our role as a court that we not seize upon the enigmatic character of the guarantee as an invitation to enact our personal predilections into law.

Although the Eighth Amendment literally reads as prohibiting only those punishments that are both "cruel" and "unusual," history compels the conclusion that the Constitution prohibits all punishments of extreme and barbarous cruelty, regardless of how frequently or infrequently imposed.

. . .

III

There are no obvious indications that capital punishment offends the conscience of society to such a degree that our traditional deference to the legislative judgment must be abandoned. It is not a punishment such as burning at the stake that everyone would ineffably find to be repugnant to all civilized standards. Nor is it a punishment so roundly condemned that only a few aberrant legislatures have retained it on the statute books. Capital punishment is authorized by statute in 40 States, the District of Columbia, and in the federal courts for the commission of certain crimes.[27] On four occasions in the last 11 years Congress had added to the list of federal crimes punishable by death.[28] In looking for reliable indicia of contemporary attitude, none more trustworthy has been advanced.

One conceivable source of evidence that legislatures have abdicated their essentially barometric role with respect to community values would be public opinion polls, of which there have been many in the past decade addressed to the question of capital punishment. Without assessing the reliability of such polls, or intimating that any judicial reliance could ever be placed on them, it need only be noted that the reported results have shown nothing approximating the universal condemnation of capital punishment that might lead us to suspect that the legislatures in general have lost touch with current social values.[29]

Counsel for petitioners rely on a different body of empirical evidence. They argue, in effect, that the number of cases in which the death penalty is imposed, as compared with the number of cases in which it is statutorily

[27] See Department of Justice, National Prisoner Statistics No. 46, Capital Punishment 1930–1970, p. 50 (Aug. 1971). Since the publication of the Department of Justice report, capital punishment has been judicially abolished in California, *People* v. *Anderson*, 6 Cal. 3d 628, 493 P. 2d 880, cert. denied, 406 U.S. 958 (1972). The States where capital punishment is no longer authorized are Alaska, California, Hawaii, Iowa, Maine, Michigan, Minnesota, Oregon, West Virginia, and Wisconsin.

[28] See Act. of Jan. 2, 1971, Pub. L. 91–644, Tit. IV, § 15, 84 Stat. 1891, 18 U. S. C. §351; Act of Oct. 15, 1970, Pub. L. 91–452, Tit. XI, § 1102(a), 84 Stat. 956, 18 U. S. C. § 844(f) (i); Act of Aug. 28, 1965, 79 Stat. 580, 18 U. S. C. § 1751; Act. of Sept. 5, 1961, § 1, 75 Stat. 466, 49 U. S. C. § 1472(i). See also opinion of MR. JUSTICE BLACKMUN, *post*, at 412–413.

[29] A 1966 poll indicated that 42% of those polled favored capital punishment while 47% opposed it, and 11% had no opinion. A 1969 poll found 51% in favor, 40% opposed, and 9% with no opinion. See Erskine, The Polls: Capital Punishment, 34 Public Opinion Quarterly 290 (1970).

available, reflects a general revulsion toward the penalty that would lead to its repeal if only it were more generally and widely enforced. It cannot be gainsaid that by the choice of juries—and sometimes judges [30]—the death penalty is imposed in far fewer than half the cases in which it is available.[31] To go further and characterize the rate of imposition as "freakishly rare," as petitioners insist, is unwarranted hyperbole. And regardless of its characterization, the rate of imposition does not impel the conclusion that capital punishment is now regarded as intolerably cruel or uncivilized.

It is argued that in those capital cases where juries have recommended mercy, they have given expression to civilized values and effectively renounced the legislative authorization for capital punishment. At the same time it is argued that where juries have made the awesome decision to send men to their deaths, they have acted arbitrarily and without sensitivity to prevailing standards of decency. This explanation for the infrequency of imposition of capital punishment is unsupported by known facts, and is inconsistent in principle with everything this Court has ever said about the functioning of juries in capital cases.

In *McGautha* v. *California, supra,* decided only one year ago, the Court held that there was no mandate in the Due Process Clause of the Fourteenth Amendment that juries be given instructions as to when the death penalty should be imposed. After reviewing the autonomy that juries have traditionally exercised in capital cases and noting the practical difficulties of framing manageable instructions, this Court concluded that judicially articulated standards were not needed to insure a responsible decision as to penalty. Nothing in *McGautha* licenses capital juries to act arbitrarily or assumes that they have so acted in the past. On the contrary, the

---

[30] The jury plays the predominant role in sentencing in capital cases in this country. Available evidence indicates that where the judge determines the sentence, the death penalty is imposed with a slightly greater frequency than where the jury makes the determination. H. Kalven & H. Zeisel, The American Jury 436 (1966).

[31] In the decade from 1961–1970, an average of 106 persons per year received the death sentence in the United States, ranging from a low of 85 in 1967 to a high of 140 in 1961; 127 persons received the death sentence in 1970. Department of Justice, National Prisoner Statistics No. 46, Capital Punishment 1930–1970, p. 9. See also Bedau, The Death Penalty in America, 35 Fed. Prob., No. 2, p. 32 (1971). Although accurate figures are difficult to obtain, it is thought that from 15% to 20% of those convicted of murder are sentenced to death in States where it is authorized. See, *e.g.,* McGee, Capital Punishment as Seen by a Correctional Administrator, 28 Fed. Prob., No. 2, pp. 11, 12 (1964); Bedau, Death Sentences in New Jersey 1907–1960, 19 Rutgers L. Rev. 1, 30 (1964); Florida Division of Corrections, Seventh Biennial Report (July 1, 1968, to June 30, 1970) 82 (1970); H. Kalven & H. Zeisel, The American Jury 435–436 (1966). The rate of imposition for rape and the few other crimes made punishable by death in certain States is considerably lower. See, *e.g.,* Florida Division of Corrections, Seventh Biennial Report, *supra,* at 83; Partington, The Incidence of the Death Penalty for Rape in Virginia, 22 Wash. & Lee L. Rev. 43–44, 71–73 (1965).

assumption underlying the *McGautha* ruling is that juries "will act with due regard for the consequences of their decision." 402 U.S., at 208.

The responsibility of juries deciding capital cases in our system of justice was nowhere better described than in *Witherspoon v. Illinois, supra:*

> [A] jury that must choose between life imprisonment and capital punishment can do little more—and must do nothing less—than express *the conscience of the community* on the ultimate question of life or death.
> And one of the most important functions any jury can perform in making such a selection is to maintain a link between contemporary community values and the penal system—a link without which the determination of punishment could hardly reflect 'the evolving standards of decency that mark the progress of a maturing society' 391 U.S., at 519 and n. 15 (emphasis added).

The selectivity of juries in imposing the punishment of death is properly viewed as a refinement on, rather than a repudiation of, the statutory authorization for that penalty. Legislatures prescribe the categories of crimes for which the death penalty should be available, and, acting as "the conscience of the community," juries are entrusted to determine in individual cases that the ultimate punishment is warranted. Juries are undoubtedly influenced in this judgment by myriad factors. The motive or lack of motive of the perpetrator, the degree of injury or suffering of the victim or victims, and the degree of brutality in the commission of the crime would seem to be prominent among these factors. Given the general awareness that death is no longer a routine punishment for the crimes for which it is made available, it is hardly surprising that juries have been increasingly meticulous in their imposition of the penalty. But to assume from the mere fact of relative infrequency that only a random assortment of pariahs are sentenced to death, is to cast grave doubt on the basic integrity of our jury system.

It would, of course, be unrealistic to assume that juries have been perfectly consistent in choosing the cases where the death penalty is to be imposed, for no human institution performs with perfect consistency. There are doubtless prisoners on death row who would not be there had they been tried before a different jury or in a different State. In this sense their fate has been controlled by a fortuitous circumstance. However, this element of fortuity does not stand as an indictment either of the general functioning of juries in capital cases or of the integrity of jury decisions in individual cases. There is no empirical basis for concluding that juries have generally failed to discharge in good faith the responsibility described in *Witherspoon*—that of choosing between life and death in individual cases according to the dictates of community values.[32]

---

[32] Counsel for petitioners make the conclusory statement that "[t]hose who are selected to die are the poor and powerless, personally ugly and socially unacceptable." Brief for Petitioner in No. 68–5027, p. 51. However, the sources cited contain

The rate of imposition of death sentences falls far short of providing the requisite unambiguous evidence that the legislatures of 40 States and the Congress have turned their backs on current or evolving standards of decency in continuing to make the death penalty available. For, if selective imposition evidences a rejection of capital punishment in those cases where it is not imposed, it surely evidences a correlative affirmation of the penalty in those cases where it is imposed. Absent some clear indication that the continued imposition of the death penalty on a selective basis is violative of prevailing standards of civilized conduct, the Eighth Amendment cannot be said to interdict its use.

· · ·

Two of the several aims of punishment are generally associated with capital punishment—retribution and deterrence. It is argued that retribution can be discounted because that, after all, is what the Eighth Amend-

---

no empirical findings to undermine the general premise that juries impose the death penalty in the most extreme cases. One study has discerned a statistically noticeable difference between the rate of imposition on blue collar and white collar defendants; the study otherwise concludes that juries do follow rational patterns in imposing the sentence of death. Note, A Study of the California Penalty Jury in First-Degree-Murder Cases, 21 Stan. L. Rev. 1297 (1969). See also H. Kalven & H. Zeisel, The American Jury 434–449 (1966).

Statistics are also cited to show that the death penalty has been imposed in a racially discriminatory manner. Such statistics suggest, at least as a historical matter, that Negroes have been sentenced to death with greater frequency than whites in several States, particularly for the crime of interracial rape. See, e.g., Koeninger, Capital Punishment in Texas, 1924–1968, 15 Crime & Delin. 132 (1696); Note, Capital Punishment in Virginia, 58 Va. L. Rev. 97 (1972). If a statute that authorizes the discretionary imposition of a particular penalty for a particular crime is used primarily against defendants of a certain race, and if the pattern of use can be fairly explained only by reference to the race of the defendants, the Equal Protection Clause of the Fourteenth Amendment forbids continued enforcement of that statute in its existing form. Cf. *Yick Wo* v. *Hopkins*, 118 U. S. 356 (1886); *Gomillion* v. *Lightfoot*, 364 U. S. 339 (1960).

To establish that the statutory authorization for a particular penalty is inconsistent with the dictates of the Equal Protection Clause, it is not enough to show how it was applied in the distant past. The statistics that have been referred to us cover periods when Negroes were systematically excluded from jury service and when racial segregation was the official policy in many States. Data of more recent vintage are essential. See *Maxwell* v. *Bishop*, 398 F. 2d 138, 148 (CA8 1968), vacated, 398 U. S. 262 (1970). While no statistical survey could be expected to bring forth absolute and irrefutable proof of a discriminatory pattern of imposition, a strong showing would have to be made, taking all relevant factors into account.

It must be noted that any equal protection claim is totally distinct from the Eighth Amendment question to which our grant of certiorari was limited in these cases. Evidence of a discriminatory pattern of enforcement does not imply that any use of a particular punishment is so morally repugnant as to violate the Eighth Amendment.

ment seeks to eliminate. There is no authority suggesting that the Eighth Amendment was intended to purge the law of its retributive elements, and the Court has consistently assumed that retribution is a legitimate dimension of the punishment of crimes. See *Williams* v. *New York*, 337 U.S. 241, 248 (1949); *United States* v. *Lovett*, 328 U.S. 303, 324 (1946) (Frankfurter, J., concurring). Furthermore, responsible legal thinkers of widely varying persuasions have debated the sociological and philosophical aspects of the retribution question for generations, neither side being able to convince the other.[33] It would be reading a great deal into the Eighth Amendment to hold that the punishments authorized by legislatures cannot constitutionally reflect a retributive purpose.

The less esoteric but no less controversial question is whether the death penalty acts as a superior deterrent. Those favoring abolition find no evidence that it does.[34] Those favoring retention start from the intuitive notion that capital punishment should act as the most effective deterrent and note that there is no convincing evidence that it does not.[35] Escape from this empirical stalemate is sought by placing the burden of proof on the States and concluding that they have failed to demonstrate that capital punishment is a more effective deterrent than life imprisonment. Numerous justifications have been advanced for shifting the burden, and they are not without their rhetorical appeal. However, these arguments are not descended from established constitutional principles, but are born of the urge to bypass an unresolved factual question.[36] Comparative deterrence is not a matter that lends itself to precise measurement; to shift the burden to the States is to provide an illusory solution to an enormously complex problem. If it were proper to put the States to the test of demonstrating the deterrent value of capital punishment, we could just as well ask them to prove the need for life imprisonment or any other punishment. Yet I know of no convincing evidence that life imprisonment is a more effective deterrent than 20 years' imprisonment, or even that a $10 parking ticket is a more effective deterrent than a $5 parking ticket. In fact, there

[33] See Hart, The Aims of the Criminal Law, 23 Law & Contemp. Prob. 401 (1958); H. Packer, The Limits of the Criminal Sanction 37–39 (1968); M. Cohen, Reason and Law 41–44 (1950); Report of Royal Commission on Capital Punishment, 1949–1953, Cmd. 8932, § 52, pp. 17–18 (1953); Hart, Murder and the Principles of Punishment: England and the United States, 52 Nw. U. L. Rev. 433, 446–455 (1957); H. L. A. Hart, Law, Liberty and Morality 60–69 (1963).

[34] See, *e.g.*, Sellin, Homicides in Retentionist and Abolitionist States, in Capital Punishment 135 *et seq.* (T. Sellin ed. 1967); Schuessler, The Deterrent Influence of the Death Penalty, 284 Annals 54 (1952).

[35] See, *e.g.*, Hoover, Statements in Favor of the Death Penalty, in H. Bedau, The Death Penalty in America 130 (1967 rev. ed.); Allen, Capital Punishment: Your Protection and Mine, in the Death Penalty in America, *supra*, at 135. See also Hart, 52 Nw. U. L. Rev. *supra*, at 457; Bedau, The Death Penalty in America, *supra*, at 265–266.

[36] See *Powell* v. *Texas*, 392 U. S. 514, 531 (1968) (MARSHALL, J.) (plurality opinion).

are some who go so far as to challenge the notion that any punishments deter crime.[37] If the States are unable to adduce convincing proof rebutting such assertions, does it then follow that all punishments are suspect as being "cruel and unusual" within the meaning of the Constitution? On the contrary, I submit that the questions raised by the necessity approach are beyond the pale of judicial inquiry under the Eighth Amendment.

• • •

Mr. Justice Powell, dissenting.

• • •

V

Petitioners seek to salvage their thesis by arguing that the infrequency and discriminatory nature of the actual resort to the ultimate penalty tend to diffuse public opposition. We are told that the penalty is imposed exclusively on uninfluential minorities—"the poor and powerless, personally ugly and socially unacceptable." [38] It is urged that this pattern of application assures that large segments of the public will be either uninformed or unconcerned and will have no reason to measure the punishment against prevailing moral standards.

Implicitly, this argument concedes the unsoundness of petitioners' contention, examined above under Part IV, that objective evidence shows a present and widespread community rejection of the death penalty. It is now said, in effect, not that capital punishment presently offends our citizenry, but that the public *would* be offended *if* the penalty were enforced in a nondiscriminatory manner against a significant percentage of those charged with capital crimes, and *if* the public were thereby made aware of the moral issues surrounding capital punishment. Rather than merely registering the objective indicators on a judicial balance, we are asked ultimately to rest a far-reaching constitutional determination on a prediction regarding the subjective judgments of the mass of our people under hypothetical assumptions that may or may not be realistic.

Apart from the impermissibility of basing a constitutional judgment of this magnitude on such speculative assumptions, the argument suffers from other defects. If, as petitioners urge, we are to engage in speculation, it is not at all certain that the public would experience deep-felt revulsion

---

[37] See, *e.g.*, K. Menninger, The Crime of Punishment 206–208 (1968).

[38] Brief of Petitioner in No. 68–5027, p. 51. Although the *Aikens* case is no longer before us . . . the petitioners in *Furman* and *Jackson* have incorporated petitioner's brief in *Aikens* by reference. See Brief for Petitioners in No. 69–5003, pp. 11–12; Brief for Petitioner in No. 69–5030, pp. 11–12.

if the States were to execute as many sentenced capital offenders this year as they executed in the mid-1930's.[39] It seems more likely that public reaction, rather than being characterized by undifferentiated rejection, would depend upon the facts and circumstances surrounding each particular case.

Members of this Court know, from the petitions and appeals that come before us regularly, that brutish and revolting murders continue to occur with disquieting frequency. Indeed, murders are so commonplace in our society that only the most sensational receive significant and sustained publicity. It could hardly be suggested that in any of these highly publicized murder cases—the several senseless assassinations or the too numerous shocking multiple murders that have stained this country's recent history— the public has exhibited any signs of "revulsion" at the thought of executing the convicted murderers. The public outcry, as we all know, has been quite to the contrary. Furthermore, there is little reason to suspect that the public's reaction would differ significantly in response to other less publicized murders. It is certainly arguable that many such murders, because of their senselessness or barbarousness, would evoke a public demand for the death penalty rather than a public rejection of that alternative. Nor is there any rational basis for arguing that the public reaction to any of these crimes would be muted if the murderer were "rich and powerful." The demand for the ultimate sanction might well be greater, as a wealthy killer is hardly a sympathetic figure. While there might be specific cases in which capital punishment would be regarded as excessive and shocking to the conscience of the community, it can hardly be argued that the public's dissatisfaction with the penalty in particular cases would translate into a demand for absolute abolition.

In pursuing the foregoing speculation, I do not suggest that it is relevant to the appropriate disposition of these cases. The purpose of the digression is to indicate that judicial decisions cannot be founded on such speculations and assumptions, however appealing they may seem.

But the discrimination argument does not rest alone on a projection of the assumed effect on public opinion of more frequent executions. Much also is made of the undeniable fact that the death penalty has a greater impact on the lower economic strata of society, which include a relatively higher percentage of persons of minority racial and ethnic group backgrounds. The argument drawn from this fact is two-pronged. In part it is merely an extension of the speculative approach pursued by petitioners, i.e., that public revulsion is suppressed in callous apathy because the

[39] In 1935 available statistics indicate that 184 convicted murderers were executed. That is the highest annual total for any year since statistics have become available. NPS, supra, n. 18. The year 1935 is chosen by petitioners in stating their thesis: "If, in fact, 184 murderers were to be executed in this year 1971, we submit it is palpable that the public conscience of the Nation would be profoundly and fundamentally revolted, and that the death penalty for murder would be abolished forthwith as the atavistic horror that it is." Brief for Petitioner in No. 68–5027, p. 26. . . .

penalty does not affect persons from the white middle class which constitutes the majority in this country. This aspect, however, adds little to the infrequency rationalization for public apathy which I have found unpersuasive.

As Mr. Justice Marshall's opinion today demonstrates, the argument does have a more troubling aspect. It is his contention that if the average citizen were aware of the disproportionate burden of capital punishment borne by the "poor, the ignorant, and the underprivileged," he would find the penalty "shocking to his conscience and sense of justice" and would not stand for its further use. *Ante*, at 365–366, 369. This argument, like the apathy rationale, calls for further speculation on the part of the Court. It also illuminates the quicksands upon which we are asked to base this decision. Indeed, the two contentions seem to require contradictory assumptions regarding the public's moral attitude toward capital punishment. The apathy argument is predicated on the assumption that the penalty is used against the less influential elements of society, that the public is fully aware of this, and that it tolerates uses of capital punishment only because of a callous indifference to the offenders who are sentenced. Mr. Justice Marshall's argument, on the other hand, rests on the contrary assumption that the public does not know against whom the penalty is enforced and that if the public were educated to this fact it would find the punishment intolerable. *Ante*, at 369. Neither assumption can claim to be an entirely accurate portrayal of public attitude; for some acceptance of capital punishment might be a consequence of hardened apathy based on the knowledge of infrequent and uneven application, while for others acceptance may grow only out of ignorance. More significantly, however, neither supposition acknowledges what, for me, is a more basic flaw.

Certainly the claim is justified that this criminal sanction falls more heavily on the relatively impoverished and underprivileged elements of society. The "have-nots" in every society always have been subject to greater pressure to commit crimes and to fewer constraints than their more affluent fellow citizens. This is, indeed, a tragic byproduct of social and economic deprivation, but it is not an argument of constitutional proportions under the Eighth or Fourteenth Amendment. The same discriminatory impact argument could be made with equal force and logic with respect to those sentenced to prison terms. The Due Process Clause admits of no distinction between the deprivation of "life" and the deprivation of "liberty." If discriminatory impact renders capital punishment cruel and unusual, it likewise renders invalid most of the prescribed penalties for crimes of violence. The root causes of the higher incidence of criminal penalties on "minorities and the poor" will not be cured by abolishing the system of penalties. Nor, indeed, could any society have a viable system of criminal justice if sanctions were abolished or ameliorated because most of those who commit crimes happen to be underprivileged. The basic problem results not from the penalties imposed for criminal conduct but from social and economic factors that have plagued humanity since the beginning of recorded history, frustrating all efforts to create in any country at any time the perfect society in which there are no "poor," no "minorities" and no "underprivileged." [40] The causes underlying this problem are unrelated to the constitutional issue before the Court.

STEVEN GOLDBERG

Does Capital Punishment Deter?

One who opposes capital punishment can terminate all discussion simply by asserting that it is morally unacceptable for a society to take the life of one of its own, and that it would be unacceptable even if it could be demonstrated that capital punishment deters some who would murder if their society did not invoke the death penalty.[1] Likewise, one who supports capital punishment can foreclose further discussion by asserting that an eye must be taken for an eye even if the taking of an eye does not deter anyone any more than would a lesser penalty. Each of these positions is as irrefutable as it is incapable of persuading anyone who does not already accept it.

The question of deterrence is, however, paramount. It is paramount not merely for those whose position would be based on capital punishment's deterrent effect—those who would favor capital punishment if it does deter, but would not if it does not—but also for those who favor and those who oppose capital punishment for any reason and wish to see their view become public policy.[2] For it seems inevitable that public policy will

An earlier version of this essay appeared in *Ethics* (October 1974; Volume 85, Number 1). Copyright 1974 by The University of Chicago Press. Reprinted with the permission of the author and the publisher.

[40] Not all murders, and certainly not all crimes, are committed by persons classifiable as "underprivileged." Many crimes of violence are committed by professional criminals who willingly choose to prey upon society as an easy and remunerative way of life. Moreover, the terms "underprivileged," the "poor" and the "powerless" are relative and inexact, often conveying subjective connotations which vary widely depending upon the viewpoint and purpose of the user.

[1] This is, of course, the position on torture taken even by most proponents of capital punishment.

[2] Three oft-heard arguments can be seen to reduce, in all respects relevant to this essay, to one or the other arguments referred to in the opening paragraph. (1) The argument that capital punishment is bad because it "creates a climate of violence" or "reduces the value put on life by the members of society" is either (A) arguing that capital punishment does not deter (indeed, that it *increases* the

be derived from the assessment of capital punishment's deterrent effect. Therefore, even those who support or oppose capital punishment categorically for purely moral reasons, and for whom the question of deterrence is irrelevant, tend to argue their positions in terms of the ability or lack of ability of capital punishment to deter. This has led to a situation in which the discussion of capital punishment has become—like the discussions of homosexuality, abortion, and pornography—a discussion in which both the proponents and opponents have raised to the level of high art the attempt to bypass logic and invent knowledge in order to make reality congruent with wish.

Those who deny the ability of capital punishment to deter invoke a number of lines of reasoning—none of which is particularly convincing. They point out, quite correctly, that the murderer often does not believe that he will be caught (so that it does not matter to the murderer whether the punishment for murder is a small fine or death). Similarly, they suggest correctly, that many murderers act out of passion and do not consider the punishment. The problem with these attempts to deny the deterrent effect of capital punishment is that no one who supports capital punishment and who has thought the problem through would predicate his support on the ability of capital punishment to deter the *murderer; by definition the murderer has not been deterred by anything.* The question that is of determinative importance, and the question that the opponents of capital punishment rarely attempt to even consider on a theoretical level, is *what is it that deters those who are deterred; that is, not the murderer, but the rest of us?*

Until the opponents of capital punishment can offer an alternative theoretical explanation of what deters the rest of us it is not likely that the assertion that capital punishment does not deter will be very persuasive. One need not, of course, accept an element as a "causative" factor simply

---

murder rate) or (B) arguing that capital punishment "reduces the value put on life" or "creates a climate of violence" in some sense that is not reflected in the murder rate and that, therefore, it is bad even if it does deter. I must admit that I have never understood in what sense capital punishment could be said to "reduce the value put on life" or "create a climate of violence" if it does deter or why anyone would care if the value put on life were reduced (or if there were an increase in the climate of violence) if this did not mean that there were, in fact, more violence. (2) The argument that capital punishment is good for the retributive reason that it reasserts the moral, social, or legal order is arguing that an eye must be taken for an eye and that capital punishment is good even if it does not deter. I must admit that I have never understood in what sense retribution could be said to reassert the moral, legal, and social order if the retribution does not even deter or why anyone would care if the moral, legal, or social order were reasserted if reassertion does not have even the empirical result of deterrence. (3) The argument that capital punishment is good because it supports the desire of a member of the society that, if he is murdered, society will avenge the injustice he suffered by meting out (what he sees as) justice is (in respects relevant to this essay) arguing that an eye must be taken for an eye.

because he cannot offer an alternative explanation, but when he denies an explanation that is both in accord with common sense and persuasive it behooves him, if he cannot present an equally persuasive alternative explanation, to demonstrate that the element which is presented as the causative factor by the explanation he denies cannot be the causative factor.[3] Opponents of capital punishment implicitly acknowledge this when they attempt to demonstrate that the death penalty is not a factor causing a lower murder rate (i.e., when they attempt to demonstrate that capital punishment does not deter). For example, these opponents have pointed out, quite correctly, that some societies that do not invoke the death penalty have lower murder rates than some that do, and have implied that this fact somehow demonstrates that capital punishment does not deter. It does not, of course, demonstrate any such thing. The fact that society A has no capital punishment and a murder rate half that of society B (which does invoke the death penalty) can just as legitimately, but no more legitimately, be interpreted as demonstrating that capital punishment does deter and that if society B did not invoke the death penalty it would have a murder rate of, say, four times that of society A. One might, in other words, argue that the very factors (whatever they are) that generate the high murder rate in society B necessitate the use of the death penalty. This is seen more clearly if we consider what would happen if we invoked the death penalty for all individuals who commit murder, except nuns. We would find that nuns had a far lower murder rate than did the rest of the population even though they comprised the only group that was not threatened with capital punishment; this can hardly be argued to demonstrate that capital punishment does not deter. (If we had the death penalty only for nuns we would still find that nuns had a lower murder

---

[3] It is, in general, true that, since most empirical variables are not closely "causally" related, the burden of "proof" is on one who claims a close relationship between two variables. This is, however, a rule of plausibility and not a rule of logic. It is important to keep the difference in mind when we consider the argument (made by those who deny that capital punishment deters) that places the burden of "proof" on those who claim that capital punishment deters. It is, it seems to me, most plausible that capital punishment deters. Both common sense and endless amounts of evidence indicate that stronger punishment tends to inculcate a stronger internal resistance to motivation for the punished behavior, and to thereby reduce the amount of the punished behavior. It would seem to me that the burden of "proof" is on those who claim that the increase from life imprisonment to death does not have the effect that every lesser increase has. (Subsequent to the writing of this essay and footnote, a number of empirical statistical studies have been published that conclude that capital punishment does deter. If the reader accepts the conclusion indicated by these studies, then he can view this essay as a theoretical explanation of the empirical relationship whose existence is demonstrated by the studies. If he does not accept the conclusion indicated by the studies then he is in the uncertain situation that existed when I wrote this essay. Perhaps the best known of the recent studies is Isaac Erlich's "Participation in Illegitimate Activities" in the May/June 1973 *Journal of Political Economy*.)

rate; this can hardly be argued to demonstrate that capital punishment does deter.) Here, in our case, it is obvious that the determinative factor is the internalized social values of the individuals and the strength with which the values have been internalized and not (primarily) the presence or absence of capital punishment. We should note, however, that the fact that another factor (in this case the values that activate or obstruct murderous behavior) is a greater influence on the murder rate than is the presence or absence of capital punishment in no way affects our discussion of capital punishment, nor does it indicate that capital punishment does not deter; the question is whether fewer members of the general population commit murder when they are socialized in the presence of the death penalty than when they are not and whether fewer nuns commit murder when *they* are socialized in the presence of the death penalty than when *they* are not and not whether other factors deter. In other words, *if* capital punishment does deter, the fact that other factors are more effective in inculcating a strong resistance to socially forbidden behavior is irrelevant and will be unless it can be demonstrated that these other factors could reduce the murder rate to zero.

Criminologists have attempted to eliminate the problem of contaminating factors by using statistics on American states, sections of states, and regions for comparisons of every conceivable combination of factors. However, while some comparisons have increased our understanding of the relative importance of various factors to murder rates (as in their demonstration of the immense importance of differing regional values to differing murder rates), I think that they encounter a problem that is insurmountable, particularly if the suggestion of how capital punishment might deter advanced in this essay is correct. All of these American states and areas are in a society that has traditionally emphasized the importance of the prohibition of murder by invoking the death penalty, and this emphasis may well have been internalized even by the populations of those states that have not invoked it. It is likely that the majority of Americans do not even know whether their respective states have the death penalty. What they do know—through movies, television, and stories—is that murder is associated with hanging and electrocution. The crucial question is whether, for a marginal group of people, this association engendered an internal resistance to the emotional and environmental incentives to murder that is sufficient to deter while an association of murder and life imprisonment would not have been sufficient.

The question of whether capital punishment deters, whether execution of the murderer prevents some people from murdering while a lesser punishment of the murderer does not, is an empirical question. I do not think that any of the empirical studies concluding that capital punishment does not deter have avoided the difficulties I have mentioned. I do not wish here to present an empirical argument claiming that capital punishment does deter. I wish to present a theoretical explanation of how capital punishment deters *if* capital punishment does deter. To be sure, if someone does present empirical evidence that overcomes the difficulties I have mentioned and that does indicate that capital punishment does not deter, then these theoretical considerations are worthless. (There is little that is of less use than a theoretical explanation of a nonexistent empirical reality.) But I would suggest that in the absence of such empirical evidence the theoretical considerations do make it seem most plausible that capital punishment does deter and that, for the reason given in footnote 3, the burden of "proof" falls on those who argue that capital punishment does not deter.

A determinative factor affecting the degree to which murder will be committed in any given society may be the strength with which the value prohibiting murder is inculcated in the society's individual members, and this strength may be a function of the penalty with which the society backs up the value. It may be that individuals give values an internal weight concomitant with the weight they perceive the value as being given by their society, and this perception may judge the weight given to the value by the society in terms of—among other things—the weight of the punishment with which the society backs up the value. This seems a reasonable explanation of why and how most individuals develop an internal resistance to murder that is sufficiently strong to deter them from acting on the basis of the emotional forces (such as anger) and the environmental forces (such as poverty) that encourage murder.

I cannot stress strongly enough that there need be no element of rational calculation on the part of the individual for us to accept the deterent capacity of capital punishment.[4] Capital punishment deters—if it does deter—not because the potential murderer weighs the potential murder against the punishment and decides that life imprisonment would be a cheap price to pay but execution is too high a price. He is deterred by capital punishment—if he is deterred by capital punishment—because he has perceived, from childhood on, that murder is the most serious of social offences.[5] He has accepted this assessment of the seriousness of murder and

---

[4] Those who are temporarily or permanently mentally disturbed have impulses and desires that are, quantitatively or qualitatively, different from those of most people. But there is no evidence against, and much evidence for, the belief that such people are affected by the early internalization of the prohibitions we have discussed. The psychotic murderer, like the normal person who murders, has, of course, failed to sufficiently internalize the prohibition against murder. But, again, this proves only what need not be proved (because it is true by definition; the murderer is one who was not deterred from murdering). The question is: what deters those, psychotic or normal, who *are* deterred?

[5] I assume here that we are considering the usual situation (murder for profit, for example) in which the seriousness of the crime as represented by the possible punishment of the death penalty is complemented by the other elements that lead to an individual's accepting the importance of the value and giving it this weight. If other factors tend to counteract this process—if, for example, murder in a particular society is punishable by death, but murder of a wife's lover is

has internalized it because (among other reasons) his society has emphasized the importance of this value by punishing it with a penalty stronger
than that which it imposes for any other crime.[6] Capital punishment
deters—if it does deter—primarily by deterring today's child from becoming
tomorrow's murderer; it deters—if it does deter—by engendering in today's
child a resistance to murder that prevents him from ever even considering
murder in the behavioral calculations he makes as an adult. There is no
reason to believe that the internal resistance is inoperative when the incentive for murder is emotional rather than environmental. When most people
feel extreme anger they yell, or punch a refrigerator, or stifle their anger.
Most people do not invoke murder in the service of their passions; their
internal resistance to murder is sufficient to deflect the passions to a permitted object. In some cases the strong sanction prevents the individual
from consciously considering the environmental possibility, or feeling the
emotion, that would serve as incentive for murder, while in other cases the
sanction channels consciously considered possibility or felt emotion into
non-murderous behavior; in either case the sanction is responsible, in some
individuals, for the prevention of murder. If this is all correct, if one develops a stronger resistance to committing murder when there is capital
punishment than when there is not, if the additional strength of resistance
thus engendered prevents some people from murdering, then we are justified in believing that capital punishment deters, and that it deters crimes
of passion as well as rational crimes.

We might see this more clearly if we consider shoplifting, rather than
murder: The two-year-old who spies a bit of shiny costume jewelery will
"shoplift" without guilt; he is unaware of the negative social sanction on

---

traditionally considered virtually justified—then the members of the society will
not, despite the presence of the death penalty, resist the pressures to commit
this crime with the strength with which they resist crimes in which the presence
of the death penalty is complemented by other factors tending to emphasize
the seriousness with which the society views the crime. (In this essay I ignore
a number of other considerations that are important in any empirical assessment
of the deterrence. For example, it must be remembered that "murder" is socially
defined (killing is the act) and one society might define a particular type of
killing as "murder" while another will not. Likewise, one society's murder rate
might be far more accurately reported than another's. Such considerations are
of practical importance in testing the hypothesis that capital punishment deters
and in assessing the theoretical points made in this essay, but they are irrelevant
to the hypotheses and theoretical points themselves.)

[6] It is possible, of course, that this reasoning is all correct, but that one weighs internalized values only in relative terms so that the internal resistance to the
emotions that would utilize murder (and the environmental factors that encourage murder) would be equally strong if life imprisonment were the most
severe penalty invoked by the society. Or it is possible that absolute severity is
crucial, but that it is so only up to a maximal threshold (ten years' imprisonment, for example) past which the individual's internal resistance no longer
increases its strength. However, one is not justified in *assuming* that either of
these possibilities in reality obtains.

such behavior. The four-year-old child, who is aware from previous observation and experience that shoplifting is considered bad, will consciously weigh alternatives before deciding whether or not to shoplift the jewelry. The twelve-year-old child, who has fully internalized the values and sanctions relevant to shoplifting, will (in most cases and most of the time) not even consider stealing the jewelery. For the twelve-year-old shoplifting is not, as it is for the four-year-old, a question of weighing satisfactions against punishments. In most cases, most of the time, *the thought and possibility of shoplifting do not even enter the twelve-year-old's mind.* Observation and experience certainly seems to justify the conclusion that the degree to which children internalize the value against shoplifting is, *ceteris paribus,* a function of the severity of the negative sanction (be it formal punishment or a harsh word). Mild sanction, such as verbal parental disapproval, will be sufficient to bring most children to the point where shoplifting does not enter the mind. But there will be some children who will not sufficiently internalize the value if the importance of the value against shoplifting is not supported by physical punishment, while they will sufficiently internalize the value if physical punishment emphasizes the importance of the value.[7] Can this not all be said of murder and capital punishment as well as of shoplifting and physical punishment and of the adults children become as well as of the children?

It is worth noting that if capital punishment does deter in the manner described here (i.e. if capital punishment increases the strength with which the social sanction is internalized and if rational calculation is of no relevance), then we would not (necessarily) expect the abolition of capital punishment to engender an immediate increase in the murder rate. The increase would not be expected to begin until the new generation (those socialized in the absence of the death penalty) reached adolescence; because rational calculation need not play a role, we would not (necessarily) expect any increase in the number of murders committed by those who had been socialized in the presence of the death penalty.

If our description of the way in which individuals develop the resistance to emotional and environmental factors encouraging murder is cor-

---

[7] There is, of course, a third category of children (those who will shoplift whether there is physical punishment or not). There is even a fourth category, children who will shoplift *only* if there is physical punishment (because, for whatever psychological reason in any given case, these children are attracted to the punishment). If the fourth category were larger than the second (i.e., if more were attracted than deterred by physical punishment) this would be identifiable from the fact that shoplifting would be *positively* correlated with physical punishment and no one would argue in favor of physical punishment as a deterrent. However, for the reason given in footnote [8], it is highly unlikely that more are attracted than deterred by an increase in punishment. (In theory, one could impose physical punishment only for category 2 individuals, but this is both impossible until such individuals can be identified and impermissible in a democratic society.)

rect, society inculcates in the individual the value prohibiting murder (or any other value) on the basis of its "saying" (through its severe punishment) that the value is a very important one and *not* primarily through the *threat* of punishment. One might argue that threat is always the initiator in the development of the individual's perception of the strength of a value, and this might well be correct, but it is important to note that this is very different from the assertion that threat deters at the time of the act. We who do not murder refrain from murdering because of the strength of the internalized value that one does not murder and not because the present threat of punishment is so great that present fear of punishment precludes our committing the murderous act.

Thus: the fact that some pickpockets picked pockets at the public hangings of pickpockets, a fact often cited as if it demonstrated the inability of the death penalty to deter, demonstrates only that some individuals who have chosen to become pickpockets will not be deterred by capital punishment. It does not even demonstrate that no pickpockets were deterred (but only that not all were, a fact no one doubts). But even if we grant that *no* pickpocket will be deterred by capital punishment, we have granted only that the *pickpocket* (i.e. the person who has already chosen to be a pickpocket) has not been deterred. The important point is that the pickpocket story avoids the central question: does the execution of pickpockets, public or private, reduce the number of people who choose to become pickpockets? *If* it does, *if* fewer people become pickpockets when pickpockets are hanged than when they are not, then we can conclude that capital punishment does deter. We can conclude that, *ceteris paribus*, capital punishment caused a marginal group of individuals to develop an internal resistance to pickpocketing that was sufficiently strong to deter them from pickpocketing at all (i.e. from becoming pickpockets), while a lesser punishment would *not* have caused them to develop a sufficiently strong internal resistance. We can conclude that we refrain from committing crimes because (among other reasons) we *feel* that the crimes are too bad to justify our committing them and that the strength of this feeling is a function of the strength of the penalty. (I have no idea whether the number of pickpockets decreases or not when pickpockets are hanged, but neither do the people who invoke this irrelevant fact about hangings and assume, with no justification, the conclusion that they claim to be proving.)

The argument I have presented does not distinguish between the emotional forces that motivate an individual to murder and the environmental forces that encourage murder; I can see no *a priori* reason to assume that the mechanism responsible for the development of the internal resistance to the passions that encourage murder is different from the mechanism responsible for the development of the internal resistance to the environmental forces that encourage murder. I see no reason to assume that the mechanism responsible for one's resisting the impulse to murder out of anger is different from the mechanism that is responsible for one's resisting the incentive to murder for profit. However, if one wishes to treat these separately nothing that I have presented need be altered. The psychiatrist who is interested in the emotions that, as Freud tells us, would "murder even for trifles" must ask why the vast majority of people possess internal resistances to such emotions sufficient to dissuade them from acting on the emotions; [8] he must ask whether there exists a marginal group of people who develop an internal resistance that is sufficiently strong to keep them from murdering when the seriousness of murder is societally emphasized by the death penalty, but who do not develop a sufficiently strong resistance when society does not so emphasize the offensiveness of the act.[9] The sociologist, who is more interested in the environmental forces that encourage murder, must ask why most people resist such environmental incentives to murder (why, for example, most poor people do not murder) [10]; he must ask whether there exists a marginal group of people equivalent to the one just mentioned.

I do not know whether capital punishment deters, but I do know that it makes sense that it would and that the arguments attempting to demonstrate that it does not are unpersuasive. Given the nature of a modern society with its heterogeneity infusing every aspect of social life and its encouragement of diversity and freedom of speech, it does not seem likely that, save perhaps the society in the throes of religious or revolutionary rebirth, any society will ever again be able to count on the strength of

[8] Throughout this essay I have assumed that if capital punishment *deters* (i.e. if there are some people who will not murder if there is capital punishment, but who will murder if there is not), then the number of people who are deterred is greater than the number of people who are *encouraged* (i.e. people who are drawn to the punishment and who will murder if there is capital punishment, but who will not murder if there is not capital punishment). I think that all human experience indicates that punishment in general deters a greater number of people than it encourages. (Whether capital punishment is, in this respect, like all other punishment, is the question of the deterrent capacity of capital punishment). However, the psychiatrists are no doubt correct in arguing that there are some people who are encouraged, even if the psychiatrists tend to overestimate the numbers of such people because such people are so overrepresented among the psychiatrists' patients. If such people do equal in number those who are deterred, then, of course, capital punishment does not deter. This will be reflected in the empirical evidence that would demonstrate that the murder rate is not reduced by capital punishment. Thus, this psychiatric argument against capital punishment is, at bottom, an empirical assertion that capital punishment does not deter (i.e. that, *ceteris paribus*, the murder rate is not lower when there is capital punishment than when there is not) and it must succeed or fail on this prediction.

[9] One could, logically, but most implausibly, argue that all individuals have internal resistances of identical strength and that individuals differ only in the strength of the forces (emotional or environmental) that motivate them to murder. However, logical or not, this view is too implausible to warrant serious consideration; clearly some people have stronger consciences than others.

[10] See "A Theoretical Postscript" for a discussion of the role of environmental pressures leading to murder.

a single shared culture and familial authority to maintain even the minimal amount of social control necessary for a society to survive. If we cannot rely on shared values and familial authority as the sole sources of social control it behooves us to understand the mechanisms that serve to permit society to survive. Such understanding is rendered impossible if we categorically assume the correctness of an explanation which may well be incorrect. This is what we do when we assert the inability of capital punishment to deter.

I suspect that we would all *like* to believe that capital punishment does not deter. This relieves us of the weight of a moral decision. The strength of human reaction reflects perceived proximity, and most of us feel the responsibility inherent in supporting the execution of real murderers more intensely than the responsibility for a hypothetical group of victims who—if capital punishment does deter—will be murdered if our opposition to capital punishment prevails but who will not be murdered if our opposition fails and capital punishment is maintained.[11] Our seeming sympathy may well be an act of moral cowardice, an acceptance of a position that caters to fears of potential guilt rather than to responsibility to real, if unnameable, people. For if the proponent of capital punishment is incorrect in his assumption that capital punishment deters and is successful in his efforts to convince his society to invoke capital punishment, he is responsible "merely" for the deaths of *guilty* individuals who, if

[11] Motivation has, of course, nothing to do with correctness of argument. But it is often the opponents of capital punishment who introduce the issue of motivation—without, I suspect, realizing that an examination of motivation casts more doubt on the goodness of the motivations of the opponent of capital punishment than on those of the proponent. This becomes clear when we consider the question frequently asked of the proponent by the opponent: would *you* "pull the switch." Now the proponent might well answer that he would not pull the switch; nor would he shoot a man who was about to kill a small child. The fact that he *could not* perform an act in no way demonstrates that the act *should not* be performed by someone who is capable of performing the act. (The proponent may think highly of the executioner, thinking the executioner one who has the fortitude to do what he believes to be right, or the proponent may despise the executioner, assuming that the executioner enjoys the execution on some level. But this has nothing to do with whether or not there should be execution and it certainly has nothing to do with whether capital punishment deters.) What the opponent's demand that the proponent pull the switch *does* indicate is the psychological importance (to one's attitude towards capital punishment) of a fear of guilt. For if the proponent is one who would have difficulty pulling the switch (as any human being should), the opponent is often one who does not merely have difficulty, but whose position on capital punishment is determined by the source of this difficulty: the fear of guilt. This is not surprising; a fear of guilt is far more easily elicited by picturing a murderer about to be executed than by trying to picture a statistical group of people who will—if capital punishment does deter—be murdered if there is no capital punishment, but who will not be murdered if there is capital punishment. Again: none of this has anything to do with whether capital punishment deters or whether—if capital punishment deters—it should be invoked.

deterrence is the rationale for execution, should not be executed. If the opponent of capital punishment, on the other hand, is incorrect in his assumption that capital punishment does not deter and is successful in his efforts to convince his society to refrain from invoking capital punishment, *he* is responsible for the deaths of *innocent* people. Moreover, the number of innocent people who would not have been murdered if the deterrent of capital punishment had been invoked will be far greater than the number of innocent people who could conceivably be executed as a result of the mistaken conviction of innocent individuals for crimes they did not commit in a society that invokes capital punishment, and considerably greater, in all probability, than the total number of individuals who will be executed (guilty plus executed by mistaken conviction) in a society that invokes capital punishment. An awareness of this reduces considerably the persuasiveness of the position that argues that since we do not know whether capital punishment deters we should not invoke it.[12]

[12] One might argue: (*a*) that no matter how great a *probability* we may someday be able to attach to the *hypothesis* that capital punishment deters, capital punishment necessitates the *certain, tangible* deaths of *specific* individuals; (*b*) that, *ipso facto*, the lives of these individuals must be given priority over the lives of the members of a *hypothetical* group of *unknown* individuals who will, in all probability, be murdered if capital punishment is not invoked (but who will, in all probability, not be murdered if capital punishment is invoked); and (*c*) that the certainty of the deaths resulting from capital punishment (that is, executions) morally precludes our invoking capital punishment no matter how much larger the *hypothetical* group than the group comprised of the executed, and despite the fact that the hypothetical group is comprised of innocent individuals while the group of the executed is comprised almost entirely of guilty individuals. This argument can be seen to be either irrelevant to this essay or unsatisfactory even if we disregard the distinction between guilty and innocent individuals. For one who so argues will be forced either: (*a*) (if he argues that certainty must *always* take priority) to deny the acceptability of every military action—in which case his argument is virtually identical with the moral assertion that the state may never take a life, a position that renders irrelevant the question of deterrence, but one that both leaves him responsible for the murders that deterrence would have prevented (if capital punishment does deter) and fails to convince anyone who rejects its moral assertion; or (*b*) (if he is not willing to take the pacifist position and is not willing to argue that certainty always takes priority over probability) to admit that capital punishment will be justified if our future knowledge does enable us to attach to the hypothesis that capital punishment deters a probability equal to that for which he would consider a military action justified even though such an action accepts *certain* deaths as justified by the probability that more lives are ultimately saved. If he takes this latter position he is merely saying that capital punishment is not *now* justified because the evidence does not *presently* allow us to attach to the hypothesis that capital punishment deters a high enough probability to morally justify our invoking capital punishment; he would have to admit that someday we may be able to attach a high enough probability to justify its invocation and that capital punishment is not, *ipso facto*, immoral. This is, incidentally, the position I take. I would not consider the (admittedly very forceful) argument that only God has the right to deny the possibility of worldly redemption (a denial inherent in the

A Theoretical Postscript and a Legal Postscript

A THEORETICAL POSTSCRIPT.   The strength with which values are internalized is a determinant of the degree to which members of a society resist external (environmental) pressures leading to the commission of crime (educational and economic discrimination, for example). It would seem time to discuss the crimes committed by members of oppressed economic and racial groups in more penetrating terms than those utilized in the superficial observation that poverty fathers crime. Poverty does, under certain conditions, father crime, of course, and the pressures leading to the commission of crime are far greater for the members of these groups than they are for members of groups for which the rewards of crime are avilable through legitimate means and in whose members the mechanisms that strengthen an individual's internal defenses against the emotional and environmental factors generating crime are more strongly represented. As long as some of the members of oppressed groups feel that they are outcasts in American society, some of the members of these groups will fail to internalize the prohibitions against crime that are inculcated in the other members of the society. But if the commission of murder is the victory of the environmental factors and the emotional forces that encourage murder over the internal forces that reflect social prohibition for every other group, then it is for members of these groups also, and our ignoring this is to treat the members of these groups as less than human as well as to limit our understanding. Without question the external factors encouraging crime and the internal anger they generate are infinitely greater for blacks than for whites, but other groups in other societies, and blacks in former times in our own, have been equally oppressed, and yet they did not always have high crime rates. Indeed, even now the overwhelming majority of blacks do not commit crimes, despite the fact that they suffer the same outrages as do those who do commit crimes. This all suggests that crimes committed by blacks, like those committed by every other group, reflect not only the external factors encouraging crime and the anger that such factors engender, but the nature of the values of the group itself and the strength of the mechanisms by which the group inculcates its values in its members—mechanisms that are the same for blacks as they are for every other group. It should be remembered that, whatever the fears and fantasies of the white majority, the overwhelming number of the victims of black crime are blacks, and it is they who are suffering as we pretend that it is only factors that are external to the black group that contribute to black crime.

We have done this often: the predictable response to the *Moynihan Report* on the black family was the fallacious attempt at refutation that

---

invocation of the death penalty) sufficiently strong to justify our ignoring a high probability that by refusing to invoke the death penalty we are condemning innocent people to death.

argued that most black families are not female headed. This is, of course, true, but it misses the point of the report—which is that a far larger number of black families are female headed than are white families. In every society it is an adult male who serves as the threat and the model by which internal resistance to the external and internal pressures encouraging crime is developed in the maturing male. If these pressures are greater for the black than for the white then it is especially important that the methods by which black resistance can be strengthened be discovered. To the extent, and it is a very great extent, that external factors encourage black crime and weaken the development of internal resistance, these external factors must be changed (as, for example, by reducing economic discrimination and those factors that encourage the deterioration of the black family), but to the extent that it is black values that contribute to the weakening of the internal resistance to the pressures encouraging crime in individual blacks it is only blacks who can bring change. It seems to me that only the black nationalists have understood all of this fully and have seen that, for example, to deny the pathological effects of the absence of the father from many black families (that is, the effect of increasing crime by weakening the forces that engender a strong internal resistance to crime) is to argue that blacks develop this resistance in some other way than do all other human beings and that, therefore, they are not human.

A LEGAL POSTSCRIPT.   One might argue that, even if capital punishment does deter, it is unjust in that, in practice, it is invoked primarily for the lower economic classes or for racial minority groups. If the members of middle- and upper-class groups are executed less often for the commission of the same crimes for which members of the oppressed groups are executed, then this is patently unjust, but it is an injustice that should be corrected not by abolishing capital punishment (it is equally unjust to put the former in prison for ten years while putting the latter in prison for life), but by equalizing the punishment. This seems to be the reasoning invoked by most of the justices of the Supreme Court in the recent decision on capital punishment. Indeed, it would seem the only possible justification for considering as "cruel and unusual" a punishment that was accepted and common when the Eighth Amendment was written and that is still favored, I assume, by a majority of the population. (If it is not so favored, then the legal question is academic; even if capital punishment does deter, it will not, and should not, be invoked if a majority manifests its moral abhorrence in legislation banning it and the question of whether it is "cruel and unusual" becomes irrelevant.) Thus the Court-imposed moratorium on capital punishment would seem to be justified when capital punishment is unfairly imposed and when there is doubt about where the public stands (though one might argue that the Court must assume that present public opinion is reflected in present laws no matter how old such laws are as long as such laws are fairly applied), but one would be hard put to find a justification for a future Court's ruling that capital punishment, fairly imposed and based on recent legislation, was "cruel and unusual."

If members of lower-class groups are executed more often than members of the middle- or upper-class groups, but only in proportion to the greater number of capital crimes they commit, then there are a number of ways in which this fact can be viewed, but, while these views will differ on whether the situation is just or unjust, none is a strong argument for the abolition of capital punishment on theoretical grounds. If the crimes that are punished by death can reasonably be argued to be more serious than those that are not (violent murders as opposed to embezzlement, for example) and if equally serious middle- and upper-class crimes (treason, for example) are also punishable by death—if, in other words, capital crimes are not capital crimes merely because they are the crimes committed by the lower class— and if all individuals who commit these crimes are treated equally, then, in a narrow sense, no injustice is present. However, one might argue that this situation is unjust in the wider sense that the groups that commit these crimes do so as a result of environmental forces over which they have no control. To a point this is unquestionably correct. However, such an environmentalist view is sustainable only if carried all the way through to describe all punishment of all types. It is to argue that all punishment is unjust because it assumes free will when there is none. Correct or incorrect, this view is perfectly logical, but no society could predicate its legal system on the central deterministic assumption; for even if all crime is in reality completely determined, i.e. even if there is no free will, the view of crime held by the members of the society (i.e. whether criminal acts are seen as the result of free will or as the effect of only deterministic factors) will be a crucial factor in determining the amount of future crime. Thus, whether or not there is, in reality, free will, the societal view of whether or not there is free will will be a monumentally important factor affecting human behavior and the amount of future crime.[13]

---

[13] Those who agree with the analysis presented in this essay often ridicule the traditional "liberal" view of murder, which sees murder as psychologically abnormal behavior and emphasizes the unhappy childhood of the murderer. In fairness to the "liberal" view the following points should be made: (1) The view presented in this essay is not necessarily discordant (or concordant) with the "liberal" view. The questions raised by this essay are unrelated to the correctness or incorrectness of the "liberal" view. Even if the liberal view is correct, it must answer the question of whether capital punishment generates in some individuals who had unhappy childhoods an internal resistance to the (irrational) act of murder that is stronger than the resistance that would be engendered by a social sanction of life imprisonment. This is another way of saying that the causation of an act of murder is often comprised of many elements (lack of love as child and/or poverty and/or the strength of the perceived evil of the act, etc.) and asking whether for some people the difference between murdering and not murdering is the perception of the evilness of the act and whether this perception is increased by the presence of

GEORGE SCHEDLER

Capital Punishment and Its Deterrent Effect

In this essay, I raise doubts of two kinds about the justification of capital punishment. First, I show how a recent argument for capital punishment is unsound.[1] This argument is extremely persuasive in so far as it admits that the relevant statistics do not support the inference that capital punishment is a superior deterrent, but concludes nevertheless that it should be retained because capital punishment runs the risk of the loss of fewer innocent lives than life imprisonment.[2] Secondly, I wish to raise doubts of

capital punishment. (2) It seems to me quite likely that in the first two-thirds of this century, the period in which the "liberal" view gained acceptance, murder was, in fact, usually the manifestation of psychological abnormality. During this period social and familial values remained quite strong and it may well have been true that murder usually represented not a weakness of superego, of conscience, but a surfeit of murderous emotions that overpowered a normal superego. It does not seem likely that most contemporary murder can be so explained. The mugger clearly has a weak superego; the formerly common response of guilt when apprehended is now rare. When there is no superego whatsoever (and there are such people) capital punishment can deter only through the fear it engenders (though even this need not be rationally or consciously calculated in order to deter). Even when the superego is weak, capital punishment can deter in the way suggested in this essay.

Reprinted from *Social Theory and Practice*, Volume 4, Number 1 (1976), 47–56, with the permission of the author and the publisher.

[1] Two versions of this argument are: Ernest van den Haag, "On Deterrence and the Death Penalty," *Journal of Criminal Law, Criminology and Police Science* 60 (June 1969): 141–47, and Steven Goldberg, "On Capital Punishment," *Ethics* 85 (October 1974): 67–74.

[2] Of course, there are those who believe that within the relevant statistics the deterrent effects can be perceived. It has been argued, for example, that there is a trade-off between the murder rate and the number of executions per conviction, such that a 1.00 percent increase in the execution rate will reduce murders by about .06 percent. See Isaac Ehrlich, "The Deterrent Effect of Capital Punishment," *American Economic Review* 65 (June 1975): 414 ff. For a criticism of this, see Peter Passell, "The Deterrent Effect of the Death Penalty: A Statistical Test," *Stanford Law Review* 65 (November 1975): 62–64. But the criticism I offer in the second part of this essay applies to both these studies. On the other hand, it has been argued that all deterrent theories (that is, those which hold that capital punishment does have a deterrent effect) must be false, for what they necessarily predict (namely, a decrease in the murder rate) is falsified by available data. See William C. Bailey, "Murder and the Death Penalty," *The Journal of Criminal Law and Criminology* 65 (September 1974): 416–25. But even this argument

a conceptual kind about the relevance of deterrence to the justification of capital punishment.

I have divided this essay into seven sections, only the last of which is devoted to this second issue. The first three sections are preliminary ones in which I explain what conditions must be satisfied before we can truly assert that capital punishment has a greater deterrent effect than any lesser penalty. The remaining sections (4, 5, and 6) are devoted to the first point above.

(1) The crucial question about the death penalty is whether we could achieve what it achieves (and avoid whatever ill effects it might have) without putting anyone to death. It is not to the point, therefore, to compare what capital punishment would accomplish with what our present practices accomplish, if those practices could be improved. We do not provide a definitive case for capital punishment if some other lesser penalty might yield the same benefits. We must, therefore, compare two hypothetical penal systems: both being similar in *all* respects except that one has capital punishment. Since it is reasonable to suppose that life imprisonment without the possibility of parole has a greater deterrent effect than the present practice of allowing parole, we shall compare the benefits of the former to the benefits of capital punishment *ceteris paribus*.

(2) Secondly, let us examine the group of murderers (or potential murderers) who are deterred by capital punishment but not by this lesser penalty.[3] We can better understand these individuals by imagining a "spectrum of deterrability" for the crime of murder. At one extreme, are individuals who will commit the crime regardless of the penalty; that is, there is no penalty severe enough to deter them. (Let us recall at this point that we are restricting our attention to those who are murderers and could not successfully assert any legal justification, such as self-defense, or any legal defense, such as insanity or duress.)[4] At the other end of the spectrum are individuals who are deterred by any penalty at all, or perhaps merely by the stigma of conviction itself; they would commit murder only if it were legalized. Obviously, the group of individuals who would be deterred by the death penalty but not by life imprisonment occupy only a small part of this spectrum. We can exclude the following from this

---

fails to rule out the possibility that something other than the existence of the death penalty causes the alleged increase in murder rates. That ruling out this possibility is crucial to any such argument is clearly shown in Goldberg's article in note 1 above.

[3] I am restricting my attention here to the question of the deterrent effect on potential murderers, not potential rapists, hijackers, or any others. What I say here might not apply *mutatis mutandis* to other categories of offenders. (For a discussion of the problems involved in deterring hijackers, see R. Chauncey, "Deterrence: Certainty, Severity, Skyjacking," *Criminology* 12 (Fall 1975): 447–73.

[4] But see James R. Browning, "The New Death Penalty Statutes: Perpetuating a Costly Myth," *Gonzaga Law Review* 9 (Spring 1974): 656–57, for a discussion of cases in which apparently insane individuals were convicted and executed.

group: (a) those who are already deterred by life imprisonment without the possibility of parole, or by any other lesser penalty; (b) those who are deterred by no penalty whatsoever; (c) those who would be deterred only by a penalty *more severe* than (a relatively quick and painless) death, such as a slow or agonizing one.

(3) Let us examine more closely those people who can be deterred only by capital punishment. (We shall call these people "the uniquely deterrable group" or "uniquely deterrable murderers.") Let us ask at this point how it might happen that a penal system with capital punishment might "misfire" in some way so that some members of this group might *not* be deterred even though the death penalty exists in the society of which they are members. At first blush this seems not possible, but let us notice that we have said of this group only that they *can* be deterred by capital punishment. If, for example, the system of mass communication in a society were extremely poor, the deterrent effect of capital punishment may be lost due to poor publicity (that it is prescribed for murder). Some members of this group will of course be deterred once the mass media informs them that the death penalty is so prescribed. But is this sufficient for everyone in this group? Is it not yet conceivable that some other people who are deterred by the death penalty might yet commit murder under these conditions? The answer is affirmative, for it is quite consistent to hold that Jones is deterred from murder by the prospect of capital punishment, but that Jones believes that the chances of actually being executed for any given murder are slim. So, for example, in a society where the death penalty is not mandatory, some individuals might commit murder although they would not if the chances of execution were better. But the mandatoriness of the death penalty is not the only factor here. An exhaustive list would be impossible, but the more important ones are:

(a) mandatoriness of the death penalty;
(b) the possibilities for the appeal of any murder conviction, especially collateral appeals;
(c) the latitude of rights accorded the accused in police interrogations and criminal proceedings;
(d) the efficiency with which police discover that crimes have been committed and carry out subsequent investigation leading to arrest.[5]

To be sure, not all of these factors will be of crucial importance to *each* member of the uniquely deterrable group. Some of them will, of course, be deterred by even the remotest prospect of death, but others, we must suppose, will not. But it is undeniable that to achieve the maximum deterrent effect, the death penalty should be widely publicized and man-

---

[5] For a discussion of some of these factors, see pages 64–66 of P. Passell's article cited in note 1 above.

datory, with a minimum of rights for the accused, and so forth. The existence of the death penalty is not sufficient of itself to deter these people—they must believe death will most likely come to *them* if they murder. Any factors which affect the probability of this occurring will be taken into account by potential murderers. (If this were not true, they are not affected by the prospect of death and are not *ipso facto* members of the uniquely deterrable group.)

Before we focus more closely on one of these factors, we should note that this analysis reveals several risks which are "absolute," in the sense that we either lose some deterrent effect of the death penalty, failing to deter some murderer and thus losing the life of an innocent victim, or we maximize the deterrent effect of capital punishment and thereby increase the probability of execution of innocent people. The mandatoriness of capital punishment, for example, is a very important factor in deterrence, but it is also one factor which increases greatly the chances of execution of the innocent. Any society with capital punishment, then, runs some risk of losing the lives of innocent people.[6]

We should note parenthetically here the moral reasons which explain why execution of the innocent is regrettable. There is no reason to suppose that the deterrent effect of the death penalty would be decreased by the occasional discovery that an innocent person had been executed. Thus, execution of the innocent is not regrettable for deterrent reasons, though it is regrettable for the same fundamental reason which makes deterrence *itself* so morally important: minimizing the loss of innocent life. The risk of that loss is increased when capital punishment has greater deterrent effect; when it does not, then the failure to deter also increases the risk that innocent people will be killed by murderers who could have been deterred by the appropriate measures ("a"–"d" above).

(4) THE EFFECTS OF PUBLICITY. By far the single most important ingredient for achieving the deterrent effect is publicity. The publicity need not take the form of public executions. It might mean that the topic of executions occupies a prominent place in daily newspapers. It might not even involve *actual* executions: in some societies, the deterrent effect might be achieved by reminders that the death penalty is prescribed for murder. Although this kind of publicity will be clearly understood by the members of the uniquely deterrable group, we must nevertheless recognize that it may trigger certain irrational responses in certain unbalanced (but not legally insane) individuals. One such group are those who have suppressed self-destructive impulses. These people would be provided with an opportunity for self-destruction that would be absent in a society without capital

---

[6] I am leaving out of account societies in which the public might be deceived into believing that executions actually take place, even though this does not happen in fact. Such societies avoid the risks under discussion here, but the justification of such a practice raises other moral questions which cannot be pursued here.

punishment. For this reason, we can attribute the deaths of both the self-destructive murderers and the murderers' victims to the publicity surrounding capital punishment. In a society without such publicity, the self-destructive impulses might remain suppressed. It is, of course, possible that such individuals might commit suicide if there were no capital punishment, but in that case we would not lose the lives of their potential victims. Furthermore, we must recognize that, although there might be few individuals with these impulses, yet the publicity surrounding capital punishment might increase the numbers through a kind of conditioning process.[7]

There are, in addition, other types of individuals for whom the message the state tries to convey has an entirely different significance. The publicity may nurture the desire to kill *other* human beings. Certain individuals might want to imitate the executioner or the murderers who are executed. These people would probably be more dangerous, since they do not desire to be apprehended, unlike the self-destructive types, and the capture of these people may cost more innocent lives.

It might be said in response that the influence of capital punishment is exaggerated in this regard—except perhaps on an oversimple or outmoded model of human behavior. Actually, however, the possibilities sketched above are quite compatible with widely held theories of human behavior. The Freudian and Jungian theories, for example, allow for various unconscious drives or instincts of a self-destructive kind—and in fact such theories give us the impression that such individuals can be found in greater numbers than we might like.[8] On a behaviorist account, too, it is possible that publicity surrounding the death penalty might positively reinforce certain tendencies towards self-destructive behavior.[9] Various theories can easily account for the existence of these tendencies, though they will disagree over how to characterize the tendencies toward

---

[7] Aside from the theoretical support for this position which I discuss in note 8 and note 9 below, there is empirical support. See Rudolf J. Gerber, "A Death Penalty We Can Live With," *Notre Dame Lawyer* 50 (December 1974): 266–68.

[8] Freud discusses this in two places: *Beyond the Pleasure Principle* and *The Ego and the Id*. The discussion in the former can be found on pages 38–41 and 46–47 in volume 18 of *The Standard Edition of the Complete Psychological Works of Sigmund Freud*, ed. James Strachey (London: 1955). The discussion in *The Ego and the Id* can be found on pages 40–46, 53–56, and 159–65. Such self-destructive impulses do not figure as prominently for Jung as they do for Freud, nevertheless, Jung discusses these in the following works: *Psychological Types, The Structure and Dynamics of the Psyche*, and *The Practice of Psychotherapy*. These discussions can be found, respectively, in the following places in *The Collected Works of C. J. Jung* (Princeton: Princeton University Press, various publication dates), volume 6, 341; volume 8, 288; and volume 16, 57.

[9] In this regard, see B. F. Skinner's discussion of the following topics in *Science and Human Behavior* (New York: Macmillan, 1953): the causes of aggressive behavior, pages 202f, 302, 372–79 and suicide, 232. See also his discussion of deferred "aversive consequences" of governmental policies in *Beyond Freedom and Dignity* (New York: Bantam Books, 1971), 31ff.

this behavior: whether it is innate or learned, whether conscious or unconscious, whether due to instincts, drives, needs, desires, and so on.

How many of these unbalanced individuals will fall into this group (we will call them "irrational" or "unbalanced" murderers) will obviously vary from one society to the next. Various social, genetic, and physiological factors, perhaps too the degree of the society's industrialization, will raise or lower the number. Not enough is known to determine the number of unbalanced murderers in a given population, let alone what factors raise or lower the number.

This is also true of the uniquely deterrable group. It is conceivable that some societies will not have any individuals who fall into that group. Other societies may have a very large number. But if there is to be any advantage to having capital punishment there must be reason to believe that there are some individuals in this group, and we must, in addition, have reason to believe that the number deterred is greater than the number of lives lost by (1) executions of innocents, including unbalanced murderers, and (2) the victims of unbalanced murders. It is crucial to notice that it is not enough to compare the *number* of uniquely deterrable murderers with the numbers in (1) and (2); we must take into account how many in the uniquely deterrable group *will actually be deterred*. This will depend upon publicity and the factors "a"–"d" which we discussed earlier.

(5) DOES CAPITAL PUNISHMENT DETER?   An affirmative answer to the question of whether the death penalty deters is not the absolute answer it has often been taken to be. To say the death penalty deters (more than a lesser penalty) is merely to say that in some societies there are individuals who fall into the uniquely deterrable group and that publicity and other factors are right. This is entirely compatible with the claim that the death penalty does *not* deter: in some societies there are no individuals who are uniquely deterrable, or, if so, the requisite publicity and other factors are not present. Different societies, or different conditions at different times in the *same* society, will warrant different answers to this question. Thus, the question has no general answer—only an answer for a certain society at a certain time.

(6) RECENT ARGUMENTS FOR CAPITAL PUNISHMENT.   The state of our knowledge of human behavior, at least in present-day American society, is such that we cannot even make good guesses at how many people, if any, fall into this group. Given this uncertainty, it has been argued recently that we should adopt the minimax strategy: we should choose the policy which will minimize the loss of life should our assumptions about deterrence be incorrect. If we incorrectly assume that capital punishment deters and we retain it, we vainly execute convicted murderers (some of whom may be innocent). On the other hand, if we incorrectly assume it does not deter and we abolish it, then the uniquely deterrable group will kill an

indefinite number of innocent people. It has been argued that the former alternative minimizes our losses, for the relative number of executed murderers (who may be innocent) will surely be smaller than the number of innocent victims. Thus, the rational alternative is to retain capital punishment.[10]

Even though this argument avoids the question of the actual numbers involved by estimating only the relative numbers, it does not take into account the (relative or absolute) number of irrational murderers and their victims that may be lost by retention but saved by abolition. Since this number is entirely independent of any deterrent effect the death penalty might have, we could never be sure we lose fewer lives by retaining capital punishment (even though it might not deter) than by abolishing it (even though it might have deterred some). If we retain it, we lose the lives of the unbalanced murderers and their victims; and if we abolish it, we save them. Both these propositions may remain true whether or not it deters. The losses of retention necessarily increase, while the losses of abolition must decrease.

It might even be the case that the number of victims of the uniquely deterrable murderers are as great as the total number of unbalanced murderers and their victims, so that even if capital punishment does deter it may not save any lives. If it did not deter, and this is the possibility relevant to the minimax strategy, the losses would be enormous: we save no innocent victims of the uniquely deterrable group, and we have lost the lives of the unbalanced murderers and their victims. Now, if we compare this to the abolition of the death penalty, even though it would have deterred, we see that we might not have lost anything, for we saved the lives of the unbalanced murderers and their victims although we lost (*ex hypothesi*) the same number of innocent people to the uniquely deterrable group.

Of course, we do not yet know what the numbers in a relative or absolute sense would be. But until we know that, we cannot possibly have reason to believe that the losses of abolition (if capital punishment would have deterred) are greater than retention (even if it does not deter).

(7) Finally, let us reflect on the reasons why viewing capital punishment in this way (that is, as a way of saving innocent lives) seems so very queer. We begin with the very reasonable position that, if capital punishment is justified at all, it must somehow save more innocent lives than any alternative. But the argument ends with the unreasonable assumption that nothing more is needed to justify capital punishment than a demonstration that fewer lives is not a sufficient condition for the justification of capital punishment, although it is necessary.

But further reflection on this also leads to odd results, for it leaves

[10] This is a summary of the argument in van den Haag's paper (see note 1 above). Goldberg's argument (also cited in note 1) is based on the same strategy, but, instead of risks to innocent life, he couches his argument in terms of the respective moral responsibilities for the loss of innocent life that retentionists and abolitionists must bear.

open the possibility that a case for the abolition of the death penalty might be made even though abolition would risk more innocent lives. But this is not an irrational risk. For it simply indicates a refusal to save more lives if doing so entails the loss of other fundamental goods, such as civil liberties. And this reveals a defect generally in any argument for—or against—capital punishment based *solely* on its superior—or inferior— deterrent effect: the basic question of the justice or injustice of capital punishment is thereby evaded entirely. Once we restrict the discussion to the probable loss of innocent life, we are treating capital punishment as a sort of tax on a course of conduct, whose justification depends upon how many will find the tax too heavy, how many will not, and how many will try to engage in the conduct hoping to escape the tax.[11] We raise, so to speak, the "price" of committing murder so high that few are willing to pay it, and, if any chooses to do so, her or his example makes it clear to others that they cannot expect to commit murders without also paying the price.[12] By viewing capital punishment in the context of a price mechanism or taxation scheme, we do not imply that the satisfaction the murderer derives from her or his crime is an absolutely illegitimate satisfaction —we suggest instead that this satisfaction is a scarce commodity of sorts, for which an extraordinarily high price must be paid.[13] But these concerns have nothing to do with the basic justice or injustice of executing those individuals who in society's eyes have committed the most serious crime. We are thus left with the conclusion that capital punishment is not justified as a *punishment*, unless, in some sense, those who have been convicted of capital crimes can be said to deserve it apart from any deterrent effects the executions will have on others. There is, then, an inescapable retributive aspect of the justification of capital punishment. The convicted murderer cannot justifiably be used merely as an example to others; what he or she receives as a punishment must somehow be deserved for having committed murder.[14]

[11] H. L. A. Hart contrasts punishment with a tax on a course of conduct on page 7 of his *Punishment and Responsibility* (Oxford: Clarendon Press, 1968).

[12] John Rawls refers to punishment as a sort of price system in his "Two Concepts of Rules," *The Philosophical Review* 64 (January 1955): 13. The analysis I present here draws upon the conception of justice Rawls presents in his *A Theory of Justice* (Cambridge, Mass.: Harvard University Press, 1971). I also emphasize an aspect of punishment which Joel Feinberg discussed in his "The Expressive Function of Punishment," *The Monist* 52 (July 1965): 397–408.

[13] Thus punishment is reduced to a price-posting mechanism. It is worth noting that those theorists who are convinced of the social worth of a "deterrence system" refer to it as a "communication system" which is a more accurate description of what deterrence is. (However, I believe there is more to it than this, since we do not, in a rational penal system, merely post "prices" in a neutral way, as though we are indifferent about the prospect that a large number of people might choose to pay the price.) See Michael R. Geerken and Walter R. Gove "Deterrence: Some Theoretical Considerations," *Law and Society Review* 9 (Spring 1975): 499 and 511.

[14] I argue that punishment as an institution cannot be justified solely on deterrent grounds in "On Telishing the Guilty," *Ethics* 86 (April 1976): 259–60.

With this last point there will no doubt be some who disagree. In reply, I can only insist that those who discuss the justification of capital punishment solely in deterrent terms cease calling it "capital punishment" and instead refer to it in a neutral way as "the death penalty," since, for them, it is no different from other penalties such as late filing of income taxes or even so-called public welfare offenses. None of these are justified because they are deserved but (usually) because of the favorable effects such fines have on those who might be tempted to commit the offense. It may even be the case that *no* punishment proper can be justified in the way I am suggesting, but we at least should not entertain the false belief that we are seeking to justify a form of punishment when, in truth, if we have justified anything at all, it is some other measure for controlling human behavior.

Selected Bibliography

ACTON, H. B. (ed.). *The Philosophy of Punishment*. New York: St. Martin's Press, Inc., 1969.

BEDAU, HUGO ADAM (ed.). *The Death Penalty in America*. Chicago: Aldine Publishing Company, 1964. Revised edition, 1967.

CEDARBLOM, J. B., and WILLIAM L. BLIZEK (eds.). *Justice and Punishment*. Cambridge, Mass.: Ballinger Publishing Company, 1977.

EZORSKY, GERTRUDE (ed.). *Philosophical Perspectives on Punishment*. Albany: State University of New York Press, 1972.

GERBER, RUDOLPH J., and PATRICK D. MCANANY (eds.). *Contemporary Punishment: Views, Explanations and Justifications*. Notre Dame, Ind.: University of Notre Dame Press, 1972.

GOLDINGER, MILTON (ed.). *Punishment and Human Rights*. Cambridge, Mass.: Schenkman Publishing Company, 1974.

HART, H. L. A. *Punishment and Responsibility: Essays in the Philosophy of Law*. Oxford: Oxford University Press, 1968.

HONDERICH, TED. *Punishment: The Supposed Justifications*. New York: Harcourt Brace Jovanovich, Inc., 1969.

MURPHY, JEFFRIE (ed.). *Punishment and Rehabilitation*. Belmont, Calif.: Wadsworth Publishing Co., Inc., 1973.

PINCOFFS, EDMUND. *The Rationale of Legal Punishment*. New York: Humanities Press, 1966.

seven

THE WORLD AT LARGE

PETER SINGER

Famine, Affluence, and Morality

As I write this, in November 1971, people are dying in East Bengal from lack of food, shelter, and medical care. The suffering and death that are occurring there now are not inevitable, not unavoidable in any fatalistic sense of the term. Constant poverty, a cyclone, and a civil war have turned at least nine million people into destitute refugees; nevertheless, it is not beyond the capacity of the richer nations to give enough assistance to reduce any further suffering to very small proportions. The decisions and actions of human beings can prevent this kind of suffering. Unfortunately, human beings have not made the necessary decisions. At the individual level, people have, with very few exceptions, not responded to the situation in any significant way. Generally speaking, people have not given

Reprinted from *Philosophy and Public Affairs*, Vol. 7, No. 3 (Spring 1972), 229–243. Copyright © by Princeton University Press. Reprinted by permission of the author and Princeton University Press.

large sums to relief funds; they have not written to their parliamentary representatives demanding increased government assistance; they have not demonstrated in the streets, held symbolic fasts, or done anything else directed toward providing the refugees with the means to satisfy their essential needs. At the government level, no government has given the sort of massive aid that would enable the refugees to survive for more than a few days. Britain, for instance, has given rather more than most countries. It has, to date, given £14,750,000. For comparative purposes, Britain's share of the nonrecoverable development costs of the Anglo-French Concorde project is already in excess of £275,000,000, and on present estimates will reach £440,000,000. The implication is that the British government values a supersonic transport more than thirty times as highly as it values the lives of the nine million refugees. Australia is another country which, on a per capita basis, is well up in the "aid to Bengal" table. Australia's aid, however, amounts to less than one-twelfth of the cost of Sydney's new opera house. The total amount given, from all sources, now stands at about £65,000,000. The estimated cost of keeping the refugees alive for one year is £464,000,000. Most of the refugees have now been in the camps for more than six months. The World Bank has said that India needs a minimum of £300,000,000 in assistance from other countries before the end of the year. It seems obvious that assistance on this scale will not be forthcoming. India will be forced to choose between letting the refugees starve or diverting funds from her own development program, which will mean that more of her people will starve in the future.[1]

These are the essential facts about the present situation in Bengal. So far as it concerns us here, there is nothing unique about this situation except its magnitude. The Bengal emergency is just the latest and most acute of a series of major emergencies in various parts of the world, arising both from natural and from man-made causes. There are also many parts of the world in which people die from malnutrition and lack of food independent of any special emergency. I take Bengal as my example only because it is the present concern, and because the size of the problem has ensured that it has been given adequate publicity. Neither individuals nor governments can claim to be unaware of what is happening there.

What are the moral implications of a situation like this? In what follows, I shall argue that the way people in relatively affluent countries react to a situation like that in Bengal cannot be justified; indeed, the whole way we look at moral issues—our moral conceptual scheme—needs to be altered, and with it, the way of life that has come to be taken for granted in our society.

In arguing for this conclusion I will not, of course, claim to be

---

[1] There was also a third possibility: that India would go to war to enable the refugees to return to their lands. Since I wrote this paper, India has taken this way out. The situation is no longer that described above, but this does not affect my argument, as the next paragraph indicates.

morally neutral. I shall, however, try to argue for the moral position that I take, so that anyone who accepts certain assumptions, to be made explicit, will, I hope, accept my conclusion.

I begin with the assumption that suffering and death from lack of food, shelter, and medical care are bad. I think most people will agree about this, although one may reach the same view by different routes. I shall not argue for this view. People can hold all sorts of eccentric positions, and perhaps from some of them it would not follow that death by starvation is in itself bad. It is difficult, perhaps impossible, to refute such positions, and so for brevity I will henceforth take this assumption as accepted. Those who disagree need read no further.

My next point is this: if it is in our power to prevent something bad from happening, without thereby sacrificing anything of comparable moral importance, we ought, morally, to do it. By "without sacrificing anything of comparable moral importance" I mean without causing anything else comparably bad to happen, or doing something that is wrong in itself, or failing to promote some moral good, comparable in significance to the bad thing that we can prevent. This principle seems almost as uncontroversial as the last one. It requires us only to prevent what is bad, and not to promote what is good, and it requires this of us only when we can do it without sacrificing anything that is, from the moral point of view, comparably important. I could even, as far as the application of my argument to the Bengal emergency is concerned, qualify the point so as to make it: if it is in our power to prevent something very bad from happening, without thereby sacrificing anything morally significant, we ought, morally, to do it. An application of this principle would be as follows: if I am walking past a shallow pond and see a child drowning in it, I ought to wade in and pull the child out. This will mean getting my clothes muddy, but this is insignificant, while the death of the child would presumably be a very bad thing.

The uncontroversial appearance of the principle just stated is deceptive. If it were acted upon, even in its qualified form, our lives, our society, and our world would be fundamentally changed. For the principle takes, firstly, no account of proximity or distance. It makes no moral difference whether the person I can help is a neighbor's child ten yards from me or a Bengali whose name I shall never know, ten thousand miles away, Secondly, the principle makes no distinction between cases in which I am the only person who could possibly do anything and cases in which I am just one among millions in the same position.

I do not think I need to say much in defense of the refusal to take proximity and distance into account. The fact that a person is physically near to us, so that we have personal contact with him, may make it more likely that we *shall* assist him, but this does not show that we *ought* to help him rather than another who happens to be further away. If we accept any principle of impartiality, universalizability, equality, or whatever, we cannot discriminate against someone merely because he is far away from us (or we are far away from him). Admittedly, it is possible that we are in a better position to judge what needs to be done to help a person near to us than one far away, and perhaps also to provide the assistance we judge to be necessary. If this were the case, it would be a reason for helping those near to us first. This may once have been a justification for being more concerned with the poor in one's own town than with famine victims in India. Unfortunately for those who like to keep their moral responsibilities limited, instant communication and swift transportation have changed the situation. From the moral point of view, the development of the world into a "global village" has made an important, though still unrecognized, difference to our moral situation. Expert observers and supervisors, sent out by famine relief organizations or permanently stationed in famine-prone areas, can direct our aid to a refugee in Bengal almost as effectively as we could get it to someone in our own block. There would seem, therefore, to be no possible justification for discriminating on geographical grounds.

There may be a greater need to defend the second implication of my principle—that the fact that there are millions of other people in the same position, in respect to the Bengali refugees, as I am, does not make the situation significantly different from a situation in which I am the only person who can prevent something very bad from occurring. Again, of course, I admit that there is a psychological difference between the cases; one feels less guilty about doing nothing if one can point to others, similarly placed, who have also done nothing. Yet this can make no real difference to our moral obligations.[2] Should I consider that I am less obliged to pull the drowning child out of the pond if on looking around I see other people, no further away than I am, who have also noticed the child but are doing nothing? One has only to ask this question to see the absurdity of the view that numbers lessen obligation. It is a view that is an ideal excuse for inactivity; unfortunately most of the major evils—poverty, overpopulation, pollution—are problems in which everyone is almost equally involved.

The view that numbers do make a difference can be made plausible if stated in this way: if everyone in circumstances like mine gave £5 to the

---

[2] In view of the special sense philosophers often give to the term, I should say that I use "obligation" simply as the abstract noun derived from "ought," so that "I have an obligation to" means no more, and no less, than "I ought to." This usage is in accordance with the definition of "ought" given by the *Shorter Oxford English Dictionary*: "the general verb to express duty or obligation." I do not think any issue of substance hangs on the way the term is used; sentences in which I use "obligation" could all be rewritten, although somewhat clumsily, as sentences in which a clause containing "ought" replaces the term "obligation."

Bengal Relief Fund, there would be enough to provide food, shelter, and medical care for the refugees; there is no reason why I should give more than anyone else in the same circumstances as I am; therefore I have no obligation to give more than £5. Each premise in this argument is true, and the argument looks sound. It may convince us, unless we notice that it is based on a hypothetical premise, although the conclusion is not stated hypothetically. The argument would be sound if the conclusion were: if everyone in circumstances like mine were to give £5, I would have no obligation to give more than £5. If the conclusion were so stated, however, it would be obvious that the argument has no bearing on a situation in which it is not the case that everyone else gives £5. This, of course, is the actual situation. It is more or less certain that not everyone in circumstances like mine will give £5. So there will not be enough to provide the needed food, shelter, and medical care. Therefore by giving more than £5 I will prevent more suffering than I would if I gave just £5.

It might be thought that this argument has an absurd consequence. Since the situation appears to be that very few people are likely to give substantial amounts, it follows that I and everyone else in similar circumstances ought to give as much as possible, that is, at least up to the point at which by giving more one would begin to cause serious suffering for oneself and one's dependents—perhaps even beyond this point to the point of marginal utility, at which by giving more one would cause oneself and one's dependents as much suffering as one would prevent in Bengal. If everyone does this, however, there will be more than can be used for the benefit of the refugees, and some of the sacrifice will have been unnecessary. Thus, if everyone does what he ought to do, the result will not be as good as it would be if everyone did a little less than he ought to do, or if only some do all that they ought to do.

The paradox here arises only if we assume that the actions in question—sending money to the relief funds—are performed more or less simultaneously, and are also unexpected. For if it is to be expected that everyone is going to contribute something, then clearly each is not obliged to give as much as he would have been obliged to had others not been giving too. And if everyone is not acting more or less simultaneously, then those giving later will know how much more is needed, and will have no obligation to give more than is necessary to reach this amount. To say this is not to deny the principle that people in the same circumstances have the same obligations, but to point out that the fact that others have given, or may be expected to give, is a relevant circumstance: those giving after it has become known that many others are giving and those giving before are not in the same circumstances. So the seemingly absurd consequence of the principle I have put forward can occur only if people are in error about the actual circumstances—that is, if they think they are giving when others are not, but in fact they are giving when others are. The result of everyone doing what he really ought to do cannot be worse than the result of everyone doing less than he ought to do, although the result of everyone doing what he reasonably believes he ought to do could be.

If my argument so far has been sound, neither our distance from a preventable evil nor the number of other people who, in respect to that evil, are in the same situation as we are, lessens our obligation to mitigate or prevent that evil. I shall therefore take as established the principle I asserted earlier. As I have already said, I need to assert it only in its qualified form: if it is in our power to prevent something very bad from happening, without thereby sacrificing anything else morally significant, we ought, morally, to do it.

The outcome of this argument is that our traditional moral categories are upset. The traditional distinction between duty and charity cannot be drawn, or at least, not in the place we normally draw it. Giving money to the Bengal Relief Fund is regarded as an act of charity in our society. The bodies which collect money are known as "charities." These organizations see themselves in this way—if you send them a check, you will be thanked for your "generosity." Because giving money is regarded as an act of charity, it is not thought that there is anything wrong with not giving. The charitable man may be praised, but the man who is not charitable is not condemned. People do not feel in any way ashamed or guilty about spending money on new clothes or a new car instead of giving it to famine relief. (Indeed, the alternative does not occur to them.) This way of looking at the matter cannot be justified. When we buy new clothes not to keep ourelves warm but to look "well-dressed" we are not providing for any important need. We would not be sacrificing anything significant if we were to continue to wear our old clothes, and give the money to famine relief. By doing so, we would be preventing another person from starving. It follows from what I have said earlier that we ought to give money away, rather than spend it on clothes which we do not need to keep us warm. To do so is not charitable, or generous. Nor is it the kind of act which philosophers and theologians have called "supererogatory"— an act which it would be good to do, but not wrong not to do. On the contrary, we ought to give the money away, and it is wrong not to do so.

I am not maintaining that there are no acts which are charitable, or that there are no acts which it would be good to do but not wrong not to do. It may be possible to redraw the distinction between duty and charity in some other place. All I am arguing here is that the present way of drawing the distinction, which makes it an act of charity for a man living at the level of affluence which most people in the "developed nations" enjoy to give money to save someone else from starvation, cannot be supported. It is beyond the scope of my argument to consider whether the distinction should be redrawn or abolished altogether. There would be many other possible ways of drawing the distinction—for instance, one might decide that it is good to make other people as happy as possible, but not wrong not to do so.

Despite the limited nature of the revision in our moral conceptual scheme which I am proposing, the revision would, given the extent of both affluence and famine in the world today, have radical implications. These implications may lead to further objections, distinct from those I have already considered. I shall discuss two of these.

One objection to the position I have taken might be simply that it is too drastic a revision of our moral scheme. People do not ordinarily judge in the way I have suggested they should. Most people reserve their moral condemnation for those who violate some moral norm, such as the norm against taking another person's property. They do not condemn those who indulge in luxury instead of giving to famine relief. But given that I did not set out to present a morally neutral description of the way people make moral judgments, the way people do in fact judge has nothing to do with the validity of my conclusion. My conclusion follows from the principle which I advanced earlier, and unless that principle is rejected, or the arguments shown to be unsound, I think the conclusion must stand, however strange it appears.

It might, nevertheless, be interesting to consider why our society, and most other societies, do judge differently from the way I have suggested they should. In a well-known article, J. O. Urmson suggests that the imperatives of duty, which tell us what we must do, as distinct from what it would be good to do but not wrong not to do, function so as to prohibit behavior that is intolerable if men are to live together in society.[3] This may explain the origin and continued existence of the present division between acts of duty and acts of charity. Moral attitudes are shaped by the needs of society, and no doubt society needs people who will observe the rules that make social existence tolerable. From the point of view of a particular society, it is essential to prevent violations of norms against killing, stealing, and so on. It is quite inessential, however, to help people outside one's own society.

If this is an explanation of our common distinction between duty and supererogation, however, it is not a justification of it. The moral point of view requires us to look beyond the interests of our own society. Previously, as I have already mentioned, this may hardly have been feasible, but it is quite feasible now. From the moral point of view, the prevention of the starvation of millions of people outside our society must be considered at least as pressing as the upholding of property norms within our society.

[3] J. O. Urmson, "Saints and Heroes," in *Essays in Moral Philosophy*, ed. Abraham I. Melden (Seattle and London, 1958), p. 214. For a related but significantly different view see also Henry Sidgwick, *The Methods of Ethics*, 7th edn. (London, 1907), pp. 220–221, 492–493.

It has been argued by some writers, among them Sidgwick and Urmson, that we need to have a basic moral code which is not too far beyond the capacities of the ordinary man, for otherwise there will be a general breakdown of compliance with the moral code. Crudely stated, this argument suggests that if we tell people that they ought to refrain from murder and give everything they do not really need to famine relief, they will do neither, whereas if we tell them that they ought to refrain from murder and that it is good to give to famine relief but not wrong not to do so, they will at least refrain from murder. The issue here is: Where should we draw the line between conduct that is required and conduct that is good although not required, so as to get the best possible result? This would seem to be an empirical question, although a very difficult one. One objection to the Sidgwick-Urmson line of argument is that it takes insufficient account of the effect that moral standards can have on the decisions we make. Given a society in which a wealthy man who gives five percent of his income to famine relief is regarded as most generous, it is not surprising that a proposal that we all ought to give away half our incomes will be thought to be absurdly unrealistic. In a society which held that no man should have more than enough while others have less than they need, such a proposal might seem narrow-minded. What it is possible for a man to do and what he is likely to do are both, I think, very greatly influenced by what people around him are doing and expecting him to do. In any case, the possibility that by spreading the idea that we ought to be doing very much more than we are to relieve famine we shall bring about a general breakdown of moral behavior seems remote. If the stakes are an end to widespread starvation, it is worth the risk. Finally, it should be emphasized that these considerations are relevant only to the issue of what we should require from others, and not to what we ourselves ought to do.

The second objection to my attack on the present distinction between duty and charity is one which has from time to time been made against utilitarianism. It follows from some forms of utilitarian theory that we all ought, morally, to be working full time to increase the balance of happiness over misery. The position I have taken here would not lead to this conclusion in all circumstances, for if there were no bad occurrences that we could prevent without sacrificing something of comparable moral importance, my argument would have no application. Given the present conditions in many parts of the world, however, it does follow from my argument that we ought, morally, to be working full time to relieve great suffering of the sort that occurs as a result of famine or other disasters. Of course, mitigating circumstances can be adduced—for instance, that if we wear ourselves out through overwork, we shall be less effective than we would otherwise have been. Nevertheless, when all considerations of this sort have been taken into account, the conclusion remains: we ought to be preventing as much suffering as we can without sacrificing something else of comparable moral importance. This conclusion is one which we may be reluctant to face. I cannot see, though, why it should be regarded as a criticism of the position for which I have argued, rather than a criticism of our ordinary standards of behavior. Since most people are self-interested to some degree, very few of us are likely to do everything that we ought to do. It would, however, hardly be honest to take this as evidence that it is not the case that we ought to do it.

It may still be thought that my conclusions are so wildly out of line with what everyone else thinks and has always thought that there must be something wrong with the argument somewhere. In order to show that my conclusions, while certainly contrary to contemporary Western moral standards, would not have seemed so extraordinary at other times and in other places, I would like to quote a passage from a writer not normally thought of as a way-out radical, Thomas Aquinas.

> Now, according to the natural order instituted by divine providence, material goods are provided for the satisfaction of human needs. Therefore the division and appropriation of property, which proceeds from human law, must not hinder the satisfaction of man's necessity from such goods. Equally, whatever a man has in superabundance is owed, of natural right, to the poor for their sustenance. So Ambrosius says, and it is also to be found in the *Decretum Gratiani*: "The bread which you withhold belongs to the hungry; the clothing you shut away, to the naked; and the money you bury in the earth is the redemption and freedom of the penniless."[4]

I now want to consider a number of points, more practical than philosophical, which are relevant to the application of the moral conclusion we have reached. These points challenge not the idea that we ought to be doing all we can do to prevent starvation, but the idea that giving away a great deal of money is the best means to this end.

It is sometimes said that overseas aid should be a government responsibility, and that therefore one ought not to give to privately run charities. Giving privately, it is said, allows the government and the noncontributing members of society to escape their responsibilities.

This argument seems to assume that the more people there are who give to privately organized famine relief funds, the less likely it is that the government will take over full responsibility for such aid. This assumption is unsupported, and does not strike me as at all plausible. The opposite view—that if no one gives voluntarily, a government will assume that its citizens are uninterested in famine relief and would not wish to be forced into giving aid—seems more plausible. In any case, unless there were a definite probability that by refusing to give one would be helping to bring about massive government assistance, people who do refuse to make

---

[4] *Summa Theologica*, II–II, Question 66, Article 7, in *Aquinas, Selected Political Writings*, ed. A. P. d'Entreves, trans. J. G. Dawson (Oxford, 1948), p. 171.

voluntary contributions are refusing to prevent a certain amount of suffering without being able to point to any tangible beneficial consequence of their refusal. So the onus of showing how their refusal will bring about government action is on those who refuse to give.

I do not, of course, want to dispute the contention that governments of affluent nations should be giving many times the amount of genuine, no-strings-attached aid that they are giving now. I agree, too, that giving privately is not enough, and that we ought to be campaigning actively for entirely new standards for both public and private contributions to famine relief. Indeed, I would sympathize with someone who thought that campaigning was more important than giving oneself, although I doubt whether preaching what one does not practice would be very effective. Unfortunately, for many people the idea that "it's the government's responsibility" is a reason for not giving which does not appear to entail any political action either.

Another, more serious reason for not giving to famine relief funds is that until there is effective population control, relieving famine merely postpones starvation. If we save the Bengal refugees now, others, perhaps the children of these refugees, will face starvation in a few years' time. In support of this, one may cite the now well-known facts about the population explosion and the relatively limited scope for expanded production.

This point, like the previous one, is an argument against relieving suffering that is happening now, because of a belief about what might happen in the future; it is unlike the previous point in that very good evidence can be adduced in support of this belief about the future. I will not go into the evidence here. I accept that the earth cannot support indefinitely a population rising at the present rate. This certainly poses a problem for anyone who thinks it important to prevent famine. Again, however, one could accept the argument without drawing the conclusion that it absolves one from any obligation to do anything to prevent famine. The conclusion that should be drawn is that the best means of preventing famine, in the long run, is population control. It would then follow from the position reached earlier that one ought to be doing all one can to promote population control (unless one held that all forms of population control were wrong in themselves, or would have significantly bad consequences). Since there are organizations working specifically for population control, one would then support them rather than more orthodox methods of preventing famine.

A third point raised by the conclusion reached earlier relates to the question of just how much we all ought to be giving away. One possibility, which has already been mentioned, is that we ought to give until we reach the level of marginal utility—that is, the level at which, by giving more, I would cause as much suffering to myself or my dependents as I would relieve by my gift. This would mean, of course, that one would reduce oneself to very near the material circumstances of a Bengali refugee. It will be recalled that earlier I put forward both a strong and a moderate version of the principle of preventing bad occurrences. The strong version, which required us to prevent bad things from happening unless in doing so we would be sacrificing something of comparable moral significance, does seem to require reducing ourselves to the level of marginal utility. I should also say that the strong version seems to me to be the correct one. I proposed the more moderate version—that we should prevent bad occurrences unless, to do so, we had to sacrifice something morally significant— only in order to show that even on this surely undeniable principle a great change in our way of life is required. On the more moderate principle, it may not follow that we ought to reduce ourselves to the level of marginal utility, for one might hold that to reduce oneself and one's family to this level is to cause something significantly bad to happen. Whether this is so I shall not discuss, since, as I have said, I can see no good reason for holding the moderate version of the principle rather than the strong version. Even if we accepted the principle only in its moderate form, how- ever, it should be clear that we would have to give away enough to ensure that the consumer society, dependent as it is on people spending on trivia rather than giving to famine relief, would slow down and perhaps disap- pear entirely. There are several reasons why this would be desirable in it- self. The value and necessity of economic growth are now being questioned not only by conservationists, but by economists as well.[5] There is no doubt, too, that the consumer society has had a distorting effect on the goals and purposes of its members. Yet looking at the matter purely from the point of view of overseas aid, there must be a limit to the extent to which we should deliberately slow down our economy; for it might be the case that if we gave away, say, forty percent of our Gross National Product, we would slow down the economy so much that in absolute terms we would be giving less than if we gave twenty-five percent of the much larger GNP that we would have if we limited our contribution to this smaller per- centage.

I mention this only as an indication of the sort of factor that one would have to take into account in working out an ideal. Since Western societies generally consider one percent of the GNP an acceptable level for overseas aid, the matter is entirely academic. Nor does it affect the question of how much an individual should give in a society in which very few are giving substantial amounts.

It is sometimes said, though less often now than it used to be, that philosophers have no special role to play in public affairs, since most pub- lic issues depend primarily on an assessment of facts. On questions of fact, it is said, philosophers as such have no special expertise, and so it has been possible to engage in philosophy without committing oneself to any posi-

---

[5] See, for instance, John Kenneth Galbraith, *The New Industrial State* (Boston, 1967); and E J. Mishan, *The Costs of Economic Growth* (London, 1967).

tion on major public issues. No doubt there are some issues of social policy and foreign policy about which it can truly be said that a really expert assessment of the facts is required before taking sides or acting, but the issue of famine is surely not one of these. The facts about the existence of suffering are beyond dispute. Nor, I think, is it disputed that we can do something about it, either through orthodox methods of famine relief or through population control or both. This is therefore an issue on which philosophers are competent to take a position. The issue is one which faces everyone who has more money than he needs to support himself and his dependents, or who is in a position to take some sort of political action. These categories must include practically every teacher and student of philosophy in the universities of the Western world. If philosophy is to deal with matters that are relevant to both teachers and students, this is an issue that philosophers should discuss.

Discussion, though, is not enough. What is the point of relating philosophy to public (and personal) affairs if we do not take our conclusions seriously? In this instance, taking our conclusion seriously means acting upon it. The philosopher will not find it any easier than anyone else to alter his attitudes and way of life to the extent that, if I am right, is involved in doing everything that we ought to be doing. At the very least, though, one can make a start. The philosopher who does so will have to sacrifice some of the benefits of the consumer society, but he can find compensation in the satisfaction of a way of life in which theory and practice, if not yet in harmony, are at least coming together.

TOM REGAN

The Moral Basis of Vegetarianism

My argument in this section turns on considerations about the natural "right to life" that we humans are sometimes said uniquely to possess, and to possess to an equal degree. My strategy here will be similar to my strategy in the previous section. What I will try to show is that arguments that might be used in defense of the claim that all human beings have this natural right, to an equal extent, would also show that animals

This material is here reprinted from Vol. 5, No. 2 of the *Canadian Journal of Philosophy* (1975), 205–213, by permission of the author and the Canadian Association for Publishing in Philosophy.
Editor's Note: Footnotes have been renumbered.

are possessors of it, whereas arguments that might be used to show that animals do not have this right would also show that not all human beings do either. Just as in the preceding section, however, so here too, a disclaimer to completeness is in order. I have not been able to consider all the arguments that might be advanced in this context; all that I have been able to do is consider what I think are the most important ones.

Let us begin, then, with the idea that all humans possess an equal natural right to life. And let us notice, once again, that it is an *equal natural* right that we are speaking of, one that we cannot acquire or have granted to us, and one that we all are supposed to have just because we are human beings. On what basis, then, might it be alleged that all and only human beings possess this right to an equal extent? Well, a number of familiar possibilities come immediately to mind. It might be argued that all and only human beings have an equal right to life because either (a) all and only human beings have the capacity to reason, or (b) all and only human beings have the capacity to make free choices, or (c) all and only human beings have a concept of "self," or (d) all and only human beings have all or some combination of the previously mentioned capacities. And it is easy to imagine how someone might argue that, since animals do not have any of these capacities, *they* do not possess a right to life, least of all one that is equal to the one possessed by humans.

I have already touched upon some of the difficulties such views must inevitably encounter. Briefly, it is not clear, first, that no nonhuman animals satisfy any one (or all) of these conditions, and, second, it is reasonably clear that not all human beings satisfy them. The severely mentally feeble, for example, fail to satisfy them. Accordingly, *if* we want to insist that they have a right to life, then we cannot also maintain that they have it because they satisfy one or another of these conditions. Thus, *if* we want to insist that they have an equal right to life, despite their failure to satisfy these conditions, we cannot consistently maintain that animals, because they fail to satisfy these conditions, therefore lack this right.

Another possible ground is that of sentience, by which I understand the capacity to experience pleasure and pain. But this view, too, must encounter a familiar difficulty—namely, that it could not justify restricting the right *only* to human beings.

What clearly is needed, then, if we are to present any plausible argument for the view that all and only human beings have an equal natural right to life, is a basis for this right that is invariant and equal in the case of all human beings and only in their case. It is against this backdrop, I think, that the following view naturally arises.[1] This is the view that the life of every human being has "intrinsic worth"—that, in Kant's terms, each of us exists as "an end in himself"—*and* that this intrinsic worth

---

[1] For an example of this kind of argument, see Gregory Vlastos' "Justice and Equality" in *Social Justice*. Edited by Richard B. Brandt. Englewood Cliffs, New Jersey: Prentice-Hall, Incorporated, 1962.

which belongs *only* to human beings, is shared *equally* by all. "Thus," it might be alleged, "it is because of the equal intrinsic worth of all human beings that we all have an equal right to life."

This view, I think, has a degree of plausibility which those previously discussed lack. For by saying that the worth that is supposed to attach to a being just because he or she is human is intrinsic, and that it is because of this that we all have an equal natural right to life, this view rules out the possibility that one human being might give this right to or withhold it from another. It would appear, therefore, that this view could make sense of the alleged *naturalness* of the right in question. Moreover, by resting the equal right to life on the idea of the equal intrinsic worth of all human beings, this view may succeed, where the others have failed, in accounting for the alleged *equality* of this right.

Despite these apparent advantages, however, the view under consideration must face certain difficulties. One difficulty lies in specifying just what it is supposed to mean to say that the life of every human being is "intrinsically worthwhile." [2] Now, it cannot mean that "each and every human being has a natural right to life." For the idea that the life of each and every human being has intrinsic worth was introduced in the first place to provide a basis for saying that each and every human being has an equal right to life. Accordingly, if say, "Jones' life is intrinsically worthwhile" ends up meaning "Jones has an equal right to life," then the claim that the life of each and every individual is equally worthwhile, judged intrinsically, cannot be construed as a *basis* for saying that each and every human being has an equal right to life. For the two claims would mean the same thing, and one claim can never be construed as being the basis for another, if they both mean the same.

But a second and, for our purposes, more important difficulty is this: On what grounds is it being alleged that each and every human being, and only human beings, are intrinsically worthwhile? Just what is there, in other words, about being human, and only about being human, that underlies this ascription of unique worth. Well, one possible answer here is that there isn't "anything" that underlies this worth. The worth in question, in short, just belongs to anyone who is human, and only to those who are. It is a worth that we simply recognize or intuit, whenever we carefully examine that complex of ideas we have before our minds when we think of the idea, "human being." I find this view unsatisfactory, both because it would seem to commit us to an ontology of value that is very difficult to defend, and because I, for one, even after the most scrupulous examination I can manage, fail to intuit the unique worth in question. I do not know how to prove that the view in question is mistaken in a few swift strokes, however. All I can do is point out the historic precedents of certain groups of human beings who have claimed to "intuit"

---

[2] This is a point that first became clear to me in discussion with Donald VanDeVeer.

a special worth belonging to their group and not to others within the human family, and say that it is good to remember that alluding to a special, intuitive way of "knowing" such things could only serve the purpose of giving an air of intellectual respectability to unreasoned prejudices. And, further, I can only register here my own suspicion that the same is true in this case, though to a much wider extent. For I think that falling into talk about the "intuition of the unique intrinsic worth of being human" would be the last recourse of men who, having found no good reason to believe that human beings have an unique intrinsic worth, would go on believing that they do anyhow.

Short of having recourse to intuition, then, we can expect those who believe that human beings uniquely possess intrinsic worth to tell us what there is about being human, in virtue of which this worth is possessed. The difficulty here, however, as can be anticipated, is that some familiar problems are going to raise their tiresome heads. For shall we say that it is the fact that humans can speak, or reason, or make free choices, or form a concept of their own identity that underlies this worth? These suggestions will not work here, anymore than they have before. For there are some beings who are human who cannot do these things, and there very well may be some beings who are not human who can. None of these capacities, therefore, could do the job of providing the basis for a kind of worth that all humans and only humans are supposed to possess.

But suppose we try to unpack this notion of intrinsic worth in a slightly different way.[3] Suppose we say that the reasons we have for saying that all and only human beings exist as ends in themselves are, first, that every human being has various positive interests, such as desires, goals, hopes, preferences and the like, the satisfaction or realization of which brings intrinsic value to their lives, in the form of intrinsically valuable experiences; and, second, that the intrinsic value brought to the life of any one man, by the satisfaction of his desires or the realization of his goals, is just as good, judged in itself, as the intrinsic value brought to the life of any other man by the satisfaction or realization of those comparable desires and goals he happens to have. In this sense, then, all men are equal, and it is because of this equality among all men, it might be alleged, that each man has as much right as any other to seek to satisfy his desires and realize his goals, so long, at least, that, in doing so, he does not violate the rights of any other human being. "Now, since," this line of argument continues, "no one can seek to satisfy his desires or realize his goals if he is dead, and in view of the fact that every man has as much right as any other to seek to satisfy his desires and realize his goals, then to take the life of any human being will always be prima facie to violate a right which he shares equally with all other human beings—namely, his right to life."

3 Vlastos, *op. cit.*

What shall we make of this argument? I am uncertain whether it can withstand careful scrutiny. Whether it can or not, however, is not a matter I feel compelled to try to decide here. What I do want to point out is that, of the arguments considered here, this one has a degree of plausibility the others lack, not only because, as I have already remarked, it addresses itself both to the alleged naturalness and the alleged equality of the right in question, but also because it rests on what I take to be a necessary condition of being human—namely, that a being must have interests. For these reasons, then, I do not think I can be accused of "straw-man" tactics by choosing this as the most plausible among a cluster of possible arguments that might be urged in support of the contention that all human beings have an equal natural right to life. At the same time, however, as can be anticipated, I believe that, whatever plausibility this argument might have in this connection, it would also have in connection with the claim that animals, too, have an equal natural right to life.

For even if it is true that this argument provides us with adequate grounds for ascribing a natural right to life equally to all human beings, there is nothing in it that could tend to show that this is a right that belongs *only* to those beings who are human. On the contrary, the argument in question would equally well support the claim that any being who has positive interests which, when satisfied, bring about experiences that are just as intrinsically valuable as the satisfaction of the comparable interests of any other individual, would have an equal right to life. In particular, then, it would support the view that animals have an equal right to life, if they meet the conditions in question. And a case can be made for the view that they do. For, once again, it seems clear that animals have positive interests, the satisfaction or realization of which would appear to be just as intrinsically worthwhile, judged in themselves, as the satisfaction or realization of any comparable interest a human being might have. True, the interests animals have may be of a comparatively low-grade, when we compare them to, say, the contemplative interests of Aristotle's virtuous man. But the same is true of many human beings: their interests may be largely restricted to food and drink, with occasional bursts of sympathy for a few. Yet we would not say that such a man has less of a right to life than another, assuming that all men have an equal right to life. Neither, then, can we say that animals, because of their "base" interests, have any less of a right to life.

One way to avoid this conclusion and, at the same time, to challenge part of the argument in Section I, is to deny that animals have interests.[4] But on what basis might this denial rest. A by now familiar basis is that animals cannot speak; they cannot use words to formulate or express anything; thus, they cannot have an interest in anything. But this

---

[4] See, for example, the essay by McCloskey, *op. cit.* McCloskey denies that animals have interests, but does not, so far as I can see, give any reason for believing that this is so.

objection obviously assumes that only those beings who are able to use words to formulate or express something can have interests, and this, even ignoring the possibility that at least some animals might be able to do this, seems implausible. For we do not suppose that infants, for example, have to learn to use a language before they can have any interests. Moreover, the behavior of animals certainly seems to attest to the fact that they not only can, but that they actually do have interests. Their behavior presents us with many cases of preferential choice and goal directed action, in the face of which, and in the absence of any rationally compelling argument to the contrary, it seems both arbitrary and prejudicial to deny the presence of interests in them.

The most plausible argument for the view that humans have an equal natural right to life, therefore, seems to provide an equally plausible justification for the view that animals have this right also. But just as in saying that men and animals have an equal right to be spared undeserved pain, so here, too, we would not imply that the right in question can never be overridden. For there may arise circumstances in which an individual's right to life could be outweighed by other, more pressing moral demands, and where, therefore, we would be justified in taking the life of the individual in question. But even a moment's reflection will reveal that we would not condone a practice which involved the routine slaughter of human beings simply on the grounds that it brought about this or that amount of pleasure, or this or that amount of intrinsically good experiences for others, no matter how great the amount of good hypothesized. For to take the lives of individuals, for this reason, is manifestly not to recognize that their life is just as worthwhile as anybody else's, or that they have just as much right to life as others do. Nor need any of this involve considerations about the amount of pain that is caused the persons whose lives are taken. Let us suppose that these persons are killed painlessly; that still would not alter the fact that they have been treated wrongly and that the practice in question is immoral.

If, then, the argument in the present section is sound; and assuming that no other basis is forthcoming which would support the view that humans do, but animals do not, have an equal right to life; then the same is true of any practice involving the slaughter of animals, and we have, therefore, grounds for responding to the two objections raised, but not answered, at the end of the first section. These objections were, first, that since the only thing wrong with the way animals are treated in the course of being raised and slaughtered is that they are caused a lot of undeserved pain, the thing to do is to desensitize them so that they don't feel anything. What we can see now, however, is that the undeserved pain animals feel is not the only morally relevant consideration; it is also the fact that they are killed that must be taken into account.

Similarly, to attempt to avoid the force of my argument for conditional vegetarianism by buying meat from farms that do not practice intensive rearing methods or by hunting and killing animals oneself . . . these expedients will not meet the total challenge vegetarians can place before their meat eating friends. For the animals slaughtered on even the most otherwise idyllic farms, as well as those shot in the wild, are just as much killed, and just as much dead, as the animals slaughtered under the most ruthless of conditions.

Unless or until, then, we are given a rationally compelling argument that shows that all and only human beings have an equal right to life; and so long as any plausible argument that might be advanced to support the view that all human beings have this right can be shown to support, to the same extent, the view that animals have this right also; and so long as we believe we are rationally justified in ascribing this right to humans and to make reference to it in the course of justifying our judgment that it is wrong to kill a given number of human beings simply for the sake of bringing about this or that amount of good for this or that number of people; given all these conditions, then I believe we are equally committed to the view that we cannot be justified in killing any one or any number of animals for the intrinsic good their deaths may bring to us. I do not say that there are no possible circumstances in which we would be justified in killing them. What I do say is that we cannot justify doing so in their case, anymore than we can in the case of the slaughter of human beings, by arguing that such a practice brings about intrinsically valuable experiences for others.

Once again, therefore, the onus of justification lies, not on the shoulders of those who are vegetarians, but on the shoulders of those who are not. If the argument of the present section is sound, it is the non-vegetarian who must show us how he can be justified in eating meat, when he knows that, in order to do so, an animal has had to be killed. It is the non-vegetarian who must show us how his manner of life does not contribute to practices which systematically ignore the right to life which animals possess, if humans are supposed to possess it on the basis of the most plausible argument considered here. And it is the non-vegetarian who must do all this while being fully cognizant of the fact that he cannot defend his way of life merely by summing up the intrinsic goods—the delicious taste of meat, for example—that come into being as a result of the slaughter of animals.

This is not to say that practices that involve taking the lives of animals cannot possibly be justified. In some cases, perhaps, they can be, and the grounds on which we might rest such a justification would, I think, parallel those outlined in the preceding section in connection with the discussion of when we might be morally justified in approving a practice that caused animals non-trivial, undeserved pain. What we would have to show in the present case, I think, in order seriously to consider approving of such a practice, is (1) that such a practice would prevent, reduce or eliminate a much greater amount of evil, including the evil that attaches to the taking of the life of a being who has as much claim as any other to an equal natural right to life; (2) that, realistically speaking, there is no other way to bring about these consequences; and (3) that we have very good reason to believe that these consequences will, in fact, obtain. Now, perhaps there are some cases in which these conditions are satisfied. For example, perhaps they are satisfied in the case of the eskimo's killing of animals and in the case of having a restricted hunting season for such animals as deer. But to say that this is (or may be) true of *some* cases is not to say that it is true of all, and it will remain the task of the non-vegetarian to show that what is true in these cases, assuming that it is true, is also true of any practice that involves killing animals which, by his actions, he supports.

Two final objections deserve to be considered before ending. The first is that, even assuming that what I have said is true of *some* non-human animals, it does not follow that it is true of *all* of them. For the arguments given have turned on the thesis that it is only beings who have interests who can have rights, and it is quite possible that, though some animals have interests, not all of them do. I think this objection is both relevant and very difficult to answer adequately. The problem it raises is how we can know when a given being has interests. The assumption I have made throughout is that this is an empirical question, to be answered on the basis of reasoning by analogy—that, roughly speaking, beings who are very similar to us, both in terms of physiology and in terms of non-verbal behavior, are, like us, beings who have interests. The difficulty lies in knowing how far this analogy can be pushed. Certain animals, I think, present us with paradigms for the application of this reasoning—the primates, for example. In the case of others, however, the situation is less clear, and in the case of some, such as the protozoa, it is very grey indeed. There are, I think, at least two possible ways of responding to this difficulty. The first is to concede that there are some beings who are ordinarily classified as animals who do not have interests and who cannot, therefore, possess rights. The second is to insist that all those beings who are ordinarily classified as animals do have interests and can have rights. I am inclined to think that the former of these two alternatives is the correct one, though I cannot defend this judgment here. And thus I think that the arguments I have presented do not, by themselves, justify the thesis that *all* animals have interests and can, therefore, possess rights. But this exaggeration has been perpetrated in the interests of style, and does not, I think, detract from the force of my argument, when it is taken in context. For the cases where we would, with good reason, doubt whether an animal has interests—for example, whether protozoa do—are cases which are, I think, irrelevant to the moral status of vegetarianism. The question of the obligatoriness of vegetarianism, in other words, can arise only if and when the animals we eat are the kind of beings who have interests. Whatever reasonable doubts we may have about which animals do and which do not have interests do not apply, I think, to those animals that are raised according to intensive rearing methods or are routinely killed, painlessly or not, preparatory to our eating them. Thus, to have it pointed out that there are or may be some animals who do not have interests does not in any way modify the obligation not to support practices that cause death or non-trivial, undeserved pain to those animals that do.

Finally, a critic will object that there are no natural rights, not even natural rights possessed by humans. "Thus," he will conclude, "no animals have natural rights either and the backbone of your argument is broken." This objection raises problems too large for me to consider here, and I must content myself, in closing, with the following two remarks. First, I have not argued that either human beings or animals do have natural rights; what I have argued, rather, is that what seem to me to be the most plausible arguments for the view that all humans possess the natural rights I have discussed can be used to show that animals possess these rights also. Thus, if it should turn out that there is no good reason to believe that we humans have any natural rights, it certainly would follow that my argument would lose some of its force. Even so, however, this would not alter the principal logical points I have endeavored to make.

But, second, even if it should turn out that there are no natural rights, that would not put an end to many of the problems discussed here. For even if we do not possess natural rights, we would still object to practices that caused non-trivial, undeserved pain for some human beings if their 'justification' was that they brought about this or that amount of pleasure or other forms of intrinsic good for this or that number of people; and we would still object to any practice that involved the killing of human beings, even if killed painlessly, if the practice was supposed to be justified in the same way. But this being so, what clearly would be needed, if we cease to invoke the idea of rights, is some explanation of why practices which are not right, when they involve the treatment of people, can be right (or at least permissible) when they involve the treatment of animals. What clearly would be needed, in short, is what we have found to be needed and wanting all along—namely, the specification of some morally relevant feature of being human which is possessed by *all* human beings and *only* by those beings who are human. Unless or until some such feature can be pointed out, I do not see how the differential treatment of humans and animals can be rationally defended, natural rights or no. And to dismiss, out of hand, the need to justify this matter, or the seriousness of doing so, would be to be a party to the 'Nazism' that Singer's Herman attributes to us all.[5]

[5] I want to thank my colleagues, W. R. Carter, Robert Hoffman and Donald VanDe-
     Veer for their helpful criticisms of an earlier draft of this paper. I am also much
     indebted to Peter Singer for bringing to my attention much of the literature and
     many of the problems discussed here.
          Lastly, John Rodman of the Political Science Department at Pitzer Col-

JOEL FEINBERG

The Rights of Animals and Unborn Generations

Every philosophical paper must begin with an unproved assumption. Mine is the assumption that there will still be a world five hundred years from now, and that it will contain human beings who are very much like us. We have it within our power now, clearly, to affect the lives of these creatures for better or worse by contributing to the conservation or corruption of the environment in which they must live. I shall assume furthermore that it is psychologically possible for us to care about our remote descendants, that many of us in fact do care, and indeed that we ought to care. My main concern then will be to show that it makes sense to speak of the rights of unborn generations against us, and that given the moral judgment that we ought to conserve our environmental inheritance for them, and its grounds, we might well say that future generations *do* have rights correlative to our present duties toward them. Protecting our environment now is also a matter of elementary prudence, and insofar as we do it for the next generation already here in the persons of our children, it is a matter of love. But from the perspective of our remote descendants it is basically a matter of justice, of respect for their rights. My main concern here will be to examine the concept of a right to better understand how that can be.

The Problem

To have a right is to have a claim [1] *to* something and *against* someone, the recognition of which is called for by legal rules or, in the case of moral rights, by the principles of an enlightened conscience. In the familiar cases of rights, the claimant is a competent adult human being, and the claimee

---

lege put me onto some dimensions of the debate over Descartes' views that I was unaware of. See his "The Dolphin Papers," *The North American Review, Vol. 259, No. 1, Spring 1974, pp. 13–26.*

Reprinted from *Philosophy and Environmental Crisis*, edited by William T. Blackstone (University of Georgia Press, Athens, Georgia, 1974) 43–68 by permission of the author and the publisher.

[1] I shall leave the concept of a claim unanalyzed here, but for a detailed discussion, see my "The Nature and Value of Rights," *Journal of Value Inquiry* 4 (Winter 1971): 263–277.

is an officeholder in an institution or else a private individual, in either case, another competent adult human being. Normal adult human beings, then, are obviously the sorts of beings of whom rights can meaningfully be predicated. Everyone would agree to that, even extreme misanthropes who deny that anyone in fact has rights. On the other hand, it is absurd to say that rocks have rights, not because rocks are morally inferior things unworthy of rights (that statement makes no sense either), but because rocks belong to a category of entities of whom rights cannot be meaningfully predicated. That is not to say that there are no circumstances in which we ought to treat rocks carefully, but only that the rocks themselves cannot validly claim good treatment from us. In between the clear cases of rocks and normal human beings, however, is a spectrum of less obvious cases, including some bewildering borderline ones. Is it meaningful or conceptually possible to ascribe rights to our dead ancestors? to individual animals? to whole species of animals? to plants? to idiots and madmen? to fetuses? to generations yet unborn? Until we know how to settle these puzzling cases, we cannot claim fully to grasp the concept of a right, or to know the shape of its logical boundaries.

One way to approach these riddles is to turn one's attention first to the most familiar and unproblematic instances of rights, note their most salient characteristics, and then compare the borderline cases with them, measuring as closely as possible the points of similarity and difference. In the end, the way we classify the borderline cases may depend on whether we are more impressed with the similarities or the differences between them and the cases in which we have the most confidence.

It will be useful to consider the problem of individual animals first because their case is the one that has already been debated with the most thoroughness by philosophers so that the dialectic of claim and rejoinder has now unfolded to the point where disputants can get to the end game quickly and isolate the crucial point at issue. When we understand precisely what *is* at issue in the debate over animal rights, I think we will have the key to the solution of all the other riddles about rights.

Individual Animals

Almost all modern writers agree that we ought to be kind to animals, but that is quite another thing from holding that animals can claim kind treatment from us as their due. Statutes making cruelty to animals a crime are now very common, and these, of course, impose legal duties on people not to mistreat animals; but that still leaves open the question whether the animals, as beneficiaries of those duties, possess rights correlative to them. We may very well have duties *regarding* animals that are not at the same time duties *to* animals, just as we may have duties regarding rocks, or buildings, or lawns, that are not duties *to* rocks, buildings, or lawns. Some legal writers have taken the still more extreme position that animals themselves are not even the directly intended beneficiaries of statutes prohibiting cruelty to animals. During the nineteenth century, for example, it was commonly said that such statutes were designed to protect human beings by preventing the growth of cruel habits that could later threaten human beings with harm too. Prof. Louis B. Schwartz finds the rationale of the cruelty-to-animals prohibition in its protection of animal lovers from affronts to their sensibilities. "It is not the mistreated dog who is the ultimate object of concern," he writes. "Our concern is for the feelings of other human beings, a large proportion of whom, although accustomed to the slaughter of animals for food, readily identify themselves with a tortured dog or horse and respond with great sensitivity to its sufferings." [2] This seems to me to be factitious. How much more natural it is to say with John Chipman Gray that the true purpose of cruelty-to-animals statutes is "to preserve the dumb brutes from suffering." [3] The very people whose sensibilities are invoked in the alternative explanation, a group that no doubt now includes most of us, are precisely those who would insist that the protection belongs primarily to the animals themselves, not merely to their own tender feelings. Indeed, it would be difficult even to account for the existence of such feelings in the absence of a belief that the animals deserve the protection in their own right and for their own sakes.

Even if we allow, as I think we must, that animals are the intended direct beneficiaries of legislation forbidding cruelty to animals, it does not follow directly that animals have legal rights, and Gray himself, for one,[4] refused to draw this further inference. Animals cannot have rights, he thought, for the same reason they cannot have duties, namely, that they are not genuine "moral agents." Now, it is relatively easy to see why animals cannot have duties, and this matter is largely beyond controversy. Animals cannot be "reasoned with" or instructed in their responsibilities; they are inflexible and unadaptable to future contingencies; they are subject to fits of instinctive passion which they are incapable of repressing or controlling, postponing or sublimating. Hence, they cannot enter into contractual agreements, or make promises; they cannot be trusted; and they cannot (except within very narrow limits and for purposes of conditioning) be blamed for what would be called "moral failures" in a human being. They are therefore incapable of being moral subjects, of acting rightly or wrongly in the moral sense, of having, discharging, or breeching duties and obligations.

But what is there about the intellectual incompetence of animals (which admittedly disqualifies them for duties) that makes them logi-

---

2 Louis B. Schwartz, "Morals, Offenses and the Model Penal Code," *Columbia Law Review* 63 (1963): 673.

3 John Chipman Gray, *The Nature and Sources of the Law*, 2d ed. (Boston: Beacon Press, 1963), p. 43.

4 And W. D. Ross for another. See *The Right and the Good* (Oxford: Clarendon Press, 1930), app. 1, pp. 48–56.

cally unsuitable for rights? The most common reply to this question is that animals are incapable of *claiming* rights on their own. They cannot make motion, on their own, to courts to have their claims recognized or enforced; they cannot initiate, on their own, any kind of legal proceedings; nor are they capable of even understanding when their rights are being violated, of distinguishing harm from wrongful injury, and responding with indignation and an outraged sense of justice instead of mere anger or fear.

No one can deny any of these allegations, but to the claim that they are the grounds for disqualification of rights of animals, philosophers on the other side of this controversy have made convincing rejoinders. It is simply not true, says W. D. Lamont,[5] that the ability to understand what a right is and the ability to set legal machinery in motion by one's own initiative are necessary for the possession of rights. If that were the case, then neither human idiots nor wee babies would have any legal rights at all. Yet it is manifest that both of these classes of intellectual incompetents have legal rights recognized and easily enforced by the courts. Children and idiots start legal proceedings, not on their own direct initiative, but rather through the actions of proxies or attorneys who are emplowered to speak in their names. If there is no conceptual absurdity in this situation, why should there be in the case where a proxy makes a claim on behalf of an animal? People commonly enough make wills leaving money to trustees for the care of animals. Is it not natural to speak of the animal's right to his inheritance in cases of this kind? If a trustee embezzles money from the animal's account,[6] and a proxy speaking in the dumb brute's behalf presses the animal's claim, can he not be described as asserting the animal's *rights?* More exactly, the animal itself claims its rights through the vicarious actions of a human proxy speaking in its name and in its behalf. There appears to be no reason why we should require the animal to understand what is going on (so the argument concludes) as a condition for regarding it as a possessor of rights.

Some writers protest at this point that the legal relation between a principal and an agent cannot hold between animals and human beings. Between humans, the relation of agency can take two very different forms, depending upon the degree of discretion granted to the agent, and there is a continuum of combinations between the extremes. On the one hand, there is the agent who is the mere "mouthpiece" of his principal. He is a "tool" in much the same sense as is a typewriter or telephone; he simply transmits the instructions of his principal. Human beings could hardly be the agents or representatives of animals in this sense, since the dumb brutes could no more use human "tools" than mechanical ones. On the other hand, an agent may be some sort of expert hired to exercise his professional judgment on behalf of, and in the name of, the principal. He may be given,

[5] W. D. Lamont, *Principles of Moral Judgment* (Oxford: Clarendon Press, 1946), pp. 83–85.

[6] Cf. H. J. McCloskey, "Rights," *Philosophical Quarterly* 15(1965): 121, 124.

within some limited area of expertise, complete independence to act as he deems best, binding his principal to all the beneficial or detrimental consequences. This is the role played by trustees, lawyers, and ghost-writers. This type of representation requires that the agent have great skill, but makes little or no demand upon the principal, who may leave everything to the judgment of his agent. Hence, there appears, at first, to be no reason why an animal cannot be a totally passive principal in this second kind of agency relationship.

There are still some important dissimilarities, however. In the typical instance of representation by an agent, even of the second, highly discretionary kind, the agent is hired by a principal who enters into an agreement or contract with him; the principal tells his agent that within certain carefully specified boundaries "You may speak for me," subject always to the principal's approval, his right to give new directions, or to cancel the whole arrangement. No dog or cat could possibly do any of those things. Moreover, if it is the assigned task of the agent to defend the principal's rights, the principal may often decide to release his claimee, or to waive his own rights, and instruct his agent accordingly. Again, no mute cow or horse can do that. But although the possibility of hiring, agreeing, contracting, approving, directing, canceling, releasing, waiving, and instructing is present in the typical (all-human) case of agency representation, there appears to be no reason of a logical or conceptual kind why that *must* be so, and indeed there are some special examples involving human principals where it is not in fact so. I have in mind legal rules, for example, that require that a defendant be represented at his trial by an attorney, and impose a state-appointed attorney upon reluctant defendants, or upon those tried in *absentia*, whether they like it or not. Moreover, small children and mentally deficient and deranged adults are commonly represented by trustees and attorneys, even though they are incapable of granting their own consent to the representation, or of entering into contracts, of giving directions, or waiving their rights. It may be that it is unwise to permit agents to represent principals without the latters' knowledge or consent. If so, then no one should ever be permitted to speak for an animal, at least in a legally binding way. But that is quite another thing than saying that such representation is logically incoherent or conceptually incongruous— the contention that is at issue.

H. J. McCloskey,[7] I believe, accepts the argument up to this point, but he presents a new and different reason for denying that animals can have legal rights. The ability to make claims whether directly or through a representative, he implies, is essential to the possession of rights. Animals obviously cannot press their claims on their own, and so if they have rights, these rights must be assertable by agents. Animals, however, cannot be represented, McCloskey contends, and not for any of the reasons already

---

[7] Ibid.

discussed, but rather because representation, in the requisite sense, is always of interests, and animals (he says) are incapable of having interests.

Now, there is a very important insight expressed in the requirement that a being have interests if he is to be a logically proper subject of rights. This can be appreciated if we consider just why it is that mere things cannot have rights. Consider a very precious "mere thing"—a beautiful natural wilderness, or a complex and ornamental artifact, like the Taj Mahal. Such things ought to be cared for, because they would sink into decay if neglected, depriving some human beings, or perhaps even all human beings, of something of great value. Certain persons may even have as their own special job the care and protection of these valuable objects. But we are not tempted in these cases to speak of "thing-rights" correlative to custodial duties, because, try as we might, we cannot think of mere things as possessing interests of their own. Some people may have a duty to preserve, maintain, or improve the Taj Mahal, but they can hardly have a duty to help or hurt it, benefit or aid it, succor or relieve it. Custodians may protect it for the sake of a nation's pride and art lovers' fancy; but they don't keep it in good repair for "its own sake," or for "its own true welfare," or "well-being." A mere thing, however valuable to others, has no good of its own. The explanation of that fact, I suspect, consists in the fact that mere things have no conative life: no conscious wishes, desires, and hopes; or urges and impulses; or unconscious drives, aims, and goals; or latent tendencies, direction of growth, and natural fulfillment. Interests must be compounded somehow out of conations; hence mere things have no interests. A *Fortiori*, they have no interests to be protected by legal or moral rules. Without interests a creature can have no "good" of its own, the achievement of which can be its due. Mere things are not loci of value in their own right, but rather their value consists entirely in their being objects of other beings' interests.

So far McCloskey is on solid ground, but one can quarrel with his denial that any animal but humans have interests. I should think that the trustee of funds willed to a dog or cat is more than a mere custodian of the animal he protects. Rather his job is to look out for the interests of the animal and make sure no one denies it its due. The animal itself is the beneficiary of his dutiful services. Many of the higher animals at least have appetites, conative urges, and rudimentary purposes, the integrated satisfaction of which constitutes their welfare or good. We can, of course, with consistency treat animals as mere pests and deny that they have any rights; for most animals, especially those of the lower orders, we have no choice but to do so. But it seems to me, nevertheless, that in general, animals *are* among the sorts of beings of whom rights can meaningfully be predicated and denied.

Now, if a person agrees with the conclusion of the argument thus far, that animals are the sorts of beings that *can* have rights, and further, if he accepts the moral judgment that we ought to be kind to animals, only one further premise is needed to yield the conclusion that some animals do in fact have rights. We must now ask ourselves for whose sake ought we to treat (some) animals with consideration and humaneness? If we conceive our duty to be one of obedience to authority, or to one's own conscience merely, or one of consideration for tender human sensibilities only, then we might still deny that animals have rights, even though we admit that they are the kinds of beings that *can* have rights. But if we hold not only that we ought to treat animals humanely but also that we should do so for the animals' own sake, that such treatment is something we owe animals as their due, something that can be claimed for them, something the withholding of which would be an injustice and a wrong, and not merely a harm, then it follows that we do ascribe rights to animals. I suspect that the moral judgments most of us make about animals do pass these phenomenological tests, so that most of us do believe that animals have rights, but are reluctant to say so because of the conceptual confusions about the notion of a right that I have attempted to dispel above.

Now we can extract from our discussion of animal rights a crucial principle for tentative use in the resolution of the other riddles about the applicability of the concept of a right, namely, that the sorts of beings who *can* have rights are precisely those who have (or can have) interests. I have come to this tentative conclusion for two reasons: (1) because a right holder must be capable of being represented and it is impossible to represent a being that has no interests, and (2) because a right holder must be capable of being a beneficiary in his own person, and a being without interests is a being that is incapable of being harmed or benefitted, having no good or "sake" of its own. Thus, a being without interests has no "behalf" to act in, and no "sake" to act for. My strategy now will be to apply the "interest principle," as we can call it, to the other puzzles about rights, while being prepared to modify it where necessary (but as little as possible), in the hope of separating in a consistent and intuitively satisfactory fashion the beings who can have rights from those which cannot.

Vegetables

It is clear that we ought not to mistreat certain plants, and indeed there are rules and regulations imposing duties on persons not to misbehave in respect to certain members of the vegetable kingdom. It is forbidden, for example, to pick wildflowers in the mountainous tundra areas of national parks, or to endanger trees by starting fires in dry forest areas. Members of Congress introduce bills designed, as they say, to "protect" rare redwood trees from commercial pillage. Given this background, it is surprising that no one [8] speaks of plants as having rights. Plants, after all, are not "mere things"; they are vital objects with inherited biological propensities deter-

[8] Outside of Samuel Butler's *Erewhon*.

mining their natural growth. Moreover, we do say that certain conditions are "good" or "bad" for plants, thereby suggesting that plants, unlike rocks, are capable of having a "good." (This is a case, however, where "what we say" should not be taken seriously: we also say that certain kinds of paint are good or bad for the internal walls of a house, and this does not commit us to a conception of walls as beings possessed of a good or welfare of their own.) Finally, we are capable of feeling a kind of affection for particular plants, though we rarely personalize them, as we do in the case of animals, by giving them proper names.

Still, all are agreed that plants are not the kinds of beings that can have rights. Plants are never plausibly understood to be the direct intended beneficiaries of rules designed to "protect" them. We wish to keep redwood groves in existence for the sake of human beings who can enjoy their serene beauty, and for the sake of generations of human beings yet unborn. Trees are not the sorts of beings who have their "own sakes," despite the fact that they have biological propensities. Having no conscious wants or goals of their own, trees cannot know satisfaction or frustration, pleasure or pain. Hence, there is no possibility of kind or cruel treatment of trees. In these morally crucial respects, trees differ from the higher species of animals.

Yet trees are not mere things like rocks. They grow and develop according to the laws of their own nature. Aristotle and Aquinas both took trees to have their own "natural ends." Why then do I deny them the status of beings with interests of their own? The reason is that an interest, however the concept is finally to be analyzed, presupposes at least rudimentary cognitive equipment. Interests are compounded out of *desires* and *aims*, both of which presuppose something like *belief*, or cognitive awareness. A desiring creature may want X because he seeks anything that is Ø, and X appears to be Ø to him; or he may be seeking Y, and he believes, or expects, or hopes that X will be a means to Y. If he desires X in order to get Y, this implies that he believes that X will bring Y about, or at least that he has some sort of brute expectation that is a primitive correlate of belief. But what of the desire for Ø (or for Y) itself? Perhaps a creature has such a "desire" as an ultimate set, as if he had come into existence all "wound up" to pursue Ø-ness or Y-ness, and his not to reason why. Such a propensity, I think, would not qualify as a desire. Mere brute longings unmediated by beliefs—longings for one knows not what—might perhaps be a primitive form of consciousness (I don't want to beg that question) but they are altogether different from the sort of thing we mean by "desire," especially when we speak of human beings.

If some such account as the above is correct, we can never have any grounds for attributing a desire or a want to a creature known to be incapable even of rudimentary beliefs; and if desires or wants are the materials interests are made of, mindless creatures have no interests of their own.

The law, therefore, cannot have as its intention the protection of their interests, so that "protective legislation" has to be understood as legislation protecting the interests human beings may have in them.

Plant life might nevertheless be thought at first to constitute a hard case for the interest principle for two reasons. In the first place, plants no less than animals are said to have needs of their own. To be sure, we can speak even of mere things as having needs too, but such talk misleads no one into thinking of the need as belonging, in the final analysis, to the "mere thing" itself. If we were so deceived we would not be thinking of the mere thing as a "mere thing" after all. We say, for example, that John Doe's walls need painting, or that Richard Roe's car needs a washing, but we direct our attitudes of sympathy or reproach (as the case may be) to John and Richard, not to their possessions. It would be otherwise, if we observed that some child is in need of a good meal. Our sympathy and concern in that case would be directed at the child himself as the true possessor of the need in question.

The needs of plants might well seem closer to the needs of animals than to the pseudoneeds of mere things. An owner may need a plant (say, for its commercial value or as a potential meal), but the plant itself, it might appear, needs nutrition or cultivation. Our confusion about this matter may stem from language. It is a commonplace that the word *need* is ambiguous. To say that A needs X may be to say either: (1) X is necessary to the achievement of one of A's goals, or to the performance of one of its functions, or (2) X is good for A; its lack would harm A or be injurious or detrimental to him (or it). The first sort of need-statement is value-neutral, implying no comment on the value of the goal or function in question; whereas the second kind of statement about needs commits its maker to a value judgment about what is good or bad for A in the long run, that is, about what is in A's interests. A being must have interests, therefore, to have needs in the second sense, but any kind of thing, vegetable or mineral, could have needs in the first sense. An automobile needs gas and oil to function, but it is no tragedy for it if it runs out—an empty tank does not hinder or retard its interests. Similarly, to say that a tree needs sunshine and water is to say that without them it cannot grow and survive; but unless the growth and survival of trees are matters of human concern, affecting human interests, practical or aesthetic, the needs of trees alone will not be the basis of any claim of what is "due" them in their own right. Plants may need things in order to discharge their functions, but their functions are assigned by human interests, not their own.

The second source of confusion derives from the fact that we commonly speak of plants as thriving and flourishing, or withering and languishing. One might be tempted to think of these states either as themselves consequences of the possession of interests so that even creatures without wants or beliefs can be said to have interests, or else as grounds independent of the possession of interests for the making of intelligible claims of rights. In either case, plants would be thought of as conceivable possessors of rights after all.

Consider what it means to speak of something as "flourishing." The verb to flourish apparently was applied originally and literally to plants only, and in its original sense it meant simply "to bear flowers: BLOSSOM"; but then by analogical extension of sense it came also to mean "to grow luxuriantly: increase, and enlarge," and then to "THRIVE" (generally), and finally, when extended to human beings, "to be prosperous," or to "increase in wealth, honor, comfort, happiness, or whatever is desirable." [9] Applied to human beings the term is, of course, a fixed metaphor. When a person flourishes, something happens to his interests analogous to what happens to a plant when it flowers, grows, and spreads. A person flourishes when his interests (whatever they may be) are progressing severally and collectively toward their harmonious fulfillment and spawning new interests along the way whose prospects are also good. To flourish is to glory in the advancement of one's interests, in short, to be happy.

Nothing is gained by twisting the botanical metaphor back from humans to plants. To speak of thriving human interests as if they were flowers is to speak naturally and well, and to mislead no one. But then to think of the flowers or plants as if they were interests (or the signs of interests) is to bring the metaphor back full circle for no good reason and in the teeth of our actual beliefs. Some of our talk about flourishing plants reveals quite clearly that the interests that thrive when plants flourish are human not "plant interests." For example, we sometimes make a flowering bush flourish by "frustrating" its own primary propensities. We pinch off dead flowers before seeds have formed, thus "encouraging" the plant to make new flowers in an effort to produce more seeds. It is not the plant's own natural propensity (to produce seeds) that is advanced, but rather the gardener's interest in the production of new flowers and the spectator's pleasure in aesthetic form, color, or scent. What we mean in such cases by saying that the plant flourishes is that our interest in the plant, not its own, is thriving. It is not always so clear that that is what we mean, for on other occasions there is a correspondence between our interests and the plant's natural propensities, a coinciding of what we want from nature and nature's own "intention." But the exceptions to this correspondence provide the clue to our real sense in speaking of a plant's good or welfare.[10] And even when there exists such a correspondence, it is often because we have actu-

---

[9] Webster's Third New International Dictionary.

[10] Sometimes, of course, the correspondence fails because what accords with the plant's natural propensities is not in our interests, rather than the other way round. I must concede that in cases of this kind we speak even of weeds flourishing, but I doubt that we mean to imply that a weed is a thing with a good of its own. Rather, this way of talking is a plain piece of irony, or else an animistic metaphor (thinking of the weeds in the way we think of prospering businessmen). In any case, when weeds thrive, usually no interests, human or otherwise, flourish.

ally remade the plant's nature so that our interests in it will flourish more "naturally" and effectively.

Whole Species

The topic of whole species, whether of plants or animals, can be treated in much the same way as that of individual plants. A whole collection, as such, cannot have beliefs, expectations, wants, or desires, and can flourish or languish only in the human interest-related sense in which individual plants thrive and decay. Individual elephants can have interests, but the species elephant cannot. Even where individual elephants are not granted rights, human beings may have an interest—economic, scientific, or sentimental—in keeping the species from dying out, and *that* interest may be protected in various ways by law. But that is quite another matter from recognizing a right to survival belonging to the species itself. Still, the preservation of a whole species may quite properly seem to be a morally more important matter than the preservation of an individual animal. Individual animals can have rights but it is implausible to ascribe to them a right to life on the human model. Nor do we normally have duties to keep individual animals alive or even to abstain from killing them provided we do it humanely and nonwantonly in the promotion of legitimate human interests. On the other hand, we do have duties to protect threatened species, not duties to the species themselves as such, but rather duties to future human beings, duties derived from our housekeeping role as temporary inhabitants of this planet.

We commonly and very naturally speak of corporate entities, such as institutions, churches, and national states as having rights and duties, and an adequate analysis of the conditions for ownership of rights should account for that fact. A corporate entity, of course, is more than a mere collection of things that have some important traits in common. Unlike a biological species, an institution has a charter, or constitution, or bylaws, with rules defining offices and procedures, and it has human beings whose function it is to administer the rules and apply the procedures. When the institution has a duty to an outsider, there is always some determinant human being whose duty it is to do something for the outsider, and when the state, for example, has a right to collect taxes, there are always certain definite flesh and blood persons who have rights to demand tax money from other citizens. We have no reluctance to use the language of corporate rights and duties because we know that in the last analysis these are rights or duties of individual persons, acting in their "official capacities." And when individuals act in their official roles in accordance with valid empowering rules, their acts are imputable to the organization itself and become "acts of state." Thus, there is no need to posit any individual superperson named by the expression "the State" (or for that matter, "the company," the

club," or "the church.") Nor is there any reason to take the rights of corporate entities to be exceptions to the interest principle. The United States
is not a superperson with wants and beliefs of its own, but it is a corporate
entity with corporate interests that are, in turn, analyzable into the interests of its numerous flesh and blood members.

Dead Persons

So far we have refined the interest principle but we have not had occasion
to modify it. Applied to dead persons, however, it will have to be stretched
to near the breaking point if it is to explain how our duty to honor commitments to the dead can be thought to be linked to the rights of the dead
against us. The case against ascribing rights to dead men can be made very
simply: a dead man is a mere corpse, a piece of decaying organic matter.
Mere inanimate things can have no interests, and what is incapable of
having interests is incapable of having rights. If, nevertheless, we grant
dead men rights against us, we would seem to be treating the interests they
had while alive as somehow surviving their deaths. There is the sound of
paradox in this way of talking, but it may be the least paradoxical way of
describing our moral relations to our predecessors. And if the idea of an
interest's surviving its possessor's death is a kind of fiction, it is a fiction
that most living men have a real interest in preserving.

Most persons while still alive have certain desires about what is to
happen to their bodies, their property, or their reputations after they are
dead. For that reason, our legal system has developed procedures to enable
persons while still alive to determine whether their bodies will be used for
purposes of medical research or organic transplantation, and to whom their
wealth (after taxes) is to be transferred. Living men also take out life
insurance policies guaranteeing that the accumulated benefits be conferred
upon beneficiaries of their own choice. They also make private agreements,
both contractual and informal, in which they receive promises that certain
things will be done after their death in exchange for some present service
or consideration. In all these cases promises are made to living persons that
their wishes will be honored after they are dead. Like all other valid
promises, they impose duties on the promisor and confer correlative rights
on the promisee.

How does the situation change after the promisee has died? Surely
the duties of the promisor do not suddenly become null and void. If that
were the case, and known to be the case, there could be no confidence in
promises regarding posthumous arrangements; no one would bother with
wills or life insurance policies. Indeed the duties of courts and trustees to
honor testimentary directions and the duties of life insurance companies to
pay benefits to survivors are, in a sense, only conditional duties before a
man dies. They come into existence as categorical demands for immediate

action only upon the promisee's death. So the view that death renders them null and void has the truth exactly upside down.

The survival of the promisor's duty after the promisee's death does not prove that the promise retains a right even after death, for we might prefer to conclude that there is one class of cases where duties to keep promises are not logically correlated with a promisee's right, namely, cases where the promisee has died. Still, a morally sensitive promisor is likely to think of his promised performance not only as a duty (i.e., a morally required action) but also as something owed to the deceased promisee as his due. Honoring such promises is a way of keeping faith with the dead. To be sure, the promisor will not think of his duty as something to be done for the promisee's "good," since the promisee, being dead, has no "good" of his own. We can think of certain of the deceased's interests, however, (including especially those enshrined in wills and protected by contracts and promises) as surviving their owner's death, and constituting claims against us that persist beyond the life of the claimant. Such claims can be represented by proxies just like the claims of animals. This way of speaking, I believe, reflects more accurately than any other an important fact about the human condition: we have an interest while alive that other interests of ours will continue to be recognized and served after we are dead. The whole practice of honoring wills and testaments, and the like, is thus for the sake of the living, just as a particular instance of it may be thought to be for the sake of one who is dead.

Conceptual sense, then, can be made of talk about dead men's rights; but it is still a wide open moral question whether dead men in fact have rights, and if so, what those rights are. In particular, commentators have disagreed over whether a man's interest in his reputation deserves to be protected from defamation even after his death. With only a few prominent exceptions, legal systems punish a libel on a dead man "only when its publication is in truth an attack upon the interests of living persons." [11] A widow or a son may be wounded, or embarrassed, or even injured economically, by a defamatory attack on the memory of their dead husband or father. In Utah defamation of the dead is a misdemeanor, and in Sweden a cause of action in tort. The law rarely presumes, however, that a dead man himself has any interests, representable by proxy, that can be injured by defamation, apparently because of the maxim that what a dead man doesn't know can't hurt him.

This presupposes, however, that the whole point of guarding the reputations even of living men is to protect them from hurt feelings, or to protect some other interests, for example, economic ones, that do not survive death. A moment's thought, I think, will show that our interests are more complicated than that. If someone spreads a libelous description of me, without my knowledge, among hundreds of persons in a remote

---

[11] William Salmond, *Jurisprudence*, 12th ed., ed. P. J. Fitzgerald (London: Sweet and Maxwell, 1966), p. 304.

part of the country, so that I am, still without my knowledge, an object of general scorn and mockery in that group, I have been injured, even though I never learn what has happened. That is because I have an interest, so I believe, in having a good reputation *simpliciter*, in addition to my interest in avoiding hurt feelings, embarrassment, and economic injury. In the example, I do not know what is being said and believed about me, so my feelings are not hurt; but clearly if I did know, I would be enormously distressed. The distress would be the natural consequence of my belief that an interest other than my interest in avoiding distress had been damaged. How else can I account for the distress? If I had no interest in a good reputation as such, I would respond to news of harm to my reputation with indifference.

While it is true that a dead man cannot have his feelings hurt, it does not follow, therefore, that his claim to be thought of no worse than he deserves cannot survive his death. Almost every living person, I should think, would wish to have this interest protected after his death, at least during the lifetimes of those persons who were his contemporaries. We can hardly expect the law to protect Julius Caesar from defamation in the history books. This might hamper historical research and restrict socially valuable forms of expression. Even interests that survive their owner's death are not immortal. Anyone should be permitted to say anything he wishes about George Washington or Abraham Lincoln, though perhaps not everything is morally permissible. Everyone ought to refrain from malicious lies even about Nero or King Tut, though not so much for those ancients' own sakes as for the sake of those who would now know the truth about the past. We owe it to the brothers Kennedy, however, as their due, not to tell damaging lies about them to those who were once their contemporaries. If the reader would deny that judgment, I can only urge him to ask himself whether he now wishes his own interest in reputation to be respected, along with his interest in determining the distribution of his wealth, after his death.

Human Vegetables

Mentally deficient and deranged human beings are hardly ever so handicapped intellectually that they do not compare favorably with even the highest of the lower animals, though they are commonly so incompetent that they cannot be assigned duties or be held responsible for what they do. Since animals can have rights, then, it follows that human idiots and madmen can, too. It would make good sense, for example, to ascribe to them a right to be cured whenever effective therapy is available at reasonable cost, and even those incurables who have been consigned to a sanatorium for permanent "warehousing" can claim (through a proxy) their right to decent treatment.

Human beings suffering extreme cases of mental illness, however, may be so utterly disoriented or insensitive as to compare quite unfavorably with the brightest cats and dogs. Those suffering from catatonic schizophrenia may be barely distinguishable in respect to those traits presupposed by the possession of interests from the lowliest vegetables. So long as we regard these patients as potentially curable, we may think of them as human beings with interests in their own restoration and treat them as possessors of rights. We may think of the patient as a genuine human person inside the vegetable casing struggling to get out, just as in the old fairy tales a pumpkin could be thought of as a beautiful maiden under a magic spell waiting only the proper words to be restored to her true self. Perhaps it is reasonable never to lose hope that a patient can be cured, and therefore to regard him always as a person "under a spell' with a permanent interest in his own recovery that is entitled to recognition and protection.

What if, nevertheless, we think of the catatonic schizophrenic and the vegetating patient with irreversible brain damage as absolutely incurable? Can we think of them at the same time as possessed of interests and rights too, or is this combination of traits a conceptual impossibility? Shocking as it may at first seem, I am driven unavoidably to the latter view. If redwood trees and rosebushes cannot have rights, neither can incorrigible human vegetables.[12] The trustees who are designated to administer funds for the care of these unfortunates are better understood as mere custodians than as representatives of their interests since these patients no longer have interests. It does not follow that they should not be kept alive as long as possible: that is an open moral question not foreclosed by conceptual analysis. Even if we have duties to keep human vegetables alive, however, they cannot be duties *to* them. We may be obliged to keep them alive to protect the sensibilities of others, or to foster humanitarian tendencies in ourselves, but we cannot keep them alive for their own good, for they are no longer capable of having a "good" of their own. Without awareness, expectation, belief, desire, aim, and purpose, a being can have no interests; without interests, he cannot be benefited; without the capacity to be a beneficiary, he can have no rights. But there may nevertheless be a dozen other reasons to treat him as if he did.

---

[12] Unless, of course, the person in question, before he became a "vegetable," left testamentary directions about what was to be done with his body just in case he should ever become an incurable vegetable. He may have directed either that he be preserved alive as long as possible, or else that he be destroyed, whichever he preferred. There may, of course, be sound reasons of public policy why we should not honor such directions, but if we did promise to give legal effect to such wishes, we would have an example of a man's earlier interest in what is to happen to his body surviving his very competence as a person, in quite the same manner as that in which the express interest of a man now dead may continue to exert a claim on us.

Fetuses

If the interest principle is to permit us to ascribe rights to infants, fetuses, and generations yet unborn, it can only be on the grounds that interests can exert a claim upon us even before their possessors actually come into being, just the reverse of the situation respecting dead men where interests are respected even after their possessors have ceased to be. Newly born infants are surely noisier than mere vegetables, but they are just barely brighter. They come into existence, as Aristotle said, with the capacity to acquire concepts and dispositions, but in the beginning we suppose that their consciousness of the world is a "blooming, buzzing confusion." They do have a capacity, no doubt from the very beginning, to feel pain, and this alone may be sufficient ground for ascribing both an interest and a right to them. Apart from that, however, during the first few hours of their lives, at least, they may well lack even the rudimentary intellectual equipment necessary to the possession of interests. Of course, this induces no moral reservations whatever in adults. Children grow and mature almost visibly in the first few months so that those future interests that are so rapidly emerging from the unformed chaos of their earliest days seem unquestionably to be the basis of their present rights. Thus, we say of a newborn infant that he has a right now to live and grow into his adulthood, even though he lacks the conceptual equipment at this very moment to have this or any other desire. A new infant, in short, lacks the traits necessary for the possession of interests, but he has the capacity to acquire those traits, and his inherited potentialities are moving quickly toward actualization even as we watch him. Those proxies who make claims in behalf of infants, then, are more than mere custodians: they are (or can be) genuine representatives of the child's emerging interests, which may need protection even now if they are to be allowd to come into existence at all.

The same principle may be extended to "unborn persons." After all, the situation of fetuses one day before birth is not strikingly different from that a few hours after birth. The rights our law confers on the unborn child, both proprietary and personal, are for the most part, placeholders or reservations for the rights he shall inherit when he becomes a full-fledged interested being. The law protects a potential interest in these cases before it has even grown into actuality, as a garden fence protects newly seeded flower beds long before blooming flowers have emerged from them. The unborn child's present right to property, for example, is a legal protection offered now to his future interest, contingent upon his birth, and instantly voidable if he dies before birth. As Coke put it: "The law in many cases hath consideration of him in respect of the apparent expectation of his birth"; [13] but this is quite another thing than recognizing a right actually

[13] As quoted by Salmond, *Jurisprudence*, p. 303. Simply as a matter of policy the potentiality of some future interests may be so remote as to make them seem un-

to be born. Assuming that the child will be born, the law seems to say, various interests that he will come to have after birth must be protected from damage that they can incur even before birth. Thus prenatal injuries of a negligently inflicted kind can give the newly born child a right to sue for damages which he can exercise through a proxy-attorney and in his own name any time *after* he is born.

There are numerous other places, however, where our law seems to imply an unconditional right to be born, and surprisingly no one seems ever to have found that idea conceptually absurd. One interesting example comes from an article given the following headline by the *New York Times*. "Unborn Child's Right Upheld Over Religion." [14] A hospital patient in her eighth month of pregnancy refused to take a blood transfusion even though warned by her physician that "she might die at any minute and take the life of her child as well." The ground of her refusal was that blood transfusions are repugnant to the principles of her religion (Jehovah's Witnesses). The Supreme Court of New Jersey expressed uncertainty over the constitutional question of whether a nonpregnant adult might refuse on religious grounds a blood transfusion pronounced necessary to her own survival, but the court nevertheless ordered the patient in the present case to receive the transfusion on the grounds that "the unborn child is entitled to the law's protection."

It is important to reemphasize here that the questions of whether fetuses do or ought to have rights are substantive questions of law and morals open to argument and decision. The prior question of whether fetuses are the kind of beings that can have rights, however, is a conceptual, not a moral, question, amenable only to what is called "logical analysis," and irrelevant to moral judgment. The correct answer to the conceptual question, I believe, is that unborn children are among the sorts of beings of whom possession of rights can meaningfully be predicated, even though they are (temporarily) incapable of having interests, because their future interests can be protected now, and it does make sense to protect a potential interest even before it has grown into actuality. The interest principle, however, makes perplexing, at best, talk of a noncontingent fetal right to be born; for fetuses, lacking actual wants and beliefs, have no actual interest in being born, and it is difficult to think of any other reason for ascrib-

---

worthy of present support. A testator may leave property to his unborn child, for example, but not to his unborn grandchildren. To say of the potential person presently in his mother's womb that he owns property now is to say that certain property must be held for him until he is "real" or "mature" enough to possess it. "Yet the law is careful lest property should be too long withdrawn in this way from the uses of living men in favor of generations yet to come; and various restrictive rules have been established to this end. No testator could now direct his fortune to be accumulated for a hundred years and then distributed among his descendants"—Salmond, ibid.

[14] *New York Times*, 17 June 1966, p. 1.

ing any rights to them other than on the assumption that they will in fact be born.[15]

Future Generations

We have it in our power now to make the world a much less pleasant place for our descendants than the world we inherited from our ancestors. We can continue to proliferate in ever greater numbers, using up fertile soil at an even greater rate, dumping our wastes into rivers, lakes, and oceans, cutting down our forests, and polluting the atmosphere with noxious gases. All thoughtful people agree that we ought not to do these things. Most would say that we have a duty not to do these things, meaning not merely that conservation is morally required (as opposed to merely desirable) but also that it is something due our descendants, something to be done for their sakes. Surely we owe it to future generations to pass on a world that is not a used up garbage heap. Our remote descendants are not yet present to claim a livable world as their right, but there are plenty of proxies to speak now in their behalf. These spokesmen, far from being mere custodians, are genuine representatives of future interests.

Why then deny that the human beings of the future have rights which can be claimed against us now in their behalf? Some are inclined to deny them present rights out of a fear of falling into obscure metaphysics, by granting rights to remote and unidentifiable beings who are not yet even in existence. Our unborn great-great-grandchildren are in some sense "potential" persons, but they are far more remotely potential, it may seem, than fetuses. This, however, is not the real difficulty. Unborn generations are more remotely potential than fetuses in one sense, but not in another. A much greater period of time with a far greater number of causally necessary and important events must pass before their potentiality can be actualized, it is true; but our collective posterity is just as certain to come into existence "in the normal course of events" as is any given fetus now in its mother's womb. In that sense the existence of the distant human future is no more remotely potential than that of a particular child already on its way.

The real difficulty is not that we doubt whether our descendants will ever be actual, but rather that we don't know who they will be. It is not their temporal remoteness that troubles us so much as their indeterminancy —their present facelessness and namelessness. Five centuries from now men and women will be living where we live now. Any given one of them will have an interest in living space, fertile soil, fresh air, and the like, but that

---

[15] In an essay entitled "Is There a Right to be Born?" I defend a negative answer to the question posed, but I allow that under certain very special conditions, there can be a "right *not* to be born." See *Abortion*, ed. J. Feinberg (Belmont, Calif.: Wadsworth, 1973).

arbitrarily selected one has no other qualities we can presently envision very clearly. We don't even know who his parents, grandparents, or great-grandparents are, or even whether he is related to us. Still, whoever these human beings may turn out to be, and whatever they might reasonably be expected to be like, they will have interests that we can affect, for better or worse right now. That much we can and do know about them. The identity of the owners of these interests is now necessarily obscure, but the fact of their interest-ownership is crystal clear, and that is all that is necessary to certify the coherence of present talk about their rights. We can tell, sometimes, that shadowy forms in the spatial distance belong to human beings, though we know not who or how many they are; and this imposes a duty on us not to throw bombs, for example, in their direction. In like manner, the vagueness of the human future does not weaken its claim on us in light of the nearly certain knowledge that it will, after all, be human.

Doubts about the existence of a right to be born transfer neatly to the question of a similar right to come into existence ascribed to future generations. The rights that future generations certainly have against us are contingent rights: the interests they are sure to have when they come into being (assuming of course that they will come into being) cry out for protection from invasion that can take place now. Yet there are no actual interests, presently existent, that future generations, presently non-existent, have now. Hence, there is no actual interest that they have in simply coming into being, and I am at a loss to think of any other reason for claiming that they have a right to come into existence (though there may well be such a reason). Support then that all human beings at a given time voluntarily form a compact never again to produce children, thus leading within a few decades to the end of our species. This of course is a wildly improbable hypothetical example but a rather crucial one for the position I have been tentatively considering. And we can imagine, say, that the whole world is converted to a strange ascetic religion which absolutely requires sexual abstinence for everyone. Would this arrangement violate the rights of anyone? No one can complain on behalf of presently non-existent future generations that their future interests which give them a contingent right of protection have been violated since they will never come into existence to be wronged. My inclination then is to conclude that the suicide of our species would be deplorable, lamentable, and a deeply moving tragedy, but that it would violate no one's rights. Indeed if, contrary to fact, all human beings could ever agree to such a thing, that very agreement would be a symptom of our species' biological unsuitability for survival anyway.

Conclusion

For several centuries now human beings have run roughshod over the lands of our planet, just as if the animals who do live there and the generations of humans who will live there had no claims on them whatever. Philosophers have not helped matters by arguing that animals and future generations are not the kinds of beings who can have rights now, that they don't presently qualify for membership, even "auxiliary membership," in our moral community. I have tried in this essay to dispel the conceptual confusions that make such conclusions possible. To acknowledge their rights is the very least we can do for members of endangered species (including our own). But that is something.

Appendix: The Paradoxes of Potentiality

Having conceded that rights can belong to beings in virtue of their merely potential interests, we find ourselves on a slippery slope; for it may seem at first sight that anything at all can have potential interests, or much more generally, that anything at all can be potentially almost anything else at all! Dehydrated orange powder is potentially orange juice, since if we add water to it, it will be orange juice. More remotely, however, it is also potentially lemonade, since it will become lemonade if we add a large quantity of lemon juice, sugar, and water. It is also a potentially poisonous brew (add water and arsenic), a potential orange cake (add flour, etc., and bake), a potential orange-colored building block (add cement and harden), and so on, *ad infinitum*. Similarly a two-celled embryo, too small to be seen by the unaided eye, is a potential human being; and so is an unfertilized ovum; and so is even an "uncapacitated" spermatozoan. Add the proper nutrition to an implanted embryo (under certain other necessary conditions) and it becomes a fetus and then a child. Looked at another way, however, the implanted embryo has been combined (under the same conditions) with the nutritive elements, which themselves are converted into a growing fetus and child. Is it then just as proper to say that food is a "potential child" as that an embryo is a potential child? If so, then what isn't a "potential child?" (Organic elements in the air and soil are "potentially food," and hence potentially people!)

Clearly, some sort of lines will have to be drawn between direct or proximate potentialities and indirect or remote ones; and however we draw this line, there will be borderline cases whose classification will seem uncertain or even arbitrary. Even though any X can become a Y provided only that it is combined with the necessary additional elements, *a, b, c, d*, and so forth, we cannot say of any given X that it is a "potential Y" unless certain further—rather strict—conditions are met. (Otherwise the concept of potentiality, being universally and promiscuously applicable, will have no utility.) A number of possible criteria of proximate potentiality suggest themselves. The first is the criterion of causal importance. Orange powder is not properly called a potential building block because of those elements needed to transform it into a building block, the cement (as opposed to any of the qualities of the orange powder) is the causally crucial one. Similarly, any pauper might (misleadingly) be called a "potential millionaire" in the sense that all that need be added to any man to transform him into a millionaire is a great amount of money.

The absolutely crucial element in the change, of course, is no quality of the man himself but rather the million dollars "added" to him.

What is causally "important" depends upon our purposes and interests and is therefore to some degree a relativistic matter. If we seek a standard, in turn, of "importance," we may posit such a criterion, for example, as that of the ease or difficulty (to some persons or other) of providing those missing elements which, when combined with the thing at hand, convert it into something else. It does seem quite natural, for example, to say that the orange powder is potentially orange juice, and that is because the missing element is merely common tap water, a substance conveniently near at hand to everyone; whereas it is less plausible to characterize the powder as potential cake since a variety of further elements, and not just one, are required, and some of these are not conveniently near at hand to many. Moreover, the process of combining the missing elements into a cake is rather more complicated than mere "addition." It is less plausible still to call orange powder a potential curbstone for the same kind of reason. The criterion of ease or difficulty of the acquisition and combination of additional elements explains all these variations.

Still another criterion of proximate potentiality closely related to the others is that of degree of deviation required from "the normal course of events." Given the intentions of its producers, distributors, sellers, and consumers, dehydrated orange juice will, in the normal course of events, become orange juice. Similarly, a human embryo securely imbedded in the wall of its mother's uterus will in the normal course of events become a human child. That is to say that if no one deliberately intervenes to prevent it happening, it will, in the vast majority of cases, happen. On the other hand, an unfertilized ovum will not become an embryo unless someone intervenes deliberately to make it happen. Without such intervention in the "normal" course of events, an ovum is a mere bit of protoplasm of very brief life expectancy. If we lived in a world in which virtually every biologically capable human female became pregnant once a year throughout her entire fertile period of life, then we would regard fertilization as something that happens to every ovum in "the natural course of events." Perhaps we would regard every unfertilized ovum, in such a world, as a potential person even possessed of rights corresponding to its future interests. It would perhaps make conceptual if not moral sense in such a world to regard deliberate nonfertilization as a kind of homicide.

It is important to notice, in summary, that words like *important, easy,* and *normal* have sense only in relation to human experiences, purposes, and techniques. As the latter change, so will our notions of what is important, difficult, and usual, and so will the concept of potentiality, or our application of it. If our purposes, understanding, and techniques continue to change in indicated directions, we may even one day come to think of inanimate things as possessed of "potential interests." In any case, we can expect the concept of a right to shift its logical boundaries with changes in our practical experience.

J. BRENTON STEARNS

Ecology and
the Indefinite Unborn

The concern people are now expressing about the human environment, ecology, pollution, and overpopulation, though admittedly legitimate from a moral point of view, has not attracted much attention from philosophers. This is notable particularly inasmuch as the United States civil rights struggle, the Vietnam War, and various responses of civil disobedience and violence to social problems have all aroused philosophers to careful thought on rights and obligations. I do not want to suggest that a social problem is interesting only if it is philosophically interesting; nor do I want to make light of the way in which the problems of waste, noise, and overcrowding have captured the popular imagination. Yes, we must protect and use wisely the human environment and natural resources. But still, saying it seems banal, and philosophers do not feed on banalities. Here we have a modern moral commandment which speaks to an urgent and serious matter but which, like "Do not steal," seems so obvious as to be trite. Yes, we must plan the world's population in a rational way. Even that commandment, though disputed by some, seems trite.

Pollution probes have given rise to much popular moralizing, but not at a highly theoretical level. Sometimes the moralist in this area urges that we consider prudential self-interest of the long run rather than of the short run. Sometimes he tries to convert us from taking a prudential point of view on the matter to taking a moral point of view. And sometimes he reminds us of the moral commitments we have already made and inspires us to act in a consistently principled way with regard to them. But we are not faced with many conflicts between moral rules and legal rules, or among obligations to the various large and small human social groups to which we belong. Furthermore, what our consciences dictate on ecology do not present striking counterexamples to any historically important philosophical theories on ethics. It is hard to find a moral theory that accounts for everything our consciences tell us about legal punishment, say, but there is no analogous problem in the ecological discussion, or so it seems.

However, there is at least one theoretical puzzle in current discussions on ecology. This paper is an attempt to be precise about the problem and to take some steps toward a solution. Very simply, the problem I find is

Reprinted from *The Monist*, Vol. 56, No. 4 (October 1972), 612–625, LaSalle, Illinois, with the permission of the author and the publisher.

that ecologists assume an obligation to future generations, an obligation which both deontological- and utilitarian-type theories are hard pressed to account for. Why should there be obligations to future generations? We have made no commitments to them. We have entered no social compacts with them. And under utilitarian theory it is hard to account for an obligation to increase the well-being of persons who do not yet exist and who, but for our reproducing ourselves, would not exist. Under any moral theory, why should there be obligations to nonexistent persons?

We will want to think carefully whether there may be some backward looking considerations that are relevant here, but it appears as if the traditional social contract idea is not useful in justifying duties to future generations. It is possible to assume an obligation to perform some service to a future person, but future persons could of course not now be parties to contracts or promises. Similarly, we could not have obligations to future persons based on their past merit or work. Future persons cannot in this sense "deserve" good or fair treatment. They could not have been benefactors to us in the past, so we could not feel indebted to them on that ground. Considerations of benevolence and noninfliction of pain seem more likely candidates for duty-making factors in this context. Indeed, utilitarian-type arguments are used almost exclusively by conservationists and ecologists. And yet, as I will try to show, utilitarian reasoning and strategy lead also to some puzzles, the solution of which will require modifications in utilitarian patterns of argument.

Before I go into the problems in detail, I do want to concede that in most cases excessive exploitation of the environment or careless use of the environment will lead to disutilities in the life-span of at least some of those now living. Even if there were no obligations to future generations there would still be good moral reason not to dump garbage into the rivers, not to burn leaves in the backyard, etc. However, not all of our concern about filth, crowded conditions, and exhaustion of natural resources or recreational areas can be handled on the basis of obligations to ourselves, our neighbors, and our children now living. I assume my readers and I are alike in our intuitive belief that it is obligatory to be economical in the use of natural resources that would not be exhausted even under noneconomical use for three generations. Perhaps we share an intuitive belief that there is at least one thing worse than producing dirty air for children now living to breathe, and that is producing still dirtier air for children not yet living to breathe at some future time. One of the things I want to do is to expose to examination the principles that lie behind these beliefs.

First I will offer a utilitarian-type answer to the problem of justifying duties to future generations. Then, after considering the difficulties in it, I will study some alternatives, and finally I will return to a modification of the original utilitarian solution. In the course of this I will take note of Jan Narveson's contributions to discussion on the topic. I will work out my own views in conversation with his. However, I am taking my own approach to the question of what utilitarianism is. I do not have time to enter a full study and evaluation of Narveson's proposal as to what form a utilitarian position should take. He, for example, thinks utilitarianism should not properly entail an obligation to produce the good, but only an obligation not to inflict suffering. I will assume to the contrary that benevolence as well as nonmaleficence is a duty-making consideration. This will make my discussion consistent with the traditional formulations of the utility principle.

A utilitarian might reply to my original query as follows. Yes, of course there are obligations of benevolence and nonmaleficence to future generations. Admittedly, were all our obligations to existent persons we should not be able to explain why we have obligations to not-yet-born people. But our obligations of benevolence are not primarily obligations to persons at all, but are at root obligations to produce future intrinsic goods, no matter who enjoys them. What is the distinction that is being made here? An obligation to a person is an obligation to an assignable individual. Having an obligation to a person entails that we can specify the individual to whom the obligation is owed. An obligation of benevolence to a person is an obligation to help a person out, or to increase his welfare, to better his lot in life, etc. However, an obligation to produce future intrinsic goods and to avoid intrinsic evils does not require the specification of individuals. Here the obligation is to increase the balance of goodness over evil in the world. Obligations to future generations may be thought of as obligations of the latter type, to produce intrinsic goods and to avoid intrinsic evils in conscious human experience in the distant future. When we are thinking in terms of the utilitarian duty to produce future intrinsic goods, we are not to consider who is to enjoy them, because the duty is abstracted from specifiable or assignable individuals. When now unborn people are to enjoy the goods, these duties are without corresponding rights. Nonexisting persons are obviously not in a position to claim rights. There is more difficulty in deciding whether rights can be claimed for or in behalf of not-yet-existing persons. Probably the most that could be said in behalf of these persons is that they will have rights. Not-yet-existing persons do not have rights now, and therefore an obligation to produce goods for them and to prevent evils for them cannot correspond to rights claims. The obligation is to produce utility per se; it is not an obligation to persons. Whether the utility will be enjoyed by people now living or by future people should make no difference in our utilitarian calculations.

Is there an obligation to reproduce, thus creating future generations? The main reason there is no obligation to do so under current conditions is that more than enough children are likely to result if people act on inclination. Where goods can be achieved by people inclined to do so, there is no reason people not so inclined should be obliged to take part in the production of those goods. On the other hand, that there be future generations is a necessary condition for the production of personal intrinsic goods in the long run. We can conceive of circumstances where it would be obligatory to reproduce. There would be a duty prima facie for some persons to do so where doing so would increase total utility and where it is necessary that at least some persons act against inclination in order to achieve the goods in question.

The issue of personal identity has nothing to do with the moral problem of planning for the future. Should the metaphysician who holds a process theory of the self feel any less committed to the future happiness of his fellow men and himself than the person who believes the self is not in flux? Under the process theory, personal identity is a quite relative sort of thing. It is relatively important over short periods of time and relatively unimportant over longer periods of time. If all duties of benevolence were duties to assignable persons, under the process view those duties would be weakened, for in every case the person who will be affected by one's action does not yet fully exist. The process metaphysician may wonder about the degree to which he is making plans for his own retirement and the degree to which he is making plans for the retirement of someone else intimately related to him by history and memory. But does it matter whether the future goods will be enjoyed by him? No, at least not from a moral point of view. It does not matter to what persons future happiness is assigned. Hence, what we have a moral interest in is future happiness, not future persons, even though happiness will be enjoyed by persons. The alternative, that there are obligations to future persons, is wrong because nonperformance of the alleged duties would not violate the just claims that can be made by and in behalf of such persons.

Although the proposal I have outlined above accounts well for the obligation we feel to unknown future generations, there are difficulties in it, and these stem mainly from the oddity of having duties that are not duties to persons. Were the duty to benevolent action a duty to produce intrinsic good per se, considerations of just distribution of goods with respect to future generations could not be admitted. If our obligation were to produce future intrinsic goods no matter who enjoys them, our duties of benevolence would have to be guided by considerations of total utility alone. We could not give thought to increasing average utility, because we do not yet have assignable persons among whom the average could be reckoned. Quite clearly, if our moral interest is in maximizing value regardless of who is the beneficiary, our interest must be in maximizing value regardless of how many are beneficiaries and how the value is distributed among the beneficiaries.

Furthermore, with total utility as our concern, we might be obliged to reproduce to the limit that the earth can sustain human life at the utility floor. That would be our duty if such a policy would increase total utility, not so otherwise. Let us suppose there is a declining return from natural resources in total utility as those resources are expended on fewer and fewer persons. Then we could utilize natural resources most efficiently in terms of total utility by using them to support as many people as we could at a standard of living where the intrinsic goods of happiness, etc., purchasable per unit of economic good is highest, which may be close to the poverty level. As we move above that level, the amount of intrinsic good purchaseable per unit of economic good would decline. True, with regard to those economic goods that will eventually be exhausted, we could use them most efficiently relative to total intrinsic goods attainable by spreading out their use over several generations. But in terms of the economic goods that are not exhausted by use, like space for living and many kinds of food production, we might do better to have them enjoyed by a great number of persons in every generation. At least, if total utility is our concern, we must be prepared to act in accord with a policy like this if empirical studies should convince us that efficiency would be served by it. Such a policy would decrease average utility, and we would be left with a most abstract kind of benevolence. We would be interested in making the world a "better place" but at the cost of decreasing average utility, at the cost of making the life of each person less fulfilled. Is it really a policy of benevolence to be committed to make things "better" but without a corollary commitment to improve the lot of people?

The problem we face is coming more clearly into focus. From a conservationist point of view, we feel obliged to protect the environment for our children's children. But it seems the only way we can defend this intuitive judgment is by saying it is an obligation to increase total utility. It is not a duty to persons, because the persons do not exist yet and, but for our reproducing, would not exist. Similarly, it is not a duty to produce the highest possible average utility, because the persons among whom we would figure the average do not yet exist and, but for our producing, would not exist.

And yet we are far from satisfied with the idea that we are obliged to produce maximum total utility no matter who enjoys it. We can think of conflicts between this principle and that of bettering the lot of assignable persons. While the total utility principle seems necessary to deal with environmental pollution, it gets us into trouble when we turn to the issue of population planning. As we have seen, considerations of total utility could, if certain empirical conditions are fulfilled, make obligatory acting on the intent of crowding the earth and allowing a low level of welfare for each person.

It seems fruitless to turn to some sort of nonutilitarian ethic, say a contractual ethic, at this point. For example, obligations to future generations cannot arise from our deciding explicitly or implicitly to reproduce. If they did, one's obligation would not extend beyond his own children, and one's moral strategy might well be different from what it would be if the obligation to be benevolent extended to all future bearers of intrinsic value. If one's obligation were to one's own children only, the justifiable strategy might be, instead of expending time and energy in social education and reform directed toward diminishing air pollution, to use one's resources in providing air conditioning of as large areas as possible for the use of one's own family. In political action the risk of futility is high, but one is engaged because the stakes are large in terms of the happiness of human beings. If our moral reasons for benevolence were limited to helping our own offspring, our moral strategy in some instances would be directed away from social action and toward producing islands of haven and safety amidst an evil world. True, in some cases the strategy would be the same, regardless of whether our benevolence were directed toward the good of all or the good only of those future persons we contract for. We might, for instance, work to prevent nuclear war even if we felt obligations only to our own children. The strategy of building bomb shelters for our own children might not be effective. However, I think it would make a strategic difference in policy on some matters, including the deployment of the environment. Obligations of a contractual sort are not strong enough to support our moral interest in leaving the world as clean as we found it.

In addition, we would have the problem that childless people who do not undertake the risks of sexual union would not have obligations to future generations under a contractual theory. Also, we might wonder whether sexual union is a deliberate enough act to incur even implicit obligations. Contractual agreements, even implicit ones, should involve deliberation and forethought. A contractual theory might limit having obligation to future generations to those who engage in some sort of rational family planning.

Some people believe they have incurred obligations to future generations by having benefitted themselves from loving care in their childhood. In our culture one normally does not do much to repay his parents for the care and expense of having been guided to adulthood, and so some people think, whether or not they engage in reproductive activities, that they have implicitly incurred an obligation to those who follow them on earth. Furthermore, there are those who think they have received such great benefits from tradition or the culture or the society, benefits that cannot be repaid to those who provided them, that they have incurred implicit obligations to succeeding generations that are analogous to repayment of debts. Some people who have enjoyed the benefits of university scholarship endowment funds see the impossibility of repaying those who endowed the funds, people who are usually by that time dead. And so they sometimes feel obliged to provide funds for future generations or, at least, to make some social contribution which would be adequate recompense for the benefits received. This obligation is a backward looking one and is not based on utility. The duty arises in virtue of the actions of a benefactor. Sometimes it is felt as not a duty to persons, strictly speaking, but rather a duty to society conceived as a system or organization of persons, or as a tradition, or as a culture—something that transcends the persons who comprise it from time to time.

Although this felt obligation has no contractual basis, it stems from a backward looking consideration which is not reducible to utility. I certainly do not want to deny that being a recipient of a cultural tradition should fill one with awe and thankfulness and should encourage one to provide a still richer tradition for those yet to come. What I question is whether this kind of consideration is sufficient for grounding the current ethic of conservation and cleanliness. There are people who do not look upon their own lives as blessings. Further, there are people who are not especially appreciative of their cultural tradition or of their own upbringing. These people can and should consider the welfare of those yet to come. Here the reasoning is totally on the ground of benevolence. And even those of us who are inspired or moved by some deontological-type reasoning—as thinking it is right and obligatory in and of itself to repay society for benefits bestowed—need to consider future utility in deciding what specific projects they shall undertake. And here we run once again into the puzzle I have set forth. A duty of benevolence to future generations is not a duty to persons but a duty to produce future intrinsic goods, and yet on that basis we cannot consider average utility nor increase in welfare for persons. We would also have difficulty in considering equality in distribution, because what is an equal distribution depends on the concept of an average or a median, neither of which could be figured without reference to the number of definite individuals among whom the goods are to be distributed.

A solution to the problem of finding an ethic of human reproduction from a utilitarian perspective is proposed by Jan Narveson.[1] What he suggests seems adequate to the problem of the population explosion, but I think his solution gets into trouble when other ecological problems are faced. Narveson denies that there is a duty of benevolence to maximize utility. He denies even that there is a moral reason to maximize utility. There is a duty of nonmaleficence, and there is a moral reason to maximize average utility. We are now in a position to decide how many people there will be in the next generation. There is a moral reason to maximize utility relative to that number of persons—to better their lot in life. There would be a duty to have children where failure to do so would cause suffering in the population already existent, unless the children to be born would suffer. There would be a moral reason to reproduce, but not a duty, if by doing so the average happiness of the total population should increase and the children to be born would not suffer. If by reproducing the average happiness should remain the same, the parents be made happy, and the child not suffer, there is a reason to have a child, but not a moral reason. If the average happiness should decrease through reproduction,

[1] "Utilitarianism and New Generations," *Mind*, 76 (1967), 62–72.

reproducing would be an act of injury to one's fellow men. There would then be a duty not to reproduce even if the child should not suffer. There is a duty not to reproduce in any case where the child will probably suffer. For Narveson the duty of nonmaleficence is very strong and overrides other considerations.

However, there is serious question as to whether Narveson's moral interest in increasing average utility takes into account more than already existent persons and persons already contracted for by existent persons. As soon as Adam and Eve decided to have a child, they were obliged to consider the welfare of that child equally with the welfare of already existent persons.[2] Narveson says that we should consider the effects of our actions with regard to persons in the distant future, persons we are not in a position to decide to produce. However, I do not see how a moral interest in increasing average utility could take such persons into account. Considering our earth's finite resources, any commitment to increase average utility must include a policy of population control, and that goes for the commitments future generations undertake as well. Man's problem is not to make some definite number of future persons happy, but to decide how many future persons there will be. Tentatively, it is Adam and Eve's having the child, or perhaps deciding to have the child, that creates a moral reason to act benevolently toward it.

Under the view that all utilitarian duties are owed to definite persons, there would be duties to existent persons and to persons already contracted for. It is more difficult to decide whether there would also be duties to persons whose future existence we can now predict. If there were duties of this type, we could account for the obligations of childless people now living to preserve a healthful environment for future generations, as well as for the similar obligations of those who expect to have children by chance over their years of fertility but who do not plan for them or contract for them in any rational way. If duties to future generations were duties to a predicted population, that would remove those duties from a contractual basis and would restore a more purely utilitarian outlook. A duty to a conceived but unborn child would not depend on the fact that we have contracted for his birth but rather on the fact that we can predict his birth as highly probable.

Admittedly a duty to a future person now contracted for is a difficult notion in itself. But I think we can say that this duty arises from the fact that the person contracted for did not ask for existence and ought to receive benevolent treatment because of our decision to reproduce. This decision may be an individual matter or it may be the result of a social policy. However, a moral interest in benevolence to persons not planned or contracted for but whose future existence can be predicted as highly probable is a still stranger notion. Clearly, no just claims can be made by

[2] Jan Narveson, *Morality and Utility* (Baltimore, Maryland: The Johns Hopkins Press, 1967), p. 50.

these persons. Not so trivially, no just claims can be made in behalf of them either. They must be considered as probable future bearers of sorrow and happiness. I would say we do have obligations with regard to a predictable future, but these obligations are not owed to assignable persons but are obligations to maximize utility. Persons existent and contracted for do have special claims upon us. They as definite individuals can either make or have made in their behalf a just claim for benevolent treatment. In considering them we must strive to advance their welfare and to increase average utility. We can predict that there will be human life on earth for many thousands of years to come. But there is no way to calculate the future probable outcome of our actions in terms of average utility or increase in welfare for these predicted persons, because part of the moral problem is deciding how many future persons there will be. The morally relevant consideration must be that of total utility only. And yet, as we have seen, this consideration is inadequate when applied to the problem of population control.

Narveson thinks we do have a duty not to reproduce in cases where we can predict that the child will suffer or where we can predict a decline in average happiness through reproduction. Foregoing children in cases where we can predict suffering for them seems reasonable enough, though admittedly this principle might clash with the ideal of maximizing average happiness. Proponents of some forms of slavery might claim that, although the system causes certain individuals to suffer, the average happiness is increased through the system. This problem could be handled by considering the claims of nonmaleficence and just distribution to outweigh those of maximizing average utility. It seems, moreover, that not every act of reproduction which decreases average utility would be morally wrong. I think we ought not to condemn acts which, though they decrease average utility somewhat, increase total utility markedly, particularly where average utility is at a high level. As I have said before, Narveson's considering average utility seems reasonable. In order to do so, however, he needs to decide who is to be included in figuring the alternative averages, and this is limited to those now living plus those we may implicitly contract for. Our utilitarian duties become duties to assignable persons, but at the cost of limiting our moral foresight to the next one hundred years.

If our commitment is to the highest average happiness of those persons now living and those we contract for, then in the decision to have a child we would be using the person as a means to the end of increasing the average happiness of other human beings. True, the presumption is that in doing so the child would be rather happy himself. And if the child in question would suffer, the duty of nonmaleficence would take precedence and the child ought not to be contracted for. However, the child's being a means to an end comes out clearly when we see that under Narveson's theory the only moral reason there could be for producing a child is increasing the average happiness of other human beings. This problem is avoided if in making moral decisions on personal action and social policies we consider all the foreseeable consequences of the possible actions open to us, not just their effects on already definite or assignable persons.

Therefore, a morality which is concerned with utilizing the human environment for human happiness in the long run must move beyond calculations of the average happiness of assignable persons, whether they be already existent, now contracted for, or now predictable. Certainly the contractual theory is weak, because it does not account for the obligations of childless persons or those who reproduce without rational design. Grounding our ecological obligations on the needs of definite predictable persons will not do, because part of our moral policy must involve a decision as to the size of future populations. In short, the moral problem of pollution transcends our love or concern for definite and assignable persons.

Now I will outline a concluding position on the problems I have exposed. First, there is an obligation to see to it that human existence continues at a high level of intrinsic value. This is not an obligation to anybody in particular, and indeed it is not an obligation to persons at all. Some people may feel particularly bound by this obligation because of thankfulness to their parents or their society or their culture for benefits received. But the obligation extends to those even who do not feel thankful, who never asked for life, and who deplore the day they were born. This obligation is not of a contractual sort and has nothing to do with whether the obligation has been voluntarily undertaken. It is a thoroughly utilitarian obligation to produce intrinsic good in conscious human experience. Since it is not an obligation to persons, it cannot be an obligation to increase average utility, but is strictly an obligation to maximize total utility. This obligation cannot be reduced to increasing average utility. First, the average at any given time may be so high that a decrease therein is not prima facie wrong. Second, some of the people in respect to whom future averages would be figured do not yet exist, and whether or not they will exist is now a matter for moral decision. When one is dealing with populations of some definite size, the act that will maximize total utility will also always maximize average utility. But that will not be the case where one seeks to maximize total utility without regard to any already definite number of persons. The indefinite unborn thus pose a unique problem for utility calculations.

However, in addition to duties to maximize total utility without regard to already definite persons, there are also duties to definite persons, those already existent and those already contracted for. These duties have a variety of grounds, some of which may not be reducible to utility. For example, it is wrong to kill people already born in an attempt to maximize either total or average utility. That would violate fundamental human rights to life and freedom. Some obligations to persons may have been deliberately undertaken through promises or contracts, and some may be considered ways of repaying parents, teachers, or the general culture for benefits received. Although duties to persons may have deontological grounds in what is demanded by fairness and adherence to agreements, the substance of duties to persons includes always the element of benevolent action toward them aimed at improving their condition. We can think of possible conflicts between duties to persons existent or contracted for and duties to maximize total utility. A policy that would increase the average happiness of the populace and the children they have decided to produce is not necessarily the same as a policy that would increase the long-range happiness of future generations. I see no formula-type answer to that kind of conflict. It must be seen as a conflict between incommensurable duties.

Here now are some general reflections on patterns of utilitarian argument. A consideration which lends strength to the utilitarian position in ethics is that being benevolent is an end of the moral life and is indeed necessary to any adequate ethical strategy. Under any theory other than utilitarian in character we must be prepared always to sacrifice benevolence in order to achieve other moral aims. Unless benevolence be our end, the right act will only contingently be benevolent. There is no way to be benevolent consistently other than to aim for it. We may think, for example, that abiding by some set of rules happens to promote benevolence. However, unless our theory is grounded directly in benevolence, we must continue to abide by the rules even when they do not produce the ends we really want. The utilitarian claims that only his theory makes the connection between morality and benevolence a necessary one. The right act is the benevolent act, and the benevolent act is the act which maximizes utility.

However, as moral philosophers have often observed, we need to be clear as to what we mean by 'benevolence'. If we understand 'benevolence' to mean 'increasing the welfare and diminishing the pain of assignable persons', we can see that a policy aimed at maximizing utility among a now indefinite population is only contingently benevolent. On the other hand, I think we have in the maximum utility principle an intuitively clear right-making consideration of high priority. I have tried to be convincing on this by showing that a maximum utility principle is assumed in the moral pronouncements on pollution which strike us as so self-evident as to be banal. Were benevolence to assignable persons to outweigh maximum utility strategies in every case, we would be committed to making life as good as possible for those now living and contracted for without regard to the indefinite unborn who will succeed us on earth.

The problem here is subtly different from the one which attends most of the confrontations between the maximum utility principle and considerations of distributive justice. The problem usually arises with reference to a definite population, and the quandary is whether to distribute widely and comparatively equally or rather to increase total utility by concentrating the benefits upon a few. But the problem of the indefinite unborn is radically prior to all issues of distributive justice, for in this case the quandary is whether to produce "consumers" of utility. Prior to the production of people or the decision to produce them no question of fair distribution can arise.

And so: (1) Yes, it is possible to act rightly but not in a way that is benevolent to definite persons; (2) The utility principle in its purest form, that which recommends as moral those acts which maximize utility, does not entail benevolence to definite persons; (3) Benevolence to definite persons is indeed a rightmaking consideration; (4) Calculations of benevolence to definite persons is incommensurable with calculations of maximum utility. The utilitarian conscience is torn between incommensurable duties prior to the problem of distribution of goods among a definite population. Conflicts in duties and the need intuitively to balance right-making factors can be found inherent in an act-utilitarian framework quite apart from the common puzzles with promises, truth-telling, and fairness.

MARK SAGOFF

On Preserving
the Natural Environment

III. A Nonutilitarian Rationale for Preserving
the Natural Environment

A

Even if nature in the rough were beautiful, this would not be an adequate reason to protect it from development, for no one has shown that beauty has any value other than the pleasure it produces, and there is usually more pleasure in exploiting a natural environment than in leaving it alone. Nor has anyone shown that pleasure taken in beauty is better than less expensive enjoyments; indeed, it is difficult to know what "better" in this context could mean. The truth is often heard that to value a woman because of her good looks is to trivialize her, to ignore her more important qualities, and to regard her only as an object of use. It is likewise true of the environment. We regard nature only as a source of recreation if we do not see the difference between a wilderness and a pretty garden. We know the difference. Let us say what it is. The respect, reverence, and benevolence many of us

Reprinted by permission of the author, *The Yale Law Journal* Company, and Fred B. Rothman & Company from *The Yale Law Journal*, Vol. 84, No. 2 (1974), 245–252, 264–267.
Editor's Note: Footnotes have been renumbered.

feel toward nature and attribute to its beauty in fact is felt for its expressive qualities. A wild area may be powerful, majestic, free; an animal may express courage, innocence, purpose, and strength. As a nation we value these qualities: the obligation toward nature is an obligation toward them.

Suppose a big company proposes to build a ski resort on a mountain top in a national park; suppose, too, it intends to construct an access highway through an untouched forest. Let us assume, moreover, that the economic benefits of this proposal are great compared to the needed investment. The benefits, of course, would extend to wildlife and to the park itself. The denizens of the forest, for example, would be fed balanced meals by the management, and their cubs, or whatever, would be checked regularly by veterinarians; the bears would sleep on foam rubber all winter in quality-controlled dens, clown with the visitors, or possibly ski themselves. The developer will be quick to point out that without proper landscaping the terrain is rough, violent, and hostile. It is not really decorative; it is not quite beautiful. Artists usually provide relief to their landscapes by including some sign of human habitation—you can pick out a country lane or church spire in the distance. A landscape as vast as a national park, however, requires more than a country road to make it beautiful; it takes a six lane highway to do the job. Few people go to church who also ski; but the rough terrain could be relieved by the graceful arches of a popular hamburger stand. And it will not cost the taxpayer a cent.

What can the environmentalist say? He can argue that the mountain will lose its fierceness, power and integrity. The wildlife will no longer be wild; it will forfeit its freedom and strength. There is no reason to think, however, that the animals value these qualities. Certainly very few people wish to confront nature on its own terms. They want an air-conditioned motel; they are glad to see the forest from a gondola after a drink. So what if they do not feel its cool hostility. Now environmentalists might begin to worry that they alone cherish the fierceness and power of nature and its integrity, or that only they and a few others value independence, power, endurance, sureness, and freedom as these are expressed by natural objects. The environmentalist will then despairingly point out that the development of a wild area, though increasing its amenity, destroys many of its expressive qualities. A protectionist policy reflects a concern with these qualities. It is justified by them and it may take on some of these qualities itself.

Let us suppose that the developer replies to this argument in the following way. A highway and a ski resort, he contends, are themselves symbols of power and freedom, not indeed the same kind of power and freedom that nature exemplifies, but the kind Americans really want. If someone reads our national literature, he might get the idea that the qualities of character Americans respect and seek are those expressed by objects in the natural environment: but this is the merest sentiment. Times have changed and the qualities we now value are symbolized by a fast pizza and a stick shift. A few snobs read books, and disagree about their meaning, but for the rest of us, who prefer magazines and watch television, the message is clear. The freshness and purity thought to be exemplified by a mountain stream now have a brand of mentholated cigarette as their symbol, and it is no longer a bear but a beverage which is wild and free. Power, as we now understand it, has nothing to do with nature. It is expressed by a hair tonic, perhaps, or by a detergent, or by a lot of engine under the hood. A century ago, natural objects were cheaper, and we could afford to use them as symbols. Now they are becoming scarce, and so we should accept a less expensive brand. Developed areas can take on the expressive function of untouched environments; the highway can replace the waterfall in our affection; the motel can take the place of the mountain.

The benefits of new symbols greatly outweigh the costs. Artificial trees can be advertised as symbols of life and integrity, and strip mines may be promoted as geological wonders—the view of the earth from the inside. Pollution exists only because we call it so; people would enjoy it if it were described as progress. The point is that we must stop attending to the literature, music, and art, written for an earlier century, which found in nature, then cheaper to preserve, the examples of important qualities. We should now believe our advertisers instead. When we realize that freedom comes with the right breakfast food, we will see that it costs much less than we expect (about 42 cents a day) to be free. From a cost-benefit standpoint you can't beat this. There is no reason that a ski lodge cannot be accepted as a symbol of all that we value. It is already. We can have our development and our aesthetic enjoyment, too.

The developer need not reply to the environmentalist in such an uncompromising manner; he could also answer in a softer way. He could agree with the environmentalist that nature does possess important aesthetic qualities, that it expresses freedom, purpose, and strength, for example, and that natural objects are more appropriate paradigms of these qualities than are breakfast foods and kitchen appliances. Accordingly, he might concede that the country has some stake in preserving or at least respecting the expressive qualities of nature, even if he is not sure what this stake may be. The developer might declare his willingness, then, to protect the aesthetic qualities of the environment as he understands them and wherever they do not simply prevent development. He might promise, for example, not to domesticate wildlife; either the animals will die or have enough room to preserve their strength and independence by fending for themselves. He might also decide not to build a pleasure palace for rich people whose only need is to amuse themselves. Nature should not be an idle spectacle; therefore he will build an arduous ski area where people will have to confront the mountain somewhat on its own terms and do rather more for their pleasure than throw a beer can out a car window. Visitors would come, then, with respect for the mountain, not to disgrace it after it has been subdued by machinery, but themselves to conquer it. In these and other ways, the developer could compromise with the environmentalist. But he must know how to determine the aesthetic qualities of various environments. He wants to understand why these qualities are so important, especially since they are often the ones which make nature least pleasant, and he needs to understand how to preserve them in a development. The problem of the symbolic aspect of nature is an important one, and it should be stated clearly and correctly.

The following pages attempt to explain the aesthetic value of natural environments. We consider only the expressive qualities of these environments and not their beauty, considered formally, or their amenity, about which enough has been said. We begin, then, by defining the expression "aesthetic quality." An "aesthetic quality" is any quality named in a metaphorical way. The distinction between the nonaesthetic and the aesthetic and the distinction between the literal and the metaphorical coincide. The distinction between the objective and the subjective is logically independent of the other distinctions: thus, a metaphorical or aesthetic quality can be objective as well. A brook, for example, may be "laughing" and "wet" in exactly the same way. Once we have these distinctions properly before us, we can understand the definition of "expression": if an object *expresses* a quality, that quality is metaphorical, the object possesses the quality, and the object exemplifies the quality.[1] Thus objects are examples or paradigms of the qualities they express. Now, paradigms have a cognitive function; they provide samples by which we learn to recognize given qualities. Change the paradigms of "freedom" and you change your understanding of what it is to be free. Thus, the question of substituting one symbol for another, and therefore one paradigm for another, is a very tricky one. It involves a change in the objects we recognize as having the quality; in other words, it changes the quality itself.

After we establish all this, we move on to determine the aesthetic qualities of nature and the natural environments to which they belong. The criterion here is our cultural history, not our advertising, and the reason is not hard to find. The business of the arts is to provide expressive objects and to represent other objects as expressive; therefore, art objects are themselves paradigms of aesthetic qualities and they represent other objects as paradigms. Just as the sciences have the function of describing the theoretical properties of things, so the arts determine, by way of providing crucial examples, aesthetic qualities. The arts, no less than the sciences describe a way the world is. This is the cognitive function of art.

Having said this much, we defend it against one objection, *viz.*, disagreements about the aesthetic properties of objects of art and nature seem to show that these properties are not objective but belong to the subject's response. This objection is not compelling; after all there can be disagreement as well about commonsense and theoretical properties. The impor-

[1] *See* N. GOODMAN, LANGUAGES OF ART 68 (1968) ("metaphorical possession is not literal possession; but possession is actual whether literal or metaphorical").

tant thing is that we have conditions for determining at least in principle when a description—aesthetic, commonsensical, or theoretical—is true or false. These conditions will be stated for the aesthetic description of nature and art.

B

An "aesthetic quality" is any quality named by a metaphorical predicate. Here are some predicates: "is laughing," "is sad," "is empty," "is free." Each of these can be used in a metaphorical and in a literal sense. When we attach the predicate "is laughing" to the subject "Mary," the predicate is used literally. Attaching it to the subject "the brook" gives us a metaphorical description. There are occasions in which a term can be predicated of an object both literally and metaphorically; then we have to determine by the context which is meant. To say that Mary is empty, for example, may characterize her personality (the metaphorical use) or assert that she has not eaten anything (her stomach is literally empty)—and one description may be true while the other is false. The difference between the metaphorical and the literal use of predicates is a matter of conventionality: the literal is the more usual, habitual, or familiar use. As a rule, metaphorical terms are transferred from their routine or literal realm of application—say, sentient beings—and applied to objects which they do not conventionally describe. Thus, when we say that a river is happy or that a mountain is hostile, we do not mean that either has feelings; we are using predicates that habitually describe sentient beings to describe inanimate things. A family of predicates has been transferred from a conventional to a less conventional realm. This is the characteristic of metaphor. A predicate which is used in a metaphorical way describes a metaphorical quality. And whether we say "metaphorical quality" or "aesthetic quality" we are talking about the same thing.

The aesthetic qualities of nature are just those qualities which are described in metaphorical terms. These terms, or predicates, very often have human beings in their literal realm or extension. When we find nature to express a metaphorical quality—e.g., freedom— it is often a quality which we literally may possess. Thus there is a connection between the ways we describe and therefore understand and experience nature and the ways we describe, understand, and experience ourselves.

In spite of the fact that the aesthetic is easily defined, as we have defined it, without any reference to the subjective, people have thought that aesthetic judgments must be or usually are subjective—and this is a mistake. Aesthetic qualities can be objective. The statement that a mountain is hostile or noble is as much a factual description as the statement that it is tall and in Spain. This is not to say, of course, that mountains are *literally* hostile or noble. On the contrary, they do not have feelings nor descend from noble blood: rather, the terms "hostile" and "noble" are used as they apply to inanimate objects and not as they apply to human beings. This use of these predicates is unconventional, of course, but not arbitrary; it is unusual, but still true or false. Metaphorical properties are not routinely ascribed to mountains, but they are correctly or incorrectly ascribed to mountains; they are actual properties nonetheless.

Why have people thought otherwise? Why is it common to believe that aesthetic descriptions are not objective but express only a subjective response? The reasons seem to be three. First, some people have thought that the aesthetic value of nature and art consists in the production or transmission of emotion in or to an audience. On this theory, a river is "happy" insofar as it causes those who see it to feel happy merely by seeing it, and a painting is "sad" insofar as it makes those who perceive it feel sad. The receipt of these emotions, on this view, explains part of the purpose of art. This theory does make aesthetic judgments subjective. Neither the mountain nor the canvas would be the logical subject of the emotional qualities. They would cause these qualities, and the subject would be the spectator himself. Second, some people have also believed that the sadness and the happiness belong as properties neither to the object nor to the subject but to a special kind of subjective or "phenomenal" entity that exists "in" experience or "in" the imagination. If this view can be understood at all, it also seems to make aesthetic qualities depend upon subjective response. Finally, the fact that people disagree concerning the aesthetic qualities they find in things also suggests that these qualities may belong or be logically tied to the subject more than to the object of experience. Since aesthetic descriptions are by definition unconventional, however, disagreement of this sort is to be expected. Nevertheless, it does raise the question whether principles for resolving such disagreements can be found.

Because these "reasons" for believing that aesthetic judgments are subjective are so widely held and respected, we shall pause to refute them. In doing so, we do not prove that aesthetic judgments and qualities are factual—only that certain reasons for believing otherwise are false. The argument for thinking that they are factual will be given later. Throughout the discussion, we shall use examples drawn from nature and from art. There is no difference between them in respect to the theory advanced here, and sometimes a painting is a less unwieldy example of a principle than is a forest or a mountain.

The belief that the function of art consists primarily in the production of emotion, although it is popular, is ludicrous. Of all art, soap operas, on such a view, become the most important, but even they are outdistanced by a roller coaster, a Baptist revival, or even a good family fight. The fact is that only preadolescents have energy for emotional thrills, and this explains their interest in hard rock; you appreciate peace and quiet after 25. Accordingly, it is hard to understand why an object that stimulates emotion is *valuable*; it would seem to be the very thing to avoid. Empathy with others, of course, is sometimes morally desirable, but for this art is no help to us. The variety of emotions with which people respond to well known works suggests that they use the occasion to feel whatever is in their own hearts and not the hearts of others. Accordingly, there can be therapy in this sort of response—we all like a good ghost story—but there is no understanding of the value of art.

It is not hard to refute the view that nature and art function aesthetically to cause pleasures and emotions in us. We need only to distinguish the emotional quality of the spectator from the emotional quality of the work. In order to recognize the passionateness of the painting the perceiver need no more become passionate than to recognize the colors of the painting he need turn red and green. This is not to deny, by the way, that the experience of a painting or of nature is emotional: we can feel *that* the painting is passionate just as we can feel *that* a person in a metaphorical sense is warm. To do this we need not ourselves become passionate or warm. We can act in the context of cognition rather than that of stimulus and response.

Of all theories of art which make it the cause of a feeling, the most heady, no doubt, is the "Formalist" thesis that "there is a particular kind of emotion provoked by works of visual art, and this . . . emotion is called the aesthetic emotion." [2] While the Formalists did not extend this hypothesis to nature, we could easily do so by holding that nature, too, proffers a special "aesthetic emotion." Clive Bell, the most vocal of the Formalists, announced that "to appreciate a work of art we need bring with us nothing from life, no knowledge of its ideas or affairs, no familiarity with its emotions." [3] Art, then, is supposed to be entertainment for the senses, when the mind is empty. But what is this "particular emotion" and why is it valuable? Needless to say, the emotion is defined in terms of the "significant form" of the painting, and vice versa, thus describing a circle, which also provokes an emotion. It need not detain us that Bell characterizes aesthetic pleasure as an ecstasy or as an exaltation, for this is said by the drunkard about alcohol, the seducer about fornication, the addict about heroin, the miser about money. They are all voluptuaries, each praising the consciousness-expanding properties of his drug. And there is no evidence that the aesthete is in fact any better for his pleasures than if he had sniffed the paint instead of looked at it. Nor need it bother us that the Formalist view makes most art before Cezanne inconsequential. Objections such as these are too easy to make, but they do teach us to avoid one perspective.

The purpose of art is not to give us a special tingle. That is the purpose of a massage. Nature and art are not mere stimuli to which we re-

[2] C. BELL, ART 6–7 (1958).
[3] *Id.* at 25.

spond with an emotion or a feeling of pleasure; they contain symbols which our perception and our tradition allow us to recognize and understand.

. . .

C

Earlier this century, conservationist groups argued with some success that governments should protect the national environment from excessive exploitation in order to safeguard and, by proper planning, to increase the benefits nature offers man. These conservationists wished to save the goose —but primarily for the sake of the golden egg. Today, environmentalists have come to see the inappropriateness and futility of this kind of argument. The argument is inappropriate because it distracts attention from the real motivation of the ecology movement, which is not to derive economic or recreational benefit from nature so much as to respect it for what it is and therefore to preserve it for its own sake. And the argument is futile, as we have said, because utility is generally to be gained by changing natural environments, not by preserving them. Accordingly, a different and, indeed, a nonutilitarian rationale is needed to support protectionist policies. This paper proposes such a rationale.

Our proposal is this: We have an obligation to protect natural environments insofar as we respect the qualities they express. We have seen that these qualities do actually belong to some environments, which are their paradigms; and the discovery or identification of these qualities is effected in our language and by our arts. Preserving an environment may be compared to maintaining an institution, for symbols are to values as institutions are to our legal and political life. The obligation to preserve nature, then, is an obligation to our cultural tradition, to the values which we have cherished and in terms of which nature and this nation are still to be described. It is difficult and indeed unnecessary to argue that fulfilling this obligation to our national values, to our history, and, therefore, to ourselves confers any kind of benefit; perhaps fulfilling a responsibility is itself a benefit, but this view requires not that we define "responsibility" in terms of "benefits," as the utilitarian does, but that we define "benefits" in terms of "responsibilities." In any case, preservation of the qualities, and accordingly the values, that this nation, as a nation, has considered peculiarly its own—and these are the qualities of nature—certainly obliges us to do otherwise than follow our pleasure and our profit. Consequently, there may be reason to think that fidelity to our historic values imposes both a "benefit" and a "cost." [4]

---

[4] About this problem Reinhold Niebuhr wrote:

"The real question is whether a religion or a culture is capable of interpreting life in a dimension sufficiently profound to understand and anticipate the sorrows and pains which may result from a virtuous regard for our responsibility;

What are the legal implications of this rationale for preserving the national environment? Can a citizen claim interest in the monuments of his nation's culture and history as such? Can he, more generally, assert legal membership in a cultural as well as political union? We believe that he can. Everyone allows that citizens have the right to vote, based on the Constitution; surely they have a right to participate in the *culture* of the nation as well. A political community does not develop independently of a cultural one, and unless people have a way of protecting their cultural as well as their political and legal institutions, eventually they may lose all of them. Now, participation in a culture must mean at least two things: individuals may contribute to it by entering the sciences or the arts, and they may become familiar with it through acquaintance with the great monuments and achievements of their nation's past. This means, of course, that people should be able to go to the National Gallery, for example, and not have Muzak piped at them, for Muzak expresses competing and distracting properties. People have a right, moreover, at least to ensure the existence of places like Sequoia National Park and to go there if they can, without having to do the usual battle with automobiles. They can demand that the mountains be left as a symbol of the sublime, a quality which is extremely important in our cultural history, rather than be turned into an expression of the soft life, which is not. The protection of the symbols— the institutions as we have said—of our cultural tradition is a condition for the maintenance of other traditions—particularly, the legal and political tradition to which our culture gives life. Accordingly, we need to respect these symbols as well as, and on the same grounds as we respect our legal and political rights. The safeguards appropriate to environmental policy, then, are not to be found in administrative codes and procedures only; we need restraints of a more dramatic and decisive kind. These must be as strong as those which protect our most fundamental rights. If restraints on the exploitation of our environment are to be adequate, then, they must be found in the Constitution itself, either as a forthright basis for statutory action [5]—placing certain national paradigms in trust,[6] for example—or simply as the national guarantor of those structures and relations necessary to maintain the American nation.[7]

---

and to achieve a serenity within sorrow and pain which is something less but also something more than 'happiness.' Our difficulty as a nation is that we must now learn that prosperity is not simply coordinated to virtue, that virtue is not simply coordinated to historic destiny, and that happiness is no simple possibility of human experience."

R. NIEBUHR, THE IRONY OF AMERICAN HISTORY 54 (1952).

[5] This, instead of the well-worn Commerce Clause. After all, it is the fact that the eagle soars in the mind's eye, and not that he may fly across state lines, which is important.

[6] *Cf.* Nantucket Islands Trust Bill, S.3536 & H.R. 15081, 93rd Cong., 2d Sess. (1974).

[7] *See* C. BLACK, JR., STRUCTURE AND RELATIONSHIP IN CONSTITUTIONAL LAW (1969).

To say that an environmental policy can be based on the Constitution[8] does not require, of course, a constitutional passage or article which directly concerns the environment; rather the argument would rest on the concept of nationhood, the structure created by the Constitution as a single instrument functioning in all of its parts. It is reasonable to think that cultural traditions and values constitute a condition—at least a causal one—of our political and legal freedom; and therefore insofar as the Constitution safeguards our nation as a political entity, it must safeguard our cultural integrity as well. Citizenship, then, can be seen to involve not only legal and political but also cultural rights and responsibilities. This possibility requires a legal argument and legal argument is not offered here. But here is a suggestion for someone else to argue. The right to cherish traditional national symbols, the right to preserve in the environment the qualities we associate with our character as a people, belongs to us as Americans. The concept of nationhood implies this right; and for this reason, it is constitutionally based.

But nothing is sacred; everything changes. It is just that changes which inhibit us from sharing our common heritage should not come at the whim of the developer. Nor should they depend on the conflicting interests of outdoors-people who like to hike and swim. Far different issues are at stake. They go to our sense of ourselves as a national community. Given this fact, it is satisfying to ground the protection of the environment on our most national legal institution. The right of our citizens to their history, to the signs and symbols of their culture, and therefore to some means of protecting and using their surroundings in a way consistent with their values is as important as the right to an equally apportioned franchise [9] or to participation in a party primary.[10] These rights are not to be denied on economic grounds. One sees too much withdrawal, aloofness, and exile in our society not to know that. As the right of the people to membership in our culture is recognized and defined, our people will become more aware and take more advantage of their membership. If with flexible constitutional structures at hand, we nonetheless forsake our national paradigms, we will not only lose once-cherished objects; we will sacrifice the values these objects express. These are the values by which we describe our national character and purpose; they are the qualities which we associate with our nation, our environment, and with the Constitution itself.[11]

---

[8] Even if such a rationale were held to provide the power by which Congress creates such trusts rather than implying the limitation itself, the recognition of this view would act as a check on governmental action. For example, public, rather than private access, is implicit; standing to sue is granted citizens once such a constitutional right has been accorded judicial recognition; interference with the protection of paradigms can be enjoined.

[9] Reynolds v. Sims, 377 U.S. 533 (1964).

[10] Smith v. Allwright, 321 U.S. 649 (1944).

[11] One afternoon last fall I was on my way to my class in Constitutional Law. I was going to lead a discussion of certain technicalities having to do with the application of

Selected Bibliography

AIKEN, WILLIAM, and HUGH LA FOLLETTE (eds.). *World Hunger and Moral Obligation*. Englewood Cliffs, N.J.: Prentice-Hall, Inc., 1977.

BLACKSTONE, WILLIAM T. (ed.). *Philosophy and Environmental Crisis*. Athens, Ga.: The University of Georgia Press, 1974.

CLARKE, RONALD O., and PETER C. LIST (eds.). *Environmental Spectrum*. New York: D. Van Nostrand Company, 1974.

MARGOLIS, JOSEPH. "Animals Have No Rights and Are Not the Equal of Humans," *Philosophic Exchange*, Vol. 1, no. 5 (1974), 119.

NARVESON, JAN. "Animal Rights," *Canadian Journal of Philosophy*, Vol. VII, no. 1 (1977), 161.

PASSMORE, JOHN. *Man's Responsibility For Nature*. London: Gerald Duckworth and Co. Ltd., 1974.

REGAN, TOM. "Narveson on Egoism and the Rights of Animals," *Canadian Journal of Philosophy*, Vol. VII, no. 1 (1977), 179.

REGAN, TOM, and PETER SINGER (eds.). *Animals Rights and Human Obligations*. Englewood Cliffs, N.J.: Prentice-Hall, Inc., 1976.

ROLSTON, H. "Is There an Ecological Ethic?" *Ethics*, Vol. 85, no. 2 (1975), 93.

STONE, CHRISTOPHER. "Should Trees Have Standing? Toward Legal Rights for Natural Objects," *Southern California Law Review*, Vol. 45 (1972), 450.

---

the Fourteenth Amendment, as implemented by acts of Congress, to voting and other rights. My head was full of section numbers in the Federal Revised Statutes. I fear I was mumbling to myself, a practice I cannot recommend to those who hold reputation dear.

I happened to look up—all the way up, over the tops of the red stone buildings into the sky as the Indians of Connecticut must have seen it before the white settlers came, with the great autumnal castles of clouds as far as imagination could reach. And somehow, very suddenly, all this illimitable expansiveness and lofty freedom connected within me with the words I was tracing from the Fourteenth Amendment through the statute books—"privileges or immunities of citizens," "due process of law," "equal protection of the laws." And I was caught for a moment by the feeling of a Commonwealth in which these words had not the narrow, culture-bound, relative meaning we are able to give them in the "real" world, but were grown to the vastness that is germinal within them.

C. BLACK, JR., THE OCCASIONS OF JUSTICE: ESSAYS MOSTLY ON LAW 29–30 (1963).

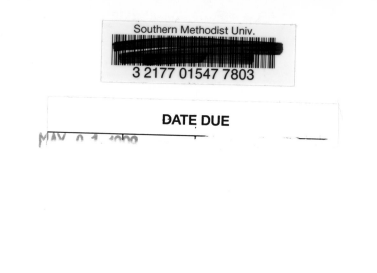